COMPUTER
NETWORKS

COMPUTER NETWORKS

ANDREW S. TANENBAUM

Vrije Universiteit
Amsterdam, The Netherlands

PRENTICE-HALL, INC.

ENGLEWOOD CLIFFS, NEW JERSEY 07632

Library of Congress Cataloging in Publication Data

Tanenbaum, Andrew S. (date)
    Computer networks.

    (Prentice-Hall software series)
    Bibliography: p.
    Includes index.
    1. Computer networks.   I. Title.   II. Series.
TK5105.5.T36   001.64'404   80-23283
ISBN 0-13-165183-8

PRENTICE-HALL SOFTWARE SERIES
Brian W. Kernighan, advisor

10 9 8 7 6 5 4 3 2 1

Printed in the United States of America

Editorial/production supervision: Nancy Milnamow
Cover design: Frederick Charles Ltd.
Manufacturing buyer: Joyce Levatino

PRENTICE-HALL INTERNATIONAL, INC., *London*
PRENTICE-HALL OF AUSTRALIA PTY. LTD., *Sydney*
PRENTICE-HALL OF CANADA, LTD., *Toronto*
PRENTICE-HALL OF INDIA PRIVATE LTD., *New Delhi*
PRENTICE-HALL OF JAPAN, INC., *Tokyo*
PRENTICE-HALL OF SOUTHEAST ASIA PTE. LTD., *Singapore*
WHITEHALL BOOKS LTD., *Wellington, New Zealand*

To Suzanne, Barbara, Marvin, and Sweetie π

CONTENTS

PREFACE

As computers have become smaller, cheaper, and more numerous, people have become more and more interested in connecting them together to form networks and distributed systems. At first these connections were made in an ad hoc way, typically with each computer regarding the other ones as terminals. However, in the past decade, a substantial body of knowledge has developed on the subject of computer networking, so that future networks and distributed systems can be designed systematically.

The key to designing a computer network was first enunciated by Julius Caesar: Divide and Conquer. The idea is to design the network as a sequence of layers, or abstract machines, each one based upon the previous one. By reducing the study of the whole to the study of its parts, the subject becomes more manageable. This book uses a model in which networks are divided into seven layers. The structure of the book follows the structure of the model to a considerable extent.

Chapter 1 provides an introduction to the subject of computer networks in general and layered protocols in particular. Chapter 2 treats a number of algorithms and heuristics for designing the topology of a network. Chapter 3 begins the study of the seven-layer model with the bottom layer (the physical layer); it covers the architecture of data communication systems, including the telephone system and satellites. Chapter 4 is primarily concerned with data link layer protocols, algorithms for reliably transmitting data over unreliable lines. Chapters 5, 6, and 7 all deal with the network layer; Chap. 5 treats point-to-point networks, Chap. 6 treats satellite and packet radio networks, and Chap. 7 treats local networks. Chapter 8 studies the transport and session layers, in particular, end-to-end protocols and internetworking. Chapter 9 is about the presentation layer, including cryptography, text compression, virtual terminal protocols, and file transfer protocols. Chapter 10 provides an introduction to some application layer issues, primarily distributed data bases and distributed operating systems. Chapter 11 contains a reading list and bibliography.

The book is intended as a text for juniors, seniors, and graduate students in computer science, electrical engineering, and related disciplines. The only prerequisites are a general familiarity with computer systems and programming, although a little knowledge of elementary calculus and elementary probability theory is useful, but not essential. Since the amount of material in the book may be too much for a one semester course, depending on the level of the students, I have made a serious attempt to make each chapter relatively independent of the other ones. This way an instructor is free to skip whichever chapters he chooses. Chapter 2, in particular, which is long and highly technical, may be omitted without loss of continuity by students who are not concerned with the topology design problem. However, if Chap. 2 is omitted, I would recommend having the students look at Eq. (2-9) and Eq (2-10), since they are used in a few places in subsequent chapters to analyze network performance.

People who have no formal computer science background, but who have had some industrial experience with minicomputers, assembly languages, system programming languages, operating systems, or data communication should have little trouble understanding the book. Even programmers or managers unfamiliar with these areas can probably understand a substantial part of the book.

Many people have helped me with this book. I would first like to thank Wiebren de Jonge for tens, if not hundreds, of hours of questions, discussions, arguments, and polemics about nearly every page of the manuscript. His impatience with my occasional indolence has shamed me into rewriting sections over and over until I finally got them right.

I would also like to thank Peter Apers, Dick Binder, Imrich Chlamtac, Dave Clark, George Conant, Ira Cotton, Rudy Cypser, Yogen Dalal, Dixon Doll, Phil Enslow, Howard Frank, Bill Franta, James P. Gray, Paul Green, Jan Hajek, Doug Jensen, Steve Johnson, Haim Kilov, Leonard Kleinrock, Simon Lam, Tony Lauck, Mike Liu, Alex McKenzie, Dave Morgan, Bob Morris, Holger Opderbeck, Robert Ryan, Paul Santos, Phil and Debbie Scherrer, Mischa Schwartz, John Shoch, Johan Stevenson, Carl Sunshine, Jim van Keulen, Stu Wecker, Barry Wessler, and Sylvia Wilbur for their help. Their collective assistance has greatly improved the book in many ways. My students, especially, Dick Biekart, Herman Gerbscheid, and Jan de Ruiter have also been very helpful.

To all the members of the Computing Science Research Center at Bell

Laboratories, thanks for many stimulating discussions during my visit there in the summer of 1979. I would especially like to thank Sandy Fraser for arranging things, Brian Kernighan and Mike Lesk for initiating me into the mysteries of the CAT, and Lorinda Cherry for causing a certain large minicomputer to comment extensively about my diction.

At this point authors normally thank their typists. Not wanting to break with this worthy tradition, I would like to thank Andy Tanenbaum for his fast and accurate typing of innumerable versions of the manuscript. Somewhat more to the point, I would like to thank Ken Thompson, Dennis Ritchie, and the other members of the Computing Science Research Center at Bell Laboratories for developing the UNIX† operating system. The UNIX text processing tools made the typing and retyping of the 1,231,788 characters comprising the final manuscript a pleasure instead of a chore.

IBM and DEC have permitted me to use material from their SNA and DECNET protocol manuals, respectively, for which I am grateful.

Last but not least, I would like to thank Suzanne, Barbara, Marvin, and Sweetie π, Suzanne for her patience, especially since she knew what she was getting in for this time, Barbara for keeping my terminal free of peanut butter, Marvin for arriving at a propitious moment, and Sweetie π for being very quiet while I was writing.

ANDREW S. TANENBAUM

---

† UNIX is a Trademark of Bell Laboratories.

COMPUTER
NETWORKS

1

INTRODUCTION

Each of the past three centuries has been dominated by a single technology. The eighteenth century was the time of the great mechanical systems accompanying the industrial revolution. The nineteenth century was the age of the steam engine. During the twentieth century, the key technology has been information gathering, processing, and distribution. Among other developments we have seen the installation of worldwide telephone networks, the invention of radio and television, the birth and unprecedented growth of the computer industry, and the launching of communication satellites.

As we move toward the final years of this century, these areas are rapidly converging, and the differences between collecting, transporting, storing, and processing information are quickly disappearing. Organizations with hundreds of offices spread over a wide geographical area routinely expect to be able to inspect the current status of even their most remote outpost at the push of a button. As our capability to gather, process, and distribute information grows, the demand for even more sophisticated information processing grows even faster.

Although the computer industry is young compared to other industries (e.g., automobiles and air transportation), computers have made spectacular progress in a short time. During the first two decades of their existence, computer systems were highly localized, usually within a single large room. Not infrequently, this room had glass walls, through which visitors could gawk at the great electronic wonder inside. A medium size company or university

1

might have had one or two computers, with large ones having had at most a few dozen. The idea that within 20 years equally powerful computers smaller than postage stamps would be mass produced by the millions was pure science fiction.

The merging of computers and communications has had a profound influence on the way computer systems are organized. The concept of the "computer center" as a room with a large computer to which users bring their work for processing is rapidly becoming obsolete. This model has not one, but two flaws in it: the concept of a single large computer doing all the work, and the idea of users bringing work to the computer, instead of bringing the computer to the users.

The old model a single computer serving all of the organization's computational needs is rapidly being replaced by one in which a large number of separate but interconnected computers do the job. These systems are called **computer networks**. The design and analysis of these networks is the subject of this book.

Throughout the book we will use the term "computer network" to mean an *interconnected* collection of *autonomous* computers. Two computers are said to be interconnected if they are capable of exchanging information. The connection need not be via a copper wire; lasers, microwaves, and earth satellites can also be used. By requiring that the computers be autonomous, we wish to exclude from our definition systems in which there is a clear master/slave relation. If one computer can forcibly start, stop, or control another one, the computers are not autonomous. An ILLIAC IV type of system, with one control unit and many slaves, is not a network. Nor is a large computer with remote card readers, printers, and terminals a network.

There is considerable confusion in the literature between a computer network and a **distributed system**. Enslow's (1978) definition requires a distributed system to have a *system-wide* operating system, with services requested by name, and not by location. In other words, the user of a distributed system should not be aware that there are multiple processors; it should look like a virtual uniprocessor. Allocation of jobs to processors, processor scheduling, allocation of files to disks, movement of files between where they are stored and where they are needed, and all other system function must be automatic.

On the other hand, Liebowitz and Carson (1978) have said: "A distributed system is one in which the computing functions are dispersed among several physical computing elements." Obviously this definition includes many systems that Enslow's excludes.

In our view a distributed system is a special case of a network, one with a high degree of cohesiveness and transparency. In essence a network may or may not be a distributed system, depending on how it is used. However, in view of the lack of any generally accepted nomenclature, we will use the term "computer network" in a generic sense, to cover both computer networks and distributed systems.

1.1. THE USES OF COMPUTER NETWORKS

Before we start to examine the technical issues in detail, it is worth devoting some time to pointing out why people are interested in computer networks, and what they can be used for.

1.1.1. Network Goals

Two forces are causing centralized computer systems to give way to networks. The first one is that many organizations already have a substantial number of computers in operation, often located far apart. For example, a company with many factories may have a computer at each location to keep track of inventories, monitor productivity, do the local payroll, and so on. Initially, each of these computers may have worked in isolation from the other ones, but at a certain time, management may have decided to connect them to be able to extract and correlate information about the entire company.

Put in slightly more general form, this goal is to make all programs, data, and other resources available to anyone on the network without regard to the physical location of the resource and the user. In other words, the mere fact that a user happens to be 1000 km away from his data should not prevent him from using the data as though it were local. Load sharing is another aspect of resource sharing. This goal may be summarized by saying it is an attempt to end the "tyranny of geography."

A second goal is to provide high reliability by having alternative sources of supply. With unconnected computers, if a machine goes down due to hardware failure, for example, the local users are out of luck, even though there may be substantial computing capacity available elsewhere. With a network, the temporary loss of a single computer is much less serious, because its users can often be accommodated elsewhere until service is restored. For military, banking, industrial process control, and many other applications, a complete loss of computing power for even a few hours due to some catastrophe, natural or otherwise, is completely intolerable.

Another important reason for distributing computing power has to do with the relative price of computing versus communication. Until about 1970, computers were relatively expensive compared to communication facilities. The reverse is now true. In some applications, data are generated at widely scattered points. For example, a government agency monitoring air pollution might collect data at various sites around the country. Prior to 1970, it was not feasible to put a computer at each location to analyze the data because computers were so expensive. Instead, all the data were transmitted to a central computer center somewhere. Now the cost of a small computer is negligible, so it becomes attractive to analyze the data at the place where it is captured, and only send occasional summaries back to the computer center, to reduce the communication cost, which now represents a larger percentage of the total cost than it used to. This approach results in a computer network.

Yet another goal of setting up a computer network has little to do with networking at all. As a side effect of its other goals, a computer network can provide a powerful communication medium among widely separated people. Using a network, it is easy for two or more people who live and work far apart to write a report. The text is kept online so that all the authors always have access to the current version. When one author makes a change, the others can get the change immediately, instead of waiting several days for a letter. Such a speed up of several orders of magnitude may make cooperation among far-flung groups of people feasible where it previously had been impossible. In the long run, the use of networks to enhance human-to-human communication may prove more important than technical goals such as improved reliability.

As we mentioned earlier, the desire to connect existing computer systems is not the only driving force behind computer networking. The other main force is the superior price/performance ratio of small computers over large ones. Mainframes are roughly a factor of 10 faster than the largest single chip microprocessors, but they cost a thousand times more. This imbalance has caused many systems designers to try to harness a collection of microcomputers to outperform the large mainframes at lower cost, much as the stagecoaches of the old west were pulled by teams of horses, not by one superhorse.

This goal leads to designs in which the system consists of many processors located close together, called a **local network**, to contrast it with the far-flung **long haul network**. In addition to a favorable price/performance ratio, local networks have other advantages over a single centralized system. For one thing, they are more reliable, since a single hardware or software failure in a well-designed network will only bring down one processor, and not affect the others. Loss of 1% of the processors should result in a slightly diminished performance for everyone, rather than leaving 1% of the users out in the cold. A related point is the ability to increase system performance gradually as the work load grows by just adding more processors.

Another major attraction of building large systems by coupling large numbers of smaller processors is the expectation of a simpler software design. In a network, it is possible to dedicate some (or all) of the processors to specialized functions, for example, data base management. Instead of having the machines be multiprogrammed (time-shared), each machine does only one thing at a time. By eliminating the multiprogramming, we can also eliminate much of the software complexity associated with the large mainframes.

In Fig. 1-1 we give a classification of multiple processor systems arranged by physical size. At the top are **data flow machines**, highly parallel computers with many functional units all working on the same program. Next come the **multiprocessors**, systems that communicate by sharing primary memory. Beyond the multiprocessors are the true networks, computers that communicate by exchanging messages. Finally, the connection of two or more distinct networks is called **internetworking**.

Interprocessor distance	Processors located in same	Example
0.1 m	Circuit board	} Data flow machine
1 m	System	} Multiprocessor
10 m	Room	
100 m	Building	} Local network
1 km	Campus	
10 km	City	
100 km	Country	} Long haul network
1000 km	Continent	
10,000 km	Planet	} Interconnection of long haul networks

Fig. 1-1. Classification of interconnected processors by physical size.

1.1.2. Applications of Networks

The major advantages of building a large system from many smaller, localized machines were discussed above: a favorable price/performance ratio, graceful degradation upon failure, and incremental growth. Normally, replacing a single mainframe by a local network located in one room does not make any new applications possible, except for a few that can take advantage of any new computing power available, but this is not an effect of the distributed nature of the system, just its total speed.

In contrast, the availability of a (public) computer network makes many new applications feasible. Some of these new applications may have important effects on society as a whole. To give an idea about some possible (future) uses for computer networks, we will now briefly look at just three examples: access to remote programs, access to remote data bases, and value added communication facilities.

A software house that has produced a valuable program may allow their clients to log in over the network and run the program. Having the customer log in on the software house's machine rather than selling the program outright is especially attractive when the program is large, written in an exotic language, machine dependent, or embedded in a web of libraries, special system calls, and other nonportable environmental features. Simulation programs often fall into this category. For example, a company might offer a model of the national or world economy. Clients could see how various projected inflation rates, interest rates, currency fluctuations, and so on, might affect their business.

Computer aided education is another possible candidate for use via a network, with many different (and competing) courses being offered. Programs that accept a description of a sick person's symptoms and make a medical diagnosis may catch on quickly in areas where doctors are scarce. They may also prove popular with patients who have seen n doctors and gotten n disjoint diagnoses. The potential of programs that could help people save money on their taxes hardly needs comment. Extremely sophisticated games and other recreational activities are likely. In short, almost any program offering a useful service to either businesses or individuals, and which is too complicated to sell outright, is a potential candidate for access via a network.

Another major area of potential network use is access to remote data bases. For example, it may someday be easy for people sitting at their terminals at home to make reservations for airplanes, trains, buses, boats, hotels, restaurants, theaters, and so on, anywhere in the world with instant confirmation. Home banking and the automated newspaper also fall in this category. Present newspapers offer a little bit of everything, but electronic ones can be easily tailored to each reader's personal taste (e.g., everything about computers, the major stories about foreign affairs, politics, and epidemics, but no football, thank you). The automated newspaper would naturally have up-to-the-second weather and stock market information. It might also have an interactive want ad section to allow readers of the antique section to ask, for example, if anyone out there has a *paper* copy of the *New York Times*.

The next step beyond automated newspapers (plus magazines and journals) is the fully automated library. Depending on the cost, size, and weight of the terminal, the printed word may become obsolete. Skeptics should take note of the effect the printing press had on the medieval illuminated manuscript.

The above applications use networking for economic reasons: calling up a distant computer via a network is cheaper than calling it directly. The lower rate is possible because a normal telephone call ties up an expensive, dedicated circuit for the duration of the call, whereas access via a network ties up long-distance lines only while data are actually being transmitted.

A third category of potential widespread network use is as a communication medium. More than half of all first class mail consists of computer-generated bills. Most, if not all, of this could be eliminated by electronic funds transfer systems, providing a huge savings to businesses and their customers. Postal services that have not changed in centuries may be in for a rude shock when the public perceives that much faster and cheaper mail service is technically feasible.

Teleconferencing is a whole new form of communication. With it, widely separated people can conduct a meeting by typing messages at their terminals. Messages may be directed at any subset of the attendees. Attendees may leave at will, and find out what they missed when they come back. Bores may be shut off at the push of a button. Summaries by person, subject, and date are instantly available. It is not even necessary for all the attendees to be present at the same time, and attendance may be anonymous.

International contacts by human beings (as opposed to governments) may be greatly enhanced by network based communication facilities. Playing bridge with your friends in Switzerland may be as easy as playing bridge with your next door neighbors. Children may learn each other's languages by communicating (or trying to communicate) with other children in foreign countries, possibly with the help of closed-circuit television, which, in principle, can also be sent over a computer network, just as digitized voice can.

It is sometimes said that there is a race going on between transportation and communication, and whichever one wins will make the other unnecessary. Using a computer network as a sophisticated communication system may reduce the amount of traveling done, thus saving energy. Home work may become popular, especially for part time workers with young children. The office and school as we now know them may disappear. Stores may be replaced by electronic mail order catalogs. Cities may disperse, since high-quality communication facilities tend to reduce the need for physical proximity. The information revolution may change society as much as the industrial revolution did.

1.2. NETWORK STRUCTURE

It is now time to turn our attention from the social implications of networking to the technical issues involved in network design. In any network there exists a collection of machines intended for running user (i.e., application) programs. We will follow the terminology of one of the first major networks, the ARPANET, and call these machines **hosts**. The hosts are connected by the **communication subnet**, or just **subnet** for short. (Some authors use the terms **transport system** or **transmission system**.) The job of the subnet is to carry messages from host to host, just as the telephone system carries words from speaker to listener. By separating the pure communication aspects of the network (the subnet) from the application aspects (the hosts), the complete network design is greatly simplified.

In nearly all networks the subnet consists of two basic components: switching elements and transmission lines. The switching elements are generally specialized computers. Again following the ARPANET terminology, we will call them **IMPs** (Interface Message Processors) throughout the book, although the terms **communication computer**, **packet switch**, **node**, and **data switching exchange** are also commonly used. Transmission lines are often called **circuits** or **channels**. In this model, shown in Fig. 1-2, each host is connected to one (or occasionally several) IMPs. All traffic to or from the host goes via its IMP.

Broadly speaking, there are two general types of designs for the communication subnet:

1. Point-to-point channels.

2. Broadcast channels.

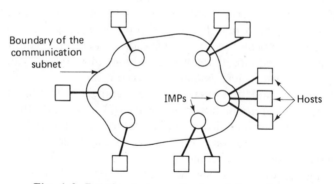

Fig. 1-2. Relation between hosts and the subnet.

In the first one, the network contains numerous cables or leased telephone lines, each one connecting a pair of IMPs. If two IMPs that do not share a cable nevertheless wish to communicate, they must do this indirectly, via other IMPs. When a message is sent from one IMP to another via one or more intermediate IMPs, the message is received at each intermediate IMP in its entirety, stored there until the required output line is free, and then forwarded. A subnet using this principle is called a **point-to-point** or **store-and-forward** subnet.

When a point-to-point subnet is used, an important design issue is what the IMP interconnection topology should look like. Figure 1-3 shows several possible topologies. Local networks that were designed as such usually have a symmetric topology. In contrast, irregular topologies usually are a result of connecting existing computers via the telephone system.

The second kind of communication architecture uses broadcasting. In this design there is a single communication channel shared by all IMPs. Inherent in broadcast systems is that messages sent by any IMP are received by all other IMPs. Something in the message itself must specify for whom it is intended. After receiving a message not intended for itself, an IMP just ignores it.

Figure 1-4 shows some of the possibilities for broadcast subnets. In a bus or cable network, at any instant one machine is the bus master and is allowed to transmit. All other machines are required to refrain from sending. A bus must have some arbitration mechanism to resolve conflicts when two or more IMPs want to transmit simultaneously. The arbitration mechanism may be centralized or distributed.

A second possibility is a satellite or ground radio system. Each IMP has an antenna through which it can send and receive. All IMPs can hear the output *from* the satellite, and in some cases they can also hear the transmissions of their fellow IMPs *to* the satellite as well.

A third broadcast system is the ring. In a ring, each bit propagates around the ring on its own, not waiting for the rest of the message to which it belongs. Typically, each bit circumnavigates the entire ring within a few bit times, often

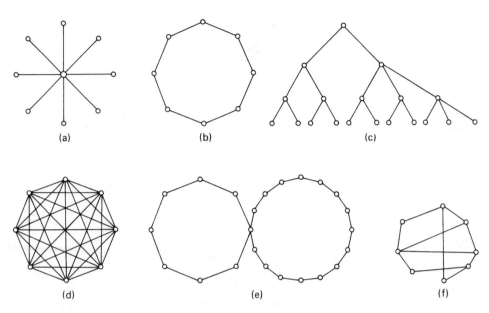

Fig. 1-3. Some possible topologies for a point-to-point subnet. (a) Star. (b) Loop. (c) Tree. (d) Complete. (e) Intersecting loops. (f) Irregular.

before the complete message has been finished. In contrast, in a loop, each message is not retransmitted by the next IMP until the entire message has been received. In a loop each line might have a different message on it, whereas in a ring this situation is unlikely unless the messages are extremely short. Like all other broadcast systems, some rule is needed for arbitrating simultaneous accesses to the channel in the ring. Be warned that our definitions of loop and ring are not universal; some authors reverse their meanings.

Broadcast subnets can be further divided into static and dynamic, depending on how the channel is allocated. A typical static allocation would be to divide time up into discrete intervals, and run a round robin, allowing each IMP to broadcast only when its time slot came up. Static allocation has the problem of wasting channel capacity when an IMP has nothing to say during its allocated slot, so some systems attempt to allocate the channel dynamically (i.e., on demand).

Dynamic allocation methods for a common channel are either centralized or decentralized. In the centralized channel allocation method, there is a single entity, for example a bus arbitration unit, which determines who goes next. It might do this by accepting requests and making a decision according to some internal algorithm. In the decentralized channel allocation method, there is no central entity; each IMP must decide for itself whether to transmit or not. You

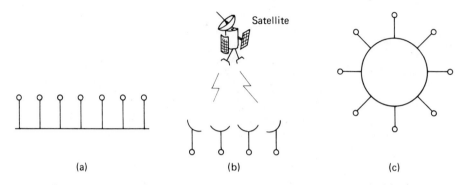

Fig. 1-4. Communication subnets using broadcasting. (a) Bus. (b) Satellite or radio. (c) Ring.

might think that this always leads to chaos, but this is not so. Later we will study many algorithms designed to bring order out of the potential chaos.

Both point-to-point and broadcast communication systems can be implemented by having a common memory shared by the processors. Usually, this type of system does not have IMPs. The details of the communication depend on the software. If there are n processors, $n(n-1)$ memory words could be allocated for communication, each word corresponding to one of the ordered pairs of processors. When a processor wants to say something to another processor, it writes a pointer to a message into the communication word. Alternatively, a broadcast-type scheme could be used, with a single communication word shared by all processors. Intermediate forms are also possible.

Several authors have attempted to produce taxonomies of computer networks. A survey of these attempts is given by Jensen et al. (1976). Unfortunately, no consensus has been achieved yet.

1.3. NETWORK ARCHITECTURES

Modern computer networks are designed in a highly structured way. In the following sections we examine the structuring technique used in some detail.

1.3.1. Protocol Hierarchies

To reduce their design complexity, most networks are organized as a series of **layers** or **levels**, each one built upon its predecessor. The number of layers, the name of each layer, and the function of each layer differ from network to network. However, in all networks, the purpose of each layer is to offer certain services to the higher layers, shielding those layers from the details of how the offered services are actually implemented.

Layer n on one machine carries on a conversation with layer n on another machine. The rules and conventions used in this conversation are collectively known as the layer n **protocol**, as illustrated in Fig. 1-5 for a seven-layer network. The entities comprising the corresponding layers on different machines are called **peer processes**. In other words, it is the peer processes that communicate using the protocol.

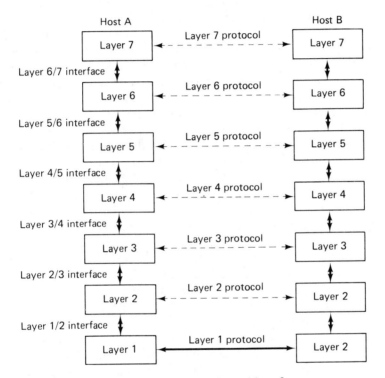

Fig. 1-5. Layers, protocols, and interfaces.

In reality, no data are directly transferred from layer n on one machine to layer n on another machine (except in the lowest layer). Instead, each layer passes data and control information to the layer immediately below it, until the lowest layer is reached. At the lowest layer there is **physical communication** with the other machine, as opposed to the **virtual communication** used by the higher layers. In Fig. 1-5 virtual communication is shown by dotted lines and physical communication by solid lines.

Between each pair of adjacent layers there is an **interface**. The interface defines which primitive operations and services the lower layer offers to the upper one. When network designers decide how many layers to include in a network and what each one should do, one of the most important considerations is having cleanly defined interfaces between the layers. Having cleanly defined interfaces, in turn, requires that each layer perform a specific collection of well understood functions. In addition to minimizing the amount of information that must be passed between layers, clean cut interfaces also make it simpler to replace the implementation of one layer with a completely different one (e.g., all the telephone lines are replaced by satellite channels), because all that is required of the new implementation is that it offers exactly the same set of services to its upstairs neighbor as the old implementation did.

The set of layers and protocols is called the **network architecture**. The specification of the architecture must contain enough information to allow an implementer to write the program for each layer so that the program will correctly obey the appropriate protocol. Neither the details of the implementation nor the specification of the interfaces are part of the architecture. In fact, it is not even necessary that the interfaces on all machines in a network be the same, provided that each machine can correctly use all the protocols. The subjects of network architectures and protocols are the principal topics of this book.

An analogy may help explain the idea of multilayer communication. Imagine two philosophers (peer processes in layer 3), one in Kenya and one in Indonesia, who want to communicate. Since they have no common language, they each engage a translator (peer processes at layer 2), each of whom in turn contacts an engineer (peer processes in layer 1). Philosopher 1 wishes to convey his affection for *oryctolagus cuniculus* to his peer. To convey his thoughts, he passes a message (in Swahili) across the 2/3 interface, to his translator, who might render it as "I like rabbits" or "J'aime les lapins" or "Ik hou van konijnen," depending on the layer 2 protocol. The translator then gives the message to his engineer for transmission, by telegram, telephone, computer network, or some other means, depending on what the two engineers have agreed on in advance (the layer 1 protocol). When the message arrives, it is translated into Indonesian and passed across the 2/3 interface to philosopher 2. Note that each protocol is completely independent of the other ones as long as the interfaces are not changed. The translators can switch from French to Dutch at will, provided that they both agree, and neither changes his interface with either layer 1 or layer 3.

Now consider a more technical example: how to provide virtual communication to the top layer of the seven-layer network in Fig. 1-6. A message, m, is produced by a process running in layer 7. The message is passed from layer 7 to layer 6 according to the definition of the layer 6/7 interface. In this example, layer 6 transforms the message in certain ways (e.g., text compression), and then passes the new message, M, to layer 5 across the layer 5/6 interface. Layer 5, in the example, does not modify the message but simply regulates the direction of flow (i.e., prevents an incoming message from being handed to layer 6 while layer 6 is busy handing a series of outgoing messages to layer 5).

In our example, as well as many actual networks, there is no limit to the size of messages accepted by layer 4, but there is a limit imposed by layer 3.

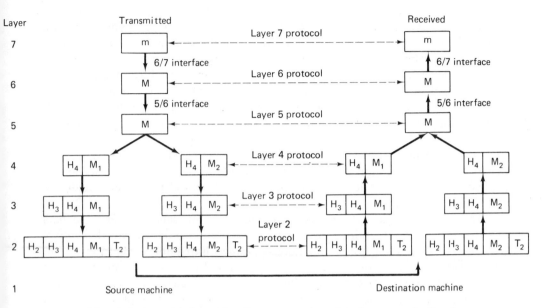

Fig. 1-6. Actual information flow supporting virtual communication in layer 7.

Consequently, layer 4 must break up the incoming messages into smaller units, prepending a **header** to each unit. The header includes control information, such as sequence numbers, to allow layer 4 on the destination machine to get the pieces back together in the right order if the lower layers do not maintain sequence. Layer 3 decides which of the outgoing lines to use, attaches its own headers, and passes the data to layer 2. Layer 2 adds not only a header to each piece, but also a trailer, and gives the resulting unit to layer 1 for physical transmission. At the receiving machine the message moves upward, from layer to layer, with headers being stripped off as it progresses. None of the headers for layers below *n* are passed up to layer *n*.

The important thing to understand about Fig. 1-6 is the relation between the virtual and actual communication and the difference between protocols and interfaces. The peer processes in layer 4, for example, conceptually think of their communication as being "horizontal," using the layer 4 protocol. Each one is likely to have a procedure called *SendToOtherSide* and a procedure *GetFromOtherSide*, even though these procedures actually communicate with lower layers across the 3/4 interface, not with the other side.

The peer process abstraction is crucial to all network design. Without this technique, it would be impossible to partition the design of the complete network, an unmanageable problem, into several smaller, manageable, design problems, namely the design of the individual layers.

1.3.2. Design Issues for the Layers

Some of the key design issues that occur in computer networking are present in several layers. Next, we describe briefly some of the common problems that must be repeatedly dealt with in the design of the different protocols.

Every layer must have a mechanism for connection establishment. Since a network normally has many computers, some of which have multiple processes, some means is needed for a process on one machine to specify who it wants to talk to. In any layer where there are multiple destinations, addressing is needed.

Closely related to the mechanism for establishing connections across the network is the mechanism for terminating them once they are no longer needed. As we will see in Chap. 8, this seemingly trivial point can actually be quite subtle.

Another set of design decisions are the rules for data transfer. Do data only travel in one direction, called **simplex** communication, or can they travel in either direction, but not simultaneously, called **half-duplex** communication, or can they travel in both directions at once, called **full duplex** communication? The protocol must also determine how many logical channels the connection corresponds to, and what their priorities are. Many networks provide at least two logical channels per connection, one for normal data and one for urgent data.

Error control is an important issue when the physical communication circuits are not perfect. Many error-detecting and error-correcting codes are known, but both ends of the connection must agree on which one is being used. In addition, the receiver must have some way of telling the sender which messages have been correctly received and which have not.

Not all communication channels preserve the order of messages sent on them. To deal with a possible loss of sequencing, the protocol must make explicit provision for the receiver to allow the pieces to be put back together properly. An obvious solution is to number the pieces, but this solution still leaves open the question of what should be done with pieces that arrive out of order.

An issue that occurs at every level is how to keep a fast sender from swamping a slow receiver with data. Various solutions have been proposed, and will be discussed later. All of them involve some kind of feedback from the receiver to the sender, either directly or indirectly, about what the receiver's current situation is.

Another problem that must be solved repeatedly at different levels is the inability of all processes to accept arbitrarily long messages. This property leads to mechanisms for disassembling, transmitting, and then reassembling messages. A related issue is what to do when processes insist upon transmitting data in units that are so small that sending each one separately is inefficient. Here the solution is to gather together several small messages heading toward a common destination into a single large message, and dismember the large message at the other side.

When it is inconvenient or expensive to set up a separate connection for each pair of communicating processes, the underlying layer may decide to use the same connection for multiple, unrelated conversations. As long as this multiplexing and demultiplexing is done transparently, it can be used by any layer. Multiplexing is needed in layer 1, for example, where all the traffic for all connections has to be sent over one, or at most, a few, physical circuits.

When there are multiple paths possible between source and destination, at some point in the hierarchy, a routing decision must be made. In fact, it is sometimes necessary to make routing decisions in two or more layers. For example, to send data from London to Rome, a high level decision might have to be made to go via France or Germany based on their respective privacy laws, and a low-level decision might have to be made to choose one of the many available circuits based on current traffic.

1.4. THE ISO REFERENCE MODEL

Now that we have discussed layered networks in the abstract at some length, it is time to look at the set of layers that will be used throughout this book. The model is shown in Fig. 1-7. This model is closely based on a proposal developed by the International Standards Organization (ISO) as a first step toward international standardization of the various protocols.

The Reference Model of Open Systems Interconnection (OSI), as ISO calls it, has seven layers. Zimmermann (1980) has described the principles that ISO applied to arrive at the seven layers. The major ones are as follows:

1. A layer should be created where a different level of abstraction is needed.

2. Each layer should perform a well defined function.

3. The function of each layer should be chosen with an eye toward defining internationally standardized protocols.

4. The layer boundaries should be chosen to minimize the information flow across the interfaces.

5. The number of layers should be large enough that distinct functions need not be thrown together in the same layer out of necessity, and small enough that the architecture does not become unwieldy.

In Sec. 1.4.1 through 1.4.7 we will discuss each layer of the architecture in turn, starting at the bottom layer. In general, we do *not* always adhere to the ISO terminology. The reason for this departure is made clear below.

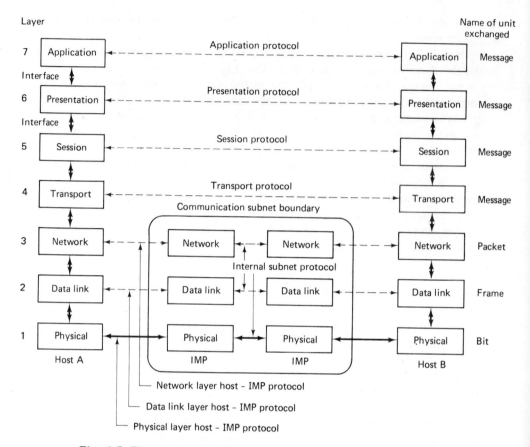

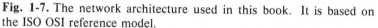

Fig. 1-7. The network architecture used in this book. It is based on the ISO OSI reference model.

1.4.1. The Physical Layer

The **physical layer** is concerned with transmitting raw bits over a communication channel. The design issues have to do with making sure that when one side sends a 1 bit, it is received by the other side as a 1 bit, not as a 0 bit. Typical questions here are how many volts should be used to represent a 1 and how many for a 0, how many microseconds a bit occupies, whether transmission may proceed simultaneously in both directions, how the initial connection is established and how it is torn down when both sides are finished, how many pins the network connector has and what each pin is used for. In some cases a transmission facility consists of multiple physical channels, in which case the physical layer can make them look like a single channel, although higher layers can also perform this function. The design issues here largely deal with mechanical, electrical and procedural interfacing to the subnet.

1.4.2. The Data Link Layer

The task of the **data link layer** is to take a raw transmission facility and transform it into a line that appears free of transmission errors to the network layer. It accomplishes this task done by breaking the input data up into **data frames**, transmitting the frames sequentially, and processing the **acknowledgement frames** sent back by the receiver. Since layer 1 merely accepts and transmits a stream of bits without any regard to meaning or structure, it is up to the data link layer to create and recognize frame boundaries. This can be accomplished by attaching special bit patterns to the beginning and end of the frame. These bit patterns can accidentally occur in the data, so special care must be taken to avoid confusion.

The term "frame" is not the official ISO term for the unit exchanged by layer 2 peer processes. The correct term is "data-link-service-data-unit." We hope our motivation for not always using the ISO nomenclature is now somewhat clearer.

A noise burst on the line can destroy a frame completely. In this case, the layer 2 software on the source machine must retransmit the frame. However, multiple transmissions of the same frame introduce the possibility of duplicate frames. A duplicate frame could be sent, for example, if the acknowledgement frame from the receiver back to the sender was destroyed. It is up to this layer to solve the problems caused by damaged, lost, and duplicate frames, so that layer 3 can assume it is working with an error-free (virtual) line. Layer 2 may offer several different services classes to layer 3, each of a different quality and with a different price.

Another issue that arises at layer 2 (and at most of the higher layers as well) is how to keep a fast transmitter from drowning a slow receiver in data. Some mechanism must be employed to let the transmitter know how much buffer space the receiver has at the moment. Typically, this mechanism and the error handling are integrated together.

If the line can be used to transmit data in both directions, this introduces a new complication that the data link layer software must deal with. The problem is that the acknowledgement frames for A to B traffic compete for the use of the line with data frames for the B to A traffic. A clever solution (piggybacking) has been devised; we will discuss it in detail later.

1.4.3. The Network Layer

The **network layer**, sometimes called the **communication subnet layer**, controls the operation of the subnet. Among other things, it determines the chief characteristics of the IMP-host interface, and how **packets**, the units of information exchanged in layer 3, are routed within the subnet. A major design issue here is the division of labor between the IMPs and hosts, in particular who should ensure that all packets are correctly received at their destinations, and in the proper order. What this layer of software does, basically, is accept messages from the source host, convert them to packets, and see to it that the packets get directed toward the destination.

A key design issue is how the route is determined. It could be based on static tables that are "wired into" the network and rarely changed. It could also be determined at the start of each conversation, for example a terminal session. Finally, it could be highly dynamic, being determined anew for each packet, to reflect the current network load.

If too many packets are present in the subnet at the same time, they will get in each others' way, forming bottlenecks. The control of such congestion also belongs to layer 3.

Since the operators of the subnet may well expect remuneration for their efforts, there is often some accounting function built into layer 3. At the very least, the software must count how many packets or characters or bits are sent by each customer, to produce billing information. When a packet crosses a national border, with different rates on each side, the accounting can become complicated.

1.4.4. The Transport Layer

The basic function of the **transport layer**, also known as the **host-host layer**, is to accept data from the session layer, split it up into smaller units, if need be, pass these to the network layer, and ensure that the pieces all arrive correctly at the other end. Furthermore, all this must be done in the most efficient possible way, and in a way that isolates the session layer from the inevitable changes in the hardware technology.

Under normal conditions, the transport layer creates a distinct network (i.e., layer 3) connection for each transport (i.e., layer 4) connection required by the session layer. However, if the transport connection requires a high throughput, the transport layer might create multiple network connections, dividing the data among the network connections to improve throughput. On the other hand, if creating or maintaining a network connection is expensive, the transport layer might multiplex several transport connections onto the same network connection, to reduce the cost. In all cases, the transport layer is required to make the multiplexing transparent to the session layer.

The transport layer also determines what type of service to provide the session layer, and ultimately, the users of the network. The most popular type of transport connection is an error-free (virtual) point-to-point channel that delivers messages in the order in which they were sent. However, other possible kinds of transport service are transport of isolated messages with no guarantee about the order of delivery, and broadcasting of messages to multiple destinations. The type of service is determined when the connection is established.

Layer 4 is a true source-to-destination or **end-to-end** layer. In other words, a program on the source machine carries on a conversation with a similar program on the destination machine, using the message headers and control messages. At the lower layers, the protocols are carried out by each machine and its immediate neighbors, and not by the ultimate source and destination machines, which may be separated by many IMPs. The difference between layers 1 through 3, which are chained, and layers 4 through 7, which are end-to-end, is illustrated in Fig. 1-7.

Many hosts are multiprogrammed, which means that multiple connections will be entering and leaving each host. There needs to be some way to tell which message belongs to which connection. The transport header (H_4 in Fig. 1-6) is one place this information could be put.

In addition to multiplexing several message streams onto one physical channel (the host-IMP channel), the transport layer must take care of establishing and deleting connections across the network. This implies some kind of naming mechanism, so that a process on one machine has a way of describing with whom it wishes to converse. There must also be a mechanism to regulate the flow of information, so that a fast host cannot overrun a slow one. Note that flow control between hosts is distinct from flow control between IMPs, although we will later see that similar principles apply to both.

Although the network architecture specifies nothing about the implementation, it is worth pointing out that the transport layer is often implemented by a part of the host operating system, which we will call a **transport station**. In contrast, the network layer is typically implemented in the host by an input/output driver. The data link and physical layers are normally implemented in hardware.

1.4.5. The Session Layer

Ignoring the presentation layer, which merely performs certain transformations on the data, the **session layer** is the user's interface into the network. It is with this layer that the user must negotiate to establish a connection with a process on another machine. Once the connection has been established, the session layer can manage the dialog in an orderly manner, if the user has requested that service.

A connection between users (technically speaking, between two two presentation-layer processes) is usually called a **session**. A session might be used to allow a user to log into a remote time-sharing system or to transfer a file between two machines. To establish a session, the user must provide the remote address he wants to connect to. Session addresses are intended for use by users or their programs, whereas transport addresses are intended for the use by transport stations, so the session layer must be able to convert a session address to its transport address, to request that a transport connection be set up.

Setting up a session is typically a complicated operation. To start with, it may be necessary that each end of the session be properly authenticated, to prove that it has the right to engage in the session and to ensure that the correct party receives the bill later. Then the two ends must agree on a variety of options that may or may not be in effect for the session, such as whether communication is to be half-duplex or full-duplex. The operation of setting up a session between two processes is often called **binding**.

Another function of the session layer is management of the session once it has been set up. For example, if transport connections are unreliable, the session layer may be required to attempt to transparently recover from broken transport connections. As another example, in many data base management systems, it is crucial that a complicated transaction against the data base never be aborted halfway, since doing so would leave the data base in an inconsistent state. The session layer often provides a facility by which a group of messages can be bracketed, so that none of them are delivered to the remote user until all of them have arrived. This mechanism ensures that a hardware or software failure within the subnet can never cause a transaction to be aborted halfway through. The session layer can also provide for ordering of messages when the transport service does not. In short, the session layer takes the bare bones bit for bit communication service offered by the transport layer and adds application-oriented functions to it.

In some networks, the session and transport layers are merged into a single layer, or the session layer is absent altogether, if all that the users want is raw communication service.

1.4.6. The Presentation Layer

The **presentation layer** performs functions that are requested sufficiently often to warrant finding a general solution for them, rather than letting each user solve the problems. These functions can often be performed by library routines called by the user. Of course, these routines can also be placed within the operating system itself, but we consider that to be a serious mistake, because the bigger the operating system is, the less likely it is to work properly.

A typical example of a transformation service that can be performed here is text compression. Most user programs do not exchange random binary bit strings. They exchange things such as people's names, city names, dates, and amounts of money. In many applications certain words or phrases are especially common, for example *withdrawal* and *deposit* in banking systems.

The presentation layer could be designed to accept ASCII strings as input and produce compressed bit patterns as output. For example, the most common 200 words could be encoded in an 8-bit byte as the numbers 0 through 199. Codes 200 through 249 could be used to indicate that the next byte contained a word code. This system allows the 200 most common words to be encoded in 1 byte, and the next 12,800 in 2 bytes. The remaining six codes, 250 through 255, could be used to indicate that an ASCII string follows, a packed decimal number (two digits per byte) follows, a 16-bit integer follows, etc. Other possibilities for compression are the elimination of repeated characters, especially multiple blanks, the use of case shifts to designate multiple alphabets (telegraph code uses 5 bits with explicit characters to shift between upper and lower case), and frequency-dependent coding.

This layer can also perform other transformations, in addition to message compression. Encryption to provide security is one possibility. Conversion between character codes, such as ASCII to EBCDIC, might often be useful. More generally, different computers usually have incompatible file formats, so a file conversion option might be useful at times. Similarly, there are many different, incompatible terminals in use throughout the world. Line and screen length, end of line convention, scroll versus page mode, character sets, and cursor addressing are but a few of the many problems. The presentation layer attempts to alleviate these problems.

1.4.7. The Application Layer

The content of the **application layer** is up to the individual user. When two user programs on different machines communicate, they alone determine the set of allowed messages and the action taken upon receipt of each. Nevertheless, there are many issues that occur here that are quite general. For example, the whole question of network transparency, hiding the physical distribution of resources from the (human) user, occurs in many applications. Another issue is problem partitioning: how can the problem be divided up among the various machines (preferably automatically), to take maximum advantage of the network. Distributed data bases also give rise to many interesting problems in the application layer. Industry specific protocols, such as for banking or airline reservation, allow computers from different companies to access each other's data bases when that is needed.

1.5. ARPANET, SNA, DECNET, AND PUBLIC NETWORKS

Throughout most of the chapters of the book, the same pattern will be followed. First comes a general discussion of the theory, insofar as this subject can be said to have any theory. Then come the examples. As examples we have chosen to use three well-known networks, the ARPANET, IBM's SNA (Systems Network Architecture), and Digital Equipment Corporation's DEC-NET. The discussions of all three will be greatly simplified; it would be possible to write an entire book about each of them, but not this book. Both due to our intentional simplification and the tendency of all three of these to change with time, the examples are given in the spirit of how things *could* be done rather than how the current implementation of any of them actually works. Furthermore, none of the examples use the ISO reference model, so we have been forced to map the layers as best we can. The approximate mapping we will use is shown in Fig. 1-8.

Layer	ISO	ARPANET	SNA	DECNET
7	Application	User	End user	Application
6	Presentation	Telnet, FTP	NAU services	
5	Session	(None)	Data flow control	(None)
4	Transport	Host-host	Transmission control	Network services
3	Network	Source to destination IMP	Path control	Transport
2	Data link	IMP-IMP	Data link control	Data link control
1	Physical	Physical	Physical	Physical

Fig. 1-8. Approximate correspondences between the various networks.

In addition to these three examples, we will also discuss some public network interface standards: X.3 and X.21 in Chap. 3, HDLC in Chap. 4, and X.25 in Chap. 5.

1.5.1. Introduction to the ARPANET

The ARPANET (McQuillan and Walden, 1977) is the creation of ARPA (now DARPA), the (Defense) Advanced Research Projects Agency of the U.S. Department of Defense. Starting in the late 1960s it began stimulating research on the subject of computer networks by providing grants to computer science departments at many U.S. universities, as well as to a few private corporations. This research led to an experimental four-node network that went on the air in December 1969. It has been operating ever since, and has subsequently grown to well over 100 computers spanning half the globe, from Hawaii to Norway. Much of our present knowledge about networking is a direct result of the ARPANET project. As a debt to this pioneering work, we have adopted some of the ARPANET terminology (e.g., host, IMP, subnet).

The original ARPANET IMPs were Honeywell DDP-516 minicomputers with 12K 16-bit words of memory. Later Honeywell DDP-316 minicomputers with 16K memories were used. More recently, a multiprocessor IMP called the Pluribus (Ornstein et al., 1975), based on the Lockheed SUE minicomputer, has been used to provide high reliability and throughput. Some of the 316s have been configured to allow up to 63 user terminals to call them directly, instead of logging into a host. These are called **TIPs**. The IMPs are mostly connected by 50 kbps leased lines, except for those in Hawaii and Norway, which use 50 and 9.6 kbps leased satellite channels, respectively. There are also some higher-speed (e.g., 230.4 kbps) leased lines in use. The original IMPs could handle one to four hosts apiece. The Pluribus IMP can handle tens of hosts and hundreds of terminals simultaneously.

The ARPANET IMP-IMP protocol really corresponds to a mixture of the layer 2 and layer 3 protocols of Fig. 1-7. Layer 3 also contains an elaborate routing mechanism. In addition, there is a mechanism that explicitly verifies the correct reception at the destination IMP of each and every packet sent by the source IMP. Strictly speaking, this mechanism is another layer of protocol, the source IMP to destination IMP protocol. However, this protocol does not exist in the ISO model. We will treat it as part of layer 3, since it is closer to that layer than to any other.

The ARPANET has not one, but two major transport protocols: the original NCP and the newer TCP. There is no session layer or presentation layer, although some of the presentation layer functions are available through specific higher level protocols, such as Telnet, the remote login facility, and FTP, the File Transfer Protocol.

1.5.2. Introduction to SNA

SNA (Cypser, 1978), is a network architecture intended to allow IBM customers to construct their own private networks, both hosts and subnet. A bank, for example, might have one or more CPUs in its data processing department and numerous terminals in each of its branch offices. Using SNA, all these isolated components could be transformed into a coherent system.

Prior to SNA, IBM had several hundred communication products, using three dozen teleprocessing access methods, with more than a dozen data link protocols alone. The basic idea behind SNA was to eliminate this chaos and to provide a coherent framework for loosely coupled distributed processing. Given the desire of many of IBM's customers to maintain compatibility with all these (mutually incompatible) programs and protocols, the SNA architecture is more complicated in places than it might have been had these constraints not been present. SNA also performs a large number of functions not found in other networks, which, although valuable for certain applications, tend to add to the overall complexity of the architecture.

SNA has evolved considerably over the years, and is still evolving. The original release, in 1974, permitted only centralized networks, that is, tree-shaped networks with only a single host and its terminals. From our point of view, that is no network at all. The 1976 release allowed multiple hosts with their respective trees, with intertree communication possible only between the roots of the trees. The 1979 release removed this restriction, allowing a more general intercommunication.

In the discussion of SNA and DECNET throughout the book, we will sometimes deviate from IBM's terminology as well as from DEC's. Each manufacturer has devised its own set of names for well-known concepts, presumably for reasons known best to itself. By sticking primarily to the ISO and ARPANET terminology, we hope to minimize confusion and be at least economically neutral.

An SNA network consists of a collection of machines called **nodes**, of which there are four types, approximately characterized as follows. Type 1 nodes are terminals. Type 2 nodes are controllers, machines that supervise the behavior of terminals and other peripherals. Type 4 nodes are front end processors, devices whose function is to relieve the main CPU of the work and interrupt handling associated with data communication. Type 5 nodes are the main hosts themselves, although with the advent of low-cost microprocessors, some controllers have acquired some host-like properties. There are no type 3 nodes.

Each node contains one or more **Network Addressable Units** or **NAUs**. A NAU is a piece of software that allows a process to use the network. An analogy may be helpful here. Consider a building with a telephone socket in every office. Each socket has a unique, hardwired address (extension number) permanently associated with it. To use the telephone system, a person plugs a telephone into a convenient socket, and thereafter can be called at the extension belonging to the socket. Similarly, each NAU has a network address. To use the network, a process must connect itself to a NAU, at which time it can be addressed and can address other NAUs. The NAUs are thus the entry points into the network for user processes.

There are three kinds of NAUs. A **logical unit** or **LU** is the usual variety to which user processes can be attached. A **physical unit** or **PU** is a special NAU associated with each node, which is used by the network to bring the node online, take it offline, test it, and perform similar administrative functions. The PU provides a way for the network to address a physical device, without reference to which processes are using it. The third kind of NAU is the **System Services Control Point** or **SSCP**, of which there is normally one per type 5 node and none in the other nodes. The SSCP has complete knowledge of, and control over, all the front ends, controllers, and terminals attached to the host. The collection of hardware and software managed by an SSCP is called a **domain**. Fig. 1-9 depicts a simple two domain SNA network.

One possible mapping of the SNA protocol hierarchy onto the ISO hierarchy is shown in Fig. 1-10. The two models do not correspond especially well, especially in layers 3, 4, and 5, so other authors may choose to map them slightly differently.

The lowest layer takes care of physically transporting bits from one machine to another. The next layer, the **data link control** layer, constructs frames from the raw bit stream, detecting and recovering from transmission errors in a way transparent to higher layers. Many networks have directly or indirectly copied

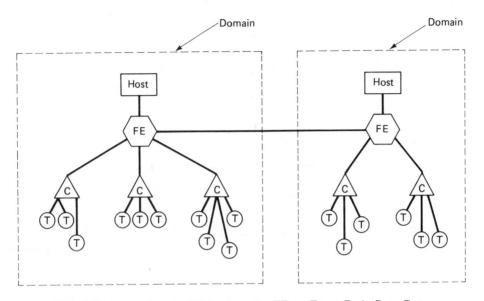

Fig. 1-9. A two domain SNA network. FE = Front End, C = Controller, T = Terminal.

their layer 2 protocol from SNA's layer 2 data communication protocol, SDLC (Synchronous Data Link Control). Layer 3 in SNA, called **path control** by IBM, is concerned with routing and congestion control within the subnet. It can block unrelated packets together into frames to enhance transmission efficiency and can deal with the hierarchical addressing used in SNA.

The next layer is **transmission control**, whose job it is to create, manage, and delete transport connections, called **sessions** in SNA. In effect, it provides a uniform interface to higher layers, independent of the properties of the subnet. Once a session has been established, it regulates the rate of flow between processes, controls buffer allocation, manages the different message priorities, handles multiplexing and demultiplexing of data and control messages for the benefit of higher layers, and performs encryption and decryption when requested to do so.

Above transmission control comes **data flow control**, which has nothing at all to do with controlling the flow of data in the usual sense. Instead, it has to do with keeping track of which end of a session is supposed to talk next, assuming that the processes want such a service. This layer is also heavily involved in error recovery. A somewhat unusual feature of the data flow control layer is the absence of a header used to communicate with the corresponding software on the other end. Instead, the information that would normally be communicated in a header is passed to transmission control as parameters and included in the transmission header.

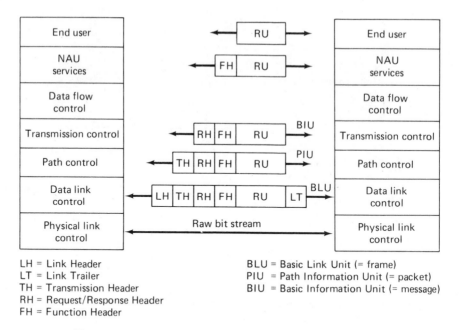

LH = Link Header
LT = Link Trailer
TH = Transmission Header
RH = Request/Response Header
FH = Function Header

BLU = Basic Link Unit (= frame)
PIU = Path Information Unit (= packet)
BIU = Basic Information Unit (= message)

Fig. 1-10. Protocol hierarchy and units exchanged in SNA.

The sixth layer within SNA, **NAU services**, provides two classes of services to user processes. First, there are **presentation services**, such as text compression. Second, there are **session services**, for setting up connections. In addition, there are **network services**, which have to do with the operation of the network as a whole.

1.5.3. Introduction to DECNET

DECNET (Wecker, 1980) is a set of programs and protocols produced by Digital Equipment Corporation for use on its computer systems. The architecture of DECNET is called DNA—Digital Network Architecture. Since it is sometimes difficult to separate the pure architecture aspects from the pure implementation aspects, we will use the term DECNET for convenience to mean DECNET and/or DNA.

The intention of DECNET is to allow any of DEC's customers to set up a private network. Thus there are many isolated DECNETs in the world, like SNA networks, in contrast to the ARPANET of which there is only one (although a number of other organizations have copied it). DECNET also differs from the ARPANET in another major respect: there is no distinction between hosts and IMPs. A DECNET is just a collection of machines (nodes), some of which may run user programs, some of which may do packet switching, and some of which may do both. The functions performed by any given machine may even change in time.

Like SNA, DECNET has evolved in time. In particular, early versions of DECNET did not have the capability for machine A to communicate with machine B unless there was a physical connection between the two machines. If A and B both had connections to a third machine C, but no direct connection with each other, the software did not allow A and B to communicate via C. To retain compatibility between the early and later versions, a distinction is made between "small" nodes and "full" nodes, the former running the old software and the latter running the new software. Small nodes can communicate only with adjacent nodes, whereas full nodes do not have this restriction.

DECNET has five layers. The physical layer, data link control layer, transport layer, and network services layer correspond almost exactly to the lowest four ISO layers. However, the agreement breaks down at layer 5, since DECNET has no session layer, and the remaining layer, the application layer, is a mixture of the ISO presentation and application layers. The relation between DECNET and the ISO model is shown in Fig. 1-8. Be sure you notice that DEC has chosen to call layer 3 the transport layer, whereas the ISO transport layer is layer 4. To avoid confusion, we will stick to the ISO nomenclature throughout the book.

Since SNA and DECNET have similar goals—to provide a general framework for networking and distributed processing—it is interesting to compare and contrast them. On the whole SNA offers more parameters, features, and options than DECNET does, and is correspondingly more complicated. For example, both SNA and DECNET have a message that is used to establish a connection between remote processes. The DECNET message, CONNECT INITIATE, has about 10 parameters. The corresponding SNA message, BIND, has three times as many parameters.

The physical layer is similar in both architectures; both can handle most of the types of lines available. Although the goals of the data link layer are the same in both architectures, the protocols differ in several ways. Frames in SNA are delimited by a special bit sequence, whereas frames in DECNET contain a character count in the header telling how long the frame is. SNA frames may be an arbitrary number of bits, whereas DECNET frames must be multiples of 8 bits. The network layers of the two architectures differ greatly. In SNA all packets belonging to a given connection follow the same route through the subnet, whereas in DECNET each packet is routed independently of all its predecessors. The transport layers provide the higher layers similar service—error free, sequenced connections—but their implementations are quite different due to the great difference in the underlying network layer. SNA has an elaborate session layer, whereas DECNET has none. Finally, the approach to the presentation layer is also different. In SNA it is possible for users to request various transformations on data passed from the application layer to the session layer, such as text compression and encryption. In DECNET these transformations are not possible, although there is a file access protocol that reads and writes remote files, providing transformations where needed.

1.5.4. Introduction to Public Networks and X.25

In many countries the government or private companies have begun to offer networking services to any organization that wishes to subscribe. The subnet is owned by the network operator, providing communication service for the customers' hosts and terminals. Such a system is called a **public network**. It is analogous to, and often a part of, the public telephone system.

Although public networks in different countries are frequently quite different internally, there are some internationally agreed upon protocols for network access, in particular the host-IMP protocols of Fig. 1-7. The existence of such agreements is desirable from the vendor's point of view, because it allows his products to be used in many countries, and is also desirable from the user's point of view, because it allows him to easily interconnect terminals and hosts from different vendors via a public network.

Three key protocols have been standardized: the physical layer, data link layer, and network layer protocols between the host and IMP. In addition, there is a set of protocols designed to allow ordinary terminals to be attached to public networks, even if they are unable to send and receive packets using the standard protocols.

The physical layer protocol, called **X.21**, specifies the physical, electrical, and procedural interface between the host and the IMP. Very few public networks actually support this standard, because it requires digital, rather than analog signaling on the telephone lines, but it will undoubtedly become more important in the future. As an interim measure, an analog interface similar to the familiar RS-232C standard has been defined. The data link layer standard has a number of (slightly incompatible) variations. They all are designed to deal with transmission errors on the telephone line between the user's equipment (host or terminal) and the public network (IMP). Finally the network layer protocol deals with addressing, flow control, delivery confirmation, interrupts and related issues. The protocols for layers 1, 2, and 3 are known collectively as **X.25**.

Because the world is still full of terminals that do not speak X.25, another set of standards has been defined that describe how an ordinary (nonintelligent) terminal communicates with an X.25 public network. In essence, the network operator installs a "black box" to which these terminals can connect. The black box is called a **PAD** (Packet Assembler Disassembler), and its function is described in an international standard known as **X.3**. A standard protocol has been defined between the terminal and the PAD, called **X.28**; another standard protocol exists between the PAD and the network, called **X.29**. We will discuss these standards later.

Given:
  Locations of the hosts and terminals
  Traffic matrix (γ_{ij})
  Cost matrix (c_{ij})

Performance constraints:
  Reliability
  Delay/Throughput

Variables:
  Topology
  Line capacities
  Flow assignment

Goal:
  Minimize cost

The hosts and terminals are the ultimate producers and consumers of information. For most design purposes hosts and terminals are equivalent, and it will often be convenient to lump them together under the term *location* or *site*. The traffic matrix tells how many packets per second on the average must be sent from site *i* to site *j*. When a new network is being designed, γ_{ij} is often unknown. In this case, a common assumption is that it is proportional to the product of the populations of the two sites, divided by the distance between them. The probability density function for packet length is assumed known and the same for all sites.

The cost matrix tells how much various speed (leased) lines from location *i* to location *j* cost per month. The cost matrix covers IMP and concentrator locations as well as customer sites. (A concentrator is a device that accepts input from several lines and feeds all the output onto one line, and vice versa. More about concentrators later.) In general the cost of a line depends on distance and speed in a highly nonlinear fashion. There is also a fixed charge (e.g., modem depreciation) that depends only on the speed, but not on the distance. The same considerations apply to leased satellite channels.

Just to complicate things further, only a discrete set of speeds are available, for example, 50, 110, 300, 600, 1200, 2400, 4800, 9600, 56,000 and 230,400 bits/sec. As a result, if the optimum speed for a line turns out to be, say, 20,000 bits/sec, the line will not be available. Either a 9600 bit/sec line or a 56,000 bit/sec line will have to be used, the former providing too little performance and the latter too high a cost. The effect of "rounding off" all the line speeds to the set of available values may produce a configuration that is far from optimal. Performing the optimization using only the allowed set of speeds is a difficult integer programming problem.

Just as an aircraft design group is given performance goals to meet (e.g., speed, range, noise level), network designers also are expected to meet prespecified goals. Two common performance requirements for networks are reliability and delay (or throughput). A reliable network will not collapse if one IMP or one line goes down. Depending on the application, it may be desirable that the network be able to sustain a loss of 2, or 3, or some other number of IMPs or lines and still function properly. The reliability constraint is often expressed in terms such as "Every pair of sites shall be able to communicate, even if an arbitrary collection of three IMPs or four lines are down."

Another common performance requirement is that the mean packet delay not exceed a given number of milliseconds. Alternatively, it might be required that 99% of the packets be delivered in less than some specified time (i.e., specification by "worst" case behavior rather than average case behavior).

The parameters that the network designers can adjust to achieve their goals are the topology (where to place IMPs, concentrators, and lines), the line capacities, and the flow assignment (routing algorithm). Notice that the designers may place *their* equipment (the IMPs and concentrators) where they want to, but they must take the customer sites as given.

Finally, the object of the entire exercise is to produce a minimum-cost design that meets all the requirements. Occasionally the problem may be turned around—there is a certain budget available and the goal is to minimize the delay subject to the available amount of money. The approach here is similar to that of the original problem, so we will not discuss this variation further.

Any way you look at it, the problem is huge. If there are n locations, there are $n(n-1)/2$ potential lines. Since each line may be present or absent, the number of potential topologies that must be considered is $2^{n(n-1)/2}$. Even for a small network with only 10 locations, there are 3×10^{13} possible topologies to be considered. If it took 1 msec per topology, which is hopelessly optimistic, it would still require 1000 years to examine all of them. Clearly, a brute-force search will not work.

2.1.2. Hierarchical Networks

Fortunately, past experience has provided a useful design strategy that can be used as a starting point. In particular, designing a computer network has many properties in common with designing a telephone network, electric power grid, natural-gas pipeline, railroad network, and many other networks. The basic principle upon which all these networks are based is that the customers are not spread around uniformly. They tend to be found mostly in cities, and not so much in rural areas.

Consequently, a hierarchical strategy seems like a reasonable approach for computer networks. In fact, the first public data networks are beginning to evolve in that direction already. The idea is to have one or more IMPs in each major city. Medium-size cities would be provided with concentrators feeding into the nearest IMP. Each customer site would have a leased (or dial-up) connection to the nearest concentrator or IMP. The IMPs would be connected by a highly redundant network of high-speed lines (including satellite connections). The concentrators would be connected to the IMPs by medium-speed lines, perhaps with or perhaps without redundancy. The customers would be connected to their concentrators by nonredundant low-speed lines. Low-, medium-, and high-speed are all relative, of course. They could be 0.3, 9.6, and 56 kbps; or 9.6, 56, and 230.4 kbps.

In this model, depicted in Fig. 2-1, there is a clear separation between the **backbone** design (interconnecting the IMPs) and the **local access** design (getting the customer's data to the backbone). By making the local access topology a tree rather than an arbitrary graph, major simplifications are possible (e.g., the routing problem vanishes, because there is only one route from customer to IMP). In the model of Fig. 2-1 we have allowed terminals to be connected using multidrop lines (i.e., not every terminal has a dedicated line to the nearest concentrator). However, each cluster of terminals is controlled by a single terminal controller, so that the entire cluster can be regarded as a single machine by the concentrator.

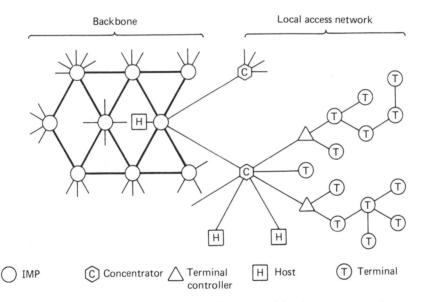

Fig. 2-1. A two-level hierarchy: backbone and local access network.

We can now break the topology design problem into several subproblems:

Backbone Design

1. What should the backbone topology be.

2. Assignment of line capacities.

3. Flow assignment.

Local Access Design

1. Where to place the concentrators.

2. Which customers to assign to which concentrators.

3. How to interconnect the terminals within a customer site.

One other subproblem that we have not included lies at the boundary between the backbone and local access designs: how to assign concentrators to IMPs. This problem is particularly nasty, because the techniques to be used for solving the backbone design assume that the total input traffic is known, which is not the case if it is not known which concentrators to assign to which IMPs. In practice, it is usually obvious which IMP is closest, and for those few cases where a concentrator lies midway between two IMPs, each assignment should be tried and the lowest cost design used.

2.2. CONNECTIVITY ANALYSIS

One of the requirements usually imposed on computer networks is that they be reliable, even in the face of unreliable IMPs and lines. To achieve high reliability with unreliable components, the network must be redundant. A sufficiently redundant network can lose a small number of components and still function properly, albeit with lower performance. In this section we examine some of the methods used to analyze the redundancy of a network. Some ideas from graph theory are useful here, so we begin with a short introduction to it. For a more lengthy introduction, see (Even, 1979).

2.2.1. Introduction to Graph Theory

A **graph** consists of a set of elements called **nodes**, and a set of **arcs** connecting the nodes. Some authors use the term **vertex** instead of node; the terms **link**, **line**, **branch**, and **edge** are also used in the literature instead of arc. We will use the various synonyms interchangeably. Two nodes are said to be **adjacent** if there is an arc directly connecting them. If they are only indirectly connected, through one or more intermediate nodes, they are not adjacent.

Graphs can have two kinds of arcs: **directed** and **undirected**. A directed arc indicates that information (or whatever commodity the graph models) can flow only in the direction indicated by the arrow on the arc. A directed arc models a simplex (unidirectional) channel. An undirected arc indicates that information can flow both ways. Undirected arcs can be used to model full-duplex channels, which can accept flow in both directions simultaneously, or half duplex channels, which can accept flow in either direction but in only one direction at a given instant. A graph containing only directed arcs is called a **directed graph**.

Similarly, a graph containing only undirected arcs is called an **undirected graph**. Mixed graphs also exist but are not of interest to us.

In many applications it is useful to assign weights to the arcs. Typically, such weights represent the carrying capacity of the arc. In a communication network this might be in bits per second or packets per second. Fig. 2-2 shows a weighted, undirected graph containing 12 nodes and 13 arcs. In some applications it is useful to allow parallel arcs between a given pair of nodes (e.g., there are multiple telephone trunks running between New York and Boston). For our purposes parallel arcs will usually be forbidden. Similarly, we will not consider graphs with self loops: arcs beginning and ending at the same node.

A graph can be easily represented by a matrix, M. The matrix element M_{ij} is equal to the capacity of the arc from i to j. If the graph is unweighted, $M_{ij} = 1$ if there is an arc from i to j, and 0 otherwise. If the lines are half-duplex or full-duplex, $M_{ij} = M_{ji}$. If self loops are forbidden, the diagonal elements, M_{ii}, are all zero.

The **degree** (or **valence**) of a node is the number of arcs ending there. In a directed graph, both incoming and outgoing arcs count. One of the oldest theorems in graph theory is due to Euler: the sum of the degrees of all the nodes in a graph is equal to twice the number of arcs. The proof is simple: each arc contributes to the degree of two nodes. A **regular** graph of degree d is one in which all nodes have degree d. From Euler's theorem we can see that there are no regular graphs of odd degree with an odd number of nodes. If such a graph existed, the sum of the degrees of its nodes would be odd (the product of two odd numbers), implying a fractional number of arcs.

A **path** is a sequence of adjacent nodes. The **length** of a path is the number of arcs it contains. In general, there may be several paths between a given pair of nodes. In Fig. 2-2, $ABCDHK$, $ABCDGFJK$, and $AEIJK$ are all paths between A and K. However, $AEIJFJK$ is not a path, since node J occurs twice in the sequence. The shortest path between a given pair of nodes is called a **geodesic**. Thus paths $DGFJ$ and $DHKJ$ are both geodesics between D and J. The **diameter** of a graph is the length of the longest geodesic. The diameter of Fig. 2-2 is 5 because there is no path between A and L of length less than 5.

A **circuit** is a sequence of adjacent nodes that comes back to the starting node. $DGFJKHD$ is an example of a circuit in Fig. 2-2. A circuit containing all the nodes of a graph is known as a **Hamiltonian circuit**. The classical "traveling salesman" problem consists of finding the shortest Hamiltonian circuit (i.e., the cheapest way for the salesman to visit all the cities in his territory).

If every node is reachable from every other node (i.e., if there is a path between every pair of nodes), the graph is said to consist of one **component**. Figure 2-2 consists of one component. A one component graph is also said to be **connected**. However, if arcs DH and JK were deleted, the graph would have two components. Reliable networks should remain connected, of course, even if some nodes and links are removed.

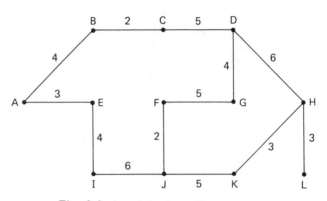

Fig. 2-2. A weighted, undirected graph.

A **spanning tree** of a graph is a subgraph containing all the nodes of the graph and some collection of arcs chosen so that there is exactly one path between each pair of nodes. If arcs *IJ* and *JK* were removed from Fig. 2-2, the resulting graph would be a spanning tree. If weights are defined for all pairs of nodes in a graph, the spanning tree with minimum total weight can be found, called the **minimum spanning tree**. (The total weight of a tree is the sum of the weights of all its arcs.) Minimum spanning trees will play an important role in the design of the local access network.

Many graph algorithms involve labeling nodes or arcs according to some rule. The labels may represent the distance from a certain node, or the amount of flow passing through the node, or various other quantities. As an example, let us consider a labeling algorithm used to find the shortest path between two specific nodes in a graph. The algorithm is due to Dijkstra (1959).

Each node is labeled (in parentheses) with its distance from the source node along the best known path. Initially, no paths are known, so all nodes are labeled with infinity. As the algorithm proceeds and paths are found, the labels may change, reflecting better paths. A label may be either tentative or permanent. Initially, all labels are tentative. When it is discovered that a label represents the shortest possible path from the source to that node, it is made permanent and never changed thereafter.

To illustrate how the labeling algorithm works, look at the weighted, undirected graph of Fig. 2-3(a), where the weights represent distance. We want to find the shortest path from *A* to *D*. We start out by marking node *A* as permanent, indicated by a filled in circle. Then we examine, in turn, each of the nodes adjacent to *A* (the working node), relabeling each one with the distance to *A*. Whenever a node is relabeled, we also label it with the node from which the probe was made, so we can reconstruct the final path later. Having examined each of the nodes adjacent to *A*, we examine all the tentatively labeled nodes in the whole graph, and make the one with the smallest label permanent, as shown in Fig. 2-3(b). This one becomes the new working node.

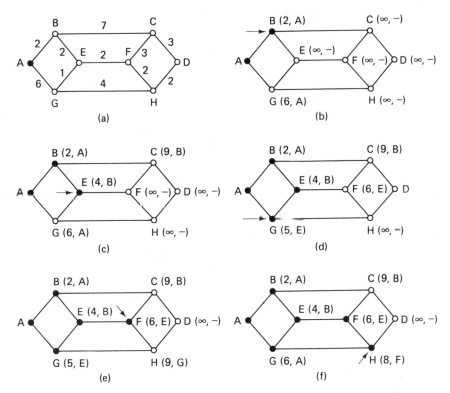

Fig. 2-3. The first five steps used in computing the shortest path from *A* to *D*. The arrows indicate the working node.

We now start at *B*, and examine all nodes adjacent to it. If the sum of the label on *B* and the distance from *B* to the node being considered is less than the label on that node, we have a shorter path, so the node is relabeled.

After all the nodes adjacent to the working node have been inspected, and the tentative labels changed if possible, the entire graph is searched for the tentatively labeled node with the smallest value. This node is made permanent, and becomes the working node for the next round. Figure 2-3 shows the first five steps of the algorithm.

To see why the algorithm works, look at Fig. 2-3(c). At that point we have just made *E* permanent. Suppose that there were a shorter path than *ABE*, say *AXYZE*. There are two possibilities: either node *Z* has already been made permanent, or it has not been. If it has, then *E* has already been probed (on the round following the one when *Z* was made permanent), so the *AXYZE* path has not escaped our attention.

Now consider the case where Z is still tentatively labeled. Either the label at Z is greater than or equal to that at E, in which case $AXYZE$ cannot be a shorter path than ABE, or it is less than that of Z, in which case Z and not E will become permanent first, allowing E to be probed from Z.

This algorithm is given in Pascal in Fig. 2-4. The only difference between the program and the algorithm described above is that in Fig. 2-4, we compute the shortest path starting at the terminal node, t, rather than at the source node, s. Since the shortest path from t to s in an undirected graph is the same as the shortest path from s to t, it does not matter at which end we begin (unless there are several shortest paths, in which case reversing the search might discover a different one). The reason for searching backwards is that each node is labeled with its predecessor rather than its successor. When copying the final path into the output variable, *path*, the path is thus reversed. By reversing the search, the two effects cancel, and the answer is produced in the correct order.

2.2.2. Cuts and Network Flow

Designers often need to be able to compute the information carrying capacity of a network. A concept from graph theory that is useful for modeling the carrying capacity of a network is the cut. An X-Y **cut** is a set of arcs whose removal disconnects node X from node Y. Four A-H cuts are shown in Fig. 2-5(a):

> cut 1: AB, AE
> cut 2: AB, ED, JF, JK
> cut 3: BC, FG, KL
> cut 4: CH, LH

The number of arcs in a cut may vary from one to all the arcs in the graph.

A **minimal cut** is one in which replacement of any of its members reconnects the graph. In other words, in a minimal cut, all of the arcs are essential. The set of arcs AB, AE, and FG form an A-H cut in Fig. 2-5(a), but the cut is not minimal, because restoring arc FG does not reconnect node A to node H. As the above example shows, there may be several minimal cuts between a pair of nodes.

In a weighted graph, each cut has a **capacity**. The capacity of a cut is the sum of the weights of the arcs in the cut. In Fig. 2-5(a), the four cuts have capacities 11, 23, 10, and 12, respectively. A cut with the minimum capacity is called a **minimum cut**.

By using the concept of a cut, we can determine the mean information flow (in bits per second) in each line of a network. To keep things simple, let us start out by considering only half-duplex lines. Thus each arc will shortly acquire an arrow, indicating which way the data are moving. Either direction is

{Find the shortest path from the source to the sink of a given graph.}

const $n = ...$;   {number of nodes}
   $infinity = ...$;   {a number larger than any possible path length}

type $node = 0 .. n$;
   $nodelist = $ **array** $[1 .. n]$ **of** $node$;
   $matrix = $ **array** $[1 .. n, 1 .. n]$ **of** $integer$;

procedure $ShortestPath(a: matrix; s,t: node;$ **var** $path: nodelist)$;
{Find the shortest path from s to t in the matrix a, and return it in $path$.}

type $lab = (perm, tent)$;   {is label tentative or permanent?}
   $NodeLabel = $ **record** $predecessor: node; length: integer; labl: lab$ **end**;
   $GraphState = array[1 .. n]$ **of** $NodeLabel$;

var $state: GraphState$; $i,k: node$; $min: integer$;
begin   {initialize}
  for $i := 1$ **to** n **do**
    with $state[i]$ **do**
      begin $predecessor := 0; length := infinity; labl := tent$ **end**;
  $state[t].length := 0$; $state[t].labl :- perm$;
  $k := t$;   {k is the initial working node}

  repeat   {is there a better path from k?}
    for $i := 1$ **to** n **do**
      if $(a[k,i] <> 0)$ **and** $(state[i].labl = tent)$ **then**   {i is adjacent & tent.}
        if $state[k].length + a[k,i] < state[i].length$ **then**
          begin
            $state[i].predecessor := k$;
            $state[i].length := state[k].length + a[k,i]$
          end;

    {Find the tentatively labeled node with the smallest label.}
    $min := infinity$; $k := 0$;
    for $i := 1$ **to** n **do**
      if $(state[i].labl = tent)$ **and** $(state[i].length < min)$ **then**
        begin
          $min := state[i].length$;
          $k := i$ {unless superseded, k will be next working node}
        end;
    $state[k].labl := perm$

  until $k = s$;   {repeat until we reach the source}

  {Copy the path into the output array.}
  $k := s$; $i := 0$;
  repeat
    $i := i + 1$;
    $path[i] := k$;
    $k := state[k].predecessor$;
  until $k = 0$
end; {ShortestPath}

Fig. 2-4. A procedure to compute the shortest path through a graph.

possible, but only one at a time. The arc will be labeled with the amount of flow. Full-duplex lines can be handled by replacing each undirected arc by a pair of directed arcs, one in each direction.

Consider a possible flow of information from node A (the source) to node H (the sink) in Fig. 2-5(a). A flow is said to be **feasible** if it meets the following conditions:

1. The source has no inward arcs (data move away from the source).

2. The sink has no outward arcs (it does not emit data).

3. No arc has more flow than its capacity (but may have less).

4. The inflow and outflow balance at all nodes except source and sink.

5. The outflow at the source must equal the inflow at the sink.

If there are multiple sources and sinks, the single source-sink graphs may be linearly superimposed. Figure 2-5(b) illustrates a feasible flow for the graph of Fig. 2-5(a). There is an outflow of seven units (e.g., kbps) from the source, A, and an inflow of seven units into the sink, H. At each intermediate node, flow is conserved. For example, at node G, there is one unit of input via FG, one unit of input via LG, and two units of output via GC.

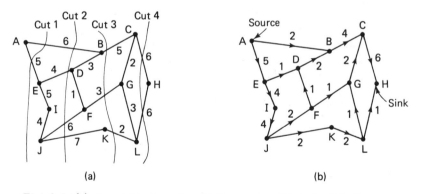

Fig. 2-5. (a) A weighted graph with four cuts. (b) A feasible flow assignment.

Although the flow of Fig. 2-5(b) is a feasible flow, it is not the maximum possible flow from A to H. Before reading further, you should try to determine the maximum feasible A-H flow by inspection of Fig. 2-5(a). Notice that it is not possible to scale the flow up linearly by multiplying the flow in each arc by the same constant, since arcs AE, GC, CH, IJ, KL and FD are already saturated.

Give up? The maximum flow can easily be found if all the cuts are known.

To see this, take a look at cut 3 (for example) in Fig. 2-5(a). To make the point clearer, the graph is redrawn as Fig. 2-6. Topologically, these two graphs are identical; they represent the same network. From Fig. 2-6 it should be obvious that all flow from node A to node H must pass through the constriction indicated by cut 3. There is no way to get any flow from the left part to the right part outside of the three arcs in the cut. Since the capacity of the cut is 10 units, there is no conceivable feasible flow pattern that can deliver more than 10 units from A to H. Any flow pattern managing to pump more data across the cut than its capacity would necessarily exceed the capacity of (at least) one of the arcs, and thus be infeasible.

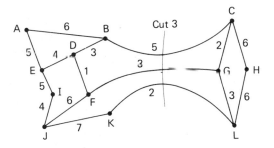

Fig. 2-6. Figure 2-5(a) redrawn.

If we were not so frugal about wasting paper, we might have provided four distorted versions of Fig. 2-5(a), one corresponding to each cut. Suffice it to say that what holds for cut 3 holds also for cuts 1, 2, and 4: no feasible A-H flow can exceed the capacity of *any* A-H cut. Because the cut with the smallest capacity forms the bottleneck, we have this important result (Ford and Fulkerson, 1962):

The maximum flow between any two arbitrary nodes in any graph cannot exceed the capacity of the minimum cut separating those two nodes.

In fact, the result is even stronger than that. It can be proven that the maximum flow is *equal* to the capacity of the minimum cut (see Frank and Frisch, 1971, for three different proofs). In other words, there is always a feasible flow that saturates the minimum cut.

To conceptualize why this is so, realize that the source is assumed capable of producing arbitrarily much flow (i.e., the flow limitation comes from the network, not from any inherent limit in the source). If the maximum flow were less than the capacity of the minimum cut, this could occur only if there were a bottleneck somewhere between the source and the cut or between the cut and the sink. One could imagine stretching the graph out in the manner of Fig. 2-6 and cutting through the bottleneck. If this new cut were saturated and had a capacity less than that of the original cut, the result still holds, only we had the wrong cut to start with. If the new cut were not saturated, then it was not really a bottleneck, because the flow could be increased. This result is widely known as the "Max-Flow Min-Cut Theorem," for obvious reasons.

2.2.3. The Max-Flow Algorithm

Although this theorem is wonderful, it does not help us much if we have no systematic way of searching for the minimum cut between a given pair of nodes. Fortunately, algorithms for finding the maximum flow and minimum cut have been a popular topic among graph theorists over the years, and several good algorithms are now known.

The max-flow algorithm we will describe is a simplified version of one published by Malhotra et al. (1978). The algorithm takes a weighted, directed graph, as input and determines the maximum feasible flow between a given source and sink. We will explain the algorithm by means of the example network of Fig. 2-7(a). In this example, between each pair of connected nodes there are two arcs, one in each direction. To keep the figure from being cluttered, we have drawn this as a single arc with two arrows.

The algorithm builds a layered network from the source, A, to the sink, F. It starts off by putting the source (alone) in layer 0. Any node connected directly to the source by a "useful" arc goes in layer 1. Any node connected to a layer 1 node by a useful arc goes in layer 2, etc. When the sink has been reached and assigned to a layer, the layering process terminates. This algorithm effectively labels each node by its distance from the source.

It is important to describe precisely what we mean by a "useful" arc. A useful (directed) arc from X to Y has either a currently assigned flow from X to Y less than the capacity or there is some flow currently assigned along the arc from Y to X. Either way, the effective (i.e., net) flow from X to Y can be augmented. In the former case by just adding more forward flow; in the latter case by canceling some reverse flow. For example, in Fig. 2-7(a) if the CD flow were 5 and the DC flow were 3, the CD arc would be useful, because the two opposing flows could be "canceled," leaving an unsaturated arc. This canceling is possible only when we are dealing with a single commodity. When there are multiple commodities, such as messages between several source-sink pairs, this canceling is not allowed.

The first layered network derived from Fig. 2-7(a) is shown in Fig. 2-7(b). Notice that the only arcs allowed are those going from layer i to layer $i + 1$. The next step is pruning off the "dead ends," those paths that do not terminate at the sink. In Fig. 2-7(b), $ABCD$, $ABGH$, IK and AJK are all dead ends. After the extraneous arcs and nodes have been pruned off, every node remaining in the layered network has one or more outgoing arcs leading to the sink and one or more incoming arcs coming from the source. In this example, only path $AILF$ survives the pruning.

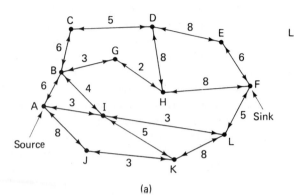

(a)

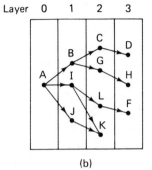

(b)

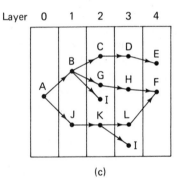

(c)

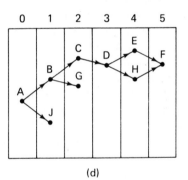

(d)

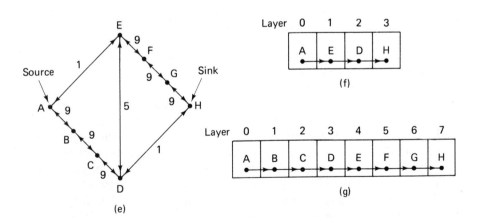

(e)

(f)

(g)

Fig. 2-7. Examples of the maximum flow algorithm.

The next step is to inspect each of the nodes in the layered network in turn to find the potential flow increase it can handle. For each outgoing arc from, say, X to Y, this is the capacity of XY minus the flow already assigned to XY, plus the flow already assigned to YX. Again realize that the net output can be increased by canceling inward flow. The total output potential is the sum of the potential of all arcs communicating with the next higher layer. The input potential can be found similarly. If, for example, the output potential is 7 and the input potential is 4, the node can accept 4 more units of flow through it (i.e., it has sufficient input capacity and sufficient output capacity).

The layered network node with the smallest potential is called the **reference node**. Its potential is called the **reference potential**. Neither the source nor the sink is eligible to be the reference node. In Fig. 2-7(b), I has an input potential of 3 and an output potential of 3, so its potential is 3. L has a potential $=$ $\min(3, 5) = 3$. The reference node is either I or L, both with reference potential 3.

The next step of the max-flow algorithm is to start at the reference node and push a flow equal to the reference potential forward toward the sink. More than one arc may be used if need be. The pushing is recursive, so when flow is pushed into a node, it must be pushed out again in the direction of the sink. Only the sink can accept extra flow without getting rid of it. In exactly the same way, we can then start at the reference node and pull (borrow) flow from the input side. It is always possible to push and pull the requisite quantity of flow from the reference node, because every other node in the layered network has at least as much potential, both input and output. It is never possible to get "stuck" in a dead end with flow that cannot be disposed of.

As a result of the previous steps, we have augmented the flow in selected arcs. We now repeat the entire process, starting with a new layered network. Figure 2-7(c) shows the next layered network. Arc AI is no longer useful because it is saturated and there is no reverse flow. After pruning, only two paths will remain: $ABGHF$ and $AJKLF$. The reference node is H (G would do equally well) and the reference potential is 2. The effect of pushing and pulling flow is to add two units to all the arcs in the path $ABGHF$. The following layered network is just the path $AJKLF$ with reference node K and reference potential 3. After that we get the layered network of Fig. 2-7(d), with reference node D and reference potential 5.

The cycle of building a layered network, finding the reference node, and augmenting the flow continues until it is not possible to build a layered network (i.e., there is no useful path from source to sink). When this happens, the current flow is the maximum flow, and the set of saturated arcs form a cut set.

Figure 2-7(e) depicts a network in which reverse flow must be pushed back to arrive at the final solution. The initial layered network is shown in Fig. 2-7(f). The first augmentation assigns 1 unit to arcs AE, ED, and DH. The next layered network is that of Fig. 2-7(g). The reference node is E and the reference potential is 6. The 6 is arrived at by adding the 5 unused capacity units from the arc *DE* to the 1 unit available by pushing the *ED* flow back to *E* and rerouting it via *FGH*. The final flow is 7 units, 5 via *ABCDEFGH*, 1 via *AEFGH*, and 1 via *ABCDH*.

A procedure to carry out the max-flow algorithm is given in Fig. 2-8. Both the capacities and the flows are represented in matrix form, for pedagogical, not efficiency reasons. The body of the procedure operates as we have described, first trying to build a layered network (including the pruning of the dead ends by *walk*), then finding the reference node *FindRefNode*, and finally by augmenting the flow in both directions from the reference node (*PushPull*). One point worth commenting on is how the pruning is done. The procedure *LayeringPossible* assigns negative numbers to nodes as it builds the layered network. The procedure *walk* then traverses the layered network starting at the sink, negating the layer numbers as it visits the nodes. When it is finished, nodes that are still negative are not reachable from the sink, and hence not part of the layered network.

As a last point, it should be pointed out that it is not necessary to rebuild the layered network until all paths from source to sink have been saturated. After having found the reference node, a check should be made to see if another node with nonzero potential can be found. In Fig. 2-7(c), for example, there are clearly two paths. However, when doing it this way, newly saturated arcs and newly unreachable nodes must be deleted before seeking the next reference node. Details are given in Malhotra et al. We have not used this method, even though it is computationally more efficient, due to the extra complexity associated with removing saturated arcs and nodes from the existing layered network. For a real application, however (as opposed to our pedagogical purposes), finding all the paths in a layered network is worth the trouble.

2.2.4. Disjoint Paths

We will now show how the max-flow min-cut theorem can be used to analyze network topologies for reliability. Our interest is in networks that can sustain the loss of one or more lines or IMPs without becoming disconnected. First we will consider the case of lines, and then the case of IMPs.

Let us define the **arc connectivity** between two nodes *X* and *Y* as the minimum number of arcs that must be removed from the graph to disconnect *X* and *Y*. In other words, the arc connectivity between two nodes is just the size of their minimum cut set. In Fig. 2-9(a), the *A*-*F* arc connectivity is 2, and the *A*-*C* arc connectivity is 3.

To calculate the arc connectivity between two nodes, we need to introduce the idea of arc-disjoint paths. Two paths are said to be **arc-disjoint** if they have no arcs in common. Arc-disjoint paths may have nodes in common, however. For example, the paths *ACF* and *ABCDEF* in Fig. 2-9(a) have no common arcs, but they do share the node *C*.

{Compute the maximum flow in a network.}

const $n = ...$;
    $unscanned = -n$;
    $infinity = ...$;

type $node = 1 .. n$;
    $xnode = -n .. n$;
    $vector = $ **array**$[node]$ **of** $xnode$;
    $matrix = $ **array**$[node, node]$ **of** $real$;
    $WhichWay = (push, pull)$;

procedure $MaxFlow(s, t$: $node$; c: $matrix$; **var** f: $matrix)$;
var $RefNode$: $node$;   {node with least excess capacity}
   $MinPotential$: $real$;   {excess capacity of the reference node}
   $layer$: $vector$;   {the layered network is defined by this array}
   i, j: $node$;   {indices}

function $min(x, y$: $real)$:$real$; **begin if** $x < y$ **then** $min := x$ **else** $min := y$ **end**;

procedure $walk(i$: $node)$;
{Traverse the layered network from t, inverting layer numbers.}
var j: $node$; li: $xnode$;
begin
   $layer[i] := -layer[i]$;
   $li := layer[i]$;
   for $j := 1$ **to** n **do**
     if $(j <> s)$ **and** $(-layer[j] = li - 1)$ **and** $((f[j,i] < c[j,i])$ **or** $(f[i,j] > 0))$
       then $walk(j)$
end; {$walk$}

function $LayeringPossible$: $boolean$;
{Is it possible to build a layered network? If so, build it.}
var i, j: $node$; k: $0 .. n$; $EmptyLayer$: $boolean$;
begin $k := 0$;   {k keeps track of layer being built}
   for $i := 1$ **to** n **do** $layer[i] := unscanned$; {initialize each node}
   $layer[s] := k$;   {source node is in layer 0}

   repeat
     $k := k + 1$;   {now locate all nodes in layer k}
     $EmptyLayer := true$;   {an empty layer stops the algorithm}
     for $i := 1$ **to** n **do**
       if $-layer[i] = k - 1$ **then**
        {i is in layer $k - 1$, its neighbors may be in layer k.}
        for $j := 1$ **to** n **do**   {check each node adjacent to i}
          if $(layer[j] = unscanned)$ **and** $((f[i,j] < c[i,j])$ **or** $(f[j,i] > 0))$
           then begin $layer[j] := -k$; $EmptyLayer := false$ **end**;
   until $(layer[t] <> unscanned)$ **or** $EmptyLayer$;
   $LayeringPossible := $ **not** $EmptyLayer$;
   $walk(t)$ {prune off the dead ends}
end; {$LayeringPossible$}

procedure *FindRefNode*(*i*: *node*);
{Traverse the layered network from *t*, seeking the reference node.}
var *j*: *node*; *li*,*lj*: *xnode*; *InCap*,*OutCap*: *real*;
begin
  li := *layer*[*i*];   *InCap* := 0;   *OutCap* := 0;
  for *j* := 1 **to** *n* **do**   {examine each node adjacent to *i*}
    begin *lj* := *layer*[*j*];
      if (*lj* = *li* − 1) **and** (*j* <> *s*) **and** ((*f*[*j*,*i*] < *c*[*j*,*i*]) **or** (*f*[*i*,*j*] > 0))
        then *FindRefNode*(*j*);
      if *lj* = *li* − 1 **then** *InCap* := *InCap* + (*c*[*j*,*i*] − *f*[*j*,*i*]) + *f*[*i*,*j*];
      if *lj* = *li* + 1 **then** *OutCap* := *OutCap* + (*c*[*i*,*j*] − *f*[*i*,*j*]) + *f*[*j*,*i*]
    end;

  if (*i* <> *s*) **and** (*i* <> *t*) **and** (*min*(*InCap*,*OutCap*) < *MinPotential*) **then**
    {Node *i* has a smaller potential than the current reference node.}
    begin *MinPotential* := *min*(*InCap*,*OutCap*); *RefNode* := *i* **end**
end; {*FindRefNode*}

procedure *PushPull*(*i*: *node*; *FlowLeft*: *real*; *p*: *WhichWay*);
{Augment the flow through *i* by pushing or pulling *MinPotential* units.}
var *j*,*k1*,*k2*,*LayerSought*: 0 .. *n*; *r*: *real*;
begin *j* := 0;

  while (*FlowLeft* > 0) **and** (*j* < *n*) **do**
    begin *j* := *j* + 1;
      if *p* = *push*
        then begin *k1* := *i*;   *k2* := *j*;   *LayerSought* := *layer*[*i*] + 1 **end**
        else begin *k1* := *j*;   *k2* := *i*;   *LayerSought* := *layer*[*i*] − 1 **end**;
      r := *min*(*FlowLeft*, *c*[*k1*,*k2*] − *f*[*k1*,*k2*] + *f*[*k2*,*k1*]); {am't of flow to move}
      if (*r* > 0) **and** (*layer*[*j*] = *LayerSought*) **then**
        begin   {push/pull some flow to/from an adjacent layer}
          FlowLeft := *FlowLeft* − *r*;
          f[*k1*,*k2*] := *f*[*k1*,*k2*] + *r* − *min*(*r*,*f*[*k2*,*k1*]);   {augment positive flow}
          f[*k2*,*k1*] := *f*[*k2*,*k1*] − *min*(*r*, *f*[*k2*,*k1*]);   {push reverse flow bkwrd}
          if (*j* <> *s*) **and** (*j* <> *t*) **then** *PushPull*(*j*,*r*,*p*)
        end
    end
end; {*PushPull*}

begin
  for *i* := 1 **to** *n* **do for** *j* := 1 **to** *n* **do** *f*[*i*,*j*] := 0;   {initially no flow}
  f[*s*,*t*] := *c*[*s*,*t*];   {if an *s*-*t* link exists, saturate it}
  while *LayeringPossible* **do**   {assign nodes to layers}
    begin *MinPotential* := *infinity*;
      FindRefNode(*t*);   {find the reference node}
      PushPull(*RefNode*, *MinPotential*, *push*);   {push flow toward *t*}
      PushPull(*RefNode*, *MinPotential*, *pull*);   {pull flow from *s*}
    end
end; {*MaxFlow*}

Fig. 2-8. A procedure for computing the maximum flow.

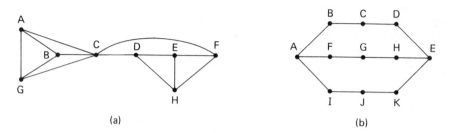

Fig. 2-9. (a) A graph with node connectivity 1, arc connectivity 2, and degree 3. (b) Three node-disjoint paths from A to E.

The importance of arc-disjoint paths to network reliability is based on the observation that if there are k arc-disjoint paths between X and Y, then at least k arcs must be removed from the graph to disconnect the nodes. This intuitive result is illustrated in Fig. 2-9(b). There are three arc-disjoint paths from A to E here, and separating these nodes requires deleting at least one arc on each of the paths.

To calculate the number of arc-disjoint paths between a given pair of nodes we can use the max-flow min-cut theorem. First replace the weights on the arcs, if any, with a weight of one on each arc. Now compute the maximum flow between the given nodes, used as source and sink. The resulting flow, which is equal to the number of arcs in the minimum cut, is also equal to the number of disjoint paths between the nodes.

To understand why this result holds, notice that flow splitting, such as that shown in node F of Fig. 2-5(b) is impossible because all arcs have unit weight, and the max-flow algorithm always finds a reference potential that is integral. For the same reason, flow combination, such as occurs at node G in Fig. 2-5(b) is also impossible. Each utilized arc emerging from the source is the start of a unique path crossing the minimum cut and ending at the sink. Conceptually one could follow each of these paths, painting each one a different color. Since each path must cross the minimum cut at some point, the number of arc-disjoint paths is just equal to the number of arcs in that cut.

Now let us define the arc connectivity of the graph as a whole, C_a, as the minimum of the arc connectivities of all pairs of nodes. If the most tenuously connected pair of nodes have only k arc-disjoint paths connecting them, then the graph has a connectivity of k (i.e., the graph is k-connected). It is possible to calculate the arc connectivity of a graph in a straightforward way. Just calculate the arc connectivity for each pair of nodes and take the minimum value found. An alternative method, computationally more efficient, will be discussed later.

Analogous to the arc connectivity between two nodes, the **node connectivity** is the minimum number of nodes whose removal will disconnect the two

nodes. If the two nodes have an arc linking them, there is no way to disconnect them by removing nodes, not even by removing all $n - 2$ of the remaining nodes in an n node graph. In this case the node connectivity is defined as
$n - 1$. Also, similar to the case of arc connectivities, the node connectivity of
the graph as a whole, C_n, is the minimum taken over all pairs of nodes.

To determine the node connectivity of a graph, we need an algorithm for
finding the node connectivity between a given pair of nodes. Fortunately, the
max-flow algorithm can be pressed into service once again. The basic idea is to
convert the problem of finding node-disjoint paths into an equivalent problem
involving arc-disjoint paths.

If there is an arc between the two given nodes, the graph can withstand the
loss of any number of intermediate nodes, in which case the node connectivity
is just $n - 1$, as mentioned above. If not, take the original (undirected) graph,
with its n nodes and a arcs, and convert it into a directed graph with $2n$ nodes
and $2a + n$ arcs. Each node, X, is replaced by a pair of nodes, X and X', with
a directed arc from X to X'. No arc goes from X' to X. If a node Y was connected to X in the original, we have the two arcs $Y'X$ and $X'Y$ in the modified
graph. In other words, all incoming arcs are attached to X and all outgoing arcs
are attached to X'.

The newly introduced arcs each have unit weight, and the original arcs are
removed. The modified graph is now complete. Figure 2-10(a) shows an
undirected graph. The modified graph produced from it is shown in Fig. 2-
10(b).

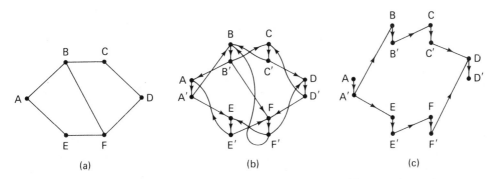

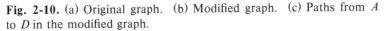

Fig. 2-10. (a) Original graph. (b) Modified graph. (c) Paths from A
to D in the modified graph.

All that remains to find the number of node-disjoint paths between the
source and sink is to run the max-flow algorithm. The maximum flow found is
equal to the number of node-disjoint paths. The reason this works is plain:
each unit weight arc can have only one path passing through it, and hence no
original node may be on two or more paths. Each path found by the max-flow

algorithm passes through a set of nodes not used by any other path. Figure 2-10(c) shows the two node-disjoint paths from A (actually A') to D found in this way.

Network designers are often confronted with the problem of whether or not a proposed network is k arc-connected or k node-connected. One way of solving the problem is just calculating the arc connectivity or node connectivity as described above and taking the minimum over all pairs of nodes. The trouble with this method is that if the network has n nodes, $n(n-1)/2$ applications of the maximum flow algorithm are needed. For large networks, this much computation is infeasible, even on large computers. Fortunately, more efficient methods are known, which we describe next.

We consider only the case of node connectivity, because that is a stronger requirement than considering arc connectivity. To see this, imagine that the reverse were true, for example, there existed some graph that could be disconnected by removing three arcs, but could not be disconnected by removing any set of three nodes. One could find the three arc cut set, and instead of removing the arcs, remove one node attached to each arc. Since removing a node also implies removing all its incident arcs, the three arc cut set would also be removed, disconnecting the graph. Since assuming that $C_n > C_a$ leads to a contradiction, it must be false. This result is part of a theorem due to Whitney (1932), which states: $C_n \leq C_a \leq d$, where d is the minimum degree taken over all nodes in the graph. That $C_a > d$ also leads to a contradiction can be easily seen by noting that any node of degree d can be isolated by removing fewer than C_a arcs, namely only d arcs.

Now let us get back to our problem of determining whether or not a given graph can withstand the loss of k nodes and remain connected. If a graph can withstand the loss of k nodes, it can also withstand the loss of k arcs, by Whitney's theorem. An algorithm due to Kleitman (1969) is as follows. Pick any node at random and call it N_1. Verify that the node connectivity between N_1 and every other node in the graph is at least $k+1$.

Now delete N_1 and all its attached arcs from the graph and choose another node, N_2. Verify that this node has at least a node connectivity of k with every other node. Next, remove N_2 and its attached arcs from the graph, and choose a third node, N_3. Verify that N_3 has at least a node connectivity of $k-1$ with each of the remaining nodes. Continue this process until you have verified that some node N_{k+1} is 1-connected to all nodes of the remaining graph. At this point the algorithm terminates.

As an example, suppose that we are presented with a network of 1000 nodes and are asked to prove that it can sustain the loss of four IMPs or lines and remain connected. We first pick a node and show that there are at least five node-disjoint paths to each of the 999 other nodes. If this node is among the 996 surviving nodes, the graph remains connected because every node can still communicate with every other node via N_1. If N_1 is among the four damaged nodes but N_2 is not, communication is still possible. We know there are four node-disjoint paths from N_2 to every other node, and that at least one of the missing nodes (N_1) does not occur on any of these four paths. Similarly, if N_1 and N_2 are both lost, we are guaranteed that N_3 has at least three node-disjoint paths to all other nodes, with only two of the bad nodes as yet unaccounted for. If N_1, N_2, and N_3 are all down, communication is still possible via N_4 because it is 2-connected to every node, and three of the four bad nodes are known not to interfere with any of its paths.

S. Even (1975) has devised another way to check for connectivity k. Number the nodes 1, 2, ..., n and then proceed as follows.

1. Form the subset consisting of the nodes 1, 2, ..., k. Check to see that each node in the subset has k node-disjoint paths to each of the other nodes in the subset. If this step succeeds, continue with step 2; otherwise, stop: the graph obviously does not have k node-disjoint paths between all pairs of nodes.

2. For each node, j, $k < j \leqslant n$, perform the following operations.
   (a) Form the subset $L = 1, 2, ..., j - 1$.
   (b) Add a new node X and connect it to each node in L.
   (c) Verify that there are k node-disjoint paths between j and X.

If for some j step 2 fails, the graph does not have k node-disjoint paths between all pairs of nodes; otherwise, it does. For a proof that this algorithm is correct, we refer you to Even's paper.

As an example of its use, we wish to see if the graph of Fig. 2-11(a) is 3-connected. Let us choose as the initial subset nodes A, B, and C. We first establish that there are three node-disjoint paths between each pair of these nodes:

A-B: AB, ACB, $AEFB$

A-C: AC, ABC, $AEDC$

B-C: BC, BAC, $BFDC$

Next we set $j = 4$ (node D) and form the set $L = \{A, B, C\}$, as shown in Fig. 2-11(b), and demonstrate the existence of three node-disjoint paths from D to X. In effect this is showing that there are three node-disjoint paths into the set $\{A, B, C\}$, which is already known to be internally 3-connected. The next two steps use $L = \{A, B, C, D\}$ and $L = \{A, B, C, D, E\}$ respectively, as shown.

For small k and large n, Even's algorithm requires n applications of the max-flow algorithm, whereas Kleitman's algorithm requires kn applications of the max-flow algorithm. Under normal circumstances, k is two or three, and n can range from tens of nodes to hundreds or even thousands of nodes, so Even's algorithm is two or three times faster.

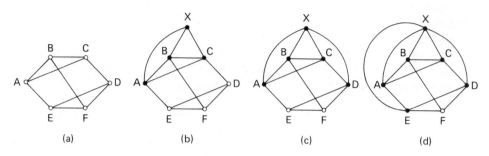

Fig. 2-11. (a) A graph. (b)-(d) Application of Even's algorithm.

2.2.5. Monte Carlo Connectivity Analysis

Kleitman's algorithm and Even's algorithm are mostly useful for analyzing the worst-case behavior of a network. For example, in a military command and control network, where the enemy is assumed to have precise knowledge of the topology, he will always strike where the network is weakest. For most applications however, it is neither necessary nor desirable that the connectivity of all IMPs be the same. The designers may be willing to have West Podunk be 1-connected, but may insist that New York be 5-connected.

With large, irregular networks, our only recourse is to simulation. A straightforward but nevertheless useful model is one in which time is divided up into uniform intervals. During each interval a link (or IMP) is either up or down, but not partly up and partly down. The probability of a link failing during any interval is p.

There are several possible metrics that can be used for network reliability. The simplest is just whether or not the network is connected. For this metric the simulation output is the probability of disconnection as a function of p. Another useful metric is the fraction of IMPs that can still communicate, again as a function of p. For many applications it may be tolerable that under normal operating conditions 99.9% (or some other percentage) of the IMP pairs can communicate.

The program of Fig. 2-12 computes the fraction of IMPs unable to communicate for various values of p. It also computes the probability that the network becomes disconnected. The assumption is that only lines fail, never IMPs, although the same principle can be used for simulating IMP failures or mixed failures. After reading in the data specifying how many simulation runs to make for each value of p, which values of p to use, and the graph (in matrix form), the program performs one simulation run on the given graph with a given p. Each arc in the graph is inspected. If a random number whose probability density function is uniform between 0.0 and 1.0 is less than p, the arc is deleted.

After the arc deletion phase is completed, we check to see which pairs of

{Check for the connectedness of a topology subject to line failures.}

program *ReliabiltySimulation* (*input*, *output*);

const $n = \ldots$;

type *matrix* = *array* [1 .. n, 1 .. n] **of** *boolean*;
var *max*, *nrounds*, *np*, *ip*, *discon*, *i*, *j*, *k*, *nr*: *integer*;
　　　　p, *NumDiscon*, *FracDiscon*, *pincr*, *seed*: *real*;
　　　　a, *b*: *matrix*;

function *random*: *real*;　　　　　　{random number from 0.0 to 1.0}
begin
　　seed := 125.0 ∗ (*seed* + 1.0);
　　seed := *seed* − 8192.0 ∗ *trunc* (*seed*/8192);
　　random := (*seed* + 0.5)/8192
end; {*random*}

begin
　　max := n ∗ (n − 1) **div** 2;　　　　{number of possible communicating pairs}
　　read (*nrounds*, *p*, *pincr*, *np*, *seed*);　　　{input data}
　　for i := 1 **to** n **do for** j := 1 **to** n **do**
　　　begin *read* (*k*); **if** $k = 0$ **then** $a[i,j] := false$ **else** $a[i,j] := true$ **end**;

　　for *ip* := 1 **to** *np* **do**　　　　　　{loop, increasing *p* each time}
　　　begin
　　　　NumDiscon := 0;　　　　　　{number of disconnected networks}
　　　　FracDiscon := 0;　　　　　　{fraction of disconnected pairs}
　　　　for *nr* := 1 **to** *nrounds* **do**　　{make multiple simulations per value of *p*}
　　　　　begin
　　　　　　b := *a*;　　　　　　　{copy the entire array *a* to *b*}
　　　　　　for i := 1 **to** n **do**　　　{destroy links at random}
　　　　　　　for j := i + 1 **to** n **do**
　　　　　　　　if $b[i,j]$ **then**
　　　　　　　　　if *random* < *p* **then begin** $b[i,j] := false$; $b[j,i] := false$ **end**;

　　　　　　for i := 1 **to** n **do**　　　{compute connectivity of the graph}
　　　　　　　for j := 1 **to** n **do**
　　　　　　　　if $b[j,i]$ **then for** k := 1 **to** n **do** $b[j,k] := b[j,k]$ **or** $b[i,k]$;

　　　　　　{Check to see how many pairs are still connected.}
　　　　　　discon := 0;　　　　　　{count disconnected pairs}
　　　　　　for i := 1 **to** n **do**
　　　　　　　for j := i + 1 **to** n **do**
　　　　　　　　if not $b[i,j]$ **then** *discon* := *discon* + 1;

　　　　　　FracDiscon := *FracDiscon* + *discon*/*max*;
　　　　　　if *discon* > 0 **then** *NumDiscon* := *NumDiscon* + 1.0
　　　　　end;

　　　　writeln (*p*: 6:2, *FracDiscon*/*nrounds*: 6:2, *NumDiscon*/*nrounds*: 6:2);
　　　　p := *p* + *pincr*　　　　　　{increase *p* to next value}
　　end
end.

Fig. 2-12. A program for computing network reliability by simulation.

nodes are connected. Note that there are only $n(n-1)/2$ possible communicating pairs in an undirected graph. We do not count the diagonal elements.

Figure 2-13 gives an example of how the reliability simulation could be used. Imagine that the network of Fig. 2-13(a) exists. The network operators feel that the reliability is inadequate and want to add some new links to reduce the disconnection probability. Since it is uneconomical to add links that will never be used, just to increase the connectivity, a study is made of where links are needed for traffic carrying purposes. It turns out that *FD*, *AJ*, *IC*, and *BH* are the best candidates, in that order. The question is: How many of these should be added to ensure a network disconnection probability of less than 1%, even if the failure rate on all the links is a pessimistic 5%? From Fig. 2-13(b) we see that the addition of *FD*, *AJ*, and *IC* will do the job.

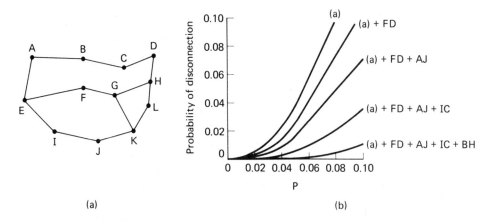

(a)   (b)

Fig. 2-13. (a) A network. (b) Probability of the network becoming disconnected as a function of link reliability.

2.3. DELAY ANALYSIS

In many design situations, there are two major constraints: reliability and delay. We have just examined reliability; now we examine delay. When network traffic is light, packet delay is primarily due to the time each IMP needs to store and forward the packet. If the distances are long, propagation delay may also play a role. However, as traffic increases, the principal delay becomes the queueing delay within each IMP, as packets must wait their turn to be sent out on a heavily used line. Consequently, our analysis of network delay will be based on a queueing theory model. In the following sections we derive the basic queueing theory results we will need later. For a more detailed treatment of the application of queueing theory to networks, see (Kleinrock, 1976).

2.3.1. Introduction to Queueing Theory

Queueing systems can be used to model processes in which customers arrive, wait their turn for service, are serviced, and then depart. Supermarket checkout stands, World Series ticket booths, and doctor's waiting rooms are examples of queueing systems. Queueing systems can be characterized by five components:

1. The interarrival-time probability density function.

2. The service-time probability density function.

3. The number of servers.

4. The queueing discipline.

5. The amount of buffer space in the queues.

It is worth explicitly noting that we are considering only systems with an infinite number of customers (i.e., the existence of a long queue does not so deplete the population of customers that the input rate is materially reduced). (In contrast, in a time-sharing system model, there are only a finite number of customers. If half of them are waiting for a response, the input rate will be significantly reduced.)

The interarrival-time probability density describes the interval between consecutive arrivals. One could imagine hiring someone (e.g., a graduate student, since they do not cost much), to watch customers arrive. At each arrival the graduate student would record the elapsed time since the previous arrival. After a sufficiently long sampling time, the list of numbers could be sorted and grouped: so many interarrival times of 0.1 sec, so many of 0.2 sec, etc. This probability density characterizes the arrival process.

Each customer requires a certain amount of the server's time. The amount of service time varies from customer to customer (e.g., one has a full shopping cart of groceries and the next has only a small box of peanut butter cookies). To analyze a queueing system, the service-time probability density function, like the interarrival density function, must be known.

The number of servers speaks for itself. Many banks, for example, have one big queue for all customers. Whenever a teller is free, the customer at the front of the queue goes directly to that teller. Such a system is a multiserver queueing system. In other banks, each teller has his or her own private queue. In this case we have a collection of independent single-server queues, not a multiserver system.

The queueing discipline describes the order in which customers are taken from the queue. Supermarkets use first come, first served. Hospital emergency rooms often use sickest first rather than first come, first served. In friendly office environments, shortest job first prevails at the photocopy machine.

Not all queueing systems have an infinite amount of buffer space. When too many customers are queued up for a finite number of slots, some customers get lost or rejected.

We will concentrate exclusively on infinite-buffer, single-server systems using first come, first served. The notation A/B/m is widely used in the queueing literature for these systems, where A is the interarrival-time probability density, B the service-time probability density, and m the number of servers. The probability densities A and B are chosen from the set

M - exponential probability density (M stands for Markov)
D - all customers have the same value (D is for deterministic)
G - general (i.e., arbitrary probability density)

The state of the art ranges from the M/M/1 system, about which everything is known, to the G/G/m system, for which no exact analytic solution is yet known.

Throughout this book we use queuing theory as one of our basic tools to analyze network performance. In particular, we usually assume the M/M/1 model. The assumption of an exponential interarrival probability is completely reasonably for any system that has a large number of independent customers. Under such conditions, the probability of exactly n customers arriving during an interval of length t is given by the Poisson law:

$$P_n(t) = \frac{(\lambda t)^n}{n!} e^{-\lambda t} \tag{2-1}$$

where λ is the mean arrival rate. (See Problem 2-6 for a derivation of the Poisson law.)

Now we will show that Poisson arrivals generate an exponential interarrival probability density. The probability, $a(t)\Delta t$, that an interarrival interval is between t and $t + \Delta t$ is just the probability of no arrivals for a time t times the probability of one arrival in the infinitesimal interval Δt:

$$a(t)\Delta t = P_0(t)P_1(\Delta t)$$

$P_0(t)$ is $e^{-\lambda t}$, and $P_1(\Delta t)$ is $\lambda \Delta t e^{-\lambda \Delta t}$. In the limit $\Delta t \to 0$, the exponential factor in P_1 approaches unity, so

$$a(t)\, dt = \lambda e^{-\lambda t}\, dt \tag{2-2}$$

Note that the integral of Eq. (2-2) from 0 to ∞ is 1, as it should be.

Although the assumption of an exponential interarrival probability density is usually reasonable, the assumption of exponential services times is harder to defend on general grounds. Nevertheless, for situations in which increasingly long service times are increasingly less likely, M/M/1 may be an adequate approximation. We leave it to the reader to show that if the probability of service finishing in some small time interval Δt is $\mu \Delta t$, then the service-time probability density function is $\mu e^{-\mu t}$, with a mean service time of $1/\mu$ sec/customer.

2.3.2. The M/M/1 Queue in Equilibrium

The state of an M/M/1 queueing system (see Fig. 2-14) is completely described by telling how many customers are currently in the system, including both queue and server. At first you might think that it would also be necessary to describe how far along the customer currently being served was, but the exponential density function has no memory: the probability of the remaining service time requiring t seconds is independent of how much service the customer has already received! The exponential function is the only one with this remarkable property, which is why queueing theorists love it so much.

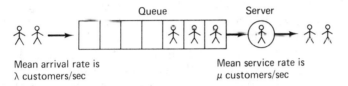

Fig. 2-14. A single-server queueing system with four customers, one in service and three in the queue.

Let p_k be the equilibrium probability that there are exactly k customers in the system (queue + server). Once we have derived these probabilities we can find the mean number of customers in the system, the expected waiting time, and other statistical properties of the system. Even when the system is in equilibrium, transitions between states take place. If the system is in state 4 (i.e., four customers in the system) and a new customer arrives, the system moves into state 5. Similarly, when a customer receives his desired service, the system moves down one state. Queueing systems in which the only transitions are to adjacent states are known in the trade as **birth-death systems**.

Figure 2-15 shows the states for a single-server queueing system, with the allowed transitions indicated by arrows. To analyze this system, we must know how many of each transition occur per second. If the mean arrival rate is λ customers/sec, the mean number of transitions/sec from state 0 to state 1 is λp_0. Suppose, for example, that 40 customers/sec arrive, there is a 20% chance of finding the system in state 0 (empty), and a 15% chance of finding the system in state 1 (one customer being served, queue empty). There will be eight transitions from 0 to 1 each second on the average, and six transitions from 1 to 2. In general, the transition rate from state k to state $k + 1$ is λp_k.

Similarly, if the server is capable of processing μ customers/sec the transition rate from state $k + 1$ to state k is μp_{k+1}. Note that the transition rate is the completion rate times the probability of the system being in the initial state,

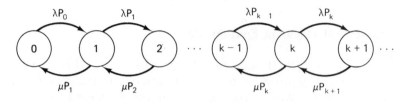

Fig. 2-15. State diagram for a single-server queueing system. The transition rates are shown as labels on the arrows.

not the final state. If you want to know how many transitions per second happen from state 4 to state 3, you need to know what the probability is of finding the system in state 4. You do not need to know what the state 3 probability is.

In equilibrium the probability of finding the system in a given state does not change with time. In particular, the probability of there being more than k customers in the system is constant. The transition from k to $k + 1$ increases this probability, and the transition from $k + 1$ to k decreases it. Therefore, these two transitions must occur at the same rate. If this were not so, the system would not be in equilibrium. If there were many transitions from, say, 4 to 5, but few transitions from 5 to 4, the mean number of customers in states above 4 would increase in time, violating our assumption about the system being in equilibrium. This principle, sometimes referred to as the principle of **detailed balancing**, is the key to solving for the state probabilities.

Looking at Fig. 2-15, we see that

$$\lambda p_0 = \mu p_1 \tag{2-3}$$

$$\lambda p_1 = \mu p_2 \tag{2-4}$$

and in general,

$$\lambda p_k = \mu p_{k+1} \tag{2-5}$$

Using Eq. (2-3), we can solve for p_1 in terms of p_0. Using Eq. (2-4), we can solve for p_2 in terms of p_1 and then use the previous result to get p_2 in terms of p_0. The solution for the general case can be found be repeating this process, yielding

$$p_k = \rho^k p_0 \tag{2-6}$$

where we have introduced $\rho = \lambda/\mu$. The variable ρ is known as the **traffic intensity**. It must be less than 1. Queueing systems that receive input faster than the server can process it are inherently unstable, and their queues grow without bound.

To eliminate p_0 from Eq. (2-6), we use the fact that the probabilities must sum to 1:

$$\sum_{k=0}^{\infty} \rho^k p_0 = 1$$

Using the well-known formula for the sum of a geometric series,

$$\sum_{k=0}^{\infty} \rho^k = \frac{1}{1 - \rho} \qquad (2\text{-}7)$$

we find that $p_0 = 1 - \rho$, and finally

$$p_k = (1 - \rho)\rho^k \qquad (2\text{-}8)$$

Notice that $\rho = 1 - p_0$ is just the probability that the system is not empty (i.e., the probability that the server is busy).

The mean number of customers in the system, N, can now be found directly from the state probabilities, Eq. (2-8):

$$N = \sum_{k=0}^{\infty} k p_k = (1 - \rho) \sum_{k=0}^{\infty} k\rho^k$$

The value of the summation can be found by differentiating both sides of Eq. (2-7) with respect to ρ and then multiplying through by ρ. Using this result, we find the mean number of customers in the system to be

$$N = \frac{\rho}{1 - \rho} \qquad (2\text{-}9)$$

As ρ approaches 1, the queue length grows very quickly.

Having found the mean number of customers in the system, we are now ready to determine the total waiting time, T, the mean interval between customer arrival and customer departure, including service time. Imagine that our friend the graduate student stops recording interarrival times once in a while, and in a fit of pique paints one of the customers shocking pink. The pink customers progress along like the other customers and are eventually disgorged from the system. Since the pink customers are in the system for an average time T (the mean time for all customers), the mean number of new arrivals subsequent to the arrival of a pink customer and just prior to his own departure is λT. This result follows directly from the fact that the arrival rate is λ customers/sec. At the instant of the pink customer's departure, all λT of these customers, and no others, are in the system. Since the mean number of customers in the system at any time is N, we have the basic result: $N = \lambda T$. This equation was first proven by D. C. Little (1961) and is known as **Little's result**.

Using Little's result and Eq. (2-9), we can now find the total waiting time, including service time:

$$T = \frac{N}{\lambda} = \frac{\rho/\lambda}{1 - \rho} = \frac{1/\mu}{1 - \rho} = \frac{1}{\mu - \lambda} \qquad (2\text{-}10)$$

This key result will be the basis of our network delay analysis.

As an example of Eq. (2-10), consider a public birdbath at which birds arrive according to a Poisson distribution. The mean arrival rate is 3 birds/min. The bathing time is exponentially distributed with a mean of 10 sec/bird. How long does a bird have to wait in the queue? The mean arrival rate is $\lambda = 0.05$ customer/sec. The mean service rate is $\mu = 0.10$ customer/sec. From Eq. (2-10) we find that $T = 20$ sec for waiting plus service. Since the mean service-time $(1/\mu)$ is 10 sec, the mean queueing time is then $20 - 10 = 10$ sec.

For the sake of generality, we will state, but not derive, the formula for the mean number of customers in the system for an M/G/1 queueing system:

$$N = \rho + \rho^2 \frac{1 + C_b^2}{2(1 - \rho)} \tag{2-11}$$

where C_b is the ratio of the standard deviation to the mean of the service time probability density function. This result, known as the **Pollaczek-Khinchine** equation, is valid for any service-time distribution. It shows that if two service-time distributions have equal means, the one with the larger standard deviation will produce a longer waiting time. For the Poisson distribution, upon which M/M/1 is based, $C_b = 1$.

2.3.3. Networks of M/M/1 Queues

The results derived above for the M/M/1 queue can be directly applied to the problem of finding the queueing delay for packets in an IMP. But first it is convenient to change the notation slightly to convert the units of service time from customers/sec to bits/sec. Let the probability density function for packet size in bits be $\mu e^{-\mu x}$ with a mean of $1/\mu$ bits/packet. Now introduce the capacity of communication channel i as C_i bits/sec. The product μC_i is then the service rate in packets/sec. The arrival rate for channel i is λ_i packets/sec. Equation (2-10) can now be rewritten for channel i as

$$T_i = \frac{1}{\mu C_i - \lambda_i} \tag{2-12}$$

where T_i includes both queueing and transmission time, as can be seen by taking the limit $\lambda_i \rightarrow 0$. Notice that the mean packet size does not depend on the channel, as the capacity and input rate do. This application of queueing theory to a communication channel was first due to Kleinrock (1964).

One problem that we face in a network is that the communication channels are not isolated. The output of one channel becomes the input to another. Several lines may converge upon a single IMP dumping packets there. Thus the input to a certain line is no longer a Poisson process outside the network, but the sum of the outputs of several other network lines. Fortunately, it has been shown (Burke, 1956) that if the outputs of several M/M/1 servers feed into the input queue of another server, the resulting input process is also a Poisson process, with mean equal to the sum of the means of the feeding processes. Even better, Jackson (1957) has shown that an open network of M/M/1 queues can be analyzed as though each one were isolated from all the others. All you need to know is the mean input rate.

However, there is still one obstacle in our way. When a packet moves around the network, it maintains its size, of course. This property introduces nonrandom correlations into the system. When a big monster packet comes along, it takes a long time to service, hence causing a noticeable gap in the arrival pattern of the queue being fed into. We can get around this problem by assuming that every time a packet arrives at an IMP, it loses its identity and a new length is chosen for it at random. This assumption, first made by Kleinrock (1964), is known as the **Independence Assumption**. Simulation and actual measurements show that it is quite reasonable to make it. Besides, if we do not make it, we cannot make any progress at all.

Let us illustrate the calculation of the mean queueing delay in a network by an example. Fig. 2-16(a) depicts a six node network using full-duplex lines. It may be helpful to think of each full-duplex line as a pair of oppositely directed simplex lines, one eastbound and one westbound. The capacities of the lines are given in kbps. The matrix of Fig. 2-16(b) has an entry for each source-destination pair. The entry for source i and destination j shows the route to be used for i-j traffic and also the number of packets/sec (γ_{ij}) to be sent from i to j. For example, there are 3 packets/sec from B to D, and they use the route BFD.

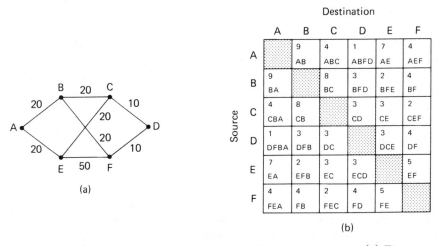

Fig. 2-16. (a) A network, with line capacities shown in bps. (b) The traffic (in packets/sec) and the routing matrix.

Given these routing and traffic matrices, it is possible to calculate the total traffic in line i, λ_i. For example, the B-D traffic contributes 3 packets/sec to the BF line and 3 packets/sec to the FD line. Similarly, the A-D traffic contributes 1 packet/sec to each of three lines. The total traffic in each east-bound line is shown in Fig. 2-17. In this example, the traffic matrix is symmetric (i.e., there is always as much traffic from X to Y as from Y to X). Furthermore, the Y-X traffic uses the exact reverse route of the X-Y traffic. We have done this to make $\lambda_{XY} = \lambda_{YX}$ for all X and Y (to simplify the example).

i	Line	λ_i (pkts/sec)	C_i (kbps)	μC_i (pkts/sec)	T_i (ms)
1	AB	14	20	25	91
2	BC	12	20	25	77
3	CD	6	10	12.5	154
4	AE	11	20	25	71
5	EF	13	50	62.5	20
6	FD	8	10	12.5	222
7	BF	10	20	25	67
8	EC	8	20	25	59

Fig. 2-17. Analysis of the network of Fig. 2-16 using a mean packet size of 800 bits. The reverse traffic (*BA*, *CB*, *DC*, etc.) is the same as the corresponding forward traffic, and has the same delay.

Figure 2-18 shows λ_i and C_i for each of the lines in Fig. 2-16. Let us now assume a mean packet size $1/\mu = 800$ bits/packet, leading to the fifth column of Fig. 2-18. With λ_i and μC_i now known, we can apply Eq. (2-12) and calculate the queueing + transmission time for each line. These times are given in the last column of Fig. 2-18.

To calculate the mean packet delay for a network with n IMPs and m lines, it is convenient to define

$$\gamma = \sum_{i=1}^{n} \sum_{j=1}^{n} \gamma_{ij} \qquad \text{and} \qquad \lambda = \sum_{i=1}^{m} \lambda_i$$

Although it might appear at first that summing the traffic between each pair of IMPs (γ) should give the same result as summing the traffic on all the lines (λ) this is not so. The reason for this seeming anomaly is that some routes use two or more hops, such as the route from A to D in Fig. 2-17. The A-D traffic contributes to the traffic in three lines. In other words, the A-D traffic is counted three times in λ but only once in γ. If every route were three hops, then λ would be three times γ. The ratio $\bar{n} = \lambda/\gamma$ is the mean number of hops per packet. Notice that $\bar{n}$ depends only on the relative traffic pattern and the routing algorithm, but not on the absolute volume of traffic. Doubling each element of γ_{ij} has no effect on $\bar{n}$.

As an aside, it is interesting to notice that λ can be related to the traffic matrix γ_{ij} by

$$\lambda = \sum_{i=1}^{n} \sum_{j=1}^{n} h_{ij} \, \gamma_{ij}$$

where h_{ij} is the number of hops in the route from IMP i to IMP j. If shortest path routing is used, as it is in our example, the λ so obtained is the theoretical minimum achievable for the given topology and traffic matrix.

The mean delay per hop is simply the sum of the individual line delays, from Eq. (2-12), weighted by the amount of traffic in the line, λ_i. To normalize the result, we divide by the total traffic, λ, yielding

$$\text{mean delay per line} = \sum_{i=1}^{m} \frac{\lambda_i T_i}{\lambda}$$

However, the mean packet delay, T, is longer, because many packets must make several hops. Remembering that $\bar{n}$ is the mean number of hops per packet, we have

$$T = \bar{n} \sum_{i=1}^{m} \frac{\lambda_i T_i}{\lambda} = \bar{n} \sum_{i=1}^{m} \frac{\lambda_i / \lambda}{\mu C_i - \lambda_i} \qquad (2\text{-}13)$$

Although we will use Eq. (2-13) repeatedly throughout this chapter, it is worth pointing out that it is only an approximation to reality. First, the assumption of exponentially distributed packet lengths may or may not be a good one in a given application. Also, we have neglected all other components to the delay, such as the time needed for the IMP to compute the software checksum (if any) and otherwise massage the packet, and the propagation delay. We have also neglected the effects of errors, retransmissions, and control packets. For a more realistic model of the delay, see Kleinrock (1970).

Using Eq. (2-13) we can now calculate the mean packet delay for our example of Fig. 2-17. For this example, $\gamma = 124$ and $\lambda = 164$ packets/sec (including the reverse traffic BA, CB, etc.). The value of $\bar{n}$ is $164/124 = 1.32$ hops/packet. The mean packet delay turns out to be 114 msec.

An important question is how much traffic a network can support using a given static routing algorithm. To see what the maximum traffic is for the routing of Fig. 2-16(b), we scale up the traffic matrix by multiplying each element by the same constant, and then recompute T. This has been done in Fig. 2-18. A scale factor of 1.0 corresponds to the traffic of Fig. 2-16(b). Higher numbers represent heavier loads, and lower numbers represent lighter loads. The second curve is for a mean packet size of 1200 instead of 800 bits.

Another interesting question is: What is the mean packet delay when the network is almost empty? It is not 0, because the transmission (service) time is included in the delay, and that is constant, independent of the load. In an unloaded network, $\mu C_i \gg \lambda_i$ so we can neglect the λ_i term in the

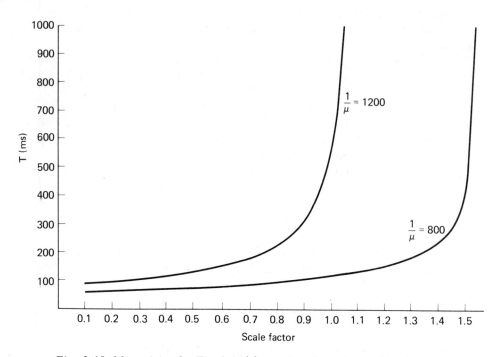

Fig. 2-18. Mean delay for Fig. 2-16(a) as a function of overall load.

denominator of Eq. (2-13) to get

$$T_0 = \bar{n} \sum_{i=1}^{n} \frac{\lambda_i/\lambda}{\mu C_i}$$

For the example of Fig. 2-16, T_0 is 57 msec. A crude approximation of the curves of Fig. 2-18 is a constant value of T_0 extending from zero load up to some critical value, which then suddenly jumps to infinity. To find the critical value, we need to know which line saturates first. The line that saturates first is the one with the lowest $\mu C_i/\lambda_i$ ratio. From Fig. 2-17 we see that line *FD* has the lowest ratio, $12.5/8 = 1.56$. As we multiply all the entries in the traffic matrix by a common scale factor, line *FD* will be the first to reach saturation. Saturation will be achieved at a scale factor of 1.56. This conclusion is also clear from Fig. 2-18.

One last remark before leaving this example concerns the true maximum flow. The capacity of the smallest cut of Fig. 2-16 is 20 kbps or 25 packets/sec. As we scale up the traffic, the smallest cut will be the first to saturate. Using the max-flow min-cut theorem we see that it should be possible to pump twenty-five 800-bit packets/sec from *A* to *D*. In reality, only 1.56 packets/sec will go from *A* to *D*.

This low value occurs because we are now dealing with multiple sources and sinks simultaneously. Just looking only at the required D-F flow (4 packets/sec, or 3.2 kbps) and the capacity exiting from D (20 kbps), we can see immediately that the scale factor cannot be much greater than 6. In other words, the D-F flow requirement affects the A-D flow. No such effect is present in the single source-sink flow problem. Nonetheless, it is still interesting to see how much traffic flows across the minimum cut by adding up the entries for CD and FD from Fig. 2-17, and then multiplying by the scale factor that saturates the network (1.56). The result is 21.8 packets/sec. To squeeze the last 15% out of the network, we would need to improve the routing, in particular, we would need to allow load splitting. Since FD saturates before CD, we could try to route some of the A-D or B-D traffic over C instead of having all of it go via F.

By now it should be clear, however, that to achieve the maximum theoretical flow, we must tolerate an infinite delay. In fact, to even achieve a flow close (say within 20%) of the theoretical limit, we must tolerate a queueing delay several times the delay of the unloaded network. From Fig. 2-18 we see that at a scale factor of 1.25 (80% of the maximum achievable with the given routing algorithm), the delay is triple the delay of an unloaded network. We can now clearly see that there is an inherent conflict between high throughput and low delay. To get the maximum throughput, we need $\mu C_i = \lambda_i$ in Eq. (2-13) for those lines that are contained in the minimum cut. But the very act of allowing the flow to approach the capacity in any line drives the delay through the roof. Since short delay times and high throughput are difficult to achieve simultaneously, it is important that the network designers clearly understand what their goals are.

2.4. BACKBONE DESIGN

Having successfully grappled with graph theory and queueing theory, we are now ready to take on the network design problem. First we deal with the backbone (the interconnection of the IMPs). Then we deal with the local access network. Our approach is that used to design the ARPANET (Frank et al., 1970; Gerla and Kleinrock, 1977b).

2.4.1. The Design Process

There are no exact solutions in this business. Trial and error plus the services of a large computer are essential. The problem is so immense that the only reasonable approach is to generate a potential network topology and then see if it obeys the connectivity and delay constraints. If not, generate another one. When a feasible topology has been found, compute its cost.

Take this topology and its cost as a starting point. From it, make small modifications ("perturbations"), yielding a number of similar networks. For each of these, check to see if any are better (i.e., feasible and cheaper). If a better network is found, use it as the base for more perturbations. This whole process is repeated using different starting topologies until the computer budget is used up. It hardly needs emphasizing that execution efficiency is of paramount importance.

Figure 2-19 shows an outline of the iteration process. The data-type *network* contains not only the connectivity matrix, including line capacities and costs, but also the assigned flows, information about which perturbations have already been tried, etc.

For each run of the program outlined in Fig. 2-19, we can find the mean delay time (which will be close to, but not always exactly the same as the input parameter), total throughput, and network cost. By running the program repeatedly with different maximum delay times, we can collect information about possible trade-offs. For example, we can plot the network cost against delay to allow the customer to see how much better response would cost, or alternatively, to see how much money could be saved by loosening the delay requirement.

Although we have primarily discussed delay as a metric of network performance, for some users (e.g., people wanting to transfer large files from place to place) throughput is more important than delay. From the output of the computer runs we could make a scatterplot of cost versus throughput, as is done in Fig. 2-20. Consider two of the minima, *A* and *B* found by the program for different values of the delay. If point *B* is below and to the right of point *A* (as shown), then point *A* is not a serious candidate, because *B* offers more throughput for less money. Thus none of the points above and to the left of *B* are viable.

B is said to *eliminate* all the local minima in the second quadrant (the shaded region in Fig. 2-20). Similarly, *C* eliminates all points in the hatched region above and to the left of it. Each local minimum found by the program may eliminate some other local minima. After each minimum has been given the chance to eliminate all the points worse than itself, the remaining points may be joined together to give a curve of cost as a function of throughput. All the points on this curve satisfy the connectivity and delay constraints and are thus feasible networks.

Considerable work has been done on this problem because an improvement of even a few percent on a large network may make a difference of thousands of dollars per month in line charges. There even exist corporations specialized in designing network topologies for their customers. Needless to say, they regard their programs as highly confidential, but some information has been published (see, for example, Boorstyn and Frank, 1977; Frank and Chou, 1972; Frank et al., 1970).

The key elements in the iteration process are as follows:

{This program contains an outline of the procedure for designing network topologies. It chooses a starting topology and then perturbs it, looking for a local optimum. The whole process is then repeated with different starting topologies.}

```pascal
program DesignTopo(input, output);

const n = ... ;                    {how many parameters}
      infinity = ... ;             {something larger than any possible cost}

type network = record ... end;     {representation, flows, capacity, variant number}
     params = array [1 .. n] of real;

var CurrentNet, TrialNet, BestNet: network;
    CurrentCost, BestCost: real;
    par: params;                   {input parameters}
    i: integer;
```

{The following procedures and functions should be defined here:
  GenerateStartingNetwork,   feasible,   PrintResults,
  GenerateVariant,   AssignCapacity,   ThereAreNoMoreVariants,
  cost,   AssignFlows,   ComputerBudgetIsUp   }

```pascal
begin
   for i := 1 to n do read(par[i]);   {go get input data}
   BestCost := infinity;
   repeat
      GenerateStartingNetwork(par, CurrentNet);        {initial topology}
      AssignFlows(CurrentNet);
      AssignCapacity(CurrentNet);
      CurrentCost := cost(CurrentNet);
      if feasible(CurrentNet) then
         begin                          {CurrentNet has met the reliability and delay constraints}

            repeat                       {try variant networks}
               GenerateVariant(CurrentNet, TrialNet);
               AssignFlows(TrialNet);
               AssignCapacity(TrialNet);
               if feasible(TrialNet) and (cost(TrialNet) < CurrentCost) then
                  begin                  {this is an improvement over the current network}
                     CurrentCost := cost(TrialNet);
                     CurrentNet := TrialNet
                  end
            until ThereAreNoMoreVariants(CurrentNet);

            if CurrentCost < BestCost then
               begin BestNet := CurrentNet; BestCost := CurrentCost end
         end
   until ComputerBudgetIsUp;
   PrintResults(BestNet)
end.
```

Fig. 2-19. Outline of the topological design process.

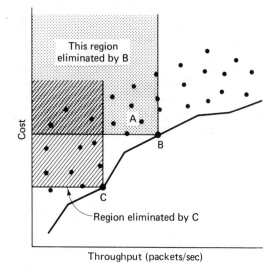

Fig. 2-20. The locus of noneliminated local minima forms the cost versus throughput curve.

1. Choosing starting topologies.

2. Assigning the flows and capacities.

3. Generating slightly modified networks from a given one.

We will now examine each of these issues in turn.

2.4.2. Generating Starting Topologies

The input to the topology generator is a list of nodes (IMPs) and their locations. The output is an initial topology, that is, a list of links or a boolean matrix A such that A_{ij} is true if there is a link between i and j, and false otherwise.

Ideally, this starting topology should also meet the connectivity constraint and take account of the cost and the delay. It is easy to generate a graph that meets the connectivity constraint—just connect every node to every other node. But we are looking for designs that do not have any more links than are really needed to meet the connectivity constraint (unless forced to by the delay constraint). Similarly, the heuristic for generating starting networks should have enough sense to try connecting Cleveland to New York before it tries connecting Cleveland to Nairobi.

One such heuristic is due to Steiglitz et al. (1969). The basic idea here is to use Whitney's theorem. If we want a k-connected network, we must ensure that every IMP has at least k links. This condition is not sufficient, but it is necessary.

Their heuristic begins by numbering the nodes at random. It is this randomization that lets the heuristic generate many topologies from the same input data. Figure 2-21(a) shows the positions of eight nodes which are now randomly numbered. Associated with each node is a number equal to the number of arcs still needed at that node. This number is called the **link deficit**. Initially, the deficit at each node is equal to the desired connectivity of the graph, k. For this example we will use a connectivity of 3.

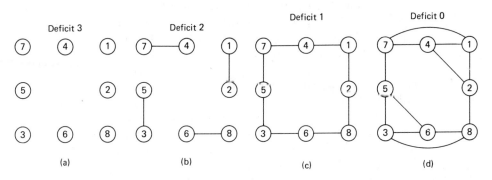

Fig. 2-21. Succeeding stages of the link-deficit algorithm.

The heuristic proceeds by adding arcs one at a time until the deficit at each node is zero or less. To add an arc XY, choose X and Y as follows:

X: Find the node with the highest deficit (i.e., the node most in need of another arc). In case of a tie, choose the node with the lowest number.

Y: Find the node not already adjacent to X with the highest deficit. In case of a tie, choose the node whose distance from X is a minimum. Distance may represent geographical distance, cost, or other metrics, of course. If several nodes with the highest deficit are at the same distance from X, take the one with the lowest number.

The first round of this process is shown in Fig. 2-21(b). Initially, all nodes have a deficit of 3. The arcs are added in the order 1-2, 3-5, 4-7, and 6-8. At this point all nodes have a deficit of 2. The next four arcs added are 1-4, 2-8, 3-6, and 5-7. At this point all nodes have a deficit of 1, and the graph is as shown in Fig. 2-21(c). The final four arcs are 1-7, 2-4, 3-8, and 5-6. The final graph is shown in Fig. 2-21(d). In some cases the heuristic will terminate with nodes having a negative deficit (e.g., if there are an odd number of nodes).

It should be emphasized that the topologies produced by this heuristic in general will *not* satisfy the connectivity constraint. It is necessary to apply the perturbation heuristics to be described later to search for a properly connected topology.

2.4.3. Flow and Capacity Assignment

To calculate the mean delay in the network, we need to know the traffic, λ_i on each link. This means that we must know the routing algorithm to derive the link traffic from the end-to-end traffic (γ_{ij}). As we shall see in Chap. 5, some algorithms are dynamic rather than static (i.e., they continually revise their routing decisions based on the current load). Consequently, it is not possible to use these algorithms to estimate the link traffic. We are left in the unfortunate position of using one routing algorithm in the design stage and possibly a completely different one during actual operation. If we are not careful, we may end up carefully optimizing the network for a traffic pattern that never exists!

Fortunately, the situation is not all that bleak. If the network is in a reasonable approximation to equilibrium (e.g., it has many small), independent customers rather than a few whoppers, the behavior of a dynamic routing algorithm may approximate that of a static one closely enough to make the model valid. In any case our only alternative at this point is to try to find the best static routing and use it to calculate the λ_is.

A straightforward way to assign the traffic flow is to use shortest-path routing. When faced with the decision of how to route the traffic between a given pair of IMPs, the shortest path is calculated and used. As the calculation proceeds, a record is kept of how much traffic has been assigned to each link so far.

At this point we have a proposed topology and a proposed set of flow assignments. The next step is to calculate the minimum cost lines needed to achieve the prescribed delay. To keep the problem manageable, we assume a linear cost function:

$$\text{total cost} = \sum_{i=1}^{m} (d_i C_i + x_i) \tag{2-14}$$

where d_i is the cost/bps for line i, C_i the capacity of line i, and x_i a constant cost associated with line i, not depending on the capacity. The d_i coefficients are given. They simply represent the price (or cost) structure for leased telephone lines, here assumed to be directly proportional to bandwidth. The constant term might represent the cost of a modem, interface, or other piece of computer equipment needed for the line, but whose price is independent of the capacity ultimately chosen for the line.

We want to minimize this cost subject to the time delay constraint

$$\frac{1}{\gamma} \sum_{i=1}^{m} \frac{\lambda_i}{\mu C_i - \lambda_i} = T \tag{2-14}$$

The solution to be presented here is due to Kleinrock (1964). It uses the method of Lagrange multipliers. Let us define the function F as

$$F = \sum_{i=1}^{m} (d_i C_i + x_i) + \beta \left(\frac{1}{\gamma} \sum_{i=1}^{m} \frac{\lambda_i}{\mu C_i - \lambda_i} - T \right)$$

The term in brackets is zero, so multiplying it by the Lagrangian variable β and adding it to the cost function will not change the nature of the minimization. We will now minimize F by setting its partial derivatives with respect to line capacities to 0:

$$\frac{\partial F}{\partial C_i} = d_i - \frac{\mu \beta \lambda_i}{\gamma} \left(\frac{1}{\mu C_i - \lambda_i} \right)^2 = 0$$

This equation can be rewritten

$$\frac{1}{\mu C_i - \lambda_i} - \sqrt{\gamma d_i / \mu \beta \lambda_i} \tag{2-15}$$

or as

$$C_i = \frac{\lambda_i}{\mu} + \sqrt{\beta} \sqrt{\lambda_i / \mu \gamma d_i} \tag{2-16}$$

To solve for β in terms of the known variables, multiply Eq. (2-16) by λ_i / γ and sum over all the lines to get

$$\frac{1}{\gamma} \sum_{i=1}^{m} \frac{\lambda_i}{\mu C_i - \lambda_i} = \frac{1}{\gamma} \sum_{i=1}^{m} \sqrt{\gamma \lambda_i d_i / \mu \beta}$$

Now notice that the left-hand side is just T, from Eq. (2-14). Collecting the $\lambda's$ inside and outside the square root, we get

$$\sqrt{\beta} = \frac{1}{T} \sum_{i=1}^{m} \sqrt{\lambda_i d_i / \mu \gamma}$$

Substituting this expression into Eq. (2-16), we finally get an expression for the optimal line capacities

$$C_i = \frac{\lambda_i}{\mu} + \frac{1}{T} \sum_{j=1}^{m} \sqrt{\lambda_j d_j / \mu \gamma} \sqrt{\lambda_i / \mu \gamma d_i}$$

This result can be simplified to

$$C_i = \frac{\lambda_i}{\mu} \left(1 + \frac{1}{\gamma T} \frac{\sum_{j=1}^{m} \sqrt{\lambda_j d_j}}{\sqrt{\lambda_i d_i}} \right) \tag{2-17}$$

Using these values for C_i we can substitute back into Eq. (2-14) to get the total cost for the network:

$$\text{total cost} = \sum_{i=1}^{m} \left(d_i \frac{\lambda_i}{\mu} + x_i \right) + \frac{1}{\gamma T} \left(\sum_{i=1}^{m} \sqrt{\lambda_i d_i / \mu} \right)^2 + x_i \qquad (2\text{-}18)$$

Although this calculation may seem complicated, you should realize that it is nevertheless a gross simplification. In particular, the assumption of a price structure in which price increases linearly with capacity is not terribly realistic. But worse yet, we have not dealt with the fact that only discrete capacities are available. For treatment of the discrete case, see Gerla and Kleinrock (1977b).

To bring the above equations back down to earth (plus or minus the height of a telephone pole), let us do a sample calculation using the network and traffic of Fig. 2-16. To keep things simple, let us assume that $d_i = 1$ and $x_i = 0$ for all i. In this way the total cost of the lines will just be the sum of their capacities. For comparison purposes, the capacities given in Fig. 2-17 added up to 170 kbps = 170 cost units. The mean packet delay, $\bar{n} \sum (\lambda_i / \lambda) T_i$, was 114 msec.

As our goal, we will find the optimal capacity assignments that produce a mean packet delay of 100 msec. Using Eq. (2-18) with a mean packet length of 800 bits we arrive at the capacity assignments and time delays shown as "optimal" in Fig. 2-22. The weighted mean packet delay is exactly 100 msec as it should be. (Remember that the mean packet delay is $\bar{n}$ times the mean link delay, since the average packet makes $\bar{n}$ hops.)

			Optimal		Uniform		Proportional	
i	Line	λ_i	C_i	T_i	C_i	T_i	C_i	T_i
1	AB	14	23.5	65	18.6	108	25.4	56
2	BC	12	21.0	70	18.6	89	21.8	66
3	CD	6	12.8	100	18.6	58	10.9	131
4	AE	11	19.7	74	18.6	82	20.0	72
5	EF	13	22.2	68	18.6	98	23.6	61
6	FD	8	15.7	86	18.6	66	14.5	99
7	BF	10	18.4	77	18.6	75	18.1	79
8	EC	8	15.7	86	18.6	66	14.5	99

Fig. 2-22. Line capacities in kbps and link delays in msec for three selected capacity assignments.

Two other capacity assignments are also shown in Fig. 2-22. Under the heading "uniform" is an assignment rule in which every line gets an equal amount of capacity, with the sum being the same as in the optimal case (149 kbps, being careful to count each line only once, even though it carries full-duplex traffic).

Under the heading "proportional" we have a capacity assignment rule in which the 149 kbps are divided up so that each line gets capacity in direct proportion to its traffic. Line 2 has twice the traffic of line 3, so it gets twice the capacity. The mean packet delay for the three cases is 100 msec, 111 msec, and 102 msec, respectively. In this example, with the traffic relatively uniform, the delay is not very sensitive to the assignment. However, if there are some lines with much heavier or much lighter traffic, the optimal assignment rule will be much better than the uniform one.

It is also instructive to compare the optimal assignment with the arbitrary one of Fig. 2-17. What are the major changes? Lines 1 and 2 each get a little bit more capacity, which improves their delay time a little bit. Line 3, which was a problem, gets 28% more capacity. Line 4 is essentially unchanged. Line 5 loses most of its excess capacity. Line 6, which was the real bottleneck, gets 57% more capacity, thus bringing its delay time within reason. The last two lines lose some unneeded capacity. Notice that the distribution of delay times in Fig. 2-22 is more uniform than in Fig. 2-17. Also note that the improved performance has been done at a lower cost. The original capacity assignments cost 170 units, versus 149 for the new one, even though the delay has been reduced from 114 msec to 100 msec.

2.4.4. Perturbation Heuristics

We have now gotten to the point of having assigned flows and capacities to the proposed network. Using Eq. (2-18), we can compute the cost of the design. If the cost is lower than the previous best cost, we accept the topology and look for variations of it. If it is more expensive than the previous best topology, we reject it, and look for more variations of the previous best one. Either way, we need ways to perturb a given network to search for local minima in the cost. Several methods for generating slightly modified networks from a given one have been proposed in the literature. Let us now examine some of them.

Branch Exchange

Some studies have shown that the basic iterative scheme is not terribly sensitive to the exact heuristic used. For this reason it is appropriate to start out with a simple method, **branch exchange**. It goes as follows:

1. Pick two links, preferably not too far apart.

2. Remove both links from the network.

3. Add two new links using another combination of the four nodes.

The branch exchange heuristic is illustrated in Fig. 2-23. The chosen links are *ED* and *FG*. There are two ways of creating new links from the four nodes *D*, *E*, *F*, and *G*: (*EG, DF*) and (*EF, DG*). The new networks formed by using each of these pairs are shown in Fig. 2-23(b) and (c) respectively.

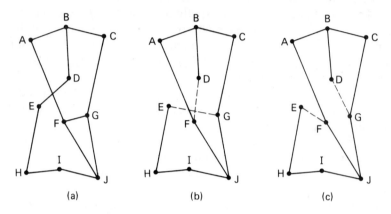

Fig. 2-23. Branch exchange heuristic. (a) Original network. (b) and (c) Derived networks.

Some simple criteria for choosing pairs of links to exchange are low utilization of the selected links, high traffic between the unconnected pairs, high cost of the selected pairs, and low cost of the nonexistent "links."

The Saturated Cut Heuristic

Gerla et al. (1974) have described a more sophisticated heuristic than branch exchange. They claim that for large networks it gives better results with less computer time. A slightly simplified version starts out like this.

1. Sort all the links by percent utilization (i.e., traffic carried/capacity).

2. Starting with the most utilized links, remove links until the network has been separated into two components.

3. Minimize this cut by tentatively putting each link in turn back into the network. If putting a link back does not reconnect the network, it is not part of the minimal cut.

4. Mark all the nodes adjacent to the cut as "primary" nodes.

5. Mark all nodes adjacent to a primary node as "secondary" nodes.

Figure 2-24 illustrates the procedure so far. Let us assume that the cut located by steps 1, 2, and 3 is (*BC, GH, OS*), shown as dashed lines. The primary nodes, *B*, *G*, *O*, *C*, *H*, and *S*, are indicated by solid circles. The secondary nodes, *A*, *E*, *F*, *N*, *R*, *P*, *T*, *D*, and *V*, are indicated by squares. The remaining nodes, which we will call the tertiary nodes, can be divided into the left tertiary and right tertiary nodes, depending on which of the two components they are in. Notice that every left tertiary node is at a distance of at least five links from the closest right tertiary node: two or more hops to the primary node, 1 hop across the cut, and two or more to the destination.

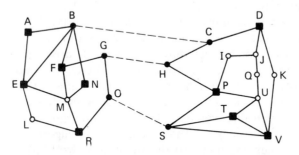

Fig. 2-24. Example of the saturated cut heuristic. The solid circles are nodes adjacent to the cut. Nodes adjacent to a solid circle are indicated by solid squares.

The heuristic provides for both adding and deleting links. You can start either with a sparse topology and add many links or a rich one and delete links or an acceptable topology and do both. When adding a link, one end should be a left tertiary node and the other a right tertiary node. They suggest two alternatives for making a choice:

1. Choose the cheapest link.

2. Choose the pair of nodes whose best path is the most saturated.

The former rule is aimed at getting the cost down, whereas the latter is aimed at improving the performance. It should be noted, however, that the heuristic may occasionally fail: there may not be any tertiaries on one side of the cut.

The other side of the coin is the heuristic for removing links. As a metric, consider the percent unused capacity in each link. When multiplied by the cost of the link, it gives the amount of money being wasted on unused capacity for that link. When removing a link, choose the link that wastes the most money, without regard to its position in relation to the cut.

The complete heuristic uses both the add and delete parts. If a proposed topology has a smaller delay time than is required, delete a link to reduce the cost. If it has a higher delay than the target delay, add a new link to reduce the delay. The heuristic is not likely to oscillate, because the links added are always long ones that are either cheap or are badly needed for their capacity, and hence are not usually immediate candidates for removal by the delete phase.

A Connectivity-restoring Algorithm

A problem with the heuristics described above is that they may inadvertently reduce the connectivity of the network. Suppose that we want to generate a network that is k-connected. At a certain point we have a proposed topology that meets the connectivity constraint. However, as the perturbation process is carried out, there is a danger that one of the variant networks will not meet the connectivity constraint.

The usual way of handling this problem is by brute force: just recompute the connectivity of each newly generated topology to see if it satisfies the constraint. It would be much nicer, however, if the heuristic used for generating perturbations always produced networks whose connectivity was as least as high as that of the original. Such a heuristic would eliminate the need to run the (time-consuming) connectivity algorithm for each new network. A transformation method has been discovered by Lavia and Manning (1975) which greatly reduces the number of times the (node) connectivity algorithm must be run.

Stronger yet, their method also restores the network diameter to its previous value. The network diameter is a graph theoretic way of measuring delay, because the longer the paths are, the more delay can be expected. A rule for perturbing a feasible network in such a way as to preserve both connectivity and diameter always yields another feasible network. Because our treatment has used queueing theory rather than graph theory for measuring the delay, we will just describe Lavia and Manning's way of restoring connectivity, referring you to the paper for the diameter part.

Network transformations can be decomposed into two basic operations: add a link, and delete a link. Adding a link can never reduce the connectivity, so any heuristic can be used: for example, one of the rules used in the cut saturation heuristic, or adding a link between the unconnected pair of nodes with the greatest end-to-end traffic.

Link deletion is where the trouble comes in. As an example, Fig. 2-25(a) shows a fragment of a formerly 3-connected network from which link XY has just been deleted. The network is now only 2-connected. What the Lavia-Manning algorithm does is add one or two new links that restore the connectivity to its old value. For convenience, let us define a **proximate** link (with respect to the deleted one) as a link that is adjacent to the deleted link at one end, and at a distance 1 from it at the other. There are five potential links proximate to XY in Fig. 2-25(a): XD, XE, YA, YB, and YC. The algorithm always chooses one or two of these to restore the connectivity.

There are two cases to consider, depending on the degrees of X and Y. From Whitney's theorem and the fact that the original graph was k-connected we know that both X and Y must be of degree k or higher. We also know that the graph left after deleting XY (call it G') is at least $(k - 1)$-connected, because the loss of one link cannot destroy two node-disjoint paths. If the deleted link does not reduce the connectivity, there is no need to restore it, so

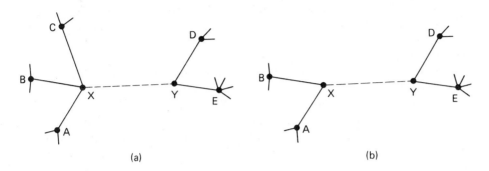

Fig. 2-25. Network fragments.

we will assume that the connectivity has been reduced.

First consider the case where one or both ends of the deleted link had a degree greater than k. Conceptually draw in the $k - 1$ node-disjoint paths between X and Y. One path might, for example, exit from X via link XA, wander around for a bit, and enter Y via EY. The second node-disjoint path still remaining in G' might exit X via XB and come into Y via DY. Since the degree of X was higher than k (3), there will always be one node adjacent to X not involved in any of the $k - 1$ node-disjoint paths from X to Y. In this example, C is the "extra" node. If the path from B to D snaked around for a while and then came into C before heading off to D, the XBC loop could be snipped off, leaving B as the extra node.

The rule for restoring the connectivity back to k is now obvious: just add a new link from Y to the extra node adjacent to X. If C is the extra node, the addition of link CY restores the connectivity because there are $k - 1$ node-disjoint paths from X to Y, none of which involve C. Path XCY is thus an additional node-disjoint path, bringing the total back up to k. The connectivity preserving transformation is therefore: delete XY and add CY.

To see which of the nodes adjacent to X to use as the extra one (i.e., which one to connect to Y), delete each one from G' in turn and see if the resulting network is still $(k - 1)$−connected. If it is, the node just tested is an acceptable candidate. There may be several acceptable candidates, but there will always be at least one.

Now let us consider the case of Fig. 2-25(b), where both X and Y had degree exactly k (3). All the nodes adjacent to both X and Y in the remaining network, G', are used for the $k - 1$ node-disjoint paths connecting them, so the method described above will not work.

Fortunately, the connectivity can be restored even in this case by adding not one, but two, new proximate links. Both of these are again chosen from the set of proximate links. One link connects X to a node adjacent to Y, and the other connects Y to a node adjacent to X. In Fig. 2-25(b) there are four possible choices: (XD, AY), (XD, BY), (XE, AY), and (XE, BY). To determine which of these choices is suitable, systematically delete a node adjacent to X and a node adjacent to Y from G', and check if the resulting graph is $(k - 1)$-connected. If so, the nodes being tested are suitable terminal points for the new links.

We need to add two links rather than only one link, because if $k - 1$ (i.e., 2) arcs are destroyed, they might just all be adjacent to X. In that case the second added link will ensure that X and Y remain connected. The same holds if all the nodes adjacent to Y are destroyed. To make our example complete, the transformation on Fig. 2-25(b) might be to delete XY and then to add XD and BY.

Other Backbone Design Methods

We have now examined several heuristic approaches to the backbone design problem in detail; now we will just mention a few more methods briefly. The approach of Gerla and Kleinrock (1977b) is to start with a fully connected network and remove uneconomical links one at a time. This process is repeated until an acceptable cost network is found. The link elimination algorithm is closely tied to a differential flow routing algorithm.

A straightforward perturbation heuristic is simply to consider in turn each pair of nodes. If a link exists between them, it is deleted; if no link exists, it is added. In either case, if the resulting topology is an improvement, it is adopted.

A related idea is to systematically examine all the links in the network, (i, j), tentatively replacing each by the pair of links (i, k) and (k, j), where k ranges over all possible nodes. Again, only improvements are adopted.

2.5. LOCAL ACCESS NETWORK DESIGN

Having finished the backbone design, it is now time to look at the problem of connecting hosts and terminals to the nearest IMP. The three basic subproblems we will tackle are concentrator location, assignment of customer sites to concentrators, and terminal layout within a site. Let us start out with the second one, because we need its solution to solve the first one.

2.5.1. Assigning Sites to Concentrators

We are given a collection of customer sites and a list of concentrator locations, as shown in Fig. 2-26(a). A customer site might be a company plant, university campus, or a single terminal. As far as the concentrator is concerned, it is a source and sink of data. Whether the data are further distributed, and if so, how, is not of interest here, although it will be later. The question is which customer sites should be attached to which concentrator. Figure 2-26(b) shows one possible solution for the customer sites and concentrators of Fig. 2-26(a).

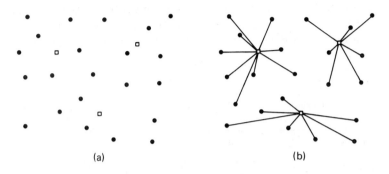

(a)   (b)

Fig. 2-26. (a) A collection of customer sites (circles) and concentrators (squares). (b) A possible assignment of sites to concentrators.

This problem (the concentrator choice problem) can be expressed as a zero-one programming problem. There are n customer sites, numbered 1 to n and m concentrators, numbered 1 to m, plus the IMP itself (often called the central site), which we will designate as concentrator location 0. The cost of connecting customer site i to concentrator j is c_{ij}. Let x_{ij} be 1 if we have actually decided to assign site i to concentrator j, and 0 otherwise. Then the total cost of a particular assignment is

$$\text{total cost} = \sum_{i=1}^{n} \sum_{j=0}^{m} x_{ij} c_{ij} \tag{2-19}$$

There are two constraints that we must impose on the solution, x_{ij}. First, each customer site is connected to exactly one concentrator:

$$\sum_{j=0}^{m} x_{ij} = 1 \qquad (i = 1, 2, \ldots, n)$$

Second, concentrator j can handle a maximum number of sites, k_j:

$$\sum_{i=1}^{n} x_{ij} \leqslant k_j \qquad (j = 0, 1, \ldots, m)$$

The limit may be the number of ports, or the processing time required for each interrupt, or some other limit. If there is no limit, k_j can be set to infinity.

What we need is an assignment of 0s and 1s to x satisfying the constraints and minimizing the cost. There are $2^{(m+1)n}$ possible assignments to x, so a full search is out of the question for all but the smallest configurations. We now present a simple heuristic for finding a feasible, suboptimal solution. For an optimal algorithm see Kershenbaum and Boorstyn (1975).

Consider the example of Fig. 2-27(a). Row *i* gives the cost of connecting site *i* to each of the concentrators. There are four concentrators, plus the central site. For this example, let k_j be 2 for all concentrators. For each row in turn, find the entry with the smallest cost. If that concentrator has room left, assign the site to that concentrator. If the concentrator is full, examine the second lowest cost, and so on. The results of running the heuristic are shown as the circled entries in Fig. 2-27(a). The total cost of this assignment is 23.

(a) Concentrator

Site	0	1	2	3	4
1	4	4	7	(2)	6
2	(1)	3	5	4	1
3	(1)	2	1	3	2
4	3	7	(6)	8	6
5	2	6	2	(1)	3
6	3	9	4	2	(3)
7	6	(2)	3	4	3
8	2	8	(7)	5	9

(b) Concentrator

Site	0	1	2	3	4
1	4	4	7	(2)	6
2	(1)	3	5	4	1
3	1	2	(1)	3	2
4	3	7	6	8	(6)
5	2	6	(2)	1	3
6	3	9	4	(2)	3
7	6	(2)	3	4	3
8	(2)	8	7	5	9

(c) Concentrator

Site	0	1	2	3	4
1	4	4	7	(2)	6
2	1	3	5	4	(1)
3	1	2	(1)	3	2
4	(3)	7	6	8	6
5	2	6	(2)	1	3
6	3	9	4	(2)	3
7	6	(2)	3	4	3
8	(2)	8	7	5	9

Fig. 2-27. The concentrator-choice problem. (a) Sites scanned in the order 12345678. (b) Sites scanned in the order 82461735. (c) Modification of (b).

Now run the heuristic again, but examining the rows in a different order. For example, make a list of the numbers 1 to *n*, randomize them, and look at the rows in that order. Figure 2-27(b) shows the result of examining the rows in the order 82461735. Here the cost is only 18. By simply repeating the procedure several times and taking the best assignment, we may get a reasonable assignment quickly.

One simple improvement that is certainly worth doing is to keep track of which concentrators were in demand after becoming full. For example, in Fig. 2-27(b), the first two assignments (rows 8 and 2) were to concentrator 0. Site 4 came next and had to settle for concentrator 4, because 0 was already full, so we mark 0 as being in demand. After all rows have been assigned, we go back and look for ties (e.g., row 2 could just as well use concentrator 4 instead of concentrator 0). By reassigning sites away from concentrators that are marked as being in demand, we can reduce the cost, as shown in Fig. 2-27(c).

The optimal solution goes further in this direction. Not only may a concentrator be reassigned to an equivalent one to make room for someone else, but it may be reassigned to a more expensive one, if the total cost is reduced.

2.5.2. The Concentrator Location Problem

Having found a heuristic or algorithm for assigning customer sites to concentrators, we can now proceed to determine where to put the concentrators. We assume that the m potential locations for concentrators are known. Clustering heuristics for this problem are discussed in McGregor and Shen (1977).

Since the number of concentrators is now a variable, we must introduce a new term into Eq. (2-19) to account for their cost:

$$\text{total cost} = \sum_{i=1}^{n} \sum_{j=0}^{m} x_{ij} c_{ij} + \sum_{j=0}^{m} y_j f_j$$

where y_j is 1 if at least one customer is using concentrator j, and 0 if no one is using it. The cost of concentrator j is f_j.

The concentrator location problem has been extensively studied by people in the field of operations research, where it is known as the warehouse location problem. Two good heuristics are ADD (Kuehn and Hamburger, 1963) and DROP (Feldman et al., 1966).

The ADD Heuristic for Locating Concentrators

Start out with all the customer sites attached to the central site. We assume that this is a feasible solution, because there is no reason why sufficient concentrators cannot be put there if need be. If for some reason having customers connected directly to the IMP is undesirable, the c_{i0} elements in the cost matrix can be made artificially high, to discourage direct connection of customer sites to the central site.

Now introduce concentrator site 1. Using some method for assigning customers to concentrators, assign each customer to either the central site or concentrator 1. With only two possibilities, the problem is simple: just assign each customer to the cheaper one. The result of this calculation will be the total cost for a system consisting of the central site and concentrator 1. If this is cheaper than having all customers hanging directly on the central site, it is an interesting possibility.

Next, reassign all customers back to the central site, eliminate concentrator 1, and consider concentrator 2. Compute the cost of this two concentrator system. Similarly, consider each of the m potential concentrators in turn, and find the one that in combination with the central site gives the minimum cost. This concentrator, say l, has now been chosen and will appear in the final configuration.

Now consider the three concentrator problem consisting of concentrators i, *l*, and the central site. Do this for each of the $m - 1$ remaining concentrators. Select the best triple and use it as the basis for solving the four concentrator problem.

Keep adding one concentrator at a time as long as the cost continues to decrease. At a certain point, the additional expense, f_j, of yet another concentrator will more than offset the small gain in line costs achieved by the addition of the new concentrator. The minimum cost configuration just found is the solution we are looking for.

The DROP Heuristic for Locating Concentrators

This heuristic is exact reverse of ADD. Start out with all the concentrators in use. Assign each customer site to one of the $m + 1$ concentrators and compute the total cost. DROP works by discarding concentrators one at a time in an attempt to get rid of uneconomical ones.

Tentatively eliminate concentrator 1. Now assign each customer site to one of the m remaining possibilities. Compute the cost of this configuration. Now put concentrator 1 back in, and remove concentrator 2. Repeat the calculation. Do this for each concentrator in turn, to discover which concentrator's demise reduces the cost the most.

In a similar manner, look for the next candidate to remove. Remove concentrators one at a time until the cost reaches a minimum and begins rising again. The cost will increase when the concentrators are so sparsely placed that the loss of even one of them causes a major increase in line costs.

2.5.3. The Terminal Layout Problem

Up until now we have just assumed that a customer site consists of a single point. If the customer site consists of a single large host computer to be attached to the network, our model is quite reasonable. However, often a customer site will actually consist of many terminals, all of which need access to the network. One solution would be to put a concentrator somewhere on the customer's premises, and run lines from the concentrator to the terminals. If each terminal has a fairly small amount of traffic, an alternative solution with several terminals sharing a line may be more economical. (How the terminals avoid getting in each other's way will be discussed in Chap. 3.)

If we define the cost of any terminal layout to be just the total length of wire used, it is clear that the cheapest solution is to connect all the terminals is a minimum spanning tree. Figure 2-28(a) gives a list of 15 terminal locations, plus the location, X, of the central site (concentrator). To illustrate two different algorithms for finding the minimum spanning tree, we will connect these 16 points together.

Prim's Minimum Spanning Tree Algorithm

Prim's algorithm starts out with only the central site in the minimum spanning tree. It then adds terminals to the tree one at a time. At each step the algorithm looks for the terminal closest to the tree, and attaches it. The distance between a terminal and the tree is the distance between the terminal and the closest node. Terminals may only be attached at nodes, that is, a terminal cannot be added to the tree by grafting it onto the middle of an arc, even if some point in the middle of the arc comes closer to the terminal than any node.

As an example, look at Fig. 2-28(b). Initially, the tree consists only of the central site. The closest terminal to the central site is J, at a distance 1, so we add it to the tree. The closest terminal to the tree now is C, at a distance 2, so it gets attached next. At this point, K is the closest, so it gets added next. The numbers on the arcs show the order in which terminals are added. When several terminals are equally close to the tree, the order in which they are added does not matter. An equivalent tree is always produced.

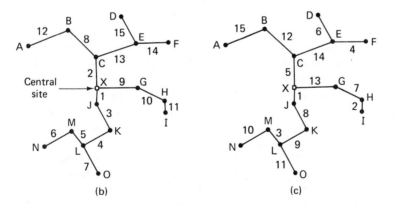

A : (1, 11) H : (11, 7)
B : (4, 12) I : (11, 6)
C : (6, 10) J : (6, 7)
D : (8, 13) K : (7, 5)
E : (9, 11) L : (5, 4)
F : (11, 11) M : (4, 5)
X : (6, 8)   N : (2, 4)
G : (9, 8)   O : (6, 2)

(a)

(b)   (c)

Fig. 2-28. (a) A list of 15 terminals' coordinates (x, y) and the concentrator, labeled X. (b) The MST produced by Prim's algorithm. (c) The MST produced by Kruskal's algorithm. The numbers indicated the order in which the arcs were added to the MST.

Kruskal's Minimum Spanning Tree Algorithm

This algorithm sorts all the interterminal distances in ascending order. Each potential line is checked, starting at the shortest. If that line can be added without forming a circuit, it is added; otherwise, it is skipped. In Fig. 2-28(c) lines *XJ* and *HI* are the shortest and are drawn in first. *LM* comes next. Just as with Prim's algorithm, when ties occur, either line may be chosen first. Like Prim's algorithm, the same tree is always produced.

Constrained Minimum Spanning Trees

In most practical situations there exist constraints that must be satisfied by a minimum spanning tree. Typically, the concentrator can handle only a maximum number of terminals per line (this has to do with the way terminals are addressed). Another obvious limitation is that the total traffic rate on a line cannot exceed the capacity of the line. To model these limitations, we assume that each terminal generates a certain amount of work per second. The tree is now constrained so that no line may handle more than k units of work per second. For example, if we have each terminal generate 1 unit of work per second, the constraint limits the number of terminals per concentrator port to k.

Neither of the algorithms described above work when the terminal layout is constrained. In fact, no practical algorithm for finding large optimal constrained minimum spanning trees is known. Instead, we must once again rely on heuristic methods.

Kruskal's algorithm can be modified to generate suboptimal solutions. Each time you are about to add a new line, check to see if the two components being merged obey the constraint. If not, do not merge them. Whenever a component grows to size k, it must be immediately connected directly to the central site via its closest node.

Prim's algorithm can also be modified appropriately. Associated with each terminal is a number, w_i, used to bias the heuristic. These numbers change as the heuristic progresses. Initially, $w_0 = 0$ and $w_i = -\infty$ $(i > 0)$. Instead of selecting a terminal to connect to the tree by using the cost, c_{ij}, we connect the terminal whose value of $c_{ij} - w_i$ is minimum, provided that such a connection does not violate the constraints. Now set $w_j = 0$. Repeat until all terminals are connected.

Kershenbaum and Chou (1974) have given a unified heuristic that can be specialized to yield Kruskal's, Prim's, and several other heuristics as well.

Tree Perturbation

The output of the constrained minimum spanning tree heuristics can often be improved by applying a variation of the branch exchange heuristic. Find the two unconnected terminals closest together (e.g. *M* and *J* in Fig. 2-28). Connect them, forming a circuit (*JKLMJ*). Now delete one of the links in this circuit (e.g., *LK*), forming a new tree. By successively deleting each of the links in the circuit, a number of new trees will be generated. Evaluate the cost and feasibility of each tree, and use the best one.

2.6. SUMMARY

Designing the topology of a network can be divided into two subproblems, the backbone design and the local access design. For the backbone design, the usual constraints are on the connectivity and delay. Techniques from graph theory are helpful for dealing with the connectivity. Among these are algorithms for finding the shortest path between two nodes of a weighted graph, and for finding the maximum possible (single commodity) flow between two nodes. The max-flow algorithm is the basis for determining the node and arc connectivity of a graph. Kleitman and Even have devised efficient algorithms for checking to see if a given graph meets a specified connectivity constraint.

In addition to graph theory, queueing theory is also a valuable tool for network design. Using the M/M/1 queueing model, it is easy to derive the mean queue length, and from the mean queue length, the mean queueing delay. Given the end-to-end traffic requirements and the routing algorithm, we have shown how to compute the mean end-to-end delay in a network.

The backbone design process is an iterative one, starting from an initial topology, and perturbing it to generate minor variations. Each variation is checked to see if it is an improvement, and if so, it is adopted as the new base topology. Branch exchange and the saturated cut set are two popular perturbation heuristics.

The local access network is also designed heuristically. First the locations for the concentrators are chosen, and then sites are assigned to concentrators. To reduce cable length, terminals can be connected to a concentrator in the form of a tree, with several constrained minimum spanning tree algorithms

Although many of the techniques presented in this chapter are empirical, in practice they work well enough to satisfy most network designers. It is fortunate that these heuristics give results close enough to the optimal values, because in many cases computing the optimal values is too costly in terms of computer time.

Research in the field of topology design now tends to focus on finding computationally efficient heuristics, and on mixed media networks. A typical example of a mixed media network is one using local access networks of the type we have described, but using a satellite to connect the IMPs instead of a point-to-point backbone network. Another example of a mixed media network is just the reverse: a common channel cable network is used for local distribution, but the long-haul portion uses a point-to-point backbone. Satellite and local cable networks are discussed at length in Chaps. 6 and 7, respectively. In general, the problems of designing integrated local, regional, national, and international networks so that they can all be used for intermixed data, voice, facsimile, and television transmission are high on the agenda for the coming decade.

PROBLEMS

1. For the graph of Fig. 2-2, give the order in which Dijkstra's shortest-path algorithm assigns permanent labels to the nodes. A is the source and G the sink.

2. What is the minimum cut between B and L in Fig. 2-7(a)?

3. For the graph shown in Fig. 2-10(a), write down the feasibility relations for the flow. (Let AB be the flow from A to B, and so on.) Given $AB = 6$, $EF = 8$, and $CD = 10$, what is the net flow from B to F?

4. What is the degree of the graph of Fig 2-7(a)? The connectivity?

5. A network has 200 nodes. The designers wish to ensure that it can withstand the loss of six nodes. How many applications of the max-flow algorithm are needed to verify that a proposed network indeed meets this requirement using
   (a) Kleitman's algorithm?
   (b) Even's algorithm?

6. Show that a queueing system with a constant arrival rate obeys Poisson statistics, in other words, that the probability of exactly k arrivals in a time t is $(\lambda t)^k e^{-\lambda t}/k!$. You will need the fact that during a short time interval of length Δt there can be 0 or 1 arrivals, but that the probability of two or more arrivals is negligible in the limit $\Delta t \rightarrow 0$. Let $P_i(x)$ be the probability of exactly i arrivals in a time interval of length x.
   (a) Compute $P_0(\Delta t)$ and $P_1(\Delta t)$.
   (b) Express $P_0(t + \Delta t)$ in terms of $P_0(t)$.
   (c) Compute $P_0(t + \Delta t) - P_0(t)$.
   (d) Divide the answer to part (c) by Δt and find $dP_0(t)/dt$.
   (e) Solve for $P_0(t)$ subject to $P_0(0) = 1$.
   (f) Compute $P_1(t + \Delta t) = P_1(t)P_0(\Delta t) + P_0(t)P_1(\Delta t)$.
   (g) Write down the differential equation for $P_1(t)$ and solve it.
   (h) Find the equation for $P_k(t)$.
   (i) Verify that $P_k(t) = (\lambda t)^k e^{-\lambda t}/k!$ solves the equation of part (h).

7. The number of programming errors made per line by the average introductory course student follows a Poisson distribution with a mean of three. What is the probability that a given line will contain exactly three errors?

8. System crashes at a certain computer center appear to follow the Poisson law, with a mean of 14 per (168 hour) week. After bringing the system back up, one of operators (Happy) told one of his colleagues (Grumpy) that he thought the system would remain up for the rest of the shift, 6 hours. Grumpy dissented and the resulting discussion resulted in a case of low-calorie freeze-dried beer being

wagered. What is the probability that Happy wins the freeze-dried beer?

9. A university cafeteria has a single customer queue with two equally slow servers, one for imitation hamburger and one for synthetic hamburger. When a server becomes free, the next customer is required to use that server (M/M/2 lunch). Write down the balance equations and then solve for the state probabilities.

10. Students queue up in front of Prof. Hatekid's office to try to get their exam grades raised. During peak periods, tearful students arrive every 6 min, on the average. To maximize their chances, they cleverly conspire to impress Prof. Hatekid by showing up in an exponential interarrival distribution. The time it takes for each student to tell his tale of woe is also varied by day of the week, to keep the professor from falling asleep. For each of the following, what is the mean queue length outside the office?
    (a) Monday: Exponential, mean = 4 min.
    (b) Tuesday: Gaussian, mean = 4 min, standard deviation = 1 min.
    (c) Wednesday: Hyperexponential, mean = 4 min, standard deviation = 8 min.

11. Intergalactic Software, Inc. has just announced release 17c of its new, improved Startrek program, featuring virtual solar systems, demand paged stars, and an Enterprise with a four speed stick shift. The day after their ad appears, the office gets 600 calls per hour. The time to place an order is exponentially distributed with a mean of 1 minute. The company wants the mean time during which the customer is put on "hold" before getting a salesbeing to be 30 sec. How many salesbeings should be assigned to the office, assuming that each being has its own private customer queue?

12. Given the network, routing algorithm, and end-to-end traffic in kbps shown below, find the mean number of hops per packet, the mean delay for the whole network, and the maximum scale factor. The traffic shown is complete; there is no reverse traffic. Each link is full-duplex and has a capacity of 50 kbps. Mean packet size is 1000 bits.

AB		10	DH via $BGFH$:	6
AC via ABC:	14	CI via $CDEI$:	10
AD via $ABCD$:	20	GB via GFB:	8
BG via BFG:	6	HD via $HFGD$:	14
BE via $BCDE$:	8	HE via HIE:	3
BI via $BFHI$:	6	IA via IHA:	10
CE via CDE:	10	IC via $IEDC$:	15

13. If the packet size of Problem 12 is now increased to 2000 bits, how are the mean number of hops, the mean time delay, and the maximum scale factor affected?

14. Given the six nodes with (x, y) coordinates shown below, draw a degree 3 starting network using the link-deficit algorithm. (Number A as 1, B as 2, and so on.)
    A: (1, 2), B: (2, 3), C: (3, 3), D: (4, 2), E: (2, 1), F: (3, 1)

15. Use the link-deficit algorithm to devise a degree 3 starting network for a group of eight nodes uniformly spaced along a straight line. The nodes are numbered 1 through 8, from left to right.

16. Three parallel transmission lines run between IMPs A and B. The three lines carry

5, 10, and 15 packets/sec, respectively. Mean packet size is 1000 bits. A total capacity of 60 kbps is available to be allocated among them. Compute the mean delay for

(a) Uniform capacity assignment.

(b) Capacity assigned proportional to traffic.

(c) Optimal assignment.

For optimal assignment, each line is first allocated what it actually needs to carry its traffic, and then the excess capacity is divided among the lines, each line getting excess capacity in proportion to its weight. The weight of a line is equal to the square root of its traffic.

17. A network has 11 nodes and 17 arcs, with traffic/capacity as follows:

AB	5/15	BC	12/20	CD	19/20	DE	7/10	EF	20/40
AG	16/30	AH	5/25	GH	2/20	BG	4/10	CH	18/30
CI	9/10	IJ	3/10	DJ	29/30	IE	7/25	EJ	2/15
JK	3/20	FK	2/10						

According to the cut saturation heuristic, which pairs are candidates to be connected? (*Note*: Each node acts as both a source and a sink, so the flow does not balance at each node.)

18. Consider again the network of Problem 17. If link *CD* were removed, how many links would have to be added to restore the connectivity? What is the set of candidates?

19. A group of four concentrators are located at coordinates (0, 3), (2, 7) (4, 1), and (4, 4). There are also 16 terminals at (1, 1), (1, 6), (2, 2), (2, 3), (2, 5), (2, 8), (3, 0), (3, 2), (3, 4), (3, 7), (4, 3), (4, 6), (5, 3), (5, 5), (5, 7), and (6, 2). No concentrator can handle more than four terminals. Find an assignment that is feasible and whose total cost is less than 30 units, where the cost of a line is simply its length. Multidrop lines are not permitted.

20. Using the same group of terminals as above, but with only a single concentrator this time, namely the one at (4, 4),

(a) Find the minimum spanning tree and its cost.

(b) Find an MST of cost < 24, (maximum four terminals per port).

21. Rewrite the maximum flow algorithm, representing the graph as a list of arcs rather than as a matrix.

22. Write a procedure that generates a random graph of degree k. Use the link-deficit algorithm or one of your own design.

23. Write a procedure to perturb a network using one of the heuristics given, or one of your own design.

24. Write a procedure to assign terminals to concentrators. The input consists of the number of concentrators and their coordinates, plus the

3

THE PHYSICAL LAYER

In this chapter we will look at the lowest layer depicted in the hierarchy of Fig. 1-7. We will begin with a theoretical analysis of data transmission, only to discover that Mother Nature puts some limits on what can be sent over a given channel. Then we move on to take a look at how the telephone system is organized, and how information is transmitted using it, including the X.21 digital interface. After that we will consider some of the issues involved with communication satellites. Next comes terminal handling, including the PAD and X.3. Finally, we will look at error-correcting and -detecting codes.

3.1. THE THEORETICAL BASIS FOR DATA COMMUNICATION

Information can be transmitted on wires by varying some physical property such as voltage or current. By representing the value of this voltage or current as a single valued function of time, say $f(t)$, we can model the behavior of the signal and subject it to mathematical analysis. This analysis is the subject of the following sections.

3.1.1. Fourier Analysis

It has been proven that any reasonably behaved periodic function, $g(t)$, with period T can be constructed by summing a (possibly infinite) number of sines and cosines:

$$g(t) = \frac{1}{2}c + \sum_{n=1}^{\infty} a_n \sin(2\pi nft) + \sum_{n=1}^{\infty} b_n \cos(2\pi nft) \qquad (3\text{-}1)$$

where $f = 1/T$ is the fundamental frequency and a_n and b_n are the sine and cosine amplitudes of the nth **harmonics** (terms). Such a decomposition is called a **Fourier series**. From the Fourier series the function can be reconstructed; i.e., if the period, T, is known and the amplitudes are given, the original function of time can be found by performing the sums of Eq. (3-1).

A data signal that has a finite duration (which all of them do) can be handled by just imagining that it repeats the entire pattern over and over forever (i.e., the interval from T to $2T$ is the same as from 0 to T, etc).

The a_n amplitudes can be computed for any given $g(t)$ by multiplying both sides of Eq. (3-1) by $\sin(2\pi kft)$ and then integrating from 0 to T. Since

$$\int_0^T \sin(2\pi kft) \sin(2\pi nft) \, dt \;=\; \begin{cases} 0 \text{ for } k \neq n \\ T/2 \text{ for } k = n \end{cases}$$

only one term of the summation survives: a_n. The b_n summation vanishes completely. Similarly, by multiplying Eq. (3-1) by $\cos(2\pi kft)$ and integrating between 0 and T, we can derive b_n. By just integrating both sides of the equation as it stands, c can be found. The results of performing these operations are as follows:

$$a_n = \frac{2}{T}\int_0^T g(t) \sin(2\pi nft) \, dt \qquad b_n = \frac{2}{T}\int_0^T g(t) \cos(2\pi nft) \, dt \qquad c = \frac{2}{T}\int_0^T g(t) \, dt$$

3.1.2. Bandwidth Limited Signals

To see what all this has to do with data communication, let us consider a specific example, the transmission of the ASCII character "b" encoded in an 8-bit byte. The bit pattern to be transmitted is 01100010. The left-hand part of Fig. 3-1(a) shows the voltage output by the transmitting computer. The Fourier analysis of this signal yields the coefficients:

$$a_n = \frac{1}{\pi n}[\cos(\pi n/4) - \cos(3\pi n/4) + \cos(6\pi n/4) - \cos(7\pi n/4)]$$

$$b_n = \frac{1}{\pi n}[\sin(3\pi n/4) - \sin(\pi n/4) + \sin(7\pi n/4) - \sin(6\pi n/4)]$$

$$c_n = 3/8$$

The root-mean-square amplitudes, $\sqrt{a_n^2 + b_n^2}$, for the first few terms are shown on the right-hand side of Fig. 3-1(a). These values are of interest because their squares are proportional to the energy transmitted at the corresponding frequency.

No transmission facility can transmit signals without losing some power in the process. If all the Fourier components were equally diminished, the resulting signal would be reduced in amplitude but not distorted [i.e., it would have the same nice squared off shape as Fig. 3-1(a)]. Unfortunately, all transmission facilities diminish different Fourier components by different amounts, thus introducing distortion into the output. Usually, the amplitudes are transmitted undiminished from 0 up to some frequency f_c [measured in cycles/sec or Hertz (Hz)] with all frequencies above this cutoff frequency strongly attenuated. In some cases this is a physical property of the transmission medium, and in other cases a filter is intentionally introduced into the circuit to limit the amount of (scarce) bandwidth available to each customer.

Now let us consider how the signal of Fig. 3-1(a) would look if the bandwidth were so low that only the lowest frequencies were transmitted [i.e., the function were being approximated by the first few terms of Eq. (3-1)]. Figure 3-1(b) shows the signal that results from a channel that allows only the first harmonic to pass through. Similarly, Fig. 3-1(c)-(e) show the spectra and reconstructed functions for higher bandwidth channels.

The time T required to transmit the character depends on both the encoding method and the signaling speed, [the number of times per second that the signal changes its value (e.g., its voltage)]. The number of changes per second is measured in **baud**. A b baud line does not necessarily transmit b bits/sec, since each signal might convey several bits. If the voltages 0, 1, 2, 3, 4, 5, 6, and 7 were used, each signal value could be used to convey 3 bits, so the bit rate would be three times the baud rate. In our example, only 0s and 1s are being used as signal levels, so the bit rate is equal to the baud rate.

Given a bit rate of b bits/sec, the time required to send 8 bits (for example) is $8/b$ sec, so the frequency of the first harmonic is $b/8$ Hz. An ordinary telephone line, often called a **voice grade line**, has an artificially introduced cutoff frequency near 3000 Hz. This restriction means that the number of the highest harmonic passed through is $24000/b$, roughly (the cutoff is not sharp). For some commonly used data rates, the numbers work out as follows:

Bps	T (msec)	First harmonic (Hz)	No. harmonics sent
300	26.67	37.5	80
600	13.33	75	40
1200	6.67	150	20
2400	3.33	300	10
4800	1.67	600	5
9600	0.83	1200	2
19200	0.42	2400	1
38400	0.21	4800	0

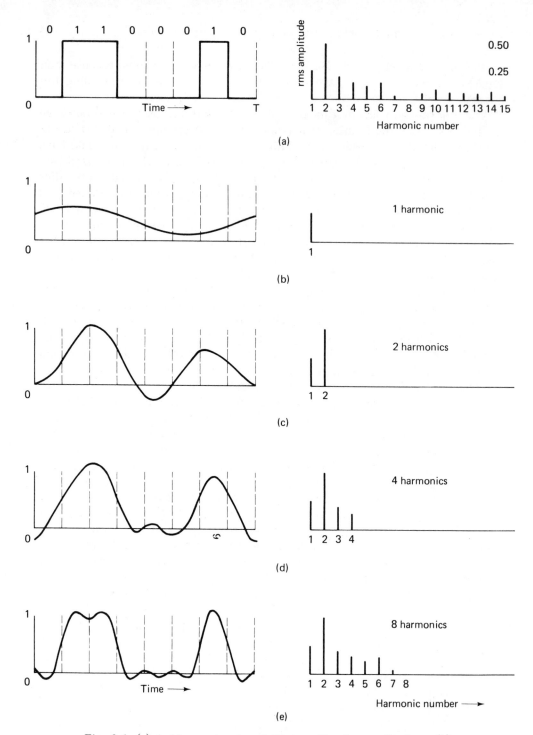

Fig. 3-1. (a) A binary signal and its rms Fourier amplitudes. (b)-(e) Successive approximations to the original signal.

From the numbers above, it is clear that trying to send at 9600 bps over a voice-grade telephone line will transform Fig. 3-1(a) into something looking like Fig. 3-1(c), making accurate reception of the original bit stream unlikely. It should be obvious that at data rates much higher than 38.4 kbps there is no hope at all, even if the transmission facility is completely noiseless. In other words, limiting the bandwidth limits the data rate, even for perfect channels.

3.1.3. The Maximum Data Rate of a Channel

As early as 1924, H. Nyquist realized the existence of this fundamental limit and derived an equation expressing the maximum data rate for a finite bandwidth noiseless channel. In 1948, C. Shannon carried Nyquist's work further and extended it to the case of a channel subject to random (thermal) noise. We will just briefly summarize their now classical results here.

Nyquist proved that if an arbitrary signal has been run through a low-pass filter of bandwidth H, the filtered signal can be completely reconstructed by making only $2H$ (exact) samples per second. Sampling the line faster than $2H$ times per second is pointless because the higher-frequency components that such sampling could recover have already been filtered out. If the signal consists of V discrete levels, Nyquist's theorem states:

$$\text{maximum data rate} = 2H \log_2 V \text{ bits/sec}$$

For example, a noiseless 3-kHz channel cannot transmit binary (i.e., two-level) signals at a rate exceeding 6000 bps (bits/sec).

So far we have considered only noiseless channels. If random noise is present, the situation deteriorates rapidly. The amount of thermal noise present is measured by the ratio of the signal power to the noise power, called the **signal-to-noise ratio**. If we denote the signal power by S and the noise power by N, the signal-to-noise ratio is S/N. Usually, the ratio itself is not quoted; instead, the quantity $10 \log_{10} S/N$ is given. These units are called **decibels** (dB). An S/N ratio of 10 is 10 dB, a ratio of 100 is 20 dB, a ratio of 1000 is 30 dB and so on. The manufacturers of stereo amplifiers often characterize the bandwidth (frequency range) over which their product is linear by giving the 3-dB frequency on each end. These are the points at which the amplification factor has been approximately halved.

Shannon's major result about noisy channels is that the maximum data rate of any channel whose bandwidth is H Hz, and whose signal-to-noise ratio is S/N, is given by

$$\text{maximum number of bits/sec} = H \log_2 (1 + S/N)$$

For example, a channel of 3000-Hz bandwidth, and a signal to thermal noise ratio of 30 dB (typical parameters of the telephone system) can never transmit more than 30,000 bps, no matter how many or few signal levels are used and no matter how often or how infrequent samples are taken. Shannon's result was derived using information-theory arguments and has very general validity. Counterexamples should be treated in the same category as perpetual motion machines. It should be noted, however, that this is only an upper bound. In practice, it is difficult to even *approach* the Shannon limit. A bit rate of 9600 bps on a voice-grade line is considered excellent, and is achieved by sending 4-bit groups at 2400 baud.

3.2. THE TELEPHONE SYSTEM

When two computers owned by the same company or organization and located close to each other need to communicate, it is often easiest just to run a cable between them. However, when the distances are large, or there are many computers, or the cables would have to pass through a public road or other public right of way, the costs of running private cables are usually prohibitive. Furthermore, in just about every country in the world, stringing private transmission lines across (or underneath) public property is also illegal. Consequently, the network designers must rely upon the existing telecommunication facilities.

These facilities, especially the switched public telephone network, were usually designed many years ago, with a completely different goal in mind: transmitting the human voice in a more-or-less recognizable form. Their suitability for use in computer-computer communication is often marginal at best, but since there is rarely an alternative, it is worth devoting some attention to them and the obstacles they present.

To see the order of magnitude of the problem, let us make a rough, but illustrative comparison of the properties of a typical computer-computer connection via a local cable and via a dial-up telephone line. A cable running between two computers can transfer data at memory speeds, typically 10^7 to 10^8 bps. The error rate is usually so low that it is hard to measure, but one error per day would be considered poor at most installations. One error per day at these speeds is equivalent to one error per 10^{12} or 10^{13} bits sent.

In contrast, a dial up line has a maximum data rate on the order of 10^4 bps and an error rate of roughly 1 per 10^5 bits sent, varying somewhat with the age of the telephone switching equipment involved. The combined bit rate times error rate performance of a local cable is thus 11 orders of magnitude better than a voice-grade telephone line. To make an analogy in the field of transportation, the ratio of the cost of the entire Apollo project, which landed men on the moon to the cost of a bus ride downtown is about 11 orders of magnitude.

The trouble, of course, is that computer systems designers are used to working with computer systems, and when suddenly confronted with another system whose performance (from their point of view) is 11 orders of magnitude worse, it is not surprising that much time and effort has been devoted to trying to figure out how to use it efficiently.

3.2.1. Who's Who in the Telecommunication World

Before looking at the technical issues involved with data communication, it is worth saying a few words about the organizations that run the telecommunication systems. The legal status of the world's telephone companies varies from country to country. At one extreme is the United States, which has 1600 separate, privately owned telephone companies. AT&T, the world's largest corporation, dominates the scene, providing telephone service to about 80% of America's telephones, spread throughout half of its geographical area, with all the other companies combined providing the remainder.

Companies in the United States that provide communication services to the public are called **common carriers**. Their offerings and prices are described by a document called a **tariff**, which must be approved by the Federal Communications Commission, for the case of interstate and international traffic, and by the state Public Utilities Commissions for intrastate traffic.

In recent years a new breed of telecommunication company has emerged to provide specialized data communication services, often in direct competition with the telephone companies. Some of these companies offer high-performance long-distance transmission facilities (e.g., using satellites), whereas others provide time-sharing, networking, or other services using transmission facilities which they themselves rent from other common carriers.

At the other extreme are countries in which the national government has a complete monopoly on all communication, including the mail, telegraph, telephone, and often radio and television as well. Most of the world falls in this category. In some cases the telecommunication authority is a nationalized company, and in others it is simply a branch of the government, usually known as the PTT (Post, Telegraph & Telephone administration).

With all these different suppliers of services, there is clearly a need to provide compatibility on a worldwide scale to ensure that people (and computers) in one country can call their counterparts in another one. This coordination is provided by an agency of the United Nations called the International Telecommunication Union, **ITU**. ITU has three main organs, two of which deal primarily with international radio broadcasting and one of which is primarily concerned with telephone and data communication systems.

The latter group is called **CCITT**, an acronym for its French name: Comité Consultatif Internationale de Télégraphique et Téléphonique. CCITT has five classes of members: A members, which are the national telecommunication administrations of the member countries (e.g., the FCC in the United States and the PTTs in Europe); B members, which are recognized private administrations (e.g., AT&T); C members, which are scientific and industrial organizations; D members, which are other international organizations; and E members, which are organizations whose primary mission is in another field but which have an interest in CCITT's work. Only A members may vote.

CCITT's task is to make technical recommendations about telephone, telegraph, and data communication interfaces. These often become internationally recognized standards. Two examples are V.24 (also known as EIA RS232 in the United States), which specifies the placement and meaning of the various pins on the connector used by most asynchronous terminals, and X.25, which specifies the interface between a computer and a computer network.

The International Standards Organization, **ISO**, is another group that tries to make the world a better place via standards. Its constituents are the national standards organizations in the member countries. On issues of telecommunication standards, ISO and CCITT *sometimes* cooperate (ISO is a *D* class member of CCITT) to avoid the irony of two official and mutually incompatible international standards.

3.2.2. Structure of the Telephone System

There are 300 million telephones in the world. From each one of them it is possible to call any of the other ones. The number of different potential connections is therefore 4.5×10^{16}. The most straightforward way of implementing the telephone network would simply be to run 300 million copper wires into everyone's house, each one leading to a different telephone. This method, although conceptually simple, has some drawbacks, to put it mildly. Consider, for example, the implications of installing a new telephone somewhere. Figure 3-2(a) illustrates the idea of a complete interconnection on a somewhat modest scale.

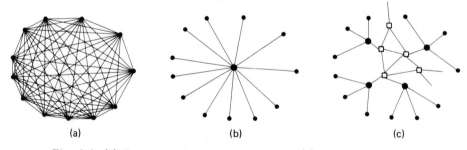

| (a) | (b) | (c) |

Fig. 3-2. (a) Fully interconnected network. (b) Centralized switch. (c) Two level hierarchy.

The next simplest approach might be to have one gigantic switch somewhere, with one line running to each of the world's telephones, as illustrated in Fig. 3-2(b). This, too, is absurd, due to the gargantuan problems of building, operating, and maintaining the switch.

In reality, the telephone system is organized as a highly redundant, multilevel hierarchy. The following description is highly simplified but gives the essential flavor nevertheless. Each telephone has two copper wires coming out of it that go directly to the telephone company's nearest **end office** (also called a **local central office**). The distance is typically 1 to 10 km, being smaller in cities than in rural areas. In the United States alone there are 25,000 end offices. The concatenation of the area code and the first three digits of the telephone number uniquely specify an end office, which is why the rate structure uses this information. The two-wire connections between each subscriber's telephone and the end office are known in the trade as the **local loop**. If the world's local loops were stretched out end to end, they would extend to the moon and back 1000 times.

If a subscriber attached to a given end office calls another subscriber attached to the same end office, the switching mechanism within the office sets up a direct electrical connection between the two local loops. This connection remains intact for the duration of the call.

If the called telephone is attached to another end office, a different procedure is used. Each end office has a number of outgoing lines to one or more nearby switching centers, called **toll offices** (or **tandem offices**). These lines are called **toll connecting trunks**. If both the caller's and callee's end offices happen to have a toll connecting trunk to the same toll office (a likely occurrence if they are relatively close by), the connection may be established within the toll office. A telephone network consisting only of end offices (the large dots) and toll offices (the squares) is shown in Fig. 3-2(c).

If the caller and callee do not have a toll office in common, the path will have to be established somewhere higher up in the hierarchy. There are sectional and regional offices that form a network by which the toll offices are connected. The toll, sectional, and regional exchanges communicate with each other via high bandwidth **intertoll trunks**. The number of different kinds of switching centers and their topology (e.g., may two sectional offices have a direct connection or must they go through a regional office?) varies from country to country depending on its telephone density. Figure 3-3 shows how a medium-distance connection might be routed.

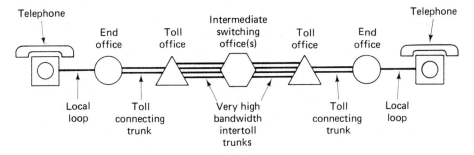

Fig. 3-3. Typical circuit route for a medium-distance call.

A variety of transmission media are used for telecommunications. Local loops consist of pairs of insulated copper wires nowadays, although at the beginning of the century, uninsulated wires spaced 25 cm apart on telephone poles were common. Between switching offices, coaxial cables, microwaves, and waveguides are used. Fiber-optics systems using lasers are also becoming more widespread, primarily because their enormous bandwidth allows a single bundle to replace many copper cables, alleviating the critical overcrowding within existing cable ducts.

3.2.3. The Local Loop

The local loop consists of a pair of copper wires running between the subscriber's telephone and an end office. If it were not for the difficulties mentioned below, such a conductor could carry traffic at 1 Mbps without any trouble. The signals used on the local loop are dc, limited by filters to the frequency range 300 to 3100 Hz. If a digital signal were to be applied to one end of the line, the received signal at the other end would not show a square wave form, owing to capacitance and inductance effects. Rather it would rise slowly and decay slowly. This effect makes baseband (dc) signaling unsuitable except at slow speeds and over short distances. The variation of signal propagation speed with frequency also contributes to the distortion.

To get around the problems associated with dc signaling, ac signaling is used. A continuous tone in the 1000- to 2000-Hz range is introduced, called a **sine wave carrier**. Its amplitude, frequency, or phase can be modulated to transmit information. In **amplitude modulation**, two different voltage levels are used to represent 0 and 1, respectively. In **frequency modulation**, also known as **frequency shift keying**, two (or more) different tones are used. In the most common form of phase modulation, the carrier wave is systematically shifted 45, 135, 225, or 315 degrees at uniformly spaced intervals. Each phase shift transmits 2 bits of information. Figure 3-4 illustrates the three forms of modulation. Mixed forms are also used. For example, four phase shifts combined with two amplitude levels provides 3 bits/baud. A device that accepts a serial stream of bits as input and produces a modulated carrier as output (or vice versa) is called a **modem** (for modulator-demodulator). The modem is inserted between the (digital) computer and the (analog) telephone system.

At the junction between the local loop, which is (usually) a two-wire circuit, and the trunk, which is a four wire circuit, echoes can occur. As an illustration of electromagnetic echoes, try shining a flashlight from a darkend room through a closed window at night. You will see a reflection of the flashlight in the window (i.e., some of the energy has been reflected at the air-glass junction and sent back toward you). The same thing happens in the end office.

The effect of the echo is that a person speaking on the telephone hears his own words after a short delay. Psychological studies have shown that this is annoying to many people, often making them stutter or become confused. To eliminate the problem of echoes, echo suppressors are installed on lines longer

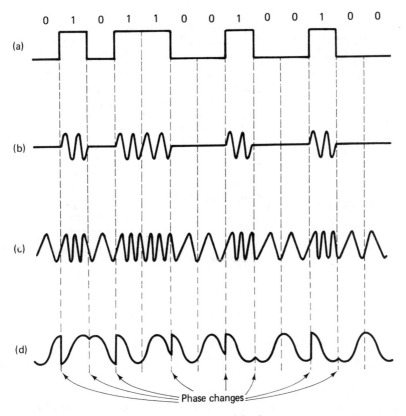

Fig. 3-4. (a) A   binary   signal.   (b) Amplitude   modulation.
(c) Frequency modulation. (d) Phase modulation.

than 2000 km. (On short lines the echoes come back so fast that people cannot detect them.) An **echo suppressor** is a device that detects human speech coming from one end of the connection and suppresses all signals going the other way.

When the first person stops talking and the second begins, the echo suppressor switches directions. While it is functioning however, information can only travel in one direction. Figure 3-5(a) shows the state of the echo suppressors while *A* is talking to *B*. Figure 3-5(b) shows the state after *B* has started talking. When echo suppressors are used, full-duplex communication is impossible.

The echo suppressors have several properties that are undesirable for data communication. First, they prevent full-duplex data transmission, which would otherwise be possible, even over the two-wire local loop (by allocating part of the bandwidth to the forward channel and part to the reverse channel). Even if half-duplex transmission is adequate, they are a nuisance because the time

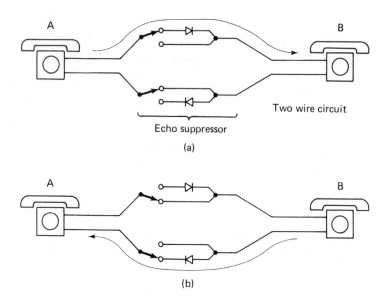

Fig. 3-5. (a) *A* talking to *B*. (b) *B* talking to *A*.

required to switch directions can be substantial. Furthermore, they are designed to reverse upon detecting human speech, not digital data, which probably will not have the desired effect.

To alleviate these problems, an escape hatch has been provided. When the echo suppressors hear a pure tone at 2100 Hz, they shut down, and remain shut down as long as a carrier is present. This arrangement is one of the many examples of **in-band signaling**, so called because the control signals that activate and deactivate internal control functions lie within the band accessible to the user (e.g., a small child keen on demonstrating her new 2100 Hz toy whistle to grandma).

In recent years a new form of local distribution has appeared on the horizon in the form of cable television. Since a television channel requires 6 MHz of bandwidth and most cable systems offer many channels, typically cables with a bandwidth of 300 MHz are used. This being orders of magnitude more than the existing telephone local loops, it bears watching in the future as a possible data transmission facility. Unlike the local loops, cable TV does not use a star pattern radiating out from an end office. Instead, everyone in the same neighborhood shares the same cable, which is like having hundreds of extension telephones on a single outgoing line. Nevertheless, high-performance data transmission systems can be built using a shared cable. We will discuss one such system (Ethernet) in Chap. 7. The basic obstacle in using these cables for home terminals is not technical, and probably not even economic, but inertia and widespread ignorance of the potential.

3.3. TRANSMISSION AND MULTIPLEXING

In the following sections we will look at some of the issues involved in transmitting information, especially in digital form.

3.3.1. Frequency Division and Time Division Multiplexing

Economies of scale play an important role in the telephone system. It costs essentially the same amount of money to install and maintain a high-bandwidth cable as a low-bandwidth wire between two switching offices (i.e., the costs come from having to dig the trench and not from the copper conductor). Consequently, telephone companies have developed elaborate schemes for multiplexing many conversations over a single physical channel.

These multiplexing schemes can be divided into two basic categories: **frequency division multiplexing** (FDM) and **time division multiplexing** (TDM). In FDM the frequency spectrum is divided up among the logical channels, with each user having exclusive possession of his frequency band In TDM the users take turns (in a round robin), each one periodically getting the entire bandwidth for a little burst of time.

AM radio broadcasting provides illustrations of both kinds of multiplexing. The allocated spectrum is about 1 MHz, roughly 500 to 1500 kHz. Different frequencies are allocated to different logical channels (stations), each operating in a portion of the spectrum, with the interchannel separation great enough to prevent interference. This system is is an example of frequency-division multiplexing. In addition (in some countries), the individual stations have two logical subchannels: music and advertising. These two alternate in time on the same frequency, first a burst of music, then a burst of advertising, then more music, etc. This situation is time-division multiplexing.

Figure 3-6 shows how three voice-grade telephone channels are multiplexed using FDM. Filters limit the usable bandwidth to about 3000 Hz per voice-grade channel. When many channels are multiplexed together, 4000 Hz is allocated to each channel to keep them well separated. First the voice channels are raised in frequency, each by a different amount. Then they can be combined, because no two channels occupy the same portion of the spectrum now. Notice that even though there are gaps (guard bands) between the channels, there is some overlap between adjacent channels, because the filters do not have sharp edges. This overlap means that a strong spike at the edge of one channel will be felt in the adjacent one as nonthermal noise.

The FDM schemes used around the world are to some degree standardized. A widespread standard is twelve 4000-Hz voice channels (3000 Hz for the user, plus two guard bands of 500 Hz each) multiplexed into the band 60 to 108 kHz. This unit is called a **group.** The 12- to 60-kHz band is sometimes used for another group. Many carriers offer a 48- to 56-kbps leased line service to customers, based on the group. Five groups (60 voice channels) can be

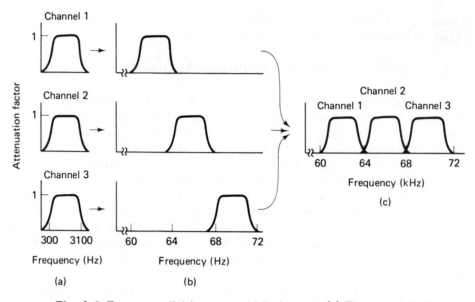

Fig. 3-6. Frequency-division multiplexing. (a) The original bandwidths. (b) The bandwidths raised in frequency. (c) The multiplexed channel.

multiplexed to form a **supergroup**. The next unit is the **mastergroup**, which is five supergroups (CCITT standard) or ten supergroups (Bell system). Other standards up to 230,000 voice channels also exist.

3.3.2. Digital Transmission

Historically, analog transmission has dominated the telecommunication industry since its inception. Signals have been sent by having some physical quantity (e.g., voltage) continuously vary as a function of time. With the advent of digital electronics and computers, the high speed intertoll trunks in industrialized countries are being converted to digital transmission (i.e., strings of 0s and 1s are transmitted instead of continuous signals). Due to the immense investment in existing facilities, it will be decades before the complete system, including all the local loops, have been converted.

Digital transmission is superior to analog transmission in several important ways. First, it potentially has a very low error rate. Analog circuits have amplifiers that attempt to compensate for the attenuation in the line, but they can never compensate exactly for it, especially if the attenuation is different for different frequencies. Since the error is cumulative, long-distance calls that go through many amplifiers are likely to suffer considerable distortion. Digital regenerators, in contrast can restore the weakened incoming signal to its original value exactly, because the only possible values are 0 and 1. Digital regenerators do not suffer from cumulative error.

A second advantage of digital transmission is that voice, data, music, television, facsimile, video telephone, and so on, can all be multiplexed together to make more efficient use of the equipment. Another advantage is that much higher data rates are possible using existing lines. As the costs of digital computers and integrated circuit chips continues to drop, digital transmission and its associated switching is likely to become much cheaper than analog transmission as well.

When a telephone subscriber attached to a digital end office makes a call, the signal emerging from his local loop is an ordinary analog signal. This analog signal is then digitized at the end office by a **codec** (coder-decoder), producing a 7- or 8-bit number. A codec is the inverse of a modem: the latter converts a digital bit stream into a modulated analog signal; the former converts a continuous analog signal into a digital bit stream. The codec makes 8000 samples per second (125 μsec/sample) because the Nyquist theorem says that this is sufficient to capture all the information from a 4-kHz bandwidth. This technique is called **pulse code modulation** (PCM).

When digital transmission began emerging as a feasible technology, CCITT was unable to reach agreement on an international standard. Consequently, there are now a variety of incompatible schemes in use around the world. International hookups between incompatible countries require (often expensive) "black boxes" to convert the originating country's system to that of the receiving country.

One method that is in widespread use is the Bell System's T1 carrier, depicted in Fig. 3-7. The T1 carrier can handle 24 voice channels multiplexed together. Usually, the analog signals are multiplexed using TDM, with the resulting analog stream being fed to the codec rather than having 24 separate codecs and then merging the digital output. Each of the 24 channels, in turn, gets to insert eight bits into the output stream. Seven of these are data, and one is for control, yielding $7 \times 8000 = 56,000$ bps of data, and $1 \times 8000 = 8000$ bps of signaling information.

A frame consists of $24 \times 8 = 192$ bits, plus one extra bit for framing, yielding 193 bits every 125 μsec. This gives a gross data rate of 1.544 Mbps. The 193rd bit is used for frame synchronization. It contains the pattern 0101010101 .... Normally, the receiver keeps checking this bit to make sure that it has not lost synchronization. If it does get out of sync, the receiver can scan for this pattern to get resynchronized. Analog customers cannot generate the bit pattern at all, because it corresponds to a sine wave at 4000 Hz, which would be filtered out. Digital customers can, of course, generate this pattern, but the odds are against it being present when the frame slips.

When CCITT finally did reach agreement, they felt that 8000 bps of signaling information was far too much, so their 1.544-Mbps standard is based upon

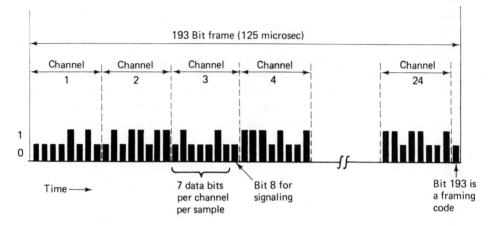

Fig. 3-7. The Bell system T1 carrier (1.544 Mbps).

an 8- rather than a 7-bit data item; that is, the analog signal is quantized into 256 rather than 128 discrete levels. Two (incompatible) variations are provided. In **common-channel signaling**, the extra bit (which is attached onto the front rather than the rear of the 193 bit frame) takes on the values 10101010 . . . in the odd frames, and contains signaling information for all the channels in the even frames.

In the other variation, **channel associated signaling**, each channel has its own private signaling subchannel. A private subchannel is arranged by allocating one of the eight user bits in every sixth frame for signaling purposes, so five out of six samples are 8 bits wide, and the other one is only 7 bits wide. CCITT also has a recommendation for a PCM carrier at 2.048 Mbps. This carrier has 32 8-bit data samples packed into the basic 125-μsec frame Thirty of the channels are used for information and two are used for signaling. Each group of four frames provides 64 signaling bits, half of which are used for channel associated signaling and half of which are used for frame synchronization or are reserved for each country to use as it wishes. Outside North America and Japan, the 2.048 Mbps carrier is in widespread use.

Just as there is little agreement on the basic carrier, there is little agreement on how it is to be multiplexed into higher bandwidth carriers. The Bell system has standards called T2, T3, and T4 at 6.132, 44.736, and 274.176 Mbps, whereas CCITT's recommendations are for 8.848, 34.304, 139.264, and 565.148 Mbps.

Once the voice signal has been digitized, it is tempting to try to use statistical techniques to reduce the number of bits needed per channel. These techniques are appropriate not only to encoding speech, but to any digitization of an analog signal (e.g., a minicomputer collecting data from a physics experiment). All of the compaction methods are based upon the principle that the signal changes relatively slowly compared to the sampling frequency, so that much of the information in the 7- or 8-bit digital level is redundant.

One method, called **differential pulse code modulation**, consists of not outputting the digitized amplitude, but the difference between the current value and the previous one. Since jumps of 32 or more on a scale of 128 are unlikely, 5 bits should suffice instead of seven. If the signal does occasionally jump wildly, the encoding logic may require several sampling periods to "catch up." For speech, the error introduced can be ignored.

A variation of this compaction method requires each sampled value to differ from its predecessor by either $+1$ or -1. A single bit is transmitted, telling whether the new sample is above or below the previous one. This technique, called **delta modulation**, is illustrated in Fig. 3-8. Like all compaction techniques that assume small level changes between consecutive samples, delta encoding can get into trouble if the signal changes too fast, as shown in the figure.

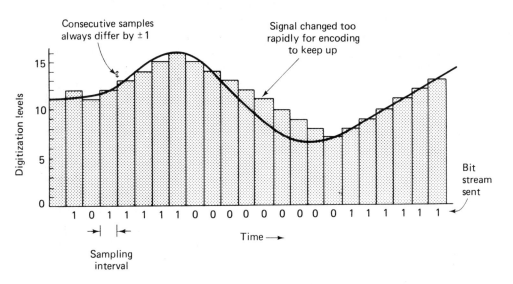

Fig. 3-8. Delta modulation.

An improvement to differential PCM is to extrapolate the previous few values to predict the next value and then to encode the difference between the actual signal and the predicted one. The transmitter and receiver must use the same prediction algorithm, of course. Such schemes are called **predictive encoding**. They are useful because they reduce the size of the numbers to be encoded, hence the number of bits to be sent.

Although PCM is beginning to be widely used on interoffice trunks, the computer user gets relatively little benefit from it if he must send his data to his end office in the form of a modulated analog sine wave at 2400 bps. It would be nice if the carrier would attach the local loop directly to the PCM trunk system, so that the computer could output digital data directly onto the local loop at 1.544 or 2.048 Mbps. The twisted pairs used for local loop distribution can handle this data rate if the loading coils used to reduce the frequency dependence of the attenuation factor at low frequencies are removed and digital regenerators are inserted every 2 km.

3.3.3. The X.21 Digital Interface

As early as 1969, CCITT realized that eventually carriers would bring true digital lines (although not necessarily at T1 speeds) onto customer premises. To encourage compatibility in their use, CCITT proposed a digital signaling interface, **X.21**, which was approved in 1976. The standard specifies how the customer's computer, or **DTE** (Data Terminal Equipment) in CCITT nomenclature, sets up and clears calls by exchanging signals with the carrier's equipment, or **DCE** (Data Circuit-Terminating Equipment) in CCITT nomenclature. For a list of other relevant CCITT standards, see (Folts, 1979).

The names and functions of the eight wires defined by X.21 are given in Fig. 3-9. The physical connector has 15 pins, but not all of them are used. The DTE uses the T and C lines to transmit data and control information, respectively. (The C line is analogous to the on hook/off hook signal in a telephone.) The DCE uses the R and I lines for data and control. The S line contains a signal stream emitted by the DCE to provide timing information, so the DTE knows when each bit interval starts and stops. At the carrier's option, a B line may also be provided to group the bits into 8-bit frames. If this option is provided, the DTE must begin each character on a frame boundary. If the option is not provided, both DTE and DCE must begin every control sequence with at least two SYN characters, to enable the other one to deduce the implied frame boundaries. In fact, even if the byte timing is provided, the DTE must send the two SYNs before control sequences, to maintain compatibility with networks that do not provide byte timing. The SYNs and all other control characters are in the International Alphabet number 5 (similar to ASCII), with odd parity.

Although X.21 is a long and complicated document, which references other long and complicated documents, the simple example of Fig. 3-10 illustrates the main features. In this example we will show how the DTE places a call to a remote DTE, and how the originating DTE clears the call when it is finished. To make the explanation clearer, we will describe the calling and clearing procedures in terms of an analogy with the telephone system.

When the line is idle (i.e., no call on it), the four signaling lines are all one. When referring to C and I, we will follow CCITT practice and call one OFF and zero ON. When the DTE wishes to place a call, it sets T to 0 and C to ON, which is analogous to a person picking up the telephone receiver to place a call. When the DCE is ready to accept a call, it begins transmitting the ASCII

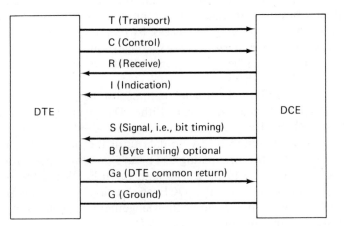

Fig. 3-9. Signal lines used in X.21.

Step	C	I	Event in telephone analogy	DTE sends on T	DCE sends on R
0	Off	Off	No connection-line idle	T = 1	R = 1
1	On	Off	DTE picks up phone	T = 0	
2	On	Off	DCE gives dial tone		R = "+ + + . . . +"
3	On	Off	DTE dials phone number	T = address	
4	On	Off	Remote phone rings		R = call progress
5	On	On	Remote phone picked up		R = 1
6	On	On	Conversation	T = data	R = data
7	Off	On	DTE says goodbye	T = 0	
8	Off	Off	DCE says goodby		R = 0
9	Off	Off	DCE hangs up		R = 1
10	Off	Off	DTE hangs up	T = 1	

Fig. 3-10. An example of X.21 usage.

"+" character on the R line, in effect, a digital dial tone, telling the DTE that it may commence dialing. The DTE "dials" the number by sending the remote DTE's address as a series of ASCII characters using the T line, 1 bit at a time. At this point the DCE sends what are called **call progress signals** to inform the DTE of the result of the call. The call progress signals, defined in CCITT recommendation X.96, consist of two digit numbers, the first of which gives the general class of the result, and the second the details. The general classes include: call put through, try again (e.g., number busy), call failed and will probably fail again next time (e.g., access barred, remote DTE out of order, DTEs incompatible), short term network congestion, and long term network congestion. If the call can be put through, the DCE sets I to ON to indicate that the data transfer may begin.

At this point a full-duplex digital connection has been established, and either side can send information at will. Either DTE can say "goodbye" by setting its C line to OFF. Having done so, it may not send more data, although it must be prepared to continue receiving data until the other DTE has finished. In step 7 of Fig. 3-10, the originating DTE says goodbye first. Its local DCE acknowledges this signal by turning its I line to OFF. When the remote DTE also has turned off its C line, the DCE at the originating side sets R to 1. Finally, the DTE sets T to 1 as an acknowledgement, and the interface is back in the idle state, waiting for another call.

The procedure for incoming calls is analogous to that for outgoing calls. If an incoming call and an outgoing call take place simultaneously, known as a **call collision**, the incoming call is canceled and the outgoing call is put through. CCITT made this decision because it may be too late at this point for some DTEs to reallocate resources already committed to the outgoing call.

Carriers are likely to offer a variety of special features on X.21 networks such as fast-connect, in which setting the C line ON is interpreted by the DCE as a request to reconnect to the number previously dialed. This feature eliminates the dialing stage, and might be useful, for example, to place a separate call to a time-sharing computer every time the person at the terminal hit return. Another possible X.21 option is the closed user group, by which a group of customers (e.g., company offices) could be prevented from call or receiving calls from anyone outside the group. Call redirection, collect calls, incoming or outgoing calls barred and caller identification are other possibilities.

3.3.4. Communication Satellites

Communication satellites have some interesting properties that make them attractive for certain applications. A communication satellite can be thought of as a big repeater in the sky. It contains one or more **transponders**, each of which listens to some portion of the spectrum, amplifies the incoming signal, and then rebroadcasts it (at another frequency, to avoid interference with the incoming signal). The downward beams can be broad, covering a substantial fraction of the earth's surface, or narrow, covering an area hundreds of kilometers in diameter.

According to Kepler's law, the orbital period of a satellite varies as the orbital radius to the 3/2 power. Near the surface of the earth, the period is about 90 min. Communication satellites at such low altitudes are not useful because they are within sight of the ground stations for too short a time interval.

However, at an altitude of 36,000 km, the satellite period is 24 hours, so it rotates at the same rate as the earth under it. An observer looking at a satellite in a circular equatorial orbit sees the satellite hang in a fixed spot in the sky, apparently motionless. Having the satellite be fixed in the sky is extremely desirable, because otherwise an expensive steerable antenna would be needed to track it.

With current technology, it is unwise to have satellites spaced much closer than 4 degrees. At smaller separations, the upward beam from a ground station illuminates not only the desired satellite, but also its neighbors. With a spacing of 4 degrees, there can only be 360/4 = 90 geosynchronous communication satellites in the sky at once. In addition to these technological limitations, there is also competition for orbit slots with other classes of users (e.g., television broadcasting, government and military use, etc.). Television satellites need to be spaced 8 degrees apart on account of their high power.

Fortunately, satellites using different parts of the spectrum do not compete, so each of the 90 possible satellites could have have several data streams going up and down simultaneously. Alternatively, two or more satellites could occupy one orbit slot if they operate at different frequencies.

To prevent total chaos in the sky, there have been international agreements about who may use which orbit slots and frequencies. The 3.7- to 4.2-GHz and 5.925- to 6.425-GHz bands (known as 4/6 GHz) have been designated as telecommunication satellite frequencies for downward and upward beams, respectively. These bands are already overcrowded because they are also used by the common carriers for terrestrial microwave links.

The next highest bands available to telecommunication are at 12/14 GHz. These bands are not (yet) congested, and at these frequencies satellites can be spaced as close as 1 degree. However, another problem exists: rain. Water is an excellent absorber of these short microwaves. Fortunately, heavy storms are usually localized, so by using several widely separated ground stations instead of just one, the problem can be gotten around at the price of extra antennas, extra cables and extra electronics to switch rapidly between stations. Frequency bands at 20/30 GHz have also been set aside for telecommunication but the equipment needed to use them is still expensive.

The first satellites had a single spatial beam that covered all the ground stations. Conventional time-division multiplexing was initially used: in turn each ground station sent a burst of traffic to the satellite. Synchronization of the ground-based transmitters was done by terrestrial cables. Because each ground station received the entire downward transmission, it just selected out those portions destined for it.

With the enormous decline in the price, size, and power requirements of microelectronics, a much more sophisticated broadcasting strategy has become possible. Each satellite is equipped with multiple antennas and multiple transponders. Each downward beam can be focused on a small geographical area, so multiple upward and downward transmissions can take place simultaneously.

These so called **spot beams** are typically elliptically shaped, and can be as small as a few hundred km.

Figure 3-11(a) illustrates a satellite with two antennas, corresponding to two geographically spaced areas. In this example, each area has two ground stations. The two stations within each area take turns broadcasting to the satellite (TDM). The numbers within the upward beams indicate the intended receiver of the message. As the messages come in, they are switched to the appropriate antenna and beamed downward. Figure 3-11(b) shows the retransmission of the messages sent upward in Fig. 3-11(a). By providing a satellite with many spot beams, one satellite can do the work of many.

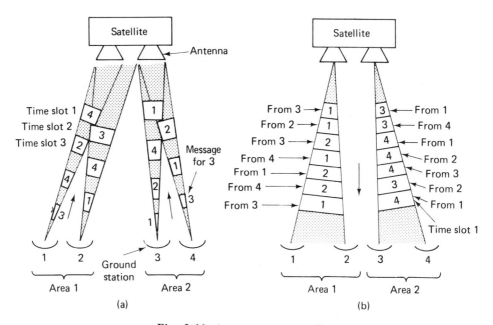

Fig. 3-11. A two antenna satellite.

A close inspection of Fig. 3-11 will show that no two ground stations ever attempt to use the same transponder at the same time. In reality, some coordination is required to ensure that such conflicts indeed do not occur. As an example of how the available bandwidth can be dynamically allocated among competing users, let us briefly look at the SPADE system used on Comsat's Intelsat satellites.

Each **SPADE** transponder is divided into 794 simplex PCM channels, each operating at 64 kbps, plus a single 128 kbps common signaling channel. The channels are multiplexed using FDM, although the same principle could have been used with TDM. Normally, a pair of simplex channels are used together to form a full-duplex channel. The common signaling channel is divided up into 50 msec time frames, with each frame containing 50 slots of 1 msec (128 bits). Each slot is permanently allocated to one of the (not more than) 50 ground stations.

When a ground station has data to send, it picks a currently unused channel at random, and writes the number of the channel in its reserved 128-bit slot. If the selected channel is still unused when the request arrives back at the earth, all stations record the selected channel as busy, and refrain from using it. If two or more stations independently request the same channel, the first request wins, and the losing stations must try again. When a station is finished transmitting, it sends a deallocation message on the common signaling channel.

Communication satellites have several properties that are radically different from terrestrial point-to-point links. To begin with, even though signals to and from a satellite travel at the speed of light (300,000 km/sec), the immense round-trip distance introduces a substantial delay. Depending on the distance between the user and the ground station, and the elevation of the satellite above the horizon, the end-to-end transit time is between 250 and 300 msec. For comparison purposes, terrestrial links have a propagation delay of roughly 6 μsec/km.

It is often said that satellite links have a longer delay than terrestrial links (especially by people operating terrestrial links). Although it is incontrovertibly true that the propagation delay is longer, the total delay depends on the bandwidth and error rate as well. For example, the total delay to send x kilobits over a 9600 bps terrestrial line is $x/9.6$ sec. To send the same message over a 5-Mbps satellite link requires $x/5000 + 0.270$ sec, including the 270 msec typical propagation delay. For messages longer than 2.6 kilobits, the satellite is faster. If we include the effect of retransmission induced delay in the calculation, the lower error rate of the satellite channel will drive the crossover point even lower.

In addition to a propagation delay that is independent of the distance between sender and receiver, satellites also have the property that the cost of transmitting a message is independent of the distance traversed. A call across the ocean costs no more to service than a call across the street. Present day common carrier price structures were developed under very different conditions, and it will be many years before the two are reconciled.

Another potentially revolutionary difference between satellites and terrestrial links is the bandwidth available. The highest speed leased lines in normal use run at 56 kbps, the bottleneck being the local loop. Rooftop to rooftop satellite transmission bypasses the local loop and can potentially offer data rates 1000 times higher. Alternatively, a cheap rooftop antenna can be used to communicate directly with a powerful satellite ground station nearby. Either way, the ability to acquire an immense bandwidth for a short time is attractive owing to the burstiness of computer traffic. Sending a magnetic tape over a 56 kbps phone line takes 7 hours; sending the same tape using a single 50-Mbps satellite transponder takes 30 sec.

Another major difference between satellite channels and terrestrial ones is the cost. Modern satellites typically have at least six transponders, each one capable of operating at 50 Mbps. This channel capacity is equivalent to roughly 100,000 voice-grade circuits. A satellite costs 20-30 million dollars, and a launching rocket a similar amount. Once launched, the satellite can be expected to function for ten years. With these parameters, a circuit costs 50 dollars per year. Furthermore, satellite costs, like computer costs, are dropping rapidly. Of course, one must figure in the cost of the ground stations, which run into tens of thousands (not millions) of dollars each, but the point should be clear. Depending upon whether one is a user, or a carrier with a huge investment in terrestrial lines, satellites can be seen either as a great boon or as a highly disruptive force.

Another interesting property of satellite broadcasting is precisely that: it is broadcasting. All stations under the downward beam can receive the transmission, including "pirate stations" the common carrier may know nothing about. The implications for privacy are obvious. Also, because a user can listen to the retransmission of his own data, he can tell whether it is in error or not. This property has important implications for error handling strategies.

It is also worth mentioning that a single optical fiber, costing a few cents, has more bandwidth than all the satellites ever launched, but because fibers are point-to-point rather than broadcast media, nearly all of the bandwidth is wasted. With a satellite, the bandwidth can be dynamically allocated to precisely those users who need it. However, as time goes on, mixed media networks using optical fibers, cable television, or the terrestrial telephone system for local distribution, and a satellite for the long-haul portion are becoming more and more common, thereby allowing small users to share a single large satellite antenna.

3.3.5. Circuit Switching and Packet Switching

Computer to computer traffic has some properties that are fundamentally different from you talking to your grandmother on the telephone. When people are talking, it is unusual for gaps in the conversation to last for many minutes. When computers are communicating, such gaps are the rule, not the exception. A burst of data will need to be sent quickly, and then there may be silence for the next 30 min. In other words, human-to-human traffic needs continuous use of a low-bandwidth channel, whereas (some) computer-to-computer traffic needs intermittent use of a high bandwidth channel. There is a difference in kind between eating an ice cream cone every day, on the one hand, and eating 365 ice cream cones on your birthday, on the other, even though the mean consumption rate is the same.

The existing telephone plant was set up for human-to-human communication, not computer-to-computer communication. A fundamentally different kind of switching is needed for data communication. In the remainder of this section we will examine this problem more closely.

Circuit Switching

When you (or your computer) places a telephone call, the switching equipment within the telephone system seeks out a physical "copper" path all the way from your telephone to the receiver's telephone. This technique is called **circuit switching** and is shown schematically in Fig. 3-12(a). Each of the six rectangles represents a carrier switching office (end office, toll office, etc.). In this example, each office has three incoming lines and three outgoing lines. When a call passes through a switching office, a physical connection is (conceptually) established between the line on which the call came in and one of the output lines, as shown by the dotted lines. In the early days of telephony, the connection was made by having the operator plug a jumper cable into the input and output sockets.

The model shown in Fig. 3-12(a) is highly simplified of course, because parts of the "copper" path between the two telephones may, in fact, be microwave links onto which thousands of calls are multiplexed. Nevertheless, the basic idea is valid: once a call has been set up, a dedicated path between both ends exists, and will continue to exist until the call is finished.

An important property of circuit switching is the need to set up an end-to-end path *before* any data can be sent. The elapsed time between the end of dialing and the start of ringing can easily be 10 sec, more on long distance or international calls. During this time interval, the telephone system is hunting for a copper path, as shown in Fig. 3-13(a). Note that before data transmission can begin, the call request signal must propagate all the way to the destination, and be acknowledged. For many computer applications (e.g., point-of-sale credit verification) long setup times are undesirable.

As a consequence of the copper path between the calling parties, once the setup has been completed, the only delay for data is the propagation time for the electromagnetic signal, about 6 msec per 1000 km. Also as a consequence of the established path, there is no danger of congestion i.e., once the call has been put through, you never get busy signals, although you might get one before the connection has been established due to lack of internal switching or trunk capacity.

Packet Switching and Message Switching

An alternative switching strategy is **message switching**, shown in Fig. 3-12(b). When this form of switching is used, no physical copper path is established in advance between sender and receiver. Instead, when the sender has a block of data to be sent, it is stored in the first switching office (i.e., IMP) and then forwarded later, one hop at a time. Each block is received in its

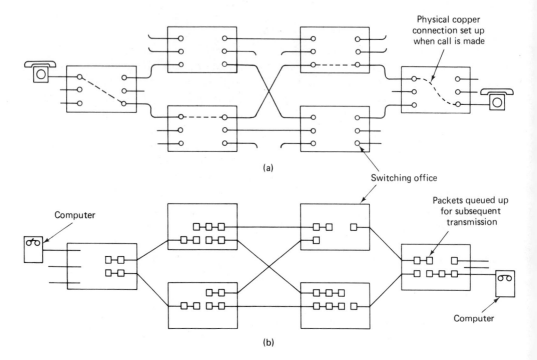

Physical copper
connection set up
when call is made

(a)

Switching office

Computer

Packets queued up
for subsequent
transmission

Computer

(b)

Fig. 3-12. (a) Circuit switching. (b) Packet switching.

entirety, inspected for errors, and then retransmitted. A network using this technique is called a **store-and-forward** network, as mentioned earlier.

Yet another possibility is **packet switching**. With message switching, there is no limit on block size, which means that IMPs must have disks to buffer long blocks. It also means that a single block may tie up an IMP-IMP line for many minutes, rendering message switching useless for interactive traffic. In contrast, packet switching networks place a tight upper limit on block size, allowing packets to be buffered in IMP main memory instead of on disk. By making sure that no user can monopolize any transmission line for more than a few tens of milliseconds, packet switching networks are well suited to handling interactive traffic. A further advantage of packet switching over message switching is shown in Fig. 3-13(b) and (c): the first packet of a multipacket message can be forwarded before the second one has fully arrived, reducing delay and improving throughput. For these reasons, computer networks are usually packet switched, occasionally circuit switched, but never message switched.

Circuit switching and packet switching differ in many respects. The key difference is that circuit switching statically reserves the required bandwidth in advance, whereas packet switching acquires and releases it as it is needed. With

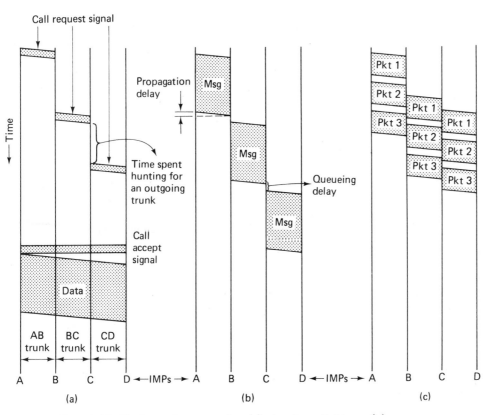

Fig. 3-13. Timing of events in (a) circuit switching, (b) message switching, (c) packet switching.

circuit switching, any unused bandwidth on an allocated circuit is just wasted. With packet switching it may be utilized by other packets from unrelated sources going to unrelated destinations, because circuits are never dedicated. However, just because no circuits are dedicated, a sudden surge of input traffic may overwhelm an IMP, exceeding its storage capacity and causing it to lose packets.

In contrast with circuit switching, when packet switching is used, it is straightforward for the IMPs to provide speed and code conversion. Also, they can provide error correction to some extent. However, in some packet-switched networks, packets may be delivered in the wrong order to the destination. Reordering of packets can never happen with circuit switching.

A final difference between the two methods is the charging algorithm. Packet carriers usually base their charge on both the number of bytes (or packets) carried and the connect time. Furthermore, transmission distance usually does not matter, except perhaps internationally. With circuit switching, the charge is based on the distance and time only, not the traffic.

Hybrid Forms

As computer and communication technology move closer together, variants and hybrid forms of circuit switching and packet switching become possible. We will now briefly touch upon four of these.

The main reason packet switching was invented is to get around the long call connection time present in the existing telephone system. A much more direct, although expensive, approach is to build a new telephone system, one in which calls are put through in milliseconds instead of seconds. With such a system, called **fast connect circuit switching** for obvious reasons, each line typed at a terminal causes the microprocessor inside the terminal to "dial" the computer, send the line, and then hang up. The Scandinavian countries have built a small-scale fast-connect (X.21) network for data communication; whether other countries will do so remains to be seen.

Just as fast-connect networks are a variation on circuit switching, there are variations on packet switching. An especially interesting one is **time-division switching**, in which each IMP scans its input lines in strict rotation. Each packet is immediately retransmitted on the correct output line, often starting as soon as the header has been read. By using fixed-size packets and a rigid time synchronization, no buffer space is needed, and the whole IMP can be reduced to a few chips. The chief virtue of time-division switching is that it offers high performance (>100 Mbps throughput) at low cost using a technology that has already proven itself in the context of the telephone system.

In a packet switching network, each packet is received in its entirety before it is forwarded. If this requirement is dropped, an hybrid form of packet switching and circuit switching becomes possible. In the hybrid, called **virtual cut through** (Kermani and Kleinrock, 1979), the packet header is examined as soon as it arrives, to determine the appropriate outgoing line. If that line is free, retransmission is begun immediately, without waiting for the complete packet. If, however, the line is busy, the packet is stored and forwarded in the usual way. Under conditions of light load, most packets will travel straight through, with no queueing delay. It is even possible for the leading edge of a packet to reach the destination before the source has finished sending the entire packet, a situation greatly resembling circuit switching.

Yet another possible switching method is based on an analogy with the public transit system. Just as subway trains followed fixed routes and fixed time schedules, picking up and discharging passengers along the way, in the TRAN network (Gerla and Destasio, 1978) packets also follow fixed routes and schedules. User data are buffered at the source, waiting for the departure of a packet going to the destination. Data from multiple users are combined in the same packet. Since the network is fully synchronous, there are no queueing delays and no congestion. By reserving a portion of each regularly scheduled packet, it is possible to give certain users a guaranteed bandwidth and a guaranteed delay.

If nothing else, all these possibilities should make clear the importance of designing networks hierarchically, as in Fig. 1-7, to insulate the higher layers from possible drastic changes in the lower ones.

3.4. TERMINAL HANDLING

For many applications the cost of communication lines exceeds the cost of the equipment connected by those lines. In an attempt to reduce communication costs, many networks provide a way for multiple terminals to share a single communication line. The conceptual model is that of Fig. 3-14, in which a **terminal controller** accepts input from a cluster of terminals, and funnels the output onto one line, as well as the reverse operation. In Fig. 3-14(a), all the terminals are wired onto the same **multidrop line**, whereas in Fig. 3-14(b), each terminal has its own **point-to-point line** to the controller. In Chap. 2 we saw this situation in connection with local access networks [see Figs. 2-1, 2-26(b), and 2-28]. In the next few pages we will examine the data communication aspects rather than the topological aspects, of terminal handling.

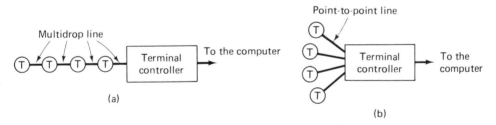

Fig. 3-14. (a) A terminal controller using one multidrop line. (b) A terminal controller using point-to-point lines.

3.4.1. Polling

Having only one output line to the computer gives rise to a problem: What happens if all the terminals try sending at once? Clearly, some method of enforcing discipline is needed. The traditional method is to require all the terminals to keep quiet until the controller says "Go ahead." The general name for this technique is **polling**.

The details of the polling differ for the point-to-point (star) controller and the multidrop controller. Let us first consider the multidrop case. Two polling methods are common. The first one, called **roll-call polling**, consists of the controller simply sending a message to each terminal in turn, inquiring whether or not the terminal has anything to say. These polling messages contain a **site address** or **station address** identifying the terminal being addressed. Each terminal knows its own address and only responds to its own polls, although it receives all polls. If the polled terminal has data to send, it sends the data. If not, it sends back a special "poll reject" message. Usually, the controller just polls all the terminals in round-robin fashion, but in some circumstances important terminals may get several polls per cycle.

On half-duplex lines each poll requires two line turnarounds, one to allow the controller to send, and one to allow the terminal to send. Since line turnaround time, including the time needed to turn the echo suppressors around is often hundreds of milliseconds, it may take a long time to complete a cycle on a line with many terminals, even if most are idle most of the time. The other polling method, **hub polling**, was designed to get around this problem. With hub polling, the controller polls the farthest terminal from it. The addressed terminal turns the line around. If it has data, it sends the data to the controller. However, if it has no data, it puts a polling message addressed to its neighbor on the line. If this terminal is also idle, it sends a poll to its neighbor (on the controller side). The poll propagates from terminal to terminal until one can be found that has something to say or until the poll gets back to the controller. The advantage here is that it is not necessary to keep turning the line around just to discover that a terminal has nothing to say. Sometimes hub polling uses a separate side channel for the polls.

For the case of a star controller, as in Fig. 3-14(b), polling is not required to avoid chaos on the lines. Nevertheless, roll-call polling is often used anyway, to allow the master to acquire input in an orderly fashion. These poll messages differ from those of the multidrop case because there are no site addresses needed; a terminal only receives those polls directed to it.

The BISYNC (binary synchronous communication) protocol, developed by IBM, is widely used in the computer industry for polling remote terminals, as well as for other applications. It is intended for lines operating in half-duplex mode, either multidrop or point-to-point. BISYNC supports three character sets: ASCII, EBCDIC, and 6-bit Transcode.

The BISYNC message format is shown in Fig. 3-15. The contents of the header field is up to the network, i.e., it is not defined by the protocol. ETB is used to terminate a block when there are more blocks to follow. ETX is used to terminate the last block. Addressing of terminals on a multidrop line is not done in the header, but by a separate control message.

When ASCII code is used, the parity bit is set and the checksum is simply a vertical parity check. With EBCDIC or 6-bit Transcode, the individual characters are not parity-checked. Instead cyclic redundancy checksums are used. These checksums will be described later in this chapter.

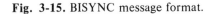

SYN = SYNchronize

SOH = Start of Header

STX = Start of TeXt

ETB = End of Transmission Block

ETX = End of TeXt

Fig. 3-15. BISYNC message format.

3.4.2. Multiplexing versus Concentration

Terminal controllers can be divided into two general classes, multiplexers and concentrators. A **multiplexer** is a device that accepts input from a collection of lines in some static, predetermined sequence, and outputs the data onto a single output line in the same sequence. Since each output time slot is dedicated to a specific input line, there is no need to transmit the input line numbers. The output line must have the same capacity as the sum of the input line capacities. Figure 3-16(a) depicts a multiplexer with four terminals. With four terminal TDM, each terminal is allocated one-fourth of the output time slots, regardless of how busy it is. If each of the terminals operates at 1200 bps, the output line must be $4 \times 1200 = 4800$ bps, since four characters *must* be sent during each polling cycle.

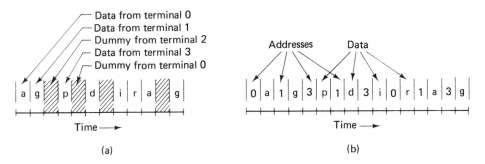

Fig. 3-16. (a) Four terminal multiplexing. (b) Four terminal concentration.

The big disadvantage of TDM is that when a terminal has no traffic, an output time slot is wasted. The output slots are filled in strict rotation, as in Fig. 3-16(a). If there are no data, dummy characters are used. It is not possible to skip a time slot, because the receiving end keeps track of which character came from which terminal by its position in the output stream. Initially, the multiplexer and the computer synchronize themselves. Both know that the order to be used, for example, is 012301230123 . . . . The data themselves carry no identification of their origin. If the multiplexer skipped a time slot when there was no data from a terminal, the receiver would get out of phase and interpret the origin of succeeding characters incorrectly.

If each terminal has traffic only a small fraction of the time, TDM makes inefficient use of the output line capacity. When the actual traffic is far below the potential traffic, most of the time slots on the output line are wasted. Consequently, it is often possible to use an output line with less capacity than the sum of the input lines. This arrangement is called **concentration**. The usual approach is to only transmit actual data and not dummy characters. However, this strategy introduces the problem of telling the receiver which character came from which input line. One solution to this problem is to send two output characters for each input character: the terminal number and the data. Figure 3-16(b) shows what the output might look like if each data character were preceded by its terminal number. Concentrators using this principle are often referred to as **statistical multiplexers** or **asynchronous time division multiplexers** or ATDMs, in contrast with the true (synchronous) multiplexers, or STDMs, although strictly speaking, a statistical multiplexer that had as much output capacity as input capacity would not be a concentrator.

Unfortunately, concentration has an inherent difficulty. If each terminal suddenly starts outputting data at its maximum rate, there will be insufficient capacity on the output line to handle it all. Some data may be lost. For this reason, concentrators are always provided with extra buffers in order to survive short data surges. The more memory a concentrator has, the more it costs but the less likely it is to lose data. Choosing the appropriate parameters for the output line bandwidth and concentrator memory size involve trade-offs. If either is too small, data may be lost. If either is too large, the whole arrangement may be unnecessarily expensive. Furthermore, the optimum choices depend on the traffic statistics, which are not always known at system design time.

3.4.3. The Packet Assembler/Disassembler

If the hosts on a packet switching network expect all packets to be in specific format (e.g., the CCITT X.25 standard), then it will not be possible to connect ordinary asynchronous terminals to the network. What is needed to connect them is a special kind of concentrator that collects individual characters from a group of terminals and periodically outputs a properly formatted packet containing the most recent character harvest. The inverse operation (splitting up packet from a host into individual characters) is also needed. A device performing these character-to-packet transformations is called a **packet assembler/disassembler** (PAD). CCITT recommendations X.3, X.28, and X.29 define the CCITT PAD interfaces. X.3 defines the PAD parameters, X.28 defines the terminal-PAD interface, and X.29 defines the PAD-computer (DTE) interface.

The (CCITT) PAD does not fit into the (ISO) protocol hierarchy very well. There is not even much agreement as to whether the PAD should be regarded as a normal host or not. In the future, many terminals will be able to send and receive complete packets using X.25 and other popular protocols, making them effectively full blown hosts, and thus eliminating the need for the PAD. We will examine the PAD here because it is related to multiplexing and concentration, not because it is really part of the physical layer.

When a terminal initially establishes contact with a PAD, the human operator or the microprocessor in the terminal, or the computer, sets up certain parameters describing the conversation between the terminal and the PAD. The parameters are numbered and so are their option values. A typical command to the PAD might be: SET 1:0, meaning set parameter 1 to value 0. Other commands are available to establish and break connections, read out the values of the parameters, reset the line, and force an interrupt. The complete list is given in Fig. 3-17.

Parameter 1 has to do with whether or not the terminal operator can change PAD parameters in the middle of a session. Parameter 2 must be set according to the terminal type.

Parameters 3 and 4 are needed because some carriers charge per packet, not per character. If a user wishes to be frugal, he will only send full packets, since they cost the same as partial packets. The trouble is, that to make intelligent use of an interactive terminal, the host must be notified every time a carriage return is typed. If the typed in characters just pile up in the PAD waiting for the packet to fill, the host will not react to them. Therefore options are provided to override the "send-only-full-packet" rule. Parameter 3 can be set to force a packet to be sent whenever a control character is typed. Parameter 4 can be set to force a packet to be sent whenever no input is received for a specified time interval. Depending on how the host has been programmed, it might be possible for the PAD to collect characters from several terminals and put them in the same packet to reduce costs.

Parameter 5 is used when the terminal also contains a paper tape reader or other relatively high speed input device. When this parameter is set to 1, the PAD may start and stop the device to regulate the flow. The ASCII control characters DC1 and DC3 are used for on and off, respectively. Parameter 6 can be used to suppress certain status reporting from the PAD. This option is useful when nontechnical personnel (e.g., bank tellers) are using the terminal. Parameter 7 tells the PAD what to do when the user types a break character. The options may be combined. Parameter 8 can be set to cause the PAD to discard computer output (e.g., after receiving a break). Parameter 9 is needed because most terminals require filler characters after a carriage return. Even some CRT terminals require fillers above 4800 bps.

Parameter 10 tells the PAD the terminal line length, so that extra long output lines can be corrected folded. Parameter 11 gives the speed. Other speeds will probably be added in the future. Parameter 12 allows the user to

Parameter	Description	Allowed values
1	Can the terminal operator escape from data transfer mode to inspect or change the PAD parameters?	0 = No (escape prohibited) 1 = Yes (escape allowed)
2	Should the PAD echo characters back to the terminal?	0 = No 1 = Yes
3	Which characters should trigger the PAD into sending a partially full packet?	0 = Only send full packets 1 = Carriage return 126 = All control chars + DEL
4	How fast should the PAD time out and send a partially full packet?	0 = No time out 1 − 255 = Time in 50 ms ticks
5	Can the PAD (temporarily) prohibit the terminal from sending characters?	0 = No (Raw mode) 1 = Yes (Flow control)
6	Is the PAD allowed to send service signals to the terminal?	0 = No (suppress signals) 1 = Yes (deliver signals)
7	What should the PAD do upon receiving a break signal from the terminal?	0 = Nothing 1 = Interrupt 2 = Reset 4 = Send a host a control packet 8 = Escape to command mode 16 = Discard output
8	Should the PAD discard computer output intended for the terminal?	0 = No (Deliver) 1 = Yes (Discard)
9	How many fill characters should the PAD insert after outputting a carriage return to the terminal?	0 = None 1 − 7 = Number of fillers
10	Should the PAD automatically fold output to prevent line overflow?	0 = No 1 − 255 (yes) line length
11	Terminal speed (bps)	0 = 110 8 = 200 1 = 134.5 9 = 100 2 = 300 10 = 50
12	Can the terminal (temporarily) prohibit the PAD from sending it output?	0 = No 1 = Yes

Fig. 3-17. The PAD parameters (from CCITT standard X.3).

temporarily shut the PAD up using DC1 and DC3, for example, to read the contents of the screen before it scrolls out of view. CCITT may add new parameters to the PAD in the future, as the need arises.

3.5. ERRORS

Transmission errors are a fact of life. Given the 40 year depreciation time on existing telephone plant, transmission errors are going to continue being a fact of life for decades to come. In the following sections we will look at some of the problems more closely and see what can be done to overcome them.

3.5.1. The Nature of Transmission Errors

Transmission errors on telephone lines are caused by a variety of different phenomena. One phenomenon that is always present is thermal noise. The electrons in the copper wires are buzzing around at high speed, producing a broad-spectrum background noise level. It is the ratio of the signal to this noise that Shannon's result deals with.

A major source of noise for data transmission is impulse noise. These pulses or spikes on the line typically have a duration of 10 msec. To the human ear, such pulses sound like little clicks. To a 9600 bps line, they sound like the death knell for 96 bits. Most of them are caused by the arcing of relays and other electromechanical wheezes at older switching offices, although lightning, clumsy telephone repairpersons, backfiring cars, surges on the power line, and telephone system signaling tones also make contributions.

Another major source of errors is the fact that the amplitude, propagation speed, and phase of signals all are frequency dependent. The telephone system in effect Fourier-analyzes all signals, distorts each frequency component separately, and then recombines them at the end. It is usually possible to lease specially conditioned lines on which the carrier has tried to minimize these effects, but such lines are more expensive than regular lines and the equalization is never perfect, anyway.

Many other sources of error also exist. Crosstalk can occur between two wires that are physically adjacent. When the echo suppressors are turned off, there will be echoes. Microwave links are subject to fading, off course birds, and the like. For voice transmission, it is desirable to compress the signal amplitude into a narrow range, because the amplifiers are not linear over wide ranges. This compression, called **companding**, can introduce errors. And finally, it is not possible to produce a perfect carrier wave. Its amplitude, frequency, and phase will always exhibit some jitter.

On PCM trunks, errors are introduced whenever the receiver gets out of sync with the transmitter. Typically, it takes a few tens of milliseconds to get back into sync, with all the data transmitted in the meanwhile delivered to the wrong destination.

As a result of the physical processes causing the noise, errors tend to come in bursts rather than singly. Having the errors come in bursts has both advantages and disadvantages over isolated single-bit errors. On the advantage side, computer data are always sent in blocks of bits. Suppose that the block size is

1000 bits, and the error rate is 0.001 per bit. If errors were independent, most blocks would contain an error. If the errors came in bursts of 100 however, only one or two blocks in 100 would be affected, on the average. The disadvantage of burst errors is that they are much harder to detect and correct than are isolated errors.

Since errors are caused by a variety of physical processes, the only way to learn about their distribution is empirically. In 1969-1970, AT&T made a major study of transmission errors on short, medium, and long lines, at various different transmission speeds (Fleming and Hutchison, 1971; Balkovic et al., 1971). They found, for example, that at 15 char/sec, with one start bit, eight data bits, and one stop bit per character, one character in 6850 was incorrect. Worse yet, one in 1467 was lost altogether. However, 1% of the calls contained more than 90% of the errors. In other words, the line quality is highly uneven.

If the mean error rate is e per character and a block contains n characters, then in the absence of error clustering, the probability that the block is transmitted perfectly is $(1 - e)^n$. The probability that the block is in error is $1 - (1 - e)^n$. If $e \ll 1$, this can be expanded using a binomial expansion to give an approximate probability of block error equal to en. The empirical data, however, gives a block error probability roughly equal to $10^{-4} n^{-0.8}$ for blocks containing n 8-bit bytes and no start or stop bits. The results vary with line length, transmission speed, and other factors, so this is just an order of magnitude estimate. Studies by European PTTs have given similar results.

3.5.2. Error-Correcting Codes

Network designers have developed two basic strategies for dealing with errors. One way is to include enough redundant information along with each block of data sent to enable to the receiver to deduce what the transmitted character must have been. The other way is only to include enough redundancy to allow the receiver to deduce that an error occurred, but not which error, and have it request a retransmission. The former strategy uses **error correcting codes** and the latter uses **error detecting codes**.

To understand how errors can be detected or corrected, it is necessary to look closely at what an error really is. Normally, a message consists of m message (i.e., useful data) bits, and r redundant, or check bits. Let the total length be n (i.e., $n = m + r$.) An n-bit unit containing data and checkbits is often referred to as an n bit **codeword**.

Given any two codewords, say, 10001001 and 10110001, it is possible to determine how many corresponding bits differ. In this case, 3 bits differ. To determine how many bits differ, just EXCLUSIVE OR the two codewords, and count the number of 1 bits in the result. The number of bit positions in which two codewords differ is called the **Hamming distance** (Hamming, 1950). Its significance is that if two codewords are a Hamming distance d apart, it will require d single-bit errors to convert one into the other.

In most data transmission applications, all 2^m possible data messages are legal, but due to the way the check bits are computed, not all of the 2^n possible codewords are used. Given the algorithm for computing the check bits, it is possible to construct a complete list of the legal codewords, and from this list find the two codewords whose Hamming distance is minimum. This distance is the Hamming distance of the complete code.

The error-detecting and error-correcting properties of a code depend on its Hamming distance. To detect d errors, you need a distance $d + 1$ code because with such a code there is no way that d single-bit errors can change a valid codeword into another valid codeword. When the receiver sees an invalid codeword, it can tell that a transmission error has occurred. Similarly, to correct d errors, you need a distance $2d + 1$ code because that way the legal codewords are so far apart that even with d changes, the original codeword is still closer than any other codeword, so it can be uniquely determined.

As a simple example of an error-detecting code, consider a code in which a single **parity bit** is appended to the data. The parity bit is chosen so that the number of 1 bits in the codeword is even (or odd). Such a code has a distance 2, since any single-bit error produces a codeword with the wrong parity. It can be used to detect single errors.

As a simple example of an error-correcting code, consider a code with only four valid codewords:

0000000000, 0000011111, 1111100000, and 1111111111

This code has a distance 5, which means that it can correct double errors. If the codeword 0000000111 arrives, the receiver knows that the original must have been 0000011111. If, however, a triple error changes 00000000000 into 00000000111, the error will not be corrected properly.

Imagine that we want to design a code with m message bits and r check bits that will allow all single errors to be corrected. Each of the 2^m legal messages has n illegal codewords at a distance 1 from it. These are formed by systematically inverting each of the n bits in the n-bit codeword formed from it. Thus each of the 2^m legal messages requires $n + 1$ bit patterns dedicated to it. Since the total number of bit patterns is 2^n we must have $(n + 1)2^m \leqslant 2^n$. Using $n = m + r$ this requirement becomes $(m + r + 1) \leqslant 2^r$. Given m, this puts a lower limit on the number of check bits needed to correct single errors.

This theoretical lower limit can, in fact, be achieved using a method due to Hamming (1950). The bits of the codeword are numbered consecutively, starting with bit 1 at the left end. The bits that are powers of 2 (1, 2, 4, 8, 16, etc.) are check bits. The rest (3, 5, 6, 7, 9, etc.) are filled up with the m data bits. Each check bit forces the parity of some collection of bits, including itself, to be even (or odd). A message bit may be included in several parity computations. To see which check bits the data bit in position k contributes to, rewrite k as a sum of powers of 2. For example, $11 = 1 + 2 + 8$ and $29 = 1 + 4 + 8 +$

16. A bit is checked by just those check bits occurring in its expansion (e.g., bit 11 is checked by bits 1, 2, and 8).

When a codeword arrives, the receiver initializes a counter to zero. It then examines each check bit, k ($k = 1, 2, 4, 8, . . .$) to see if it has the correct parity. If not, it adds k to the counter. If the counter is zero after all the check bits have been examined (i.e., if they were all correct), the codeword is accepted as valid. If the counter is nonzero, it contains the number of the incorrect bit. For example, if check bits 1, 2, and 8 are in error the inverted bit is 11, because it is the only one checked by bits 1, 2, and 8. Figure 3-18 shows some 7-bit ASCII characters encoded as 11-bit codewords using a Hamming code. Remember that the data are found in bit positions 3, 5, 6, 7, 9, 10, and 11.

Char.	ASCII	Check bits
H	1001000	00110010000
a	1100001	00111001001
m	1101101	01101010101
m	1101101	01101010101
i	1101001	11101011001
n	1101110	01101010110
g	1100111	11111001111
	0100000	10011000000
c	1100011	01111000011
o	1101111	00101011111
d	1100100	11111001100
e	1100101	10111000101

Order of bit transmission

Fig. 3-18. Use of a Hamming code to correct burst errors.

Hamming codes can only correct single errors. However, there is a trick that can be used to permit Hamming codes to correct burst errors. A sequence of k consecutive codewords are arranged as a matrix, one codeword per row. Normally, the data would be transmitted one codeword at a time, from left to right. To correct burst errors, the data should be transmitted one column at a time, starting with the leftmost column. When all k bits have been sent, the second column is sent, and so on. When the message arrives at the receiver, the matrix is reconstructed, one column at a time. If a burst error of length k occurs, 1 bit in each of the k codewords will have been affected, but the Hamming code can correct one error per codeword, so the entire block can be restored. This method uses kr check bits to make blocks of km data bits immune to a single burst error of length k or less.

3.5.3. Error-Detecting Codes

Error correcting codes are sometimes used for data transmission, for example when the channel is simplex, so retransmissions cannot be requested, but most often error detection followed by retransmission is preferred because it is more efficient. As a simple example, consider a channel on which errors are isolated and the error rate is 10^{-6} per bit. Let the block size be 1000 bits. To provide error correction for 1000-bit blocks, 10 check bits are needed; a megabit of data would require 10,000 check bits. To merely detect a bad block, a single parity bit per block will suffice. Once every 1000 blocks an extra block (1001 bits) will have to be transmitted. The total overhead for the error detection + retransmission method is only 2001 bits per megabit of data, versus 10,000 for a Hamming code.

If a single parity bit is added to a block and the block is badly garbled by a long burst error, the probability that the error will be detected is only 0.5, which is hardly acceptable. The odds can be improved considerably by regarding each block to be sent as a rectangular matrix n bits wide and k bits high. A parity bit is computed separately for each column and affixed to the matrix as the last row. The matrix is then transmitted one row at a time. When the block arrives, the receiver checks all the parity bits. If any one of them is wrong, it requests a retransmission of the block.

This method can detect a single burst of length n, since only 1 bit per column will be changed. A burst of length $n + 1$ will pass undetected, however, if the first bit is inverted, the last bit is inverted, and all the other bits are correct. (A burst error does not imply that all the bits are wrong, it just implies that at least the first and last are wrong.) If the block is badly garbled by a long burst or by multiple shorter bursts, the probability that any of the n columns will have the correct parity, by accident, is 0.5, so the probability of a bad block being accepted when it should not be is 2^{-n}.

Although the above scheme may be adequate sometimes, in practice, another method is in widespread use: the **polynomial code** (also known as a **cyclic redundancy code** or CRC code). Polynomial codes are based upon treating bit strings as representations of polynomials with coefficients of 0 and 1 only. A k-bit message is regarded as the coefficient list for a polynomial with k terms, ranging from x^{k-1} to x^0. Such a polynomial is said to be of degree $k - 1$. The high-order (leftmost) bit is the coefficient of x^{k-1}; the next bit is the coefficient of x^{k-2}, and so on. For example, 110001 has 6 bits and thus represents a six term polynomial with coefficients 1, 1, 0, 0, 0, and 1: $x^5 + x^4 + x^0$.

Polynomial arithmetic is done modulo 2, according to the rules of algebraic field theory. There are no carries for addition or borrows for subtraction. Both addition and subtraction are identical to EXCLUSIVE OR. For example:

```
  10011011      00110011      11110000      01010101
+ 11001010    + 11001101    - 10100110    - 10101111
  --------      --------      --------      --------
  01010001      11111110      01010110      11111010
```

Long division is carried out the same way as it is in binary except that the subtraction is done modulo 2, as above. A divisor is said "to go into" a dividend if the dividend has as many bits as the divisor.

When the polynomial code method is employed, the sender and receiver must agree upon a **generator polynomial**, $G(x)$, in advance. Both the high- and low-order bits of the generator must be 1. To compute the **checksum** for some message with m bits, corresponding to the polynomial $M(x)$ the message must be longer than the polynomial. The basic idea is to append a checksum to the end of the message in such a way that the polynomial represented by the checksummed message is divisible by $G(x)$. When the receiver gets the checksummed message, it tries dividing it by $G(x)$. If there is a remainder, there has been a transmission error.

The algorithm for computing the checksum is as follows:

1. Let r be the degree of $G(x)$. Append r zero bits to the low-order end of the message, so it now contains $m + r$ bits, and corresponds to the polynomial $x^r M(x)$.

2. Divide the bit string corresponding to $G(x)$ into the bit string corresponding to $x^r M(x)$ using modulo 2 division.

3. Subtract the remainder (which is always r or fewer bits) from the bit string corresponding to $x^r M(x)$ using modulo 2 subtraction. The result is the checksummed message to be transmitted. Call its polynomial $T(x)$.

Figure 3-19 illustrates the calculation for a message 1101011011 and $G(x) = x^4 + x + 1$.

It should be clear that $T(x)$ is divisible (modulo 2) by $G(x)$. In any division problem, if you diminish the dividend by the remainder, what is left over is divisible by the divisor. For example, in base 10, if you divide 210278 by 10941, the remainder is 2399. By subtracting off 2399 from 210278, what is left over (207879) is divisible by 10941.

Now let us analyze the power of this method. What kinds of errors will be detected. Imagine that a transmission error occurs, so that instead of the polynomial for $T(x)$ arriving, $T(x) + E(x)$ arrives. Each 1 bit in $E(x)$ corresponds to a message bit that has been inverted. If there are k 1 bits in $E(x)$, k single-bit errors have occurred. A single burst error is characterized by an initial 1, a mixture of 0s and 1s, and a final 1, with all other bits being 0.

Upon receiving the checksummed message, the receiver divides it by $G(x)$; that is, it computes $[T(x) + E(x)]/G(x)$. $T(x)/G(x)$ is always 0, so the result of the computation is simply $E(x)/G(x)$. Those errors that happen to correspond to polynomials containing $G(x)$ as a factor will slip by unnoticed, but all other errors will be caught.

If there has been a single-bit error, $E(x) = x^i$, where i determines which

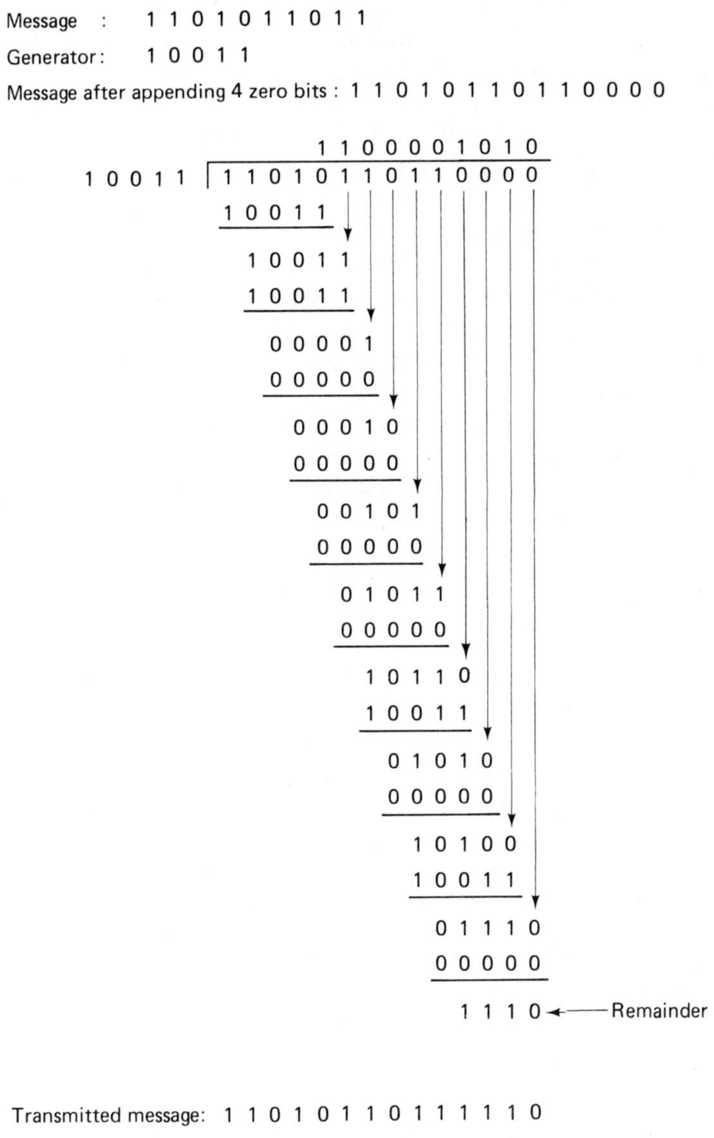

Message   :   1 1 0 1 0 1 1 0 1 1

Generator: 1 0 0 1 1

Message after appending 4 zero bits : 1 1 0 1 0 1 1 0 1 1 0 0 0 0

```
                            1 1 0 0 0 0 1 0 1 0
        1 0 0 1 1   1 1 0 1 0 1 1 0 1 1 0 0 0 0
                    1 0 0 1 1
                    ‾‾‾‾‾‾‾‾‾
                      1 0 0 1 1
                      1 0 0 1 1
                        0 0 0 0 1
                        0 0 0 0 0
                          0 0 0 1 0
                          0 0 0 0 0
                            0 0 1 0 1
                            0 0 0 0 0
                              0 1 0 1 1
                              0 0 0 0 0
                                1 0 1 1 0
                                1 0 0 1 1
                                  0 1 0 1 0
                                  0 0 0 0 0
                                    1 0 1 0 0
                                    1 0 0 1 1
                                      0 1 1 1 0
                                      0 0 0 0 0
                                        1 1 1 0  ◄——— Remainder
```

Transmitted message: 1 1 0 1 0 1 1 0 1 1 1 1 1 0

Fig. 3-19. Calculation of the polynomial code checksum.

bit is in error. If $G(x)$ contains two or more terms, it will never divide $E(x)$, so all single-bit errors will be detected.

If there have been two isolated single-bit errors, $E(x) = x^i + x^j$, where $i > j$. Alternatively, this can be written as $E(x) = x^j(x^{i-j} + 1)$. If we assume that $G(x)$ is not divisible by x, a sufficient condition for all double errors to be detected is that $G(x)$ does not divide $x^k + 1$ for any k up to the maximum value of $i - j$ (i.e., up to the maximum message length). Simple, low-degree polynomials that give protection to long messages are known. For example, $x^{15} + x^{14} + 1$ will not divide $x^k + 1$ for any k below 32768.

If there are an odd number of bits in error, $E(X)$ contains an odd number of terms (e.g., $x^5 + x^2 + 1$, but not $x^2 + 1$). Interestingly enough, there is no polynomial with an odd number of terms that has $x + 1$ as a factor in the modulo 2 system. By making $x + 1$ a factor of $G(x)$, we can catch all errors consisting of an odd number of inverted bits.

To see that no polynomial with an odd number of terms is divisible by $x + 1$, assume that $E(x)$ has an odd number of terms and is divisible by $x + 1$. Factor $E(x)$ into $(x + 1) Q(x)$. Now evaluate $E(1) = (1 + 1)Q(x)$. Since 1 $+ 1 = 0$ (modulo 2), $E(1)$ must be zero. If $E(x)$ has an odd number of terms, substituting 1 for x everywhere will always yield 1 as result. Thus no polynomial with an odd number of terms is divisible by $x + 1$.

Finally, and most important, a polynomial code with r check bits will detect all burst errors of length $\leqslant r$. A burst error of length k can be represented by $x^i(x^{k-1} + \ldots + 1)$, where i determines how far from the right hand end of the received message the burst is located. If $G(x)$ contains an x^0 term, it will not have x^i as a factor, so if the degree of the parenthesized expression is less than the degree of $G(x)$, the remainder can never be zero.

If the burst length is $r + 1$, the remainder of the division by $G(x)$ will be zero if and only if the burst is identical to $G(x)$. By definition of a burst, the first and last bits must be 1, so whether it matches depends on the $r - 1$ intermediate bits. If all combinations are regarded as equally likely, the probability of such an incorrect message being accepted as valid is $\frac{1}{2}^{r-1}$.

It can also be shown that when an error burst longer than $r + 1$ bits occurs, or several shorter bursts occur, the probability of a bad message getting through unnoticed is $\frac{1}{2}^r$ assuming that all bit patterns are equally likely.

Three polynomials have become international standards:

$$\text{CRC-12} = x^{12} + x^{11} + x^3 + x^2 + x^1 + 1$$
$$\text{CRC-16} = x^{16} + x^{15} + x^2 + 1$$
$$\text{CRC-CCITT} = x^{16} + x^{12} + x^5 + 1$$

All three contain $x + 1$ as a prime factor. CRC-12 is used when the character length is 6 bits. The other two are used for 8-bit characters. A 16-bit checksum, such as CRC-16 or CRC-CCITT, catches all single and double errors, all errors with an odd number of bits, all burst errors of length 16 or less, 99.997% of 17-bit error bursts, and 99.998% of 18-bit and longer bursts.

Although the calculation required to compute the checksum may seem complicated, Peterson and Brown (1961) have shown that a simple shift register circuit can be constructed to compute and verify the checksums in hardware. In practice, this hardware is nearly always used.

3.6. SUMMARY

The laws of nature put two fundamental limits on the data rate of a channel. The Nyquist limit restricts the number of independent samples per second to twice the bandwidth but does not restrict the precision of those samples or the total data rate. The Shannon limit, in contrast, limits the total data rate to a quantity dependent on the bandwidth and the signal-to-noise ratio.

The telephone system contains three major components: the local loops, the switching offices, and the interoffice transmission trunks. The local loops are 3000-Hz, two-wire, dedicated channels, whereas the interoffice trunks are high-bandwidth coaxial cable, microwave, waveguide, fiber-optic, or satellite channels onto which many voice-grade channels are multiplexed. Historically, trunks have carried analog signals, using frequency-division multiplexing, but there is a worldwide trend toward digital signaling and time-division multiplexing.

Computer networks use circuit switching, packet switching, or a hybrid of the two. With circuit switching, the user is given a dedicated channel from source to destination for the duration of the call. X.21 is an international standard interface for circuit-switched networks. With packet switching there is no dedicated circuit; instead, each block of data is stored and forwarded at each intermediate switching office as it travels to the destination.

Terminals can be connected to a network via a multiplexer or concentrator, to reduce the number of communication lines needed. A multiplexer has the same output capacity as the sum of its input capacities. A concentrator has less output capacity than input capacity, and relies on the fact that not all the input lines will be busy all the time.

Transmission lines are often subject to nonthermal spikes, causing burst errors. These errors can be corrected using error-correcting codes, although in practice it is more common to simply detect the errors and have the bad blocks retransmitted.

PROBLEMS

1. Compute the Fourier coefficients for the function $f(t) = t$ $(0 \leqslant t \leqslant 1)$.

2. A noiseless 4-kHz channel is sampled every millisecond. What is the maximum data rate?

3. Television channels are 6 MHz wide. How many bits/sec can be sent if four-level digital signals are used?

4. If a binary signal is sent over a 3000-Hz channel whose signal-to-noise ratio is 20 dB, what is the maximum achievable data rate?

5. What signal-to-noise ratio is needed to put a T1 carrier on a 50 kHz line?

6. A simple telephone system consists of two end offices and a single toll office to which each end office is connected by a 1-MHz full-duplex trunk. The average telephone is used to make four calls per 8-hour workday. The mean call duration is 6 min. Ten percent of the calls are long-distance (i.e., pass through the toll office). What is the maximum number of telephones an end office can support? (Assume 4 kHz per circuit.)

7. A digital switchboard serves an office building with a huge number of telephones and k outgoing trunk lines. Intercall times are distributed exponentially, with a mean interval $1/\lambda$ sec between calls. Call lengths are also distributed exponentially, with a mean length of $1/\mu$ sec. If no trunk lines are available, the call is automatically queued in a single FCFS queue. Derive an expression giving the probability that a call will be queued because all lines are blocked. (*Note:* It is this problem that ultimately led to the development of queueing theory.)

8. What is the percent overhead on a T1 carrier, that is, what percent of the 1.544 Mbps are not delivered to the end user?

9. Compare the maximum data rate of a noiseless 4-kHz channel using:
   (a) Dibit phase encoding (analog).
   (b) The T1 PCM system (digital).

10. What is the difference, if any, between the demodulator part of a modem and the coder part of a codec? (After all, both convert analog signals to digital ones.)

11. A signal is transmitted digitally over a 4000 Hz noiseless channel with one sample every 125 μsec. How many bits per second are actually sent for each of these encoding methods?
   (a) CCITT 2.048 Mbps standard.
   (b) DPCM with a 4-bit relative signal value.
   (c) Delta modulation.

12. A pure sine wave of amplitude A is encoded using delta modulation, with x samples/sec. An output of $+1$ corresponds to a signal change of $+A/8$, and an output signal of -1 corresponds to a signal change of $-A/8$. What is the highest frequency that can be tracked without cumulative error?

13. Figure 3-10 depicts the events happening at the calling DTE during call setup but does not show what the sequence is at the receiving DTE. Make a proposal for a scheme that would allow the receiving DTE to answer calls, accepting or rejecting reverse charging if requested.

14. Compare the delay in sending an x-bit message over a k-hop path in a circuit-switched network and in a (lightly loaded) packet-switched network. The circuit set up time is s sec, the propagation delay is d sec per hop, the packet size is p bits, and the data rate is b bps. Under what conditions does the packet network have a lower delay?

15. Suppose that x bits of user data are to be transmitted over a k-hop path in a packet-switched network as a series of packets, each containing p data bits and h header bits, with $x \gg p + h$. The bit rate of the lines is b bps and the propagation delay is negligible. What value of p minimizes the total delay?

16. A concentrator controls a group of n 300 bps terminals. It is connected to a computer over a 1200 bps synchronous line. All messages from the terminals are exactly 28 bytes. Output messages from the concentrator are 30 bytes (the data plus 2 bytes giving the terminal number). Each terminal produces messages randomly, with a mean of three per minute. Use an M/D/1 queueing model to derive a relation between the number of terminals and the mean amount of buffer space needed within the concentrator, including space for the message being transmitted.

17. What is the distance of the following code?
000000 001101 110100 111111 101010 110011

18. Compute the checksum for the message 11001010101 using the polynomial $x^4 + x^3 + x + 1$.

19. The message 101011000110 arrives using the polynomial $x^6 + x^4 + x + 1$. Is it correct?

20. Write a procedure that computes the value of a periodic function after it has been passed through a low-pass filter. The function itself, its period, and the cutoff frequency are parameters to your procedure.

21. Write a procedure that encodes an input function using delta modulation. The number of digitization levels and the interval between layers should be given as procedure inputs. Use half the levels for positive and half for negative values. The sampling interval should also be a parameter.

22. Write a procedure that accepts a bit vector as input and computes the checksum using CRC-CCITT.

23. Write a program to simulate the behavior of a concentrator with n input lines. Assume a Poisson arrival pattern but fixed-length messages. Simulate the concentrator for various loads, and compare the measured mean queue length with that predicted by queueing theory.

4

THE DATA LINK LAYER

In this chapter we will study the design of layer 2, the data link layer. This study deals with the algorithms for achieving reliable, efficient communication between two adjacent IMPs (or between a host and an IMP). By adjacent, we mean that the two IMPs are physically connected by a communication channel that acts conceptually like a wire (e.g., a coaxial cable, a telephone line, fiber optics, lasers, even a leased satellite channel). The essential property of a channel that makes it "wire-like" is that the bits are delivered in exactly the same order in which they are sent.

At first you might think this problem is so trivial that there is no software to study—IMP *A* just puts the data on the wire, and IMP *B* just takes it off. Unfortunately, real-world communication circuits have the nasty property of making errors now and then, which causes transmitted data to get mangled or even get lost altogether. Furthermore, the communication channel has only a finite data rate, and there is a nonzero propagation delay between the time a bit is sent and the time it is received. These limitations, coupled with the finite processing speed of the IMPs and hosts, have important implications for the efficiency of the data transfer. The algorithms used by adjacent IMPs must take all these factors into consideration.

4.1. ELEMENTARY DATA LINK PROTOCOLS

To introduce the subject of protocols, we will begin by looking at three protocols of increasing complexity.

4.1.1. Some Declarations Needed by the Protocols

In our model of a multilevel protocol hierarchy (Fig. 1-7), the user process passes some information to layer 6, which then gives it to layer 5, the session layer, which gives it in turn to layer 4, the transport layer. The transport layer software splits the data up into messages if need be, and attaches a transport header to the front of each message. It then passes these messages to its IMP. The IMP removes the host's packet and frame headers, and attaches its own headers to the front of each message, thus forming an IMP-IMP packet. The layer 3 IMP-IMP packet header might contain the source and destination addresses, routing information, etc. Eventually, the packet gets down to layer 2, where a frame header and frame trailer are attached for transmission, and the frame is sent to the next IMP. This general model is depicted in Fig. 4-1(a).

In this chapter we are only interested in the layer 2 protocols, so we will use the simplified model of Fig. 4-1(b) instead. We will ignore the packet layer altogether, as well as the intermediate IMPs, and just deal with messages and frames. The basic idea of this chapter is that the layer 2 software gets some input that it must transmit without error, even over noisy lines. Whether the input comes from layer 3 or layer 4 is immaterial.

Our initial conceptual model is that host A wants to send a long stream of data to host B. Later, we will consider the case where host B also wants to send data to host A simultaneously, but for the time being just consider simplex data transmission from A to B.

Host A is assumed to have an infinite supply of data ready to send and never has to wait for data to be produced. When the IMP asks for data, the host is always able to comply immediately. (This restriction, too, will be dropped later.) As far as the layer 2 software is concerned, a host message is pure data, every single bit of which is to be delivered to the other host. The fact that the receiving host may interpret part of the data it is given as a header is of no concern to the layer 2 software.

When an IMP accepts a message, it uses the message to construct a frame. The frame usually contains certain control information in addition to the message itself. The frame is then transmitted to the other IMP. We will assume that there exist suitable library procedures *sendf* to send a frame and *getf* to receive a frame. The transmitting hardware computes and appends the checksum, so that the IMP software need not worry about it. The polynomial algorithm discussed in Chap. 3 might be used, for example.

Initially, the receiver has nothing to do. It just sits around waiting for something to happen. In the example protocols of this chapter we indicate that an IMP is waiting for something to happen by the procedure call *wait*(*event*). This procedure only returns when something has happened, (e.g., a frame has arrived). Upon return, the variable *event* will tell what happened. The set of possible events differs for the various protocols to be described and will be

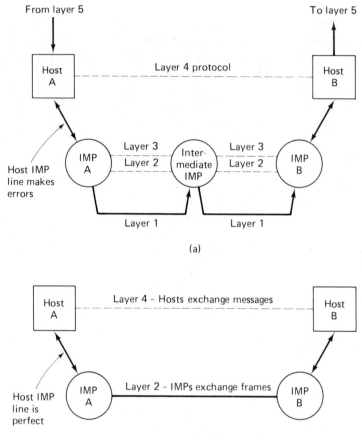

Fig. 4-1. (a) Layer 2, 3, and 4 protocols in the general case. (b) Simplified model used in this chapter.

defined separately for each protocol. Note that in a more realistic situation the IMP will not sit in a tight loop waiting for an event, as we have suggested, but will receive an interrupt, which will cause it to stop whatever it is doing and go handle the incoming frame. Nevertheless, for simplicity we will ignore all the details of parallel activity within the IMP and assume that it is dedicated full time to handling just our one channel.

When a frame arrives at the receiver, the hardware computes the checksum. If the checksum is incorrect (i.e., there was a transmission error), the IMP is so informed (*event* = *CksumErr*). If the inbound frame arrived undamaged, the IMP is also informed (*event* = *FrameArrival*), so it can acquire the frame for inspection using *getf*. As soon as the receiving IMP has acquired an undamaged frame, it checks the control information in the header, and if everything is all right, the message portion is passed to the host. Under no circumstances is a frame header ever given to a host.

There is a good reason why the host must never be given any part of the frame header: to keep the host and IMP protocols completely separate. As long as none of the hosts know anything at all about the data link protocol or the frame format, these things can be changed without requiring changes to the host's software.

Providing a rigid interface between host and IMP greatly simplifies the software design, because the communication protocols and host protocols can evolve independently. It would be terrible if every little change to the lower-layer protocols required changing all the host operating systems. Since the IMPs in most networks are generally identical pieces of hardware, changing the IMP software merely requires changing one program and then shipping it out to all the IMP sites (via the network itself, naturally). Changing the host protocol is much more complicated if, as is often the case, the hosts are not all identical. Such a change requires modifying every operating system present on the network, a vastly more complex task than changing one mini- or microcomputer program.

Figure 4-2 shows some declarations common to many of the protocols to be discussed later. Five data structures are defined there: *bit*, *SequenceNr*, *message*, *FrameKind*, and *frame*. A *bit* is a 0 or a 1. A *SequenceNr* is a small integer used to number the frames in order to tell them apart. The constant *MaxSeq* is defined together with each protocol. A *message* is the unit of information between a host and an IMP, or a host and a host. In our model it always contains exactly *LastBit* + 1 bits, but more realistically would be of variable length, from 0 to *LastBit* + 1 bits.

A *frame* is composed of four fields: *kind*, *seq*, *ack*, and *info*, the first three of which contain control information, and the last of which may contain actual data to be transferred. These control fields are collectively called the **frame header**. The *kind* field tells whether or not there are any data in the frame, because some of the protocols distinguish frames containing exclusively control information from those containing data as well. The *seq* and *ack* fields are used for sequence numbers and acknowledgements, respectively; their use will be described in more detail later. The *info* field of a data frame contains a single transport message; the *info* field of a control frame is not used. A more realistic implementation would use a variable-length *info* field, omitting it altogether for control frames.

A number of procedures are also listed in Fig. 4-2. These are library routines whose details are implementation-dependent and whose inner workings

{Some data types and procedures common to a number of the protocols.}

```
const LastBit = ... ;                {determines message size}
      doomsday = false;              {used to repeat forever}
      MaxSeq = ... ;                 {MaxSeq = highest seq = 2↑n − 1}

type bit = 0 .. 1;
     SequenceNr = 0 .. MaxSeq;    {used to number the frames}
     message = packed array [0 .. LastBit] of bit;    {a host-host message}
     FrameKind = (data, ack, nak);
     frame = packed record
       kind: FrameKind;
       seq: SequenceNr;
       ack: SequenceNr;
       info: message
     end;
```

procedure *wait*(**var** *event*: *EvType*);
begin {Wait for an event to happen; return its type in *event*.} **end**;

procedure *FromHost*(**var** *m*: *message*);
begin {Fetch information from the host for transmission on the channel.} **end**;

procedure *ToHost*(*m*: *message*);
begin {Deliver information from an inbound frame to the host.} **end**;

procedure *getf*(**var** *r*: *frame*);
begin {Go get an inbound frame and copy it to *r* for the receiver.} **end**;

procedure *sendf*(*s*: *frame*);
begin {Transmit the frame *s* over the communication channel.} **end**;

procedure *StartTimer*(*k*:*SequenceNr*);
begin {Start the clock running and enable *TimeOut* event.} **end**;

procedure *StopTimer*(*k*:*SequenceNr*);
begin {Stop the clock and disable *TimeOut* event.} **end**;

procedure *StartAckTimer*;
begin {Start an auxiliary timer for sending separate acks.} **end**;

procedure *StopAckTimer*;
begin {Stop the auxiliary timer and disable *HostIdle* event.} **end**;

procedure *EnableHost*;
begin {Allow the host to cause a *HostReady* event.} **end**;

procedure *DisableHost*;
begin {Forbid the host from causing a *HostReady* event.} **end**;

procedure *inc*(**var** *k*: *SequenceNr*);
begin {Increment *k* circularly.} **if** $k < MaxSeq$ **then** $k := k + 1$ **else** $k := 0$ **end**;

Fig. 4-2. Some definitions needed in the examples to follow.

will not concern us further here. The procedure *wait* sits in a tight loop waiting for something to happen, as mentioned earlier. The procedures *ToHost* and *FromHost* are used by the IMP to pass messages to the host and accept messages from the host, respectively. Note that *getf* and *sendf* are used for exchanging frames between the IMPs, whereas *ToHost* and *FromHost* are used for exchanging messages between IMP and host.

In most of the protocols we assume an unreliable channel that loses entire frames upon occasion. To be able to recover from such calamities, the sending IMP must start an internal timer or clock whenever it sends a frame. If no reply has been received within a certain predetermined time interval, the clock times out and the IMP receives an interrupt signal.

In our protocols this is handled by allowing the procedure *wait* to return *event = TimeOut*. The procedures *StartTimer* and *StopTimer* are used to turn the timer on and off, respectively. Timeouts are possible only when the timer is running. It is explicitly permitted to call *StartTimer* while the timer is running; such a call simply resets the clock to cause the next timeout after a full timer interval has elapsed (unless it is reset or turned off in the meanwhile).

The procedures *StartAckTimer* and *StopAckTimer* are used to control an auxiliary timer used to generate acknowledgements under certain conditions.

The procedures *EnableHost* and *DisableHost* are used in the more sophisticated protocols, where we no longer assume that the host always has messages to send. When the IMP enables its host, the host is then permitted to interrupt when it has a message to be sent. We indicate this with *event = HostReady*. When a host is disabled, it may not cause such events. By being careful about when it enables and disables its host, an IMP can prevent an active host from swamping it with messages for which it has no buffer space.

Frame sequence numbers are always in the range 0 to *MaxSeq* (inclusive), where *MaxSeq* is different for the different protocols. It is frequently necessary to advance a sequence number by 1 circularly (i.e., *MaxSeq* is followed by 0). The procedure *inc* performs this incrementing.

The declarations of Fig. 4-2 are part of each of the protocols to follow. To save space and to provide a convenient reference, they have been extracted and listed together, but conceptually they should be merged with the protocols themselves.

4.1.2. An Unrestricted Simplex Protocol

As an initial example we will consider a protocol that is as simple as can be. Data are transmitted in one direction only. Both the transmitting and receiving hosts are always ready. Processing time can be ignored. Infinite buffer space is available. And best of all, the communication channel between the IMPs never damages or loses frames. This thoroughly unrealistic protocol, which we will nickname "Utopia," is shown in Fig. 4-3.

The protocol consists of two distinct procedures, a sender and a receiver.

{Protocol 1 ("utopia") provides for data transmission in one direction only, from sender to receiver. The communications channel is assumed to be error free, and the receiver is assumed to be able to process all the input infinitely fast. Consequently, the sender just sits in a loop pumping data out onto the line as fast as it can.}

type *EvType* = (*FrameArrival*);

```
procedure sender1;
var s: frame;                          {buffer for an outbound frame}
    buffer: message;                   {buffer for an outbound message}
begin
  repeat
    FromHost(buffer);                  {go get something to send}
    s.info := buffer;                  {copy it into s for transmission}
    sendf(s);                          {send it on its way}
  until doomsday                       {tomorrow, and tomorrow, and tomorrow,
                                        creeps in this petty pace from day to day,
                                        to the last syllable of recorded time;
                                                    — Macbeth, V, v}

end;  {sender1}


procedure receiver1;
var r: frame;
    event: EvType;                     {filled in by wait, but not used here}
begin
  repeat
    wait(event);                       {only possibility is FrameArrival}
    getf(r);                           {go get the inbound frame}
    ToHost(r.info)                     {pass the data to the host}
  until doomsday
end;  {receiver1}
```

Fig. 4-3. An unrestricted simplex protocol.

The sender runs on the transmitting IMP, and the receiver runs on the receiving IMP. No sequence numbers or acknowledgements are used here, so *MaxSeq* is not needed. The only event type possible is *FrameArrival*, (i.e., the arrival of an undamaged frame).

The sender is in an infinite loop bracketed by **repeat until** *doomsday*, just pumping data out onto the line as fast as it can. The body of the loop consists of three actions: go fetch a message from the (always obliging) host, construct an outbound frame using the variable *s*, and send the frame on its way. Only the *info* field of the frame is used by this protocol, because the other fields have to do with error and flow control, and there are no errors or flow control restrictions here.

The receiver is equally simple. Initially, it waits for something to happen, the only possibility being the arrival of an undamaged frame. Eventually, the frame arrives and the procedure *wait* returns, with *event* set to *FrameArrival* (which is ignored anyway). The call to *getf* removes the newly arrived frame from the hardware buffer and puts it in the variable *r*. Finally the data portion is passed on to the host and the IMP settles back to wait for the next frame.

4.1.3. A Simplex Stop-and-Wait Protocol

Now we will drop the most unrealistic restriction used in protocol 1: the ability of the receiving host to process incoming data infinitely fast (or equivalently, the presence in the receiving IMP of an infinite amount of buffer space in which to store all incoming frames while they are waiting their respective turns). The communication channel is still assumed to be error-free however, and the data traffic is still simplex.

The main problem we have to deal with here is how to prevent the sender from flooding the receiver with data faster than the latter is able to process it. In essence, if the receiver requires a time *t* to execute *getf + ToHost*, the sender must transmit at an average rate less than one frame per time *t*. Stronger yet, if we assume that there is no automatic buffering and queueing done within the receiver's hardware, the sender must never transmit a new frame until the old one has been fetched by *getf*, lest the new one overwrite the old one.

In certain restricted circumstances (e.g., synchronous transmission and a receiving IMP fully dedicated to processing the one input line), it might be possible for the sender to simply insert a delay into protocol 1 to slow it down sufficiently to keep from swamping the receiver. However, more usually, each IMP will have several lines to attend to, and the time interval between a frame arriving and its being processed may vary considerably. If the network designers can calculate the worst-case behavior of the receiver, they can program the sender to transmit so slowly that even if every frame suffers the maximum delay, there will be no overruns. The trouble with this approach is that it is too conservative. It leads to a bandwidth utilization that is far below the optimum (unless the best and worst cases are almost the same (i.e., the variation in the IMPs reaction time is small).

A more general solution to this dilemma is to have the receiver provide feedback to the sender. After having passed a message to its host, the receiver sends a little dummy frame back to the sender which, in effect, gives the sender permission to transmit the next frame. After having sent a frame, the sender is required by the protocol to bide its time until the little dummy (i.e., acknowledgement) frame arrives.

Protocols in which the sender sends one frame and then waits for an acknowledgement before proceeding are called **stop-and-wait**. Figure 4-4 gives an example of a simplex stop-and-wait protocol. As in protocol 1, the sender starts out by fetching a message from the host, using it to construct a frame,

{Protocol 2 ("stop-and-wait") also provides for a one directional flow of data from sender to receiver. The communications channel is once again assumed to be error free, as in protocol 1. However, this time, the receiver has only a finite buffer capacity and a finite processing speed, so the protocol must explicity prevent the sender from flooding the receiver with data faster than it can be handled.}

```
type EvType = (FrameArrival);

procedure sender2;
var s: frame;
    buffer: message;
    event: EvType;
begin
  repeat
    FromHost(buffer);            {fetch information from the host}
    s.info := buffer;            {copy it into s,for subsequent transmission}
    sendf(s);                    {bye bye little frame}
    wait(event);                 {do not proceed until given go ahead}
  until doomsday
end;  {sender2}

procedure receiver2;
var r,s: frame;
    event: EvType;
begin
  repeat
    wait(event);                 {only possibility is FrameArrival}
    getf(r);                     {go get the frame}
    ToHost(r.info);              {give the message to the host}
    sendf(s);                    {send a dummy frame as a go ahead signal}
  until doomsday
end;  {receiver2}
```

Fig. 4-4. A simplex stop-and-wait protocol.

and sending it on its way. Only now, unlike in protocol 1, the sender must wait until an acknowledgement frame arrives before looping back and fetching the next message from the host. The sending IMP need not even inspect the incoming frame: there is only one possibility.

The only difference between *receiver1* and *receiver2* is that after delivering a message to the host, *receiver2* sends an acknowledgement frame back to the sender before entering the wait loop again. Because only the arrival of the frame back at the sender is important, not its contents, the receiver need not put any particular information in it.

Although data traffic in this example is simplex, going only from the sender to the receiver, frames do travel in both directions. Consequently, the communication channel between the two IMPs needs to be capable of bidirectional information transfer. However, this protocol entails a strict alternation of flow: first the sender sends a frame, then the receiver sends a frame, then the sender sends another frame, then the receiver sends another one, and so on. A half-duplex physical channel would suffice here.

4.1.4. A Simplex Protocol for a Noisy Channel

Now let us consider the unfortunately all-too-realistic situation of a communication channel that makes errors. Frames may be either damaged or lost completely. However, we assume that if a frame is damaged in transit, the receiver hardware will detect this when it computes the checksum. If the frame is damaged in such a way that the checksum is nevertheless correct, an exceedingly unlikely occurrence, this protocol (and all other protocols) can fail (i.e., deliver an incorrect message to the host).

At first glance it might seem that a minor variation of protocol 2 would work. The sender would send a frame, but the receiver would only send an acknowledgement frame if the data were correctly received. If a damaged frame arrived at the receiver, it would be discarded. After a while the sender would time out and send the frame again. This process would be repeated until the frame finally arrived intact.

The above scheme has a fatal flaw in it. Think about the problem and try to discover what might go wrong before reading further.

To see what might go wrong, remember that it is the task of the communication subnet to provide error free, transparent communication between hosts. Host A gives a series of messages to its IMP, and the subnet must guarantee that the identical series of messages are delivered to host B by IMP B, in the same order. In particular, host B has no way of knowing that a message has been lost or duplicated, so the subnet must guarantee that no combination of transmission errors, no matter how unlikely, can cause a duplicate message to be delivered to a host.

Consider the following scenario:

1. Host A gives message 1 to its IMP. The message is correctly received at B and passed to host B. IMP B sends an acknowledgement frame back to IMP A.

2. The acknowledgement frame gets lost completely. It just never arrives at all. Life would be a great deal simpler if the channel only mangled and lost data frames and not control frames, but sad to say, the channel is not very discriminating.

3. IMP A eventually times out. Not having received an acknowledgement, it (incorrectly) assumes that its data frame was lost or damaged and sends the frame containing message 1 again.

4. The duplicate frame also arrives at IMP B perfectly and is also

unwittingly passed to host B. If A is sending a file to B, part of the file will be duplicated (i.e., the copy of the file made by B will be incorrect and the error will not have been detected). In other words, the protocol will fail.

Clearly, what is needed is some way for the receiver to be able to distinguish a frame that it is seeing for the first time from a retransmission. The obvious way to achieve this is to have the sender put a sequence number in the header of each frame it sends. Then the receiver can check the sequence number of each arriving frame to see if it is a new frame or a duplicate to be discarded.

Since a small frame header is desirable, the question arises: What is the minimum number of bits needed for the sequence number? The only ambiguity in this protocol is between a frame, m, and its direct successor, $m + 1$. If frame m is lost or damaged, the receiver will not acknowledge it, so the sender will keep trying to send it. Once it has been correctly received, the receiver will send an acknowledgement back to the sender. It is here that the potential trouble crops up. Depending upon whether the acknowledgement frame gets back to the sender correctly or not, the sender may try to send m or $m + 1$.

The event that triggers the sender to start sending $m + 2$ is the arrival of an acknowledgement for $m + 1$. But this implies that m has been correctly received, and furthermore that its acknowledgement has also been correctly received by the sender (otherwise, the sender would not have begun with $m + 1$, let alone $m + 2$). As a consequence, the only ambiguity is between a frame and its immediate predecessor or successor, not between the predecessor and successor themselves.

A 1-bit sequence number (0 or 1) is therefore sufficient. At each instant of time, the receiver expects a particular sequence number next. Any arriving frame containing the wrong sequence number is rejected as a duplicate. When a frame containing the correct sequence number arrives, it is accepted, passed to the host, and the expected sequence number is incremented modulo 2 (i.e., 0 becomes 1 and 1 becomes 0).

An example of this kind of protocol is shown in Fig. 4-5. Protocols in which the sender waits for a positive acknowledgement before advancing to the next data item are often called PAR—Positive Acknowledgement with Retransmission. Like protocol 2, this one also transmits data only in one direction. Although it can handle lost frames (by timing out), it requires the timeout interval to be long enough to prevent premature timeouts. If the sender times out too early, while the acknowledgement is still on the way, it will send a duplicate.

When the previous acknowledgement finally does arrive, the sender will mistakenly think that the just sent frame is the one being acknowledged and will not realize that there is potentially another acknowledgement frame somewhere "in the pipe." If the next frame sent is lost completely but the extra

{Protocol 3 ("par") allows data to be transmitted in one direction over a noisy communications channel that garbles and even loses frames.}

const *MaxSeq* = 1;

type *EvType* = (*FrameArrival*, *CksumErr*, *TimeOut*);

procedure *sender3*;
var *NextFrameToSend*: *SequenceNr*;   {sequence number of next outgoing frame}
    s: *frame*;   {scratch variable}
    buffer: *message*;   {buffer for outbound message}
    event: *EvType*;
begin
    NextFrameToSend := 0;   {initialize outbound sequence numbers}
    FromHost (*buffer*);   {fetch first message}
    repeat
      s.info := *buffer*;   {construct frame for transmission}
      s.seq := *NextFrameToSend*;   {insert sequence number in frame}
      sendf (*s*);   {send it on its way}
      StartTimer (*s.seq*);   {if answer takes too long, time out}
      wait (*event*);   {possibilities: *FrameArrival, CksumErr, TimeOut* }
      if *event* = *FrameArrival* **then**
        begin   {an acknowledgement has arrived intact}
          FromHost (*buffer*);   {fetch the next one to send}
          inc (*NextFrameToSend*);   {invert *NextFrameToSend*}
        end
    until *doomsday*
end;   {*sender3*}

procedure *receiver3*;
var *FrameExpected*: *SequenceNr*;   {*FrameExpected* = 0 or 1}
    r,*s*: *frame*;   {scratch variables}
    event: *EvType*;
begin
    FrameExpected := 0;
    repeat
      wait (*event*);   {possibilities: *FrameArrival, CksumErr*}
      if *event* = *FrameArrival* **then**
        begin   {a valid frame has arrived}
        getf (*r*);   {accept inbound frame}
        if *r.seq* = *FrameExpected* **then**
          begin   {this is what we have been waiting for}
            ToHost (*r.info*);   {pass the data to the host}
            inc (*FrameExpected*) {next time expect the other sequence nr}
          end;
          sendf (*s*)   {none of the fields are used!}
        end
    until *doomsday*
end;   {*receiver3*}

Fig. 4-5. A Positive Acknowledgement/Retransmission protocol.

acknowledgement arrives correctly, the sender will not attempt to retransmit the lost frame, and the protocol will fail. In later protocols the acknowledgement frames will contain information to prevent just this sort of trouble. For the time being, the acknowledgement frames will just be dummies, and we will assume a strict alternation of sender and receiver.

Protocol 3 differs from its predecessors in that both sender and receiver have a variable whose value is remembered while the IMP is in wait state. The sender remembers the sequence number of the next frame to send in *NextFrameToSend*; the receiver remembers the sequence number of the next frame expected in *FrameExpected*. Each protocol has a short initialization phase before entering the infinite loop.

After transmitting a frame, the sender starts the timer running. If it was already running, it will be reset to allow another full timer interval. The time interval must be chosen to allow enough time for the frame to get to the receiver, for the receiver to process it in the worst case, and for the acknowledgement frame to propagate back to the sender. Only when that time interval has elapsed is it safe to assume that either the transmitted frame or its acknowledgement has been lost, and to send a duplicate.

After transmitting a frame and starting the timer, the sender waits for something exciting to happen. There are three possibilities: an acknowledgement frame arrives undamaged, a damaged acknowledgement frame staggers in, or the timer goes off. If a valid acknowledgement comes in, the sender fetches the next message from its host and puts it in the buffer, overwriting the previous message. It also advances the sequence number. If a damaged frame arrives or no frame at all arrives, neither the buffer nor the sequence number are changed, so that a duplicate can be sent.

When a valid frame arrives at the receiver, its sequence number is checked to see if it is a duplicate. If not, it is accepted, passed to the host, and an acknowledgement generated. Duplicates and damaged frames are not passed to the host.

4.2. SLIDING WINDOW PROTOCOLS

In the previous protocols, data were transmitted in only one direction. In most practical situations, there is a need for transmitting data in both directions. Typically, there will be several independent processes on host *A* that want to send data to host *B*, and in addition, several processes on host *B* that want to send to host *A*.

One way of achieving full-duplex data transmission would be to have two separate communication channels, and use each one for simplex data traffic (in different directions). If this were done, we would have two separate physical circuits, each with a "forward" channel (for data) and a "reverse" channel (for acknowledgements). In both cases the bandwidth of the reverse channel would be almost entirely wasted. In effect, the user would be paying the cost of two circuits but only using the capacity of one.

A better idea is to use the same circuit for data in both directions. After all, in protocols 2 and 3 it was already being used to transmit frames both ways, and the reverse channel has the same capacity as the forward channel. In this model the data frames from A to B are intermixed with the acknowledgement frames from A to B. By looking at the *kind* bit in the header of an incoming frame, the receiver can tell whether the frame is data or acknowledgement.

Although interleaving data and control frames on the same circuit is an improvement over having two separate physical circuits, yet another improvement is possible. When a data frame arrives at an IMP, instead of immediately sending a separate control frame, the IMP restrains itself and waits until the host passes it the next message. The acknowledgement is attached to the outgoing data frame (using the *ack* field in the frame header). In effect, the acknowledgement gets a free ride on the next outgoing data frame. The technique of temporarily delaying outgoing acknowledgements so that they can be hooked onto the next outgoing data frame is widely known as **piggybacking**.

The principal advantage of piggybacking over having distinct acknowledgement frames is a better use of the available channel bandwidth. The *ack* field in the frame header only costs a few bits, whereas a separate frame would need a header, the acknowledgement, and a checksum. In addition, fewer frames sent means fewer "frame arrived" interrupts, and perhaps fewer buffers in the receiver, depending on how the receiver software is organized. In the next protocol to be examined, the piggyback field costs only 1 bit in the frame header. Rarely does it cost more than a few bits.

Piggybacking also introduces a complication not present with separate acknowledgements. How long should the IMP wait for a message onto which to piggyback the acknowledgement? If the IMP waits longer than the sender's timeout period, the frame will be retransmitted, defeating the whole purpose of having acknowledgements. If the IMP were an oracle and could foretell the future, it would know when the next host message was going to come in, it could decide either to wait for it or send a separate acknowledgement immediately, depending on how long the projected wait was going to be. Of course, the IMP cannot foretell the future, so it must resort to some ad hoc scheme, such as waiting a fixed number of milliseconds. If a new host message arrives quickly, the acknowledgement is piggybacked onto it; otherwise, if no new host message has arrived by the end of this time period, the IMP just sends a separate acknowledgement frame.

In addition to it being only simplex, protocol 3 can deadlock if the sender times out too early. It would be nicer to have a protocol that remained synchronized in the face of any combination of garbled frames, lost frames, and premature timeouts. The next three protocols are all highly robust and continue to function properly even under pathological conditions. All three belong to a class of protocols often referred to as **sliding window** protocols. The three differ among themselves in terms of efficiency, complexity, and buffer requirements, as discussed later.

In all sliding window protocols, each outbound frame contains a sequence number, ranging from 0 up to some maximum. The maximum is usually $2^n - 1$ so the sequence number fits nicely in an n bit field. The stop-and-wait sliding window protocol uses $n = 1$, restricting the sequence numbers to 0 and 1, but more sophisticated versions can use arbitrary n.

The essence of all sliding window protocols is that at any instant of time, the sender maintains a list of consecutive sequence numbers corresponding to frames it is permitted to send. These frames are said to fall within the **sending window**. Similarly, the receiver also maintains a **receiving window** corresponding to frames it is permitted to accept. The sending window and the receiving window need not have the same lower and upper limits, or even have the same size.

Although these protocols give the IMPs more freedom about the order in which they will send and receive frames, we have most emphatically not dropped the requirement that the protocol must deliver messages to the destination host in the same order that they were passed to the source IMP by the source host. Nor have we changed the requirement that the IMP-IMP communication channel is "wire-like," (i.e., must deliver frames in the order sent).

The sequence numbers within the sender's window represent frames sent but as yet not acknowledged. Whenever a new message arrives from the host, it is given the next highest sequence number, and the upper edge of the window is advanced by one. When an acknowledgement comes in, the lower edge is advanced by one. In this way the window continuously maintains a list of unacknowledged frames.

Since frames currently within the sender's window may ultimately be lost or damaged in transit, the sender must keep all these frames in its memory for possible retransmission. Thus if the maximum window size is n, the sender needs n buffers to hold the unacknowledged frames. If the window ever grows to its maximum size, the sending IMP must forcibly shut off the host until another buffer becomes free.

The receiving IMP's window corresponds to the frames it may accept. Any frame falling outside the window is discarded without comment. When a frame whose sequence number is equal to the lower edge of the window is received, it is passed to the host, an acknowledgement is generated, and the window is rotated by one. Unlike the sender's window, the receiver's window always remains at its initial size. Note that a window size of 1 means that the IMP only accepts frames in order, but for larger windows this is not so. The host, in contrast, is always fed data in the proper order, regardless of the IMP's window size.

Figure 4-6 shows an example with a maximum window size of 1. Initially, no frames are outstanding, so the lower and upper edges of the sender's window are equal, but as time goes on, the situation progresses as shown.

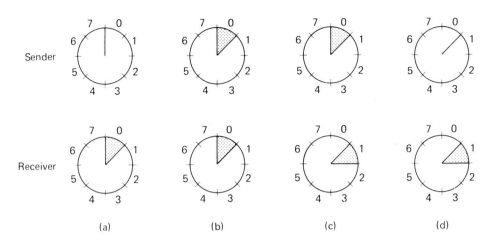

Fig. 4-6. A sliding window of size 1, with a 3-bit sequence number. (a) Initially. (b) After the first frame has been sent. (c) After the first frame has been received. (d) After the first acknowledgement has been received.

4.2.1. A One Bit Sliding Window Protocol

Before tackling the general case, let us first examine a sliding window protocol with a maximum window size of 1. Such a protocol uses stop-and-wait, since the sender transmits a frame and waits for its acknowledgement before sending the next one.

Figure 4-7 depicts such a protocol. *NextFrameToSend* tells which frame the sender is trying to send. Similarly, *FrameExpected* tells which frame the receiver is expecting. In both cases, 0 and 1 are the only possibilities.

Normally, one of the two IMPs goes first. In other words, only one of the IMP programs should contain the *sendf* and *StartTimer* procedure calls outside the main loop. In the event both IMPs start off simultaneously, a peculiar situation arises, which is discussed later. The starting IMP fetches the first message from its host, builds a frame from it, and sends it. When this (or any) frame arrives, the receiving IMP checks to see if it is a duplicate, just as in protocol 3. If the frame is the one expected, it is passed to the host and the receiving window is slid up.

The acknowledgement field contains the number of the last frame received without error. If this number agrees with the sequence number of the frame the sender is trying to send, the sender knows it is done with the frame stored in *buffer* and can fetch the next message from its host. If the sequence number disagrees, it must continue trying to send the same frame. Whenever a frame is received, a frame is also sent back.

{Protocol 4 ("sliding window") is bidirectional, and more robust than protocol 3. It can withstand any combination of errors and timeouts without losing or duplicating host messages.}

const *MaxSeq* = 1;

type *EvType* = (*FrameArrival*, *CksumErr*, *TimeOut*);

procedure *protocol4*;
var *NextFrameToSend*: *SequenceNr*; {0 or 1 only}
       FrameExpected: *SequenceNr*;   {0 or 1 only}
       r,*s*: *frame*;   {scratch variables}
       buffer: *message*;   {current message being sent}
       event: *EvType*;

begin
  NextFrameToSend := 0;   {initialize outbound stream}
  FrameExpected := 0;   {initialize inbound stream}
  FromHost(*buffer*);   {fetch message from host}
  s.info := *buffer*;   {prepare to send initial frame}
  s.seq := *NextFrameToSend*; {frame sequence number}
  s.ack := 1 − *FrameExpected*; {piggybacked ack}
  sendf(*s*);   {transmit the frame}
  StartTimer(*s.seq*);   {start the timer running}

  repeat
     wait(*event*);   {possibilities: *FrameArrival*, *CksumErr*, *TimeOut*}
     if *event* = *FrameArrival* **then**
        begin   {an inbound frame made it without error}
          getf(*r*);   {go get it}

          if *r.seq* = *FrameExpected* **then**
             begin   {handle inbound frame stream}
               ToHost(*r.info*); {pass the message to the host}
               inc(*FrameExpected*) {invert the receiver seq number}
             end;

          if *r.ack* = *NextFrameToSend* **then**
             begin   {handle outbound frame stream}
               FromHost(*buffer*); {fetch a new message from host}
               inc(*NextFrameToSend*) {invert sender seq number}
             end

        end;

     s.info := *buffer*;   {construct outbound frame}
     s.seq := *NextFrameToSend*; {insert sequence number into it}
     s.ack := 1 − *FrameExpected*; {this is seq number of last received frame}
     sendf(*s*);   {transmit a frame}
     StartTimer(*s.seq*)   {start the timer running}
  until *doomsday*

end; {*protocol4*}

Fig. 4-7. A 1-bit sliding window protocol.

Now let us examine protocol 4 to see how resilient it is to pathological scenarios. Assume that *A* is trying to send its frame 0 to *B* and that *B* is trying to send its frame 0 to *A*. Suppose that *A* sends a frame to *B*, but *A*'s timeout interval is a little too short. Consequently, *A* may time out repeatedly, sending a series of identical frames, all with *seq* = 0 and *ack* = 1.

When the first valid frame arrives at *B*, it will be accepted, and *FrameExpected* set to 1. All the subsequent frames will be rejected, because their sequence numbers will be wrong. Furthermore, since all the duplicates have *ack* = 1 and *B* is still waiting for an acknowledgement of 0, *B* will not fetch a new message from its host.

After every rejected duplicate comes in, *B* sends *A* a frame containing *seq* = 0 and *ack* = 0. Eventually, one of these arrives correctly at *A*, causing *A* to begin sending the next message. No combination of lost frames or premature timeouts can cause the protocol to deliver duplicate messages to either host, or to skip a message, or to get into a deadlock.

However, a peculiar situation arises if both sides simultaneously send an initial message. This synchronization difficulty is illustrated by Fig. 4-8. In part (a), the normal operation of the protocol is shown. In (b) the peculiarity is illustrated. If *B* waits for *A*'s first frame before sending one of its own, the sequence is as shown in (a), and every frame is accepted. However, if *A* and *B* simultaneously initiate communication, their first frames cross, and the IMPs then get into situation (b). In (a) each frame arrival brings a new message for the host; there are no duplicates. In (b) half of the frames contain duplicates, even though there are no transmission errors.

4.2.2. A Protocol with Pipelining

Until now we have made the tacit assumption that the transmission time required for a frame to arrive at the receiver plus the transmission time for the acknowledgement to come back is negligible. Sometimes this assumption is patently false. In these situations the long round-trip time can have important implications for the efficiency of the bandwidth utilization. As an example, consider a 50 kbps satellite channel with a 500-msec round-trip propagation delay. Let us imagine trying to use protocol 4 to send 1000-bit frames via the satellite. At $t = 0$ the sender starts sending the first frame. At $t = 20$ msec the frame has been completely sent. Not until $t = 270$ msec has the frame fully arrived at the receiver, and not until $t = 520$ msec has the acknowledgement arrived back at the sender, under the best of circumstances (no waiting in the receiver and a short acknowledgement frame). This means that the sender was blocked during 500/520 or 96% of the time (i.e., only 4% of the available bandwidth was used). Clearly, the combination of a long transit time, high bandwidth and short frame length is disastrous in terms of efficiency.

The problem described above can be viewed as a direct consequence of the

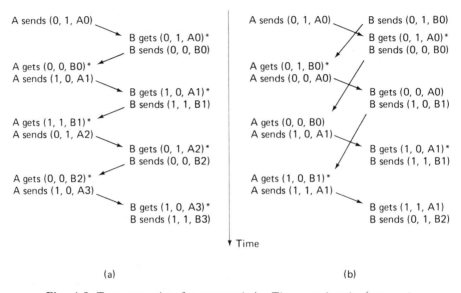

Fig. 4-8. Two scenarios for protocol 4. The notation is (seq, ack, message number). An asterisk indicates where a host accepts a message.

rule requiring a sender to wait for an acknowledgement before sending another frame. If we relax that restriction, much better efficiency can be achieved. Basically the solution lies in allowing the sender to transmit up to w frames before blocking, instead of just 1. With an appropriate choice of w the sender will be able to continuously transmit frames for a time equal to the round-trip transit time without filling up the window. In the example above, w should be at least 26. The sender begins sending frame 0 as before. By the time it has finished sending 26 frames, at $t = 520$, the acknowledgement for frame 0 will have just arrived. Thereafter, acknowledgements will arrive spaced by 20 msec, so the sender always gets permission to continue just when it needs it. At all times, 25 or 26 unacknowledged frames are outstanding. Put in other terms, the sender's maximum window size is 26.

This technique is known as **pipelining**. If the channel capacity is b bits/sec, the frame size l bits, and the round-trip propagation time R sec, the time required to transmit a single frame is l/b sec. After the last bit of a data frame has been sent, there is a delay of $R/2$ before that bit arrives at the receiver, and another delay of at least $R/2$ for the acknowledgement to come back, for a total delay of R. In stop-and-wait the line is busy for l/b and idle for R, giving a line utilization of $l/(l + bR)$. If $l < bR$ the efficiency will be less than 50%. Since there is always a finite delay for the acknowledgement to propagate back, in principle pipelining can be used to keep the line busy during this interval, but if the interval is small, the additional complexity is not worth the trouble.

Pipelining frames over an unreliable communication channel raises some serious issues. First, what happens if a frame in the middle of a long stream is damaged or lost? Large numbers of succeeding frames will arrive at the receiver before the sender even finds out that anything is wrong. When a damaged frame arrives at the receiver, it obviously should be discarded, but what should the receiver do with all the correct frames following it? Remember that the receiving IMP is obligated to handmessages to the host in sequence.

There are two basic approaches to dealing with errors in the presence of pipelining. One way, often called **go back n**, is for the receiver simply to discard all subsequent frames, sending no acknowledgements, This strategy corresponds to a receive window of size 1. In other words, the IMP refuses to accept any frame except the next one it must give to the host. If the sender's window fills up before the timer runs out, the pipeline will begin to empty. Eventually, the sender will time out and retransmit all unacknowledged frames in order, starting with the damaged or lost one. This approach, shown in Fig. 4-9(a), can waste a lot of bandwidth if the error rate is high.

The other general strategy for handling errors when frames are pipelined, called **selective repeat**, is to have the receiving IMP store all the correct frames following the bad one. When the sender finally notices that something is wrong, it just retransmits the one bad frame, not all its successors, as shown in Fig. 4-9(b). If the second try succeeds, the receiving IMP will now have many correct frames in sequence, so they can all be handed off to the host quickly and the highest number acknowledged.

This strategy corresponds to a receiver window larger than 1. Any frame within the window may be accepted and buffered until all the preceding ones have been passed to the host. This approach can require large amounts of IMP memory if the window is large.

These two alternative approaches are trade-offs between bandwidth and IMP buffer space. Depending on which resource is more valuable, one or the other can be used. Figure 4-10 shows a pipelining protocol in which the receiving IMP only accepts frames in order; frames following an error are discarded. In this protocol, for the first time, we have now dropped the assumption that the host always has an infinite supply of messages to send. When the host has a message it wants to send, it can cause a *HostReady* event to happen. However, in order to enforce the flow control rule of no more than *MaxSeq* unacknowledged frames outstanding at any time, the IMP must be able to prohibit the host from bothering it with more work. The procedures *EnableHost* and *DisableHost* perform this function.

Note that a maximum of *MaxSeq* frames and not *MaxSeq* + 1 frames may be outstanding at any instant, even though there are *MaxSeq* + 1 distinct sequence numbers: 0, 1, 2, . . . , *MaxSeq*. To see why this restriction is needed, consider the following scenario with *MaxSeq* = 7.

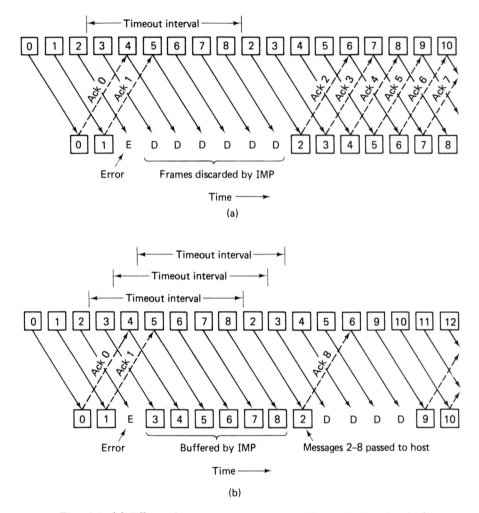

Fig. 4-9. (a) Effect of an error when the receiver window size is 1. (b) Effect of an error when the receiver window size is large.

1. The sender sends frames 0 through 7.

2. A piggybacked acknowledgement for frame 7 eventually comes back to the sender.

3. The sender sends another eight frames, again with sequence numbers 0 through 7.

4. Now another piggybacked acknowledgement for frame 7 comes in.

The question is: did all eight frames belonging to the second batch arrive successfully, or did all eight get lost (counting discards following an error as lost)? In both cases the receiver would be sending frame 7 as the acknowledgement. The sender has no way of telling. For this reason the maximum number of outstanding frames must be restricted to *MaxSeq*.

Although protocol 5 does not buffer the frames arriving after an error, it does not escape the problem of buffering altogether. Since a sender may have to retransmit all the unacknowledged frames at a future time, it must hang on to them until it knows for sure that they have been accepted by the receiver. When an acknowledgement comes in for frame *n*, frames $n - 1$, $n - 2$, and so on, are also automatically acknowledged. This property is especially important when some of the previous acknowledgement bearing frames were lost. Whenever any acknowledgement comes in, the IMP checks to see if any buffers can now be released. If buffers can be released (i.e., there is some room available in the window), a previously blocked host can now be allowed to cause more *HostReady* events.

Because this protocol has multiple outstanding frames, it logically needs multiple timers, one per outstanding frame. Each frame times out independently of all the other ones. All of these timers can easily be simulated in software, using a single hardware clock that causes interrupts periodically. The pending timeouts form a linked list, with each node of the list telling how many clock ticks until the timer goes off, the frame being timed, and a pointer to the next node.

As an illustration of how the timers could be implemented, consider the example of Fig. 4-11. Assume that the clock ticks once every 100 msec. Initially the real time is 10:00:00.0 and there are three timeouts pending, at 10:00:00.5, 10:00:01.3, and 10:00:01.9. Every time the hardware clock ticks, the real time is updated and the tick counter at the head of the list is decremented. When the tick counter becomes zero, a timeout is caused and the node removed from the list, as shown in Fig. 4-11(b). Although this organization requires the list to be scanned when *StartTimer* or *StopTimer* is called, it does not require much work per tick. In protocol 5, both of these routines have been given a parameter, indicating which frame is to be timed.

Grange and Mussard (1978) have pointed out that protocol efficiency can be improved by putting the piggyback field in the trailer rather than the header. That way, if an inbound frame arrives while the outbound line is being used to transmit a data frame, it is not too late to hook the acknowledgement onto the current frame instead of having to wait for the next one.

4.2.3. A Protocol That Accepts Frames Out of Order

Protocol 5 works well if errors are rare, but if the line is poor it wastes a lot of bandwidth on retransmitted frames. An alternative strategy to handling errors is to allow the receiver to accept and buffer the frames following a damaged or lost one, as in Fig. 4-9(b). Figure 4-12 illustrates our last, and most

{Protocol 5 ("pipelining") allows multiple outstanding frames. The sender may transmit up to *MaxSeq* frames without waiting for an acknowledgement. In addition, unlike the previous protocols, the host is not assumed to have a new message all the time. Instead, the host causes *HostReady* events when there is a message to be sent.}

type *EvType* = (*FrameArrival, CksumErr, TimeOut, HostReady*);

procedure *protocol5*;
var *NextFrameToSend*: *SequenceNr*; {*MaxSeq* > 1; used for outbound frame stream}
    AckExpected: *SequenceNr*;   {oldest frame as yet unacknowledged}
    FrameExpected: *SequenceNr*; {next frame expected on inbound stream}
    r,s: *frame*;   {scratch variables}
    buffer: **array**[*SequenceNr*] **of** *message*; {buffers for the outbound stream}
    nbuffered: *SequenceNr*;   {how many buffer slots are currently in use}
    i: *SequenceNr*;   {used to index into buffer}
    event: *EvType*;

function *between*(*a,b,c*: *SequenceNr*): *boolean*;
{Return true if $a <= b < c$ circularly, false otherwise.}
begin
  if ((*a* <= *b*) **and** (*b* < *c*)) **or** ((*c* < *a*) **and** (*a* <= *b*)) **or** ((*b* < *c*) **and** (*c* < *a*))
    then *between* := *true*
    else *between* := *false*
end; {*between*}

procedure *SendData*(*FrameNr*: *SequenceNr*);
{Construct and send a data frame.}
begin
  s.info := *buffer*[*FrameNr*];   {insert message into frame}
  s.seq := *FrameNr*;   {insert seq into frame}
  s.ack := (*FrameExpected* + *MaxSeq*) **mod** (*MaxSeq* + 1); {piggyback ack}
  sendf(*s*);   {transmit the frame}
  StartTimer(*FrameNr*)   {start the timer running}
end; {*SendData*}

begin
  EnableHost;   {allow host to cause *HostReady* events}
  NextFrameToSend := 0;   {initialize}
  AckExpected := 0;   {next ack expected on inbound stream}
  FrameExpected := 0;   {next data frame expected inbound}
  nbuffered := 0;   {initially no messages are buffered}

  repeat
    wait(*event*);   {possibilities: *FrameArrival, CksumErr, TimeOut, HostReady*}
    case *event* **of**

```
      HostReady:                     {the host has a message to send}
        begin                        {accept, save and transmit a new frame}
          FromHost(buffer[NextFrameToSend]);      {accept message from host}
          nbuffered := nbuffered + 1;     {one more frame buffered now}
          SendData(NextFrameToSend);      {transmit the frame}
          inc(NextFrameToSend)     {expand sender's window}
        end;

      FrameArrival:                  {a data or control frame has just arrived}
        begin
          getf(r);                   {fetch the frame from the operating system}

          if r.seq = FrameExpected then
            begin                    {frames are only accepted in proper order}
              ToHost(r.info);        {pass message to host}
              inc(FrameExpected)     {advance inbound window}
            end;

          {ack n implies n − 1, n − 2, etc.; check for this}
          while between(AckExpected, r.ack, NextFrameToSend) do
            begin                    {handle the piggybacked ack}
              nbuffered := nbuffered − 1;     {one frame fewer buffered}
              StopTimer(AckExpected);     {frame not lost, stop timer}
              inc(AckExpected)     {contract sender's window}
            end

        end;

      CksumErr: ;                    {just ignore bad frames}

      TimeOut:                       {trouble; retransmit all outstanding frames}
        begin
          NextFrameToSend := AckExpected; {start retransmitting here}
          for i := 1 to nbuffered do
            begin
              SendData(NextFrameToSend);
              inc(NextFrameToSend)
            end
        end
      end;
      if nbuffered < MaxSeq then EnableHost else DisableHost
    until doomsday
  end; {protocol5}
```

Fig. 4-10. A sliding window protocol with multiple outstanding frames.

general, protocol. This protocol does not discard frames merely because an earlier frame was damaged or lost.

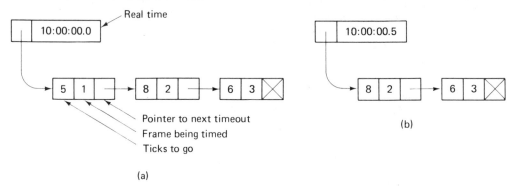

Fig. 4-11. Simulation of multiple timers in software.

In this protocol, both sender and receiver maintain a window of acceptable sequence numbers. The sender's window size starts out at 0 and grows to some predefined maximum, *MaxSeq*. The receiver's window, in contrast, is always fixed in size and equal to *MaxSeq*. The receiver has a buffer reserved for each sequence number within its window. Associated with each buffer is a bit (*arrived*) telling whether the buffer is full or empty. Whenever a frame arrives, its sequence number is checked by the function *between* to see if it falls within the window. If so, and if it has not already been received, it is accepted and stored. This action is taken without regard to whether or not it contains the next message expected by the host. Of course, it must be kept within the IMP and not passed to the host until all the lower numbered frames have already been delivered to the host in the correct order.

Nonsequential receive introduces certain problems not present in protocols in which frames are only accepted in order. We can illuminate the trouble most easily with an example. Suppose that we have a 3-bit sequence number, so that the sender is permitted to transmit up to seven frames before being required to wait for an acknowledgement. It sends frames 0 through 6. Meanwhile, the receiver's window allows it to accept any frame with sequence number between 0 and 6 inclusive. If all seven transmitted frames arrive correctly, the receiver will acknowledge them, and advance its window to allow receipt of 7, 0, 1, 2, 3, 4, or 5. All seven buffers are marked empty.

It is at this point that disaster strikes in the form of a lightning bolt hitting the telephone pole, and wiping out all the acknowledgements. The sender eventually times out and retransmits frame 0. When this frame arrives at the receiver, a check is made to see if it is within the receiving window. Unfortunately, it is within the new window, so it will be accepted. The receiver sends a piggybacked acknowledgement for frame 6, since 0 through 6 have been received.

The sender is happy to learn that all its transmitted frames did actually arrive correctly, so it advances its window and immediately sends frames 7, 0, 1, 2, 3, 4, and 5. Frame 7 will be accepted by the receiver and passed directly to the host. Immediately thereafter, the receiving IMP checks to see if it has a valid frame 0 already, discovers that it does, and passes the frame to the host. Consequently, the host gets an incorrect message, and the protocol fails.

The essence of the problem is that after the receiver advanced its window, the new range of valid sequence numbers overlapped the old one. The following batch of frames might be either duplicates (if all the acknowledgements were lost) or new ones (if all the acknowledgements were received). The poor receiver has no way of distinguishing these two cases.

The way out of this dilemma lies in making sure that after the receiver has advanced its window, there is no overlap with the original window. To ensure that there is no overlap, the maximum window size should be at most half the range of the sequence numbers. For example, if 4 bits are used for sequence numbers, these will range from 0 to 15. Only eight unacknowledged frames should be outstanding at any instant. That way, if the receiver has just accepted frames 0 through 7 and advanced its window to permit acceptance of frames 8 through 15, it can unambiguously tell if subsequent frames are retransmissions (0 through 7) or new ones (8 through 15). In general, the window size for protocol 6 will be $(MaxSeq + 1)/2$.

An interesting question is: How many buffers must the receiver have? Under no conditions will it ever accept frames whose sequence numbers are below the lower edge of the window or frames whose sequence numbers are above the upper edge of the window. Consequently, the number of buffers needed is equal to the window size, not the range of sequence numbers. In the above example of a 4-bit sequence number, eight buffers, numbered 0 through 7, are needed. When frame i arrives, it is put in buffer i mod 8. Notice that although i and $(i + 8)$ mod 16 are "competing" for the same buffer, they are never within the window at the same time, because that would imply a window size of 9.

For the same reason, the number of timers needed is equal to the number of buffers, not the size of the sequence space. Effectively, there is a timer associated with each buffer. When the timer runs out, the contents of the buffer is retransmitted.

In protocol 5, there is an implicit understanding that the channel is heavily loaded. When a frame arrives, no acknowledgement is sent immediately. Instead, the acknowledgement is piggybacked onto the next outgoing data frame. If the reverse traffic is light, the acknowledgement will be held up for a long period of time. If there is a lot of traffic in one direction and no traffic in the other direction, only $MaxSeq$ messages are sent, and then the protocol blocks. In protocol 6 this problem is fixed. After an in sequence data frame arrives, an auxiliary timer is started by $StartAckTimer$. If no reverse traffic has presented itself before this timer goes off, a separate acknowledgement frame is

{Protocol 6 ("nonsequential receive") accepts frames out of order, but passes messages to the host in order. Associated with each outstanding frame is a timer. When the timer goes off, only that one frame is retransmitted, not all the outstanding frames, as in protocol 5.}

```
const NrBufs = ... ;                    {NrBufs = (MaxSeq + 1) div 2}
      MaxBuf = ... ;                    {MaxBuf = NrBufs − 1}

type bufnr = 0 .. MaxBuf;
     EvType = (FrameArrival, CksumErr, TimeOut, HostReady, HostIdle);

procedure protocol6;
var AckExpected: SequenceNr;        {lower edge of transmitter window}
    NextFrameToSend: SequenceNr;        {upper edge of transmitter window + 1}
    FrameExpected: SequenceNr;      {lower edge of receiver window}
    TooFar: SequenceNr;             {upper edge of receiver window + 1}
    OldestFrame: SequenceNr;        {which frame timed out?}
    i: bufnr;                       {index into buffer pool}
    r,s: frame;                     {scratch variables}
    OutBuf: array[bufnr] of message;       {buffers for outbound stream}
    InBuf: array[bufnr] of message;  {buffers for inbound stream}
    arrived: array[bufnr] of boolean;      {inbound bit map}
    nbuffered: SequenceNr;          {how many output buffers currently used}
    NoNak: boolean;                 {set to false when a nak is sent}
    event: EvType;

function between(a,b,c: SequenceNr): boolean;
begin
    if ((a <= b) and (b < c)) or ((c < a) and (a <= b)) or ((b < c) and (c < a))
      then between := true
      else between := false
end; {between}

procedure SendFrame(fk: FrameKind; FrameNr: SequenceNr);
{Construct and send a data, ack, or nak frame.}
begin s.kind := fk;                     {kind = data, ack, or nak}
    if fk = data then s.info := OutBuf[FrameNr mod NrBufs];
    s.seq := FrameNr;                   {only meaningful for data frames}
    s.ack := (FrameExpected + MaxSeq) mod (MaxSeq + 1);
    if fk = nak then NoNak := false;        {one nak per frame, please}
    sendf(s);                           {transmit the frame}
    if fk = data then StartTimer(FrameNr mod NrBufs);
    StopAckTimer                        {no need for separate ack frame}
end; {SendFrame}

begin
    EnableHost;                         {here begins the initialization}
    NextFrameToSend := 0;   AckExpected := 0;   FrameExpected := 0;
    TooFar := NrBufs;       nbuffered := 0;      NoNak := true;
    for i := 0 to MaxBuf do arrived[i] := false;

    repeat
       wait(event);
       case event of
```

```
HostReady:                        {accept, save, and transmit a new frame}
  begin
    nbuffered := nbuffered + 1;          {expand window}
    FromHost(OutBuf[NextFrameToSend mod NrBufs]); {fetch new message}
    SendFrame(data, NextFrameToSend);          {transmit frame}
    inc(NextFrameToSend) {advance upper window edge}
  end;

FrameArrival:                     {a data or control frame has arrived}
  begin getf(r);                  {fetch frame from operating system}
    if r.kind = data then
    begin                         {an undamaged data frame has arrived}
      if (r.seq <> FrameExpected) and NoNak then SendFrame(nak,0);
      if between(FrameExpected, r.seq, TooFar) and
        (arrived[r.seq mod NrBufs] = false) then
      begin                       {frames may be accepted in any order}
        arrived[r.seq mod NrBufs] := true;      {mark buffer as full}
        InBuf[r.seq mod NrBufs] := r.info;      {insert data in buffer}
        while arrived[FrameExpected mod NrBufs] do
        begin                     {pass frames and advance window}
          ToHost(InBuf[FrameExpected mod NrBufs]);
          NoNak := true;
          arrived[FrameExpected mod NrBufs] := false;
          inc(FrameExpected);          {advance lower edge of receiver window}
          inc(TooFar);          {advance upper edge + 1 of receiver window}
          StartAckTimer;          {to see if separate ack needed}
        end
      end
    end; {end of code for data frame}

    if (r.kind = nak) and
      between(AckExpected, (r.ack + 1) mod (MaxSeq + 1), NextFrameToSend) then
      SendFrame(nak, (r.ack + 1) mod (MaxSeq + 1));

    while between(AckExpected, r.ack, NextFrameToSend) do
      begin nbuffered := nbuffered - 1;          {handle piggybacked ack}
        StopTimer(AckExpected mod NrBufs);     {frame arrived intact}
        inc(AckExpected)          {advance lower window edge}
      end

  end; {end of FrameArrival code}

CksumErr: if NoNak then SendFrame(nak,0);     {damaged frame received}

TimeOut: SendFrame(data, OldestFrame);          {we timed out}

HostIdle: SendFrame(ack, 0)     {host idle too long, send ack}

  end; {end of case}

  if nbuffered < NrBufs then EnableHost else DisableHost
until doomsday
end; {protocol6}
```

Fig. 4-12. A sliding window protocol with nonsequential receive.

sent. An interrupt due to the auxiliary timer is called a *HostIdle* event. With this arrangement, one-directional traffic flow is now possible, because the lack of reverse data frames onto which acknowledgements can be piggybacked is no longer an obstacle.

Protocol 6 uses a more efficient strategy than protocol 5 for dealing with errors. Whenever the receiver has reason to suspect that an error has occurred, it sends a negative acknowledgement (NAK) frame back to the sender. Such a frame is a request for retransmission of the frame specified in the NAK. There are two cases when the receiver should be suspicious: a damaged frame has arrived or a frame other than the expected one arrived (potential lost frame). To avoid making multiple requests for retransmission of the same lost frame, the receiver should keep track of whether a NAK has already been sent for a given frame. The variable *NoNak* in protocol 6 is true if no NAK has been sent yet for *FrameExpected*. If the NAK gets mangled or lost, no real harm is done, since the sender will eventually time out and retransmit the missing frame anyway.

If the time required for a frame to propagate to the IMP, be processed there, and an acknowledgement returned is (nearly) constant, the sender can adjust its timer to be just slightly larger than the normal time interval expected between sending a frame and receiving its acknowledgement. However, if this time is highly variable, the sender is faced with the choice of either setting the interval to a small value, and risking unnecessary retransmissions, thus wasting bandwidth, or setting it to a large value, going idle for a long period after an error, thus also wasting bandwidth. If the reverse traffic is sporadic, the time to acknowledgement will be irregular, being shorter when there is reverse traffic and longer when there is not. Variable processing time within the receiver can also be a problem here. In general, whenever the standard deviation of the acknowledgement interval is small compared to the interval itself, the timer can be set "tight" and NAKs are not useful. Otherwise, the timer must be set "loose," and NAKs can appreciably speed up retransmission of lost or damaged frames.

Closely related to the matter of timeouts and NAKs is the question of determining which frame caused a timeout. In protocol 5 it is always *AckExpected*, because it is always the oldest. In protocol 6, there is no trivial way to determine who timed out. Suppose that frames 0 through 4 have been transmitted, meaning that the list of outstanding frames is 01234, in order from oldest to youngest. Now imagine that 0 times out, 5 (a new frame) is transmitted, 1 times out, 2 times out, and 6 (another new frame) is transmitted. At this point the list of outstanding frames is 3405126, from oldest to youngest. If all inbound traffic is lost for a while, the seven outstanding frames will time out in that order. To keep the example from getting even more complicated than it already is, we have not shown the timer administration. Instead, we just assume that the variable *OldestFrame* is set upon timeout to indicate which frame timed out.

4.3. EXAMPLES OF THE DATA LINK LAYER

Having treated the general principles of data link protocols, it is now time to see what these protocols look like in practice. We will present three detailed examples: ARPANET, SNA, and DECNET. These three examples are especially interesting because each one uses a completely different method for delimiting frames. The data link layer used in public networks is essentially the same as in SNA.

4.3.1. The Data Link Layer in the ARPANET

When an IMP wants to send a frame to an adjacent IMP, it sets it up in a memory buffer and then starts the transmission hardware. When the complete frame has been sent (1008 bits at 50 kbps takes about 20 msec) an interrupt is generated. Before sending the first character in the buffer, the transmission hardware sends a SYN (SYNchronize), a DLE (Data Link Escape) and an STX (Start of TeXt). These three characters serve to define the start of the frame for the receiver. Then the contents of the IMP buffer is transmitted, 1 bit at a time. Finally the hardware automatically transmits a DLE and an ETX (End of TeXt) followed by a 24 bit CRC checksum and then another SYN character. If there is no new frame to transmit, the hardware keeps sending SYNs.

If a DLE ETX sequence happened to occur in the data, the receiver would be confused, so the hardware automatically inserts an extra DLE in front of any DLE in the text. This method for achieving data transparency is known as **character stuffing** and is shown in Fig. 4-13. The receiving hardware strips off the extra DLEs. In this manner arbitrary binary text can be transmitted through the network. If data transparency were not achieved (e.g., if the code DLE could not be sent), binary programs could not be transmitted, because this code may occur. In particular, the new versions of the IMP program could not be distributed over the network, as they regularly are.

Although character stuffing does not at first glance appear to increase the chance of an undetected error, it actually does. Imagine that a single-bit error changes the DLE STX into P STX (DLE = 20 octal and P = 120 octal). The receiver will not recognize end of frame. Instead, it will merge the bad frame and the following one into a single long frame. Normally, the checksum computation will detect this error, but there is a small chance that by accident the merged frame will have the same checksum as the frame following the bad one. If this happens, a single-bit error will not be detected. The use of a frame length field in the header can eliminate this problem, however.

The ARPANET has both single frame and multiframe messages. For the time being we will restrict our attention to the single-frame (i.e., single-packet) case, corresponding to messages up to 1008 bits long. When a message comes into an IMP from a host, the IMP first builds a 128 bit header and attaches it to the front of the message, forming a packet. The routing algorithm then takes

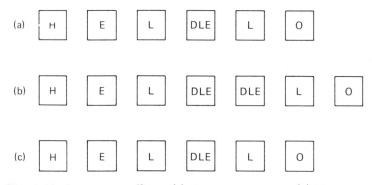

Fig. 4-13. Character stuffing. (a) The original data. (b) The data as they appear on the line. (c) The data as they are stored in the receiver's memory after destuffing.

over and decides which output line to use. When the packet has worked its way to the front of its queue, the IMP hardware transmits it, encased by the frame header and trailer, as shown in Fig. 4-14. Control, routing, tracer and other special packets have different formats.

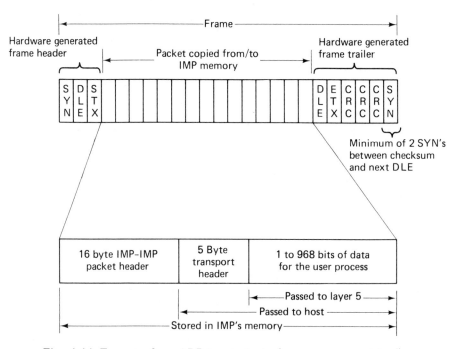

Fig. 4-14. Format of an ARPA net single frame message while "on the wires."

The IMP software multiplexes eight logically independent, full-duplex channels onto each physical line (16 in the case of the satellite links, owing to the long delay). Each of these logical channels operates using a 1-bit sliding window (i.e., a stop-and-wait protocol). Each IMP maintains a table containing 3 bits per logical channel [i.e., 24 bits per physical line (48 bits for satellite links)]. The 3 bits tell whether or not there is an outstanding packet on that logical channel, the sequence number of the next packet to send, and the sequence number of the next packet expected. When a packet needs to be sent, the lowest idle logical channel is marked busy and used. When the acknowledgement comes in, it is marked idle again.

When the sender wants to send a packet, it chooses the lowest idle logical channel and includes the current sequence number in the packet header. If this sequence number is one higher (modulo 2) than the last packet accepted, the receiver accepts this one, increments the sequence number (modulo 2), and sends an acknowledgement. If the incoming packet's sequence number matches the receiver's variable, the packet is a duplicate and is discarded. When the acknowledgement gets back to the transmitter, it is checked against the last sequence number sent. If the numbers agree, the transmit sequence number is complemented and the logical channel is marked idle.

Each packet sent contains in its header the last packet received on each of the logical channels rather than just an acknowledgement bit for the logical channel to which this packet belongs. Doing it this way ensures that even if a packet is lost, the next one will convey the complete acknowledgement status. When no reverse traffic exists, a special acknowledgement packet is sent.

The IMP-IMP protocol does not use NAKs. If a packet comes in damaged, it is just ignored. The sender will time out in 125 msec, and send it again. However, the use of eight distinct stop-and-wait logical channels rather than a 3-bit sliding window achieves the same effect as having NAKs: a damaged packet will be repeated quickly, without regard to the other seven packets.

We will discuss the details of the IMP-IMP packet header in Chap. 5 because some of its fields are related to the layer 3 protocol rather than the layer 2 protocol. Suffice it to say that the header contains three fields used directly for exchanging frames between adjacent IMPs:

1. A 1-bit sequence number for the stop-and-wait protocol.

2. A 3-bit logical channel number.

3. An 8-bit acknowledgement field.

4.3.2. The Data Link Layer in SNA and X.25

In this section we will examine a group of closely related protocols that are widely used throughout the world. They are all derived from the data link protocol used in SNA. In the early days of the networking, most protocols were character-oriented. That is, a frame consisted of a group of characters in some character code (e.g., ASCII, EBCDIC). IBM's BISYNC protocol and the ARPANET IMP-IMP protocol are examples of character-oriented protocols.

In a character-oriented protocol, a frame is composed of an integral number of characters in the chosen code (e.g., 6- or 8-bit characters in BISYNC). This means that a computer with a 9-bit character cannot send arbitrary messages in BISYNC to another computer with 9-bit characters unless the characters are chopped up and repacked in units of 6 or 8 bits. In addition to the length problem, achieving data transparency by having a special transparent mode in which character stuffing is used is character-code-dependent.

As networks developed, the disadvantages of embedding the character code in the protocol design became more and more obvious. In the early 1970s the time was ripe for a new generation of protocols. IBM developed **SDLC** (Synchronous Data Link Control), which is now used in SNA, and submitted it to ANSI and ISO for acceptance as U.S. and international standards, respectively. ANSI modified it to become **ADDCP** (Advanced Data Communication Control Procedure), and ISO modified it to become **HDLC** (High-level Data Link Control). CCITT then adopted and modified HDLC for its **LAP** (Link Access Procedure) as part of the X.25 network interface standard, but later modified it again to **LAPB**, to make it more compatible with a later version of HDLC. The nice thing about standards is that you have so many to choose from; furthermore, if you do not like any of them, you can just wait for next year's model.

All of these protocols are based on the same principles. All are bit-oriented. They differ only in minor, but nevertheless irritating, ways. The discussion of bit-oriented protocols that follows is intended as a general introduction. For the specific details of any one protocol, please consult the appropriate definition.

The reason that these protocols are referred to as "bit-oriented" is that each one allows data frames containing an arbitrary number of bits. The frame size need not be an integral multiple of any specific character size. Traditional protocols (e.g., BISYNC) recognized the end of frame by some special character, such as ETB or ETX. Since bit-oriented frames to not have to contain an integral number of characters, a new method is needed to delimit frame yet preserve data transparency (i.e., allow arbitrary data, including the frame delimiter pattern).

The data transparency method used by all the new protocols is called **bit stuffing**. Each frame begins and ends with a special bit pattern, namely 01111110. Whenever the transmitting hardware encounters five consecutive ones in the data, it automatically stuffs a 0 bit into the outgoing bit stream. Bit stuffing is analogous to character stuffing, in which a DLE is stuffed into the outgoing character stream before each control character. When the receiver sees five consecutive incoming 1 bits, followed by a 0 bit, it automatically destuffs (i.e., deletes) the 0 bit. Just as character stuffing is completely transparent to the software in both computers, so is bit stuffing. If the user data contained the flag pattern 01111110, it would be transmitted as 011111010 but stored in the receiver's memory as 01111110. Figure 4-15 gives an another example of how bit stuffing works.

(a)   0 1 1 0 1 1 1 1 1 1 1 1 1 1 1 1 1 1 0 0 1 0

(b)   0 1 1 0 1 1 1 1 1 0 1 1 1 1 1 0 1 1 1 1 1 0 1 0 0 1 0
                                   Stuffed bits

(c)   0 1 1 0 1 1 1 1 1 1 1 1 1 1 1 1 1 1 1 1 0 0 1 0

Fig. 4-15. Bit stuffing. (a) The original data. (b) The data as they appear on the line. (c) The data as they are stored in the receiver's memory after destuffing.

All the bit-oriented protocols use the frame structure shown in Fig. 4-16. The *Address* field is primarily of importance on multidrop lines, where it is used to identify one of the terminals. For point-to-point lines, it is sometimes used to distinguish commands from responses.

Bits	8	8	8	⩾ 0	16	8
	01111110	Address	Control	Data	Checksum	01111110

Fig. 4-16. Frame format for bit-oriented protocols.

The *Control* field is used for sequence numbers, acknowledgements, and other purposes, as discussed below.

The *Data* field may contain arbitrary information. It may be arbitrarily long, although the efficiency of the checksum falls off with increasing frame length due to the greater probability of multiple burst errors.

The *Checksum* field is a minor variation on the well-known cyclic redundancy code, using CRC-CCITT as the generating polynomial. The variation is to allow lost flag bytes to be detected.

The frame is delimited with another flag sequence (01111110). On idle point-to-point lines, flag sequences are transmitted continuously, just as SYN characters are usually transmitted during idle periods when BISYNC is used. The minimum frame contains three fields and totals 32 bits, excluding the flags on either end.

There are three kinds of frames: **Information**, **Supervisory**, and **Unnumbered**. The contents of the *Control* field for these three kinds are shown in Fig. 4-17. The protocol uses a sliding window, with a 3-bit sequence number.

Up to seven unacknowledged frames may be outstanding at any instant. The *Seq* field in Fig. 4-17(a) is the frame sequence number. The *Next* field is a piggybacked acknowledgement. However, all the protocols adhere to the convention that instead of piggybacking the number of the last frame received correctly, they use the number of the first frame not received (i.e., the next frame expected). The choice of using the last frame received or the next frame expected is arbitrary; it does not matter which convention is used, provided that it is used consistently of course.

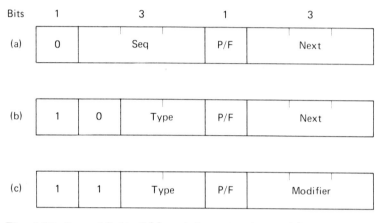

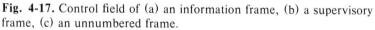

Fig. 4-17. Control field of (a) an information frame, (b) a supervisory frame, (c) an unnumbered frame.

The *P/F* bit stands for *Poll/Final*. It is used when a computer (or concentrator) is polling a group of terminals. When the computer wants to transmit data to a terminal, it sends a poll message with the *P/F* bit set to 1. The terminal responds with a frame containing the *P/F* bit also 1. Then the computer sends a series of data frames, only the last of which has *P/F* set to 1, to indicate that it is the final frame.

In some of the protocols, the *P/F* bit is used to force the other machine to send a Supervisory frame immediately rather than waiting for reverse traffic onto which to piggyback the window information. The bit also has some minor uses in connection with the Unnumbered frames.

The various kinds of Supervisory frames are distinguished by the *Type* field. Type 0 is an acknowledgement frame (officially called RECEIVE READY) used to indicate the next frame expected. This frame is used when there is no reverse traffic to use for piggybacking.

Type 1 is a negative acknowledgement frame (officially called REJECT). It is used to indicate that a transmission error has been detected. The *Next* field indicates the first frame in sequence not received correctly (i.e., the frame to be retransmitted). The sender is required to retransmit all outstanding frames starting at *Next*. This strategy is similar to our protocol 5 rather than our protocol 6.

Type 2 is RECEIVE NOT READY. It acknowledges all frames up to but not including *Next*, just as Receive Ready, but it tells the sender to stop sending. RNR is intended to signal certain temporary problems with the receiver, such as a shortage of buffers, and not as an alternative to the sliding window flow control. When the condition has been repaired, the receiver sends a Receive Ready, Reject, or certain control frames.

Type 3 is the SELECTIVE REJECT. It calls for retransmission of only the frame specified. In this sense it is like our protocol 6 rather than 5 and is therefore most useful when the sender's window size is half the sequence space size, or less. Thus if a receiver wishes to buffer out of sequence frames for potential future use, it can force the retransmission of any specific frame using Selective Reject. HDLC and ADCCP allow this frame type, but SDLC and LAPB do not allow it (i.e., there is no Selective Reject), and type 3 frames are undefined.

The third class of frame is the Unnumbered frame. It is used for control purposes. The various bit-oriented protocols differ considerably here, in contrast with the other two kinds, where they are nearly identical. Five bits are available to indicate the frame type, but not all 32 possibilities are used.

All the protocols provide a command, DISC (DISConnect), that allows a machine to announce that it is going down (e.g., for preventive maintenance). They also have a command that allows a machine that has just come back on line to announce its presence and force all the sequence numbers back to zero. This command is called SNRM (Set Normal Response Mode). Unfortunately, "Normal Response Mode" is anything but normal. It is an unbalanced (i.e., asymmetric) mode in which one end of the line is the master and the other the slave. SNRM dates from a time when data communication meant a terminal talking to a host, which clearly is asymmetric. To make the protocol more suitable when the two partners are equals, HDLC and LAPB have an additional command, SABM (Set Asynchronous Balanced Mode), which resets the line and declares both parties to be equals. They also have commands SABME and SNRME, which are the same as SABM and SNRM, respectively, except that they enable an extended frame format that uses 7-bit sequence numbers instead of 3-bit sequence numbers.

A third command provided by all the protocols is FRMR (FRaMe Reject), used to indicated that a frame with a correct checksum but impossible semantics arrived. Examples of impossible semantics are a type 3 Supervisory frame in LAPB, a frame shorter than 32 bits, an illegal control frame, and an acknowledgement of a frame that was outside the window, etc. FRMR frames contain a 24-bit data field telling what was wrong with the frame. The data include the control field of the bad frame, the window parameters, and a collection of bits used to signal specific errors.

Control frames may be lost or damaged, just like data frames, so they must be acknowledged too. A special control frame is provided for this purpose, called UA (Unnumbered Acknowledgement). Since only one control frame may be outstanding, there is never any ambiguity about which control frame is being acknowledged.

The remaining control frames deal with initialization, polling, and status reporting. There is also a control frame that may contain arbitrary information, UI (Unnumbered Information). These data are not passed to the user, but are for the receiving IMP itself.

4.3.3. The Data Link Layer in DECNET

The data link protocol in DECNET is called DDCMP (Digital Data Communications Message Protocol). It is quite unusual, in that frames are not delimited by some bit pattern as in SDLC, but by including an explicit character count in the header. If this count should ever be corrupted by transmission errors, the protocol can get out of synchronization and lose track of the frame boundaries. To minimize the chance of a bad count field, the frame header has its own private checksum, distinct from the data checksum.

DDCMP uses a sliding window, with up to 255 packets outstanding in the extreme case. Acknowledgements can be piggybacked if there is reverse traffic. The maximum packet size is 16383 bytes versus 1008 bits (equivalent to 126 bytes) in the ARPANET, and no explicit maximum in SNA. Since there is no preemption, if a long packet is being sent over a slow line, all other traffic will just have to wait.

Like SNA, and unlike the ARPANET, DECNET can handle half-duplex lines and multidrop lines as well as full-duplex lines. Several machines may share a multidrop line. When half-duplex lines are being used, one side is explicitly the master until it announces that it is done sending, at which time the other side can begin to send. When multidrop lines are being used, one site is designated as the master and all the others are slaves. All communication is from or to the master. Direct slave-slave communication is not possible.

The format used for data packets in DDCMP is shown in Fig. 4-18. The names of some fields have been changed from the DEC documents to conform to the nomenclature we have been using so far. The *SOH* field indicates Start of Header. It is always the constant 129 to indicate that a data packet follows.

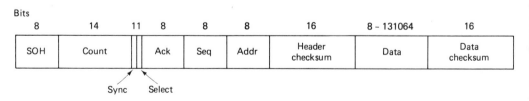

Fig. 4-18. Data format used by DDCMP.

The *Count* field gives the length of the data field in bytes. Minimum is 1, maximum is 16383. Note that the packet must be an integral number of 8-bit bytes, whereas neither SNA nor the ARPANET has this restriction.

The *Sync* field is used to synchronize both sides of the line if necessary.

The *Select* field is only used on half-duplex or multidrop lines. This bit is set to indicate that the current sender has no more packets to send. On half duplex lines, this information permits the other side to begin transmitting. On multidrop lines, the bit toggles control between master and slave.

The *Ack* field contains the number of the last packet correctly received in sequence. It is the piggybacked acknowledgement.

The *Seq* field is the sequence number of this packet, 0-255.

The *Addr* field is used on multidrop lines to indicate the machine to whom the packet is addressed. On point-to-point lines this field is not needed, and is always 1.

The *Header checksum* field is a cyclic redundancy checksum using the CRC-16 polynomial. It checks only the header fields (i.e., *SOH* through *Addr*). As mentioned above, the reason for a separate checksum for the header is the sensitivity of count-delimited protocols to errors. If a packet whose true length was a few bytes was inadvertently received with a count of thousands, the receiver would continue listening even after the packet fully arrived. Eventually, the sender would time out and transmit a repeat or query, but this would also just calmly be accepted by the receiver. After many attempts the sender might falsely conclude that the receiver was down, whereas in fact it was just merrily accumulating data. The ARPANET does not have this problem because DLE ETX always indicates end of packet, so there is no danger of a receiver collecting many packets thinking them all part of one giant packet. Also the small upper bound on packet length prevents this from happening. The flag sequence used in SNA also makes it unlikely that many frames will ever be merged by accident.

The *Data* field contains the true data. Any combination of bytes is legal. Due to the byte count, there is no need to use character stuffing on DLE or any other character, which simplifies the hardware.

The *Data checksum* field is the checksum for the data part of the packet.

In addition to the data packets, there are also control packets. The most important of these are ACK, NAK, REP, START, and STARTACK. ACK is used to convey acknowledgements when there is no reverse traffic to piggyback onto. NAK is used to indicate that a packet was not received correctly. NAK also implicitly acknowledges correct receipt of all packets up to the bad one. The REP packet is sent when a transmitter times out. It inquires about the status of the packet just sent. The receiver is required to answer with either an ACK or NAK, depending upon whether or not the packet in question was received correctly or not. The REP is used because with such long packets permitted, automatic retransmission would be highly undesirable if the receiver were merely a little bit late in sending an acknowledgement. The START and

STARTACK control packets are used to initialize a sender-receiver pair.

The DDCMP layer accepts four principal commands from higher layers of software: initialize a line, close a line down, send a packet, and receive a packet. These commands are used by the network layer to get messages sent. We will examine the network layer in Chap. 5.

4.4. ANALYSIS OF PROTOCOLS

In principle, protocols 4, 5, and 6 are all equally good. They all serve to convert a line that makes errors into a virtual error free channel. In practice they can differ substantially in terms of performance. In the following section, we will examine some aspects of protocol performance. Then we will look at some formal methods for investigating protocol behavior.

4.4.1. Protocol Efficiency

Many factors influence the efficiency of a protocol. Among them are whether frames are of fixed or variable length, whether piggybacking is used or not, whether the protocol is pipelined or stop-and-wait, whether the line is half- or full-duplex, and the statistical characteristics of the transmission errors. For our protocol 1, for example, the channel efficiency is 100%, because the sender just keeps sending full blast. However, the other protocols are less efficient because they must occasionally wait for acknowledgements, or retransmit frames a second time.

As an example, let us analyze a one directional stop-and-wait protocol with fixed-length frames and no piggybacking, such as our protocol 3. The basic approach we will use to determine the channel efficiency of any protocol, is to determine how much bandwidth is actually tied up to send the statistically average frame, taking account of all its retransmissions and timeouts. For the derivation we will need the following notation:

A = number of bits in an ACK frame

C = channel capacity in bps

D = number of data bits per frame

E = probability of a bit being in error

$F = D + H$ (total frame length)

H = number of bits in the frame header

I = interrupt and IMP service time + propagation delay

L = probability that a frame or its ACK is lost or damaged

P_1 = probability that a data frame is lost or damaged

P_2 = probability that an ACK frame is lost or damaged

R = mean number of retransmissions per data frame

T = timeout interval

U = channel utilization (efficiency)

W = window size

Before considering the effects of errors, let us see what the channel utilization would be for a perfect line. Surprisingly enough, it can be far below 100%. Denote the time that the sender begins to send a frame as time 0. At time F/C the last bit has been sent. At time $(F/C) + I$ the last bit has arrived at the receiver, the interrupt has been serviced, and the IMP is ready to start sending the acknowledgement frame. At time $(F/C) + I + (A/C)$ the last bit of the acknowledgement frame has been sent. At time $(F/C) + I + (A/C) + I$, the sender has processed the acknowledgement and is ready to send the next data frame. The bandwidth occupied by this frame is C multiplied by the time taken, or $F + A + 2CI$. The number of data bits actually transferred is D, so the channel efficiency is $D/(H + D + A + 2CI)$. If the header and acknowledgements are negligible, the bandwidth low, and the propagation and service times are short, the channel utilization will be high; otherwise, not.

Now let us consider the effects of transmission errors. If a frame is damaged or lost, the sender will time out T sec after the last bit has been sent. Thus an unsuccessful transmission uses $F + CT$ bits worth of transmission capacity. If the mean number of retransmissions per frame is R, the total channel capacity used for the R bad frames and one good one is $R(F + CT) + (F + A + 2CI)$.

Now it remains to compute the mean number of retransmissions per frame. A frame is successful if both the data and acknowledgement are correctly received. The probability of success is $(1 - P_2)(1 - P_1)$. Therefore, the probability of failure is $L = 1 - (1 - P_2)(1 - P_1)$. The probability that exactly k attempts are needed (i.e., $k - 1$ retransmissions) is $(1 - L)L^{k-1}$. This result yields an expected number of transmissions per frame of $1/(1 - L)$ and an expected number of retransmissions one less, or $R = L/(1 - L)$.

Using this value of R, we arrive at a channel utilization

$$U = \frac{D}{(L/(1 - L))(F + CT) + (F + A + 2CI)}$$

If the receiving IMP's service time has a low variance, the sender can set its timeout interval just above the time required for the acknowledgement to arrive: $T = A/C + 2I$ (approximately). The channel efficiency then becomes

$$U = \frac{D}{H + D} \times (1 - P_1)(1 - P_2) \times \frac{1}{1 + CT/(H + D)}$$

The first factor represents the loss due to header overhead. The second factor represents the loss due to errors. The third factor represents the loss due to stop-and-wait.

To proceed further, we need a model relating the probability of a frame's being in error to its length. To start with, let us make the (not terribly realistic) assumption that each bit has a probability E of being in error, independent of the preceding and succeeding bits. With this assumption and $A = H$ we find that the channel utilization is given by the formula

$$U = \frac{D}{H + D} \times (1 - E)^{H + D}(1 - E)^{H} \times \frac{1}{1 + CT/(H + D)} \quad (4\text{-}1)$$

An interesting and important question now arises: What is the optimum frame size? If the frames are too short, the efficiency will be low due to the header overhead. If the frames are too long, the probability of a frame being received without error will be low, so the efficiency will drop due to the many retransmissions. This reasoning suggests that there must be an optimum frame size, with the optimum depending on the header size, error rate, raw bandwidth, and timeout interval. To find the optimum, take the partial derivative of U with respect to D and set it equal to zero. As Field (1976) has shown, this leads to the equation

$$D^2 + D(H + CT) + \frac{H + CT}{\ln (1 - E)} = 0$$

with solution

$$D_{\text{opt}} = \frac{H + CT}{2}\left[\sqrt{1 - 4/[(H + CT)\ln (1 - E)]} - 1\right]$$

If E is very small, which is commonly the case, $\ln(1 - E)$ can be accurately approximated by $-E$. Furthermore, a small E means that both the 1 under the radical and the 1 following the radical can be ignored, yielding the approximation

$$D_{\text{opt}} = \sqrt{(H + CT)/E} \quad (4\text{-}2)$$

Notice that $H + CT$ is the overhead due to headers and timeouts. As the line quality improves (i.e., $E \to 0$), the optimum frame size increases, as it should. If there are no errors, the only overhead comes from headers and the stop-and-wait protocol, both of which argue for as long a frame as possible. On the other hand, a high error rate drives the frame size down, to avoid retransmission of long frames.

To analyze the channel efficiency for frame sizes close to the optimum, let $D = xD_{\text{opt}}$, so values of x close to 1.0 represent frames close to the optimum size. Now substitute Eq. (4-2) into Eq. (4-1) and make the approximation $(1 - E)^D = 1 - ED$ to get

$$U = (1 - 2HE) \; \frac{1 - x\sqrt{(H + CT)E}}{1 + \dfrac{1}{x}\sqrt{(H + CT)E}}$$

As long as the radical remains relatively small, the channel utilization is not terribly sensitive to small deviations from the optimum frame size.

Actual measurements of the error characteristics of the telephone system show that errors do not befall individual bits at random. Instead, errors tend to come in bunches. Thus the model $P_1 = 1 - 1 - E)^{H + D}$ is not an accurate one. Experimentally, it appears that $P_1 = k(H + D)^\alpha$ provides a better fit. Finding the optimum frame size and channel efficiency for this model can be done using the method shown above.

Other protocols can also be analyzed using this procedure. As an example, consider protocol 5 under conditions of heavy traffic (i.e., there is always work to be done). Also assume that the window size is large enough that the sender never has to block because the window is full (unless there are errors, of course). For simplicity, assume that the piggybacked acknowledgements are free, and can be ignored in the analysis.

When an error occurs, the sender runs to the end of its window and then begins timing out. The bandwidth wasted during the timeout will be CT. After the timeout, the full window of W frames must be retransmitted. If the mean number of retransmissions is R, the total bandwidth occupied per successfully received frame is $H + D + R[W(H + D) + CT]$. The channel efficiency is then D divided by this amount of bandwidth.

For a more comprehensive analysis of protocol efficiency, see Field (1976) and Fraser (1977).

4.4.2. Protocol Verification

Realistic protocols, and the programs that implement them, are often quite complicated. Consequently, some computer scientists have advocated making formal mathematical models of protocols so that they can be proven correct (e.g., Bochmann and Sunshine, 1980; Danthine, 1980; Merlin, 1979; Sunshine, 1979). In this section we will look at some of the models and techniques that have been proposed.

Finite State Machine Models

A key concept used in many protocol models is the **finite state machine**. With this technique, each **protocol machine** (i.e., sender or receiver) is always in a specific state at every instant of time. Its state consists of all the values of its variables, including the program counter.

In most cases, a large number of states can be grouped together for purposes of analysis. For example, considering the receiver in protocol 3, we could abstract out from all the possible states two important ones: waiting for frame 0 or waiting for frame 1. All other states can be thought of as transient, just steps on the way to one of the main states. Typically, the states are chosen to be those instants that the protocol machine is waiting for the next event to happen [i.e., executing the procedure call *wait*(*event*) in our examples]. At this point the state of the protocol machine is completely determined by the states of its variables. The number of states is then 2^n, where n is the number of bits needed to represent all the variables combined.

The state of the complete system is the combination of all the states of the two protocol machines and the channel. The state of the channel is determined by its contents. Using protocol 3 again as an example, the channel has four possible states: a zero frame or a one frame moving from sender to receiver, an acknowledgement frame going the other way, or an empty channel. If we model the sender and receiver as each having two states, the complete system has 16 distinct states.

A word about the channel state is in order. The concept of a frame being "on the channel" is an abstraction, of course. What we really mean is that a frame has been partially transmitted, partially received, but not yet processed at the destination. A frame remains "on the channel" until the protocol machine executes *getf* and processes it.

From each state, there are zero or more possible **transitions** to other states. Transitions occur when some event happens. For a protocol machine a transition might occur when a frame is sent, when a frame arrives, when a timer goes off, when a host interrupt occurs, etc. For the channel, typical events are insertion of a new frame onto the channel by a protocol machine, delivery of a frame to a protocol machine, or loss of a frame due to a noise burst. Given a complete description of the protocol machines and the channel characteristics, it is possible to draw a directed graph showing all the states as nodes and all the transitions as directed arcs.

One particular state is designated as the **initial state**. This state corresponds to the description of the system when it starts running, or some convenient starting place shortly thereafter. From the initial state, some, perhaps all, of the other states can be reached by a sequence of transitions. Using well-known techniques from graph theory (e.g., computing the transitive closure of a graph), it is possible to determine which states are reachable and which are not. This analysis can be helpful in determining if a protocol is correct or not.

As an example of a state machine graph, consider Fig. 4-19(a). This graph corresponds to protocol 3 as described above: each protocol machine has two states and the channel has four states. Each state is labeled by three characters, *XYZ*, where *X* is 0 or 1, corresponding to the frame the sender is trying to send, *Y* is also 0, 1, corresponding to the frame the receiver expects, and *Z* is 0, 1, *A*, or empty (−), corresponding to the state of the channel. In this example the initial state has been chosen as (000). In other words, the sender has just sent frame 0, the receiver expects frame 0, and frame 0 is currently on the channel.

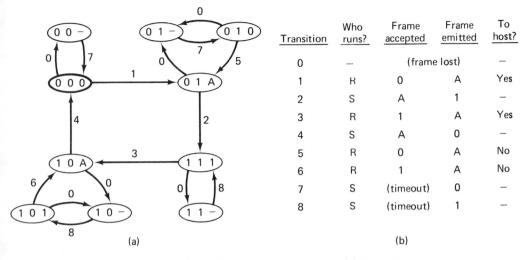

Transition	Who runs?	Frame accepted	Frame emitted	To host?
0	—	(frame lost)		—
1	R	0	A	Yes
2	S	A	1	—
3	R	1	A	Yes
4	S	A	0	—
5	R	0	A	No
6	R	1	A	No
7	S	(timeout)	0	—
8	S	(timeout)	1	—

(a)   (b)

Fig. 4-19. (a) State diagram for protocol 3. (b) Transitions.

Nine kinds of transitions are shown in Fig. 4-19. Transition 0 consists of the channel losing its contents. Transition 1 consists of the channel correctly delivering frame 0 to the receiver, with the receiver then changing its state to expect frame 1 and emitting an acknowledgement. Transition 1 also corresponds to the receiver delivering frame 0 to its host. The other transitions are listed in Fig. 4-19(b). The arrival of a frame with a checksum error has not been shown because it does not change the state (in protocol 3).

During normal operation, transitions 1, 2, 3, and 4 are repeated in order over and over. In each cycle two frames are correctly delivered, bringing the sender back to the initial state of trying to send a new frame with sequence number 0. If the channel ever loses frame 0, it makes a transition from state (000) to state (00−). Eventually, the sender times out (transition 7) and the system moves back to (000). The loss of an acknowledgement is more complicated, requiring two transitions, 7 and 5, or 8 and 6, to repair the damage.

One of the properties that a protocol with a 1-bit sequence number must have is that no matter what sequence of events happen, the receiver never delivers two odd frames to the host without and intervening even frame, and vice versa. From the graph of Figure 4-19 we see that this requirement can be stated more formally as "there must not exist any paths from the initial state on which two occurrences of transition 1 occur without an occurrence of transition 3 between them, or vice versa." From the figure it can be seen that the protocol is correct in this respect.

Another, similar requirement is that there not be any paths on which the sender changes state twice (e.g., from 0 to 1 and back to 0) while the receiver state remains constant. Were such a path to exist, then in the corresponding sequence of events two frames would be irretrievably lost, without the receiver noticing. The message sequence delivered to the receiving host would have an undetected gap of two messages in it.

Yet another important property of a protocol is the absence of deadlocks. A **deadlock** is a situation in which the protocol can make no more forward progress (i.e., deliver messages to the host) no matter which events happen. In terms of the graph model, a deadlock is characterized by the existence of a subset of states that is reachable from the initial state and which has two properties:

1. There is no transition out of the subset.

2. There are no transitions in the subset that cause forward progress.

Once in the deadlock situation, the protocol remains their forever. Again, it is easy to see from the graph that protocol 3 does not suffer from deadlocks.

Now let us consider a variation of protocol 3, one in which the half-duplex channel is replaced by a full-duplex channel. In Fig. 4-20 we show the states as the product of the states of the two protocol machines and the states of the two channels. Note that the forward channel now has three states: frame 0, frame 1, or empty, and the reverse channel has two states, A or empty. The transitions are the same as in Fig. 4-19(b), except that when a data frame and an acknowledgement are on the channel simultaneously, there is a slight peculiarity. The receiver cannot remove the data frame by itself, because that would entail having two acknowledgements on the channel at the same time, something not permitted in our model (although it is easy to devise a model that does allow it). Similarly, the sender cannot remove the acknowledgement, because that would entail emitting a second data frame before the first had been accepted. Consequently, both events must occur together, for example, the transition between state (000A) and state (111A), labeled as 1 + 2 in the figure.

In Fig. 4-20(a) there exist paths that cause the protocol to fail. In particular, there are paths in which the sender repeatedly fetches new frames, even though the previous ones have not been delivered correctly. The problem arises because it is now possible for the sender to timeout and send a new frame without disturbing the acknowledgement on the reverse channel. When this acknowledgement arrives, it will be mistakenly regarded as referring to the current transmission and not the previous one.

One state sequence causing the protocol to fail is shown in Fig. 4-20(b). In the fourth and sixth states of this sequence, the sender changes state, indicating that it fetches a new frame from its host, while the receiver does not change state, that is, does not deliver any frames to the receiving host.

Petri Net Models

The finite-state machine is not the only technique that can be used to model protocols. Another model is the **Petri net** (Danthine, 1977, 1980; Merlin, 1976). A Petri net has four basic elements: places, transitions, arcs, and tokens. A **place** represents a state which (part of) the system may be in.

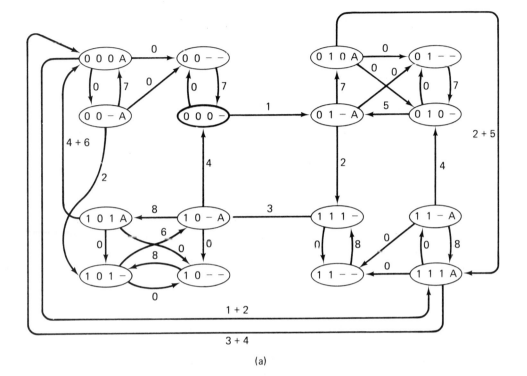

(a)

$(0\ 0\ 0\ -), (0\ 1\ -\ A), (0\ 1\ 0\ A), (1\ 1\ 1\ A), (1\ 1\ -\ A), (0\ 1\ 0\ -), (0\ 1\ -\ A), (1\ 1\ 1\ -)$

(b)

Fig. 4-20. (a) State graph for protocol 3 and a full-duplex channel. (b) Sequence of states causing the protocol to fail.

Figure 4-21 shows a Petri net with two places, A and B, both shown as circles. The system is currently in state A, indicated by the **token** (heavy dot) in place A. A **transition** is indicated by a horizontal or vertical bar. Each transition has zero or more **input arcs**, coming from its input places, and zero or more **output arcs**, going to its output places.

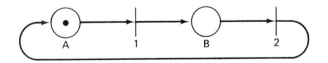

Fig. 4-21. A Petri net with two places and two transitions.

A transition is **enabled** if there is at least one input token in each of its input places. Any enabled transition may **fire** at will, removing one token from each input place and depositing a token in each output place. If the number of input arcs and output arcs differ, tokens will not be conserved. If two or more transitions are enabled, any one of them may fire. The choice of a transition to fire is indeterminate, which is why Petri nets are useful for modeling protocols. The Petri net of Fig. 4-21 is deterministic, and can be used to model any two-phase process (e.g., the behavior of a baby: eat, sleep, eat, sleep, and so on). As with all modeling tools, unnecessary detail is suppressed.

Figure 4-22 gives the Petri net model of Fig. 4-20. Unlike the finite-state machine model, there are no composite states here; the sender's state, channel state, and receiver's state are represented separately. Transitions 1 and 2 correspond to transmission of frame 0 by the sender, normally, and on a timeout respectively. Transitions 3 and 4 are analogous for frame 1. Transitions 5, 6, and 7 correspond to the loss of frame 0, an acknowledgement, and frame 1, respectively. Transitions 8 and 9 occur when a data frame with the wrong sequence number arrives at the receiver. Transitions 10 and 11 represent the arrival at the receiver of the next frame in sequence and its delivery to the host.

Petri nets can be used to detect protocol failures in a way similar to the use of finite-state machines. For example, if some firing sequence included transition 10 twice without transition 11 intervening, the protocol would be incorrect. The concept of a deadlock in a Petri net is also similar to its finite state machine counterpart.

Petri nets can be represented in convenient algebraic form resembling a grammar. Each transition contributes one rule to the grammar. Each rule specifies the input and output places of the transition, for example, transition 1 in Fig. 4-22 is $BD \rightarrow AC$. The current state of the Petri net is represented as an unordered collection of places, each place represented in the collection as many times as it has tokens. Any rule all whose left-hand side places are present can be fired, removing those places from the current state, and adding its output places to the current state. The marking of Fig. 4-22 is ACG, so rule 10 ($CG \rightarrow DF$) can be applied but rule 3 ($AD \rightarrow BE$) cannot.

Before terminating our discussion of protocol verification, it is probably worthwhile to state what is probably obvious: the graph corresponding to a realistic protocol, such as HDLC, is immense. For this reason, much of the current work in protocol verification is concerned with managing the "state explosion." For details, see the references.

Another approach is that of Hajek (1978, 1979). Hajek has developed a program, APPROVER, which mechanically generates all states reachable from a given initial state and checks the validity of user specified conditions in each state. The program is fast enough to be useful for verifying many realistic protocols, and has even found errors in protocols claimed to have been proven correct by hand (Hajek, 1979).

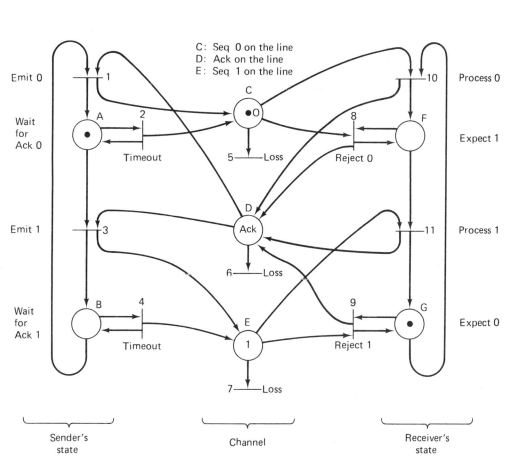

Fig. 4-22. A Petri net model for protocol 3.

4.5. SUMMARY

The task of the data link layer is to convert noisy lines into communication channels free of transmission errors for use by the network layer. To accomplish this goal, the data are broken up into frames, each of which is transmitted as many times as necessary to ensure that it has been received correctly. To prevent a fast sender from overrunning a slow receiver, the data link protocol always provides for flow control. The sliding window mechanism is widely used to integrate error control and flow control in a convenient way.

Sliding window protocols can be categorized by the size of the sender's window and the size of the receiver's window. When both are equal to 1, the protocol is stop-and-wait. When the sender's window is greater than 1, for example to prevent the sender from blocking on a circuit with a long propagation delay, the receiver can be programmed either to discard all frames other than the next one in sequence (protocol 5) or buffer out-of-order frames until they are needed (protocol 6).

Many networks use one of the bit-oriented protocols—SDLC, HDLC, ADCCP, or LAPB—at the data link level. All of these protocols use flag bytes to delimit frames, and bit stuffing to prevent flag bytes from occurring in the data. All of them also use a sliding window for flow control.

Protocols can be analyzed for a variety of properties, for example, performance and correctness. Examples of each are presented in this chapter.

PROBLEMS

1. Can you think of any circumstances under which an open-loop protocol, (e.g., a Hamming code) might be preferable to the feedback type protocols discussed throughout this chapter?

2. A channel has a bit rate of 4 kbps and a propagation delay of 20 msec. For what range of frame sizes does stop-and-wait give an efficiency of at least 50%?

3. A 3000-km long T1 trunk is used to transmit 64-byte frames using protocol 5. If the propagation speed is 6 μsec/km, how many bits should the sequence numbers be?

4. Imagine a sliding window protocol using so many bits for sequence numbers that wraparound never occurs. What relations must hold among the four window edges and the window size?

5. Frames of 1000 bits are sent over a 1-Mbps satellite channel. Acknowledgements are always piggybacked onto data frames. The headers are very short. Three bit sequence numbers are used. What is the maximum achievable channel utilization for
   (a) Stop-and-wait.
   (b) Protocol 5.
   (c) Protocol 6.

6. If the procedure *between* in protocol 5 checked for the condition $a \leqslant b \leqslant c$ instead of the condition $a \leqslant b < c$, would that have any effect on the protocol's correctness or efficiency? Explain.

7. Imagine that you are writing the data link layer software for a line used to send data to you, but not from you. The other end uses HDLC, with a 3-bit sequence number and a window size of seven frames. You would like to buffer as many out of sequence frames as possible to enhance efficiency, but you are not allowed to modify the software on the sending side. Is it possible to have a receiver window greater than one, and still guarantee that the protocol will never fail? If so, what is the largest window that can be safely used?

8. Consider the operation of protocol 6 over a 1 Mbps error-free line. The maximum frame size is 1000 bits. New host messages are generated about one second apart.

IMP service time is negligible. The timeout interval is 10 msec. If the special acknowledgement timer were eliminated, unnecessary timeouts would occur. How many times would the average message be transmitted?

9. In protocol 6 the code for *FrameArrival* has a section used for NAKs. This section is invoked if the incoming frame is a NAK and another condition is met. Give a scenario where the presence of this other condition is essential.

10. In protocol 6 $MaxSeq = 2^n - 1$. While this condition is obviously desirable to make efficient use of header bits, we have not demonstrated that it is essential. Does the protocol work correctly for $MaxSeq = 4$, for example?

11. Compute the fraction of the bandwidth that is wasted on overhead (headers and retransmissions) for protocol 6 on a heavily loaded 50 kbps satellite channel with data frames consisting of 40 header and 3960 data bits. ACK frames never occur. NAK frames are 40 bits. The error rate for data frames is 1%, and the error rate for NAK frames is negligible. The sequence numbers are 8 bits.

12. Each of the N hosts attached to an IMP generates messages with a Poisson arrival pattern having a mean of λ messages/sec. The probability that a message has length m bits $(1 \leqslant m < \infty)$ is P_m. Each message acquires h bits of frame header while on the IMPs one and only IMP-IMP line. The line has a data rate of b bps. The probability that a bit will be received in error is e. Acknowledgements come back instantly, and occupy negligible bandwidth. If all traffic is to distant hosts, what is the maximum value of N?

13. Discuss the potential advantages and disadvantages of the ARPANET eight logical channel IMP-IMP protocol versus a 3-bit HDLC sliding window protocol.

14. If the bit string 0111101111101111110 is subjected to bit stuffing, what is the output string?

15. Redraw Fig. 4-20 for a full-duplex channel that never loses frames. Is the protocol failure still possible?

16. Give the firing sequence for the Petri net of Fig. 4-22 corresponding to the state sequence (000), (01A), (01−), (010), (01A) in Fig. 4-19. Explain in words what the sequence represents.

17. Given the transition rules $AC \rightarrow B$, $B \rightarrow AC$, $CD \rightarrow E$, and $E \rightarrow CD$, draw the Petri net described. From the Petri net, draw the finite state graph reachable from the initial state ACD. What well-known computer science concept do these transition rules model?

18. In Fig. 4-22, transition 9 is $EG \rightarrow DG$. Under what conditions, if any, can the rule be simplified to $E \rightarrow D$?

19. Write a program to simulate the communication of protocol 6. The program should read in the following parameters: transmission rate of the channel, length of a data frame, length of an ACK or NAK frame, probability of a frame being lost, propagation time of the channel, and mean rate at which a host produces new messages (assume an exponential interarrival distribution). For each set of parameters, the program should print out the effective date rate achieved.

20. Write a program to stochastically simulate the behavior of a Petri net. The program should read in the transition rules as well as a list of states corresponding to the host issuing a new message or the host accepting a new message. From the initial state, also read in, the program should pick enabled transitions at random and fire them, checking to see if two a host ever accepts two messages without the other host emitting a new one in between.

5

THE NETWORK LAYER I:

POINT-TO-POINT NETWORKS

Having looked at how adjacent IMPs reliably exchange frames over unreliable lines (Chap. 4), it is now time to move up one layer in the protocol hierarchy of Fig. 1-7 to see how the network layer works. Since the subnet extends only up as far as layer 3, the primary interface between hosts and subnet occurs in this layer. There are three main design issues we must face in layer 3:

1. What does the subnet-host interface look like?

2. How are packets routed within the subnet?

3. How are congestion and deadlocks prevented?

In this chapter we will examine each of these issues in turn.

5.1. VIRTUAL CIRCUITS AND DATAGRAMS

To simplify the software design, networks are organized hierarchically. Every host has the illusion that it can converse with every other host via some kind of communication channel. In fact, the host is really communicating with the IMP, which in turn communicates with other IMPs, and eventually the destination host. The illusion that hosts can talk to one another is maintained by the communication subnet. This situation is sketched in Fig. 5-1(a).

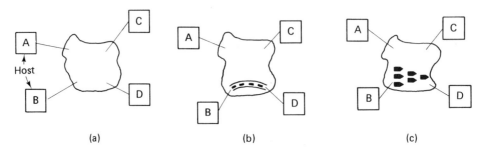

Fig. 5-1. (a) The communication subnet. (b) Artist's conception of a virtual circuit. (c) Artist's conception of six datagrams. The pointy part is the address.

5.1.1. The Service Provided by the Network Layer

One of the most important (and controversial) design questions is the nature of the service provided to the transport layer by the network layer. Alternatively put, what properties should the subnet have, when viewed by the hosts? To make this somewhat philosophical point more concrete, if a host sends a message to another host, should it be able to count on the message arriving properly? In other words, should the subnet make error detection and correction transparent to the hosts? Every subnet handles data link errors in a transparent way, but other errors can still occur, principally lost and duplicate packets due to faulty IMP hardware or software.

A second example of a function that the network layer *might* perform is making sure that packets arrive in the same order they were sent. In fact, there are a number of other possible options as well, but in practice, two conceptual models dominate. In the **virtual circuit** model, the network layer provides the transport layer with a perfect channel: no errors, all packets delivered in order, etc. In the **datagram** model, the network layer simply accepts messages from the transport layer and attempts to deliver each one as an isolated unit. Messages may arrive out of order, or not at all.

Some analogies may make clearer the distinction between a network layer offering virtual circuit service and one offering datagram service. The public telephone network provides its customers with virtual circuit service (if we ignore its high error rate). As with all virtual circuit services, the telephone customer must first set up the virtual circuit (dial the call), then transmit the data (talk), and finally close down the circuit (hang up). Although what happens inside the telephone system or subnet is undoubtedly very complicated, the two users are provided with the illusion of a dedicated point-to-point channel between themselves. In particular, information is delivered to the receiver in the same order in which it is transmitted by the sender.

The appropriate analogy for the datagram model is the postal (or telegraph) system. Each letter or telegram is transported as an isolated entity, and as such must carry the complete destination address. If a letter carrier loses a letter, the postal system does not time out and automatically send a duplicate; error control is the user's responsibility. Finally, letters do not necessarily arrive in the order mailed.

By now the difference between virtual circuit service and datagram service should be clear (see Fig. 5-2). In the former, there is an explicit setup procedure, followed by a data transfer phase, and then an explicit shutdown procedure. Once the circuit has been established, individual data items do not have to carry destination addresses, because the destination was specified during setup. With datagrams there is no setup. Each datagram is carried independently from every other one, and the network layer makes no attempt to do error recovery.

Issue	Virtual circuit	Datagram
Destination address	Only need during setup	Needed in every packet
Error handling	Transparent to host (done in the subnet)	Explicitly done by the host
End-to-end flow control	Provided by the subnet	Not provided by the subnet
Packet sequencing	Messages always passed to the host in the order sent	Messages passed to the host in the order they arrive
Initial setup	Required	Not possible

Fig. 5-2. Summary of the major differences between virtual circuit and datagram service.

5.1.2. Comparison of Virtual Circuit and Datagram Service

The decision to have the network layer provide datagram service, virtual circuit service, or both is usually dictated by the layer 3 interface the carrier offers between the subnet and hosts. To emphasize this fact in the following discussion, we will use the term "subnet" to mean network layer and the term "host" to mean transport layer.

Datagram service is the more primitive of the two services. When it is provided by the subnet, the hosts generally add error and sequence control so as to provide virtual circuits to their user processes. The key issue here is: Who provides the error and sequence control—the subnet or the hosts? That is, is end-to-end error control, sequence control (and possibly flow control), done in layer 3 or at layer 4? Different networks have different answers to this question. Let us now look at some of the arguments each way.

Virtual circuits have the advantage that the hosts do not have to go to the trouble of ordering the messages since they come in in order. However, this advantage turns into a disadvantage if a particular user process does not care about the ordering. For example, if one machine is sending a disk image to another, sector by sector, with each message identifying the sector, it does not matter what order the sectors come in, but holding up one sector because its predecessor needs to be retransmitted is inefficient.

A similar situation holds with error control. With virtual circuit service the host need not worry about errors, but there are situations where automatic retransmission is undesirable. An obvious example is digitized real-time speech. It is far better for the listener to hear an incorrect packet (a fraction of a word garbled) than to hear a 2 sec pause while waiting for timeout and retransmission.

In the example above, the user might consider the error control provided by the subnet "too good." In other situations, the user might consider it too weak. Banks, in particular, tend to get quite upset if 1 dollar becomes 4097 dollars due to a 1-bit transmission error. Those applications requiring better accuracy than the subnet provides (essentially longer checksums) may end up superimposing their own error-detecting scheme on top of the subnet's by computing and transmitting checksums within the data itself. In this case it is clearly inefficient to have the subnet duplicate what the user insists upon doing for himself anyway.

In addition to providing automatic sequencing and error control, virtual circuits also provide flow control. As in the other cases, there may be users who can handle very high data rates and do not want the subnet to impede them. For example if one of the hosts is a minicomputer collecting real time data at high speed, and another is a dedicated mini whose job it is to store the data as fast as it comes in, datagrams may be able to provide substantially higher throughput than a compulsory flow control scheme based on a sliding window. This conclusion is especially true if the subnet forces a standard window size on all customers.

Yet another potential advantage of datagrams for the sophisticated user is the ability to do his own packet switching. A host might take packets from the public network as they come and reinject them into a local private network. If the private network uses datagrams internally, there is hardly any point in forcing them to come out of the public one in sequence, only to be randomized milliseconds later anyway. Yet if the public network only offers virtual circuit service, there will surely be a performance penalty to be paid.

For transaction oriented systems, such as point-of-sale credit verification, the cost of setting up and later clearing the virtual circuit can easily dwarf the cost of sending the single message.

From these examples you can see that datagrams provide sophisticated users with great flexibility in handling sophisticated applications. The supporters of virtual circuits would argue that most network applications (e.g., remote login, file transfer) prefer sequential, error free, flow controlled communication channels. Most existing user programs and most existing operating systems understand this class of device, which makes interfacing to them easier.

Also, by putting the sequencing, error control, and flow control in the subnet, the code only has to be written once. If these functions are in the hosts, each host operating system has to be modified, resulting in much more work. Replacing bits and pieces of code in everybody's operating system is a task to be favorably compared only with Hercules cleaning out the Augean stables. If the subnet designers are computer network experts and the computer centers owning the hosts relative newcomers to networking, the argument for having the subnet designers do as much of the work as possible becomes even stronger.

Another argument for putting as much of the data communication work as possible in the subnet is that the IMPs are minis or micros, and invariably better suited to that kind of work than the hosts. Furthermore, the price/performance ratio nowadays strongly favors smaller machines, so the IMPs can probably do the job cheaper as well.

Before leaving this subject, it is worth saying a few words about the political implications of the subnet service. For public networks, the subnet is provided by the common carrier and the hosts are the property of the users. A datagram interface in essence tells the carrier that its task is to move bits around, and nothing else. This hardly seems unreasonable. Carriers are basically in the communication business after all. In fact, in many countries, the carrier is forbidden from being in any other business.

Nevertheless, some carriers regard the data processing market as an extremely attractive one, which they would dearly like to be in. Providing virtual circuits is an obvious extension to the basic communication function. Remote terminal handling (polling, code translation, local editing, etc.) is an obvious extension of the virtual circuit facility.

Having gotten control of one end of the virtual circuit (the terminal), the carrier's attention might just turn to the other end, often a data base system. Some carriers have already begun providing Viewdata service (user queries concerning a carrier maintained data base). By offering to hold the users' data, the carrier could expand the Viewdata service to allow queries about these data as well. The next step, already taken in some countries, would be carrier supplied terminals and modems, analogous to carrier supplied telephones.

At this point the carrier has the terminal, modem, communication line, computer, and data base in hand. All that is left to do to complete the transfer is to arrange for legislation legally barring any competition in the areas in which the carrier is now firmly entrenched. In countries where the carrier just happens to be the government (e.g., all of Europe), the temptation to fight the (foreign) data processing industry via this route may be especially great. Readers who are intrigued or appalled by this scenario should read (Pouzin 1976a, 1976b) for more details.

5.1.3. The Internal Structure of the Subnet

Having looked at the two classes of service the subnet can provide to its customers, it is time to see how the subnet works inside. Interestingly enough, the same two models, virtual circuit and datagram, can be used for internal transport. When virtual circuits are used, a route is chosen from source IMP to destination IMP when the circuit is set up. That route is used for all traffic flowing over the virtual circuit.

If packets flowing over a given virtual circuit always take the same route through the subnet, each IMP must remember where to forward packets for each of the currently open virtual circuits passing through it. Every IMP must maintain a table with one entry per open virtual circuit. Virtual circuits not passing through IMP X are not entered in X's table, of course. Each packet traveling through the subnet must contain a virtual circuit number field in its header, in addition to sequence numbers, checksums, and the like. When a packet arrives at an IMP, the IMP knows on which line it arrived and what the virtual circuit number is. Based only on this information, the packet must be forwarded to the correct IMP.

When a user process tells its host's operating system that it wants to talk to a process in another machine, the local host chooses a virtual circuit number not already in use on that machine for the conversation. Since each host chooses virtual circuit numbers independently, the same virtual circuit number is likely to be in use on two different paths through some intermediate IMP, leading to ambiguities.

Consider the subnet of Fig. 5-3(a). Suppose that a process in A's host wants to talk to a process in D's host. Host A chooses virtual circuit 0. Let us assume that route $ABCD$ is chosen. Simultaneously, a process in B decides it wants to talk to a process in D (not the same one as A). If there are no open virtual circuits starting in B at this point, host B will also choose virtual circuit 0. Further assume that route BCD is selected as the best one. After both virtual circuits have been set up, the process at A sends its first message to D, on virtual circuit 0. When the packet arrives at D, the poor host does not know which user process to give it to.

To solve this problem, whenever a host wants to create a new outbound virtual circuit, it chooses the lowest circuit number not currently in use. The IMP (say X) does not forward this setup packet to the next IMP (say Y) along

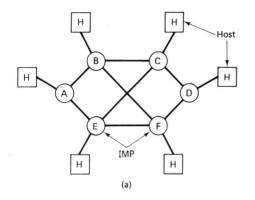

8 Simplex virtual circuits

Originating at A	Originating at B
0 - ABCD	0 - BCD
1 - AEFD	1 - BAE
2 - ABFD	2 - BF
3 - AEC	
4 - AECDFB	

(a)   (b)

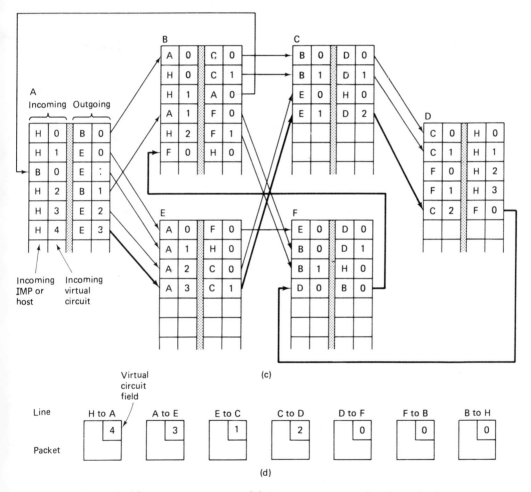

(c)

(d)

Fig. 5-3. (a) Example subnet. (b) Eight virtual circuits through the subnet. (c) IMP tables for the virtual circuits in (b). (d) The virtual circuit changes as a packet progresses.

193

the route as is. Instead, X looks in its table to find all the circuit numbers currently being used for traffic to Y. It then chooses the lowest free number and substitutes that number for the one in the packet, overwriting the number chosen by the host. Similarly, IMP Y chooses the lowest circuit number free between it and the next IMP.

When this setup packet finally arrives at the destination, the IMP there chooses the lowest available inbound circuit number, overwrites the circuit number found in the packet with this, and passes it to the host. As long as the destination host always sees the same circuit number on all traffic arriving on a given virtual circuit, it does not matter that the source host is consistently using a different number.

Figure 5-3(b) gives eight examples of virtual circuits pertaining to the subnet of part (a). Part (c) of the figure shows the IMPs' tables, assuming the circuits were created in the order: $ABCD$, BCD, $AEFD$, BAE, $ABFD$, BF, AEC, and $AECDFB$. The last one ($AECDFB$) may seem somewhat roundabout, but if lines AB, BC, and EF were badly overloaded when the routing algorithm ran, this might well have been the best choice.

Each entry consists of an incoming and an outgoing part. Each of the two parts has an IMP name (used to indicate a line) and a virtual circuit number. When a packet arrives, the table is searched on the left (incoming) part, using the arrival line and virtual circuit number found in the packet as the key. When a match is found, the outgoing part of the entry tells which virtual circuit number to insert into the packet and which IMP to send it to. H stands for the host, both on the incoming and outgoing sides.

As an example, consider a packet traveling from host A to host B on virtual circuit 4 (i.e., route $AECDFB$). When IMP A gets a packet from its own host, with circuit 4, it searches its table, finding a match for $H4$ at entry 5 (the top entry is 0). The outgoing part of this entry is $E3$, which means replace the circuit 4 with circuit 3 and send it to IMP E. IMP E then gets a packet from A with circuit 3, so it searches for $A3$ and finds a match at the third entry. The packet now goes to C as circuit 1. The sequence of entries used is marked by the heavy line. Figure 5-3(d) shows this sequence of packet numbers.

Because virtual circuits can be initiated from either end, a problem occurs when call setups are propagating in both directions at once along a chain of IMPs. At some point they have arrived at adjacent IMPs. Each IMP must now pick a virtual circuit number to use for the (full-duplex) circuit it is trying to establish. If they have been programmed to choose the lowest number not already in use on the link between them, they will pick the same number, causing two unrelated virtual circuits over the same physical line to have the same number. When a data packet arrives later, the receiving IMP has no way of telling whether it is a forward packet on one circuit or a reverse packet on the other. If circuits are simplex, there is no ambiguity.

You should realize that every process must be required to indicate when it is through using a virtual circuit, so that the virtual circuit can be purged from the IMP tables to recover the space. In public networks the motivation is the stick rather than the carrot: users are invariably charged for connect time as well as for data transported.

So much for the use of virtual circuits internal to the subnet. The other possibility is to use datagrams internally. When datagrams are used, the IMPs do not have a table with one entry for each open virtual circuit. Instead, they have a table telling which outgoing line to use for each possible destination IMP. These tables are also needed when virtual circuits are used internally, to determine the route for a setup packet.

Each datagram must contain the full destination address (the machine, and some indication of which process on that machine). When a packet comes in, the IMP looks up the outgoing line to use and sends it on its way. Nothing in the packet is modified. Also, the creation and destruction of Transport layer virtual circuits do not require any special work on the part of the IMPs.

5.1.4. Comparison of Virtual Circuits and Datagrams within the Subnet

Both virtual circuits and datagrams have their supporters and their detractors. We will now attempt to summarize the arguments both ways. Be sure to remember that with public networks the subnet is owned and operated by the carrier and the hosts are owned by the customer.

Inside the subnet the main trade-off between virtual circuits and datagrams is between IMP memory space and bandwidth. Virtual circuits allow packets to contain circuit numbers instead of full destination addresses. If the packets tend to be fairly short, a full destination address in every packet may represent a significant amount of overhead, and hence wasted bandwidth. The use of virtual circuits internal to the subnet becomes especially attractive when many of the "hosts" are actually interactive terminals with only a few characters per packet. The price paid for using virtual circuits internally is the table space within the IMPs. Depending upon the relative cost of communication circuits versus IMP memory, one or the other may be cheaper.

For transaction processing systems, the overhead required to set up and clear a virtual circuit may easily dwarf the use of the circuit, as mentioned above. If the majority of the traffic is expected to be of this kind, the use of virtual circuits inside the subnet makes little sense.

Virtual circuits also have a vulnerability problem. If an IMP crashes and loses its memory, even if it comes back up a second later, all the virtual circuits passing through it will have to be aborted. In contrast, if a datagram IMP goes down, only those users whose packets were queued up in the IMP at the time will suffer, and maybe not even all those, depending upon whether they have already been acknowledged or not. The loss of a communication line is fatal to virtual circuits using it, but can be easily compensated for if datagrams are used. Datagrams also allow the IMPs to balance the traffic throughout the subnet, since routes can be changed halfway through a conversation.

5.1.5. Independence of Subnet Service and Subnet Structure

Since the choice between virtual circuit and datagram as an interface and as an internal strategy are independent, there are four possible combinations. These are shown in Fig. 5-4. The simplest possibility is datagram service implemented by using datagrams inside the subnet. DECNET uses this approach. Each packet contains the full destination address. Error control, sequencing, and flow control are done by the transport layer. The subnet accepts and transports isolated packets, and nothing else.

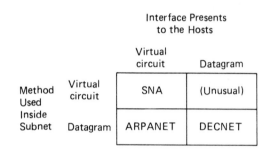

Fig. 5-4. Combinations of subnet interface and subnet internal operation.

At the other extreme is SNA, which uses virtual circuits inside the subnet to provide virtual circuit service to the transport layer. Many public networks also use this approach, for example the French PTT's public network, TRANSPAC (Danet et al., 1976).

The ARPANET uses a mixture of the virtual circuit and datagram methods. The hosts see the subnet as a virtual circuit system, but the subnet itself uses datagrams inside. Messages put into the subnet come out at the other end in the same order.

The fourth combination is a somewhat strange one: datagrams on the outside and virtual circuits on the inside. This arrangement might be of use in a situation where an existing operating system constructed messages containing full destination addresses and sent them off as isolated units. If long sequences to the same address were expected, the IMP might be programmed to set up a virtual circuit upon seeing a new destination. Virtual circuits unused for a long period of time would time out and be scrapped automatically.

5.2. ROUTING ALGORITHMS

The **routing algorithm** is that part of the layer 3 software responsible for deciding which output line an incoming packet should be transmitted on. If the subnet uses datagrams internally, this decision must be made anew for every arriving data packet. However, if the subnet uses virtual circuits internally, routing decisions are made only when a new virtual circuit is being set up. Thereafter, data packets just follow the previously established route. The latter case is often called **session routing**, because a route remains in force for an entire user session (e.g., a login session at a terminal or a file transfer).

Regardless of whether routes are chosen independently for each packet or just at the start of new sessions, there are certain properties that are desirable in a routing algorithm: correctness, simplicity, robustness, stability, fairness, and optimality. Correctness and simplicity hardly require comment, but the need for robustness may be less obvious at first. Once a major network comes on the air, it may be expected to run continuously for years without system-wide failures. During that period there will be hardware and software failures of all kinds. Hosts, IMPs, and lines will go up and down repeatedly, and the topology will change many times. The routing algorithm must be able to cope with changes in the topology and traffic without requiring all jobs in all hosts to be aborted and the network to be rebooted every time some IMP crashes.

Stability is also an important goal for the routing algorithm. As we shall see shortly, there exist routing algorithms that never converge to equilibrium, no matter how long they run. Fairness and optimality may sound like Motherhood and Apple Pie—surely no one would oppose them—but as it turns out, they are often contradictory goals. As a simple example of this conflict, look at Fig. 5-5(a). Suppose that there is enough traffic between A and A', between B and B', and between C and C' to saturate the horizontal links. To maximize the total flow, the X to X' traffic should be shut off altogether. Unfortunately, X and X' may not see it that way. Evidently, some compromise between global efficiency and fairness to individual connections is needed.

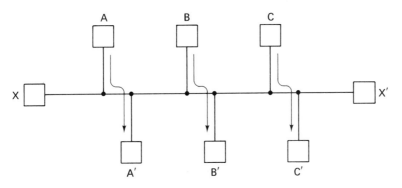

Fig. 5-5. Conflict between fairness and optimality.

Before we can even attempt to find trade-offs between fairness and optimality, we must decide what it is we seek to optimize. Minimizing mean packet delay is an obvious candidate, but so is maximizing total network throughput.

Furthermore, these two goals are also in conflict, since operating any queueing system near capacity ($\rho \rightarrow 1$) implies a long queueing delay. As a compromise, many networks attempt to minimize the number of hops a packet must make, because reducing the number of hops tends to improve the delay and also reduce the amount of bandwidth consumed, which tends to improve the throughput as well.

Routing algorithms can be grouped into two major classes: nonadaptive and adaptive. Nonadaptive algorithms do not base their routing decisions on measurements or estimates of the current traffic and topology, whereas adaptive ones do. If an adaptive algorithm manages to adapt well to the traffic, it will naturally outperform an algorithm that is oblivious to what is going on in the network, but adapting well to the traffic is easier said than done. Adaptive algorithms can be further subdivided into centralized, isolated, and distributed (McQuillan, 1974), all of which are discussed in detail below.

5.2.1. Flooding

One of the simplest routing algorithms is **flooding**, in which every incoming packet is sent out on every outgoing line except the one it arrived on. Flooding obviously generates vast numbers of duplicate packets, in fact, an infinite number unless some measures are taken to damp the process. One such measure is to have a hop counter contained in the header of each packet, which is decremented at each hop, with the packet being discarded when the counter reaches zero. Ideally, the hop counter should be initialized to the length of the path from source to destination. If the sender does not know how long the path is, it can initialize the counter to the worst-case, namely, the full diameter of the subnet.

An alternative technique for damming the flood is to have the source IMP put a sequence number in each packet it receives from its hosts. Each IMP then needs a list per source IMP telling which sequence numbers originating at that source have already been seen. To prevent the list from growing without bound, each list should be augmented by a counter, k, meaning that all sequence numbers through k have been seen. When a packet comes in, it is easy to check if the packet is a duplicate; if so, it is discarded.

Flooding is not practical in most applications, but it does have some uses. For example, in military applications, where large numbers of IMPs may be blown to bits at any instant, the tremendous robustness of flooding is highly desirable. In distributed data base applications, it is sometimes necessary to update all the data bases concurrently, in which case flooding can be be useful. A third possible use of flooding is as a metric against which other routing algorithms can be compared. Flooding always chooses the shortest path, because it chooses every possible path in parallel. Consequently, no other algorithm can produce a shorter delay (if we ignore the overhead generated by the flooding process itself).

A variation of flooding that is slightly more practical is **selective flooding**. In this algorithm the IMPs do not send every incoming packet out on every line, only on those lines that are going approximately in the right direction. There is usually little point in sending a westbound packet on an eastbound line unless the topology is extremely peculiar.

Yet another nonadaptive algorithm is random walk. The IMP simple picks a line a random and forwards the packet on it. Here, also, the IMP can make some attempt to get the packet heading in roughly the right direction. If the subnet is richly interconnected, this algorithm has the property of making excellent use of alternative routes. It is also highly robust.

5.2.2. Static Routing

Static or **directory routing** is a simple algorithm and one of the most widely used. Each IMP maintains a table with one row for each possible destination IMP. A row gives the best, second best, third best, etc. outgoing line for that destination, together with a relative weight. Before forwarding a packet, an IMP generates a random number and then chooses among the alternatives, using the weights as probabilities. The tables are worked out manually by the network operators, loaded into the IMPs before the network is brought up, and not changed thereafter.

As an example, consider the subnet of Fig. 5-6(a). IMP J's routing table is given in Fig. 5-6(b). If J receives a packet whose destination is A, it uses the row labeled A. Here three choices are presented. The line to A is the first choice, followed by the lines to I and H respectively. To decide, J generates a random number between 0.00 and 0.99. If the number is below 0.63, line A is used; if the number is between 0.63 and 0.83, I is used; otherwise, H is used. The three weights are therefore the respective probabilities that A, I, or K will be used.

In this example, the weights are somewhat ad hoc. A better, although more complicated, way to choose the routes is to explicitly minimize the mean packet time given by Eq. (2-13). Given the routing tables, it is easy to calculate λ_i for each line, and hence T. An iterative procedure exists to adjust a given flow pattern toward the one minimizing T, but due to its complexity, we will not describe it here. For details, see Gerla and Kleinrock (1977b).

Even without knowing the details of the subnet topology and traffic, it is possible to make some general statements about the optimum routes. One such statement is known as the **optimality principle**. It states that if IMP J is on the optimal path from IMP I to IMP K, then the optimal path from J to K also falls along the same route. To see this, call the part of the route from I to J r_1 and the rest of the route r_2. If a route better than r_2 existed from J to K, it could be concatenated with r_1 to improve the route from I to K, contradicting our statement that $r_1 r_2$ is optimal.

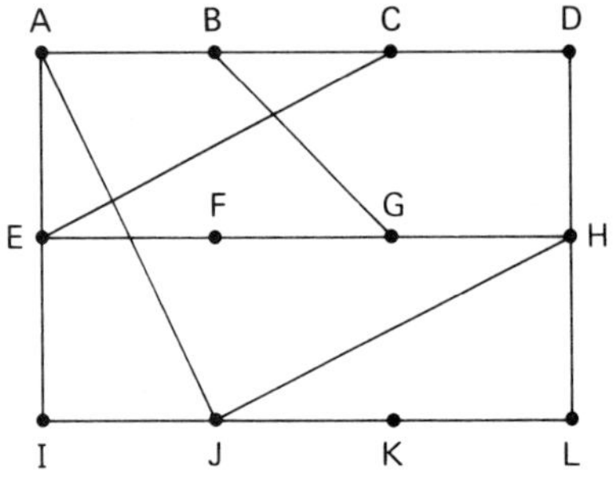

Destination	First choice		Second choice		Third choice	
A	A	0.63	I	0.21	H	0.16
B	A	0.46	H	0.31	I	0.23
C	A	0.33	I	0.33	H	0.34
D	H	0.50	A	0.25	I	0.25
E	A	0.40	I	0.40	H	0.20
F	A	0.33	H	0.33	I	0.34
G	H	0.46	A	0.31	K	0.23
H	H	0.63	K	0.21	A	0.16
I	I	0.65	A	0.22	H	0.13
—						
K	K	0.67	H	0.22	A	0.11
L	L	0.42	H	0.42	A	0.16

(a)   (b)

Fig. 5-6. (a) An example subnet. (b) Routing table for node J.

As a direct consequence of the optimality principle, we can see that the set of optimal routes from all sources to a given destination form a tree rooted at the destination. Such a tree is called a **sink tree** and is illustrated in Fig. 5-7. Since the sink tree is indeed a tree, it does not contain any loops, so each packet will be delivered within a finite and bounded number of hops.

The main attraction of nonadaptive algorithms is that they are simple: simple to understand and simple to implement. Static directory routing can give good performance if the topology and traffic do not change much. It also makes good use of existing bandwidth by using alternative routes.

5.2.3. Centralized Routing Algorithms

The main problem with nonadaptive algorithms (such as static routing) is just that—they do not adapt. If the traffic levels in different parts of the subnet change dramatically and often, static algorithms are unable to cope with these changes. Unfortunately, much computer traffic is bursty in nature: a user may ask to have a large file sent between two machines, putting a heavy load on portions of the subnet for a few minutes, and may then abstain from using the subnet for the next several hours. Static routing tables must be designed based

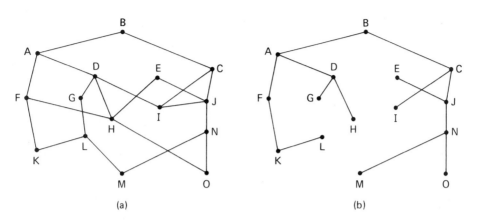

Fig. 5-7. (a) A subnet. (b) The sink tree for IMP B, using number of hops as metric.

on mean traffic conditions, but for bursty traffic, such means are not very useful.

Centralized routing is similar to static directory routing in that each IMP maintains a table telling how to forward packets. This table may or may not contain alternate routes, just as static directory routing. The difference between static and centralized routing lies in how the routing tables inside the IMPs are constructed. In static routing the network designers or managers calculate the best routes in advance, based on their expectations of average traffic. The tables are loaded into the IMPs before the network comes up and remain fixed forevermore (or more likely, for long periods of time). Changing the routing tables is done manually.

When centralized routing is used, somewhere within the network there is a **routing control center** (RCC). Periodically, each IMP sends status information to the RCC (e.g., a list of its neighbor's that are up, current queue lengths, amount of traffic processed per line since the last report, etc.). The RCC collects all this information, and then, based upon its global knowledge of the entire network, computes the optimal routes from every IMP to every other IMP, for example using the shortest path algorithm of Fig. 2-4. From this information it can build new routing tables and distribute them to all the IMPs.

At first glance centralized routing is attractive: since the RCC has complete information, it can make perfect decisions. Another advantage of it is that it relieves the IMPs of the burden of the routing computation.

Unfortunately, centralized routing also has some serious, if not fatal, drawbacks. For one thing, if the subnet is to adapt to changing traffic, the routing calculation will have to be performed fairly often. For a large network, the calculation will take many seconds, even on a substantial CPU. If the purpose of the running the algorithm is to adapt to changes in the topology rather than changes in the traffic, however, running it every minute or so may be adequate.

A more serious problem is the vulnerability of the RCC. If it goes down or becomes isolated by line failures, the subnet is suddenly in big trouble. One solution is to have a second machine available as a backup, but this amounts to wasting a large computer. An arbitration method is also needed to make sure that the primary and backup RCCs do not get into a fight over who is the boss.

Yet another problem with centralized routing concerns distributing the routing tables to the IMPs. The IMPs that are close to the RCC will get their new tables first and will switch over to the new routes before the distant IMPs have received their tables. Inconsistencies may arise here, so packets may be delayed. Among the packets delayed will be the new routing tables for the distant IMPs, so the problem feeds upon itself.

If the RCC computes the optimal route for each pair of IMPs and no alternates, the loss of even a single line or IMP will probably cut some IMPs off from the RCC, with disastrous consequences. If the RCC does use alternate routing, the argument in favor of having an RCC in the first place, namely that it can find the optimum routes, is weakened.

A final problem with centralized routing is the heavy concentration of routing traffic on the lines leading into the RCC. Figure 5-8 illustrates this problem. The figure was drawn by tracing the shortest path from each machine to the RCC, and placing an arrow on each line. A line with n arrows mean that n IMPs are reporting to the RCC via it. The heavy load and consequent vulnerability of lines near the RCC is apparent.

5.2.4. Isolated Routing

All these problems with centralized routing algorithms suggest that decentralized algorithms might have something to offer. In the simplest decentralized routing algorithms, the IMPs make routing decisions based only upon information they themselves have gleaned; they do not exchange routing information per se with other IMPs. Nevertheless, they try to adapt to changes in topology and traffic. These are usually called **isolated adaptive** routing algorithms.

One simple isolated adaptive algorithm is Baran's (1964) **hot potato** algorithm. When a packet comes in, the IMP tries to get rid of it as fast as it can, by putting it on the shortest output queue. In other words, when a packet arrives, the IMP counts the number of packets queued up for transmission on each of the output lines. It then attaches the newly arrived packet to the end of the shortest output queue, without regard to where that line leads. In Fig. 5-9, the inside of IMP J from Fig. 5-6(a) is shown at a certain instant of time. There are four output queues, corresponding to the four output lines. Packets are queued up on each line waiting for transmission. In this example, queue I is the shortest, with only one packet queued up. The hot potato algorithm would therefore put the newly arrived packet on this queue.

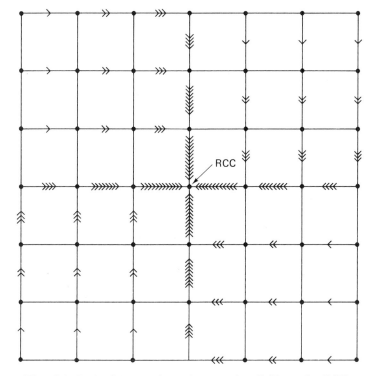

Fig. 5-8. Paths followed from the outgoing IMPs to the RCC.

A variation of this idea is to combine static directory routing with the hot potato algorithm. When a packet arrives, the routing algorithm takes into account both the static weights of the lines and the queue lengths. One possibility is to use the best static choice, unless its queue exceeds a certain threshold. Another possibility is to use the shortest queue, unless its static weight is too low. Yet another way is to rank order the lines in terms of their static weights, and again in terms of their queue lengths, taking the line for which the sum of the two ranks is lowest. Whatever algorithm is chosen should have the property that under light load the line with the highest static weight is usually chosen, but as the queue for this line builds up, some of the traffic is diverted to less busy lines.

Another isolated routing algorithm, also due to Baran, is **backward learning**. In the 1950s and 1960s, when newspaper reporters from Western countries were rarely allowed to visit China, it was common to see news stories beginning with "According to travelers recently arriving in Hong Kong from China . . . . " The idea was that instead of the reporter going to place X, she could talk to people who just came from X and ask them what was going on there. The backward learning algorithm does the same thing.

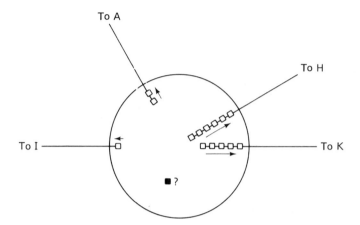

Fig. 5-9. Queueing within the IMP.

One way to implement backward learning is to include the identity of the source IMP in each packet, together with a counter that is incremented on each hop. If an IMP sees a packet arriving on line k from IMP H with hop count 4, it knows that H cannot be more than four hops away via line k. If its current best route to H is estimated at more than four hops, it marks line k as the choice for traffic to H and records the estimated distance as four hops. After a while, every IMP will discover the shortest path to every other IMP.

Alas, there is a fly in the ointment. Since IMPs only record changes for the better, if a line goes down or becomes overloaded, there is no mechanism for recording the fact. Consequently, IMPs must periodically forget everything they have learned and start all over again. During the new learning period, the routing will be far from optimal. If the tables are purged frequently, the IMPs route a substantial number of packets using routes of unknown quality; if the tables are purged rarely, the adaptation process is slow.

Rudin (1976) has described an interesting hybrid between centralized routing and isolated routing, which he calls **delta routing**. In this algorithm, each IMP measures the "cost" of each line (i.e., some function of the delay, queue length, utilization, bandwidth, etc.) and periodically sends a packet to the RCC giving it these values.

Using the information sent to it by the IMPs, the RCC computes the k best paths from IMP i to IMP j, for all i and all j, where only paths that differ in their initial line are considered. Let C_{ij}^1 be the total cost of the best i-j path, C_{ij}^2 be the total cost of the next best path, etc. If $C_{ij}^n - C_{ij}^1 < \delta$, path n is declared to be equivalent to path 1, since their costs differ by so little. When the routing computation is finished, the RCC sends each IMP a list of all the equivalent paths for each of its possible destinations. (Actually, only the initial lines are needed, not the full paths.)

To do actual routing, the IMP is permitted to choose any of the equivalent paths. It may decide among them at random or use the *current* measured value of the line costs, that is, choose the path from the allowed set whose current initial line is cheapest. By adjusting k and δ, the network operators can transfer authority between the RCC and the IMPs. As $\delta \rightarrow 0$, all other paths are deemed inferior to the best path, and the RCC makes all the decisions. However, as $\delta \rightarrow \infty$, all the paths considered will be deemed equivalent, and the routing decisions are made in the IMPs based on local information only. Rudin's simulations have shown that δ can be chosen to provide better performance than either pure centralized routing or pure isolated routing. The French public packet switching network, Transpac (Simon and Danet, 1979), uses delta routing.

5.2.5. Distributed Routing Algorithms

In this class of routing algorithms, each IMP periodically exchanges explicit routing information with each of its neighbors. Typically, each IMP maintains a routing table indexed by, and containing one entry for, each other IMP in the subnet. This entry contains two parts: the preferred outgoing line to use for that destination, and some estimate of the time or distance to that destination. The metric used might be number of hops, estimated time delay in milliseconds, estimated total number of packets queued along the path, excess bandwidth, or something similar.

The IMP is assumed to know the "distance" to each of its neighbors. If the metric is hops, the distance is just one hop. If the metric is queue length, the IMP simply examines each queue. If the metric is delay, the IMP can measure it directly with special "echo" packets that the receiver just timestamps and sends back as fast as it can.

As an example, assume that delay is used as a metric and that the IMP knows the delay to each of its neighbors. Once every T msec each IMP sends to each neighbor a list of its estimated delays to each destination. It also receives a similar list from each neighbor. Imagine that one of these tables has just come in from neighbor X, with X_i being X's estimate of how long it takes to get to IMP i. If the IMP knows that the delay to X is m msec, it also knows that it can reach IMP i via X in $X_i + m$ msec via X. By performing this calculation for each neighbor, an IMP can find out which estimate seems the best, and use that estimate and the corresponding line in its new routing table. Note that the old routing table is not used in the calculation.

This updating process is illustrated in Fig. 5-10. Part (a) shows a subnet. The first four columns of part (b) show the delay vectors received from the neighbors of IMP J. A claims to have a 12-msec delay to B, a 25-msec delay to C, a 40-msec delay to D, etc. Suppose that J has measured or estimated its delay to its neighbors, A, I, H, and K as 8, 10, 12, and 6 msec, respectively.

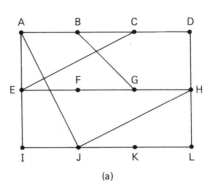

(a)

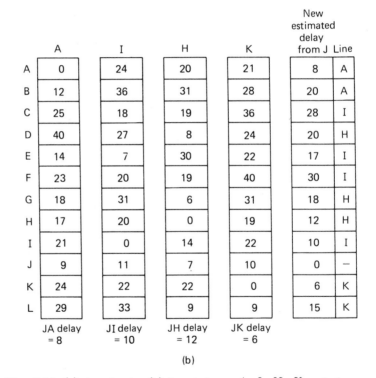

	A		I		H		K		New estimated delay from J	Line
A	0		24		20		21		8	A
B	12		36		31		28		20	A
C	25		18		19		36		28	I
D	40		27		8		24		20	H
E	14		7		30		22		17	I
F	23		20		19		40		30	I
G	18		31		6		31		18	H
H	17		20		0		19		12	H
I	21		0		14		22		10	I
J	9		11		7		10		0	—
K	24		22		22		0		6	K
L	29		33		9		9		15	K

JA delay = 8	JI delay = 10	JH delay = 12	JK delay = 6

(b)

Fig. 5-10. (a) A subnet. (b) Input from *A, I, H, K* and the new routing table for *J*.

Consider how *J* computes its new route to IMP *G*. It knows that it can get to A in 8 msec, and *A* claims to be able to get to *G* in 18 msec, so *J* knows it can count on a delay of 26 msec to *G* if it forwards packets bound for *G* to *A*. Similarly, it computes the delay to *G* via *I*, H, and *K* as 41 (31 + 10), 18

$(6 + 12)$, and 37 $(31 + 6)$ msec respectively. The best of these values is 18, so it makes an entry in its routing table that the delay to G is 18 msec, and that the route to use is via H. The same calculation is performed for all the other destinations, with the new routing table shown in the last column of the figure.

5.2.6. The Topology Update Problem

The distributed adaptive routing algorithm discussed above (and all others of its type) have the property of reacting quickly to good news but slowly to bad news. This point is discussed at great length in McQuillan's thesis (1974), which is the basis for what follows. Consider the situation of an IMP whose best route to some other IMP is very bad. If the IMP suddenly learns that there is a short delay via some other, totally unexpected line (e.g., a previously down IMP has just come up), it will switch over to the new route immediately. When an IMP comes up, the time it takes for other IMPs to learn about it and begin using it is a small multiple of the routing table exchange period. As an example, consider the simple subnet of Fig. 5-11, where the delay metric is the number of hops. Initially A is down, and all the other IMPs know this (i.e., have a delay of infinity to A). When A comes up, the other IMPs learn about it via the routing packet exchange. Let us consider this exchange in detail. For the time being, assume that there is a gigantic gong out there somewhere that sounds periodically, causing all IMPs to send out their routing packets on all lines simultaneously (i.e., packet transmission is synchronized).

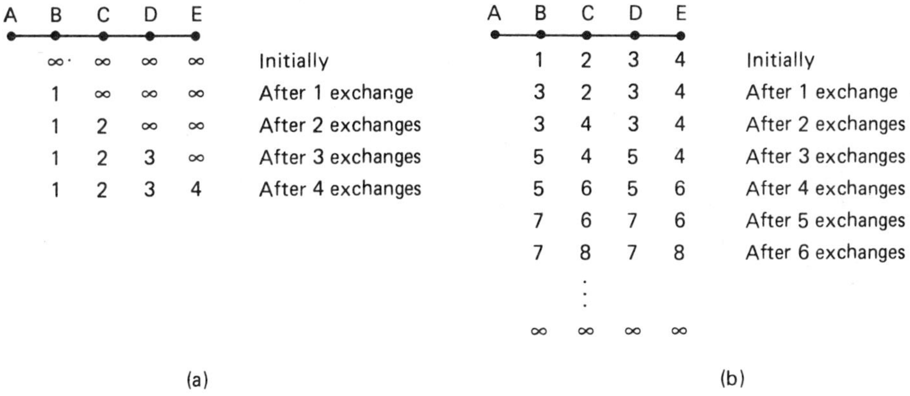

A	B	C	D	E	
●—	●—	●—	●—	●	
	∞·	∞	∞	∞	Initially
	1	∞	∞	∞	After 1 exchange
	1	2	∞	∞	After 2 exchanges
	1	2	3	∞	After 3 exchanges
	1	2	3	4	After 4 exchanges

(a)

A	B	C	D	E	
●—	●—	●—	●—	●	
	1	2	3	4	Initially
	3	2	3	4	After 1 exchange
	3	4	3	4	After 2 exchanges
	5	4	5	4	After 3 exchanges
	5	6	5	6	After 4 exchanges
	7	6	7	6	After 5 exchanges
	7	8	7	8	After 6 exchanges
	.				
	.				
	∞	∞	∞	∞	

(b)

Fig. 5-11. The topology update problem.

At the time of the first packet exchange B learns that its left neighbor has zero delay to A. B makes an entry in its routing table that A is one hop away. All the other IMPs still think A is down. At this point the table entries are as shown in the second row of Fig. 5-11(a). C learns about A as a result of the next packet exchange, and makes an entry in its tables that A is two hops away. D and E know nothing yet. However within two more exchanges, both of them know too. The word is spreading at the rate of one hop per exchange period.

Now let us consider the situation of all IMPs initially up, with A suddenly crashing. At first B, C, D and E have entries of 1, 2, 3, and 4, respectively. At the first packet exchange, B does not hear anything from A, but C announces that it has a path to A that is two hops long. B has no way of knowing that C's path is via B. For all B knows, C might have 20 outgoing lines, all of which have independent paths to A, each of which is of length 2. As a result, B now thinks it can reach A via C with a total path length of 3. Similarly, C uses B's routing packet in which B claims to have a one hop path to A as the basis for its routing table entry, which remains at two hops. D and E do not change yet.

At the next exchange, B hears that C has a path of length 2, so B's entry remains stable at 3. C however hears from both of its neighbors, B and D, that they each have a path of length three. It chooses one of them as the preferred line, but in any case its estimate of the delay to A is now four hops. Subsequent exchanges produce the history shown in Fig. 5-11(b).

From this figure it should be clear why bad news travels slowly: no IMP ever has a value more than one worse than the minimum of all its neighbors. Gradually all the IMPs work their way up to infinity, but the number of exchanges required is equal to the numerical value used for infinity. For this reason it is wise to set infinity to the lowest value that is not possible as a legitimate value. If the number of hops is the metric, infinity should be set to the longest path + 1. If the metric is time delay, there is no sharp limit, so infinity must be set much higher than any value every expected to occur in the worst-case. If an actual value ever does reach infinity by accident, that IMP will be treated as if it were unreachable.

It should be clear that some method is needed to make the subnet respond faster to bad news, especially loss of an IMP or a line. One interesting heuristic, called **hold down**, is due to W. Crowther and is described by McQuillan (1974). It works as follows. When the previous best route suddenly worsens (i.e., the delay this time is more than it was last time), the routing table entry is set to the current value received along the line that was until now the best route. For example, if the route to IMP X via line 3 previously had a delay of 30 msec, and now it has a delay of 50 msec, the routing table entry is set to current value of the previously best line, line 3 (i.e., the entry is set to 50). This change is made even if the expected delay via some other route is shorter. If an IMP or line goes down altogether, the IMP detecting the failure should inject into itself a dummy routing packet containing infinity for all entries, and proceed as if it came from the bad line.

It is important that the hold down time be long enough. Consider the example of Fig. 5-12, in which the arrows show the best route to A. The metric here might be delay; it is obviously not number of hops. If the line from B to C suddenly goes down, C will begin holding down. It will later tell D that it has an infinite delay to C. D will pass this tidbit on to E, which gives it to F.

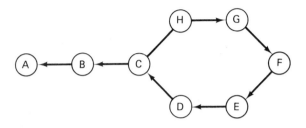

Fig. 5-12. An example where hold down fails if the count is too short.

So far, H is still routing traffic via G. The hold down has not affected it, because its best route is via G, and this route has not gotten worse. That C has been announcing that it (C) is in trouble does not bother H, because H is not routing anything via C.

Suppose that at this point C's hold down counter runs out. C and H exchange packets; C tells H that it has infinite delay to A, while H gives its previous value to C. Needless to say, C is overjoyed and begins routing traffic for A via H. Worse yet, it tells D about the good news. The word spreads like wildfire, and within a few more exchanges everyone has forgotten that B is inaccessible. Packets may loop until B comes back up.

Because the entire hold down mechanism is rather ad hoc, researchers have been looking for better ways to propagate information about changes in the topology. Several algorithms that explicitly use the concept of the sink tree (Fig. 5-7) have been proposed. We will now outline one due to Chu (1978).

The problem with the basic distributed adaptive algorithm is that when an IMP learns that a neighbor has a route to a distant destination, the IMP has no way of knowing whether the route passes through itself. In Chu's algorithm the IMPs keep track of precisely this information, to avoid shuttling packets back and forth over a line.

In general, if traffic from IMP X passes through IMP Y as it flows along the sink tree to the destination, X is said to be **upstream** from Y and Y is said to be **downstream** from X. To illustrate these notions, consider the subnet of Fig. 5-13(a), with the sink tree for destination H shown in Fig. 5-13(b). (Throughout this example we will use shortest path routing, with ties broken alphabetically; for example, B routes to H via $BCEH$ rather than $BDGH$ because $BCEH < BDEH$.)

With the sink tree in mind, the problem becomes much clearer: when a line goes down, blocking the path to a certain destination, an IMP cannot simply divert its traffic to another IMP that is upstream from it with respect to that

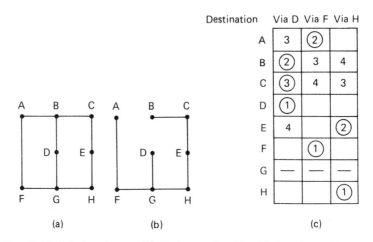

Fig. 5-13. (a) A subnet. (b) Sink tree for H. (c) Routing table used by G.

destination. It must seek out a neighbor that is attached to another (independent) branch of the sink tree. In Chu's algorithm, each IMP maintains a routing table with one row per destination, as in Fig. 5-13(c). Each column gives the number of hops to the destination via a specific output line. For IMP G, the output lines are D, F, and H. The best route in indicated by a circle. Entries that refer to upstream IMPs are left blank. Note that the sink tree used to determine who is upstream and who is downstream is different for each row of the table.

Now let us see what happens if line GH fails. IMP G starts out by marking all the entries in column H as unusable. It then checks each row for which the best route has been wiped out to see if an alternative route is available. For destination E, for example, an alternative route is available via D. (Remember that in this example D routes to E via B because $DBCE < DGHE$.)

For destination H the situation is worse because both neighbors are upstream from G. Consequently, G sends each of them a control packet saying "I cannot reach H any more. Please help me." Upon receiving the packet each neighbor checks to see if it has an alternative (previously suboptimal) route. D has such an alternative, and sends a reply back announcing it. F, however, has no alternative, because its only other neighbor, A, is upstream from it, so it acts in much the same way that it would have if line FG had gone down, namely, by asking A for help. Control packets continue propagating upstream until someone finds an alternate route. When G finally receives replies from all its upstream neighbors, it can make new entries in its routing table and choose the best. The only condition under which the algorithm fails is when none of the IMPs upstream from the failed link can make contact with any IMP on another branch of the sink tree. This condition occurs only when the subnet has been broken into two separate components.

Segall (1979) has devised several algorithms similar in spirit to Chu's, but which adapt the sink trees to changes in traffic as well as changes in topology. Segall's algorithms can also be shown to be loop-free, even while the algorithm is running and not all the tables have been updated. In short, sink trees are changed when the destination itself has become aware of the need to change. It then sends control packets up the tree. When an IMP discovers that it has no upstream neighbors with respect to the destination named in the control packet (i.e., it is at the end of a branch), it changes its tables and sends a reply packet down to the destination. Since changes to the tables are triggered by the reply packets, the changes occur in a well defined order, and this ordering is used to maintain the loop-free property.

5.2.7. Hierarchical Routing

As networks grow in size, the IMP routing tables grow proportionally. Not only is IMP memory consumed by ever increasing tables, but more CPU time is needed to scan them and more bandwidth is needed to send status reports about them. At a certain point the network may grow to the point where it is no longer feasible for every IMP to have an entry for every other IMP, so the routing will have to be done hierarchically, as it is in the telephone network.

When hierarchical routing is used, the IMPs are divided into **regions**, with each IMP knowing all the details about how to route packets to destinations within its own region, but knowing nothing about the internal structure of other regions. When different networks are connected together, it is natural to regard each one as a separate region in order to free the IMPs in one network from having to know the topological structure of the other ones.

For huge networks, a two-level hierarchy may be insufficient; it may be necessary to group the regions into clusters, the clusters into zones, the zones into groups, and so on, until we run out of names for aggregations. As an example of a multilevel hierarchy, consider how a packet might be routed from Berkeley, California to Malindi, Kenya. The Berkeley IMP would know the detailed topology within California, but would send all out-of-state traffic to the Los Angeles IMP. The Los Angeles IMP would be able to route traffic to other domestic IMPs, but would send foreign traffic to New York. The New York IMP would be programmed to direct all traffic to the IMP in the destination country responsible for handling foreign traffic, say in Nairobi. Finally, the packet would work its way down the tree in Kenya until it got to Malindi.

Figure 5-14 gives a quantitative example of routing in a two-level hierarchy with five regions. The full routing table for IMP $1A$ has 17 entries, as shown in Fig. 5-14(b). When routing is done hierarchically, as in Fig. 5-14(c), there are entries for all the local IMPs as before, but all other regions have been condensed into a single IMP, so all traffic for region 2 goes via the $1B-2A$ line, but the rest of the remote traffic goes via the $1C-3B$ line. Hierarchical routing has reduced the table from 17 to 7 entries. As the ratio of the number of regions to the number of IMPs within a region grows, the savings in table space grow proportionally.

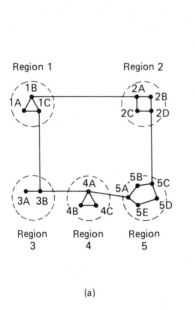

Full table for 1A

Dest.	Line	Hops
1A	—	—
1B	1B	1
1C	1C	1
2A	1B	2
2B	1B	3
2C	1B	3
2D	1B	4
3A	1C	3
3B	1C	2
4A	1C	3
4B	1C	4
4C	1C	4
5A	1C	4
5B	1C	5
5C	1B	5
5D	1C	5
5E	1C	5

Hierarchical table for 1A

Dest	Line	Hops
1A	—	—
1B	1B	1
1C	1C	1
2	1B	2
3	1C	2
4	1C	3
5	1C	3

(a)   (b)   (c)

Fig. 5-14. Hierarchical routing.

Unfortunately, these gains in space are not free. There is a penalty to be paid, and this penalty is in the form of increased path length. For example, the best route from $1A$ to $5C$ is via region 2, but with hierarchical routing all traffic to region 5 goes via region 3, because that is a better choice for most destinations in region 5.

When a single network becomes very large, an interesting question is how many levels should the hierarchy have? For example, consider a subnet with 720 IMPs. If there is no hierarchy, each IMP needs 720 routing table entries. If the subnet is partitioned into 24 regions of 30 IMPs each, each IMP needs 30 local entries plus 24 remote entries for a total of 54 entries. If a three-level hierarchy is chosen, with eight clusters, each containing 9 regions of 10 IMPs, each IMP needs 10 entries for local IMPs, 9 entries for routing to other regions within its own cluster, and eight entries for distant clusters, for a total of 27 entries. Kleinrock and Kamoun (1977) and Kamoun and Kleinrock (1979) have discovered that the optimal number of levels for an N IMP subnet is ln N, requiring a total of e ln N entries per IMP. They have also discovered that the increase in effective mean path length caused by hierarchical routing is sufficiently small that it is not objectionable.

5.2.8. Broadcast Routing

For some applications, hosts need to send messages to all other other hosts. Typical examples might be for scheduling: a host wants to find out which other hosts are willing and able to perform a certain task for it, or distributed data base updates. In some networks the IMPs may also need such a facility, for example to distributed routing table updates. Sending a packet to all destinations simultaneously is called **broadcasting**, and various methods have been proposed for implementing it. Our treatment is based on the work of Dalal and Metcalfe (1978).

One broadcasting method that requires no special features from the subnet is for the source to simply send a distinct packet to each destination. Not only is the method wasteful of bandwidth but it also requires the source to have a complete list of all destinations. In practice this may be the only possibility, but it is the least desirable of the methods.

Flooding is another obvious candidate. Although flooding is ill-suited for ordinary point-to-point communication, for broadcasting it might rate serious consideration, especially if none of the methods described below are applicable. The problem with flooding as a broadcast technique is the same problem it has as a point-to-point routing algorithm: it generates too many packets and consumes too much bandwidth.

A third algorithm is **multidestination routing**. If this method is used, each packet contains either a list of destinations or a bit map indicating the desired destinations. When a packet arrives at an IMP, the IMP checks all the destinations to determine the set of output lines that will be needed. (An output line is needed if it is the best route to at least one of the destinations.) The IMP generates a new copy of the packet for each output line to be used and includes in each packet only those destinations that are to use the line. In effect, the destination set is partitioned among the output lines. After a sufficient number of hops, each packet will carry only one destination and can be treated as a normal packet. Multidestination routing is like separately addressed packets, except that when several packets must follow the same route, one of them pays full fare and the rest ride for free.

A fourth broadcast algorithm makes explicit use of the sink tree for the IMP initiating the broadcast, or any other convenient spanning tree for that matter. If each IMP knows which of its lines belong to the spanning tree, it can copy an incoming broadcast packet onto all the spanning tree lines except the one it arrived on. This method makes excellent use of bandwidth, generating the absolute minimum number of packets necessary to do the job. The only problem is that each IMP must have knowledge of some spanning tree for it to be applicable, and many of the routing algorithms we have studied do not have such knowledge.

Our last broadcast algorithm is an attempt to approximate the behavior of the previous one, even when the IMPs do not know anything at all about spanning trees. The idea is remarkably simple once it has been pointed out. When a broadcast packet arrives at an IMP, the IMP checks to see if the packet arrived on the line that is normally used for sending packets *to* the source of the broadcast. If so, there is an excellent chance that the broadcast packet itself followed the best route from the IMP and is therefore the first copy to arrive at the IMP. This being the case, the IMP forwards copies of it onto all lines except the one it arrived on. If, however, the broadcast packet arrived on a line other than the preferred one for reaching the source, the packet is discarded as a likely duplicate.

An example of the algorithm, called **reverse path forwarding**, is shown in Fig. 5-15. Part (a) shows a subnet, part (b) shows a sink tree for IMP I of that subnet, and part (c) shows how the reverse path algorithm works. On the first hop, I sends packets to F, H, J, and N, as indicated by the second row of the tree. Each of these packets arrives on the preferred path to I (assuming that the preferred path falls along the sink tree) and is so indicated by a circle around the letter. On the second hop, eight packets are generated, two by each of the IMPs that received a packet on the first hop. As it turns out, all eight of these arrive at previously unvisited IMPs, and all but one arrive along the preferred line. Of the eight packets generated on the third hop, only two arrive on the preferred path (at C and L), and so only these generate further packets. After five hops and 23 packets, the broadcasting terminates, compared with four hops and 14 packets had the sink tree been followed exactly.

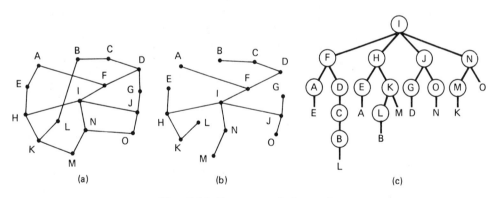

Fig. 5-15. Reverse path forwarding.

The principal advantage of reverse path forwarding is that it is both reasonably efficient and easy to implement. It does not require IMPs to know about spanning trees, nor does it have the overhead of a destination list of bit map in each broadcast packet as does multidestination addressing. Nor does it require any special mechanism to stop the process, as flooding does (either a hop counter in each packet and a priori knowledge of the subnet diameter, or a list of packets already seen per source).

5.3. CONGESTION

When too many packets are present in (a part of) the subnet, performance degrades. This situation is called **congestion**. Figure 5-16 depicts the symptom. When the number of packets dumped into the subnet by the hosts is within its carrying capacity, they are all delivered (except for a few that are afflicted with transmission errors), and the number delivered is proportional to the number sent. However, as traffic increases too far, the IMPs are no longer able to cope, and they begin losing packets. This tends to make matters worse. At very high traffic, performance collapses completely, and almost no packets are delivered.

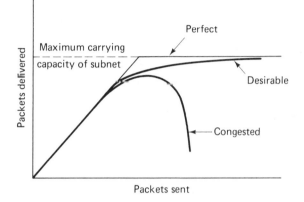

Fig. 5-16. When too much traffic is offered, congestion sets in, and performance degrades sharply.

Congestion can be brought about by several factors. If the IMPs are too slow to perform the various bookkeeping tasks required of them (queueing buffers, updating tables, etc.), queues can build up, even though there is excess line capacity. On the other hand, even if the IMP CPU is infinitely fast, queues will build up whenever the input traffic rate exceeds the capacity of the output lines. This can happen, for example, if three input lines are delivering packets at top speed, all of which need to be forwarded along the same output line. Either way, the problem boils down to not enough IMP buffers. Given an infinite supply of buffers, the IMP can always smooth over any temporary bottlenecks by just hanging onto all packets for as long as necessary. Of course, for stable operation, the hosts cannot indefinitely pump packets into the subnet at a rate higher than the subnet can absorb.

Congestion tends to feed upon itself and become worse. If an IMP has no free buffers, it must ignore newly arriving packets. When a packet is discarded, the IMP that sent the packet will time out and retransmit it, perhaps ultimately many times. Since the sending IMP cannot discard the packet until it has been acknowledged, congestion at the receiver's end forces the sender to refrain from releasing a buffer it would have normally freed. In this manner, congestion backs up, like cars approaching a toll booth.

We will now examine five strategies for dealing with congestion:

1. Preallocation of resources to avoid congestion.

2. Allowing IMPs to discard packets at will.

3. Restricting the number of packets allowed in the subnet.

4. Using flow control.

5. Choking off input when congestion occurs.

In the following sections we will deal with each of these methods in turn.

5.3.1. Preallocation of Buffers

If virtual circuits are used inside the subnet, it is possible to solve the congestion problem altogether, as follows. When a virtual circuit is set up, the call request packet wends its way through the subnet, making table entries as it goes. When it has arrived at the destination, the route to be followed by all subsequent data traffic has been determined and entries made in the routing tables of all the intermediate IMPs.

Normally, the call request packet does not reserve any buffer space in the intermediate IMPs, just table slots. However, a simple modification to the setup algorithm could have each call request packet reserve one or more data buffers as well. If a call request packet arrives at an IMP and all the buffers are already reserved, either another route must be found or a "busy signal" must be returned to the caller. Even if buffers are not reserved, some aspiring virtual circuits may have to be rerouted or rejected for lack of table space, so reserving buffers does not add any new problems that were not already there.

By permanently allocating buffers to each virtual circuit in each IMP, there will always be a place to store any incoming packet until it can be forwarded. First consider the case of a stop-and-wait IMP-IMP protocol. One buffer per virtual circuit per IMP is sufficient for simplex circuits, and one for each direction is sufficient for full-duplex circuits. When a packet arrives, the acknowledgement is not sent back to the sending IMP until the packet has been forwarded. In effect, an acknowledgement means that the receiver not only received the packet correctly, but also that it has a free buffer and is willing to accept another one. If the IMP-IMP protocol allows multiple outstanding packets, each IMP will have to dedicate a full window's worth of buffers to each virtual circuit to completely eliminate the possibility of congestion.

When each virtual circuit passing through each IMP has a sufficient amount of buffer space dedicated to it, packet switching becomes quite similar to circuit switching. In both cases an involved setup procedure is required. In both cases substantial resources are permanently allocated to specific connections, whether or not there is any traffic. In both cases congestion is impossible because all the resources needed to process the traffic have already been reserved. And in both cases there is a potentially inefficient use of resources, because resources not being used by the connection to which they are allocated are nevertheless unavailable to anyone else.

Because dedicating a complete set of buffers to an idle virtual circuit is expensive, some subnets may use it only where low delay and high bandwidth are essential, for example on virtual circuits carrying digitized speech. For virtual circuits where low delay is not absolutely essential all the time, a reasonable strategy is to associate a timer with each buffer. If the buffer lays idle for too long, it is released, to be reacquired when the next packet arrives. Of course, acquiring a buffer might take a while, so packets would have to be forwarded without dedicated buffers until the chain of buffers could be set up again.

5.3.2. Packet Discarding

Our second congestion control mechanism is just the opposite of the first one. Instead of reserving all the buffers in advance, nothing is reserved in advance. If a packet arrives and there is no place to put it, the IMP simply discards it. If the subnet offers datagram service to the hosts, that is all there is to it: congestion is resolved by discarding packets at will. If the subnet offers virtual circuit service, a copy of the packet must be kept somewhere so that it can be retransmitted later. One possibility is for the IMP sending the discarded packet to keep timing out and retransmitting the packet until it is received. Another possibility is for the sending IMP to give up after a certain number of tries, and require the source IMP to time out and start all over again.

Discarding packets at will can be carried too far. It is clearly stupid in the extreme to ignore an incoming packet containing an acknowledgement from a neighboring IMP. That acknowledgement would allow the IMP to abandon a by-now-received packet and thus free up a buffer. However, if the IMP has no spare buffers, it cannot acquire any more incoming packets to see if they contain acknowledgements. The solution is to permanently reserve one buffer per input line to allow all incoming packets to be inspected. It is quite legitimate for an IMP to examine a newly arrived packet, make use of any piggybacked acknowledgement, and then discard the packet anyway. Alternatively, the bearer of good tidings could be rewarded by keeping it, using the just freed buffer as the new input buffer.

If congestion is to be avoided by discarding packets, a rule is needed to tell when to keep a packet and when to discard it. Irland (1978) studied this problem and came up with a simple, yet effective heuristic for discarding packets. In the absence of any explicit rule to the contrary, a single output line might hog all the available buffers in an IMP, since they are simply assigned first come, first served. Figure 5-17(a) shows an IMP with a total of 10 buffers. Three of these are permanently assigned to the input lines. The remaining seven are holding packets queued for transmission on one of the output lines.

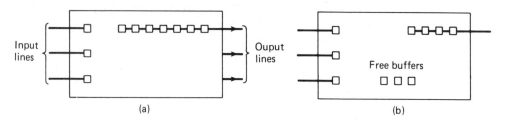

Fig. 5-17. Congestion can be reduced by putting an upper bound on the number of buffers queued on an output line.

Even though two output lines are idle, any incoming packets destined for these lines must be discarded because there are no spare buffers. This is obviously wasteful. Irland's idea is to limit the number of buffers that may be attached to any one output queue. For example, if the limit were set at four, the situation of Fig. 5-17(b) would prevail: three unassigned buffers. A newly arrived packet wanting to go out on the first output line would be discarded rather than allowing it to increase the queue length to five.

This strategy is not really as drastic as it may appear. After all, that output line is already running at maximum capacity. Having seven packets queued instead of four will not pump the bits out any faster, but it will allow traffic for the other lines to be forwarded immediately, possibly doubling or tripling the output rate of the IMP. In any case, the discarded packet will be retransmitted shortly. If the system is well tuned, it will even be retransmitted before the queue empties, so its initial rejection will not even be noticed.

Irland studied several different algorithms for determining maximum queue length, m, for an IMP with k buffers (buffers permanently dedicated for input do not count). The uncontrolled case is $m = k$. If there are s output lines, the case $m = k/s$ effectively means that each buffer is dedicated to a given output line. No line may borrow even one buffer from an idle line, ever. Intuitively this is not efficient, and the study bears this out.

It turns out that the optimal value of m is a complicated function of the mean traffic. Although the IMP could attempt to measure its traffic and continually adjust m, if the traffic were bursty, this probably would not work well. Irland did, however, discover a simple rule of thumb that usually gives good, but not optimal, performance: $m = k/\sqrt{s}$. For example, for seven pool buffers and three lines, $m = 7/\sqrt{3} = 4$.

A related idea, due to Kamoun (1976), directly prevents any line or lines from starving: a minimum number of buffers is dedicated to each line. If there is no traffic, the empty buffers are reserved. Irland's method can be combined with Kamoun's by having a minimum and a maximum number of buffers for each line. The ARPANET uses this method.

Although discarding packets is easy, it has some disadvantages. Chief among these is the extra bandwidth needed for the duplicates. If the probability of a packet being discarded is p, the expected number of transmissions before it is accepted is $1/(1 - p)$. A related issue is how long the timeout interval should be. If it is too short, duplicates will be generated when they are not needed, making the congestion worse. If it is too long, the delay will suffer.

One way to minimize the amount of bandwidth wasted on the retransmission of discarded packets is to systematically discard packets that have not yet traveled far and hence do not represent a large investment in resources. The limiting case of this strategy is to discard newly arrived packets from hosts in preference to discarding transit traffic. Kamoun (1979), Lam and Reiser (1977), and Schwartz and Saad (1979) have all studied this method, and come to the conclusion that it is sound. Their models differ slightly, but the basic idea is that IMPs should refuse or discard new packets from attached hosts whenever the number of buffers tied up by new packets (or total packets) exceeds some threshold.

5.3.3. Isarithmic Congestion Control

Congestion occurs when there are too many packets in the subnet. A direct approach to controlling it is to limit the number of packets in the subnet. Davies (1972) proposed a method that enforces precisely such a limit.

In this method, called **isarithmic** because it keeps the number of packets constant, there exist permits, which circulate about within the subnet. Whenever an IMP wants to send a packet just given to its by it host, it must first capture a permit and destroy it. When the destination IMP finally removes the packet from the subnet, it regenerates the permit. These simple rules ensure that the number of packets in the subnet will never exceed the number of permits initially present.

However, this method has some problems. First, although it does guarantee that the subnet as a whole will never become congested, it does not guarantee that a given IMP will not suddenly be swamped with packets.

Second, how to distribute the permits is far from obvious. To prevent a newly generated packet from suffering a long delay while the local IMP tries to scout up a permit, the permits must be uniformly distributed, so that every IMP has some. On the other hand, to permit high-bandwidth file transfer, it is undesirable for the sending IMP to have to go hunting all over the place to find enough permits. It would be nicer if they were all centralized, so that requests for substantial numbers could be honored quickly. Some compromise must be found, such as having a maximum number of permits that may be present at any IMP, with excess permits required to hunt for an IMP with space. Note that the random walk of the excess permits itself puts a load on the subnet.

Third, and by no means least, if permits ever get destroyed for any reason, (e.g., transmission errors, malfunctioning IMPs, being discarded by a congested IMP), the carrying capacity of the network will be forever reduced. There is no easy way to find out how many permits still exist while the network is running.

5.3.4. Flow Control

There is some confusion in the literature between flow control and congestion control. Most authors use flow control to mean the mechanism by which a receiver throttles a sender to prevent data from arriving at a rate faster than the receiver can handle it. Stop-and-wait and the sliding window are two well-known flow control mechanisms. All flow control mechanisms either require the sender to stop sending at some point and wait for an explicit go-ahead message, or permit the receiver to simply discard messages at will with impunity.

Congestion control, in contrast, deals with the problem of more packets arriving at an IMP than there are buffers to store them all. Flow control is an end-to-end phenomenon, whereas congestion control deals with problems occurring at intermediate IMPs as well.

The reason some writers have confused the two topics is not hard to find. Some networks (notably the ARPANET) have attempted to use flow control mechanisms to eliminate congestion. Although flow control schemes can be used by the transport layer to keep one host from saturating another, and flow control schemes can be used to prevent one IMP from saturating its neighbors, it is difficult to control the total amount of traffic in the network using end-to-end flow control rules.

Flow control cannot really solve congestion problems for a good reason: computer traffic is bursty. Most of the time an interactive user sits at his terminal scratching his head, but once in a while he may want to scan a large file. The potential peak traffic is vastly higher than the mean rate. Any flow control scheme which is adjusted so as to restrict each user to the mean rate will provide bad service when the user wants a burst of traffic. On the other hand, if the flow control limit is set high enough to permit the peak traffic to get through, it has little value as congestion control when several users demand the peak at once. (If half the people in the world suddenly picked up their telephones to call the other half, there would be a lot of busy signals; the telephone system is also designed for average traffic, not worst-case.)

When flow control is used in an attempt to quench congestion, it can apply to It can limit the traffic between pairs of:

1. User processes (e.g., one outstanding message per virtual circuit).

2. Hosts, irrespective of the number of virtual circuits open.

3. Source and destination IMPs, without regard to hosts.

In addition, the number of virtual circuits open can be restricted. We will discuss the details of the ARPANET approach later in this chapter.

5.3.5. Choke Packets

Although limiting the volume of traffic between each pair of IMPs or hosts may indirectly alleviate congestion it does so at the price of potentially reducing throughput even when there is no threat of congestion. What is really needed is a mechanism that is triggered only when the system is congested.

One such mechanism is discussed in (Majithia et al., 1979). Each IMP monitors the percent utilization of each of its output lines. Associated with each line is a real variable, u, whose value, between 0.0 and 1.0, reflects the recent utilization of that line. To maintain a good estimate of u, a sample of the instantaneous line utilization, f (either 0 or 1), can be made periodically and u updated according to

$$u = au + (1 - a)f$$

where the constant a determines how fast the IMP forgets recent history.

Whenever u moves above the threshold, the output line enters a "warning" state. Each newly arriving packet is checked to see if its output line is in warning state. If so, the IMP sends a **choke packet** back to the source host, giving it the destination found in the packet. The packet itself is tagged (a header bit is turned on) so that it will not generate any more choke packets later, and is forwarded in the usual way.

When the source host gets the choke packet, it is required to reduce the traffic sent to the specified destination by X percent. Since other packets aimed at the same destination are probably already under way and will generate yet more choke packets, the host should ignore choke packets referring to that destination for a fixed time interval. After that period has expired, the host listens for more choke packets for another interval. If one arrives, the line is still congested, so the host reduces the flow still more and begins ignoring choke packets again. If no choke packets arrive during the listening period, the host may increase the flow again. The feedback implicit in this protocol should prevent congestion, yet not throttle any flow unless trouble occurs.

Several variations on this congestion control algorithm has been proposed. For one, the IMPs could maintain two critical levels. Above the first level, choke packets are sent back. Above the second, incoming traffic is just discarded, the theory being that the host has probably been warned already. Without extensive tables it is difficult for the IMP to know which hosts have been warned recently about which destinations, and which hosts have not.

Another variation is to use queue lengths instead of line utilization as the trigger signal. The same exponential weighting can be used with this metric as with u, of course. Yet another possibility is to have the IMPs propagate congestion information along with routing information, so that the trigger is not based on only one IMPs observations, but on the fact that somewhere along the path there is a bottleneck. By propagating congestion information around the subnet, choke packets can be sent earlier, before too many more packets are under way.

5.3.6. Deadlocks

The ultimate congestion is a **deadlock**, also called a **lockup**. The first IMP cannot proceed until the second IMP does something, and the second IMP cannot proceed because it is waiting for the first IMP to do something. Both IMPs have ground to a complete halt and will stay that way forever. Deadlocks are not considered a desirable property to have in your network.

The simplest lockup can happen with two IMPs. Suppose that IMP A has five buffers, all of which are queued for output to IMP B. Similarly, IMP B has five buffers, all of which are occupied by packets needing to go to IMP A [see Fig. 5-18(a)]. Neither IMP can accept any incoming packets from the other. They are both stuck. This situation is called **direct store and forward lockup**. The same thing can happen on a larger scale, as shown in Fig. 5-18(b). Each IMP is trying to send to a neighbor, but nobody has any buffers available to receive incoming packets. This situation is called **indirect store and forward lockup**. Note that when an IMP is locked up, all its lines are effectively blocked, including those not involved in the lockup.

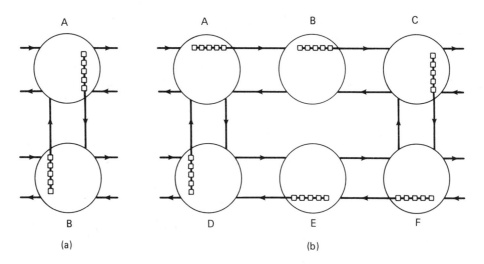

Fig. 5-18. Store-and-forward lockup. (a) Direct. (b) Indirect.

Merlin and Schweitzer (1980a, 1980b) have presented a solution to the problem of store-and-forward lockup. In their scheme, a directed graph is constructed, with the buffers being the nodes of the graph. Arcs connect pairs of buffers in the same IMP or adjacent IMPs. The graph is constructed in such a way that if all packets move from buffer to buffer along the arcs of the graph, then no deadlocks can occur.

As a simple example of their method, consider a subnet with N IMPs in which the longest route from any source to any destination is of length M hops. Each IMP needs $M + 1$ buffers, numbered from 0 to M. The buffer graph is now constructed by drawing an arc from buffer i in each node to buffer $i + 1$ in each of the adjacent nodes. The legal routes from buffer i at IMP A are those to a buffer labeled $i + 1$ at IMPs adjacent to A, and then to a buffer labeled $i + 2$ at IMPs two hops from A, etc.

A packet from a host can only be admitted to the subnet if buffer 0 at the source IMP is empty. Once admitted, this packet can only move to a buffered labeled 1 in an adjacent IMP, and so on, until either it reaches its destination and is removed from the subnet, or it reaches a buffer labeled M, in which case it is discarded. (If M is chosen longer than the longest route, then only looping packets will be discarded.) A packet in buffer i in some IMP may only be moved if buffer $i + 1$ in the IMP chosen by the routing algorithm is free. Note that numbering the buffers does not restrict the choice of routing algorithm, which can be static or dynamic.

To see that this algorithm is deadlock free, consider the state of all buffers labeled M at some instant. Each buffer is in one of three states: empty, holding a packet destined for a local host, or holding a packet for distant host. In the second case the packet can be delivered, in the third case the packet is looping and must be dropped. In all three cases the buffer can be made free. Consequently, all the packets in buffers labeled $M - 1$ can now moved forward, one at a time, to be delivered or discarded. Once all the buffers labeled $M - 1$ are free, the packets in buffers labeled $M - 2$ can be moved forward and delivered or discarded. Eventually, all packets can be delivered or discarded. If the routing algorithm guarantees that packets cannot loop, then M can be set to the longest path length, and all packets will be correctly delivered with no discards and no deadlocks.

Merlin and Schweitzer have also presented many improvements to this simple strategy to reduce the number of buffers needed and to improve the performance. For example, a packet that has already made i hops i.e., is currently in a buffered labeled i, can be put in any available higher numbered buffer at the next hop, not just in buffer $i + 1$. As long as the sequence of buffer numbers is monotonically increasing, there can be no deadlocks. Other improvements involve path switching and common buffer pools.

Store-and-forward lockups are not the only kind of deadlocks that plague the subnet. Consider the situation of an IMP with 20 buffers and lines to four other IMPs, as shown in Fig. 5-19. Four of the buffers are dedicated to the four input lines, to help alleviate congestion. Assume that a sliding window protocol is being used, with window size seven. Further, assume that packets are accepted out of order by the IMP, but must be delivered to the host in order. At the time of the snapshot, five virtual circuits, 0, 1, 2, 3, and 4, are open between the host and other hosts.

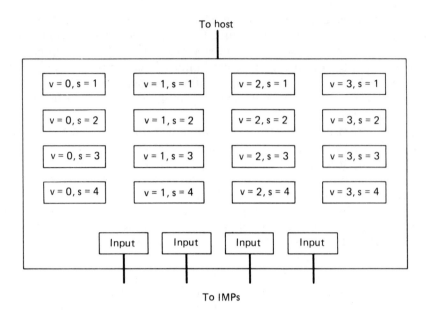

Fig. 5-19. Reassembly lockup.

Rather than dedicate a full window load of buffers to each open virtual circuit, buffers are simply assigned on a first come, first served basis. As soon as the next sequence number expected by the host becomes available, that packet is passed to the host (with each virtual circuit independent of all the others). However higher number packets within the window are buffered in the usual way.

In Fig. 5-19, v and s indicate the virtual circuit and sequence number of each packet, respectively. The host is waiting for sequence number 0 on all four virtual circuits, but none of them have arrived undamaged yet. Nevertheless, all the buffers are occupied.

If packet 0 should arrive, it would have to be discarded due to lack of buffer space. As a result, no more packets can be passed to the host and no buffers freed. This deadlock occurred in the ARPANET in a slightly different form, and was called **reassembly lockup**.

In the ARPANET there are multipacket messages (i.e., messages too large to fit into a single packet). By allowing hosts to pass relatively large chunks of information to the IMPs in a single transfer, the number of host interrupts could be reduced. The sending IMP splits multipacket messages into individual packets and sends each one separately. The destination IMP must put all the pieces together before passing the reassembled message to the host. If pieces of several multipacket messages have managed to commandeer all the available buffer space in the destination IMP, the missing pieces will have to be rejected and the IMP (and host) will be deadlocked. To see that this deadlock is essentially the same as the sliding window one, just think of the full window as a multipacket message.

The ARPANET solution is to have the source IMP ask the destination IMP permission to send a multipacket message. The destination IMP then dedicates enough buffers to reassemble the full message before telling the source to go ahead. The sliding window version of the deadlock can only be prevented by dedicating a full window's worth of buffers to each open virtual circuit. The reason this strategy is more attractive in the ARPANET case is that there most (96%) messages are single packet, not multipacket, whereas in the sliding window case, in effect, all messages are multipacket.

Two other problems discovered in the ARPANET are worth mentioning here. Both were caused by malfunctioning IMPs. All of a sudden, one IMP announced that it had zero delay to all other IMPs in the entire subnet. The adaptive routing algorithm spread the good news far and wide. The other IMPs were ecstatic. Within a few seconds, practically all of the traffic in the entire subnet was headed toward the only IMP that was not working properly. Although not a deadlock, this certainly brought the whole network to a grinding halt.

The other problem was also caused by a failing memory. One fine day the Aberdeen IMP (on the East Coast) decided that it was the UCLA IMP (on the West Coast). The consequences of this case of mistaken identity can be easily imagined, especially for the UCLA and Aberdeen hosts.

The fix applied to the IMP software was to have each IMP periodically compute a software checksum of its own code and tables, in hopes of discovering ailing memory words, such as those that caused the above problems. Nevertheless the nagging question of how you prevent one bad IMP from bringing the whole network down remains. One of the arguments in favor of computer networking is that higher reliability can be achieved so: if one machine goes down, there are still plenty of others around. However, if a single failure at one site often pollutes the entire nationwide (or worldwide) system, there may be no advantage at all.

5.4. EXAMPLES OF THE NETWORK LAYER

The above material should give you a good feeling for the choices and options available to subnet designers. In the remainder of this chapter we will examine our three example networks to see what choices their designers actually made in practice. We will also look at the layer 3 protocol used in public networks.

5.4.1. The Network Layer in the ARPANET

The ARPANET communication subnet uses datagrams inside but provides virtual circuit service to the hosts. Datagram service is also available, but is used less often. Each host's operating system is responsible for breaking the user's data stream into messages prefixed by 40-bit transport headers. These messages (up to 8063 bits) are transmitted transparently by the subnet, and delivered bit for bit the same to the receiving host. If two hosts agree to exchange ancient Babylonian parking tickets in EBCDIC, that is their business; the subnet will not complain.

How the host actually gets its message into the IMP is a somewhat involved story. Suffice it to say here that the host attaches a 96-bit host-IMP **leader** to the front of each message. The leader tells the IMP to which virtual circuit the message belongs, to which host it is to be sent, and a few other things the IMP needs to know. Data are sent from host to IMP one bit at a time with an explicit (hardware) go ahead signal after each bit. This signal is needed because the host and IMP may have different word lengths, and hence may have to pause to reference memory at different times. For most host-IMP pairs, the maximum data rate is about 10^5 bits/sec. The leader is stripped off by the IMP and is not transmitted, although the destination IMP constructs a new leader when passing the message to the destination host.

As the message pours into the IMP, it is split up into a maximum of eight packets each of which is a maximum of 1008 bits. The network designers expected there to be two distinct classes of traffic, interactive and file transfer. The interactive messages, coming from or going to a terminal, are usually single-packet, whereas the file transfer traffic is usually multipacket. The packets of a multipacket message may well be sent over different routes, in order to provide high throughput.

In order to offer virtual circuit service with a subnet that uses datagrams inside, the ARPANET layer 3 protocol contains provision for explicit end-to-end acknowledgements within the subnet. When a message enters the source IMP it is assigned a number. If an acknowledgement for this message fails to arrive from the destination IMP within the timeout interval, the source IMP assumes that something bad has happened (such as one of the intermediate IMPs crashing) and takes corrective action. The acknowledgement is called an **RFNM** (Request For Next Message).

This end-to-end acknowledgement is in addition to the IMP-IMP packet acknowledgements. You might think that the RFNM packets were superfluous, since adjacent IMPs will keep transmitting over and over until the packet gets through, but an IMP could crash after having acknowledged receipt of a packet but before having forwarded it. To recover from this situation, the source IMP must hold a copy of each message it originates until the corresponding RFNM has come in. If there has been no response for 30 sec, the source IMP sends a query to the destination IMP. Depending on the answer, if any—the destination IMP might have crashed—the source IMP may retransmit the message. The protocol has been designed to withstand losing RFNMs, as well as the queries and their responses.

In addition to its role as an end-to-end acknowledgement within the subnet, the RFNM plays a major role in the congestion control mechanism. All the congestion control methods tried, attempted to limit what a source IMP, acting as agent for its hosts, could send to a destination IMP, acting as agent for its hosts. In other words, they operated on an end-to-end basis within the subnet. This situation is different from the simple line protocol used by adjacent IMPs, and also different from the flow control enforced by the hosts themselves.

In the first version of the subnet, a host was permitted to have only one outstanding message per virtual circuit. In other words, once a message had been sent, the host-IMP line was blocked, and the source IMP would not send any more messages on that virtual circuit until the RFNM came in. This scheme did not work very well as congestion control, and quickly gave way to another one.

In the second version, there was no restriction on the number of outstanding messages per virtual circuit per se, but each pair of source-destination IMPs were not allowed to have more than four outstanding messages total. In addition, an explicit mechanism was introduced to eliminate the by-then all-too-obvious problem of reassembly lockup.

The general principle was: before a source IMP sent a message to a destination IMP, it was required to first send a little packet reserving the appropriate number of buffers. Only after receiving an ALLOCATE packet was it allowed to go ahead and send the message. If the destination IMP did not have any buffer space, it just queued the request and sent the ALLOCATE packet later, when space became available. Meanwhile, the source IMP just sat around waiting. To provide good response for single-packet messages, a special mechanism was provided: a single-packet message served as its own allocation request. If the destination IMP had room, it just accepted the message and sent back an RFNM immediately. If it did not have any room, it discarded the packet but remembered the request for later.

To provide high bandwidth for file transfers, after a multipacket message arrived at its destination, the IMP did not just send an RFNM and then release the buffers. Instead it held the buffers and told the source IMP it was doing so by piggybacking an ALLOCATE packet onto the RFNM. As long as the source host kept sending multipacket messages rapidly, it could hang onto the destination buffers more or less indefinitely. However, if the source host failed to send another multipacket message within 250 msec, the source IMP would give the allocation back.

In the third version of the congestion control mechanism, the rule about four outstanding messages per source-destination IMP pair was replaced by a limit of eight messages between each pair of hosts. Notice that the designers tried all three possibilities for controlling flow: first on a per virtual circuit basis, then on a source IMP—destination IMP pair basis, then on a host pair basis.

Although the IMP transmitting hardware automatically generates checksums that are verified by the receiving IMPs hardware, these checksums exist only while the packet is "on the wires." To guard against errors caused by bad memory words in an IMP, the source IMP computes a software checksum by simply adding up all the words in a packet and then adding the packet length to the sum. This checksum is transported along with the packet. At each intermediate IMP along the way, the software checksum is explicitly verified by the IMP program before sending the IMP-IMP acknowledgement. With 16 bits of software checksum and 24 bits of hardware checksum per packet, the mean time between undetected errors should be centuries.

To enhance security, the subnet is broken up into 16 logically distinct subnets. Each host has a bit map telling it which subnet it belongs to and which of the other logical subnets it may communicate with. In this way an installation may set up a host so that its users may not divulge information to arbitrary sites on the network.

Originally, routing in the ARPANET was done with the distributed adaptive algorithm described earlier, including hold down. Every 640 msec each IMP exchanged delay information with its neighbors. As the 1160-bit routing messages came in, each IMP updated its routing tables. In addition, a separate check was made to see which IMPs were unreachable by using hop count as a metric. On lines slower than 50 kbps, the routing messages were exchanged less frequently, to save scarce bandwidth.

In 1979, this famous algorithm was put out to pasture because it adapted too slowly, occasionally caused packets to loop for long periods of time, did not use alternate routes at all, and because the ARPANET had grown to the size where the routing packets were interfering with the regular traffic. The replacement algorithm (McQuillan et al., 1980; Rosen, 1980), maintains at each IMP a representation of the entire ARPANET, including the delays on each line. Using this data base, every IMP computes the shortest path to every other IMP, with delay being the metric for distance. These paths are used for routing. Since every IMP runs the shortest path calculation on (almost) the same data base, the paths are consistent and there is little looping.

To provide adaptation to traffic changes, each IMP measures the delay on each of its lines averaged over a 10 sec period. The results of these measurements, together with an update sequence number, are then broadcast to all other IMPs using a flooding algorithm.

Although routing is the principal function of layer 3 in our model, the ARPANET protocols do not make a clear distinction between layers 2 and 3, and furthermore, the ARPANET also has the subnet end-to-end protocol, as mentioned above. Consequently, the 128-bit IMP-IMP packet header (see Fig. 4-14 as well as Fig. 5-20) contains fields relating to layer 2, layer 3, and the end-to-end subnet protocol. For example, the *Seq*, *Logical channel number*, and *Acknowledgement bits* fields belong to the data link protocol; most of the rest are used by the source IMP to destination IMP (subnet end-to-end) portion of the protocol.

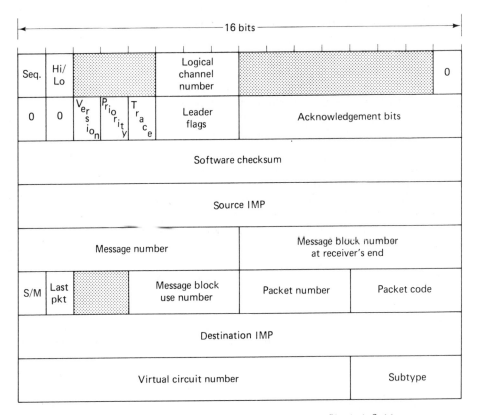

Fig. 5-20. Format of an ARPANET data packet. Shaded fields are reserved for future use.

The *Seq* field is the 1-bit sequence number used by the stop-and-wait protocol between adjacent IMPs.

The *Hi/Lo* field is used to tell which end of the line the packet came from. Nearly all the time, when an IMP sends a packet, it is delivered to the IMP at the other end. However, once in a rare while the carrier needs to take a line out of service for maintenance. The maintenance includes looping the line back onto itself, so data sent arrive back at the sender. If the IMP should decide to transmit a packet while the line was looped back, it would receive its own packet, inspect the acknowledgement bits, and behave incorrectly. The Hi/Lo bit enables each IMP to tell when a line is looped back. This may sound like an unimportant point, but it shows to what lengths the designers have gone to ensure extremely high reliability.

The *Logical channel number* tells which of the eight stop-and-wait channels available on the IMP-IMP line this packet belongs to.

The *Version* bit is needed because new versions of the IMP program are distributed and installed while the subnet is running. Since successive versions may differ in details, the IMPs must know whether a just arrived packet was generated by the current or previous version of the IMP program. Again you can see here the tremendous efforts the designers have made to make sure the subnet never goes down, not even for changing the IMP program. As a point of reference, how many computer manufacturers are able to switch over to a new version of the operating system without stopping the machine, and without affecting the jobs running during the changeover? Answer: not very many.

The *Priority* bit is used by the host to indicate which messages it considers important. The IMP just takes the bit at face value, so there has to be a gentlemen's agreement not to abuse it. Usually, hosts use it for transport protocol control messages or interactive traffic.

The *Trace* bit tells the subnet to trace the packet so that the network management can learn how it was routed, etc.

The *Leader flags* are passed by the source host to the source IMP, propagated through the subnet, and eventually transmitted to the destination host. These have to do with the host-IMP protocol.

The *Acknowledgement bits* give the sequence number of the last packet received on each of the eight logical channels. These are the piggybacked bits going back home.

The *Software checksum* is computed by the source IMP and verified by each IMP along the way in order to detect IMP memory failures as well as transmission errors.

The *Source IMP* field speaks for itself. This format allows for up to 65K IMPs in the subnet.

The *Message number* is assigned by the source IMP. Consecutive messages between host *A* and host *B* are numbered consecutively. The RFNMs and source IMP to destination IMP protocol packets refer to this field.

The *Message block number* is used by the destination IMP as an index into its tables to find the variables pertaining to the traffic for this host-host pair.

The *S/M* field indicates single- or multiple-packet message.

The *Last packet bit* tells the destination IMP that this is the last piece of a multipacket message. Without it, the IMP would not know how long the message was.

The *Message block use number* is needed because message blocks are scarce resources. If a host-host pair has no traffic for a substantial period of time, the message blocks being used for that pair may be reclaimed and used for another host-host pair. If the former owner now suddenly starts sending traffic, this will be inserted into the data stream to which the message block now belongs. To prevent this, there is a 4-bit counter associated with each message block. This counter is incremented upon each use of the message block, so it is possible to detect sudden activity from long dormant transport pairs, by seeing that the message use number does not agree with the current one.

The *Packet number* numbers the packets of a message. Four bits have been provided to allow longer messages in the future.

The *Packet code* indicates the type of message. The code 0 is used for normal data; the remaining control codes are as follows:

1. Request for buffer allocation at destination IMP (single or multipacket).

2. Source IMP returning multipacket allocation it does not need.

3. Incomplete message? Query from source IMP to destination IMP when no RFNM, Dead Destination, or other response has arrived with a prescribed timeout period.

4. RFNM (from destination IMP to source IMP acknowledging a message).

5. RFNM + ALLOCATE (allows source to immediately send another message of the same kind—single or multipacket).

6. Dead destination (from destination IMP if host was down).

7. Incomplete reply. This code is the response to the packet code 3 query.

The *Destination IMP* field tells where to send the packet.

The *Virtual circuit number* is taken from the host-IMP leader at the source and reinserted into the IMP-host leader at the destination. The destination host needs this information in order to demultiplex the many virtual circuits entering it.

The *Subtype* field is used to distinguish normal packets from datagrams. Datagrams do not use the source IMP to destination IMP protocol, are not necessarily delivered in order, and are not flow controlled. Once the source IMP has sent a datagram, that is the last it ever hears of the datagram. The only checking is the normal IMP-IMP checksum.

5.4.2. The Network Layer in SNA

The path control layer in SNA provides virtual circuit service to the transmission control layer. In this respect it encompasses not only the network layer in the ISO model, but also some transport layer functions as well. It accomplishes this goal by using session routing, with an elaborate system of alternate routes and backup routes. In essence, the network managers hand prepare a table giving a list of routes from each source to each destination, with the network dynamically choosing from among the static choices. Below we will describe briefly the routing and congestion control algorithms. For more details, see (Ahuja, 1979; Atkins, 1980; Gray and McNeill, 1979).

For the purposes of routing, an SNA network is divided up into **subareas**, each of which contains one or more NAUs. Each NAU has a two-part address: its subarea, and its address within the subarea. Each subarea is under the control of a type 4 or type 5 node. In effect, the subareas form a backbone onto which the type 1 and type 2 nodes are attached, as shown in Fig. 5-21. This model is similar to that of Fig. 2-1.

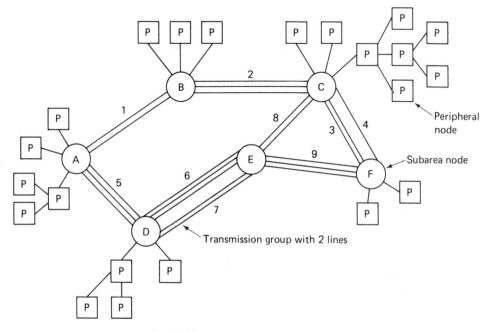

Fig. 5-21. An example SNA network.

When a session is established the source selects a virtual route for the session. A **virtual route** is an ordered list of subareas from the source subarea to the destination subarea. In Fig. 5-21, *ABCF*, *ADEF*, and *ADECF* are all virtual routes from subarea *A* to subarea *F*. (In our terminology, a virtual route is just the list of IMPs that form the path.)

The decision to chose one virtual route or another is based on two pieces of information, the current load assigned to the various virtual routes, and the service class desired for the session. Possible **service classes** are interactive, remote job entry, file transfer, secure, real time, etc. Service classes typically differ in their delay, throughput, or security requirements (e.g., satellite links are more subject to eavesdropping than terrestrial links). Up to eight alternative virtual routes can be provided for each of three service classes, for a total of 24 possibilities. Multiple, unrelated sessions may use the same virtual route.

The concept of a virtual route is needed because there may be multiple lines between subareas. These lines are divided into **transmission groups.** For example, in Fig. 5-21, there are five lines between D and E, divided into two transmission groups. Transmission groups generally contain homogeneous lines; for example, two subareas might have three transmission groups between them, one a single leased satellite channel, the second a group of two 56-kbps digital (PCM) lines, and the third a group of four 9600 bps analog lines. Each transmission group has a single transmission queue, with the first packet taking the next available line in the group (that is, the lines are interchangeable). The idea of having multiple lines in a group is primarily to provide higher bandwidth than that of a single line. The idea of having multiple transmission groups is to provide highly disjoint paths, both for different service classes and for high reliability.

As part of establishing a session, the virtual route chosen by the source is mapped onto an **explicit route**, which is a sequence of transmission groups. For example, in Fig. 5-21, 5683, 5783, 5684, and 5784 are all possible explicit routes for the virtual route $ADECF$. When a packet comes into a subarea, the routing process examines the destination and explicit route number, consults its explicit route tables, and queues the packet for the appropriate transmission group. The data link layer decides which line to use within that group. If all transmission groups consisted of a single line, packets would be kept in sequence from source to destination. However, due to multiple (unreliable) lines per group, packets can arrive at the next subarea in the wrong order. Unlike the ARPANET, which does packet resequencing only at the destination, SNA resequences at each subarea.

If all the lines in a transmission group fail, all the explicit routes using that group must be rerouted using another explicit route corresponding to the chosen virtual route. If none can be found, another virtual route must be chosen. If no virtual routes are available, the session must be aborted. As transmission groups come up and down, control packets are sent around the network, so that each subarea knows which explicit routes are currently available and which are not.

To increase transmission efficiency, several unrelated packets that happen to be queued for the same transmission group may be blocked together into a **basic transmission unit**, as shown in Fig. 5-22. When the frame arrives at the next subarea, it is broken down and all the packets are individually queued on the appropriate outgoing transmission groups. Thus blocking and deblocking is done on a hop-by-hop rather than end-to-end basis. The packets in a block may well all have different sources and different destinations. This facility is most commonly used between hosts (type 5 nodes) and front end communication controllers (type 4 nodes), to reduce the number of CPU interrupts. SNA also allows it on SDLC links, but since merging two SDLC frames into one only saves 5 bytes, it is hardly worth the trouble.

Flow control in layer 3 is done per virtual route, without regard to the

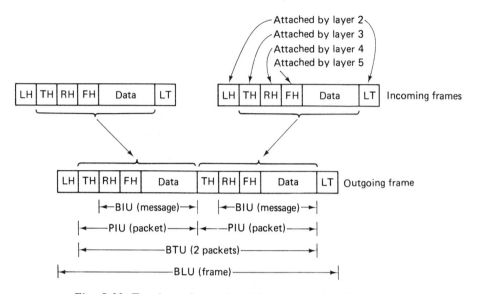

Fig. 5-22. Two incoming packets blocked together for output.

number of sessions using the virtual route. Upon receipt of transmit authorization from the receiver, the sender is permitted to send a window of n packets, the first of which will normally contain a request to send n more packets. When the receiver has sufficient buffer space available, it returns an authorization for the next group of n packets. This mechanism, called **pacing**, is different from sliding window flow control, but if the receiver maintains $2n - 1$ buffers and always returns transmit authorizations immediately, a continuous flow of data can be maintained.

Congestion control is achieved by dynamically adjusting the pacing parameter, n. Associated with each virtual route are a minimum window size, n_{low}, and a maximum window size, n_{high}. The minimum window size is usually equal to the number of hops in the route, and the maximum window size is some small multiple thereof, for example $n_{high} = 3n_{low}$. Each packet header contains 2 bits that are set to 0 by the sender. If an intermediate IMP is moderately congested, it sets 1 of the bits to one. If it is badly congested, it sets the other bit to 1. If it is not congested, it leaves the bits alone.

When each packet arrives at its destination, the state of these bits tells how much congestion there is along the path. Based on the amount of congestion, n for the corresponding virtual route can be increased or decreased. For moderate congestion, the window size is reduced by one; for severe congestion it is set to n_{low}. If there is no congestion, it is increased by one. Under all conditions $n_{low} \leqslant n \leqslant n_{high}$. The pacing count is also reduced when congestion is present. This congestion control technique is similar to using choke packets.

Path control uses several different TH formats. Abbreviated headers are used within the source and destination areas, with conversion to the full header done when the packet is first queued for transmission out of the source subarea or into the destination subarea. The idea behind this two header system is to spare simple terminals and their controllers the trouble of managing the somewhat involved intersubarea header. The simple header used between terminals and controllers is shown in Fig. 5-23.

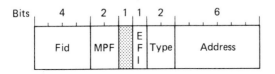

Fig. 5-23. Transmission header used within a subarea.

The *Fid* field identifies the header type (0011 in this case).

The *MPF* field is the mapping field and tells whether the PIU contains a whole BIU or only part, and if part, whether the first part, a middle part, or the last part.

The *EFI* bit indicates whether the flow is to be expedited or not.

The *Type* field indicates the session type: LU-LU, LU-SSCP, PU-LU, or PU-SSCP.

Finally, the *Address* field identifies the element of the subarea.

Before leaving SNA, it is interesting to note that although the ARPANET and SNA originally had radically different routing algorithms, in the course of time they have moved closer. The original ARPANET algorithm was completely dynamic, with routing decisions made without any knowledge of the global topology. The original SNA algorithm was completely static, with routing decisions made manually, based on knowledge of the complete topology. After some experienced had been gained, the ARPANET designers changed the algorithm to base the routing on explicit knowledge of the topology, and the SNA designers moved in the direction of making the algorithm more dynamic. The conclusion seems to be that good routing algorithms should be dynamic and based on knowledge of the topology.

5.4.3. The Network Layer in DECNET

The network layer in DECNET provides pure datagram service to the transport layer. Packets may or may not be delivered in sequence, or delivered at all for that matter. Packets may loop, may be duplicated, and may be discarded by the congestion control algorithm. In short, all the problems that may occur in the ARPANET may also occur in DECNET, except that the ARPANET has an end-to-end protocol within the subnet to hide them from the hosts and DECNET does not.

The routing algorithm used in DECNET is essentially a copy of the original ARPANET algorithm. Each IMP (i.e., node that does packet switching), maintains two vectors for each outgoing line, indexed by destination. One vector contains the estimated path length to each destination via that line; the other vector contains the estimated cost to each destination via that line. When a packet comes in, the outgoing line with the lowest cost to the required destination is chosen.

The routing tables are updated in much the same way as the original ARPANET algorithm, except that DECNET only attempts to adjust for topology changes, not for traffic fluctuations. Instead of delay, the inverse of the line bandwidth is used as distance metric. In addition to periodic table updates, routing packets are sent to neighboring IMPs whenever certain critical events happen. Among these events are lines coming up or going down, the cost of a line changing, and so on. By making the updating process event driven, the frequency of the periodic updates can be considerably reduced (e.g., once per 15 sec instead of once per 0.64 sec). The routing packets contain 16 bits per destination, 11 bits giving the line cost, and 5 bits giving the hop count.

Since each IMP maintains the estimated cost and path length for each outgoing line, unlike the ARPANET, which only maintained it for the best line, the possibility of load splitting is present.

Congestion control is achieved using the choke packet method described above. Each IMP maintains two vectors per destination for use by the congestion-control algorithm: the credit vector and the usage vector. The credit vector tells how many units of traffic the IMP may send to each destination, and the usage vector tells how many have already been sent. The traffic units are arbitrary, but each packet has a value. At no time may an IMP have more usage than it has credit to any destination. If it runs out of credit, it must discard all packets to that destination. Initially, each credit counter is set to a standard value, and each usage counter is set to a low, but positive value. The intention, of course, is to dynamically adjust the credit and usage counters to shut off flow when congestion builds up.

To know when congestion has become serious enough to warrant adjusting the counters, each IMP monitors the queue length and utilization of each line, keeping track of a weighted average of the previous average and the current value. When either metric rises above a threshold, a choke packet is generated and sent back to the source of the packet that triggered the event. The choke packet causes the source to multiply the current value of its usage counter by a constant factor, effectively reducing its available credit for future transmissions to the same destination. Periodically, all credit counters are increased by a constant amount, and all usage counters are decremented by a constant amount, to allow the network to gradually forget past congestion.

The final aspect of the congestion control algorithm is the rule used for discarding packets. The choking mechanism does not guarantee that an IMP will never run out of buffers. It merely attempts to gradually slow down the flow when the network gets into trouble. The discard rule is Irland's square root heuristic: When an output queue has reached a length equal to the number of buffers divided by the square root of the number of output lines, packets that need to go in that queue are discarded.

In addition to its routing and congestion control functions, the network layer of DECNET ensures that packets do not live forever. Each packet has a hop counter in the network layer header. Every time the packet is forwarded, the hop counter is incremented by one. When the counter reaches a threshold value, the packet is discarded. The threshold value is normally set just above the length of the longest path through the network. There is no attempt to have a different threshold for each source-destination pair.

The network header used for data packets is shown in Fig. 5-24. The *Version* bit tells which version of the protocol generated the packet. The *Return request* bit indicates that an undeliverable packet should be returned to the sender. When a packet is on its return journey, the *Returning* bit is turned on. The *Choke* bit indicates that the packet is a choke packet rather than an ordinary data packet. The *Destination* and *Source* fields tell which machine the packet is going to and came from. Finally, the *Hops* counter is used to kill off old packets.

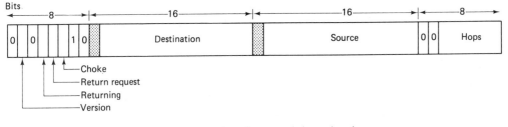

Fig. 5-24. DECNET network layer header.

5.4.4. The Network Layer in X.25

To prevent networks in different countries from developing mutually incompatible interfaces, CCITT has proposed international standard network access protocols for layers 1, 2, and 3, or levels 1, 2, and 3, as CCITT calls them. These standards are collectively known as **X.25** (Rybczynski, 1980). Within a short time X.25 will dominate all international network activity as well as national networking in every country in the world except possibly the United States. However, even in the U. S., X.25 will play a large role, especially in corporations that need international communication (including communication to Canada, which already has a major X.25 network, Datapac).

X.25 defines the interface between the host, called a **DTE** (Data Terminal Equipment) by CCITT, and the carrier's equipment, called a **DCE** (Data

Circuit-terminating Equipment) by CCITT. An IMP is known as a **DSE** (Data Switching Exchange). In this section we will adhere to the CCITT terminology because it is in widespread use in public network circles. X.25 defines the format and meaning of the information exchanged across the DTE - DCE interface for the layer 1, 2, and 3 protocols (see Fig. 5-25). Since this interface separates the carrier's equipment (the DCE) from the user's equipment (the DTE), it is important that the interface be very carefully defined.

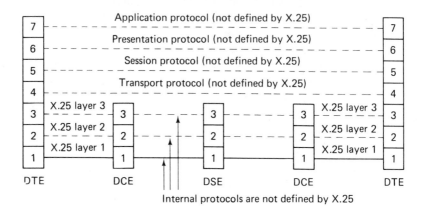

Fig. 5-25. The place of X.25 in the protocol hierarchy.

The X.25 standard defines three layers (levels) of communication: the physical layer, the frame layer, and the packet layer. The physical layer deals with how 0s and 1s are represented, how contact is established with the network, timing aspects, and so forth. Actually, X.25 does not define these things, but rather references two other standards, X.21 and X.21 *bis*, which define the digital and analog interfaces, respectively. We discussed X.21 in Chap. 3 and will not discuss it further here. X.21 *bis* is an interim standard to be used on analog networks until digital networks become widely available.

The frame layer is what ISO calls the data link layer. Its job is to ensure reliable communication between DTE and DCE, even though they may be connected by a noisy telephone line. The protocols used are LAP and LAPB, as discussed in Chap. 4.

The third, or packet layer, which ISO calls the network layer, is concerned with the format and meaning of the data field contained within each frame. All the packets discussed below are contained in the data field of the frame of Fig. 4-16. The packet layer provides for routing and virtual circuit management.

An outline of X.25 goes something like this. When a DTE wants to communicate with another DTE, it must first set up a virtual circuit between them. To do this, the DTE builds a CALL REQUEST packet and passes it to its DCE. The subnet then delivers the packet to the destination DCE, which then gives it to the destination DTE. If the destination DTE wishes to accept the call, it sends a CALL ACCEPTED packet back. When the originating DTE receives the CALL ACCEPTED packet, the virtual circuit is established. At this point both DTEs may use the full-duplex virtual circuit to exchange data packets. When either side has had enough, it sends a CLEAR REQUEST packet to the other side, which then sends a CLEAR CONFIRMATION packet back as an acknowledgement.

The originating DTE may choose any idle virtual circuit number for the conversation. If this virtual circuit number is in use at the destination DTE, the destination DCE must replace it by an idle one before delivering the packet. Thus the choice of circuit number on outgoing calls is determined by the DTE, and on incoming calls by the DCE. It could happen that both simultaneously choose the same one, leading to a **call collision**. X.25 specifies that in the event of a call collision, the outgoing call is put through and the incoming one is canceled. Many networks will attempt to put the incoming call through shortly thereafter using a different virtual circuit.

In addition to these virtual calls, X.25 also provides for permanent virtual circuits. These are analogous to leased lines in that they always connect two fixed DTEs and do not need to be set up.

The format of the CALL REQUEST packet is shown in Fig. 5-26(a). This packet, as well as all other X.25 packets, begins with a 3-byte header. (CCITT calls bytes **octets**.)

The *Group* and *Channel* fields together form a 12-bit virtual circuit number. Virtual circuit 0 is reserved for future use, so in principle, a DTE may have up to 4095 virtual circuits open simultaneously. The *Group* and *Channel* fields individually have no particular significance.

The *Type* field in the CALL REQUEST packet, and in all other control packets, identifies the packet type. The *Control* bit is set to 1 in all control packets and to 0 in all data packets. By first inspecting this bit the DTE can tell whether a newly arrived packet contains data or control information.

We are now finished with the (3-byte) header. The remaining fields of Fig. 5-26(a) are unique to the CALL REQUEST packet. The next two fields tell how long the calling and called addresses are, respectively. Both addresses are encoded as decimal digits, 4 bits per digit. Old habits die hard in the telephone industry.

The *Facilities length* field tells how many bytes worth of facilities field follows. The *Facilities* field itself is used to request special features for this virtual circuit. The specific features available may vary from network to network. One possible feature is reverse charging (collect calls). This facility is especially important to organizations with thousands of remote terminals that initiate calls to a central computer. If all terminals always request reverse charging, the organization only gets one "network phone bill" instead of thousands of them. High-priority delivery is also a possibility. Yet another feature is a simplex, instead of a full-duplex, virtual circuit.

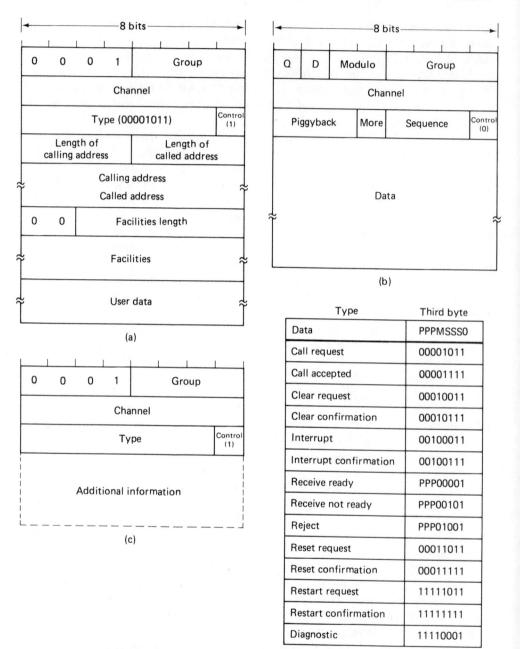

Fig. 5-26. X.25 packet formats. (a) Call request format. (b) Control packet format. (c) Data packet format. (d) Type field (P = Piggyback, S = Sequence, M = More).

The caller can also specify a maximum packet length and a window size rather than using the defaults of 128 bytes and two packets, respectively. If the callee does not like the proposed maximum packet length or window size he may make a counterproposal in the facilities field of the CALL ACCEPTED packet. The counterproposal may only change the original one to bring it closer to the default values, not further away.

Some facilities must be selected when the customer becomes a network subscriber rather than on a call-by-call basis. These include closed user groups (no user can call outside the group, for security reasons), maximum window sizes smaller than seven (for terminals with limited buffer space), line speed (e.g. 2400 bps, 4800 bps, 9600 bps), and prohibition of outgoing calls or incoming calls (terminals place calls but do not accept them).

The *User data* field allows the DTE to send up to 16 bytes of data together with the CALL REQUEST packet. The DTEs can decide for themselves what to do with this information. They might decide, for example, to use it for indicating which process in the DTE the caller wants to be connected with. Alternatively, it might contain a login password.

The format of the other control packets is shown in Fig. 5-26(b). In some cases they consist only of a header. In other cases they have an additional byte or two tacked on. The fourth byte of the CLEAR REQUEST packet, for example, tells why the circuit is being cleared. CLEAR REQUEST packets are automatically generated by the subnet when a CALL REQUEST cannot be put through. When this happens, the cause is recorded here. Typical causes are: callee refuses to accept reverse charging, the number is busy, the destination is down, or the network is congested.

Because X.25 makes a distinction between CLEAR REQUEST and CLEAR CONFIRMATION, there is the possibility of a **clear collision**, (i.e., both sides decide to terminate the virtual circuit simultaneously). However, because it is always obvious what is happening, there is no ambiguity, and the virtual circuit can be cleared without delay.

The data packet format is shown in Fig. 5-26(c). The Q bit indicates Qualified data. The standard is silent as to what distinguishes qualified from unqualified data, but the intention is to allow protocols in the transport and higher layers to set this bit to one to separate their control packets from their data packets. The *Control* field is always 0 for data packets. The *Sequence* and *Piggyback* fields are used for flow control, using a sliding window. The sequence numbers are modulo 8 if *Modulo* is 01, and modulo 128 if *Modulo* is 10. (00 and 11 are illegal.) If modulo 128 sequence number are used, the header is extended with an extra byte to accommodate the longer *Sequence* and *Piggyback* fields. The meaning of the *Piggyback* field is determined by the setting of the D bit. If $D = 0$, a subsequent acknowledgement means only that the local DCE has received the packet, not that the remote DTE has received it. If $D = 1$, the acknowledgement is a true end-to-end acknowledgement, and means that the packet has been successfully delivered to the remote DTE.

Even if delivery is not guaranteed (i.e., $D = 0$), the *Piggyback* field can be useful. Consider, for example, a carrier that offers a high delay service for bargain hunters. Incoming packets are written onto a magnetic tape, which is then mailed to the destination the next day. In this case the *Piggyback* field is used strictly for flow control. It tells the DTE that the DCE is prepared to accept the next packet, and nothing more.

One point worth noting about acknowledgements in X.25 is that instead of returning the number of the last packet correctly received (as in our examples of Chap. 4), the DTEs are required to return the number of the next packet expected (i.e., one higher). This choice is an arbitrary one, but to be X.25-compatible, DTEs must play the game according to CCITT's rules.

The *More* field allows a DTE to indicate that a group of packets belong together. For example, to send a long message, each packet except the last one would have the *More* bit on. Only a full packet may have this bit set. The subnet is free to repackage data in different length packets if it needs to, but it will never combine data from different messages (as indicated by the *More* bit) into one packet.

The standard says that all carriers are required to support a maximum packet length of 128 data bytes. However, it also allows carriers to provide optional maximum lengths of 16, 32, 64, 256, 512, and 1024 bytes. In addition, maximum packet length can be negotiated when a virtual circuit is set up. The point of maximum packet lengths longer than 128 is for efficiency. The point of maximum packet lengths shorter than 128 is to allow terminals with little buffer space to be protected against long incoming packets.

The other kinds of control packets are listed in Fig. 5-26(d). INTERRUPT packets allow a short (1 byte) signal to be sent out of sequence. Since control packets do not bear sequence numbers, they can be delivered as soon as they arrive, without regard to how many sequenced data packets are queued up ahead of them. A typical use for this packet is to convey the fact that a terminal user has hit the quit or break key. An INTERRUPT packet is acknowledged by an INTERRUPT CONFIRMATION packet.

The RECEIVE READY packet is used to send separate acknowledgements when there is no reverse traffic to piggyback onto. The PPP field tells which packet is expected next. When sequence numbers are modulo 128, an extra byte is needed for this packet.

The RECEIVE NOT READY packet allows a DTE to tell the other side to stop sending packets to it for a while. RECEIVE READY can then be used to tell the DCE to proceed.

The REJECT packet allows a DTE to request retransmission of a series of packets. The PPP field indicates the sequence number at which retransmission is to begin.

The RESET and RESTART packets are used to recover from varying degrees of trouble. A RESET REQUEST applies to a specific virtual circuit and has the effect of reinitializing the window parameters to 0. A common use of

RESET REQUEST is for the DCE to inform the DTE that the subnet has crashed. After receiving a RESET REQUEST, the DTE has no way of knowing if packets that were outstanding at the time have been delivered. Recovery must be done by the transport layer. Up to two extra bytes in the RESET REQUEST packet allows the requester to try to explain what the cause of the reset is. The DTE can also initiate a RESET REQUEST, of course.

A RESTART is much more serious. It is used when a DTE or DCE has crashed and is forced to abandon all of its virtual circuits. A single RESTART REQUEST is equivalent to sending a RESET REQUEST separately for each virtual circuit.

A DIAGNOSTIC control packet is also provided, to allow the network to inform the user of problems, including errors in the packets sent by the user (e.g., an illegal *Type* field).

The X.25 standard contains several state diagrams to describe event sequences such as call setup and call clearing. The diagram of Fig. 5-27 shows the subphases of call setup. Initially, the interface is in state *P1*. A CALL REQUEST or INCOMING CALL (i.e., incoming CALL REQUEST) changes the state to *P2* or *P3*, respectively. From these states the data transfer state, *P4*, can be reached, either directly, or via *P5*. Similar diagrams are provided for call clearing, resetting, and restarting.

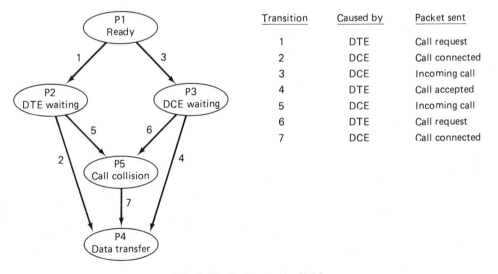

Transition	Caused by	Packet sent
1	DTE	Call request
2	DCE	Call connected
3	DCE	Incoming call
4	DTE	Call accepted
5	DCE	Incoming call
6	DTE	Call request
7	DCE	Call connected

Fig. 5-27. Call setup in X.25.

The original (1976) X.25 standard was more-or-less as we have described it so far (minus the *D* bit, DIAGNOSTIC packet, and the packet length and window size negotiation). However, there was considerable demand for a datagram facility, in addition to the virtual circuits. Both the United States and Japan made (conflicting) proposals for the architecture of the datagram service. In the great tradition of international bureaucracies, CCITT accepted *both* of them, making the protocol even more complicated than it already was.

Both datagram facilities are minor variations on the CALL REQUEST packet. In what is referred to as the true datagram packet (U.S. proposal), the format is the same as the CALL REQUEST packet of Fig. 5-27(a), except that the third byte is replaced with a *Sequence* field and a *Piggyback* field, just as in data packets. The *More* and *Control* bits are both zero. The user data field is also expanded to a maximum of 128 bytes, the first two of which are the **datagram identification**. Each datagram is sent independently of all other datagrams. In the facilities field of a datagram, a request can be made for explicit notification of delivery (or lack thereof). The notification packet, called a **datagram service signal** packet, then tells whether the datagram was delivered or not, and if not delivered, why not (destination address incorrect, network congestion, etc.). The datagram is identified by the datagram identification.

The flow control parameters do not have end-to-end meaning (i.e., D must be 0). Their purpose is to prevent the DTE from trying to send datagrams faster than the DCE can accept them. Datagrams can use any virtual circuit number not in use for a virtual call or permanent virtual circuit. The RESET REQUEST, RESTART REQUEST, RR, RNR, and DIAGNOSTIC packets retain their normal meaning on datagram circuits.

In the other datagram facility (Japanese proposal), called **fast select**, the CALL REQUEST packet is also expanded to include 128 bytes of user data, but the third byte remains the way it was. Fast select is requested as a facility. As far as the network is concerned, the packet really is an attempt to establish a virtual circuit. When fast select is used, the called DTE may reject the attempted call with a CLEAR REQUEST packet, which has also been expanded to include 128 bytes of reply data. However, it may also accept the call, in which case the virtual circuit is set up normally. For more details about datagrams and fast select, see (Folts, 1980b).

Before leaving the subject of X.25, there are a few more points worth making. First, there is some controversy about whether the X.25 packet layer corresponds to the network layer or transport layer in the ISO Open Systems Reference Model. When there is no end-to-end significance for the acknowledgements (i.e., $D = 0$), it is incontrovertibly a network layer protocol, and another layer of protocol is needed on top of it to ensure that messages really do arrive at the other side. On the other hand, when $D = 1$, the acknowledgements really do mean that the destination DTE has accepted the message, so X.25 is functioning as a transport protocol. No additional transport protocol is required unless the "quality of service" is inadequate e.g., the user expects the transport service to recover from network resets and restarts transparently, or to have a lower rate of undetected errors than the carrier provides.

The original X.25 standard had only $D = 0$ packets and aroused so much controversy that CCITT added end-to-end significance in 1980. However, not all carriers allow $D = 1$ packets. Being able to use X.25 as a transport protocol is unquestionably a convenience to the users but considerably more work for the implementers. Also, if the acknowledgements are *not* end-to-end, more pipelining is possible—DCEs can issue acknowledgements immediately. They never have to wait for anything to propagate back from the destination DTE, so the sender will rarely be blocked by the flow control window.

A second point worth making about X.25 is that data packets contain a short (only 3-byte) header, which suggests that the X.25 designers were more worried about transmission bandwidth than about DCE table space. Although X.25 does not even mention the DCE-DCE protocols, it was clear when X.25 was designed that many carriers intended to use virtual circuits within the subnet, as in Fig. 5-3. In this case the X.25 packet can be used as is, internally as well as externally. Although this approach is costly in terms of DCE memory, computer memory prices are dropping much faster than transmission bandwidth costs, so this may be a wise decision.

A third noteworthy point is the considerable redundancy in X.25. Setting up a connection requires two addresses, the address of the packet switching network itself, used in the X.21 protocol, and the address of the remote DTE, used in the X.25 packet layer. Once the connection has been established, there are two separate flow control windows, in layers 2 and 3. An alternative, and simpler design would be to have the address used in the X.21 layer be the address of the remote DTE, thus eliminating the need for CALL REQUEST and CALL ACCEPTED packets. Using the X.21 clearing sequence to terminate DTE-DTE connections would eliminate the CLEAR REQUEST and CLEAR CONFIRMED packets as well. Furthermore, the redundancy inherent in having flow control in both the frame and packet layers is wasteful for terminals and other DTEs that have only a single virtual circuit open at any time. For these simple DTEs, the packet layer could be dispensed with altogether.

5.5. SUMMARY

A key issue in the design of a packet switching network is the nature of the service provided to the hosts, that is, the division of labor between hosts and IMPs. If virtual circuit service is provided, the subnet is taking on the responsibility for transparent error correction. If datagram service is provided, the hosts must do the work.

Another important design issue is whether the subnet itself uses virtual circuits or datagrams internally. This decision affects the reliability, performance, and cost of the subnet.

Routing within the subnet can be done using statically or dynamically. Static routing uses fixed tables within the IMPs to do routing and does not adjust to traffic patterns. Dynamically routing algorithms build their own routing tables and can adjust the flows as the traffic changes.

Congestion can occur when there is too much traffic in the subnet. Various techniques for preventing it have been proposed, including using flow control, choke packets, and permits.

The ARPANET uses datagrams inside to provide virtual circuit service to the hosts. SNA uses virtual circuits inside to provide virtual circuit service to the host. DECNET uses datagrams inside to provide datagram service to the hosts. The three networks differ in many other ways as well. X.25 defines protocols for both virtual circuit service and datagram service, although not all carriers implement both of them. The internal protocols used by public networks are not specified.

PROBLEMS

1. Are there any circumstances when a virtual circuit service will (or should) deliver packets out of order? Explain.

2. Referring to Fig. 5-3, what new table entries would be needed to add a path *AEFD*?

3. Consider the following design problem concerning implementation of virtual circuit service. If virtual circuits are used internal to the subnet, each data packet must have a 3-byte header, and each IMP must tie up 8 bytes of storage for circuit identification. If datagrams are used internally, 15-byte headers are needed but no IMP table space is required. Transmission capacity costs 1 cent per 10^6 bytes, per hop. IMP memory can be purchased for 1 cent per byte and is depreciated over 2 years (business hours only). The statistically average session runs for 1000 sec, in which time 200 packets are transmitted. The mean packet requires four hops. Which implementation is cheaper, and by how much?

4. Assuming that all IMPs and hosts are working properly and that all software in both is free of all errors, is there any chance, however small, that a packet will be delivered to the wrong destination?

5. What is the difference, if any, between static routing using two equally weighted alternatives, and selective flooding using only the two best paths?

6. A certain network uses hot potato routing, that is, incoming packets are put on the shortest queue. One of the IMPs has only two outgoing lines, hence two queues. If the queues are equally long, packets are put on a queue at random. Write down the equation expressing the conservation of flow into and out of the state in which the length of queue 1 is i and the length of queue 2 is j, with $i > j + 1$ and $j > 1$.

7. Propose a good routing algorithm for a network in which each IMP knows the path length in hops to each destination for each output line, and also the queue lengths for each line. For simplicity assume that time is discrete and that a packet can move one hop per time interval.

8. An IMP uses a combination of hot potato and static routing. When a packet comes in, it goes onto the first choice queue if and only if that queue is empty and the line is idle; otherwise it uses the second-choice queue. There is no third choice. If the arrival rate at the IMP for a certain destination is λ packets/sec and the service rate is μ packets/sec, what fraction of the packets get routed via the first choice queue? Assume Markov arrivals and service times.

9. If delays are recorded as 8-bit numbers in a 50 IMP, degree 3 network, and delay vectors are exchanged twice a second, how much bandwidth per (full-duplex) line is chewed up by the distributed routing algorithm?

10. The updating done in Fig. 5-11 is left-right symmetric in that each IMP instantaneously reads its neighbors' values and then adjusts its own. In practice it may be difficult to achieve the necessary synchronization. Redraw both parts of the figure assuming:
    (a) First the leftmost IMP updates, then the next leftmost, and so on.
    (b) First the rightmost IMP updates, then the next rightmost, and so on.

11. For hierarchical routing with 4800 IMPs, what region and cluster sizes should be chosen to minimize the size of the routing table for a three layer hierarchy?

12. Looking at the subnet of Fig. 5-7, how many packets are generated by a broadcast from B, using
    (a) reverse path forwarding?
    (b) the sink tree?

13. Irland's method for controlling congestion requires discarding packets if the required queue exceeds a certain length. Use an M/M/1 finite buffer queueing model to derive an expression telling what fraction of the packets will be discarded.

14. As a possible congestion control mechanism in a subnet using virtual circuits internally, an IMP could refrain from acknowledging a received packet until (1) it knows its last transmission along the virtual circuit was received successfully and (2) it has a free buffer. For simplicity, assume that the IMPs use a stop-and-wait protocol and that each virtual circuit has a one buffer dedicated to it for each direction of traffic. If it takes T sec to transmit a packet (data or acknowledgement), and there are n IMPs on the path, what is the rate at which packets are delivered to the destination host? Assume that transmission errors are rare, and that the host-IMP connection is infinitely fast.

15. A datagram subnet allows IMPs to drop packets whenever they need to. The probability of an IMP discarding a packet is p. Consider the case of a source host connected to the source IMP, which is connected to the destination IMP, and then to the destination host. If either of the IMPs discards a packet, the source host eventually times out and tries again. If both host-IMP and IMP-IMP lines are counted as hops, what is the mean number of
    (a) hops a packet makes per transmission?
    (b) transmissions a packet makes?
    (c) hops required per received packet?

16. Does the Merlin-Schweitzer buffering algorithm guarantee that every packet will be delivered within a finite time? If so, prove it, if not, what is needed to fix it?

17. Why do you think CCITT provided flow control in the X.25 frame layer and the X.25 packet layer instead of just in one layer?

18. When an X.25 DTE and DCE both decide to put a call through at the same time, a call collision occurs and the incoming call is canceled. When both sides try to clear simultaneously, the clear collision is resolved without canceling either request. Do you think that simultaneous resets are handled like call collisions or clear collisions? Defend your answer.

19. Write a program to simulate routing using flooding. Each packet should contain a counter that is decremented on each hop. When the counter gets to zero, the packet is discarded. Time is discrete, with each line handling one packet per time interval. Make three versions of the program: all lines are flooded, all lines except the input line are flooded, and only the (statically chosen) best k lines are flooded. Compare flooding with deterministic routing $(k = 1)$ in terms of delay and bandwidth used.

20. Simulate routing using a combination of hot potato and static routing. Time is discrete as above. Use the statically best route unless the queue length is k or more, in which case use the next best route, etc. Investigate the effect of k on mean delay.

21. Write a program that simulates a computer network using discrete time. The first packet on each IMP queue makes one hop per time interval. Each IMP has only a finite number of buffers. If a packet arrives and there is no room for it, it is discarded and not retransmitted. Instead, there is an end-to-end protocol, complete with timeouts and acknowledgement packets, that eventually regenerates the packet from the source IMP. Plot the throughput of the network as a function of the end-to-end timeout interval, parametrized by error rate.

6

THE NETWORK LAYER II:

SATELLITE AND PACKET RADIO NETWORKS

In the preceding chapter we examined layer 3 of the classical store-and-forward subnet at considerable length. This kind of network consists of a collection of IMPs hosts, concentrators, and terminals that are connected in some irregular topology by point-to-point lines (e.g., leased telephone circuits). Each line connects exactly two locations.

Now we will examine a radically different kind of subnet, one in which every packet sent is automatically received by every site. Each receiver must select out that part of the input addressed to it. In this system there are no point-to-point telephone lines. Instead, there is a single shared transmission medium for which the various machines contend. Only one packet may be in flight at any instant, which means that a high-bandwidth medium must be used to make the whole arrangement practical.

Much of the present research in computer networking is focused on alternatives to store-and-forward subnets, so it is likely that the material in this chapter will become increasingly important in the future. When packet broadcasting is used, it replaces layer 3 in the hierarchy of Fig. 1-7. In other words, Chap. 6 is an alternative to Chap. 5. Broadcast networks must have a data link frame format e.g., HDLC, but the principles for designing such (layer 2) frames are similar to those of point-to-point networks, so we will not devote special attention to them (for some details, see Jacobs, et al., 1978, 1979). Similarly, broadcast networks must have a transport layer, but there is no reason for the transport layer of a broadcast network to differ from the broadcast layer of a store-and-forward network. Stronger yet, the transport layer should be designed to work with any possible network layer, to allow one type to be replaced by another type.

6.1. SATELLITE PACKET BROADCASTING

When communication satellites were first launched, they were used in exactly the same way terrestrial cables were used—for point-to-point communication. A transatlantic satellite connected carrier offices on either side of the ocean. The carrier could route a particular call over the satellite link or over the cable (or one way above the ocean and the other way under it in order to halve the round-trip delay). The satellite was just a big cable in the sky.

This mode of satellite usage had obvious advantages at that time. First, a satellite ground station cost tens of millions of dollars, making it unlikely that many people would decide to buy one of their own. Second, because the satellite was used only only to interconnect the carriers' switching offices, its use was more-or-less transparent to the user (except for the delay). Third, and by no means least, circuit switching using point-to-point lines had totally dominated telecommunication since its inception a century ago. Using the new medium to simulate an old one seemed like the most natural thing in the world.

In a mere two decades the situation has changed completely. Ground station costs have dropped by three orders of magnitude, making the private antenna an economically attractive proposition for many corporate users. Additionally, the cost of the (micro)computer that is needed to interface an ordinary terminal to the antenna, although still positive, is barely so. Finally, the growth of telecommunication for transmitting data has been enormous, bringing with it a demand for communication channels with a much higher bandwidth and a much lower error rate than has been traditional in telephony.

The confluence of these developments suggests a different mode of operation for the satellite. Each company plant, university campus, government building, etc., could have its own rooftop antenna communicating directly with the satellite, or with a large satellite ground station nearby. The satellite just acts as a repeater, amplifying and rebroadcasting everything that comes in. Consequently, the model we will adopt for discussing such systems is that of a group of N independent users, each of whom wishes to communicate with one or more of the other ones.

The key ingredient in this model is that the users are uncoordinated and have no other means of communication other than the satellite channel. In particular, the decision of how to allocate the satellite channel must be made using the channel itself. As we shall demonstrate shortly, this is easier said than done. Another thing to keep in mind is that a satellite is inherently a broadcast medium. Anyone who cares to erect an antenna can listen to everyone else's messages. (The implications of this obvious fact for privacy will be discussed in Chap. 9.) Although the broadcast property was not used by the original applications, it is essential in achieving the necessary coordination among the users, as will become clear later.

The key question in a system having a single communication channel that must be shared efficiently and fairly among a large number of widely dispersed, uncoordinated users is how to share the channel. All of our analysis of satellite packet broadcasting will revolve about this one issue. If everyone just begins transmitting whatever he wants to whenever he wants to, without regard to what other users are doing, chaos will result, and there will be almost no communication at all.

To emphasize this important point, we now state a fundamental assumption explicitly: if two users broadcast simultaneously, the satellite will rebroadcast the sum of the two incoming signals, resulting in garbage. We therefore assume that each packet contains a checksum strong enough to permit the receiver to detect all collisions, so damaged packets can be discarded.

Another important property of satellite packet broadcasting is that the sender can listen for his own packet, one round-trip time after sending it. Since the sender can tell from this whether or not a collision has occurred, there is no need for explicit destination to source acknowledgements. If the packet was garbled, the sender learns of the problem simultaneously with the receiver and can take appropriate action without having to be told.

Before describing satellite packet broadcasting in detail, it is worth mentioning some of the advantages it has over conventional store-and-forward networks that use terrestrial telephone lines. First, the protocols are much simpler because no acknowledgements are needed. Second, the entire routing problem vanishes into thin air. Third, it is no longer possible for some lines to be badly congested while others are idle. Fourth, increasing the scale of the network is just a matter of adjusting one parameter, the satellite bandwidth rather than performing a complicated heuristic topology optimization. Fifth, mobile users can easily be accommodated. The principal disadvantages of satellite networks are the longer propagation times and the need for expensive antennas.

6.1.1. Conventional Channel Allocation Methods

Allocation of a single channel among competing users happens in contexts other than satellite packet broadcasting. It is instructive to examine those situations to see if their solutions are applicable here. One common situation in which a single channel is shared is a multidrop line connecting a group of terminals. The method normally used there to bring order out of chaos is polling. The central site sends short poll messages to each terminal in turn giving it permission to send any data it has. Terminals are expected to be seen and not heard in the absence of a poll.

Polling using a satellite can be implemented in two ways: either an onboard computer issues the polls or one of the ground stations acts as a central site. If the satellite itself issues the polls, it takes 270 msec for the satellite to discover that a polled user has nothing to say. With N users, the full polling cycle takes $0.270N$ sec. With $N = 100$ users, it takes 27 sec to go around once. Such a response time is not likely to go down well with people using interactive terminals. If a ground station issues the polls, the situation is even worse, since a poll/answer sequence now takes 540 instead of 270 msec.

The transit time is not the only problem with polling. Another problem is: How does the satellite know who it should poll? A satellite carrier might have hundreds or thousands of customers, only a small fraction of whom are logged in at any moment.

Since polling from a satellite is clearly inappropriate for a large number of terminals, we must look at other channel allocation strategies. The traditional way of using a satellite is frequency-division multiplexing (FDM). If there are N users, the bandwidth is divided up into N equal sized portions (with guard bands between them), each user being assigned one portion. Since each user has his own private frequency band to use, there is no interference between users, and the system operates without error. When there are only a small and fixed number of ground stations, each of which has a heavy (buffered) load of traffic (e.g., carriers' switching offices), FDM is a simple and efficient allocation mechanism. (When the number of stations is fixed, but all have bursty traffic, the SPADE system, described in Chap. 3, is attractive.)

However, when the number of stations is large and continuously varying, FDM presents some problems. If the spectrum is cut up into N regions, and fewer than N users are currently logged in, a large piece of valuable spectrum will be wasted. If more than N users want to log in, some of them will be denied permission, for lack of bandwidth, even if some of the logged in users hardly ever transmit or receive anything.

But even assuming that the number of users could somehow be held constant at N, dividing the single available channel up into static subchannels is inherently inefficient, and there is no way to get around this. The basic problem is that when some users are quiescent, their bandwidth is simply lost. They are not using it, and no one else is allowed to use it. It is just wasted. Furthermore, in most computer systems, data traffic is extremely bursty (peak traffic to mean traffic ratios of 1000:1 are common). Consequently, most of the channel will be idle most of the time.

Exactly how bad static FDM is can easily be seen from a simple queueing theory calculation. Let us start from Eq. (2-12), which expresses the mean time delay for a channel of capacity C bps, when λ packets/sec arrive, each packet having a length drawn from an exponential probability density function with mean $1/\mu$ bits/packet:

$$T = \frac{1}{\mu C - \lambda}$$

Now let us divide the single channel up into N independent subchannels, each with capacity C/N bps. The mean input rate on each of the subchannels will now be λ/N. Substituting above, we get

$$T_{\text{FDM}} = \frac{1}{\mu(C/N) - (\lambda/N)} = \frac{N}{\mu C - \lambda} = NT \qquad (6\text{-}1)$$

The mean packet delay using FDM is N times worse than if all the packets were somehow magically orderly arranged in a big central queue.

Precisely the same arguments that apply to FDM also apply to synchronous time-division multiplexing. Each user is statically allocated every Nth time slot. If a user does not use his allocation, it just lies fallow.

At first it might appear that asynchronous time-division multiplexing (concentration) could be used, but there is a problem here, too. In the traditional ATDM scheme, each terminal has a private (dedicated) port into the concentrator. If two terminals decide to send characters simultaneously, each one is loaded into a different memory location in the concentrator for queueing and subsequent transmission. Even if all terminals transmit at once, there will be no collisions at the concentrator. If there is sufficient memory, all terminals may send continuously indefinitely with no data loss. With uncoordinated, geographically dispersed users who have only a single shared channel to communicate on, there is no private port, and two simultaneous transmissions will collide. To avoid conflicts we could give each user a private portion of the spectrum, but this is just FDM, which we have already shown to be inefficient with many bursty users. None of the traditional data communication methods work here. We need a genuinely new channel allocation method.

6.1.2. Pure ALOHA and Slotted ALOHA

In the early 1970s, Norman Abramson (1970, 1973a, 1973b, 1977) and his colleagues at the University of Hawaii devised a new and elegant method to solve this problem. Their work has been extended by many researchers since then (Binder et al., 1975; Carleial and Hellman, 1975; Ferguson, 1975b; Lam, 1974; and Roberts, 1973, to name just a few). Although Abramson's work, called the ALOHA system, used ground based radio packet broadcasting rather than satellite packet broadcasting, the basic idea is applicable to any system in which uncoordinated users are competing for the use of a single shared channel. Nevertheless, there are some important differences between ground radio packet broadcasting and satellite packet radio broadcasting (notably the propagation delay). We will examine ground radio in general, and the University of Hawaii ALOHA system in particular, later in this chapter.

The basic idea of an ALOHA system is simple: just let the users transmit whenever they have data to be sent. There will be collisions, of course, and the colliding packets will be destroyed. However, due to the perfect feedback property of packet broadcasting, the sender of a packet can always find out whether or not his packet was destroyed by just listening to the downward rain of packets one round-trip time after sending the packet. If the packet was destroyed, the sender just waits a random amount of time and sends it again. The waiting time must be random or the same packets will collide over and over, in lockstep. Systems in which multiple users share a common channel is a way that can lead to conflicts are widely known as **contention** systems.

A sketch of packet generation in an ALOHA system is given in Fig. 6-1. We have made the packets all the same length because it has been shown that the throughput of ALOHA systems is maximized by having a uniform packet size rather than allowing variable length packets (Abramson, 1977; Ferguson, 1975a; Gaarder, 1972).

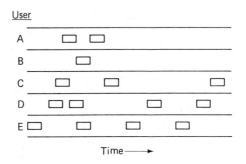

Fig. 6-1. In pure ALOHA, packets are transmitted at completely arbitrary times.

Whenever two packets try to occupy the channel at the same time there will be a collision and both will be garbled. You should realize that if the first bit of a new packet overlaps with just the last bit of a packet almost finished, both packets will be totally destroyed, and both will have to be retransmitted later. The checksum cannot (and should not) distinguish between a total loss and a near miss. Bad is bad.

A most interesting question is: What is the throughput of an ALOHA channel? Let us first consider an infinite collection of interactive users sitting at their terminals. A user is always in one of two states: thinking or blocked. Initially, all users are in the thinking state. Whenever someone decides what to do next, he types a line of text followed by a carriage return. At this point he is blocked and stops thinking. The microcomputer inside the terminal immediately locks the keyboard to prevent any more input. It then sends a packet containing the line to the satellite and waits R sec to see if it was successful. If so, the user's keyboard is unlocked. If not, the keyboard remains locked, and the packet is retransmitted over and over until it is successfully sent.

Let the "packet time" denote the amount of time needed to transmit the standard, fixed-length packet (i.e., the packet length divided by the bit rate). At this point we assume that the infinite-population of users generates new packets according to a Poisson distribution with mean S packets per packet time. (The infinite-population assumption is needed to ensure that S does not decrease as users become blocked.) If $S > 1$, the user community is generating packets at a higher rate than the channel can handle, and nearly every packet will suffer a collision. For reasonable throughput we would expect $0 < S < 1$.

In addition to the new packets, the users also generate retransmissions of packets that previously suffered collisions. Let us further assume that the probability of k transmission attempts per packet time, old and new combined, is also Poisson, with mean G per packet time. Clearly, $G \geqslant S$. At low load (i.e., $S = 0$), there will be few collisions, hence few retransmissions, so $G = S$. At high load there will be many collisions, so $G > S$. Under all loads, the throughput is just the offered load, G, times the probability of a transmission being successful that is, $S = GP_0$, where P_0 is the probability that a packet does not suffer a collision.

A packet will not suffer a collision if no other packets are sent within one packet time of its start, as shown in Fig. 6-2. Under what conditions will the shaded packet arrive undamaged? If any other user has generated a packet between t_0 and $t_0 + t$ the end of that packet will collide with the beginning of the shaded one. In fact, the shaded packet's fate was already sealed even before the first bit was sent, but due to the long propagation delay, it has no way of knowing that another packet was already underway. Similarly, any other packet started between $t_0 + t$ and $t_0 + 2t$ will bump into the end of the shaded packet.

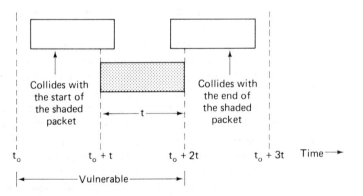

Fig. 6-2. Vulnerable period for the shaded packet.

The probability that k packets are generated during a given packet time is given by the Poisson distribution:

$$\Pr[k] = \frac{G^k e^{-G}}{k!} \tag{6-2}$$

so the probability of zero packets is just e^{-G}. In an interval two packet times long, the mean number of packets generated is $2G$. The probability of no other traffic being initiated during the entire vulnerable period is thus given by $P_0 = e^{-2G}$. Using $S = GP_0$, we get

$$S = Ge^{-2G}$$

This result was first derived by Abramson (1970).

The throughput-offered traffic relation is shown in Fig. 6-3. The maximum throughput occurs at $G = 0.5$, with $S = 1/(2e)$, which is about 0.184. In other words, the best we can hope for is a channel utilization of 18%. This result is not very encouraging, but with everyone transmitting whenever he wants to, we could hardly have expected a 100% success rate.

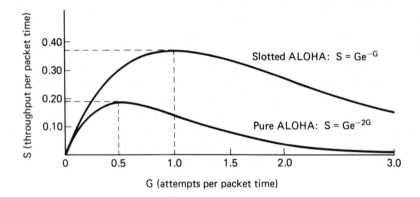

Fig. 6-3. Throughput versus offered traffic for ALOHA systems.

In 1972, Roberts published a method for doubling the capacity of an ALOHA system. His proposal was to divide time up into discrete intervals, each interval corresponding to one packet. One way to achieve synchronization among the users would be to have the satellite emit a pip at the start of each interval, like a clock. Although the pips would arrive down at the earth 270 msec later, each user would receive the signal at about the same time. By making the time slots slightly larger than the packet times, the variation in propagation time with position on the earth could be compensated for.

In Roberts method, which has come to be known as **slotted ALOHA**, in contrast to Abramson's **pure ALOHA**, a terminal is not permitted to send whenever a carriage return is typed. Instead, it is required to wait for the beginning of the next slot. Thus the continuous pure ALOHA is turned into a discrete one. Since the vulnerable period is now reduced in half, the probability of no other traffic during the same slot as our test packet is e^{-G} which leads to

$$S = Ge^{-G} \qquad (6\text{-}3)$$

As you can see from Fig. 6-3, slotted ALOHA peaks at $G = 1$, with a throughput of $S = 1/e$ or about 0.368, twice that of pure ALOHA. If the system is operating at $G = 1$, the probability of an empty slot is 0.368 (from Eq. 6-2). The best we can hope for using slotted ALOHA is 37% of the slots empty, 37% successes, and 26% collisions. Operating at higher values of G reduces the number of empties but increases the number of collisions exponentially. To see how this rapid growth of collisions with G comes about, consider the transmission of a test packet. That probability that it will avoid a collision is e^{-G}, the probability that all the other users are silent in that slot. The probability of a collision is then just $1 - e^{-G}$. The probability of a transmission requiring exactly k attempts, (i.e., $k - 1$ collisions followed by one success) is

$$P_k = e^{-G}(1 - e^{-G})^{k-1}$$

The expected number of transmission per carriage return typed, E, is then

$$E = \sum_{k=1}^{\infty} kP_k = \sum_{k=1}^{\infty} ke^{-G}(1 - e^{-G})^{k-1} = e^G$$

As a result of the exponential dependence of E upon G, small increases in the channel load can drastically reduce its performance.

6.1.3. Finite Population ALOHA

The above results have been obtained using the assumption of an infinite number of users. Abramson (1973a) also analyzed slotted ALOHA systems with a finite number of users. We now briefly summarize his results.

Let S_i be the probability of a successful transmission generated by user i. Remember that at equilibrium the throughput rate must equal the rate at which new packets are generated. Let G_i be the total transmission probability (per slot) of user i, including both new packets and retransmissions. Clearly, $S_i \leqslant G_i$. The probability that a given slot will contain a successful packet sent by user i is the probability that user i sends a packet, times the probability that none of the $N - 1$ other users sends a packet:

$$S_i = G_i \prod_{j \neq i} (1 - G_j) \tag{6-4}$$

Let us now specialize Eq. (6-4) to the case of N identical users, each having a throughput of $S_i = S/N$ packets/slot and a total transmission rate of $G_i = G/N$ packets/slot, where $G = \sum G_i$. Substituting into Eq. (6-4), we get

$$S = G\left(1 - \frac{G}{N}\right)^{N-1}$$

As $N \rightarrow \infty$, we can use the fact that

$$\lim_{k \to \infty} \left(1 + \frac{x}{k}\right)^k = e^x$$

to arrive at Eq. (6-3).

From Fig. 6-3 we see that the maximum throughput for an infinite-population slotted ALOHA system occurs at $G = 1$. Abramson (1973a) has shown that this intuitively reasonable result also holds for systems with a finite number of users. The condition for maximum throughput is

$$\sum_{i=1}^{N} G_i = 1 \tag{6-5}$$

Now let us consider two classes of users, for example file transfer users and interactive users. Let there be N_1 of the first kind and N_2 of the second, with throughput S_1 and S_2 respectively (per user). Then Eq. (6-4) reduces to

$$S_1 = G_1(1 - G_1)^{N_1 - 1}(1 - G_2)^{N_2} \tag{6-6}$$

and

$$S_2 = G_2(1 - G_2)^{N_2 - 1}(1 - G_1)^{N_1} \tag{6-7}$$

For maximum throughput we must obey the constraint of Eq. (6-5), which becomes

$$N_1 G_1 + N_2 G_2 = 1 \tag{6-8}$$

We now have three equations in four unknowns (S_1, S_2, G_1, G_2). By using Eq. (6-8), we can eliminate G_2 from the two class throughput equations [Eq's. (6-6) and (6-7)] to yield parametric equations for the throughput, parametrized by G_1.

As a first example, consider $N_1 = 1$ and $N_2 = 1$. This leads to $S_1 = G_1^2$ and $S_2 = (1 - G_1)^2$. S_1, S_2 and $S = S_1 + S_2$ are plotted in Fig. 6-4(a). Notice that when G_1 is close to 0, user 1 hardly ever attempts to send, and user 2 is free to use nearly every slot, so the total throughput is close to one packet per slot. The worst case is when both users attempt to send on every slot with a probability of 0.5. If that happens there is a 25% chance that user 1 will try and user 2 will refrain. Similarly, there is a 25% chance that user 2 will try and user 1 will refrain. The total throughput is therefore 0.5 packet per slot. The conclusion to be drawn from this example is that an asymmetric situation yields a higher throughput than does a symmetric one.

Next let us specialize Eq's. (6-6) and (6-7) to the case of $N_1 = 1$ and $N_2 = \infty$. User 1 might be trying to transfer a large file, whereas the remaining users are doing interactive work. To keep the total traffic finite, we must let $G_2 \to 0$ in such a way that $G = N_2 G_2$ remains finite. Letting $S = N_2 S_2$ we get

$$S_1 = G_1 e^{-G}$$

and

$$S = Ge^{-G}(1 - G_1)$$

The condition for maximum total throughput is now $G_1 + G = 1$, which allows

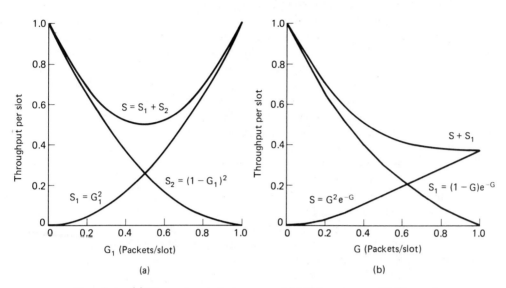

Fig. 6-4. (a) Throughput of a two-user ALOHA system.   (b) Throughput of an ALOHA system with one large and many small users.

us to plot S_1, S, and the total throughput, $S_1 + S$, as a function of G. This plot is given in Fig. 6-4(b). When G is small, the interactive users are not doing much, and the single "large" user can continuously send packets without collisions, thus achieving a very high total channel utilization. As G increases, the interactive traffic claims a larger portion of the available bandwidth and the large user is forced to send less to maintain the total offered traffic at one packet per slot.

6.1.4. Delay and Throughput of Slotted ALOHA

The throughput is not the only parameter we are interested in. The mean packet delay is also important, especially for interactive users. Just as with store-and-forward networks, we shall discover that high throughput and low delay are inherently in conflict. Good performance on one of them can be achieved only at the expense of the other.

In store-and-forward networks, the delay comes from queueing within the IMPs. In ALOHA, the delay comes from collisions, forcing some packets to be retransmitted over and over. Due to the long round-trip propagation delay, R, each collision introduces a delay of at least R, because it takes that long to determine whether or not the packet transmission was successful. If a packet collides three times, the delay between first transmission and successful delivery will be at least $4R$. Depending on how long the wait between a collision and the retransmission is, the delay may be considerably more.

To study the distribution of delay times, we will adopt the following model. N identical users each generate *new* packets according to a Poisson distribution with a mean $p \ll 1$ packets per slot when not blocked. Retransmissions are not counted in p. If the mean think time is T_1 and the slot time is T_2, then $p = T_2/T_1$. Alternatively, p can be thought of as the probability of a given (unblocked) user generating a packet in a given slot. Since the *total* traffic, new packets plus retransmissions, must be one packet/slot for maximum throughput, the total rate at which new packets are introduced into the system must be less than 1 (i.e. $Np < 1$).

When a user types a line, he is blocked and stops thinking, as in our previous model. We could allow the terminal to buffer several packets in order to allow the user to continue immediately, but this complicates the analysis. Furthermore, it affects the system stability adversely, as we shall see later. Our goal is to compute the mean time between a user typing a carriage return and the packet being correctly received by the remote computer. We have used the model of people sitting at terminals (rather than having all nodes be computers) for its anthropomorphic value, but the analysis is identical for computer-computer communication, of course. However, for the sake of generality, we will use the neutral term "stations" from now on.

A key parameter in the model is how the station randomizes its waiting times before attempting a retransmission. In slotted ALOHA the waiting time consists of an integral number of slots to be skipped before trying again. If the mean number of slots skipped is short, the chance for the same collision occurring again is large. For example, if two stations collide and each waits either zero or one slot with equal probability, the chance for an identical collision the second time is 0.5. On the other hand, if the retransmissions are spread out uniformly over the next 100 slots, the chance of the same packets colliding again is 0.01. Of course, the mean delay in the latter case will be much greater than in the former. This is the heart of the throughput-delay trade-off for ALOHA systems.

A reasonable algorithm to use for deciding how many slots to skip is to redistribute packets uniformly into the next L slots. Allowing for a round-trip propagation delay of R slots, the number of slots between the first and second transmission may be $R + 1$, $R + 2$, $\ldots$, $R + L$, each with probability $1/L$.

Unfortunately, this randomization strategy is difficult to model, largely on account of the satellite propagation delay. Instead, we will adopt a probabilistic model in which a previously collided packet (called a "backlogged" packet henceforth) is retransmitted with probability α in all slots following the original transmission until it is sent. In this model the mean delay before retransmission is geometrically distributed, with the probability of a k slot delay given by $\alpha(1 - \alpha)^{k-1}$. The mean delay before retransmission is

$$\sum_{k=1}^{\infty} \alpha k (1 - \alpha)^{k-1} = \frac{1}{\alpha}$$

Notice that we are including the retransmission slot itself in the delay. Also remember that this delay is not the time the station is blocked, because a packet may have to be retransmitted many times and this delay corresponds only to the interval between consecutive retransmissions; it does not take into account how many such intervals are needed.

Using simulation, Lam (1974) has shown that the final result is sensitive to the assumed mean delay between retransmission attempts but not to the shape of the curve. By equating the mean delay in the probabilistic model to the mean delay in reality,

$$\frac{1}{\alpha} = R + \frac{L + 1}{2}, \tag{6-9}$$

we can use the probabilistic model, determine the optimal value for α, and later deduce the appropriate value of L to use in reality.

The state of the ALOHA system can be completely described by telling how many stations are blocked. In state k, there are k packets backlogged. Each of the backlogged stations may decide to retransmit its one and only backlogged packet, with the probability of transmission being α and the probability of skipping the current slot being $1 - \alpha$. In addition to the mean retransmission traffic of $k\alpha$ packets per slot, the $N - k$ unblocked stations are busy generating new packets at a collective rate of $(N - k)p$ packets per slot.

The state of the system varies from slot to slot as new packets become backlogged and as backlogged packets are finally transmitted successfully. Unlike our earlier derivation of the M/M/1 queueing system, this is not a birth-death process, because state changes are not always to adjacent states. For example, three new packets could become backlogged during one slot. Figure 6-5 shows the allowed transitions for a three station system. Although the state may increase by more than one during a given slot, decreases are always in units of one, since the backlog can be reduced by at most one during a single slot. Interestingly enough, the transition from 0 to 1 is impossible, because if there is no backlog and exactly one station decides to transmit, the transmission will always be successful.

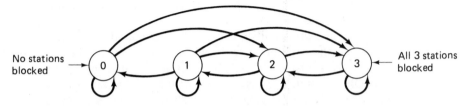

Fig. 6-5. Allowed transitions for a three state Markov model of slotted ALOHA.

An ALOHA system that moves around among a finite number of discrete states in discrete time steps can be modeled using a Markov process (Carleial and Hellman, 1975; Kleinrock and Lam, 1975).

To analyze the behavior of a Markov process, we need to calculate the probability, p_{ij}, that a system in state i moves to state j in the next time slot. For convenience, we introduce the notation that n represents the total number of *new* packets generated by the $N - i$ unblocked stations during the current slot, with $0 \leqslant n \leqslant N - i$. Similarly, r represents the number of retransmissions attempted by the i backlogged stations during the same time interval, with $0 \leqslant r \leqslant i$. Thus $\Pr[n = 0]$ is the probability that no new packets are generated during the current slot, and $\Pr[r \geqslant 1]$ is the probability that one or more of the backlogged stations attempt a retransmission during the current slot. With this notation, the transition probabilities can be written as in Fig. 6-6(a). The event probabilities are given in Fig. 6-6(b) both for the case of finite N and p and for the limit $N \to \infty$, $p \to 0$, $Np \to S$.

As an example, consider a slotted ALOHA system with three users, $p = 0.1$, and $\alpha = 0.2$. The transition probabilities are given in Fig. 6-7(a). Notice that each row sums to 1.000 because the probability that the system moves from its current state to *some* state is unity.

Initially, the system starts in state 0, with all stations unblocked. As time goes on, it approaches equilibrium. This does not mean that it is always in the same state, only that the probability of finding the system in state k does not depend on time (as it does in the early history). To solve for the equilibrium probability, e_k, of finding the system in state k, we must solve the simultaneous linear equations

$$e_k = \sum_{i=0}^{N} e_i p_{ik} \qquad (k = 0, \ldots, N)$$

subject to the constraint that $\Sigma e_k = 1$. Consider one of the equations for $N = 3$:

$$e_0 = e_0 p_{00} + e_1 p_{10} + e_2 p_{20} + e_3 p_{30}$$

Each term on the right-hand side corresponds to the probability of making the transition to state 0 from one of the states (including 0). The $N + 1$ equations are not independent, which is why the additional constraint of requiring the probabilities to sum to unity is needed.

The equilibrium state probabilities can also be calculated in another way. If we take the matrix p_{ij} and multiply it by itself, we get a new matrix, $p_{ij}^{(2)}$, which represents the two-step transition probabilities. For example, $p_{03}^{(2)}$ is the probability that an ALOHA system that is in state 0 during a certain slot will be in state 3 two slots later. By multiplying p_{ij} by itself repeatedly, we can get the n-step transition probabilities, each matrix multiplication adding one new step. For a well behaved Markov process such as ours, successively higher powers of the transition matrix rapidly approach $p_{ij}^{(\infty)}$ which gives the probability of being in state j given that the system was in state i long ago. Obviously this is

$$p_{ij} \quad = \quad 0 \quad (j \leqslant i - 2)$$

$$p_{i,i-1} \quad = \quad \Pr[n = 0] \Pr[r = 1]$$

$$p_{ii} \quad = \quad \Pr[n = 0] \Pr[r \neq 1] + \Pr[n = 1] \Pr[r = 0]$$

$$p_{i,i+1} \quad = \quad \Pr[n = 1] \Pr[r \geqslant 1]$$

$$p_{ij} \quad = \quad \Pr[n = j - i] \quad (j \geqslant i + 2)$$

(a)

Event		Finite case	Infinite case
$\Pr[n = 0]$	$=$	$(1 - p)^{N-i}$	e^{-S}
$\Pr[n = 1]$	$=$	$(N - i)p(1 - p)^{N-i-1}$	Se^{-S}
$\Pr[n = j - i]$	$=$	$\binom{N-i}{j-i} p^{j-i}(1 - p)^{N-j}$	$\dfrac{S^{j-i}}{(j - i)!} e^{-S}$
$\Pr[r = 0]$	$=$	$(1 - \alpha)^i$	$(1 - \alpha)^i$
$\Pr[r = 1]$	$=$	$i\alpha(1 - \alpha)^{i-1}$	$i\alpha(1 - \alpha)^{i-1}$
$\Pr[r \neq 1]$	$=$	$1 - i\alpha(1 - \alpha)^{i-1}$	$1 - i\alpha(1 - \alpha)^{i-1}$
$\Pr[r \geqslant 1]$	$=$	$1 - (1 - \alpha)^i$	$1 - (1 - \alpha)^i$

(b)

Fig. 6-6. (a) State transition probabilities. (b) Probabilities for various events

independent of i, so all the elements in a column of $p_{ij}^{(\infty)}$ are identical. In other words, all the rows are the same, and each one gives the equilibrium state probabilities.

Given the equilibrium state probabilities, we can now find the mean backlog (i.e., the expected number of stations blocked waiting for retransmission):

$$\text{mean backlog} = \sum_{k=0}^{N} k e_k$$

To find the mean throughput of the system, we need to find the throughput for each of the possible states of the system, and then weight them by the equilibrium state probabilities. The throughput in state k is just the probability that a packet is successfully sent given that k stations are blocked and $N - k$

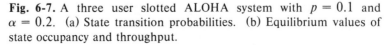

	New state					At equilibrium			
	0	1	2	3		0	1	2	3
0	0.972	0.000	0.027	0.001		0.760	0.131	0.095	0.014
Original state 1	0.162	0.792	0.036	0.010			Throughput		
2	0.000	0.288	0.676	0.036		0	1	2	3
3	0.000	0.000	0.384	0.616		0.243	0.306	0.352	0.384

(a)   (b)

Fig. 6-7. A three user slotted ALOHA system with $p = 0.1$ and $\alpha = 0.2$. (a) State transition probabilities. (b) Equilibrium values of state occupancy and throughput.

are unblocked. A successful transmission can happen in one of two ways:

1. One unblocked station sends a new packet; no retransmissions.

2. No new packets; exactly one retransmission attempted.

The probability of this occurring is just

$$f_k = \Pr[n = 1]\ Pr[r = 0] + Pr[n = 0]\ Pr[r = 1] \qquad (6\text{-}10)$$

The mean throughput can now be found:

$$\text{mean throughput} = \sum_{k=0}^{N} e_k f_k$$

The equilibrium state probabilities and throughputs for our three station example are shown in Fig. 6-7(b).

We now have enough information to find the mean delay as well. It is just the mean backlog divided by the mean throughput i.e.

$$\frac{\displaystyle\sum_{k=0}^{N} k e_k}{\displaystyle\sum_{k=0}^{N} f_k e_k}$$

This is essentially Little's result in disguise. Suppose, for example, that the mean backlog is eight packets and the mean throughput is 0.25 packet/slot. If the stations queued up nicely, it would take 32 slots for a newly blocked station to work its way to the front of the queue. Nevertheless, the system can be seen as a single-server queue in which the queueing discipline is not first come, first served. Instead, a random customer is plucked from the middle of the queue each time and served.

Figure 6-8 shows the throughput as a function of G, the delay as a function of G, and finally the throughput-delay trade-off, using the Markov model. What is important to note is that the delay is small as long as G is small. However, as soon as the system begins operating at too high a G value, the delay skyrockets due to collisions, and the throughput falls back. Notice the resemblance of Fig. 6-8(a) to the infinite-population model of Fig. 6-3, as well as the resemblance of Fig. 6-8(b) to our earlier result $E = e^G$ (also for infinite population).

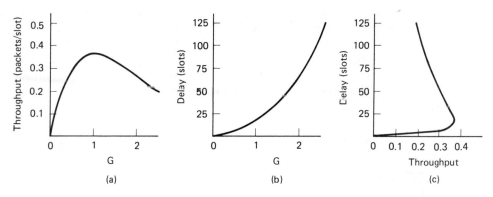

Fig. 6-8. Throughput and delay computed from the Markov model with $N = 25$ and $\alpha = 0.1$.

6.1.5. Stability of Slotted ALOHA

Some ALOHA systems are inherently stable and others are inherently unstable. Due to random statistical fluctuations, once in a while an unusually large number of unblocked stations will attempt to send during the same slot. There will be a collision and all the packets will become backlogged. Due to the large number of backlogged packets, there will be many collisions in the succeeding slots and the throughput will be less than normal. As new packets are generated, most of them also become backlogged. Eventually, all N stations become backlogged, and from Eq. (6-10) we get

$$\text{throughput} = N\alpha(1 - \alpha)^{N-1} \tag{6-11}$$

Equation (6-11) suggests that by making α small, we can achieve non-negligible throughput even when the system is badly backlogged. This observation is true, but the price we must pay is long delay times. By Eq. (6-9) a small value of α corresponds to a large value of L. In other words, the random time waited between retransmissions rises quickly with decreasing α. If 1000 backlogged stations spread their retransmissions out over a million slots, the chance of a collision will be negligible, but the price paid is terrible response.

To investigate the stability of slotted ALOHA, we need a relation between mean backlog and mean throughput. Typically p is a given quantity i.e., the slot time divided by the mean think time of the user population. Using Eq. (6-10), it is straightforward to calculate the throughput as a function of the backlog. Figure 6-9(a) shows a typical throughput-backlog relationship. When the backlog has reached 60 packets, at $\alpha = 0.1$ we are attempting to retransmit 6.0 packets/slot, not to mention any new packets. Thus it is not surprising that the throughput is low. For 60 backlogged stations and $\alpha = 0.02$, the retransmitted packets represent a load of only 1.2 packets/slot, which is only slightly higher than the optimal value of G.

As more stations become backlogged, the rate of new packet generation drops linearly. With k stations backlogged, the input rate is $(N - k)p$. The input rate as a function of the backlog is shown in Fig. 6-9(b) for the case of $p = 0.002$ and $N = 100$. Such a plot is referred to as a **load line** (Kleinrock and Lam, 1975). The slope of the load line is $-p$; its x intercept is N.

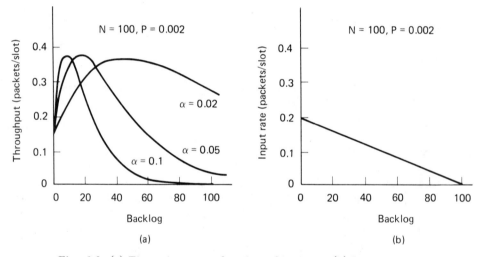

Fig. 6-9. (a) Throughput as a function of backlog. (b) Input rate as a function of backlog.

At equilibrium, the throughput rate must equal the input rate. By drawing the throughput curve and the load line on the same graph, we can find their intersections, as shown in Fig. 6-10. Four cases are depicted in Fig. 6-10. In the first case, N is small, the system is lightly loaded, and equilibrium is achieved with a low backlog. So little traffic is offered that packets nearly always get through the first time and no backlog builds up.

Nevertheless, it is important to realize what happens if a sudden fluctuation in input moves the system to a high backlog, as shown by the dotted vertical

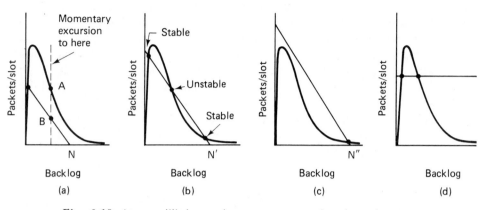

Fig. 6-10. At equilibrium, input rate equals throughput rate.
(a) Stable, low delay. (b) Bistable. (c) Stable, high delay.
(d) Unstable.

line. The throughput is now at point *A* and the input is at point *B*. Since *A* is higher than *B*, the throughput exceeds the input rate, which drives the backlog down to the equilibrium point. Any excursion above equilibrium produces a throughput higher than the rate at which new packets are generated. Similarly, an excursion to the left drops the throughput so sharply that the backlog builds up again. No matter what the backlog is, there are forces driving the system inexorably back to the equilibrium point. If the load line crosses the throughput curve in exactly one place, the system is globally stable and will always return to the equilibrium point after any excursion, no matter how big it may be. Lam (1974) has shown that the values of backlog and throughput at the equilibrium point are excellent approximations to the true mean backlog and mean throughput calculated by forming a weighted sum over all possible system states.

Now let us be greedy and increase the number of users, so that the load line moves up to the position of Fig. 6-10(b). The load line intersects the throughput curve in three places. At all three points the input rate equals the throughput rate, so each one represents a possible equilibrium point. However, only two of them are stable. First consider the low backlog equilibrium point. For small excursions either way, the situation of Fig. 6-10(a) prevails and the system is stable. At the middle equilibrium point, the situation is exactly reversed. If the backlog increases momentarily, the throughput drops faster than the input rate, so the backlog becomes even larger. The situation feeds upon itself until the system reaches the high backlog equilibrium point, which is again stable. Figure 6-10(b) is bistable. The two equilibrium points correspond to nearly no one backlogged and nearly everyone backlogged, respectively.

Being even more greedy, as in Fig. 6-10(c), is like killing the goose that laid the golden egg. The channel is now completely overloaded. The only equilibrium point is when the input rate and throughput are both very close to zero. When there are an infinite number of users, the input rate does not drop as the backlog increases, so we get the situation of Fig. 6-10(d): one stable and one unstable equilibrium point. If the system ever manages to get into a high backlog state, the input rate will continue to exceed the throughput rate and the backlog will grow without bound.

Carleial and Hellman (1975) have expressed the stability problem in a slightly different form. They pointed out that the mean drift of the system in state i is

$$\sum_{j=0}^{N} (j - i)p_{ij}$$

States with a drift of 0 are equilibrium points. If the slope of the drift curve at the equilibrium point is negative, the equilibrium is stable, because increases in the backlog tend to make the system drift downward, and vice versa.

An interesting question about the bistable situation of Fig. 6-10(b) is: What is the chance of the system getting itself into the high backlog stable state? Intuitively, the farther down the "hill" the low backlog stable equilibrium point is, the less likely it is that a momentary burst of activity will push the system past the point of no return.

To calculate the probability of an initially empty system being near the unstable equilibrium point after a given number of slots, proceed as follows. Take the state-transition matrix and make state k absorbing by setting $p_{kk} = 1$ and all the other elements of row k to 0. With this new matrix if the system ever gets to state k, it will stay there. This model is an approximation, because the chance of spontaneously escaping from the unstable region, however small, is not zero. By computing successive powers of the transition matrix, we get the multistep transition probabilities. The element p_{0k} gives the probability of the system having reached state k starting from an empty system. By plotting p_{0k} against the power of the transition matrix, we get the probability of reaching the unstable state with the corresponding time interval.

Figure 6-11(a) shows the throughput rate, input rate, and load line for 25 stations and $p = 0.01$. The corresponding multistep transition probabilities, p_{0N} are shown in Fig. 6-11(b). With $\alpha = 0.25$ there is a 50% chance that the backlog will grow to 25 within 10,000 slots. With $\alpha = 0.40$ the 50% point has dropped to 1000 slots. With these parameters, the system will collapse within seconds of being started up. By adjusting α it is possible to trade off stability against delay. Since the mean delay is closely approximated by the backlog divided by the throughput at the equilibrium point, from Fig. 6-11 it is easy to see that the stability is more sensitive to α than the delay. Consequently, system designers have some latitude in choosing a value of α that is small enough to provide good stability, without extracting too heavy a price in terms of excessive delay.

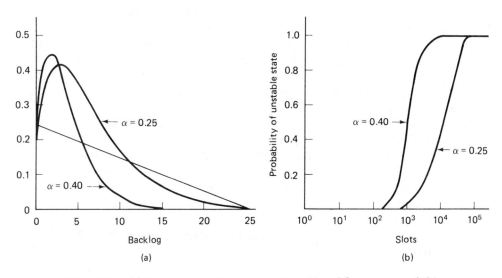

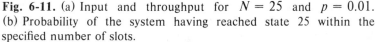

Fig. 6-11. (a) Input and throughput for $N = 25$ and $p = 0.01$. (b) Probability of the system having reached state 25 within the specified number of slots.

6.1.6. Controlled ALOHA

The only way to guarantee a stable system with a fixed α is to restrict the number of users to such a low value that the load line crosses the throughput curve in only one place. Doing so is often uneconomical, because it gears the system to worst-case behavior. Put in other words, setting the parameters so as to guarantee stable operation until all circumstances, no matter how unlikely, restricts the number of users to a value so small that the system may cost to be economically justified. However, as we can see from Fig. 6-9(a), α has an important influence on the shape of the throughput curve, and hence on the stability. If we could somehow decrease α when the system got into trouble, we could raise the throughput curve above the load line and make the system stable. Ideally, we would like α large when the backlog is small (to get rid of packets quickly and achieve a short delay time), and small when the backlog is large (to drive the backlog down).

Several methods have been proposed (Lam and Kleinrock, 1975) for controlling α dynamically in order to achieve short delays when the system is lightly loaded and stable behavior when it is not. One method is simply to have each station keep track of how many retransmissions the packet currently in the output buffer has to its credit. When a packet is first generated, the counter is set to zero. Upon each collision, it is increased by one. The value of the counter can be used as a crude measure of the channel load. The station could have a series of (fixed) retransmission probabilities, α_i (i.e., randomization intervals, L_i), subject to $\alpha_{i+1} \leqslant \alpha_i$. As the channel load increases, every station attempting to transmit will automatically wait longer and longer between successive retransmissions. This method has the advantage that it relies only on information directly available to the station (i.e., it does not require the station to monitor the channel other than to see if its own packets have collided). It has the disadvantage, however, that each packet must learn about the channel load all over again.

Lam and Kleinrock (1975) have studied another controlled ALOHA method that does retain some history, so that new packets can profit from their predecessors' experience. In his scheme, there are only two values for α, a large one that is used when the system is operating properly, and a small one that is used when the system gets into trouble. Whenever the collision rate exceeds a certain threshold value, all stations switch to the lower value and continue to use it until things are back to normal.

A more direct approach to the control problem is based on Abramson's observation that the throughput is maximized at $G = 1$. The goal of this method is to have each station estimate G and adjust its own value of α upward if $G < 1$ and downward if $G > 1$.

To estimate G, we can use Eq. (6-2). The probability of an empty slot, P_0, is $G^0 e^{-G}/0!$ which is just e^{-G}. Taking logarithms, we have $G = -\ln P_0$. P_0 can be easily estimated by noting the fraction of slots that were empty during the recent past. This requires a shift register with 1 bit per slot. The observation period should be longer than the round-trip time, to prevent instabilities.

When the channel is lightly loaded, we would like α as large as possible, subject to the constraint of Eq. (6-10). When the channel is heavily loaded, we want α to become small. There exist many functions of G that are suitable for computing α from G, for example $\alpha = e^{-G}/(R + 1)$. This function ensures that we do not attempt to reduce L below 1, even when the channel is idle. The function is also easy to compute, because e^{-G} is just the fraction of the shift register positions containing 0 (no collision).

Gerla and Kleinrock (1977a) have proposed another method based on estimating G. Their method is designed to handle the case of stations that do not block when a packet is generated, but just keep on going. As a result, two queues may build up in each station: virgin packets that have not been sent yet and packets that are waiting for retransmission. Different probabilities are used for these queues. They propose that each packet header contain the probabilities currently in use at the sender's station. In this way each station can set its parameters to be equal to the mean of everyone else's, plus a correction term of the form $(1 - G)\Delta$, where Δ is an experimentally determined constant. When $G > 1$, the correction term is negative, decreasing the appropriate α; when $G < 1$, α is increased. The feedback inherent in this proposal ensures that the probabilities only change slowly and, furthermore, that no station gets too far out of step with the others.

6.1.7. Reservation ALOHA

Even the most clever, dynamically adjusted control scheme will never get the throughput of a slotted ALOHA channel above $1/e$ (except for small N). However, at high channel loads, there are other methods for making good use of a single shared channel, in particular, time-division multiplexing. Several researchers have proposed control schemes that act like normal or nearly normal slotted ALOHA at low channel utilization, and move gradually over to some kind of TDM as the channel load grows.

All these methods have one feature in common: some slots are reserved for specific stations. Stations are required to refrain from attempting to use a slot reserved for somebody else. The methods differ in the way reservations are made and released. For comparison, remember that in TDM the slots are organized into frames of N slots, with each slot permanently reserved for a specific station.

Binder (1975) proposed a method that starts out with the basic TDM model and adapts to slotted ALOHA for low channel utilization. As in TDM, N consecutive slots are grouped together into a frame, with each station "owning" one frame position. If there are more slots than stations, the extra slots are not assigned to anyone. If the owner of a slot does not want it during the current frame, he does nothing. An empty slot is a signal to everyone else that the owner has no traffic. During the next frame, the slot becomes available to anyone who wants it, on a contention basis. If the owner wants to retrieve "his" slot, he transmits a packet, thus forcing a collision (if there was other traffic). After a collision, everyone except the owner must desist from using the slot. Thus the owner can always begin transmitting within two frame times in the worst case. At low channel utilization the system does not perform as well as normal slotted ALOHA, since after each collision, the collidees must abstain for one frame to see if the owner wants the slot back. Figure 6-12(a) shows a frame with eight slots, seven of which are owned.

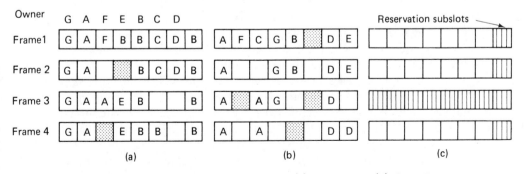

Fig. 6-12. Reservation   schemes.   (a) Binder.   (b) Crowther. (c) Roberts. The shaded boxes indicate collisions.

One slight inefficiency with this method is that whenever the owner of a slot is through with it, the position must go idle during the next frame to announce that its owner is done. To eliminate this wasted slot, an extra bit could be added to the header of all packets to announce that the owner did or did not have any more data for the next frame.

A much more serious problem, however, is that the number of users must be known in advance, or at least bounded from above. If this is not the case, several users could be assigned to the same slot, in the hope that it will not occur too often that both of them claim the slot simultaneously. To arbitrate when this does happen, each user could be given a static priority, with lower-priority users deferring to higher ones in the case of conflict.

Crowther et al. (1973) have proposed a different reservation method that is applicable even when the number of stations is unknown and varying dynamically. In their method, slots do not have permanent owners, as in Binder's, but instead, whenever a transmission is successful, the station making the successful transmission is entitled to that slot in the next frame as well. Thus as long as a station has data to send, it can continue doing so indefinitely (subject to some "Please-do-not-be-a-pig" rules). Since it is unlikely that all stations will have long runs of data to send simultaneously, this method works well even when the number of slots per frame is far less than the number of stations. In essence the proposal allows a dynamic mix of slotted ALOHA and TDM, with the number of slots devoted to each varying with demand. Figure 6-12(b) shows a frame with eight slots. Initially, E is using the last slot, but after two frames, it no longer needs it. It lies idle for one frame, and then D picks it up and keeps it until he is done.

A third scheme, due to Roberts (1973), requires stations to make advance requests before transmitting. Each frame contains one special slot [the last one in Fig. 6-12(c)], which is divided into V smaller subslots used to make reservations. When a station wants to send data, it broadcasts a short request packet during one of the reservation subslots. If the reservation is successful, (i.e., no collision), then the next regular slot (or slots) is reserved. At all times everyone must keep track of the queue length, so that when any station makes a successful reservation it will know how many data slots to skip before transmitting. Stations need not keep track of *who* is queued up; they merely need to know how long the queue is. When the queue length drops to zero, all slots revert to reservation subslots, to speed up the reservation process.

To see if satellite packet broadcasting worked as well in practice as it does in theory, starting in 1975, DARPA (née ARPA) began supporting an experimental packet broadcasting system using a 64 kbps Intelsat IV satellite channel (Chu et al., 1979; Jacobs et al., 1978; Jacobs et al., 1979; Kahn, 1979). The paper by Kahn is especially interesting; it describes the legal hurdles faced by DARPA, even though the project was clearly a research experiment, and was sponsored by the U. S. government.

The satellite network, known as SATNET, uses large ground stations in

Etam, West Virginia; Goonhilly, England; and Tanum, Sweden; and a smaller ground station in Clarksburg, Maryland. The protocol used, called **PODA** (Priority Oriented Demand Assignment), has two variants, **FPODA** (Fixed PODA), which is essential TDM, and **CPODA** (Contention PODA), which is a sophisticated version of Roberts' reservation scheme.

Each frame is divided into a data part and a control part for reservations. The relative sizes of the two parts are dynamically adjusted depending on the load. A portion of the data part is reserved for FPODA, providing guaranteed bandwidth for those processes needing it. The rest of the data part is used by CPODA. An interesting feature of CPODA is the ability to piggyback reservation requests onto data packets, with the consequence that heavy users of the channel do not have to keep fighting for reservation slots. The reservation information includes the size of the packet to be sent and the priority, and this information is used in the scheduling of the channel rather than simply using first come, first served. A sophisticated scheduling algorithm is needed since packet speech is transmitted, as well as data.

6.2. PACKET RADIO

Ground radio packet broadcasting differs from satellite packet broadcasting in several ways. In particular, stations have limited range, introducing the need for radio repeaters, which in turn affects the routing and acknowledgement schemes. Also, the propagation delay is much less than for satellite broadcasting. In the following sections we will look at some of the ways in which ground radio differs from satellite packet broadcasting. More details are provided in (Gitman et al., 1976; Kahn, 1977, Kahn et al., 1978; and Tobagi, 1980b, 1980c).

6.2.1. The University of Hawaii ALOHA System

The first computer system to employ radio instead of point-to-point wires for its communication facility was the ALOHA system at the University of Hawaii. The system first went on the air in 1971, and has been evolving ever since. Since this system is the ancestor of all packet broadcasting systems, we describe it below in some detail. For a more complete description, see (Abramson 1970, 1973b; and Binder et al., 1975).

The ALOHA system was begun to allow people at the University of Hawaii, who were spread out over seven campuses on four islands, to access the main computer center on Oahu without using telephone lines, which were expensive and unreliable. Communication is provided by equipping each station with a small FM radio transmitter/receiver with sufficient range (30 km) to talk to the computer center's transmitter/receiver. Later, a powerful repeater was introduced, increasing the theoretical range to 500 km.

All communication is either from a station to the computer center or from the computer center to a station. There is no station-to-station communication. When a packet is received at the computer center, it is processed there. It is not retransmitted for all other stations to hear. This arrangement is fundamentally different from the satellite broadcasting model, in which the satellite is merely a big repeater in the sky. Since incoming packets are not rebroadcast, a station has no way of knowing whether or not its transmission was received correctly by the central site. As a result, explicit acknowledgements are needed, just as in point-to-point connections.

After overcoming some initial skepticism about the unusual communication mechanism, the project was assigned two bands in the UHF part of the spectrum. One frequency band, at 407.350 MHz, is used for inbound traffic, from stations to the central site. The other frequency band, at 413.475 MHz, is used for outbound traffic, from the central site to the stations. Transmission is at 9600 bps. The use of distinct channels for inbound and outbound traffic has important implications for the whole system organization. After several years of experience, the research group concluded that a single channel probably would have been a better idea.

The original rationale for having two distinct channels was the fundamental difference in the inbound and outbound traffic. Inbound, many uncoordinated users are competing for access to a shared resource. Outbound, a single site is in complete control of the channel, so there is no contention and no collisions. The basic idea is to use the inbound channel on a random access (what is now called pure ALOHA) basis, and the outbound channel on a straight broadcasting basis, with each station extracting those packets directed to it from the output stream.

Figure 6-13 shows the essential elements of the ALOHA system. At the central site is a 32K HP 2100 minicomputer, called the Menehune (the Hawaiian word for "imp") that is connected to the antenna. All data in or out of the central site passes through it. The Menehune, in turn, is connected to two large computers, an IBM 370 and the BCC 500, as well as to two other networks, ARPANET and PACNET. Each station has a control unit that buffers some text and handles retransmissions. The original control units were hardwired, but later Intel 8080s were used to provide more flexibility. Some stations are connected to concentrators to reduce transmitter/receiver costs.

Packets consist of four parts. First comes a 32-bit header, containing, among other things, the user identification and the packet length. To provide good reliability, the header is followed by a 16-bit checksum. Next comes the data, up to 80 bytes (640 bits), followed by another checksum. The maximum packet is $32 + 16 + 640 + 16 = 704$ bits. At 9600 bps, the transmission time for the longest packet is 73 msec.

When a station has data to send, it just goes ahead and sends. This way of operating is ALOHA at its purest. When the Menehune correctly receives a packet, it inserts an acknowledgement packet into the output stream. If a

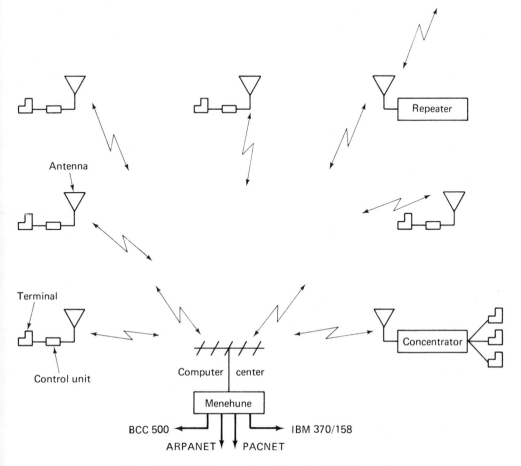

Fig. 6-13. The University of Hawaii ALOHA system.

station does not receive an acknowledgement within a preset time, it assumes that the packet suffered a collision, and retransmits it. The retransmission intervals are distributed between 200 and 1500 msec, with various distributions having been tried (e.g., uniform, three shorts and then a long, etc.).

Although control of the outbound channel might at first seem trivial, there are some important design issues here too. For one thing, transmitting packets on a first come, first served basis is not a good idea, because if an acknowledgement packet is delayed too long, the station will assume that a collision has occurred and send the packet again. Under conditions of heavy load, many unnecessary retransmissions will occur, making the situation even worse. Consequently, the Menehune maintains a separate queue for acknowledgement packets and gives this queue priority over the data queue.

The use of store-and-forward repeaters (to amplify signals and thus increase their range) introduces some problems. The repeaters use the same frequency for output as for input. This means that a repeater cannot start the retransmission until the input has been completely received and stored; otherwise, they would overlap and be unintelligible. If the Menehune broadcasted a new packet while a repeater was still forwarding an old one, stations within range of both the repeater and the Menehune would receive the superposition of the two packets, which is meaningless. Furthermore, while forwarding a packet, the repeater is not able to accept new packets. Consequently, the Menehune must be careful about the order in which it sends packets, and it must take the repeater geometry into account when making scheduling decisions.

Another problem unique to ALOHA is the way in which errors are handled. Because packets are not rebroadcast for all to hear, the Menehune must send acknowledgement packets back to the stations. Doing so is straightforward and causes no problems. What does cause problems is the Menehune's lack of knowledge about whether or not its transmissions are being correctly received. In an urban area, such as around Honolulu, there are many electrical devices that can cause static on an FM radio.

The obvious solution is to have the stations acknowledge reception of computer data, as well as vice versa. The trouble is, these acknowledgements must be sent in the random access channel, where it's dog eat dog. The probability of an acknowledgement being delayed for a substantial period of time due to collisions and timeouts is much greater than on a point-to-point line. If the acknowledgement is delayed too long, the Menehune times out and tries again, wasting valuable bandwidth.

The worst part of it is, the station has no way of knowing whether or not its acknowledgement has gotten through. One solution would be to have the acknowledgements themselves be acknowledged. This solution is not used. Instead, output packets are numbered. The Menehune simply refrains from sending a new output packet until the previous one has been acknowledged. When a station receives a new output packet, it knows that its last acknowledgement has arrived.

Yet another peculiar property of packet broadcasting that was first noticed in the ALOHA system is the need to decouple the transmission speed from the station speed. In a conventional time-sharing system, the computer knows the speed of all the stations and sends data to them at the correct speed. It does not try to force feed 300 bps hardcopy matrix printers at 9600 bps. There is also no need to, because each station has a dedicated line connecting it to the computer.

In ALOHA, the situation is different. The Menehune could keep track of the printing speed of the recipient of each packet and adjust its bit rate accordingly, but sending a page of output at 300 bps would be a tremendous waste of bandwidth and would adversely affect all other users, even those with fast CRTs. The solution used is to have the Menehune always broadcast at 9600 bps with local buffering provided at the station. Nevertheless, the Menehune must keep track of the actual printing speed, to avoid sending more data before the old data have a chance to be printed.

An alternative solution would be to have the station refrain from sending its acknowledgement until it had finished printing. The trouble with this is that if the acknowledgement were delayed substantially due to collisions, the printer would lie idle, even when there was plenty of work for it. By sending the acknowledgement as quickly as possible (i.e., as soon as the data are received), the printer can be kept busy at the expense of some complexity in the Menehune.

6.2.2. Design Issues for Packet Radio Networks

In the preceding section we looked at the original ALOHA system as an example of a ground radio packet broadcasting system. In this section we will examine some additional design problems often present in these systems. The introduction of a large number of repeaters, in particular (to increase the geographic coverage of the system), brings with it a number of complications because repeaters store incoming packets and then rebroadcast them on the same frequency. Simultaneous reception and transmission is therefore impossible.

Let us first look at the conceptual model of a packet radio system. There are (at least) three situations in which packet radio is attractive as a method of local distribution from a central site to remote stations.

1. The stations are located in areas where the telephone system is poorly developed or nonexistent: nearly all rural areas, and most of the Third World falls into this category. Automated weather and seismic data collection stations are often parachuted into jungles, deserts, and hostile mountain terrain, which frequently lack the amenities of civilization, such as telephone poles.

2. The stations are mobile. A fleet of ships is a good example of a group of users that is inherently mobile. Police cars, ambulances, fire engines, and taxis are other examples.

3. The stations have a high peak-to-average traffic ratio, or a low data rate. In both cases, the cost of a dedicated line may make the application uneconomic. Packet radio offers the possibility of sharing a single channel instead of having a large number of channels with fixed (and mostly wasted) capacity. Equation (6-1) tells the whole story.

Although portable FM radio transmitters are usually equipped with a simple whip antenna, which makes them omnidirectional, repeaters may be equipped with omnidirectional or directional antennas, as needed. Repeaters may also be able to adjust their broadcasting power, to increase or decrease their range. If a substantial number of repeaters are battery powered, the system design must be sufficiently redundant to cope with repeaters whose batteries have gone dead, since this will be a regular occurrence.

When a packet radio system contains multiple repeaters, routing becomes an issue again, just as in point-to-point store-and-forward networks. The most naive routing strategy, just having each repeater act as a transponder, storing and forwarding all incoming packets, does not work at all. Every packet would just bounce back and forth between adjacent repeaters forever, clogging up the channel.

When a repeater receives a packet, it must make a decision. To forward, or not to forward, that is the question. The choice of forwarding or discarding is analogous to an IMP's choice of output line in a point-to-point network. The goals of the routing procedure are the same as in all networks, of course: to achieve a high probability of delivering packets to the ultimate destination and to consume the minimum resources in the process.

Gitman et al. (1976) have suggested three possible routing strategies. The first algorithm is a modified version of flooding. Each repeater just forwards all incoming packets, subject to two restraints. The first restraint is a hop counter, which is included in the header of each packet. Each time the packet is forwarded, the hop counter is decremented by one. When this counter gets to zero, the packet is discarded. This rule by itself is sufficient to guarantee that no packet lives forever.

The choice of the initial value of the counter is an important design parameter. If it is too small, packets destined for outlying areas may never arrive. If it is too large, vast numbers of useless duplicates may be generated, wasting precious bandwidth. The problem is complicated by the fact that the central site may only have an approximate idea of the topology, if that much. In Fig. 6-14(a) the shortest path from the station to the central site is two hops, but if the battery in repeater A has become sufficiently drained, it may not have enough power to reach the central site. In that case a hop limit of two in the packet would prevent the packet from ever arriving. With a hop limit of four, the packet could take the other route. The problem of choosing the hop count is closely connected with the problem of ensuring that a point-to-point network has k node disjoint paths between each pair of nodes. As the hop count is allowed to increase, more and more alternate paths become feasible, thereby making the network less and less vulnerable to repeater failures. If each station has a reasonable idea of how many hops it is from the central site, it can choose a hop limit appropriate to its distance rather than having all stations use the worst-case value.

A second restraint that is needed to make flooding a practical algorithm is for repeaters to be able to recognize reruns of packets that they have recently forwarded. Consider the example of Fig. 6-14(b). Suppose that the maximum number of hops for the station shown is set at four. When the packet is

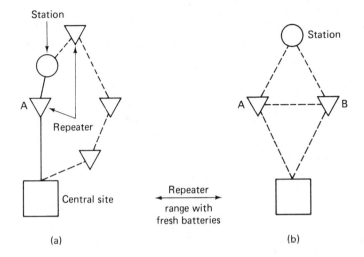

Fig. 6-14. (a) The shortest route from the station to the central site is shown as a solid line. An alternate route is shown as a dashed line. (b) Another repeater topology.

initially transmitted, both *A* and *B* receive and forward it. Each of them hears the other's retransmission (after any collisions have been resolved) and retransmits it again. This goes on for a while until the hop count has been exhausted. The result is a substantial amount of wasted bandwidth.

To alleviate this situation, each repeater can maintain a first-in first-out (FIFO) queue of the most recent *m* packets retransmitted. Whenever a packet comes in, it is checked against the available history and discarded if it is a duplicate. Each new packet causes the oldest one in the FIFO queue to be pushed off the end and lost. Rather than remembering the entire packet, it is sufficient to remember some unique identifier, such as the concatenation of source, destination, and sequence number.

With these two extra rules, flooding is a reasonable algorithm to use in the case of highly mobile stations and/or repeaters. Its attractiveness lies in the fact that it does not depend on any repeater knowing the location of any other one. Nor does it assume any fixed assignment of stations to repeaters. The obvious disadvantage is the large amount of bandwidth it consumes.

The second of the routing algorithms proposed by Gitman et al. is hierarchical routing. The repeaters are organized into a tree, with the central site at the root. (They also consider the case of multiple "central sites," but we will restrict ourselves to just one.) This algorithm requires that the central site be aware of the complete topology. This information can be acquired by having the central site send broadcast probe packets periodically. Each repeater responds to a probe by sending an answer packet. When a repeater forwards an answer packet due to another repeater, it appends its identification to the packet. From the returned answers, the central site can easily determine the shortest path to each repeater. Upon learning the new topology, the central site then informs each repeater of its new label. A label is just a path description, as shown in Fig. 6-15.

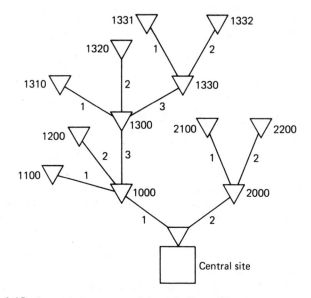

Fig. 6-15. A repeater tree and its labeling. The largest path is four hops, so labels have four fields, with trailing zeros if need be.

Once the repeater tree has been formed, each data packet sent by the central site can contain the label of the repeater to which the station has been assigned. The packet must also contain a pointer telling which field in the label is the current one. When a packet arrives at a repeater, the repeater checks to see if it is named in the current field. If so, it advances the pointer by one field and forwards the packet. If not, it just discards the packet.

To see why this mechanism is needed, consider a packet directed to repeater 1310 in Fig. 6-15. The central site initializes the pointer to the first 1 and broadcasts it. Repeater 1000 knows that it must forward it, and any other repeaters that hear the packet do not forward it. By the time repeater 1300 forwards the packet, the pointer is now pointing at the second 1. Were it not for the pointer, repeater 1000 might detect the packet, see that it was on the path, and forward it again.

If a repeater along the required path has failed, all is not lost. The repeater, failing to get an acknowledgement, could set a bit in the header telling all repeaters to adopt the flooding algorithm for the packet. It could also announce the failure to the central site (assuming that it was still connected), requesting the central site to conduct another probe and relabel the tree.

The broadcast nature of packet radio makes a completely different strategy also possible: the repeater could simply advance the pointer one field, turn up its power, blast away, and hope to skip over the failed repeater. This strategy implies a conservative design, in which repeaters normally operate at less than full power. One problem, however, is that although the correct repeater may receive the packet, it may be too weak to get the acknowledgement all the way back.

In the third routing algorithm, a repeater only forwards a packet if it is closer to the destination than the last repeater that forwarded the packet. Each repeater is assumed to know its distance in hops from every other repeater. This information can be acquired by having each repeater broadcasts its distance table periodically. Each data packet contains the identification of the destination and the sender's distance from that destination. At each hop there is a new sender, and hence a new distance. When a packet arrives at a repeater, the program checks to see if it is closer to the destination than the sender. If so, the packet is heading the right way and is forwarded. If not, the packet is heading the wrong way and is discarded.

As an example, consider Fig. 6-16. When the central site sends a packet to A, it indicates that the distance is three hops. Both J and K receive the initial transmission. J knows that it is only two hops from A, so it forwards the packet, changing the distance in the header to two hops. K knows that it is just as far away as the sender, so it discards the packet. The packet sent by J is received by F, G, H, and K. Of them, F and G are the only ones closer than two hops, so they alone forward the packet, each one changing the distance in the header to 1. A will eventually get two copies of the packet. This algorithm always uses the shortest path, but it is more robust than the previous one, because it concurrently tries all alternate paths whose length are equal to the minimum length. It also consumes more bandwidth. This algorithm is also applicable to station-station traffic rather than just station-central site traffic. A last point in its favor is its ability to easily adapt to mobile repeaters. the ARPANET algorithm adapts to new topologies.

An important design issue that must be resolved no matter which routing algorithm is chosen is the way packets are acknowledged. There is a basic distinction between hop-by-hop acknowledgement and end-to-end acknowledgement. When the error rate is low, the end-to-end scheme may be sufficient, but when the error rate is high, as it is likely to be in a packet broadcasting environment, hop-by-hop should be used in order to detect lost packets as quickly as possible. One property a network of packet repeaters has in common with satellite broadcasting is the ability of a repeater to tell whether or not its neighbor received the packet correctly by just listening to the retransmission. In many cases this may eliminate the need for an explicit acknowledgement. However, some kind of acknowledgement is still needed at the end of the path, because neither the station nor the central site retransmits its input.

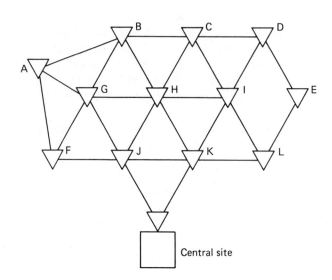

Fig. 6-16. A repeater network. The lines indicate which repeaters are in the range of each other.

Up until now we have made the assumption that when two packets collide, both will be lost. In fact, this is overly pessimistic, since many FM receivers are able to extract the stronger of two overlapping packets without error. This phenomenon is known as the **capture effect**. To see how this influences the system performance, imagine that there are two classes of stations, one broadcasting at high power, and one at low power, (or one group close by and one group far away, both at the same power). If two overlapping packets both originate from the same group, the receiver cannot disentangle them, and both are lost. If, however, they originate from different groups, the stronger one will be accepted. In half the cases, what was previously counted as a collision is now a success! An interesting property of the capture effect is that under conditions of heavy load, stations close to the central site may generate so much traffic that stations farther out are locked out completely. This occurs because when a close in and a far out station collide, the close in station has a stronger signal and always wins. Metzner (1976) has analyzed the capture effect quantitatively.

6.3. SUMMARY

Communication satellites are fundamentally different from terrestrial store-and-forward networks in that they offer a single channel that must be allocated among the users. When there are many bursty users, FDM and TDM are inefficient ways to use the channel, which leads to the ALOHA approach. In

ALOHA systems, stations broadcast at will, detect the presence or absence of collisions themselves, and retransmit if necessary. The key difference between ALOHA and other protocols for controlling a single channel is that in ALOHA there is no centralized channel allocator.

Slotted ALOHA can be modeled as a Markov process. From this Markov model, we can find the equilibrium state occupancies, the mean throughput, and the mean delay, as well as analyzing the stability. To prevent bistable ALOHA systems from moving into the low throughput state, the retransmission probability can be dynamically adjusted. By using various reservation techniques, the throughput can be increased well above the $1/e$ limit of slotted ALOHA.

Packet radio is similar to satellite broadcasting, with the problem of the long propagation delay replaced by the problem of the repeater topology. Routing becomes an issue again, just as in point-to-point networks, and some of the same techniques can be applied to dealing with it.

Be sure you realize how the material of this chapter fits into the layered model of Fig. 1-7. The ALOHA protocols discussed here are alternatives to the point-to-point routing protocols that we studied in Chap. 5. The transport layer, which we will study in Chap. 8, is the same, whether the transmission subsystem uses store-and-forward or packet broadcasting techniques.

PROBLEMS

1. A group of N stations share a 56 kbps pure ALOHA channel. Each station outputs a 1000-bit packet on an average of once every 100 sec, even if the previous one has not yet been sent (e.g., the stations are buffered). What is the maximum value of N?

2. An infinite-population slotted ALOHA system has a packet time equal to k slot times. A packet can begin in any slot. The channel load is G packets per packet time. What is the throughput in packets per packet time? Find the throughput in the limiting cases of $k = 1$ and $k \rightarrow \infty$, and interpret these results.

3. Ten thousand airline reservation stations are competing for the use of a single slotted ALOHA channel. The average station makes 18 requests/hour. A slot is 125 μsec. What is the approximate total channel load?

4. A large population of ALOHA users manages to generate 50 requests/sec, including both originals and retransmissions. Time is slotted in units of 40 msec.
   (a) What is the chance of success on the first attempt?
   (b) What is the probability of exactly k collisions and then a success?
   (c) What is the expected number of transmission attempts needed?

5. Measurements of an infinite user slotted ALOHA channel show that 10% of the slots are idle.

(a) What is the channel load, G?

(b) What is the throughput?

(c) Is the channel underloaded or overloaded?

6. In an infinite-population slotted ALOHA system, the mean number of slots a station waits between a collision and its retransmission is 4. Plot the delay versus throughput curve for this system.

7. A small slotted ALOHA system has only k customers, each of whom has a probability $1/k$ of transmitting during any slot (originals + retransmissions combined). What is the channel throughput as a function of k? Evaluate this expression numerically for $k = 2, 3, 4, 5, 10$ and lim $k \rightarrow \infty$.

8. A slotted ALOHA system has four stations, with transmission rates $G_1 = 0.1$, $G_2 = 0.5$, $G_3 = 0.2$, and $G_4 = 0.2$ packet/slot respectively.

(a) What are the individual throughput rates for each user?

(b) What is the total throughput?

(c) What fraction of the slots are empty?

9. Show that the maximum throughput of a finite population system with identical stations occurs at $G = 1$.

10. To reduce contention on its dispatcher's radio, a taxicab company has decided to slot time into 1-sec intervals. The company then begins hiring unemployed computer science Ph.D's as drivers, since the new system requires its users to speak digitally, in 1 sec bursts. Late one night, only two digital speaking drivers are out, both talking to the dispatcher. The probability that a driver has something to say during a slot is 0.3. In the event of a collision, each one repeats during the succeeding slots with a probability 0.2. Calculate the mean number of slots required per successful transmission. (The night dispatcher speaks only analog, and says nothing.)

11. Consider the behavior of a slotted ALOHA station that does not block when a packet is generated. Instead, the packet is put into the (infinite) transmission queue, and the program continues running. The probability of a packet being generated in any slot is p, irrespective of the queue length. Whenever the queue is nonempty, the station transmits with probability α. The channel load due to other stations is G packets/slot. What is the mean queue length?

12. The value of the throughput in Fig. 6-9 for backlog = 0 appears to be independent of α. Is this generally true? Explain.

13. For a certain $p = 0.01$ ALOHA system, the throughput versus backlog (b) curve can be roughly approximated by $f(b) = b^5 e^{-b}/50$. Draw the curve and from it estimate

(a) the maximum number of users a monostable system can support.

(b) the mean backlog if there are 10 users.

(c) the mean backlog if there are 50 users.

14. In the example of Fig. 6-10(a), the load line crosses the throughput curve before the peak. Are there examples of stable systems in which the load line crosses after the peak? Defend your answer.

15. A slotted ALOHA system with an infinite population has a hardware shift register built into each station to record whether a given slot was used (1) or not (0). The shift register reads: 01101001100000101000. What are the estimates of G and S?

16. A packet radio system using repeaters has the topology shown in Fig. 6-16, where an arc indicates who is within range of whom. A packet is initially broadcast by the central site. During the next slot, J and K rebroadcast it. If flooding is used with a hop count of four, how many repeater-time slots will be occupied if
    (a) repeaters do not have any memory?
    (b) repeaters remember packets they have seen before?
    A repeater-time slot is the use of one repeater for one time slot. Ignore collisions.

17. Referring to Fig. 6-16 again, a packet is sent from the central site to D. Using the third routing algorithm discussed in the text, tell which repeaters forward during which slots, assuming no collisions.

18. A group of $2N$ stations communicate using a slotted ALOHA satellite. The satellite uses the capture effect to resolve collisions. The $2N$ stations are divided into N signal strength classes, each with two members. If each station has a probability p of transmitting during a slot, what is the throughput in the limit $N \to \infty$? Plot the throughput as a function of p and explain in words why the curve has the shape it does.

19. Write a program to simulate slotted controlled ALOHA. Each station should monitor the channel load and increment its value of α by X percent whenever $G < 1$ and decrement it by the same amount if $G > 1$. Assume negligible propagation delay. Examine how X and the length of the shift register affect system performance.

20. Write a program to analyze a Markov model of a two-user slotted ALOHA system with $p = 0.1$ and $\alpha = 0.5$.
    (a) Compute the transition matrix, P.
    (b) Compute the multistep transition matrix, P^i, for $i = 2$ through 10.
    (c) Solve for the equilibrium probabilities and compare with part (b).

7

THE NETWORK LAYER III:

LOCAL NETWORKS

In this chapter we continue our study of alternatives to the classical store-and-forward packet switching subnet of Chap. 5. Like Chap. 6, this chapter deals with broadcast rather than point-to-point media. Also like Chap. 6, the material of this chapter corresponds primarily to layer 3 in the model of Fig. 1-7. However, unlike Chap. 6, we will now restrict ourselves to the case of geographically local networks. This distinction is crucial, as will become apparent shortly.

As a start, let us say what we mean by a local network. Local networks generally have three distinctive characteristics:

1. A diameter of not more than a few kilometers.

2. A total data rate exceeding 1 Mbps.

3. Ownership by a single organization.

Most local networks use broadcasting in their subnets, so it is this type that we will emphasize.

Why is anyone interested in building a local network? Basically there are two reasons, and they are the same reasons that people are interested in networks in general. One reason is to connect together a collection of computers, terminals, and peripherals located in the same building or in adjacent buildings, not only to allow them all to intercommunicate, but also to allow all of them to access a remote host or other network. In the absence of the local network, separate connections would be needed between the remote facility and each of the local machines, whereas with the local network the remote facility need only tap onto the local network in one place. This approach is typically motivated by the prior existence of a large collection of minicomputers that need to talk to each other and to some central computer center.

The other reason there is interest in local networks is to exploit the advantages of functionally distributed computing. In this approach, some of the machines are dedicated to perform specific functions, such as file storage, data base management, terminal handling, and so on. By having different machines perform different tasks, the goal is to make the implementation simpler or more efficient.

Local networks differ from their long-haul cousins in several ways. The key difference is that the designers of long-haul networks are often forced by economic or legal reasons to use the public telephone network, regardless of its technical suitability. In contrast, nothing prevents the designers of a local net from laying their own high-bandwidth cable(s), which they nearly always do. From this one difference spring numerous advantages. To start with, bandwidth is no longer the precious resource it was in the long-haul case, so the designers do not have to stand on their heads to optimize its use. For example, a pipelined subnet protocol becomes unnecessary; stop-and-wait, which is much simpler, will do fine. Similarly, the idea of sending a call setup packet (as in X.25) just to avoid putting full source and destination addresses in each data packet needs rethinking. In fact, many local networks include not only the machine number, but also the process number in both source and destination fields of all packets. Once the setup packet has been eliminated, datagrams become a much more attractive way of operating than they were in the long-haul case. Another major attraction of local nets is the ability of each station (terminal or computer) to sense the state of a common broadcast channel before attempting to use it. This makes all the difference in the world, as we shall see.

In this chapter we will discuss three types of local networks: carrier sense networks, ring networks, and shared-memory networks. Carrier sense and ring networks are conceptually similar to the satellite networks of Chap. 6, although they are technically different. Shared-memory systems are not only technically different from carrier sense, ring, satellite, and radio networks, but conceptually different as well, since all processes in the entire system can share a common address space if they so desire.

Although we will concentrate on the three types of local networks mentioned above, it is worth pointing out that there are some other possibilities too. For example, store-and-forward packet switching—the ARPANET in miniature —is certainly feasible. Time division switching is used as the basis for Datakit (Chesson and Fraser, 1980). Another possibility is a time-division multiplexed bus, a bus with a fixed number of stations operating as a round robin. In turn, each station has permission to transmit a fixed-size packet. HDXP (Jensen, 1978) is a sophisticated implementation of this idea. In HDXP each station has a circular shift register with a read head over one bit position. Any station currently having a 1 bit under its read head may send. The (manual) initialization of the shift registers with exactly one station having a 1 bit in each position avoids conflicts, and allows some stations to have higher priority than others, by giving them more 1 bits.

7.1. CARRIER SENSE NETWORKS

The most common transmission media for carrier sense networks are coaxial cable, twisted pairs, and fiber optics. Coaxial cable and twisted pairs typically are operated in the 1- to 10-Mbps region. Fiber optic systems can run at higher speeds, but they are more difficult to tap onto without weakening the signal appreciably.

Different cable topologies are possible. Four of these are shown in Fig. 7-1. The simplest way to organize a cable network is just to snake a single cable around the building and let each station tap onto it at the nearest point. The disadvantage of this method is that the cable may become very long. Long cables not only complicate the engineering of layer 1, but the performance of the protocols are also affected, as we will show later. To reduce cable length, some cable networks have a vertical "spine" running from the basement to the roof, with a horizontal cable for each floor tapping onto it, as shown in Fig. 7-1(b). The most general possible topology is the tree, as in Fig. 7-1(c), since a network in which there were two paths between some pairs of stations would suffer from interference between the two signals.

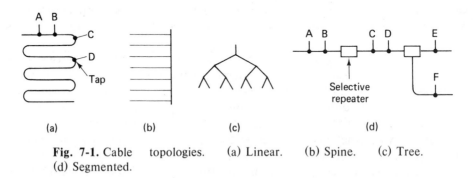

Fig. 7-1. Cable topologies. (a) Linear. (b) Spine. (c) Tree. (d) Segmented.

An alternative way to organize a cable network is as a collection of separate segments. In an unsegmented cable, only one station may transmit at a time, but in a segmented cable, there may be one transmission in progress on each segment simultaneously, because the cables are not directly connected.

Instead, there are **selective repeaters** between segments, which store and then forward packets destined for a segment farther down the line. For example, in Fig. 7-1(d), communication could take place between stations A and B, C and D, as well as E and F simultaneously. Obviously, the repeaters have to know the locations of all stations in order to know whether or not to repeat a given packet onto a given segment, but a station's segment can easily be made part of its address. Notice that a segmented cable consists of segments whose addressing and protocol structures are identical. The more difficult problem of interconnecting heterogeneous networks will be studied in Chap. 8.

7.1.1. Persistent and Nonpersistent CSMA

Packet broadcasting systems that do not suffer from the long propagation delay inherent with geosynchronous satellites differ in many ways from their heavenly cousins. One major difference is that the shorter delay time provides better feedback to the stations about the system state, thus allowing the channel utilization to be pushed way above the $1/e$ limit imposed by slotted ALOHA. In particular, if the propagation delay is short compared to the packet transmission time, a station can listen before sending. It can then base its actions on whether the channel is busy or not. Protocols in which stations listen for a carrier (i.e., a transmission) and act accordingly are called **carrier sense protocols**. Tobagi (1974) has analyzed several such protocols in detail. Below we present a few of his results for slotted and unslotted systems. The result are also given in (Kleinrock and Tobagi, 1975).

All of Tobagi's analyses are based on the following assumptions:

1. All packets are of constant length.

2. There are no errors, except those caused by collisions.

3. There is no capture effect.

4. The random delay after a collision is uniformly distributed and large compared to the packet transmission time.

5. Packet generation attempts (new ones plus retransmissions) form a Poisson process with mean G packets per packet time.

6. A station may not transmit and receive simultaneously.

7. Each station can sense the transmissions of all other stations.

8. The propagation delay is small compared to the packet transmission time, and identical for all stations.

9. Sensing the state of the channel can be done instantaneously.

The first carrier sense protocol is 1-persistent CSMA (Carrier Sense

Multiple Access). When a station has data to send, it first listens to the channel to see if anyone else is transmitting. If the channel is busy, the station waits until it becomes idle. When the station detects an idle channel, it transmits a packet. If a collision occurs, the station waits a random amount of time and starts all over again. The protocol is called 1-persistent because the station transmits with a probability of 1 whenever it finds the channel idle.

The propagation delay has an important effect on the performance of the protocol. There is a small chance that just after a station begins sending, another station will become ready to send and sense the channel. If the first station's signal has not yet reached the second one, the latter will sense an idle channel and will also begin sending, resulting in a collision. The longer the propagation delay is, the more important this effect becomes, and the worse the performance of the protocol.

Even if the propagation delay is zero, there will still be collisions. If two stations become ready in the middle of a third station's transmission, both will wait politely until the transmission ends and then both will begin transmitting exactly simultaneously, resulting in a collision. If they were not so greedy, there would be fewer collisions. Even so, this protocol is far better than pure ALOHA, because both stations have the decency to desist from interfering with the third station's packet. Intuitively, this will lead to a higher performance than pure ALOHA. Exactly the same holds for slotted ALOHA.

Be sure that you realize why 1-persistent CSMA cannot be used with satellite packet broadcasting. If a station listened before sending, it would learn whether or not anyone had any data to send 270 msec ago. That is all well and good but tells nothing at all about whether anyone else has any data to send now. It is like looking at a star in the sky 1000 light-years distant. What you see now is what was going on there 1000 years ago.

For the case of zero propagation time the throughput, (i.e., channel utilization), S, is given by

$$S = \frac{Ge^{-G}(1 + G)}{G + e^{-G}}$$

This result also holds for slotted systems in which the slot time is much smaller than the packet time, and packets can occupy multiple slots. At low G values, the throughput is low due to the presence of G as a factor in the numerator. If no one tries to send, the throughput will be low. As $G \to \infty$, $S \to Ge^{-G}$, which tends to zero.

A second carrier sense protocol is nonpersistent CSMA. In this protocol, an attempt is made to be less greedy than in the previous one. Before sending, a station senses the channel. If no one else is sending, the station begins doing so itself. However, if the channel is already in use, the station does not continually sense it for the purpose of seizing it immediately upon detecting the end of the previous transmission. Instead, it waits a random period of time and then repeats the algorithm. Intuitively this algorithm should lead to better channel utilization and longer delays than 1-persistent CSMA. For the case of zero propagation delay, both the slotted and unslotted versions give the same throughput as a function of demand:

$$S = \frac{G}{1 + G}$$

The last protocol is p-persistent CSMA. It applies to slotted channels and works as follows. When a station becomes ready to send, it senses the channel. If it is idle, it transmits with a probability p. With a probability $q = 1 - p$ it defers until the next slot. If that slot is also idle, it either transmits or defers again, with probabilities p and q. This process is repeated until either the packet has been transmitted or another station has begun transmitting. In the latter case, it acts as if there had been a collision (i.e., it waits a random time and starts again). If the station initially senses the channel busy, it waits until the next slot and applies the above algorithm.

The analysis of this protocol is far more complicated than that for the other two. For zero propagation delay, the throughput is given by

$$S = \frac{Ge^{-G}(1 + pGX)}{G + e^{-G}}$$

where

$$X = \sum_{k=0}^{\infty} \frac{(qG)^k}{(1 - q^{k+1})k!}$$

For all $p > 0$, the throughput drops to 0 as $G \to \infty$. For $p = 0$, the asymptotic throughput is 1.0 but the delay becomes infinite. Figure 7-2 shows the throughput versus offered traffic for all three protocols, as well as pure and slotted ALOHA.

Tobagi also investigated another situation: What happens to the performance if some of the stations are hidden from other stations, for example by hills, buildings, etc. This amounts to dropping assumption 9 above. Not surprisingly, as more and more stations become separated, the performance drop, because a station may think the channel is idle when actually a hidden station is transmitting. For the case where there is a central site visible from all stations, he proposed and analyzed a solution to this problem. Whenever any station begins to transmit, the central site should begin broadcasting a "busy tone" on another channel. By sensing this busy tone a station can tell that a hidden station is transmitting, and thus refrain from doing so itself.

The only complication is that the busy-tone channel also requires some bandwidth. If this bandwidth is kept small, to avoid reducing the normal channel too much, there will be a nonnegligible delay in sensing the busy tone. This delay makes the busy-tone scheme less satisfactory than the case where all stations are within line of sight of each other, but better than the case of just ignoring hidden stations.

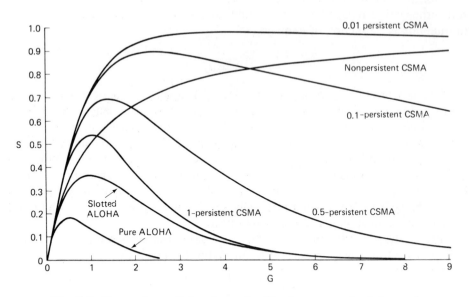

Fig. 7-2. Comparison of the channel utilization versus load for various random access protocols.

7.1.2. Ethernet

Although the carrier sense protocols described above are clearly improvements on pure ALOHA, they, too, can be considerably improved. The main problem with them is that if two stations begin transmitting at the same instant, each will transmit its complete packet, thus wasting the channel for an entire packet time. In 1976, Metcalfe and Boggs of Xerox PARC published a description of a coaxial cable network, **Ethernet**, in which all stations monitor the cable (the ether) during their own transmission, terminating transmission immediately if a collision is detected. This strategy greatly reduces the amount of bandwidth wasted on colliding packets.

The Ethernet mechanism is modeled in Fig. 7-3. At the point marked t_0 a station has finished transmitting its packet. Any other station having a packet to send may now attempt to do so. If two or more stations decide to transmit simultaneously, there will be a collision. Each will detect the collision, abort its transmission, wait a random period of time, and then try again, assuming that no other station has started transmitting in the meantime. Our model for Ethernet will therefore consist of alternating contention and transmission periods, with idle periods occurring when all stations are quiet (e.g., for lack of work).

Now let us look closely at the details of the contention algorithm. Suppose that two stations both begin transmitting at exactly time t_0. How long will it

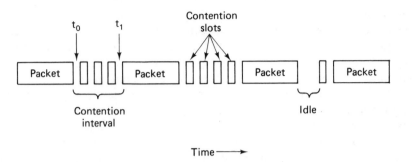

Fig. 7-3. Ethernet can be in one of three states: contention, transmission, or idle.

take them to realize that there has been a collision? The answer to this question is vital to determining how long the contention period will be, and hence what the delay and throughput will be. The minimum time to detect the collision is then just the time it takes the signal to propagate from one station to the other.

Based on this reasoning, you might think that a station not hearing a collision for a time equal to the full cable propagation time after starting its transmission could be sure it had seized the cable. By "seized" we mean that all other stations knew it was transmitting and would not interfere. This conclusion is wrong. Consider the following worst-case scenario. Let the time for a signal to propagate between the two farthest stations be τ. At t_0 one station begins transmitting. At $\tau - \epsilon$, an instant before the signal arrives at the most distant station, that station also begins transmitting. Of course, it detects the collision almost instantly and stops, but the little noise burst caused by the collision does not get back to the original station until time $2(\tau - \epsilon)$. In other words, in the worst case a station cannot be sure that it has seized the channel until it has transmitted for 2τ without hearing a collision. For this reason we will model the contention interval as a slotted ALOHA system with slot width 2τ. On a 1 km long coaxial cable, $\tau = 5\,\mu$sec. For simplicity we will assume that each slot contains just 1 bit. Once the channel has been seized, a station can transmit at any rate it wants to, of course, not just at 1 bit per τ sec.

It is important to realize that collision detection is an *analog* process. The station's hardware must listen to the cable while it is transmitting. If what it reads back is different from it is putting out, it knows a collision is occurring. The implication is that the signal encoding must allow collisions to be detected (e.g., a collision of two 0 volt signals may well be impossible to detect). For engineering reasons its is sometimes desirable for stations always to output a 1 bit when trying to acquire the ether rather than the first actual data bit, which may be 1 or 0.

Metcalfe and Boggs have described an adaptive randomization strategy to minimize delay under light loads and yet be stable under heavy loads. After a packet is successfully transmitted, all stations may compete for the first contention slot. If there is a collision, all colliding stations set a local parameter, L, to 2 and choose one of the next L slots for retransmission. Every time a station is involved in a collision, it doubles its value of L. In effect, after k collisions, a fraction 2^{-k} of the stations will attempt to retransmit in each of the succeeding slots. As the Ethernet becomes more and more heavily loaded, the stations automatically adapt to the load, thus preventing the kind of bistable behavior that we saw earlier in uncontrolled slotted ALOHA. This heuristic is called **binary exponential backoff**. There are obviously many variations on this theme, such as increasing the randomization interval by a constant amount, instead of a constant factor, upon collision. Both of these schemes have the problem that with each new packet the station forgets everything and must learn about the load all over again.

As described so far, Ethernet provides no acknowledgements at all. Since the mere absence of collisions certainly does not guarantee that bits were not garbled by noise spikes on the cable, for reliable communication the destination must verify the checksum, and if correct, send an acknowledgement packet back to the source. Normally, this acknowledgement would just be another packet as far as the Ethernet protocol is concerned, and would have to fight for channel time just like a data packet. However, a simple modification to the contention algorithm allows speedy confirmation of packet receipt and thus improves throughput (Tokoro and Tamaru, 1977). All that is needed is to reserve the first contention slot following successful transmission for the destination station. Using this mechanism, acknowledgements come back so fast that a stop-and-wait protocol is completely adequate, simplifying the entire network design.

Now let us briefly examine the performance of Ethernet under conditions of heavy and constant load, that is, k stations always ready to transmit. If each station transmits during a contention slot with probability p, the probability, A, that some station acquires the ether during that slot is

$$A = kp(1 - p)^{p-1} \qquad (7\text{-}1)$$

A is maximized when $p = 1/k$, with $A \rightarrow 1/e$ as $k \rightarrow \infty$. The probability that the contention interval has exactly j slots in it is $A(1 - A)^{j-1}$, so the mean number slots per contention is given by

$$\sum_{j=0}^{\infty} jA(1 - A)^{j-1} = \frac{1 - A}{A}$$

Since each slot has a duration 2τ, the mean contention interval, w, is $2\tau(1 - A)/A$. Assuming optimal p, the mean number of contention slots is never more than $e - 1$, so w is at most $2\tau(e - 1) = 3.4\tau$.

If the mean packet takes P sec to transmit, when many stations have packets to send,

$$\text{channel efficiency} = \frac{P}{P + 3.4\tau}$$

Here we see where the maximum cable distance between any two stations enters into the performance figures, giving rise to topologies other than that of Fig. 7-1(a). The longer the cable, the longer the contention interval. In Fig. 7-4, the channel efficiency is plotted versus number of ready stations for $\tau = 5 \ \mu\text{sec}$ and a data rate of 10 Mbps.

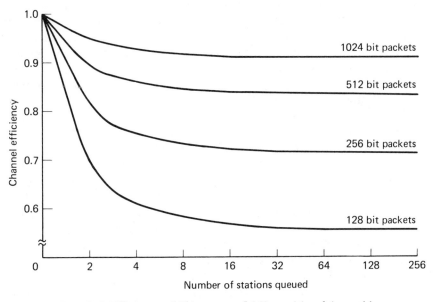

Fig. 7-4. Efficiency of Ethernet at 5 Mbps with a 1 km cable.

To determine the mean number of stations ready to transmit under conditions of high load, we can use the following (crude) observation. Each packet ties up the channel for one contention period and one packet transmission time, for a total of $P + w$ sec. The number of packets per second is therefore $1/(P + w)$. If each station generates packets at a mean rate of λ packets/sec, when the system is in state k the total input rate of all unblocked stations combined is $(N - k)\lambda$ packets/sec. Since in equilibrium the input and output rates must be identical, we can equate these two expressions and solve for k. (Note that w is a function of k.)

Lam (1980) has used the theory of imbedded Markov chains to analyze the performance of an adaptive Ethernet protocol that maintains a constant mean load on the channel. Franta and Bilodeau (1980) have also analyzed contention networks. Some experimental measurements of the performance of the Xerox PARC Ethernet are given in (Shoch and Hupp, 1980).

7.1.3. Collision-Free Protocols

Although collisions do not occur on the Ethernet once a station has unambiguously seized the channel, they can still occur during the contention period. These collisions do adversely affect the system performance, especially when the cable is long and the packets short. In this section we will examine some protocols that resolve the contention for the ether without any collisions at all, not even during the contention period.

In all the protocols to be described, we make the assumption that there are N station addresses. In other words, each station has a station address from 0 to $N - 1$ "wired" into it. That some stations may be inactive part of the time does not matter. The basic question remains: Which station is allocated the channel after a successful transmission? We continue using the model of Fig. 7-3, with its discrete contention slots.

A Bit-Map Protocol

In our first collision-free protocol, the basic bit-map method, each contention period consists of exactly N slots. If station 0 has a packet to send, it transmits a 1 bit during the first slot. No other station is allowed to transmit during this slot. Regardless of what station 0 does, station 1 gets the opportunity to transmit a 1 during slot 1, again only if it has a packet queued. In general, station j may announce the fact that it has a packet to send by inserting a 1 bit into slot j. After all N slots have passed by, each station has complete knowledge of which stations wish to transmit. At that point they begin transmitting, in numerical order (see Fig. 7-5). Since everyone agrees on who goes next, there will never be any collisions. After the last ready station has transmitted its packet, an event all stations can easily monitor, another N bit contention period is begun. Note that if a station becomes ready just after its bit slot has passed by, it is out of luck and must remain silent until everyone has had his say and the bit map comes around again.

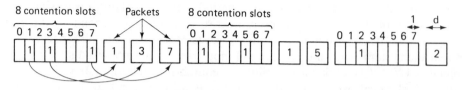

Fig. 7-5. The basic bit-map protocol.

Let us briefly analyze the performance of this protocol. For convenience, we will measure time in units of the contention bit slot, with data packets consisting of d time units. Under conditions of low load, the bit map will simply be repeated over and over, for lack of data packets.

Consider the situation from the point of view of a low-numbered station, such as 0 or 1. Typically, when it becomes ready to send, the "current" slot will be somewhere in the middle of the bit map. On the average, the station will have to wait $N/2$ slots for the current scan to finish and another full N slots for the following scan to run to completion before it may begin transmitting.

The prospects for high-numbered stations are brighter. Generally these will only have to wait half a scan ($N/2$ bit slots) before starting to transmit. High numbered stations rarely have to wait for the next scan. Since low-numbered stations must wait on the average $1.5N$ slots and high-numbered stations must wait on the average $0.5N$ slots, the mean for all stations is N slots. The channel efficiency at low load is easy to compute. The overhead per packet is N bits, and the amount of data is d bits, for an efficiency of $d/(N + d)$.

At high load, when all the stations have something to send all the time, the N bit contention period is prorated over N packets, yielding an overhead of only 1 bit per packet, or an efficiency of $d/(d + 1)$. The mean delay for a packet is equal to the sum of the time it queues inside its station, plus an additional $N(d + 1)/2$ once it gets to the head of its internal queue.

BRAP—Broadcast Recognition with Alternating Priorities

The basic bit-map protocol has several drawbacks, the most blatant of which is the asymmetry with respect to station number: higher-numbered stations get better service than lower-numbered ones. Another drawback is that under conditions of light load a station must always wait for the current scan to be finished (at the very least) before it may transmit. Our next protocol eliminates both these problems. It was discovered independently by Scholl (1976) and Chlamtac (1976). Chlamtac's version is called BRAM (Broadcast Recognition Access Method); Scholl's version is called MSAP (Mini Slotted Alternating Priorities). As a compromise, we will adopt the name BRAP. Hansen and Schwartz (1979) have described a related scheme.

In BRAP, as soon as a station inserts a 1 bit into its slot, it begins transmission of its packet immediately thereafter. In addition, instead of starting the bit scan with station 0 each time, it is started with the station following the one that just transmitted. In effect, permission to send rotates among the stations in a round-robin fashion. Any station wishing to exercise its permission to send simply does so without further ado. Any station not wishing to send just lets its bit slot go idle. BRAP is illustrated in Fig. 7-6, with the same pattern of ready stations as in Fig. 7-5. Notice that each contention period always consists of a run of (zero or more) empty slots, terminated by a single 1 bit. As soon as someone announces that he wants the channel, he gets it immediately.

BRAP can also be described in a slightly different form. Going back to the original Ethernet, we could say that BRAP consists of having each station delay its attempt to seize the channel, with the delay time being proportional to the

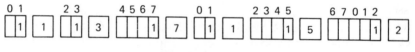

Fig. 7-6. BRAP.

difference between the station's number and the number of the last successful transmission, modulo N. Since the delays are staggered, there are no collisions.

Although the channel efficiency of BRAP is identical to the basic bit-map method, its delay characteristics are better. In particular, at low load a station only has to wait an average of $N/2$ bit slots before starting (for large N), versus N for the earlier protocol. At high load, BRAP and the basic method are similar, since the major delay comes from the packets, not the contention slots.

MLMA—The Multi-Level Multi-Access Protocol

The problem with BRAP is not with the channel utilization, which is excellent in the case of high load, but with the delay when the system is lightly loaded. When no stations are ready, there are no data packets, and the N-bit headers just go on and on until some station inserts a 1 bit in its bit slot. On the average, a station will have to wait N bit slots before it may begin sending.

Rothauser and Wild (1977) have devised a method that is nearly as efficient under conditions of high channel load but has a shorter delay under conditions of low channel load. In their method, a station announces that it wants to send by broadcasting its address in a particular format. We will illustrate the idea by means of an example using radix 10 arithmetic and $N = 1000$. An address in this system consists of three decimal digits, each decimal digit represented by a group of 10 bits called a "decade." For example, 472 is represented by setting bit 4 in the first decade, bit 7 in the middle decade, and bit 2 in the last decade.

If only one station attempts to transmit during a packet slot, it uses the 30-bit header to announce itself and then it sends its packet. The trouble arises when two or more stations try to insert their addresses into the same header. To disambiguate all the addresses, the stations behave as follows. The first decade in every packet slot corresponds to the hundreds place in the station number. After the first decade is finished, stations that have not transmitted a bit must remain silent until all the stations that did set a bit have transmitted their data. Call the highest occupied bit position in the first decade x. In the second decade, all stations with x as their leading digit announce their tens place. Call the highest occupied bit here y. In the third decade, all the stations whose addresses begin with xy may set the bit corresponding to their last digits. There are at most 10 of them.

This example is illustrated in Fig. 7-7 for five stations, with addresses 122, 125, 705, 722, and 725. Here $x = 7$ and $y = 2$. After decade 2, all stations now know that 722 and 725 want to send, and that furthermore one or more stations with addresses between 700 and 709, and one or more stations with addresses between 100 and 199 also want to send. Decade three identifies 705. Decade four is used for the tens place of all stations in the highest "century" not yet fully identified. In this case the 100 series stations get to broadcast their tens places next. If station 342 had also set its bit in decade 0, decade 4 would have been devoted to the 300 series stations instead of the 100 series. After the 100 series stations have broadcast their tens places, everyone knows that the highest (and only) remaining group of stations is 120-129, so the following decade is used to separate them out. Finally, the data are sent, in numerical order of the station addresses.

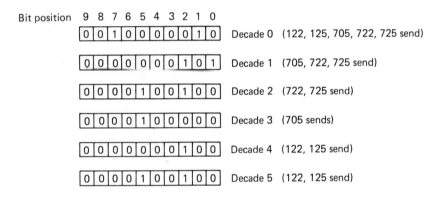

Fig. 7-7. MLMA. The recognition of stations 122, 125, 705, 722, and 725 requires 60 bits.

The number of decades needed to resolve conflicts depends on the addresses themselves. To separate 122 and 129 requires only three decades, but to separate 122 and 229 requires five decades. If all 1000 stations want to send, decade 0 is for the 900 series, decade 1 is for 990-999, decade 2 is for 980-989, etc. Decade 10 is for 900-909, decade 11 is for the tens place of the 800 series stations, etc. In all, 111 decades are needed for the header (the initial one, the 10 "centuries," and the 100 decades that differentiate on the ones place).

The channel efficiency is difficult to calculate exactly, but for a minimum channel load, 30 bits of header are needed, giving an efficiency of $d/(d + 30)$. In the limit of a very heavy load, a frame consists of 111 decades of header and 1000 data packets, for an efficiency of $d/(d + 1.11)$, which is close to the efficiency of the bit-map method. The mean delay under conditions of light load is just 25 bits (if station 485 becomes ready just after the first 5 bits of the first decade have gone idle, it is not too late to capture the slot).

By now it should be clear that the choice of radix 10 was an arbitrary choice. Any other radix would do, also. For example, with radix 2 and 1000 stations, 10 levels are needed, each containing 2 bits. The first "decade" (bicade?) is used to separate stations 0-511 from stations 512-1000. To minimize the number of bits in the header for the case of only one request per frame, consider some radix, r, with l levels ("decades"). The number of levels for a given r is the smallest value of l such that $r^l \geqslant N$. We seek to minimize the number of bits in the header, lr, subject to the constraint $r^l \geqslant N$. The minimum occurs at $r = e$. For 1000 stations, $r = 2$ and $l = 10$ is best, but for 2000 stations the optimum radix is 3, with seven levels.

Binary Countdown

The limiting case of MLMA consists of having 1 bit at each level. For N stations, the number of levels needed is $\log_2 N$ rounded upward to an integer. To signal that it wants to send, a station writes its address into the header as a binary number. We will call this protocol **binary countdown**. However, to avoid conflicts, the usual arbitration rule must be applied: as soon as a station sees that a high-order bit position that is 0 in its address has been overwritten with a 1, it gives up. After the winning station has transmitted its address, there is no information available telling how many other stations want to send, so the algorithm begins all over with the next packet. The channel efficiency of this method, $d/(d + \ln N)$, is better than decimal MLMA when there are many bursty stations, but slightly less under a full load. If, however, the packet format has been cleverly chosen so that the sender's address is the first field in the packet, even these $\ln N$ bits are not wasted.

Mok and Ward (1979) have described a variation of binary countdown using a parallel rather than a serial interface. They also suggest using virtual station numbers, with the virtual station numbers from 0 up to and including the successful station being circularly permuted after each transmission, to give priority to stations that have been silent unusually long. For example, if stations A, B, C, D, E, F, G, and H have virtual station numbers 4, 2, 7, 5, 1, 0, 3, and 6, respectively, a successful transmission by station D will assign to the eight stations 5, 3, 7, 0, 2, 1, 4, and 6, respectively. Station D will now only be able to acquire the channel if no other station wants it.

7.1.4. Limited-Contention Protocols

We have now considered two basic strategies for channel acquisition in a cable network: contention, as in the original Xerox PARC Ethernet, and collision-free methods. Each strategy can be rated as to how well it does with respect to the two important performance measures, delay at low load and channel efficiency at high load. Under conditions of light load, contention (i.e., pure or slotted ALOHA) is preferable due to its low delay. As the load increases, contention becomes increasingly less attractive, because the overhead associated with channel arbitration becomes greater. Just the reverse is true for the collision-free protocols. At low load they have high delay, but as the load increases, the channel efficiency improves rather than getting worse as it does for contention protocols.

Obviously, it would be nice if we could combine the best properties of the contention and collision-free protocols, arriving at a new protocol that used contention at low loads to provide low delay, but used a collision-free technique at high load to provide good channel efficiency. Such protocols, which we will call **limited contention protocols**, do, in fact, exist, and will conclude our study of carrier sense networks.

Up until now the only contention protocols we have studied have been symmetric, that is, each station attempts to acquire the channel with some probability, p, with all stations using the same p. Surprisingly enough, the overall system performance can be improved by using a protocol that assigns different probabilities to different stations, rotating the assignments on each slot to ensure fairness.

Before looking at the asymmetric protocols, let us quickly review the performance of the symmetric case. Equation (7-1) gives the probability that some station successfully acquires the channel during a given slot if there are k stations contending for it, each transmitting with probability p. To find the optimal value of p, we differentiate A with respect to p, set the result to zero, and solve for p. Doing so, we find that the best value of p is $1/k$. Substituting $p = 1/k$ into Eq. (7-1), we get

$$\Pr[\text{success with optimal } p] = \left(\frac{k-1}{k}\right)^{k-1} \qquad (7\text{-}2)$$

This probability is plotted in Fig. 7-8. For small numbers of stations the chances of success are good, but as soon as the number of stations reaches even five, the probability has dropped close to its asymptotic value of $1/e$.

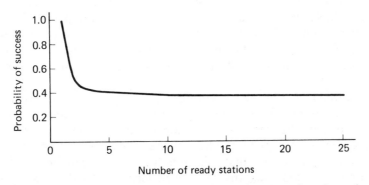

Fig. 7-8. Acquisition probability for a symmetric contention channel.

From Fig. 7-8 it is fairly obvious that the probability of some station acquiring the channel can be increased only by decreasing the amount of competition. The limited-contention protocols do precisely that. They first divide the stations up into (not necessarily disjoint) groups. Only the members of group 0 are permitted to compete for slot 0. If one of them succeeds, it acquires the channel and transmits its packet. If the slot lies fallow or if there is a collision, the members of group 1 contend for slot 1, etc. By making an appropriate division of stations into groups, the amount of contention for each slot can be reduced, thus operating each slot near the left end of Fig. 7-8.

The trick is how to assign stations to slots. Before looking at the general case, let us consider some special cases. At one extreme, each group has but one member. Such an assignment guarantees that there will never be collisions, because at most one station is contending per slot. We have seen this protocol before; it is just BRAP. The next special case is to assign two stations per group. The probability that both will try to transmit during a slot is p^2, which for small p is negligible. Assigning two stations per slot reduces the number of slots in the BRAP bit map from $N/2$ to $N/4$, halving the delay. As more and more stations are assigned to the same slot, the probability of a collision grows, but the length of the bit map scan needed to give everyone a chance shrinks, as discussed by Chlamtac et al. (1979). The limiting case is a single group containing all stations (i.e., slotted ALOHA). What we need is a way to assign stations to slots dynamically, with many stations per slot when the load is low and few (or even just one) station per slot when the load is high.

The Adaptive Tree Walk Protocol

One particularly simple way of performing the necessary assignment is to think of the stations as being organized in a binary tree (Capetanakis, 1979a, 1979b). as illustrated in Fig. 7-9. In the first contention slot following a successful packet transmission, slot 0, all stations are permitted to try to acquire the channel. If one of them does so, fine. If there is a collision, then during slot 1 only those stations falling under node B may compete. If one of them acquires the channel, the slot following the packet is reserved for those stations under node C. If, on the other hand, two or more stations under node B want to transmit, there will be a collision during slot 1, in which case it is node D's turn during slot 2.

In essence, if a collision occurs during slot 0, the entire tree is searched, depth first, to locate all ready stations. Each bit slot is associated with some particular node in the tree. If a collision occurs, the search continues recursively with the left and right children of that node. If a bit slot goes idle or if there is exactly one station that transmits into it, the searching of its node can stop, because all ready stations have been located. (If there were more than one, there would have been a collision.)

When the load on the system is heavy, it is hardly worth the effort to dedicate slot 0 to node A, because that makes sense only in the unlikely event that

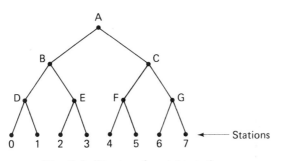

Fig. 7-9. The tree for eight stations.

precisely one station has a packet to send. Similarly, one could argue that nodes B and C should be skipped as well for the same reason. Put in more general terms, at what level in the tree should the search begin? Clearly, the heavier the load, the farther down the tree the search should begin. For the time being, let us assume that each station has a good estimate of the number of ready stations, q. We will come back to the question of how to obtain such estimates later.

To proceed, let us number the levels of the tree from the top, with node A in Fig. 7-9 at level 0, nodes B and C at level 1, etc. Notice that each node at level i has a fraction 2^{-i} of the total tree below it. If the q ready stations are uniformly distributed, the expected number of them below a specific node at level i is just $2^{-i}q$. Intuitively, we would expect the optimal level to begin searching the tree as the one at which the expected number of contending stations per slot is 1, that is, the level at which $2^{-i}q = 1$. Solving this equation we find that $i = \log_2 q$.

The Urn Protocol

Kleinrock and Yemini (1978) and Yemini (1978) have described another protocol that is similar to the tree walk protocol, but uses an urn rather than a tree as its basis. Like the tree walk protocol, it limits the number of stations entitled to transmit during each slot in such a way as to maximize the probability of getting exactly one ready station per contention slot.

In this protocol, an analogy is made between the stations and the balls in an urn. (Why probability theorists always use urns, and never basins, buckets, cauldrons, chalices, crocks, pots, pails, or tubs for ball storage is a question we leave to the linguistically minded reader.) Green balls correspond to stations that are ready (have a packet to send). Red balls correspond to stations that do not have a packet to send.

The probability of selecting exactly x green balls from the urn if we withdraw n balls without replacement is

$$\frac{\binom{k}{x}\binom{N-k}{n-x}}{\binom{N}{n}}$$

The first factor in the numerator is the number of ways of selecting x green balls from among the k green balls in the urn. The second factor in the numerator is the number of ways of selecting $n - x$ red balls from among the $N - k$ red balls in the urn. The denominator is the number of ways of selecting n balls from the N balls in the urn.

What we are really interested in is the probability of drawing exactly one green ball, since that is the only way a successful transmission can occur. When $x = 1$, the probability of success is maximized by choosing $n = N/k$ (truncated down to an integer). The mean number of green balls in the sample is equal to the sample size, n, times the probability that a given ball is green, k/N. This value is always close to 1 (it is not exactly 1 due to the truncation). Figure 7-10 shows the probability of getting exactly one green ball for the case $N = 100$. For $k > N/2$, only one ball will be sampled, and the throughput will be equal to the fraction of stations wanting to transmit.

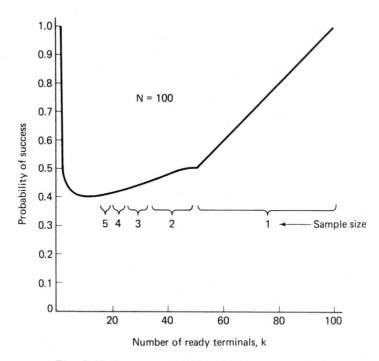

Fig. 7-10. Success probability with the urn method.

After having determined what n should be, the next question is which stations are to be chosen. This decision must be made in a distributed way, and all stations must agree on the decision for the method to work. Several methods have been proposed (Yemini, 1978). A particularly attractive one is as follows. The stations are imagined to be arranged in numerical order along the circumference of a hypothetical circle. A window of size n rotates around the circle. During each slot, those stations inside the window are given permission to send. (Being in the window is analogous to being under the node in Fig. 7-9 that owns the current slot.) If there was a successful transmission or no transmission at all, the window is advanced N positions. If there was a collision, the window is shrunk back to half its size, and the process is repeated until the collision ceases. (Shrinking the window is analogous to recursively walking one of the subtrees of a Fig. 7-9 node.)

Let us consider how the entire algorithm works under two conditions, light load and heavy load. If the estimate of the number of ready stations is 1 or fewer, the window size will be N. In other words, the window will go all the way around, and all stations will be allowed to send at will. Under these conditions, the protocol degenerates to uncontrolled slotted ALOHA. If the estimate of k remains stable at 2 for a while, n will be $N/2$ and the stations will be partitioned into two groups, with half the stations operating under uncontrolled slotted ALOHA in the odd slots, and the other half operating the same way in the even slots. Finally, if $k \geqslant N/2$, the sample size (i.e., the window size) will be 1. During each slot, exactly one station will be given permission to send, so there will be no collisions. The position of the lucky station will rotate around the circle. In this limit, the system becomes identical to synchronous time-division multiplexing. Thus the urn method acts like slotted ALOHA at low load and automatically goes over to STDM at high load.

It is worth pointing out that a variant of BRAM, parametric BRAM (Chlamtac et al., 1979), also adjusts the number of stations per slot dynamically. A detailed simulation has shown the optimum number of stations per slot for varying loads. Each station simply looks up an entry in an internal table to determine the correct number for the current load.

All of the limited-contention protocols assume that each station has an estimate of the number of stations wanting to transmit. One way for stations to estimate the system state is to have a logically separate subchannel used for signaling state changes. Such a subchannel can be obtained by traditional multiplexing. For example, by allocating a narrow frequency band on the cable for signaling only (FDM), or by setting aside the first contention slot following each successful packet transmission for signaling only (TDM). Either way, we assume that the signaling subchannel is slotted.

Each station must maintain a running estimate of the number of ready stations. This estimate must be updated when either one of two events happens: a successful transmission occurs (state is decremented), or a new station becomes ready (state is incremented). The former is easy to detect because all stations can easily keep track of successful transmissions. The latter is trickier and is the reason the separate subchannel is needed. When a station becomes ready, it announces itself on the signaling subchannel. If only one station becomes ready during a signaling slot, this can be unambiguously detected by everyone else. However, if two or more become ready during one signaling slot, there will be a collision.

At this point we explicitly assume that these collisions can be detected. When a collision occurs on the subchannel, all the stations know that two or more stations have become ready, but they do not know exactly how many. To make an estimate of the mean number of newly ready stations represented by each collision, let us assume that the number of stations that become ready in each slot is a Poisson process with mean m. The probability of zero stations becoming ready in a given slot is e^{-m}, by Eq. (6-2). Similarly, the probability of one station becoming ready in a signaling slot is me^{-m}. Both of these quantities can be accurately estimated by recording the fraction of subchannel slots containing zero or one "I am ready" messages. From this information, two estimates of m can be made and then the average used.

With an estimate of m known, we can now deduce the probability that exactly r stations become ready using Eq. (6-2). Using the formula for conditional probabilities,

$$\text{Pr}[A \text{ given } B] = \frac{\text{Pr}[A \text{ and } B]}{\text{Pr}[B]}$$

we find that

$$\text{Pr}[\text{exactly r stations in a collision}] = \frac{m^r e^{-m} / r!}{1 - e^{-m} - me^{-m}}$$

Given the probabilities, we can find the mean. In general the mean number of stations in a collision will not be an integer, so the running estimate of the system state will also take on continuous rather than integer values. This is not a problem as long as we force n to be an integer.

Although we have presented both the collision-free and limited-contention protocols in the context of channel acquisition in carrier sense networks, it is important to realize that they are equally applicable to slotted ALOHA systems of the type described in Chap. 6. For example, after a collision is detected in slotted ALOHA, the adaptive tree walk protocol could be used, that is, only the lower half of the stations may compete for the next slot. The point is that after a successful packet transmission, the contention for the bit slots is exactly the process as contention for normal data slots, only on a smaller scale. (Of course, satellite propagation delays may affect the performance, but not the principle.)

7.2. RING NETWORKS

Having finished our study of carrier sense networks, it is time to move on to another popular kind of local network, the **ring network**. Ring nets also use cables, either twisted pair or coaxial, just like carrier sense networks, but the organization is fundamentally different. Whereas a carrier sense network is basically a passive, electrically connected cable onto which all stations tap, a ring net is actually a series of point-to-point cables between consecutive stations. Also, the interfaces used on ring nets are active rather than passive.

A major issue in the design and analysis of ring nets is the "physical length" of a bit. If the data rate of the ring is R Mbps, a bit is emitted every $1/R$ μsec. (Bits are transmitted serially, just as with the Ethernet.) With a typical signal propagation speed of 200 m/μsec, each bit occupies $200/R$ meters on the ring. This means, for example, that a ring whose circumference is 1000 meters can contain only 5 bits on it at once. The implications of the number of bits on the ring will become clearer later.

In all rings there is a need for the conceptual equivalent of a master clock telling each station to read one input bit and write one output bit. Since centralized components are a no-no in this book, we will just point out that the same effect can be achieved by encoding 0 bits as a positive pulse followed by a negative pulse, and 1 bits as a negative pulse followed by a positive pulse (or vice versa). This way an idle ring still has a well defined bit pattern on it (all zeros), and timing is provided by the leading edges of the data bits themselves, without a master clock.

Many researchers have designed and implemented ring nets (e.g., Clark et al., 1978; Farber and Larson, 1972; Farmer and Newhall, 1969; Fraser, 1975; Liu, 1978; Needham, 1979; Pierce, 1972). In the follow sections we will discuss, in turn, four of the major types of rings.

7.2.1. Token Rings

The oldest, and still most popular, kind of ring net is what we will call a **token ring** (Farber and Larson, 1972). In this kind of ring a special bit pattern, called the **token**, circulates around the ring whenever all stations are idle. Typically, the token will be a special 8-bit pattern, for example, 11111111. Bit stuffing is used to prevent this pattern from occurring in the data.

When a station wants to transmit a packet, it is required to seize the token and remove it from the ring before transmitting. To remove the token, the ring interface, which connects the station to the ring (see Fig. 7-11), must monitor all bits that pass by. As the last bit of the token passes by, the ring interface inverts it, changing the token (e.g., 11111111) into another bit pattern, known as a **connector** (e.g., 11111110). Immediately after the token has been so transformed, the station making the transformation is permitted to begin transmitting.

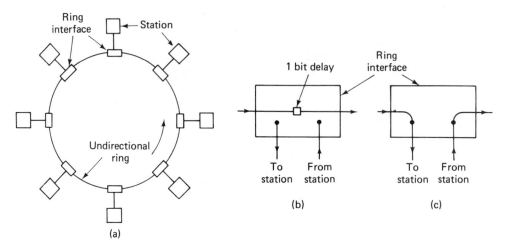

Fig. 7-11. (a) A ring net. (b) Listen mode. (c) Transmit mode.

This organization has several important implications for the ring design. To start with, after reading all but the last bit of a (potential) token, the interface must be able to read the last bit and decide whether or not to invert it before forwarding any part of the bit. If the preceding bit pattern is a token, the final bit must be inverted. However, if the final bit shows that the bit pattern is not a token, that is, it is just some data, the final bit must not be inverted. This requirement means that each arriving bit must be stored in its entirety, and then a new bit generated, thereby creating a 1-bit delay in each ring interface. If there are many stations on the ring, the cumulative affect of these 1-bit delays has an important impact on the performance of the ring.

Another implication of the token ring design is that the ring itself must have a sufficient delay to contain a complete token to circulate when all stations are idle. The delay has two components: the 1-bit delay introduced by each station, and the signal propagation delay. In almost all rings, the designers must assume that stations may be powered down at various times, especially at night. If the interfaces are powered from the ring, shutting down the station has no effect on interface, but if the interfaces are powered externally, they must be designed to connect the input to the output when power goes down, thus removing the 1-bit delay. The point here is that on a short ring an artificial delay may have to be inserted into the ring at night to ensure that a token can be contained on it.

Ring interfaces have two operating modes, listen and transmit. In listen mode, the input bits are simply copied to output, with a delay of one bit time, as shown in Fig. 7-11(b). In transmit mode [Fig. 7-11(c)], which is entered only after the token has been seized, the interface breaks the connection between input and output, entering its own data onto the ring. To be able to switch from listen to transmit mode in 1 bit time, the interface usually needs to buffer one or more packets itself rather than having to fetch them from the station on such short notice.

As bits that have propagated around the ring come back, they are removed from the ring by the sender. The sending station can either save them, to compare with the original data to monitor ring reliability, or discard them. This ring architecture puts no limit on the size of the packets, because the entire packet never appears on the ring at one instant. After a station has finished transmitting the last bit of its packet, it must regenerate the token. When the last bit of the packet has gone around and come back, it must be removed, and the interface must switch back into listen mode immediately, to avoid removing the token or connector that follows.

It is straightforward to handle acknowledgements on a token ring. The packet format need only include a 1-bit field for acknowledgements, initially zero. When the destination station has received a packet, it need only invert the bit. Of course, if the acknowledgement means that the checksum has been verified, the bit must follow the checksum, and the ring interface must be able to verify the checksum as soon as its last bit has arrived. When a packet is broadcast to multiple stations, a more complicated acknowledgement mechanism must be used (if any is used at all).

When traffic is light, the token will spend most of its time idly circulating around the ring. Occasionally a station will convert it to a connector, followed by a packet and then a new token. However, when the traffic is heavy, so that there is a queue at each station, as soon as a station finishes its transmission and regenerates the token, the next station downstream will see and remove the token. In this manner the permission to send rotates smoothly around the ring, in round-robin fashion. Since there is only one token, there is never any contention as in the Ethernet. Higher level protocols decide whether a station must regenerate the token after one packet, or whether it may empty its entire queue first.

In a certain respect, ring nets are similar to systems that use hub polling, as described in Chap. 3. In both cases the control token is passed in a unidirectional manner from station to station. The major difference is that with conventional hub polling there is a master station that initiates the poll, whereas in a ring net all stations are equals. Also, hub polling usually occurs on a multidrop line rather than on a circular one.

Now let us now briefly analyze the performance of a token ring. Assume that packets are generated according to a Poisson process, and that when a station receives permission to send, it empties itself of all queued packets, with the mean queue length being q packets. The total arrival rate of all N stations combined is λ packets/sec. Each station contributes λ/N. As usual, we will call the service rate (the number of packets/sec that a station can transmit) μ. The time it takes for a bit to go all the way around an idle ring, or **walk time**, consisting of both the one bit-per-station delays and the signal propagation delay, plays a key role in the mean delay. Denote the walk time by w. The quantity we intend to compute is the **scan time**, s, the mean interval between token arrivals at a given station.

Each scan time is divided into two parts, the walk time, w, and the time required to service each of the Nq requests queued up to service, each of which requires $1/\mu$ sec. Algebraically,

$$s = w + \frac{Nq}{\mu} \qquad (7\text{-}3)$$

The mean queue length is easy to derive, since it is just the number of requests that pile up during an interval of length s when the arrival rate is λ/N, namely $q = \lambda s/N$. Substituting into Eq. (7-3) we get

$$s = w + \frac{\lambda s}{\mu}$$

Introducing $\rho = \lambda/\mu$ and solving for s we find

$$s = \frac{w}{1 - \rho} \qquad (7\text{-}4)$$

The channel-acquisition delay is about half the scan time, so we now have one of the basic performance parameters. Notice that the delay is always proportional to the walk time, both for low load and high. Also note that ρ represents the utilization of the entire ring, not the utilization of a single station, which is ρ/N.

The other key performance parameter is the channel efficiency under heavy load. The only overhead is the walk time between stations. If every station has data to send, this overhead is w/N, compared to the transmission time per station, Nq/μ. Using these times the channel efficiency can be found.

Although the token ring and Ethernet differ in many details, they also have many things in common. Since they use similar technologies, they can operate at similar data rates. In both cases stations must first acquire the channel before transmitting, with channel acquisition done by waiting for the token in one case and by contention in the other. Both systems have a channel efficiency determined by this wait time and transmission time. As the data rate is dramatically increased, say by using a fiber-optics medium, both networks' channel efficiency drops toward zero, because the channel-acquisition time in both cases depends on signal propagation speed, and this is not affected by increasing the data rate. Because the propagation time enters into the channel-acquisition time, both networks suffer from increased cable length, Ethernets due to increased contention slot size and token rings due to increased walk time. Under conditions of heavy load the ring operates as a round robin, as do most of the Ethernet protocols (e.g., BRAP, adaptive tree walk, urn), although the Ethernet protocols must be quite sophisticated to achieve this effect, whereas it happens automatically on the ring.

7.2.2. Contention Rings

As long as 100% of the hardware and software functions flawlessly, the token ring works fine. However, if the token is ever accidentally lost, the system is in deep trouble. The traditional approach to solving the missing-token problem is to have each interface start a timer immediately prior to its searching for a token. The timer must be set to the worst case, namely all $N - 1$ other stations have a maximum length packet to transmit. If the timer goes off, the interface knows that there has been a mishap, so it puts a token onto the ring and hopes for the best. Unfortunately, two or more interfaces may put tokens onto the ring at the same time, making the problem even worse.

The regeneration of lost tokens is essentially the same arbitration problem as channel allocation in the Ethernet. This observation led Clark et al. (1978) to suggest a new kind of ring net, called a **contention ring**, which utilizes the contention mechanism required for token recovery to eliminate the channel-acquisition delay when the load is light.

Unlike the token ring, which contains a circulating token when there is no traffic, the contention ring contains nothing at all when there is no traffic. In this respect it is like the Ethernet. When a station has a packet to transmit, it checks to see if a bit is currently passing through its interface. If there is no traffic, it just starts transmission. At the end of its packet, it puts a token onto the ring, just as the token ring does. However, unlike the token ring, it also removes the token when the packet comes around again.

Now consider how a station behaves when it notices traffic on the ring at the time it wants to send. It just waits for the token, and as in the token ring, inverts the last bit, thus converting it to a connector. Directly following the connector it begins transmitting its own packet. Since the token is now missing, no other station can seize it, so there is no contention. Once the ring is completely full of bits (e.g. when the load is high), no station will ever transmit unless it has acquired the token. Consequently, under conditions of high load, the contention ring acts just like a token ring.

Alas, there is a fly in the ointment. If exactly one station decides to begin transmitting onto an idle ring, the situation is as depicted in Fig. 7-12(a). One station puts data onto the ring and the same station removes it. So far, so good. The trouble comes when two stations simultaneously decide to transmit onto an idle ring, as shown in Fig. 7-12(b). The data that each station absorbs are the data the other station put onto the ring. Depending on the positions of the two stations, the packet may well be removed before it gets to the destination, hardly an acceptable situation. Fortunately each station can recognize that what it is receiving is not what it sent, especially if packets begin with the sender's address. When a station detects that such a collision has occurred, it terminates its transmission but keeps on absorbing data until there is no more. Eventually, the ring becomes quiet again, both stations wait random amounts of time, and the contention begins anew.

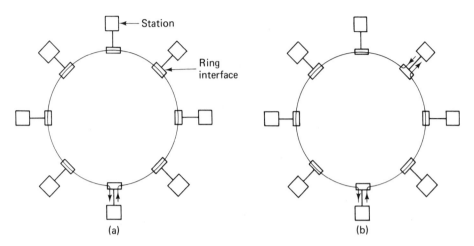

Fig. 7-12. A contention ring. (a) Normal operation. (b) Collision.

In summary, the contention ring has low channel-acquisition delay when it is lightly loaded, and the properties of the token ring when it is heavily loaded, the price paid being the occurrence of contention even when the hardware is functioning properly. Another point is the inability of a station to know whether or not it has acquired the channel until its first few bits have passed all the way around, been absorbed, and analyzed. In contrast, a token ring station knows immediately when it has captured the token, and an Ethernet station knows whether it has been successful within one round-trip propagation time. Note that the walk time of the ring is often far more than the round-trip propagation time of the Ethernet due to the 1-bit delays in each station, so the contention ring has the longest channel-acquisition time of the three systems. A plus point for the contention ring over the Ethernet is that it uses only digital logic. It detects collisions by looking at bit patterns, not by analyzing analog waveforms as the Ethernet does.

7.2.3. Slotted Rings

Each of the previous rings normally operates with only one packet on the ring at a time. The next two rings normally operate with multiple packets on the ring. The first of these is the **slotted ring** (Pierce, 1972), so-called because it is slotted into a number of fixed-size packets. Unless the physical distance around the ring is very large or there are many stations, it is unlikely that there will be enough delay to hold several packets, so artificial delays are needed. These can be obtained easily by putting shift registers in the ring interfaces. Instead of the 1-bit delay of Fig. 7-11(b), there are multiple-bit delays. Figure 7-13 shows a conceptual model of a slotted ring.

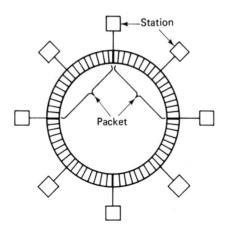

Fig. 7-13. A slotted ring.

Each packet slot contains a bit that tells whether the slot is full or empty. When a station wishes to transmit, it simply waits for an empty slot to come around, marks it as full, and puts its data in the slot. Of course, packets must be small enough to fit in a packet slot, in contrast to the token and contention rings, both of which support packets of arbitrarily large size.

7.2.4. Register Insertion Rings

The last kind of ring, the **register insertion ring**, is a more sophisticated version of the slotted ring. The design described below was developed by Liu (1978).

To understand how the register insertion ring works, we must examine the ring interface, shown in Fig. 7-14. The interface contains two registers, a shift register and an output buffer. When a station has a packet to transmit, it loads the packet into the output buffer. Packets may be variable length, up to the size of the output buffer.

When the ring is started up, the input pointer shown in Fig. 7-14 points to the rightmost bit position in the shift register, meaning that all the bit slots including and to the left of where it is pointing are empty. When a bit arrives from the ring, it is placed at the position pointed to by the input pointer, and the pointer is moved 1 bit to the left. As soon as the address field of the packet has arrived, the interface can determine whether or not the packet is addressed to it. If so, the rest of the packet is diverted to the station, removing the packet from the ring. The input pointer is then reset to the extreme right.

If, however, the packet is not addressed to the local station, the interface begins forwarding it. As each new bit arrives, it is put in the place pointed to by the input pointer. The entire contents of the shift register is then shift right

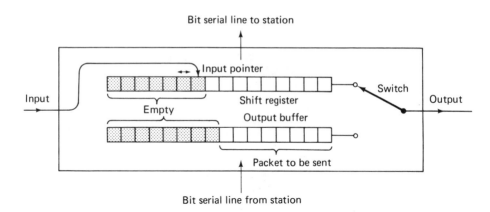

Fig. 7-14. Interface of a register insertion ring.

one position, pushing the rightmost bit out onto the ring. The input pointer is not advanced. If no new input arrives, for example due to an interpacket gap, the contents of the shift register can be reduced by 1 bit and the input pointer moved right one position.

Now let us see how output from the station happens. Whenever the shift register has pushed out the last bit of a packet, it checks to see if (1) there is an output packet waiting, and (2) the number of empty slots in the shift register is at least as large as the output packet. Only if both conditions are met can output proceed, in which case the output switch is flipped and the output buffer is now shifted out onto the ring, 1 bit at a time, in synchronization with the input. New input is accumulated in the shift register, which is why there must be enough empty slots there to accommodate all the input while the output buffer is being emptied. Not all the slots may be needed, since an interpacket gap may arrive during output, but the interface must be prepared for the worst case. As soon as the output buffer has been emptied, the switch is flipped again, and the shift register is emptied (if it has anything in it).

An interesting property of this ring architecture is the way it prevents a station from monopolizing the ring. If the ring is idle, the shift register will be empty when an output packet has been finished, so the next output packet can be sent as soon as it can be loaded into the output buffer by the station. In effect, if the ring is idle, any station can have the entire bandwidth if it so desires. If the ring is busy, however, after sending a packet the station will not be allowed to send another one because there will usually be insufficient empty slots in the shift register. Only when enough interpacket gaps have been saved up can output occur again. In essence, to send a b-bit packet, the interface must accumulate b bits worth of empty space on the ring in which to insert the packet. The b bits need not be consecutive, however, because the interpacket gaps are accumulated in the left-hand portion of the shift register.

7.3. SHARED MEMORY SYSTEMS

Local networks are generally more tightly coupled than are long-haul networks. The ultimate in tight coupling is a collection of processors that share a common address space or use the same main memory. Some authors refer to these systems as **multiprocessors**, distinguishing them from networks and distributed systems. In our view, however, shared-memory is simply another alternative for the communication architecture, along with rings, Ethernets, satellites, radio, and point-to-point architectures rather than something fundamentally different. Of course, the properties of shared-memory systems differ from those of point-to-point networks, but so do those of Ethernets and rings. Because shared memory is a technique applicable only to processors physically separated by no more than a few meters, it is less generally applicable than are the more loosely coupled technologies, so our treatment will be correspondingly brief. For a comprehensive annotated bibliography on multiprocessors see (Satyanarayanan, 1980).

7.3.1. Processor-Memory Interconnection

The three basic methods of connecting processors and memory are illustrated in Fig. 7-15. In all cases we will assume that the memory is split up into several modules to increase the number of simultaneous memory accesses. Although modules may have multiple input lines, as a rule requests are serviced sequentially rather than in parallel. Multiple modules therefore increase the system throughput.

The simplest interconnection scheme is the time-shared bus of Fig. 7-15(a). In this organization all the processors and all the memories are connected to a common bus. Minicomputers often use this arrangement, even when there is only one processor. The bus usually consists of a flat ribbon cable with more than 50 lines. Some lines are dedicated to (memory) addresses, other lines are dedicated to data, and still other lines are for control and arbitration among the competing processors.

A subtle, but important, point is the difference between the communication architecture of shared memory implemented with a time-shared bus on the one hand, and the Ethernet on the other. In a shared-memory system a processor communicates with another by writing a message in memory, which the other one subsequently finds and reads. No messages are sent directly from one processor to another as in the Ethernet. The shared-memory system allows multiple processors to operate on the same set of global variables simultaneously, which the message based Ethernet does not.

As with all systems that share a common communication channel, there must be some mechanism to allocate the bus when two or more processors want it simultaneously. The usual method is a centralized bus arbiter, but even this architecture has three variations.

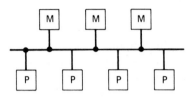

(a)

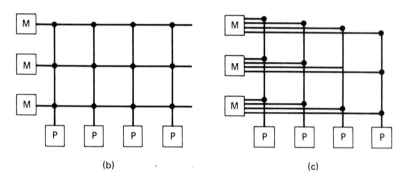

(b)   (c)

Fig. 7-15. Processor-memory interconnection methods. (a) Time-shared bus. (b) Crosspoint switch. (c) Multiported memory.

First, each processor could have a dedicated request line and a dedicated grant line into the arbiter. Such an arrangement is very flexible, allowing the arbiter to pick and choose among the requests, but it requires two dedicated wires per processor. Not only does this lead to an expensive bus, but it also fixes the number of processors at the time the bus is designed.

In the second approach, there is a single bus request line and a single bus grant line, onto which all processors are attached in parallel. When a request comes in to the arbiter, it polls the processors to see which one wants service. The polling messages can put on the address lines, or the processors can be distinguished by timing.

The third approach is known as **daisy chaining**. It consists of having a single bus request line onto which all processors are tapped in parallel, and a bus grant line, which runs serially through all the processors. As soon as the arbiter sees a bus request come in, it puts its reply on the bus grant line. Processors that did not request the bus just pass the grant signal downstream to the next processor. The first processor that requested the bus assumes the grant is for it and does not pass the signal downstream. The other processors have to try again later.

An alternative to a central arbiter is to have the bus be operated as a time-division multiplexer. With N processors, every Nth bus cycle is dedicated to a specific processor. No arbiter is needed, but substantial bus capacity will be wasted unless all processors are equally active.

In a large system, the bus is likely to be a bottleneck. The obvious solution is to have multiple buses. One common approach is to have a separate bus going into each memory module, with each processor attached to each memory bus, as shown in Fig. 7-15(b). In this design the rectangular grid of buses and interconnections is called a **crosspoint switch**. Each of the heavy dots in the figure represents a switch that can be opened and closed by one processor. As in the case of a single bus, some arbitration mechanism is needed to prevent two processors from trying to access the same bus at the same time. As the number of processors increases, it is necessary to increase the number of memories accordingly; otherwise, bus access will continue to be a problem, just as in the case of a single bus. This observation means that the complexity of the crosspoint switch grows quadratically with system size, an extremely undesirable situation.

Yet a third interconnection organization is the multiported memory, shown in Fig. 7-15(c). Here each processor has a private input line to each memory. The number of crosspoints is, in fact, exactly the same as the centralized crosspoint switch, the only difference being that the switch is no longer centralized but divided up among the memory modules. Depending on implementation considerations, one or the other organization may be more practical.

7.3.2. Examples of Shared Memory Systems

Although many computer manufacturers offer a product based on a small number of processors sharing a common memory, these are rarely expandable to even 10 processors. On the other hand, several research systems have been constructed with an eye to investigating the problems inherent in tightly coupled systems with many processors. We will now look at two of these, both constructed at Carnegie-Mellon University.

The Carnegie-Mellon multi-mini-processor, C.mmp (Wulf, 1972), was historically the first of the two, so we will begin with it. The architecture is shown in Fig 7-16. C.mmp consists of 16 processors, all of them PDP-11s, together with 16 memory modules and a 16×16 crosspoint switch. Each PDP-11 has its own private Unibus, just as normal, stand alone PDP-11 does. On these private Unibuses are a small amount of local memory and the various I/O devices. By allowing each processor a small amount of local memory, for use by the currently executing program, the number of references to the shared memory can be reduced thus reducing the contention for the switch, speeding up execution.

A PDP-11 has a 16-bit address space. The common memory has a 25-bit address space (32M bytes). To allow each processor to read and write anywhere in the common memory, the 16-bit processor addresses must be mapped onto memory addresses. This mapping is accomplished by a map inserted

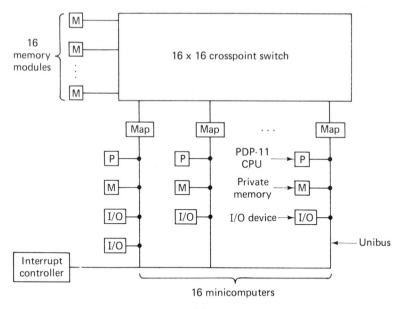

Fig. 7-16. C.mmp.

between the Unibuses and the crosspoint switch. Each PDP-11 has its address space divided up in eight pages of 8K bytes each. The common memory is divided up in 4096 pages of 8K bytes each. Each map contains registers mapping the eight pages of processor address space on the common memory. Thus each processor can only directly address 64K bytes of memory at any instant, but its operating system can change the map, subject to certain protection rules of course. The small size of the processor address space turned out to be a major headache for the system designers, but there was little choice given their desire to use the then available off-the-shelf minicomputers.

Our second example of a shared-memory system is Cm* (Swan et al., 1977a, 1977b; Jones et al., 1977). This system, shown in Fig. 7-17, uses a bus hierarchy to reduce bus contention. The basic building block of Cm* is a module consisting of an LSI-11 processor connected through a switch to a bus, on which hangs some local memory and I/O devices. Each memory module hangs on the bus of some processor; there is no "free standing" memory as in C.mmp.

The modules are clustered together onto buses called Kmap buses. Each Kmap bus has a centralized bus arbiter, the Kmap, whose job it is to resolve contention for the bus. In addition to the LSI-11 buses and the Kmap buses, there are also intercluster buses, used by the Kmaps to communicate among themselves.

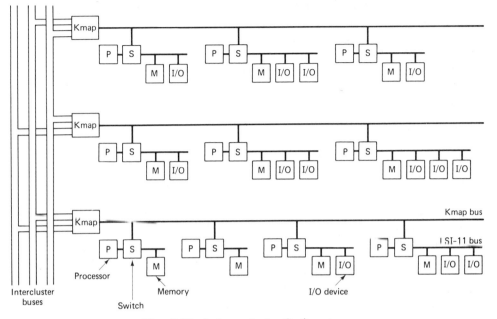

Fig. 7-17. A three cluster Cm* system.

All the memory modules in the complete system together form a single common address space, just like C.mmp, although the size of the address space is 2^{28} bytes rather than 2^{25} bytes. Like the PDP-11s, the LSI-11s have 16-bit address spaces, although in Cm* they were split up into 16 pages of 4K instead of eight pages of 8K.

When a processor references its address space, the local switch to which it is connected looks the page number up in a table, much like the map in C.mmp. If the address requested happens to map onto a location in the local memory, the access is put through immediately. If, however, the address is not local, the Kmap is invoked. If the needed word is local to the cluster, the Kmap can perform the access, because it can communicate with all the switches on its bus. If the access is in another cluster, a packet is sent to the appropriate Kmap via an intercluster bus. Thus we have the amazing situation of a communication architecture that looks to the users like shared memory being implemented by packet switching.

The idea behind Cm* is that under normal conditions the program and local data (stack frame) being executed by each LSI-11 will be in its own local memory, thus avoiding the time-consuming necessity of using the Kmap. Furthermore, the operating system attempts to assign tasks to processors in such a way as to minimize the number of intercluster references. As long as programs exhibit a high degree of locality, a Cm* system can be expanded more-or-less indefinitely, with clusters being added as the work load increases.

Although we do not have the space to go into the details here, we do wish to mention that Cm* is an unusual system in that it is capability based. Access to each data structure in the system is controlled by a capability. Operations can be defined on data structures, with the operations being carried out by the Kmap microcode. These properties give processes on Cm* the power to interact tightly when needed, yet protect themselves completely when interaction is not desired. For more information, consult the references.

7.4. SUMMARY

Unlike long-haul networks, which must use common-carrier provided transmission facilities out of necessity, local networks are free to choose their own transmission technology. The most common technologies all use a single broadcast channel, such as the satellite broadcasting systems of Chap. 6. The key difference between the local and satellite networks is the local network's ability to avoid collisions by sensing the channel before transmitting on it. The long propagation delay makes such methods impractical with satellite networks.

The simplest protocols are the CSMA protocols, which continue to transmit the current packet even when a collision is occurring. The Ethernet protocols are better, aborting transmission as soon as a collision is detected. A variety of protocols are available to minimize collisions during the contention period. We examined binary exponential backoff, the bit-map protocol, BRAP, MLMA, binary countdown, adaptive tree walk, and the urn protocol. It should be emphasized that all of these are also suitable for use with ordinary slotted ALOHA systems, provided that the worst-case signal propagation time between stations is short compared to the bit time.

An alternative to the Ethernet is the ring net. There are four basic kinds of ring nets as well as numerous minor variations. The four kinds are the token ring, with its circulating token, the contention ring, which is a hybrid of the token ring and Ethernet, the slotted ring, which has discrete slots into which packets can be placed, and the register insertion ring.

Shared memory is another alternative for the communication architecture of local networks. It can be implemented using a shared bus, a crosspoint switch, or multiported memory.

It should be kept in mind that all of these different kinds of networks use the basic multilayer protocols of Fig. 1-7. The protocols described in this chapter correspond to the network layer, in that they provide a less than 100% reliable datagram service to the higher layers. The transport, presentation, and application protocols discussed in the following chapters apply equally well to local networks as to long-haul networks.

PROBLEMS

1. A seven story office building has 15 adjacent offices per floor. Each office contains a wall socket for a terminal in the front wall, so the sockets form a rectangular grid in the vertical plane, with a separation of 4 m between sockets, both horizontally and vertically. Assuming that it is feasible to run a straight cable between any pair of sockets, horizontally, vertically, or diagonally, how many meters of cable are needed to connect all sockets using
   (a) a star configuration with a single IMP in middle?
   (b) an Ethernet?
   (c) a ring net?

2. A 1 km long, 10 Mbps Ethernet has a propagation speed of 200 m/μsec. Data packets are 256 bits long, including 32 bits of header, checksum and other overhead. The first bit slot after a successful transmission is reserved for the receiver to capture the channel to send a 32-bit acknowledgement packet. What is the effective data rate, excluding overhead, assuming that there are no collisions (e.g., urn protocol at heavy load)?

3. Two Ethernet stations are each trying to transmit long (multipacket) files. After each packet is sent, they contend for the channel using the binary exponential backoff algorithm. What is the probability that the contention ends on round k, and what is the mean number of rounds per contention period?

4. How many "octades" does MLMA need to resolve all the conflicts if the stations whose octal addresses are 4052, 3052, 2162, 7722, 2712, 3662, and 3663 all decide to send at once?

5. Prove that at low channel load, the MLMA header is minimized when the radix of the system, r, is equal to e.

6. In the binary countdown protocol, stations with higher addresses have higher priority, and presumably higher throughput than do stations with lower addresses. Analyze this effect using a discrete time Markov model. During each time slot each station is either ready (has a packet to send) or is idle (has no packet to send). Thus the state of an N station system can be given by an N bit vector, telling who is ready and who is idle. When two or more stations are ready, the one with the highest number wins and becomes idle. The probability that an idle station becomes ready in any slot is p. For the case of $N = 2$:
   (a) Write down the transition rates between all pairs of states.
   (b) Solve for the equilibrium state probabilities.
   (c) Find the throughput of each station.
   (d) Plot the throughput ratio for $0 \leqslant p \leqslant 1$.
   Before solving the problem mathematically, make a rough sketch of what you expect the curve of part (d) to look like, to test your intuition about how the system behaves.

7. An Ethernet uses Mok and Ward's version of binary countdown. At a certain instant, the ten stations have the virtual station numbers 8, 2, 4, 5, 1, 7, 3, 6, 9, and 0. The next three stations to send are 4, 3, and 9, in that order. What are the new virtual station numbers after all three have finished their transmissions?

8. Sixteen stations are contending for the use of a shared channel using the adaptive tree walk protocol discussed in section 7.1.4. If all the stations whose addresses are prime numbers suddenly become ready at once, how many bit slots are needed to resolve the contention?

9. A collection of 2^n stations use the adaptive tree walk protocol to arbitrate access to a shared cable. At a certain instant two of them become ready. What are the minimum, maximum, and mean number of slots to walk the tree if $2^n \gg 1$?

10. A biology student minoring in computer science has built a microprocessor-based, all-digital mousetrap in order to recapture one or more of the eight microprocessor-based, all-digital mice that have escaped from their cages. Unfortunately, there are also 11 ordinary, plain old analog mice in the lab. When the trap has reached its capacity of three mice, of either genre, the microprocessor emits an ASCII "Control G" character to alert the student. What is the probability of his having captured exactly one digital mouse?

11. If the urn protocol is used with 200 users, of whom 40 are ready to send, what is the probability of a collision? Of success?

12. At a transmission rate of 5 Mbps and a propagation speed of 200 m/μsec, how many meters of cable is the 1-bit delay in a token ring interface equivalent to?

13. A very heavily loaded 1 km long, 10-Mbps token ring has a propagation speed of 200 m/μsec. Fifty stations are uniformly spaced around the ring. Data packets are 256 bits, including 32 bits of overhead. Acknowledgements are piggybacked onto the data packets and are thus effectively free. The token is 8 bits. Compare the maximum effective data rate with that of the Ethernet of Problem 2.

14. In a token ring the sender removes the packet. What modifications to the system would be needed to have the receiver remove the packet instead, and what would the consequences be?

15. In an N-station contention ring, exactly one of the stations has just begun to transmit. What is the probability that the station captures the ring if the walk time is w sec and the arrival of packets at each station from processes within its computer is Poisson with mean λ?

16. A large slotted ring contains 1024 bits, grouped in 32 packets slots. If 60% of the packet slots are empty on the average, what is the chance that a newly generated packet will have to wait more than two slots to get onto the ring?

17. A computer system uses a single bus for communication between its processors and memories. Bus arbitration is done using daisy chaining. The performance of this system is similar to one of the Ethernet protocols. Which one?

18. In a Cm* type system, a local memory reference takes 1 μsec, an intracluster memory reference takes 5 μsec, and an intercluster memory reference takes 10 μsec. If measurements show that two-thirds of all memory references are local, and of the nonlocal ones, nine-tenths are intracluster, how much could a computation be speeded up by moving all the code and data to the local memory?

19. Write a program to simulate a 1-persistent unslotted ALOHA system, and plot the throughput versus the channel load.

20. Write a program to simulate BRAP. Both the contention slots and the data (bit) slots are 1 μsec long. During each slot, the probability of an unblocked station generating a packet (and becoming blocked) is p. Let the packet transmission times be exponentially distributed with a mean of n μsec. Compute and plot the throughput in packets/sec, as well as the mean delay, both as a function of p for 100 stations and $n = 100$ μsec.

21. In Prob. 6 you were asked to analyze a two station binary countdown system analytically. Now write a program to determine numerically the throughput for each station in an N-station binary countdown system.

22. Write a program to simulate the behavior of a token black. Use the program to see how sensitive Eq. (7-4) is to changes in the model. Try variable packet lengths, non-Poisson arrivals, etc.

8

THE TRANSPORT AND SESSION LAYERS

Having completed our study of the physical, data link, and network layers, it is time to turn our attention to the transport layer. The lowest three layers are concerned with the transmission, framing, and routing of packets between adjacent machines (with the understanding that in a broadcast network, all machines are adjacent). The transport layer, in contrast, has the task of providing a reliable and efficient end-to-end transport service between (user) processes rather than just between machines.

Throughout this chapter we will continue to use the conceptual model of Fig. 1-7. In this model, the subnet interface extends up only as far as layer 3. In other words, the programs that comprise the transport layer run only on the hosts and not on the IMPs, in contrast to the lower three layers, which are present on both hosts and IMPs. In the future, some networks will offer transport layer service within the subnet, but such a development will only change the terminology that should be used in this chapter, not the content, because the technical issues of ensuring reliable end-to-end communication are the same, no matter whether the customer or the carrier is administratively responsible for it. These issues center on the user interface to the transport layer: naming and addressing of users, connection establishment and termination, buffering and flow control, multiplexing, error recovery, and synchronization.

After a detailed discussion of transport protocols, we will take a careful look at the problems involved in connecting two or more networks. Many of the difficulties encountered in internetworking can be greatly alleviated by proper design of the transport protocol, so these two topics are intimately related.

After finishing the transport layer, we will say a few words about the session layer and then examine the transport layers of our usual example networks.

8.1. TRANSPORT PROTOCOL DESIGN ISSUES

The most important single factor affecting transport protocol design is the kind of service the subnet provides. If the subnet provides virtual circuit service, guaranteeing that messages are delivered in order from sender to receiver, without error, loss, or duplication, the transport protocol becomes relatively simple, because the subnet is in fact doing all the work. If, however, the subnet provides datagram service, it is up to the hosts to make sure that messages are delivered in order without error, loss, or duplication. This situation requires a much more sophisticated transport protocol.

It is worth mentioning that although a packet carrier may claim to provide virtual circuit service, some users may be skeptical. If a group of users does not believe that the carrier is technically capable of living up to its promise of 100% reliable service, they may decide to treat the subnet as a high-quality datagram system, and superimpose their own end-to-end error and flow control on top of the carrier's.

It is also worth pointing out that X.25 does not offer virtual circuit service despite its virtual circuit interface because the network can send RESET (or RESTART) packets to the hosts at will. After a RESET packet arrives at a host, there is no way provided within X.25 for the host to inquire about the status of packets still outstanding. Both the next sequence number to use and the next acknowledgement to expect must immediately be set to zero at both ends. Recovery must be done by a higher layer, namely the transport layer. Put in other words, users who like to live dangerously can use X.25 as though it were a transport protocol, but users who want to be sure that data are never lost or duplicated must put another layer of protocol on top of X.25.

The design of the transport protocol is different from the design of the data link protocol due to a major difference between the environment in which the two protocols operate. This difference is illustrated in Fig. 8-1. At the data link layer, two IMPs communicate directly via a physical channel, whereas at the transport layer, this physical channel is replaced by the entire subnet. This difference has many important implications for the protocols. For one thing, in the data link layer, it is not necessary for an IMP to specify which IMP it wants to talk to—each outgoing line uniquely specifies a particularly IMP. In the transport layer, explicit addressing of destinations is required. For another thing, the process of establishing a connection over the wire of Fig. 8-1(a) is simple: the other end is always there (unless it has crashed, it which case it is not there). Either way, there is not much to do. In the transport layer, initial connection establishment is more complicated, as we will see.

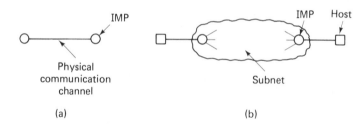

Fig. 8-1. (a) Environment of the data link layer. (b) Environment of the transport layer.

A third, and exceedingly annoying, difference between the data link layer and the transport layer is the existence of storage capacity in the subnet. When an IMP sends a frame, it may arrive or be lost, but it cannot bounce around for a while and then suddenly emerge at an inopportune moment 30 sec later. If the subnet uses datagrams and adaptive routing inside, there is a nonnegligible probability that a packet may be stored for a number of seconds and then delivered later. The consequences of this ability of the subnet to store packets can be disastrous.

A final difference between the data link and transport layers is one of amount rather than of kind. Buffering and flow control are needed in both layers, but the presence of a large and dynamically varying number of connections in the transport layer may require a different approach than we used in Chap. 4.

8.1.1. Transport Service

Collectively, layers 1 through 4 provide a **transport service**, shielding the higher layers from the technical details of how the communication is achieved. The operating system on each host provides a collection of system (or library) calls to allow users to communicate with remote processes. It is up to the transport layer to bridge the gap between what the operating system offers to its users, the transport service, and what the subnet actually provides. If the subnet service is modified, the transport layer will also have to be modified, to implement the old system calls using the new subnet service, but software above the transport layer will not be affected. The characteristics of the transport service are network dependent, but most networks offer at least error-free delivery of messages in sequence.

The transport layer defines a set of **transport addresses** or **sockets** through which communication occurs. The transport addresses form a network-wide name space that allow processes to refer to one another. To ensure that all transport addresses are globally unique, the transport addresses consist of a network number, a host number, and a **port** assigned by the host. For example, the ARPANET TCP protocol provides 32 bits for network + host and 16 bits for ports, whereas CCITT's numbering plan provides four decimal digits for network number and 10 decimal digits for host + port. Users of the transport service can request a **transport connection** to be established between a local transport address and one on a remote machine, as illustrated in Fig. 8-2. The paths *CGJSPL* and *DHJSOK* are two example transport connections.

The network layer also defines a set of addresses, called **network addresses**, which the transport layer uses to create transport connections. For example, if the network of Fig. 8-2 uses X.25, the network addresses *E*, *F*, *G*, and *H* might correspond to X.25 virtual circuits 1, 2, 3, and 4. In the figure, each transport connection uses a different X.25 virtual circuit, but multiple transport connections could be multiplexed onto a single virtual circuit, as will be discussed later. Be sure to note the difference between a "transport connection" and a "virtual circuit" in what follows, the former referring to layer 4 and the layer to layer 3.

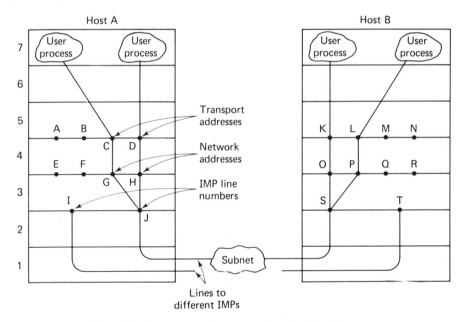

Fig. 8-2. Transport addresses and network addresses.

Although multiplexing of transport connections onto virtual circuits is not done in this example, multiplexing of virtual circuits onto physical circuits is done. Virtual circuits *GJSP* and *HJSO* both use line *J*, although a second connection to the subnet, via *I*, is also available.

At host *B*, the network layer must demultiplex incoming traffic, indicating which packets belong to virtual circuit *O* and which to *P* for the benefit of the transport layer. This demultiplexing normally consists of just stripping the header from the incoming packets and passing the data up to the transport layer, together with some indication of the network address of each one.

To illustrate what a typical transport service might offer its users, we will postulate a simple set of system calls that user programs may make (layers 5 and 6 are ignored here for simplicity):

connum = CONNECT(local, remote)
connum = LISTEN(local)
status = CLOSE(connum)
status = SEND(local, buffer, bytes)
status = RECEIVE(local, buffer, bytes)

The CONNECT call takes two parameters, a local transport address, *local*, and a remote transport address, *remote*, and tries to establish a transport connection between the two transport addresses. If it succeeds, it returns in *connum* a nonnegative number used to identify the connection on subsequent calls. If it fails, the reason for failure is put in *connum* as a negative number. In our simple model, each transport address may participate in only one transport connection, so a possible reason for failure is that one of the transport addresses is currently in use. Some other reasons are: remote host down, illegal local address, and illegal remote address.

The LISTEN call announces the caller's willingness to accept connection requests directed at the indicated address. Depending on the implementation, the caller may be suspended until a CONNECT is performed on the address being listened to, or the caller may continue executing, with the connection attempt indicated by a signal or interrupt from the operating system. In our model, the caller is suspended.

The CLOSE call terminates a transport connection. The parameter *connum* tells which one. Possible errors are: *connum* belongs to another process, or *connum* is not a valid connection identifier.

The SEND call transmits the contents of the buffer as a message on the indicated transport connection. Possible errors, returned in *status*, are: no connection, illegal buffer address, or negative count.

The RECEIVE call indicates the caller's desire to accept data. The size of the incoming message is placed in *bytes*. If the remote process has closed the connection or the buffer address is illegal (e.g., outside the user's program), *status* is set accordingly.

Please be sure to realize that this example is analogous to the early examples presented in Chap. 4: it is more for pedagogical purposes than a serious proposal. After we have finished studying it, we will then discuss various issues that are oversimplified here. Figure 8-3 gives an example program for implementing our transport service. Such a program, often called a **transport station**, may be part of the host's operating system or it may be a package of library routines running within the user's address space. In some cases it may even run on a front end processor external to the host itself. For simplicity, the example of Fig. 8-3 has been programmed as though it were a library package, but the changes needed to make it part of the operating system are minimal (primarily how user buffers are accessed). In an operating system implementation, the issues of multiprogramming several users also arises, whereas our model only deals with a single user. The user may have multiple transport connections open at once, of course.

Although this transport station is simple, it is nevertheless instructive to examine it closely. Basically it provides a means for user programs to establish, use and terminate sequenced, error-free connections. Messages sent may be arbitrarily long, even though the underlying network has a maximum packet size, *MaxPkt*. The network service used by the transport station is assumed to be reliable (to keep the example short) and to have an X.25 interface.

The interface to the network layer is via the procedures *ToNet* and *FromNet* (not shown). Each has six parameters: the connection identifier, which maps one-to-one onto network virtual circuits; the X.25 *Q* and *M* bits, which indicate control message and more data from this messages follows in the next packet, respectively; the packet type, chosen from the set CALL REQUEST, CALL ACCEPTED, CLEAR REQUEST, CLEAR CONFIRMED, DATA, and CREDIT; a pointer to the data itself; and the number of bytes of data. *ToNet* and *FromNet* interface to procedures such as *FromHost* and *ToHost* in Chap. 4.

On calls to *ToNet*, the transport station fills in all the parameters for the network layer to read; on calls to *FromNet*, the network layer dismembers an incoming packet for the transport station. By passing information as procedure parameters rather than passing the actual outgoing or incoming packet itself, the transport layer is shielded from the details of the network layer protocol. When the transport station attempts to send a packet when the underlying virtual circuit's sliding window is full, it is put to sleep (suspended) within *ToNet* until there is room in the window. This sleep/wakeup mechanism is transparent to the transport station and is controlled by the network layer using the *EnableHost* and *DisableHost* commands described in the protocols of Chap. 4. The management of the X.25 packet layer window is also done by the network layer.

In addition to this transparent sleep/wakeup, there are also explicit *sleep* and *wakeup* procedures (not shown) called by the transport station. The procedure *sleep* is called when the transport station is logically blocked waiting for an external event to happen, generally the arrival of a packet. After *sleep* has been called, the transport station (and user process, of course) stop executing. However, if a packet arrives or the clock ticks, an interrupt will be generated, and the appropriate interrupt handler, *PacketArrival* or *clock*, will be run. The interrupt handlers always run to completion without being interrupted themselves, and may call *wakeup*, in which case the sleeping transport station is awakened as soon as the interrupt handler returns. Interrupts can only occur

```
const MaxConn = ... ;   MaxMsg = ... ;   MaxPkt = ... ;
      TimeOut = ... ;
      q0 = 0; q1 = 1;
      m0 = 0; m1 = 1;
      cred = ... ;
      ok = 0;
      ErrFull = −1;   ErrReject = −2;   ErrClosed = −3;   LowErr = −3;

type bit = 0..1;
      TransportAddress = integer;
      ConnId = 1 .. MaxConn;        {connection identifier}
      PktType = (CallReq, CallAcc, ClearReq, ClearConf, DataPkt, credit);
      cstate = (idle, listening, waiting, queued, open, sending, receiving, closing);
      message = array [0 .. MaxMsg] of 0 .. 255;
      msgptr = ↑message;            {pointer to a message}
      ErrorCode = LowErr .. 0;
      ConnIdOrErr = LowErr .. MaxConn;
      PktLength = 0 .. MaxPkt;
      packet = array[PktLength] of 0 .. 255;

var ListenAddress: TransportAddress;          {local address being listened to}
      ListenConn: ConnId;                     {connection identifier for listen}
      data: packet;                           {scratch area for packet data}
      conn: array[ConnId] of record
        LocalAddress, RemoteAddress: TransportAddress;
      MsgsSent, MsgsReceived: integer;
      state: cstate;                          {state of this connection}
      UserBufferAddress: msgptr;              {pointer to receive buffer}
      ByteCount: 0 .. MaxMsg;                 {send/receive count}
      ClrReqReceived: boolean;                {set when CLEAR REQ packet received}
      timer: integer;                         {used to time out CALL REQUEST packets}
      credits: integer;                       {number of messages that may be sent}
      end;

function listen(t: TransportAddress): ConnIdOrErr;
{User wants to listen for a connection.}
var i: integer; found: boolean;
begin i := 1;  found := false;
  while (i < = MaxConn) and not found do
    if (conn[i].state = queued) and (conn[i].LocalAddress = t)
      then found := true
      else i := i + 1;

  if not found then begin ListenAddress := t;  sleep;  i := ListenConn end;
  conn[i].state := open;
  conn[i].timer := 0;
  listen := i;
  ListenConn := 0;                  {0 is assumed to be an invalid address}
  ToNet(i, q0, m0, CallAcc, data, 0)     {accept the connection}
end; {listen}
```

```
function connect(l, r: TransportAddress): ConnIdOrErr;
{User wants to connect to a remote process.}
var i: integer;
begin i := MaxConn;                    {search table backwards}
    data[0] := r;   data[1] := l;      {CALL REQUEST packet needs these}
    while (conn[i].state <> idle) and (i > 1) do i := i - 1;
    if conn[i].state = idle then
        with conn[i] do
            begin MsgsSent := 0;  MsgsReceived := 0;
                LocalAddress := l;  RemoteAddress := r;   state := waiting;
                ClrReqReceived := false;  credits := 0;   timer := 0;
                ToNet(i, q0, m0, CallReq, data, 2);
                sleep;
                if state = open then connect := i;
                if ClrReqReceived then
                    begin
                        connect := ErrReject;
                        state := idle;
                        ToNet(i, q0, m0, ClearConf, data, 0)
                    end
            end
    else connect := ErrFull
end; {connect}

function send(cid: ConnId; bufptr: msgptr; bytes: integer): ErrorCode;
{User wants to send a message.}
var i, count: integer;   m: bit;
begin
    with conn[cid] do
        begin state := sending;
            ByteCount := 0;
            if (not ClrReqReceived) and (credits = 0) then sleep;
            if not ClrReqReceived then
                begin
                    repeat
                        if bytes - ByteCount > MaxPkt
                            then begin count := MaxPkt;  m := 1 end
                            else begin count := bytes - ByteCount;  m := 0 end;
                        for i := 0 to count - 1 do data[i] := bufptr↑[ByteCount + i];
                        ToNet(cid, q0, m, DataPkt, data, count);
                        ByteCount := ByteCount + count;
                    until ByteCount = bytes;
                    MsgsSent := MsgsSent + 1;
                    credits := credits - 1;
                    send := ok
                end
            else send := ErrClosed;
            state := open
        end
end; {send}
```

```
function receive(cid: ConnId; bufptr: msgptr; var bytes: integer): ErrorCode;
{User is prepared to receive a message.}
begin
  with conn[cid] do
    begin
      if not ClrReqReceived then
        `begin state := receiving;
           UserBufferAddress := bufptr;    ByteCount := 0;
           data[0] := cred;   data[1] := 1;
           ToNet(cid, q1, m0, DataPkt, data, 2);
           sleep;
           bytes := ByteCount;
           MsgsReceived := MsgsReceived + 1;
           bytes := ByteCount
        end;
      if ClrReqReceived then receive := ErrClosed else receive := ok;
      state := open
    end
end; {receive}

function close(cid: ConnId): ErrorCode;
{User wants to close a connection.}
begin
  with conn[cid] do
    if ClrReqReceived
      then begin state := idle;   ToNet(cid, q0, m0, ClearConf, data, 0) end
      else begin state := closing;   ToNet(cid, q0, m0, ClearReq, data, 0) end;
  close := ok
end; {close}

procedure PacketArrival;
{A packet has arrived, get and process it.}
var cid: ConnId;                    {connection on which packet arrived}
    q, m: bit;
    ptype: PktType;                 {CallReq, CallAcc, ClearReq, ClearConf, DataPkt, credit}
    data: packet;                   {data portion of the incoming packet}
    count: PktLength;               {number of data bytes in packet}
    i: integer;                     {scratch variable}
begin
  FromNet(cid, q, m, ptype, data, count);  {go get it}
  with conn[cid] do
  case ptype of
  CallReq:
    begin LocalAddress := data[0];   RemoteAddress := data[1];
      if LocalAddress = ListenAddress
        then begin ListenConn := cid; state := open; wakeup end
        else begin state := queued; timer := TimeOut end;
      MsgsSent := 0;   MsgsReceived := 0;
      ClrReqReceived := false;   credits := 0
    end;
```

CallAcc:
  begin
    state := *open*;
    wakeup
  end;

ClearReq:
  begin
    ClrReqReceived := *true*;
    if *state* = *closing* **then** *state* := *idle*; {clear collision}
    if *state* **in** [*waiting*, *receiving*, *sending*] **then** *wakeup*
  end;

ClearConf:
  state := *idle*;

credit:
  begin
    credits := *credits* + *data*[1];
    if *state* = *sending* **then** *wakeup*
  end;

Datapkt:
  begin
    for *i* := 0 **to** *count* − 1 **do** *UserBufferAddress*↑[*ByteCount* + *i*] := *data*[*i*];
    ByteCount := *ByteCount* + *count*;
    if *m* = 0 **then** *wakeup*
  end
  end;
end; {PacketArrival}

procedure *clock*;
{The clock has ticked, check for timeouts of queued connect requests.}
var *i*: *ConnId*;
begin
  for *i* := 0 **to** *MaxConn* **do**
    with *conn*[*i*] **do**
      if *timer* > 0 **then**
        begin
          timer := *timer* − 1;
          if *timer* = 0 **then**
            begin
              state := *closing*;
              ToNet(*i*, *q0*, *m0*, *ClearReq*, *data*, 0)
            end
        end
end; {clock}

Fig. 8-3. A simple transport station.

when the user is executing code outside the transport station or when the transport station is sleeping. This property is crucial to the correct functioning of the transport station.

The existence of the Q (Qualifier) bit in the X.25 header allows us to avoid the overhead of a transport protocol header. Ordinary data messages are sent as X.25 data packets with $Q = 0$. Transport protocol control messages, of which there is only one (CREDIT) in our example, are sent as X.25 data packets with $Q = 1$. These control messages are detected and processed by the receiving transport station, of course.

The main data structure used by the transport station is the array *conn*, which has one record for each potential connection. The record maintains the state of the connection, including the transport addresses at either end, the number of messages sent and received on the connection, the current state, the user buffer pointer, the number of bytes of the current messages sent or received so far, a bit indicating that the remote user has done a CLOSE, a timer, and a permission counter used to enable sending of messages. Not all of these fields are used in our simple example, but a complete transport station would need all of them, and perhaps more. Each *conn* entry is assumed initialized to the *idle* state.

When the user calls CONNECT, the network layer is instructed to send a CALL REQUEST packet to the remote machine, and the user is put to sleep. When the CALL REQUEST packet arrives at the other side, the transport station is interrupted so that it can check to see if the local user is listening on the specified address. If so, a CALL ACCEPTED packet is sent back and the remote user is awakened; if not, the CALL REQUEST is queued for *TimeOut* clock ticks. If a listen is done within this period, the connection is established; otherwise, it times out and is rejected with a CLEAR REQUEST packet. This mechanism is needed to prevent a process from blocking forever in the event that the remote process does not want to connect to it.

To avoid having to provide and manage buffers within the transport station, a flow control mechanism different from the traditional sliding window is used here. Instead, when a user calls RECEIVE, a special **credit message** is sent to the transport station on the receiving machine and is recorded in the *conn* array. When SEND is called, the transport station checks to see if a credit has arrived on the specified connection. If so, the message is sent (in multiple packets if need be) and the credit decremented; if not, the transport station puts itself to sleep until a credit arrives. This mechanism guarantees that no message is ever sent unless the other side has already done a RECEIVE. As a result, whenever a message arrives there is guaranteed to be a buffer available into which it can be put. The scheme can easily be generalized to allow receivers to provide multiple buffers and request multiple messages.

You should keep the simplicity of Fig. 8-3 in mind. A realistic transport station would normally check all user supplied parameters for validity, handle recovery from network resets, deal with call collisions, and support a more general transport service including such facilities as interrupts, datagrams, and nonblocking versions of the SEND and RECEIVE calls.

8.1.2. Addressing and Connection Establishment

In a computer network, hosts have resources that can be accessed remotely by other hosts. Typical examples of such resources are processes, files, mailboxes, terminals, and unique peripheral devices. Throughout our discussion of naming, and addressing it will be convenient to focus on one kind of resource, the **generic service**, as a prototype. A generic service performs some set of actions for its customers. Some possible services are: time of day, Pascal compilation, file storage and retrieval, and data base management. Associated with each service is a process called a **server**, whose task it is to provide the service to any (authorized) process that requests it.

One way to implement services is to have each server process execute a LISTEN call on some transport address. To use a service, a user then does a CONNECT specifying the appropriate remote transport address. The question then arises, how does the user know which server is listening to which transport address? Also, how does a server know which transport address to listen to?

At this point it is useful to distinguish between a *name* that is, which service the user wants, and an *address*, that is, which transport address the server is listening to (Shoch, 1978). A name is generally a character string intended for use by people rather than machines. Consequently, a mapping must be done between the name and the address. The mapping may be accomplished by consulting a **name server**, analogous to the telephone system's directory assistance server. In some cases servers may listen to so-called **well-known addresses**, which are widely known and rarely changed, so they can be published in printed books. The address of the name server must never be changed, since the name server cannot be used to locate itself, just as people cannot use the telephone operator to ask how to call the operator. (If you think the latter is obvious, try it in a foreign country some time.)

In any event, once a name, such as *time-of-day*, has been mapped onto an address, such as 2102780001, the transport station must set up a connection with the process listening to that address. Although there are no general rules about how services are named, the naming being possibly local to each host or specific to each application, there are two general strategies for allocating transport addresses, **hierarchical addresses** and **flat addresses**.

With a hierarchical address space, the address consists of a sequence of fields, used to disjointly partition the space. For example, a truly universal addressing scheme might be

<address> = <galaxy> <star> <planet> <country> <network> <host> <port>

With hierarchical addresses, knowledge of an address tells where the server is located.

With flat naming, this is not the case. Flat names have no particular relationship to geography or any other hierarchy. Conceivably, flat addresses could be allocated by having a single system-wide counter that could be read and incremented any time a new address was needed. In this way addresses would be unique, but not related to location.

To make the difference between hierarchical and flat addresses clearer, let us consider an analogy between telephone numbers and (U.S.) social security numbers. The set of international telephone numbers form a hierarchical address space. For example, a number such as 19076543210 can be parsed as 1-907-654-3210, where 1 is a "country" code (U.S. + Canada), 907 is an area code (Alaska), 654 designates an end office, and 3210 designates a specific "port" (subscriber line) within that central office. In contrast, a social security number such as 290380002 cannot be broken down into a state code + a county code + a city code to tell where its bearer is currently to be found. Therefore, social security numbers form a flat address space.

CCITT, in recommendation X.121, has decreed that public computer networks will use a numbering system similar to the public switched telephone network, with each host identified by a decimal number consisting of a country code, a network code, and an address within the specified network. The full address may contain up to 14 decimal digits, of which the first three indicate the country, and the next one indicates the network number. For countries expected to have many public networks engaged in international traffic, multiple country codes have been allocated e.g., the United States has been allocated country codes 310 through 329, allowing up to 200 international networks, Canada has been allocated 302 through 307, allowing up to 60 international networks, but the Kingdom of Tonga has been allocated only code 539, allowing for 10 networks. Country codes with initial digits of 0 and 1 are reserved for future use, and initial digits 8 and 9 are used for connecting to the public telex and telephone networks, respectively.

The division of the remaining 10 digits is not specified by X.121, permitting each network to allocate the 10 billion addresses itself. Figure 8-4 shows a possible division of these 10 digits: seven digits to indicate the host and three digits to indicate the port. This division makes it possible to have 10 million hosts per network, each with up to 1000 addresses. If 10 digits do not provide enough resolution (and they do not for networks that use 32-bit transport addresses), the user data field at the end of the X.25 CALL REQUEST packet can be used to provide **subaddressing**, essentially, more address bits.

Both hierarchical and flat addressing have advantages and disadvantages. Hierarchical addressing makes routing easy, since, for example, each country need only know how to get packets to every other country, and need not know anything about that country's innards. Another advantage of hierarchical addressing is the ease of creating new ports. Each country can decide how it wants to assign hosts to networks without having to ask any central authority for permission. Similarly, each host has a set of ports it can allocate as it sees

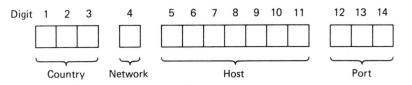

Fig. 8-4. Possible X.121 numbering scheme using 14 digits.

fit, without any need for coordinating its allocations with any other hosts. A third advantage is the ability to default the high-order bits of a port, just as you need not dial the country and area codes for local telephone calls.

Hierarchical addressing also has some disadvantages. For one, if a process migrates to a new machine, it cannot take its address with it. Another problem is that hierarchical addressing allocates an equal number of addresses to each country code, each network code, and so on. This may not always be desirable. Another danger is overspecification of the route. For example, if the address contains an <IMP> field in addition to all the others listed above, it becomes difficult for a host to achieve high reliability by attaching to two IMPs. Any attempt to connect to the host will specify which IMP is to be used, thus ruling out the other one, even if the first is down. When only the host is specified, the subnet retains the freedom to seek out which IMP to use.

Flat addressing has just the reverse properties from hierarchical addressing. Routing is much harder, but a mobile process can take its address with it. Assigning addresses is more complicated, however, due to the need to make sure that every address is unique. One shudders at the mere prospect of a centralized address allocator. A more realistic possibility is to have each host assign addresses using a hierarchical name, but not expect that a process can be located using its address. This method has the disadvantage of requiring a host to remember which addresses it has already assigned, since it cannot tell by just looking at what it currently has. If a host crashes and forgets its history, there is a danger of duplicate addresses. By using the current time of day as the port part, crashes are no longer so serious, but there are other problems, to be described later.

To summarize, users normally access generic services by name, not by address. The local host must use the name to find the transport address of a process willing to do the work. Once the address of such a process is known, contact can be established with it using the CONNECT primitive or its equivalent. However, a difficulty arises when a host potentially offers a very large variety of services. For example, if a time-sharing system has a thousand programs available, it is not feasible to have each one perpetually listening on a well-known address on the off chance that some remote user wants to use it. Among other reasons, each process requires some table space within the operating system, and such space is a scarce resource. Furthermore, multiple instances of many programs would be needed, in case several remote users wanted to run the same program at the same time.

This problem occurred during the early days of the ARPANET and was solved in an elegant way, which has become known as the ARPANET **initial connection protocol**. We will now describe an equivalent, but simpler mechanism. Instead of every conceivable server listening at a well-known address, each host that wishes to offer service to remote users has a special **process server** (or **logger**) through which all services must be requested. Whenever the process server is idle, it listens to a well-known address. Potential users of any service must begin by doing a CONNECT, specifying the address of the process server. Once the connection has been established, the user sends the process server a message telling which program it wants to run. The process server then chooses an idle address and spawns a new process, telling the new process to listen to the chosen address. Finally, the process server sends the remote user the chosen address, terminates the connection (with CLOSE), and goes back to listening on its well-known address.

At this point the new process is listening on an address that the user now knows, so it is possible for the user to close the connection to the process server and CONNECT to the new process. Once this connection has been set up, the new process executes the desired program, the name of which was passed to it by the process server, together with the address to listen to. The entire protocol is illustrated in Fig. 8-5.

8.1.3. Flow Control and Buffering

In some ways the flow control problem at the transport layer is the same as at the data link layer, but in other ways it is different. The basic similarity is that in both layers a sliding window or equivalent scheme is needed on each connection to keep a fast transmitter from overrunning a slow receiver. The main difference is that the IMP usually has relatively few lines whereas the host may have numerous connections. This difference makes it impractical to implement the data link buffering strategy in the transport layer.

In the data link protocols of Chap. 4, frames were buffered at both the sending IMP and at the receiving IMP. In protocol 6, for example, both sender and receiver are required to dedicate $MaxSeq + 1$ buffers to each line, half for input and half for output. For a host with a maximum of, say, 64 connections and a 4-bit sequence number, this protocol would require 1024 buffers.

In the data link layer, the sending side must buffer outgoing frames because they might have to be retransmitted. If the subnet provides datagram service, the sending transport station must also buffer, and for the same reason. If the receiver knows that the sender buffers all messages until they are acknowledged, the receiver may or may not dedicate specific buffers to specific connections, as it sees fit. The receiver may, for example, maintain a single buffer pool shared by all connections. When a message comes in, an attempt is

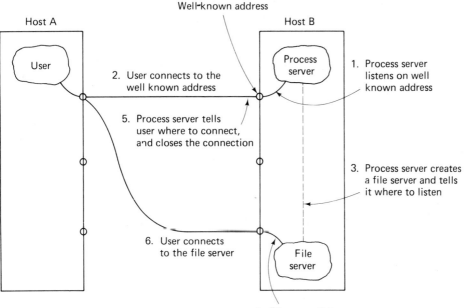

Fig. 8-5. How a user in host *A* connects to a file server in host *B*.

made to dynamically acquire a new buffer. If one is available, the message is accepted, otherwise it is discarded. Since the sender is prepared to retransmit messages lost by the subnet, no harm is done by having the receiver drop messages. The sender just keeps trying until it gets an acknowledgement. However, if this strategy is used, the receiver must be careful to avoid reassembly lockup.

In summary, if the subnet is unreliable, the sender must buffer all messages sent, just as in the data link layer. Remembering our earlier comments about X.25 RESET packets, it is clear that if a host wants to offer truly reliable service using a subnet that can reset virtual circuits at will, the sending host has to buffer all outstanding messages until they are acknowledged by the receiving host.

On the other hand, if the subnet really is reliable (e.g., a projected mean time between resets of 1000 years), other trade-offs become possible. In particular, if the sender knows that the receiver always has buffer space, it need not retain copies of the messages it sends. However, if the receiver cannot guarantee that every incoming message will be accepted, the sender will have to buffer anyway. In the latter case, the sender cannot trust the subnet's acknowledgement, because the acknowledgement means only that the message arrived, not that it was accepted. We will come back to this important point later.

Even if the receiver has agreed to do the buffering, there still remains the question of the buffer size. If most messages are nearly the same size, it is natural to organize the buffers as a pool of identical size buffers, with one message per buffer, as in Fig. 8-6(a). However, if there is wide variation in message size, from a few characters typed at a terminal to thousands of characters from file transfers, a pool of fixed-sized buffers presents problems. If the buffer size is chosen equal to the largest possible message, space will be wasted whenever a short message arrives. If the buffer size is chosen less than the maximum message size, multiple buffers will be needed for long messages, with the attendant complexity.

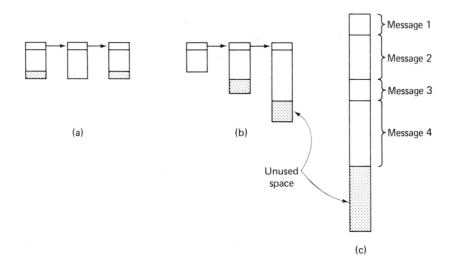

Fig. 8-6. (a) Chained fixed-size buffers. (b) Chained variable-size buffers. (c) One large circular buffer per connection.

Another approach to the buffer size problem is to use variable-size buffers, as in Fig. 8-6(b). The advantage here is better memory utilization, at the price of far more complicated buffer management. A third possibility is to dedicate a single large circular buffer per connection, as in Fig. 8-6(c). This system also makes good use of memory, provided that all connections are heavily loaded, but is poor if some connections are lightly loaded.

The optimum trade-off between source buffering and destination buffering depends on the type of traffic carried by the connection. For low-bandwidth, sporadic traffic, such as that produced by an interactive terminal, it is better not to dedicate any buffers, but rather to acquire them dynamically at both ends. Since the sender cannot be sure the receiver will be able to acquire a buffer, the sender must retain a copy of the message until it is acknowledged. On the other hand, for file transfer and other high-bandwidth traffic, it is better if the receiver does dedicate a full window of buffers, to allow the data to flow at maximum speed. Thus for low-bandwidth, bursty traffic it is better to buffer at the sender, and for high-bandwidth smooth traffic it is better to buffer at the receiver.

As connections are opened and closed, and as the traffic pattern changes, the sender and receiver need to dynamically adjust their buffer allocations. Consequently, the transport protocol should allow a sending host to request buffer space at the other end. Buffers could be allocated per connection, or collectively, for all the connections running between the two hosts. Alternatively, the receiver, knowing its buffer situation (but not knowing the offered traffic), could tell the sender "I have reserved X buffers for you." If the number of open connections should increase, it may be necessary for an allocation to be reduced, so the protocol should provide for this possibility.

A reasonably general way to manage dynamic buffer allocation is to decouple the buffering from the acknowledgements, in contrast to the sliding window protocols of Chap. 4. Dynamic buffer management means, in effect, a variable-sized window. Initially, the sender requests a certain number of buffers, based on its perceived needs. The receiver then grants as many of these as it can afford. Every time the sender transmits a message, it must decrement its allocation, stopping altogether when the allocation reaches zero. The receiver then separately piggybacks both acknowledgements and buffer allocations onto the reverse traffic.

Figure 8-7 shows an example of how dynamic window management might work in a datagram network with 4-bit sequence numbers. Assume that buffer allocation information travels in separate messages, as shown, and is not piggybacked onto reverse traffic. Initially, A wants eight buffers, but is only granted four of these. It then sends three messages, of which the third is lost. Message 6 acknowledges receipt of all messages up to and including sequence number 1, thus allowing A to release those buffers, and furthermore informs A that it has permission to send three more messages starting beyond 1, (i.e., messages 2, 3, and 4). A knows that it has already sent number 2, so it thinks that it may send messages 3 and 4, which it proceeds to do. At this point it is blocked, and must wait for more buffer allocation. Timeout induced retransmissions (line 9), however, may occur while blocked, since they use buffers that have already been allocated. In line 10, B acknowledges receipt of all messages up to and including 4, but refuses to let A continue. Such a situation is impossible with the fixed window protocols of Chapter 4. The next message from B to A allocates another buffer and allows A to continue.

Potential problems with buffer allocation schemes of this kind can arise in datagram networks if control messages can get lost. Look at line 16. B has now allocated more buffers to A, but the allocation message was lost. Since control messages are not sequenced or timed out, A is now deadlocked. To prevent this situation, each host should periodically send control messages giving the acknowledgement and buffer status on each connection. That way, the deadlock will be broken, sooner or later.

	A	Message	B	Comments
1	→	< request 8 buffers >	→	A wants 8 buffers
2	←	< ack = 15, buf = 4 >	←	B grants messages 0-3 only
3	→	< seq = 0, data = m0 >	→	A has 3 buffers left now
4	→	< seq = 1, data = m1 >	→	A has 2 buffers left now
5	→	< seq = 2, data = m2 >	...	Message lost but A thinks it has 1 left
6	←	< ack = 1, buf = 3 >	←	B acknowledges 0 and 1, permits 2-4
7	→	< seq = 3, data = m3 >	→	A has 1 buffer left
8	→	< seq = 4, data = m4 >	→	A has 0 buffers left, and must stop
9	→	< seq = 2, data = m2 >	→	A times out and retransmits
10	←	< ack = 4, buf = 0 >	←	Everything acknowledged, but A still blocked
11	←	< ack = 4, buf = 1 >	←	A may now send 5
12	←	< ack = 4, buf = 2 >	←	B found a new buffer somewhere
13	→	< seq = 5, data m5>	→	A has 1 buffer left
14	→	< seq = 6, data = m6 >	→	A is now blocked again
15	←	< ack = 6, buf = 0 >	←	A is still blocked
16	...	< ack = 6, buf = 4 >	←	Potential deadlock

Fig. 8-7. Dynamic buffer allocation. The arrows show the direction of transmission. An ellipsis (...) indicates a lost message.

Up until now we have tacitly assumed that the only limit imposed on the sender's data rate is the amount of buffer space available in the receiver. As memory prices continue to fall dramatically, it may become feasible to equip hosts with so much memory that lack of buffers is rarely, if ever, a problem.

When buffer space no longer limits the maximum flow, another bottleneck will appear: the carrying capacity of the subnet. If adjacent IMPs can exchange at most x frames/sec and there are k disjoint paths between a pair of hosts, there is no way that those hosts can exchange more than kx messages/sec, no matter how much buffer space is available at each end. If the sender pushes too hard (i.e., sends more than kx messages/sec), the subnet will become congested, because it will be unable to deliver messages as fast as they are coming in.

What is needed is a flow control mechanism based on the subnet's carrying capacity rather than on the receiver's buffering capacity. Clearly, the flow control mechanism must be applied at the sender, to prevent it from having too many unacknowledged messages outstanding at once. Belsnes (1975) has proposed using a sliding window flow control scheme in which the sender dynamically adjusts the window size to match the network's carrying capacity. If the network can handle c messages/sec and the cycle time (including transmission, propagation, queueing, processing at the receiver, and return of the acknowledgement) is r, then the sender's window should be cr. With a window of this size the sender normally operates with the pipeline full. Any small decrease in network performance will cause it to block.

In order to adjust the window size periodically, the sender could monitor both parameters and then compute the desired window size. The carrying capacity can be determined by simply counting the number of messages acknowledged during some time period and then dividing by the time period. During the measurement, the sender should send as fast as it can, to make sure that the network's carrying capacity, and not the low input rate, is the factor limiting the acknowledgement rate. The time required for a transmitted message to be acknowledged can be measured exactly and a running mean maintained. Since the capacity of the network depends on the amount of traffic in it, the window size should be adjusted frequently, to track changes in the carrying capacity.

8.1.4. Multiplexing

Multiplexing several conversations onto connections, virtual circuits, and physical links plays a role in several layers of the network architecture. In the transport layer the need for multiplexing can arise in a number of ways. For example, in networks that use virtual circuits within the subnet, each open connection consumes some table space in the IMPs for the entire duration of the session. If buffers are dedicated to the virtual circuit in each IMP as well, a user who left his terminal logged into a remote machine during a coffee break is nevertheless consuming expensive resources. Although this implementation of packet switching defeats one of the main reasons for having packet switching in the first place—to bill the user based on the amount of data sent, not the connect time—a number of PTTs have chosen this approach, presumably because it so closely resembles the circuit switching model to which they have grown accustomed over the decades.

The consequence of a price structure that heavily penalizes installations for having many virtual circuits open for long periods of time is to make multiplexing of different transport connections onto the same network connection attractive. This form of multiplexing, called **upward multiplexing**, is shown in Fig. 8-8(a). In this figure, four distinct transport connections all use the same virtual circuit to the remote host. When connect time forms the major component of the carrier's bill, it is up to the transport layer to group transport connections according to their destination and map each group onto the minimum number number of virtual circuits. If too many connections are mapped onto one virtual circuit, the performance will be poor, because the window will usually be full, and users will have to wait their turn to send one message. If too few connections are mapped onto one virtual circuit, the service will be expensive. When upward multiplexing is used with X.25, we have the ironic (tragic?) situation of having to identify the connection using a field in the transport header, even though X.25 provides more than 4000 virtual circuit numbers expressly for that purpose.

Multiplexing can also be useful in the transport layer for another reason, related to carrier technical decisions rather than carrier pricing decisions.

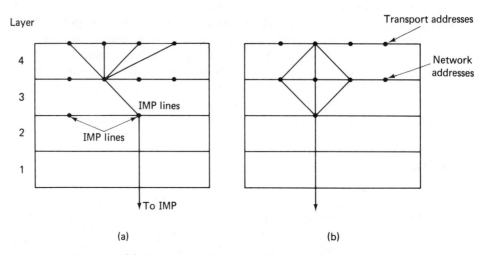

Fig. 8-8. (a) Upward multiplexing. (b) Downward multiplexing.

Suppose, for example, that a certain important user needs a high-bandwidth connection from time to time. If the subnet enforces a sliding window flow control with a 3-bit sequence number, the user must stop sending as soon as seven packets are outstanding, and must wait for the packets to propagate to the remote host and be acknowledged. If the physical connection is via a satellite, the user is effectively limited to seven packets every 540 msec. With 128-byte packets, the usable bandwidth is about 14 kbps, even though the physical channel bandwidth is more than 1000 times higher.

The solution is to have the transport layer open multiple network connections, and distribute the traffic among them on a round-robin basis, as indicated in Fig. 8-8(b). This modus operandi is called **downward multiplexing**. The transmission group idea in SNA (Fig. 5-21) is an implementation of downward multiplexing. With k network connections open, the effective bandwidth is increased by a factor of k. With X.25, 128-byte packets, and a 3-bit sequence number, it is theoretically possible to achieve data rates in excess of 50 Mbps. Of course, this performance can be achieved only if the host-IMP line can support 50 Mbps, because all 4095 virtual circuits are still being sent out over one physical line, at least in Fig. 8-8(b). If multiple host-IMP lines are available, downward multiplexing can also be used to increase the performance even more.

Multiplexing also occurs in some other contexts in the transport layer. For example, a host might have multiple, independent transport stations, each using different transport protocols (e.g., to talk to a variety of incompatible remote hosts). When there are two or more transport stations, the interface between layers 3 and 4 must be multiplexed, so layer 3 will know which transport station to give an incoming packet to. In an X.25 network, the network layer would have to remap the transport stations' choice of virtual circuit numbers, since each transport station is free to choose the same numbers as the others.

Another use for multiplexing is the ability to distinguish between high- and low-priority data sent on the same connection. In effect, several subconnections with different priorities are being multiplexed onto the same transport connection. In addition to the date itself, there may also be control information to be multiplexed along with the data.

8.1.5. Synchronization in the Presence of Delayed Packets

When two user processes wish to communicate, each one must connect to a local transport address using the appropriate system call. Then the two transport stations set up and properly initialize a connection between the users. In this section we will demonstrate that setting up connections is easier said than done when the subnet can store packets for an indefinite period of time. This effect is most pronounced in networks using datagrams inside, but to allow interconnection to datagram networks, even pure virtual circuit networks must be prepared to deal with the problem or suffer the consequences.

Delayed duplicates occur when the routing algorithm gets into a loop (A thinks the best route is via B, and B thinks the best route is via A), or when congestion simply causes a long delay. Either way, the sending host eventually times out and retransmits. If the new packet takes a different route it may arrive before the original, at which time both sender and receiver forget about the extra packet. After a while the sequence numbers will wrap around. If the delayed packet now shows up at the receiver, it will be accepted, and the correct packet will be rejected as a duplicate. The transport station will deliver incorrect data to the user, and the error will not be detected.

The delayed duplicate problem can be attacked in various ways, none of them very satisfactory. One way is to use throwaway transport addresses. In this approach, each time a transport address address is needed, a new, unique address is generated, typically based on the current time. When a connection is closed, the addresses are discarded forever. This strategy makes the process server model of Fig. 8-5 impossible. A variation on the idea is never to let the source address be reused, but to permit reuse of the destination address. Yet another variation is merely to forbid the same combination of address to be linked up again. Still another possibility is to make the sequence number space so large that it never recycles. For example, 48 bits will allow 1000 packets per second for 8000 years before recycling.

All these ideas have the same basic flaw: they require each host to maintain a certain amount of history information indefinitely. If a host crashes and loses its memory, it will no longer know which addresses are allowed or which sequence number comes next. Instead, we need to take a different tack. Rather than allowing packets to live forever within the subnet, we must devise a mechanism to kill off very old packets that are still wandering about. If we can ensure that no packet lives longer than some known time, the problem becomes somewhat more manageable.

Packet lifetime can be restricted to a known maximum using one of the following techniques:

1. Restricted subnet design.

2. Putting a hop counter in each packet.

3. Time stamping each packet.

The first method includes any method that prevents packets from looping, combined with some way of bounding congestion delay over the (now known) longest possible path. The second method consists of having the data link protocol simply discard any packet whose hop counter has exceeded a certain value. The third method requires each packet to bear the time it was created, with the IMPs agreeing to discard any packet older than some agreed upon time. This latter method requires the IMP clocks to be synchronized, which itself is a nontrivial task unless synchronization is achieved external to the network, for example by listening to WWV or some other radio station that broadcasts the exact time periodically.

In practice, we will need to guarantee not only that a packet is dead, but also that all acknowledgements to it are also dead, so we will now introduce T, which is some small multiple of the true maximum packet lifetime. The multiple is protocol-dependent and simply has the effect of making T longer. If we wait a time T after a packet has been sent, we can be sure that all traces of it are now gone and that neither it nor its acknowledgements will suddenly appear out of the blue.

A consequence of having storage in the subnet is that hosts may not send data as fast as they wish. If a host ever cycled through its sequence space within the packet lifetime, two packets with the same sequence number could be outstanding simultaneously, leading to disaster. If the sequence numbers have k bits, this requirement implies that no host may ever send more than 2^k packets within any time interval of duration T.

With maximum packet lifetimes bounded, there are several ways to deal with delayed duplicates. One way is to wait for T sec after closing a connection before allowing another connection to be opened with the same connection identifier (connection number or pair of addresses). This guarantees that all packets from all previous incarnations of the connection have been quenched. This method has two serious disadvantages however. Requests to open connections may have to be delayed until T has expired, and hosts must maintain information about connections that no longer exist (for a time T after each was closed).

There is also a way of preventing old duplicates from causing trouble, which does not required delaying new connections, although it, too, requires that hosts keep information about closed connections for a time T after closing. Instead of always initializing each new connection to begin with message 0, each host remembers the last sequence number used for each connection for a time T beyond when the connection was closed. If the connection is reopened while old packets may still exist, there will be no overlap between old and new sequence numbers, so there will be no confusion. However, this approach, like the preceding one, requires hosts to remember information about closed connections, but it does not require a delay upon opening a new connection.

A minor variation on the above strategy is to include an incarnation number in each packet. Each time a connection identifier is reused, the incarnation number is incremented. This way packets from previous incarnations can be distinguished from current ones. In essence, the incarnation number is really just part of the sequence number, just like the current sequence number, it is vulnerable to being lost in a crash.

All three of these methods require hosts to maintain some information about each previously closed connection for a time T after it was closed. In the event of a host crash, the only safe way to come back on the air is to wait a time T before reopening any connection. The problem with this whole approach is that when designing a protocol to be used internationally with networks as yet unknown, it is difficult to make a good estimate of T. Under such conditions the designers should be conservative and assume that a large value of T will be needed, which makes all of the preceding methods unattractive.

For our final attempt to deal with delayed duplicates, we will now describe a synchronization method due to Tomlinson (1975) that solves many of these problems, but introduces some peculiarities of its own. The method was further refined by Sunshine and Dalal (1978).

To get around the problem of a host losing all memory of where it was after a crash, Tomlinson proposed equipping each host with a time of day clock. The clocks at different hosts need not be synchronized. Each clock is assumed to take the form of a binary counter that increments itself at uniform intervals. Furthermore, the number of bits in the counter must equal or exceed the number of bits in the message sequence numbers. Last, and most important, the clock is assumed to continue running even if the host goes down.

The basic idea is to ensure that two identically numbered packets (messages) are never outstanding at the same time. When a connection is set up, the low-order k bits of the clock are used as the initial sequence number (also k bits). Thus, unlike our protocols of Chap. 4, each connection starts numbering its messages with a different sequence number. This linear relation between time and initial sequence numbers is shown in Fig. 8-9. Once both hosts have agreed on the initial sequence number, any sliding window protocol can be used for data flow control. In reality, the initial sequence number curve (shown by the heavy line) is not really linear, but a staircase, since the clock advances in discrete steps. For simplicity we will ignore this detail.

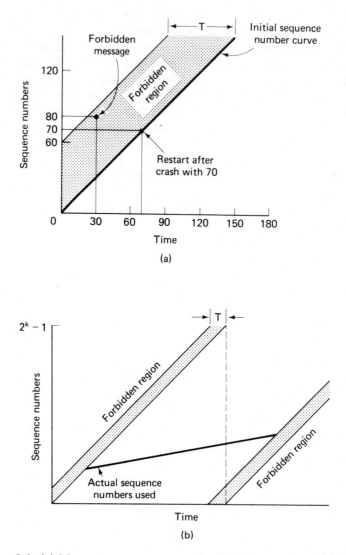

Fig. 8-9. (a) Messages may not enter the forbidden region. (b) The resynchronization problem.

To avoid requiring hosts to wait for T sec after a crash, it is necessary to introduce a new restriction on the use of sequence numbers. We can best see the need for this restriction by means of an example. Let T, the maximum packet lifetime be 60 sec, and let the clock tick once per second. As shown in Fig. 8-9, the initial sequence number for a connection opened at time x will be x. Imagine that at $t = 30$ sec, an ordinary data message being sent on (a previously opened) connection 5 is given sequence number 80. Call this message X. Immediately after sending message X, the host crashes and then quickly restarts. At $t = 60$, it begins reopening connections 0 through 4. At $t = 70$, it reopens connection 5, using initial sequence number 70 as required. Within the next 15 sec it sends data messages 70 through 80. Thus at $t = 85$ a new message with sequence number 80 and connection 5 has been injected into the subnet. Unfortunately, message X has not yet expired. If it should arrive at the receiver before the new message 80, it will be accepted and the correct message rejected.

To prevent such problems, we must prevent sequence numbers from being used (i.e., assigned to new messages) for a time T before their potential use as initial sequence numbers. The illegal combinations of time and sequence number are shown as the **forbidden region** in Fig. 8-9(a). Before sending any message on any connection, the transport station must read the clock and check to see that it is not in the forbidden region.

The protocol can get itself into trouble in two different ways. If a host sends too much data too fast on a newly opened connection, the actual sequence number versus time curve may rise more steeply than the initial sequence number versus time curve. This means that the maximum data rate on any connection is one message per clock tick. It also means that the transport station must wait until the clock ticks before opening a new connection after a crash restart, lest the same number be used twice. Both of these points argue for a short clock tick.

Unfortunately, entering the forbidden region from underneath by sending too fast is not the only way to get into trouble. From Fig. 8-9(b) it should be clear that at any data rate less than the clock rate, the curve of actual sequence numbers used versus time will eventually run into the forbidden region from the left. The greater the slope of the actual sequence number curve, the longer this event will be delayed. As we stated above, just before sending every message, the transport station must check to see if it is about to enter the forbidden region, and if so, either delay the message for T sec or resynchronize the sequence numbers.

The clock based method solves the delayed duplicate problem for data packets, but for this method to be useful, a connection must first be established. Since control packets may also be delayed, there is a potential problem in getting both sides to agree on the initial sequence number. Suppose, for example, that connections are established by having one host, A, send a SYN1 message containing the proposed initial sequence number and destination port number to the other host, B. The receiving host, B, then acknowledges this request by sending a SYN2 message back. If the SYN1 message is lost but a delayed duplicate SYN1 suddenly shows up at B, the connection will be established incorrectly.

To solve this problem, Tomlinson (1975) has introduced the **three-way handshake**. This establishment protocol does not require both hosts to begin sending with the same sequence number, so it can be used with synchronization methods other than the global clock method. The setup procedure when A initiates is shown in Fig. 8-10. A chooses a sequence number somehow, say x, and sends it to B, as indicated by the two rightward arrows. B replies with a SYN2 message acknowledging x and announcing its own initial sequence number, y (which may be equal to x, of course). Finally, A acknowledges B's choice of an initial sequence number in its first data message.

#	A	Packet	B	Comment
1	→	< type = SYN1, seq = x >	→	A wishes to initiate
2	←	< type = SYN2, seq = y, ack = x >	←	B accepts A's request
3	→	< type = DATA, seq = x, ack = y >	→	A acks B and starts transmission

(a)

#	A	Packet	B	Comment
1	. . .	< type = SYN1, seq = x >	→	Delayed duplicate SYN1 arrives at B
2	←	< type = SYN2, seq = y, ack = x >	←	B accepts A's request
3	→	< type = REJECT, ack = y >	→	A rejects B's connection

(b)

#	A	Packet	B	Comment
1	. . .	< type = SYN1, seq = x >	→	Delayed duplicate SYN1 arrives at B
2	←	< type = SYN2, seq = y, ack = x >	←	B accepts it
3	. . .	< type = DATA, seq = x, ack = z >	→	Delayed duplicate. B sees that z ≠ y
4	→	< type = REJECT, ack = y >	→	A rejects B's attempt as before

(c)

Fig. 8-10. The three-way handshake. (a) Normal operation. (b) Delayed SYN1. (c) Delayed SYN1 and delayed acknowledgement.

Now let us see how the three-way handshake works in the presence of delayed duplicate control messages. In Fig. 8-10(b), the first message is a delayed duplicate SYN1 from a connection since closed. This message arrives at B without A's knowledge (indicated by . . . in A's column). B reacts to this message by sending A a SYN2 message, in effect asking for verification that A was indeed trying to set up a new connection. When A rejects B's attempt to establish, B realizes that it was tricked by a delayed duplicate and abandons the connection.

The worst case is when both a delayed SYN1 and an acknowledgement to a SYN2 are floating around in the subnet. This case is shown in Fig. 8-10(c). As in the previous example, B gets a delayed SYN1 and replies to it. At this point it is crucial to realize that B has proposed using y as the initial sequence number for B to A traffic, knowing full well that no messages containing sequence number y or acknowledgements to y are still in existence. When the second delayed message arrives at B, the fact that z has been acknowledged rather than y tells B that this, too, is an old duplicate.

Gracefully terminating an already established connection is somewhat easier than setting up a new one because CLOSE requests can be numbered in sequence. Ideally, each host should send a CLOSE request and then wait until it has received both an acknowledgement, and an in sequence CLOSE request from the other side. That way it knows that all its transmitted data have been received, and furthermore that there are no more incoming data. However, since the CLOSE acknowledgements themselves are not acknowledged, if one of them gets lost the sender will not know that it should retransmit it; hence, the intended recipient will never close. Sunshine and Dalal (1978) discuss this problem in more detail.

8.1.6. Crash Recovery

For the most part, the transport protocol need not concern itself with errors. Transmission errors are supposed to be detected and corrected transparently by the lower layers of protocol. However, if the hosts do not trust the packet carrier's claimed error rate or require a lower one, they are free to compute, transmit, and verify their own checksums within the transport header. In addition to reducing the number of undetected errors, such an end-to-end checksum also serves to check for transmission errors on the host-IMP lines, as well as potential software bugs in the subnet. If the subnet fragments and then reassembles host messages, an end-to-end checksum can also be designed to check to see that the pieces got put back together in the proper order.

Transmission errors are not the only problem that the hosts have to deal with. Crash recovery is another one. If the the subnet goes down, it will probably lose information about the status of packets currently in transit. An X.25 network, for example, indicates loss of information by sending RESET or RESTART packets to the hosts. In principle, hosts can recover from subnet crashes if the transport protocol has been designed to allow one host to inquire about the status of the other. In effect, after a crash host A can ask host B: "I have four unacknowledged messages outstanding, 2, 3, 4, and 5; have you received any of them?" Based on the answer, A can retransmit the appropriate messages, provided that it has kept copies of them. If the host simply assumes that the subnet is reliable and does not keep copies, it will not be able to recover in this manner.

A more troublesome problem is how to recover from host crashes. To illustrate the difficulty, let us assume that one host, the sender, is sending a long file to another host, the receiver, using a simple stop-and-wait protocol. The operating system on the receiving host simply passes the incoming messages to the user, one by one. Part way through the transmission the receiver crashes. When it comes back up, its tables are reinitialized, so it no longer knows precisely where it was.

In an attempt to recover its previous status, the receiver might send a broadcast message to all other hosts, announcing that it had just crashed and requesting the other hosts to inform it of the status of all open connections. The sender can be in one of two states: one message outstanding, $S1$, or no messages outstanding, $S0$. Based on only this state information, the sender must decide whether or not to retransmit the most recent message.

At first glance it would seem obvious that the sender should retransmit only if it has an unacknowledged message outstanding (i.e., is in state $S1$) when it learns of the crash. However, a closer inspection reveals difficulties with this naive approach. Consider, for example, the situation when the receiving host first sends an acknowledgement, and then when the acknowledgement has been sent performs the write. Writing a message onto the output stream and sending an acknowledgement are considered as two distinct indivisible events that cannot be done simultaneously. If a crash occurs after the acknowledgement has been sent, but before the write has been done, the other host will receive the acknowledgement and thus be in state $S0$ when the crash recovery announcement arrives. The sender will therefore not retransmit, thinking the message has arrived correctly, leading to a missing message.

At this point you may be thinking: "That problem can be solved easily. All you have to do is reprogram the transport station to first do the write, and then send the acknowledgement." Try again. Imagine that the write has been done but the crash occurs before the acknowledgement can be sent. The sender will be in state $S1$ and thus retransmit, leading to an undetected duplicate message in the output stream.

No matter how the sender and receiver are programmed, there are always situations where the protocol fails to recover properly. The receiver can be programmed in one of two ways: acknowledge first or write first. The sender can be programmed in one of four ways: always retransmit the last message, never retransmit the last message, retransmit only in state $S0$, or retransmit only in state $S1$. This gives eight combinations, but as we shall see, for each combination there is some set of events that makes the protocol fail.

Three events are possible at the receiver: sending an acknowledgement (A), writing to the output process (W), and crashing (C). The three events can occur in six different orderings: $AC(W)$, AWC, $C(AW)$, $C(WA)$, WAC, and $WC(A)$, where the parentheses are used to indicate that neither A nor W may follow C (i.e., once it has crashed, it has crashed). Figure 8-10 shows all eight combinations of sender and receiver strategy and the valid event sequences for each one. Notice that for each strategy there is some sequence of events that causes the protocol to behave incorrectly. For example, if the sender always retransmits, the AWC event will generate an undetected duplicate, even though the other two events work properly.

Making the protocol more elaborate does not help. Even if the sender and

Strategy used by receiving host

	First ACK, then write			First write, then ACK		
Strategy used by sending host	AC(W)	AWC	C(AW)	C(WA)	W AC	WC(A)
Always retransmit	OK	DUP	OK	OK	DUP	DUP
Never retransmit	LOST	OK	LOST	LOST	OK	OK
Retransmit in S0	OK	DUP	LOST	LOST	DUP	OK
Retransmit in S1	LOST	OK	OK	OK	OK	DUP

OK   = Protocol functions correctly
DUP = Protocol generates a duplicate message
LOST = Protocol loses a message

Fig. 8-11. Different combinations of sender and receiver strategy.

receiver exchange several messages before the receiver attempts to write, so that the sender knows exactly what is about to happen, the sender has no way of knowing whether a crash occurred just before or just after the write. The conclusion is inescapable: under our ground rules of no simultaneous events, host crash/recovery cannot be made transparent to higher layers.

Put in more general terms, this result can be restated as recovery from a layer N crash can only be done by layer $N + 1$, and then only if the higher layer retains enough status information. As mentioned above, the transport layer can recover from failures in the network layer, provided that each end of a connection keeps track of where it is.

This problem gets us into the issue of what a so-called end-to-end acknowledgement really means. In principle, the transport protocol is end-to-end and not chained like the lower layers. Now consider the case of a user entering requests for transactions against a remote data base. Suppose that the remote transport station is programmed to first pass messages to the next layer up, and then acknowledge. Even in this case, the receipt of an acknowledgement back at the user's machine does not necessarily mean that the remote host stayed up long enough to actually update the data base. A truly end-to-end acknowledgement, whose its receipt means that the work has actually been done, and lack thereof means that it has not, is probably impossible to achieve.

8.2. INTERCONNECTION OF PACKET-SWITCHING NETWORKS

Having examined how two hosts communicate when they are both in the same network, we now turn to the problem of how they communicate when they are in separate, but interconnected, networks. These two cases can be quite different. In particular, even if the sender's network and the receiver's network both provide virtual circuit service, packets from one network to the other may have to pass through an intermediate datagram network on the way. If that network resolves its own congestion problems, for example, by discarding packets willy-nilly, the hosts had better be prepared to do their own end-to-end error control, virtual circuits or no virtual circuits. For this reason, some transport protocols designed with internetworking in mind assume worst case and put the full responsibility for error and flow control in the hosts.

A key design requirement when connecting two networks is to minimize the impact on both of them. If a proposal to connect two networks together requires either of them to make major changes to its hardware, software, or protocols, it is unlikely that the proposal will be accepted. Furthermore, since most traffic is internal, any interconnection scheme that imposes heavy cost or performance penalties on intranet traffic for the benefit of the small volume of internet traffic is not likely to be well received. Thus we are faced with a dilemma: two machines cannot communicate unless they use the same protocols, yet we want two machines with incompatible protocols to communicate, nevertheless.

8.2.1. Gateways

The solution to this dilemma is to insert a "black box" between the networks. The black box is called a **gateway**. The function of the gateway is to convert packets from one protocol to another, analogous to a United Nations interpreter who can accept Chinese input and produce English output.

A gateway may be bilateral or multilateral, that is,, it may connect to two or more networks, just as an interpreter may be able to convert between any combination of English, Chinese, Swahili, and Dutch. Figure 8-12(a) depicts seven isolated networks that are to be interconnected. To achieve this interconnection, let us put six gateways (for example) among the networks, connected as shown in Fig. 8-12(b). In this example, A, C, and D are bilateral gateways, whereas B, E, and F are trilateral gateways.

There is an interesting way of looking at a collection of gateways and networks that provides a useful model for routing and other aspects of internetworking. Consider the collection of gateways and networks as an undirected graph, with the gateways as the nodes and the networks as the arcs. (The link between a gateway and a network is considered to be part of the network.) Such a graph is shown in Fig. 8-12(c). Notice that parallel arcs are possible, as between E and F, since these two gateways have two distinct routes between each other. Another peculiar property of these **supernetworks** is that each "line" may have a different speed, delay, price, and protocol.

An alternative to the bilateral and multilateral gateways of Fig. 8-12(b) is the design of Fig. 8-13. In this approach, a completely new network is built exclusively for the purpose of carrying internet traffic. Each of the "IMPs" in the new network is actually a gateway, which communicates with one or more

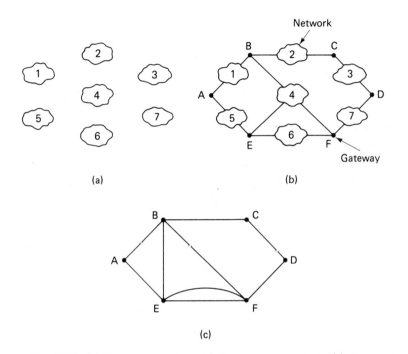

Fig. 8-12. (a) Seven networks. (b) Six gateways added. (c) Supernet formed by the gateways.

networks. Whenever a packet must be passed from one network to another, the source network delivers it to the interconnection network, where it is routed internally among the gateways until it is delivered to the destination network. Since the interconnection network's only subscribers are the carrier's who run the individual networks, the interconnection network is sometimes called a **carrier's carrier**.

The construction of interconnection networks is a logical outgrowth of the hierarchical model of Fig. 2-1. At the top level is the interconnection network, which connects the national networks. At the middle level are the national networks themselves. At the lowest level are the customers' local networks. These three levels might well use three different technologies, for example, satellite broadcasting (see Chap. 6) for the international network, store-and-forward packet switching (see Chap. 5) for the national networks, and rings or Ethernets (see Chap. 7) for the local networks. In Europe, for example, the EEC (Common Market) has constructed an international network, Euronet, which *could* serve the role of an interconnection network. Whether it ever *will* or not is a political issue, because a number of PTTs are loathe to give up any of their power to a European authority and hence prefer the approach of Fig. 8-12(b), which does not contain any central authority.

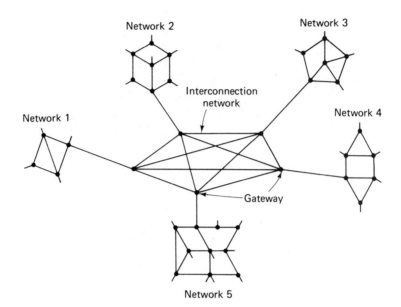

Fig. 8-13. An interconnection network.

One way of programming a gateway is to have it simply convert incoming packets to the format of the outgoing network. For a bilateral gateway, there are two possible conversions (1-2 or 2-1). For a trilateral gateway, there are six possible conversions. The supernet of Fig. 8-12(b) requires 24 different conversions.

If the supernet has a high degree of connectivity, something that is desirable for both performance and reliability reasons, writing all the gateway software will be a major undertaking. However, there is another approach, which is simpler. First, most or all of the networks must agree on a standard internetwork packet format to be used *between* networks. This format is not used *inside* any network, so it does not require any network to modify its own protocols.

Once an internet packet has been adopted, a gateway can be constructed as in Fig. 8-14(a). Four processes run in the gateway. Each of these processes performs one of the four conversions: net 1 to internet, net 2 to internet, internet to net 1, or internet to net 2. When a packet comes in from net 1, it is converted to the internet format and put in the buffer. Eventually, the internet to net 2 process takes it out of the buffer, converts it, and transmits it. If there are n networks, this method requires writing $2n$ routines (from each network format to the internet format, and vice versa), whereas the pairwise method described earlier might require as many as $n(n-1)$ routines, depending on the connectivity. This approach is reminiscent of the UNCOL (Steel, 1960) idea for implementing *m* languages on *n* machines. The supernet of Fig. 8-12(b) requires only 14 conversion routines using this approach rather than 24 using the pairwise method.

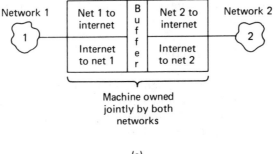

(a)

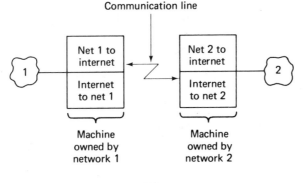

(b)

Fig. 8-14. (a) A Full gateway. (b) Two half-gateways.

Even if it is impossible to get all the networks to agree to a single internet packet format, there is much to be gained if most of them agree. The networks that have agreed to a standard internet packet can use it, whereas connections to other networks will have to be made pairwise.

One nontechnical problem that often arises when two networks are connected, is: Who owns, operates, and maintains the gateway? When the two networks are in different countries, as is often the case, we may have the awkward situation of two governments jointly owning a small minicomputer worth perhaps a few thousand dollars. A lot of finger pointing can be avoided by adopting the design of Fig. 8-14(b). Each network operates a **half-gateway**, responsible only for converting to and from its internal format. Since the half-gateway software is intimately related to the local network software, it may be possible to put it in one of the IMPs or hosts, thus avoiding a special machine altogether. The half-gateway approach makes each network responsible for converting all outbound traffic to the internet format and all inbound traffic to its internal format. The network maintains complete control over its own protocols and can change them whenever it wishes, without having to get anyone else to agree to such changes.

8.2.2. The Level of Interconnection

An important internetwork design issue (Sunshine, 1977) is the gateway level: Should it be an IMP or a host? These choices are illustrated in Fig. 8-15(a) and (b), respectively. For simplicity we will refer to "gateway" rather than "gateway or half-gateways" henceforth, but both are intended.

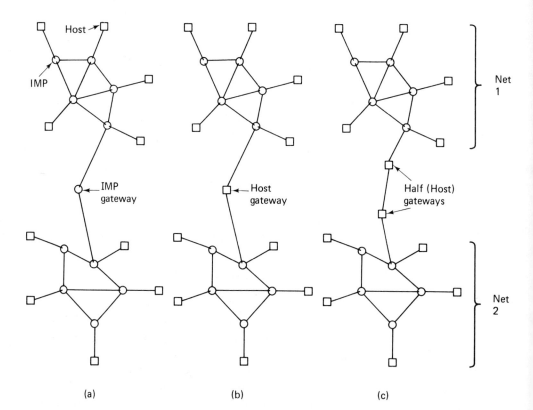

Fig. 8-15. (a) Interconnection at the IMP level. (b) Interconnection at the host level. (c) Interconnection at the host level with half-gateways.

Let us first consider making the gateway an IMP. If both networks have identical data link protocols, the gateway can almost pass the packets through unmodified. We say "almost" because there is one small problem: addressing. Assume that the network 1 IMPs are numbered from 0 to $n - 1$. Similarly, the IMPs of network 2 are numbered from 0 to $m - 1$. When an IMP in network 1 wants to send a packet to IMP k in network 2, it will have to specify that it means IMP k in network 2 and not in network 1. To do this requires an extra bit in the packet header. If there are many networks accessible (e.g., one or more per country), a new field will have to be added to the header of every packet, including the vast majority that begin and end in the same network. This violates both the principle of not requiring existing networks to change their protocols and the principle of not degrading intranet traffic for the benefit of internet traffic.

If the two networks being connected have different subnet protocols, either data link, routing, or end-to-end, there are even more problems. For example, suppose that in network 1 the subnet takes great care never to generate duplicate packets, so its hosts do not worry about duplicates at all, but in network 2 the subnet makes no effort to filter out duplicates, so its hosts do the work. Traffic from 2 to 1 runs the danger of having duplicates sneak through undetected. Another problem occurs if one network has an end-to-end protocol within the subnet and the other does not, or if they both do, but they differ, or even if the protocols are identical but the timeout intervals are very different, there will be insurmountable difficulties. In short, connecting two networks by inserting a new IMP between them is almost impossible.

In contrast, inserting a new host between them, as in Fig. 8-15(b) or (c) is much easier. Since the gateway is indistinguishable from an ordinary customer (host) as far as the subnet is concerned, internetworking requires no changes to the data link layer. Consequently, the existence of internet traffic does not penalize intranet traffic. In principle, two networks could be connected without the packet carrier even knowing about the connection, although doing so is illegal just about everywhere.

To send an internetwork message, a host just addresses the message to the gateway that, the same way it would send a message to any other host—using the standard transport protocol. The gateway then converts the message to the format of the second network, and addresses it to the next gateway using the second network's transport protocol. When the model of Fig. 8-15(c) is being used, the gateway converts the message to the format agreed upon for the gateway-to-gateway line.

8.2.3. The X.75 Model versus the Datagram Model

As we mentioned earlier, the type of service offered to the transport layer by the network layer has a major impact on the design of the transport layer. This conclusion holds for the internetwork case as strongly as for the intranetwork case. As usual, the network layer can offer a virtual circuit service to the transport layer, or it can offer a pure datagram service. Two radically different approaches to internetworking have come into existence, one based on each of these models. The CCITT internetwork protocol, called **X.75**, is based on the virtual circuit model, whereas the research community (e.g., DARPA, Xerox PARC) prefers the datagram model. We will now examine each of these models in turn. More details can be found in (DiCiccio et al., 1979; Edge, 1979; Grossman et al., 1979; Boggs et al., 1980; Postel, 1980).

The CCITT X.75 model is based on the idea of building up an internetwork connection by concatenating a series of intranetwork and half-gateway to half-gateway virtual circuits. The model is shown in Fig. 8-16(a). The connection between the source host, in one network, and the destination host, in another network, is composed of five adjacent virtual circuits, marked VC 1-5. VC 1 goes from the source host to a half-gateway (called a **signaling terminal** or **STE** by CCITT), in its own network. VC 2 goes from the half-gateway in the source network to a half-gateway in an intermediate network, assuming that there is no direct connection between the source and destination networks. VCs 3 and 5 are also intranet, like VC 1, and VC 4 is internet, like VC 2.

In this model the transport layer sets up a connection by building a CALL REQUEST message and passing it to the network layer, together with the destination address. The network layer, either in the host or the in the IMP, then chooses an appropriate (half) gateway and a virtual circuit to it is built. The first gateway records the existence of the virtual circuit in its tables and proceeds to build another virtual circuit to the next gateway. This process continues until the destination host has been reached. The resulting path is much like the chaining of layers 1 through 3 in Fig. 1-7: The network layer is chained, but the transport layer is end-to-end.

Once data packets begin flowing along the path, each gateway relays incoming packets, converting between packet formats and virtual circuit numbers as needed. Clearly all data packets must traverse the same sequence of gateways, although VCs 1, 3, and 5 in Fig. 8-16(a) might be implemented internally using datagrams, so that not all packets need follow precisely the same route from source to destination.

The essential feature of this approach is that the transport layer explicitly asks the network layer to open a connection to a specific destination, which results in a sequence of virtual circuits being set up. Each gateway maintains tables telling which virtual circuits pass through it, where they are to be routed, and what the new virtual circuit number is. To close a connection, the transport layer must given an explicit command. The whole arrangement is similar to the fixed routing of Fig. 5-3, except that only the sequence of gateways is fixed, not (necessarily) the full sequence of IMPs.

Figure 8-17 shows the protocols used on the various lines when two X.25 networks are connected. The source host talks to the subnet using X.25, as usual. The internal IMP-IMP protocol is not specified by CCITT and probably will be different in every network. The protocol used between the gateways and

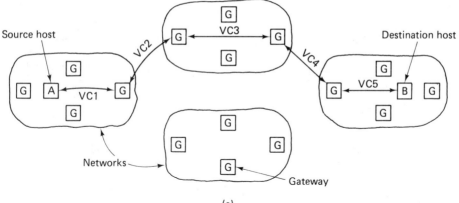

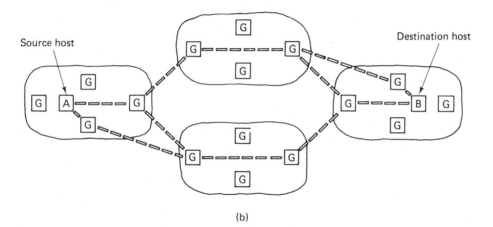

Fig. 8-16. (a) Internetworking using concatenated virtual circuits.
(b) Internetworking using datagrams.

the rest of the subnet is also left open, but here there are clearly two distinct
choices: the internal IMP-IMP protocol, or X.25. If this protocol is the IMP-
IMP protocol, the network regards the gateway as an IMP, as in Fig. 8-15(a),
except that here we have used two half-gateways instead of one full gateway. If
the gateway-to-subnet protocol is X.25, the subnet regards the gateway as a
host, and Fig. 8-15(c) prevails.

Although the X.75 protocol itself only applies to the gateway-to-gateway
lines, it effectively dictates the concatenated virtual circuit architecture by
requiring all packets on a connection to pass over the same gateway-to-gateway
virtual circuit in sequence. It is hard to see how different packets could use
different gateways and still meet this requirement. The X.75 protocol is

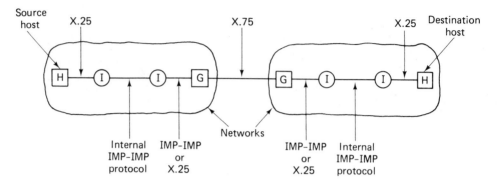

Fig. 8-17. Protocols in the CCITT internetwork model.

practically identical with X.25. The only important difference is the presence of a *Network utilities* just prior to the *Facilities* in the CALL REQUEST packet [see Fig. 5-26(a)]. Like the facilities, it begins with a byte giving the length of the field, again 0 to 63 bytes, followed by the utilities themselves. The contents of this field are not defined by X.75, except for the requirement that as a CALL REQUEST packet propagates from source to destination, each network transited must record its four digit X.121 number in the field. Other utilities will no doubt be added as they are needed.

The alternative internetwork model to CCITT's is the datagram model, shown in Fig. 8-16(b). In this model, the only service the network layer offers to the transport layer is the ability to inject datagrams into the subnet, and hope for the best. There is no notion of a virtual circuit at all in the network layer, let alone a concatenation of them. Neither is there any concept of a CALL REQUEST packet in the network layer, although the transport layer clearly must have messages for CONNECT and OPEN. This model does not require all packets belonging to one connection to traverse the same sequence of gateways. In Fig. 8-16(b) datagrams from *A* to *B* are shown taking a wide variety of different routes through the internetwork. On the other hand, it also does not guarantee that the packets arrive at the destination in order, assuming that they arrive at all.

In both the concatenated virtual circuit model and the datagram model, the transport messages undergo a series of wrappings and unwrappings as they move from network to network. In Fig. 8-18, for example, we show how a datagram might be modified as it progresses from host *A* to host *B*. The basic unit moved is the datagram (also-called an **internet packet**), which contains a transport message inside it, as well as its own datagram header, *DGH*. The datagram header contains the complete source and destination addresses, as well as a sequence number used to put the datagrams back into sequence at the destination host. If each network has its own datagram header, the gateways will have to perform the appropriate translations. In addition, each network has its own requirements for host-IMP and IMP-IMP data link headers and trailers, as do the gateways.

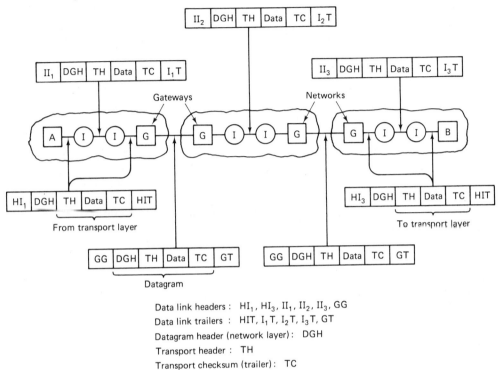

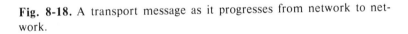

Data link headers : HI_1, HI_3, II_1, II_2, II_3, GG
Data link trailers : HIT, I_1T, I_2T, I_3T, GT
Datagram header (network layer): DGH
Transport header : TH
Transport checksum (trailer): TC

Fig. 8-18. A transport message as it progresses from network to network.

The concatenated virtual circuit and datagram approaches have different strengths and weaknesses. The concatenated virtual circuit model has essentially the same advantages as session (i.e., fixed) routing within a single subnet: buffers can be reserved in advance to ease congestion, sequencing can be guaranteed, short headers can be used, and the troubles caused by delayed duplicate packets can be avoided. It also has the same disadvantages: table space required in the gateways for each open connection, whether or not there is any traffic, no alternate routing to avoid congested areas, and vulnerability to gateway failures anywhere along the path. It also has the disadvantage or being difficult, if not impossible, to implement if one of the networks involved is an unreliable datagram network.

The properties of the datagram approach to internetworking are the same as those of datagram subnets: more potential for congestion, but also more potential for adapting to it, robustness in the face of gateway failures, and longer headers needed.

An issue somewhat related to that of virtual circuits versus datagrams is the question of who should do the routing through the internet. Clearly, hosts cannot be expected to know the internal topology of remote networks, so some form of hierarchical routing is needed. However, the routing problem is more complex than that described in Chap. 5, because each network traversed may have a different effective bandwidth, delay error rate, and even charging algorithm.

One routing strategy is to have the source host or source IMP choose the initial gateway and let the gateways take over from there. Another routing strategy is **source routing**, that is, having the source host determine the complete route to be used.

For routing within a single homogeneous network, source routing has little to offer, but in the context of international internetworking it may be important to some users. The U. S. Dept. of Defense, for example, may prefer its top secret traffic to England to go via Canada rather than via Cuba, if a choice must be made. A Scandinavian company may not want to send its payroll file from Norway to Denmark via Sweden, for fear of violating Sweden's strict laws about exporting information about Swedish citizens from Sweden. As we saw in Chap. 4, the optimum packet size depends on the technical characteristics of the network, so a user wishing to use the optimum size needs a way to ensure the route he has optimized for is the the route that is actually taken.

8.2.4. Internetwork Packet Fragmentation

Each network imposes some maximum size on its packets. These limits have various causes, among them:

1. Hardware (e.g., the width of a TDM transmission slot).

2. Operating system (e.g., all buffers are 512 bytes).

3. Protocols (e.g., the number of bits in the packet length field).

4. Compliance with some (inter)national standard.

5. Desire to reduce error induced retransmissions to some level.

6. Desire to prevent one packet from occupying the channel too long.

Some typical examples of maximum packet lengths are:

1. HDLC: in principle infinite.

2. X.25: networks are permitted packets as long as 8192 bits.

3. ARPA Packet Radio Network: 2032 bits.

4. X.25: networks are encouraged to use 1024 bits as the limit.

5. ARPANET: 1008 bits.

6. University of Hawaii ALOHANET: 640 bits.

7. Bell Labs Spider: 256 bits.

An obvious problem appears when a large packet wants to travel through a network whose maximum packet size is too small. This problem has received a great deal of attention in the literature (see e.g., Shoch, 1979), and some proposals for solving it have been made.

One solution is to make sure the problem does not occur in the first place. In other words, the supernet should use a routing algorithm that avoids sending packets through networks that cannot handle them. However, this solution is no solution at all. What happens if the original source packet is too large to be handled by the destination network? The routing algorithm can hardly bypass the destination. Nevertheless, intelligent routing can minimize the extent of the problem.

Basically, the only solution to the problem is to allow gateways to break packets up into **fragments**, sending each fragment as a separate internet packet. However, as every parent of a small child knows, converting a large object into small fragments is considerably easier than the reverse process. (Physicists have even given this effect a name: the second law of thermodynamics.) Packet-switching networks, too, have trouble putting the fragments back together again.

The ARPANET message/packet interaction provides a useful analogy. An IMP will cheerfully accept a host message up to eight times the maximum packet length. The subnet fragments the message into packets, ships them off individually, and recombines the pieces at the destination. The destination host is totally unaware of the fact that the subnet cannot handle messages larger than 1008 bits without breaking them up. Of course, the destination IMP is only too painfully aware of the fragmentation, because it has to deal with a complicated buffering strategy designed to prevent reassembly lockup.

Two opposing strategies exist for recombining the fragments back into the original packet. The first strategy is to make fragmentation caused by a "small packet" network transparent to any subsequent networks through which the packet must pass on its way to the ultimate destination. This option is shown in Fig. 8-19(a). When an oversized packet arrives at a gateway, the gateway breaks it up into fragments. Each fragment is addressed to the same exit gateway, where the pieces are recombined. In this way passage through the small packet network has been made transparent. Subsequent networks are not even aware that fragmentation has occurred.

Transparent fragmentation is simple but has some problems. For one thing, the exit gateway must know when it has received all the pieces, so that either a count field or an "end of packet" bit must be included in each packet.

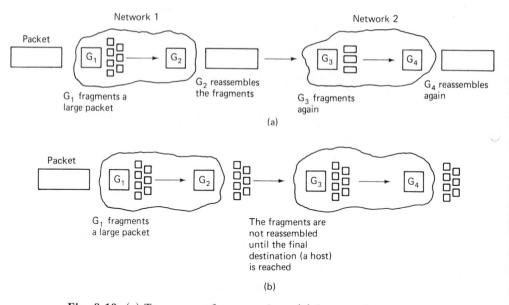

Fig. 8-19. (a) Transparent fragmentation. (b) Internet fragmentation.

For another thing, all packets must exit via the same gateway. By not allowing some fragments to follow one route to the ultimate destination, and other fragments a disjoint route, some performance may be lost. A third problem is possible reassembly lockup at the exit gateway. A last problem is the overhead required to repeatedly reassemble and then refragment a large packet passing through a series of small packet networks.

The other fragmentation strategy is to refrain from recombining fragments at any intermediate gateways. Once a packet has been fragmented, each fragment is treated as though it were an original packet. All fragments are passed through the exit gateway (or gateways), as shown in Fig. 8-19(b). Recombination occurs only at the destination host.

Nontransparent fragmentation also has some problems. For example, it requires *every* host to do reassembly. Yet another problem is that when a large packet is fragmented the total overhead increases, because each fragment must have a header. Whereas in the first method this overhead disappears as soon as the small packet network is exited, in this method the overhead remains for the rest of the journey. An advantage of this method, however, is that multiple exit gateways can now be used. Of course, if the concatenated virtual circuit model is being used, this advantage is of no use.

Shoch (1979) has proposed having each packet carry a bit specifying whether or not the ultimate destination is prepared to reassemble fragments. If it is not, any gateway fragmenting a packet must arrange for some other gateway to reassemble the pieces. If the ultimate destination is prepared to do reassembly itself, fragmentation may or may not be transparent, at each gateway's discretion.

When a packet is fragmented, the fragments must be numbered in such a way that the original data stream can be reconstructed. One way of numbering the fragments is to use a tree. If packet 0 must be split up, the pieces are called 0.0, 0.1, 0.2, etc. If these fragments must themselves be fragmented at a subsequent gateway, the pieces are numbered 0.0.0, 0.0.1, 0.0.2, . . . , 0.1.0, 0.1.1, 0.1.2, etc. If enough fields have been reserved in the header for the worst case and if there are no duplicates generated anywhere, this scheme is sufficient to ensure that all the pieces can be correctly reassembled at the destination, no matter what order they arrive in.

However, if even one network loses or discards packets, there is a need for end-to-end retransmissions, with unfortunate effects for the numbering system. Suppose that a 1024-bit packet is initially fragmented into four equal-sized fragments, 0.0, 0.1, 0.2, and 0.3. Fragment 0.1 is lost, but the other parts arrive at the destination. Eventually, the source times out and retransmits the original packet again. Only this time the route taken passes through a network with a 512-bit limit, so two fragments are generated. When the new fragment 0.1 arrives at the destination, the receiver will think that all four pieces are now accounted for and reconstruct the packet, incorrectly.

A completely different (and better) numbering system is for the internetwork protocol to define an elementary fragment size small enough that the elementary fragment can pass through every network (Cerf and Kahn, 1974). When a packet is fragmented, all the pieces are equal to the elementary fragment size except the last one, which may be shorter. An internet packet may contain several fragments, for efficiency reasons. The internet header must provide the original packet number, and the number of the (first) elementary fragment contained in the frame. As usual, there must also be a bit indicating that the last elementary fragment contained within the internet packet is the last one of the original packet.

This approach requires two sequence fields in the internet header: the original packet number, and the fragment number. There is clearly a trade off between the size of the elementary fragment and the number of bits in the fragment number. Because the elementary fragment size is presumed to be acceptable to every network, subsequent fragmentation of an internet packet containing several fragments causes no problem. The ultimate limit here is to have the elementary fragment be a single bit or byte, with the fragment number then being the bit or byte offset within the original packet, as shown in Fig. 8-20.

Some internet protocols take this method even further, and consider the entire transmission on a virtual circuit to be one giant packet, so that each fragment contains the absolute byte number of the first byte within the fragment.

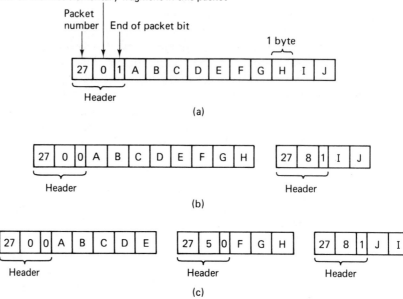

Fig. 8-20. Fragmentation when the elementary data size is 1 byte. (a) Original packet, containing 10 data bytes. (b) Fragments after passing through a network with maximum packet size of 8 bytes. (c) Fragments after passing through a size 5 gateway.

8.3. THE SESSION LAYER

In this section we will briefly look at some of the functions performed by the session layer. The session layer does not rate its own chapter in this book because there is so little to say about it. Many networks (e.g., the ARPANET) do not even have one. The basic task of the session layer is to take the bare transport service, which just moves raw bits from machine *A* to machine *B*, and add user oriented services to it.

One service that all networks must provide is a way for remote users to identify themselves. When messages begin arriving from the outside world the host must first determine who sent them. Once the identity of the sender is known, the operating system can determine what privileges the user is allowed. Incoming messages typically indicate their origin by giving a machine number and a process number, but not the identification of the (human) user. In the case where a person simply wants to log onto a remote machine, the authentication mechanism need not be different than if the user had called up the remote machine directly on the telephone. However, when a process (rather than a person) decides that it wants to use a remote machine for a short time, for example, to fetch a record in a file, it is annoying to force the person at the terminal to go through the login sequence. Instead, the session layer can go through it for him.

For some applications one side of a connection sends data, waits for a response, then sends more data. Managing the alternation, if required, is also part of session management.

Synchronization, checkpointing, and crash recovery are also possible session control functions. For example, if a user is sending a long file over the network, one that takes hours of transmission time, and the virtual circuit is wiped out by an IMP crash near the end, who pays for the retransmission, the carrier or the user? If the carrier were to take responsibility, it would probably find that after every crash some users would claim the crash cost them six days work, and they wanted six days of free network time. One way to solve the problem is to have the session management software automatically segment file transfers and use an acknowledgement protocol so that if a crash occurs, at most one segment has to be retransmitted.

More generally, the session layer could do its best to make transport connection failures transparent to higher layers. Whenever a transport connection broke, the session layer could automatically set up a new transport connection, resynchronize both ends of the connection, and continue from where it left off. In this way, batch users would notice nothing at all, and interactive users would only notice a short delay while a new transport connection was being set up and the status was being verified.

8.4. EXAMPLES OF THE TRANSPORT AND SESSION LAYERS

To make the principles of transport layer design discussed above more concrete, we now turn to our usual example networks.

8.4.1. The Transport Layer in the ARPANET

In the original ARPANET design, the subnet was assumed to offer virtual circuit service (i.e., be perfectly reliable). The first transport layer protocol, **NCP** (Network Control Protocol), was designed with a perfect subnet in mind. It just passes messages to the network layer and assumes that they will all be delivered in order to the destination. Experience has shown that the ARPANET is indeed reliable enough for this protocol to be completely satisfactory for traffic within the ARPANET itself.

However, as time went on, DARPA became interested in interconnecting the ARPANET to unreliable datagram networks, for example a packet radio network set up in the San Francisco Bay area. This forced a major change in the transport layer and led to the gradual introduction of a new transport layer protocol, **TCP**, which has been specifically designed to tolerate an unreliable subnet. Associated with TCP is a new layer 3 as well, variously called the **datagram** or **internet** layer, whose job is to route datagrams around the network or networks, fragmenting datagrams and then reassembling them transparently for delivery to the destination transport station. NCP and TCP transport stations can coexist simultaneously within the same host. First we will describe NCP and then TCP.

NCP (Network Control Protocol)

The basic transport service provided by NCP to its users is an error-free, sequenced, simplex connection. To achieve full-duplex communication, two connections are required. Each connection connects a specific port at one end to a specific port at the other end. Ports are 32-bit numbers, with even numbers used for receiving and odd numbers for sending. The low-order bit of a port is called its **gender**. Each connection must have one even port and one odd port.

To establish a connection, two messages must be exchanged, analogous to CALL REQUEST and CALL ACCEPTED in X.25. These setup messages are RTS (Receiver To Sender) and STR (Sender To Receiver), as shown in Fig. 8-21. Most hosts have transport service primitives LISTEN and INIT, which allow users to passively wait for a connection and actively attempt to open one, respectively. LISTEN specifies a local port to listen to, and optionally a remote transport address it expects to hear from. INIT must specify both transport addresses.

When a user does an INIT, the transport station inspects the genders of the ports to determine whether the connection is for outbound or inbound traffic. Armed with this knowledge it sends an RTS or STR to the remote host. When the request for connection arrives at the remote host, the transport station there checks to see if anyone is listening on the specified port. If so, an STR or RTS is sent back; if not the transport station may choose to queue the request for a while, or it may reject the connection attempt using the CLS (CLoSe) message. Once a connection has been established, it is assigned an 8-bit connection number (*Link* in Fig. 8-21) to eliminate the need to send two 32-bit ports in every message.

Data messages contain a 40-bit header with four fields, two of which must be zero. The other two contain the number of bits in a "byte" and the number of such bytes in the message. These fields are useful when the source and destination hosts have different word lengths. The link number is passed to layer 3 as a parameter. The link number is included in the IMP-IMP header (*Virtual circuit number* in Fig. 5-20) and passed up to the destination NCP as a parameter. Logically, the link number could have been included in the NCP header. It was decided not to do so to allow the IMPs to keep track of which message belonged to which link. (An early version of the congestion-control algorithm restricted hosts to one outstanding message per link.)

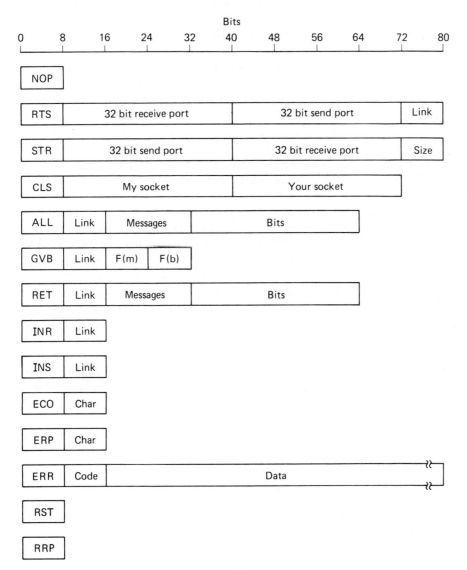

Fig. 8-21. ARPANET NCP control messages.

Note that NCP does not have any acknowledgement scheme at all; it simply assumes that the subnet can handle all errors transparently, and that all messages are delivered in sequence, exactly as sent.

Connections are closed by having the transport stations exchange CLS messages. Since there is no distinction between CLEAR and CLEAR CONFIRMATION, as in X.25, there is no clear collision problem. If both sides decide to close simultaneously, each one will interpret the other's initial request as an answer to its own request, and be satisfied.

In contrast to nearly all the other protocols we have studied, NCP does not use a sliding window for flow control. Instead, it has an explicit buffer allocation mechanism, which uses three control messages: ALL (ALLocate), GVB (GiVe Back), and RET (RETurn). When a connection is initially established, the sending host is forbidden from sending anything. It is required to wait until the receiving host sends an ALL message for that connection. The ALL message itself, like all control messages, is sent on link 0, and not on the link it refers to. In other words, the buffer allocation is done on a host pair basis, not per connection. The ALL message specifies both a message limit and a bit limit. If it specified only, say, a limit of 1000 bits, some wiseguy host might send 1000 messages of 1 bit each, potentially causing problems.

Even the most conservative host may, at times, be forced by lack of buffer space to try to reclaim allocations previously granted. For example, if a host has already dedicated all its buffer space to some collection of connections, none of which are being used heavily, and suddenly a large number of new connections are set up. To request that a sender return some of its allocation, the receiver sends a GVB message to it. This message gives the fraction of the allocated messages $F(m)$ and bits $F(b)$ that the receiver wants back. Both quantities are in units of 1/128 of the total. The sender is expected to comply by using the RET message. In practice, GVB is rarely used; many hosts have not even implemented it.

Like X.25, NCP provides for an out of band interrupt mechanism. However, unlike X.25, there is no data associated with the INR (INterrupt by Receiver) and INS (INterrupt by Sender) messages, the former of which is used by receivers and the latter by senders.

The ECO (EChO) message can be used by a host to see if another host is currently running. It requests the specified character to be echoed, using the ERP (Echo RePly) message. This message can also be used for making timing measurements.

If either host discovers an error, it can report this with the ERR (ERRor) message. Such messages help the network operators debug the software. Some of the potential errors are:

1. Undefined NCP control message.

2. Control message with too few parameters detected.

3. Control message with invalid parameters.

4. Unknown port or link.

5. Invalid transport header.

The *Code* field of the ERR message tells which error was detected, and the *Data* field gives the details (e.g., the bad parameters).

The last two messages, RST (ReSTart) and RRP (Restart RePly), are the same as RESTART and RESTART CONFIRMATION in X.25. In other words, they purge all links. These messages are used after one of the hosts has crashed.

TCP (Transmission Control Protocol)

As we mentioned above, TCP was designed to deal with lossy subnets. It is by far the most complicated protocol we have examined so far and is the only one designed to deal correctly with pathological situations such as the delayed duplicate problem of Fig. 8-10.

A TCP transport station accepts arbitrarily long **letters** from user processes, breaks them up into pieces not exceeding 65K bytes, and sends each piece as a separate datagram. The network layer gives no guarantee that datagrams will be delivered properly, so it is up to TCP to time out and retransmit them as need be. Datagrams that do arrive may well do so in the wrong order; it is up to TCP to reassemble them into letters in the proper sequence. Of course, intranet traffic within the ARPANET is highly reliable, so this robustness is not needed, but other interconnected networks may be less reliable.

Every byte of data transmitted by TCP has its own private sequence number. The sequence number space is 32 bits wide to make sure that old duplicates have long since vanished by the time the sequence numbers have wrapped around. TCP does, however, explicitly deal with the problem of delayed duplicates when attempting to establish a connection, using the three-way handshake for this purpose.

Figure 8-22 shows the headers used by TCP and the underlying datagram protocol. The first thing that strikes one is that the minimum TCP + datagram header is 40 bytes. Bytes, not bits. Let us dissect this large beast top down, starting with the TCP header. The *Source port* and *Destination port* fields identify the ultimate user processes communicating. Each host may decide for itself how to allocate its ports.

The *Sequence number* and *Piggyback acknowledgement* fields perform their usual functions. They are 32 bits long because every byte of data is numbered in TCP.

The *TCP header length* tells how many 32-bit words are contained in the TCP header. This information is needed because the *Options* field is variable length.

Next come six 1-bit flags. *URG* is set to 1 if the *Urgent pointer* is in use. The *Urgent pointer* is used to indicate a byte offset from the current sequence number at which urgent data are to be found. This facility is in lieu of interrupt messages. The *SYN* bit is used to establish connections. The connection request (which we have called *SYN1*) has *SYN* = 1 and *ACK* = 0 to indicate

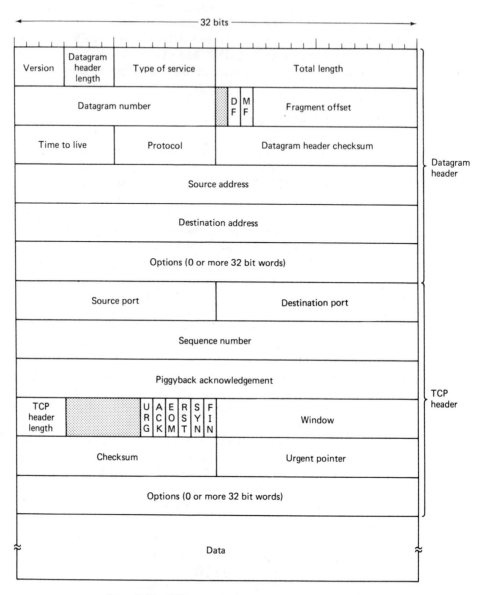

Fig. 8-22. TCP and the internet datagram headers.

that the piggyback acknowledgement field is not in use. The connection reply (which we have called *SYN2*) does bear an acknowledgement, so it has *SYN* = 1 and *ACK* = 1. In essence the *ACK* bit is used to distinguish *SYN*1 from *SYN*2. The *FIN* bit is used to close a connection. It specifies that the sender has no more data. After closing a connection, a process may continue to receive data indefinitely. The *RST* bit is used to reset a connection that has become confused due to delayed duplicate *SYN*s or host crashes. The *EOM* bit indicates End Of Message.

Flow control in TCP is handled using a variable-size sliding window. Only here a long field is needed, because *Window* tells how many bytes may be sent beyond the byte acknowledged, not how many messages.

A *Checksum* is also provided for extreme reliability. The checksum algorithm is simply to add up all the data, regarded as 16-bit words, and then to take the 1's complement of the sum.

The *Options* field is used for miscellaneous things, for example to communicate buffer sizes during the setup procedure.

When the transport layer has attached its header to the user data, the datagram layer takes over, attaching its header to the front and transmitting the resulting bit stream to the IMP using the host-IMP protocol. Logically, we should have described the datagram header in Chap. 5, because it belongs to layer 3, but we have delayed the discussion until now because the protocol was motivated by the needs of internetworking, for example fragmentation, and was actually part of TCP until 1979.

The *Version* field keeps track of which version of the protocol the datagram belongs to. By including the version in each datagram, the possibility of changing protocols while the network is operating is not excluded. An analogous field is present in the ARPANET IMP-IMP header.

Just as the TCP header has a variable-length field at the end, so does the datagram header. For this reason its header length must also be specified.

The *Type of service* field allows the host to tell the subnet what kind of service it wants. Various combinations of reliability and speed are possible. For digitized voice, fast delivery is far more important than correcting transmission errors. For file transfer, accurate transmission is far more important than speedy delivery. A variety of other combinations are also provided for.

The *Total length* includes everything in the datagram—both headers and all the data. The maximum length is 65,536 bytes.

The *Datagram number* field is needed to allow the destination host to determine which datagram a newly arrived fragment belongs to.

DF stands for Don't Fragment. It is an order to the gateways not to fragment the datagram because the destination is incapable of putting the pieces back together again.

MF stands for More Fragments. All fragments except the last one must have this bit set. This bit should not be confused with the *EOM* bit in the TCP layer. Messages are divided into datagrams, and datagrams are divided into fragments, and each layer needs to indicate the end of the current unit.

The *Fragment offset* tells where in the current datagram this fragment belongs. All fragments except the last one in a datagram must be a multiple of 8 bytes, the elementary fragment unit. Since 13 bits are provided, there are a maximum of 8192 fragments per datagram, giving a maximum datagram length of 65536 bytes, in agreement with the *Total length* field.

The *Time to live* field is a counter used to limit packet lifetimes. When it becomes zero, the packet is destroyed. The unit of time is the second, allowing a maximum lifetime of 255 sec.

When the datagram layer has assembled a complete datagram, it needs to be told what to do with it. Notice that there are no port numbers within the datagram header. Instead, the *Protocol* field tells which of the various layer 4 transport stations the datagram belongs to. TCP is certainly one possibility, but there may be others.

The *Datagram header checksum* verifies the header only. Such a checksum is useful because the header may change at a gateway (e.g., fragmentation may occur). The checksum algorithm is the same as in the TCP header.

The *Source address* and *Destination address* indicate the network number (8 bits) and host number (24 bits). The *Options* field is used for security, source routing, error reporting, time stamping, and other information. Basically it provides an escape to allow subsequent versions of the protocol to include information not present in the original design, to allow experimenters to try out new ideas, and to avoid allocating header bits to information that is rarely needed.

The difference in size and information content of the TCP header and say, the X.25 header, is so great that it bears a few words. The difference is caused by a fundamentally different view of the world held by CCITT and the research community. [Several other well-known network architectures coming from research labs, e.g., Xerox PARC (Boggs et al., 1980) are similar in spirit to that of datagram/TCP.] The research view is that many organizations in the future will have numerous small computers connected by Ethernets, ring nets, packet radio nets, and other local networks providing datagram service. In this view, most communication will be local e.g., between a secretary and the local phototypesetter, with use of the long-haul network relatively rare. Operating systems for local networks tend to be datagram (message) oriented. Local networks usually have plenty of bandwidth, so minimizing the header for the benefit of the occasional long-haul packet is not an overriding criterion. Providing considerable flexibility for dealing with unforeseen future applications is considered more important.

The CCITT view, in contrast, is more concerned with the use of public networks to allow terminals to access large central computers, and to permit widely separately computers to transfer large files. It is also more attuned to the existing telephone system, in which bandwidth is an expensive resource. These factors led CCITT to choose a design expected to be economically viable as quickly as possible, and to interface well to existing systems and existing applications. Hence the emphasis on virtual circuits and short headers. Datagrams were only added to the X.25 standard in late 1980, and many carriers cannot handle them.

Although digitized packet speech did not play a major role in the development of either TCP or X.25, it will no doubt become more important in time.

Digitized speech needs low overhead and guaranteed bandwidth. Clearly, the X.25 call setup mechanism makes it simple to implement virtual circuits with reserved buffers within the subnet, whereas the datagram style and large headers of TCP and the Xerox Pup architecture make it harder. Only time will tell if the research and CCITT approaches will eventually converge.

8.4.2. The Transport and Session Layers in SNA

The primary function of the transport layer is to establish, manage, and delete reliable end-to-end connections between processes and to provide a uniform interface to higher layers for requesting these functions. In SNA they are carried out by a combination of the path control and transmission control layers. The path control layer provides for end-to-end reliability, but transport connections are established and deleted by the transmission control layer. The data flow control layer (layer 5) adds certain user oriented services to the bare transport connection. We will discuss each of these in turn.

When one process wants to communicate with another, it must ask the SSCP controlling its domain to set up the connection (session). Since each process (NAU) always has a session with the SSCP, the process can make the request over that session. If the request refers to the remote process by a symbolic name, the SSCP maps it onto the network address.

The two ends of a session are not symmetric. One end is designated as the **primary** and the other as the **secondary**. The primary usually has more power and responsibility than the secondary. Remember that in the original SNA release there was only one host in the entire network, so the host was the primary and the terminal the secondary. The same asymmetry is present in SDLC.

The details of how sessions are set up depend on whether the source and destination are in the same domain or not, whether it is the primary or secondary or a third party that initiates the session and whether both ends are available when the request is made, among other factors. As a simple example, consider the situation of Fig. 8-23, in which the secondary requests a session with an available primary in another domain.

Fourteen control messages (including responses i.e., acknowledgements) are required to establish the session. First the secondary tells its SSCP that it wants a session. The SSCP then tells the remote SSCP that one of its users wishes to initiate a session, and provides the user's password for authentication (message 2). If the remote SSCP is prepared to set up the session (i.e., the password is correct, the SSCP has a path to the primary, the primary is not already at its session limit, etc.), the remote SSCP lets the initiating SSCP know (message 3). After acknowledging receipt of the original request message to its user, the secondary's SSCP sends a formal request to **bind** to the primary's SSCP (message 5)

Binding is one of the key operations in SNA. The bind command (message

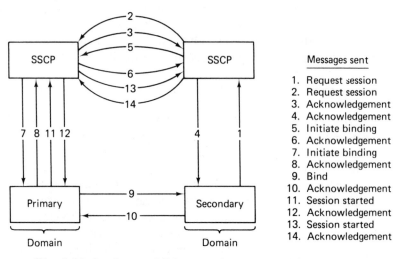

Fig. 8-23. Session establishment when requested by secondary.

9), which is always sent from a primary to a secondary, is several dozen bytes long and specifies many parameters for the coming session, such as protocols to be used, dialog control, flow control parameters, and so on. Once binding is complete, the primary tells its SSCP that it has succeeded (message 11), and the primary SSCP tells the secondary SSCP. Like the bind message, data messages go directly from the source to the destination, bypassing the SSCPs.

In addition to setting up and tearing down sessions, the transmission control layer in SNA ensures that all messages are delivered to higher layers in the proper order, unless the bind message specified otherwise. The sequence numbers are not contained in the RH header but are passed as parameters to path control, together with the data.

The flow control algorithm used by the transmission control layer is the same one used by the path control layer, except that here it is applied separately to each session, and not to the full set of sessions between two hosts. Flow control in the transmission control layer is independent of flow control in the path control layer. To request permission to send another n messages, the sender turns on a bit in the RH header. When the other end sets the corresponding bit in its acknowledgement, the sender may go ahead and send another n messages.

Although the rate of flow in a session is managed by the transmission control layer, the direction of flow is managed by the data flow control layer. This function, which we will call **dialog control**, corresponds to the session layer in the ISO model. To understand why dialog control is needed, you should realize that sending a message does not necessarily cause a process to go to sleep (as it does in Fig. 8-3), and that messages, including acknowledgements, from the other end can arrive and cause interrupts at arbitrary and inconvenient times.

Dialog control provides a facility for grouping messages into **chains** for error recovery and other purposes. It can be arranged to have a failure in the middle of a chain cause the entire chain to be retransmitted. Also, a process can request to have interrupts for acknowledgements of the front of the chain inhibited until the entire chain has been sent, in effect causing strict alternation of chains by sender and receiver.

SNA distinguishes requests that require an acknowledgement from those that do not. A source and receiver can also agree on the semantics of an acknowledgement, for example, message was received, message was received and processing started, or message was received and fully processed. Since processing of messages may take a considerable amount of time, there is a danger that responses that merely acknowledge the arrival of a later message may come back before the acknowledgement of completed processing of an earlier message. Dialog control can ensure that acknowledgements are delivered to the user in the same order in which the requests were sent, simplifying the user program. Stronger yet, dialog control can even force a user to operate in stop-and-wait mode by blocking it until each message it sends is acknowledged.

Yet another feature of dialog control is the ability to group a series of requests and responses in both directions into a unit called a **bracket**. A typical example might be the series of messages in both directions needed to reserve a seat on an airplane. Bracketing could be used prevent messages from other customers from getting through to the airline data base manager until the original transaction was completed. When each end of a session is capable of initiating complex transactions, bracketing is useful to prevent one side from initiating a new transaction until the other side has finished.

Session management and dialog control are carried out using the **request-response** or **RH** header (see Fig. 1-10), as well as with special transport control messages. The format of the RH is shown in Fig. 8-24.

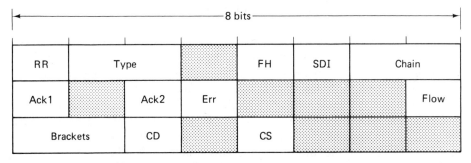

Fig. 8-24. The SNA Request-Response header.

The *RR* field is 0 for a request and 1 for a response.

The *Type* field tells what to do with the message: 00 = pass to NAU services layer, bypassing dialog control, 10 = pass to dialog control for normal processing, 11 = control message pertaining to this session, 01 = network control message.

The *FH* field tells whether or not an FH header is included in the data portion. The *SDI* fields tells whether or not a 4-byte sense data field is present in the message. Sense data are used for error reporting.

The *Chain* field gives chaining information: 10 = start of chain, 00 = middle of chain, 01 = end of chain, 11 = single message chain.

The two *Ack* fields and the *Err* field are used in requests for specifying the kind of acknowledgement desired, and in responses for reporting back. The exact meaning of the bits is determined by higher layers of software.

The *Flow* field is used by senders to ask permission to transmit another group of *n* messages, and by receivers to grant or deny that permission.

The *Brackets* field delimit the bracket structure, analogous to the *Chain* field.

When dialog control is being used to simulate a half-duplex link, the *CD* field is used to change direction.

Finally, when a session is bound, the two ends can agree to use a main character code and an alternate one (e.g., EBCDIC and ASCII). The *CS* field selects one code or the other.

8.4.3. The Transport Layer in DECNET

The transport layer in DECNET is clean and simple, much in the same spirit as our example of Sec. 8.1.1, although a little more elaborate. Like our example, its primary function is to establish, manage, and terminate sequenced, flow controlled, error-free connections for the exchange of arbitrary length user messages. Like our example (and like the ARPANET and unlike SNA), the transport service is used directly by user programs, with no intervening session or presentation layers. However, unlike our example, the DECNET transport station must deal with (an unreliable) pure datagram service at the network layer.

To get a better understanding of the transport layer and its protocol, **NSP** (Network Services Protocol), let us examine the transport service commands and their actions. The manner in which the commands are invoked is implementation dependent, being system calls on some machines and library routine calls on others. To establish a full-duplex transport connection (called a **link** by DEC), the user executes a CONNECT REQUEST, providing as parameters the destination machine's address, the process name in the destination machine, the sender's identity, the connection identifier to be used for outgoing traffic, a buffer for returned data, and a few other items. Note that there is no uniform space of transport addresses. Instead, remote processes are identified by machine number, chosen from a uniform 15 bit address space, and a process name, which is determined by the naming conventions at the destination. The

CONNECT REQUEST causes an NSP message CONNECT INITIATE to be sent to the remote process.

A process that wants to listen for incoming CONNECT INITIATE messages must do a LISTEN (called RECEIVE CONNECT by DEC), providing a buffer for the incoming message. Once a CONNECT INITIATE has arrived, the user may accept or reject it using ACCEPT CONNECT or REJECT CONNECT, respectively, both of which can provide return information to the other process. If the connection is accepted, the accepting process provides its own connection identifier for outgoing traffic. NSP uses CONNECT CONFIRM and DISCON-NECT INITIATE messages to accept and reject incoming requests, the same as X.25 uses CALL ACCEPTED and CLEAR REQUEST. However, since the network layer provides only datagram service and may suffer from old duplicates, the initiating transport station acknowledges the response. Even with this three-way handshake, connection establishment in DECNET is simpler than in SNA (see Fig. 8-23).

Two forms of SEND (TRANSMIT) and RECEIVE are provided, one for transferring messages in a single contiguous buffer (of arbitrary size), and one for transferring messages piecemeal, a segment (packet) at a time. In the latter case the user must indicate whether a segment is the start, middle, or end of a message on output, and the transport station provides this information for incoming segments. The segmented versions of the primitives allow messages larger than the process's address space to be sent and received.

Three options are provided for flow control to and from the user. One option is no flow control by the transport layer; the users must arrange their own. The other two options are flow control on a message or segment basis, respectively, corresponding to the message and segment SEND/RECEIVE primitives. Both of the latter options use credits, like Fig. 8-3, but in DEC-NET, processes may provide multiple buffers for both whole messages and segments.

The transport service also includes primitives to send and receive interrupts and to close the connection.

8.5. SUMMARY

The function of the transport layer is to provide a subnet-independent transport service to the users. The transport service normally includes primitives to establish connections, send and receive messages, and terminate connections. Many networks offer much more elaborate services as well.

The transport layer must also implement the transport service so defined using the service the subnet provides. Among the main issues in transport protocol design are naming and addressing (e.g., hierarchical versus flat), connection establishment and termination, flow control, buffering, multiplexing and error recovery. When duplicate packets can exist in the subnet for substantial periods of time, special care (e.g., three-way handshakes) must be taken to ensure that they do not pop up unexpectedly and wreak havoc.

As more and more networks come into existence, the need to interconnect them arises. Interconnection can be accomplished by inserting a black box (gateway) between pairs or larger groups of networks. Typically, the gateway operates as a host. Two radically different approaches to internetworking have been tried: concatenated virtual circuits and datagrams. When networks with different maximum packet sizes are interconnected, there is a need to fragment large packets and then reassemble the pieces later. Depending on the details of the internetwork strategy adopted, the transport layer may be considerably or only marginally affected by the requirements of internetworking.

The ARPANET has two transport protocols, NCP and TCP. NCP is for intranet traffic and is based on the assumption of a reliable subnet. TCP is for internet traffic and is based on the assumption of an unreliable subnet. The ARPANET does not have a session layer. In contrast, SNA makes no provision for interconnecting to non-SNA networks, but has an elaborate session layer, reflecting a more production oriented and less experimental approach than the ARPANET. DECNET has a clean and simple transport layer, designed to provide reliable connections with an unreliable subnet.

PROBLEMS

1. Consider the use of X.25 as a transport protocol (with the D bit on). Its control packets do not carry sequence numbers. Could this possibly cause trouble in networks using datagrams inside?

2. Are deadlocks possible with the transport station described in the text?

3. What happens when the user of the transport station given in Fig. 8-3 sends a zero length message? Discuss the significance of your answer.

4. Out of curiosity, the implementer of the transport station of Fig. 8-3 has decided to put counters inside the *sleep* procedure to collect statistics about the *conn* array. Among these are the number of connections in each of the eight possible states, n_i ($i = 1, \ldots, 8$). After writing a massive FORTRAN program to analyze the data, our implementer discovered that the relation $\sum n_i = MaxConn$ appears to always be true. Are there any other invariants involving only these eight variables?

5. For each event that can potentially occur in the transport station of Fig. 8-3, tell whether it is legal or not when the user is sleeping in *sending* state.

6. The "truly universal" transport address numbering scheme given in the text specifies the network and host but not the IMP. What are the advantages and disadvantages of including the IMP number in the address?

7. The setup procedure of Fig. 8-5 applies to a subnet offering virtual circuit service. Describe the analogous setup procedure for a datagram subnet.

8. The dynamic buffer allocation scheme of Fig. 8-7 tells the sender how many buffers it has beyond the acknowledged message. An alternative way of conveying the same information would be for the buffer field to simply tell how many additional buffers, if any, had been allocated. In this method the sender maintains a counter that is incremented by the contents of the buffer field in arriving messages, and decremented when a message is sent for the first time. Are the two methods equally good?

9. A user process sends a stream of 128-byte messages to another user process over a connection. The receiver's main loop consists of two actions, fetch message and process message. The time required to fetch and process a message has an exponential probability density, with mean 10 msec. The window mechanism allows up to 16 outstanding messages at any instant. All communication lines in the subnet are 230 kbps, but due to delays in the subnet, the arrival pattern at the receiver is approximately Poisson. Measurements show that the time for an acknowledgement to get back to the sender, measured from the first bit of transmission, is 200 msec. What is the mean number of bytes of buffer space required at the receiving host?

10. A group of N users located in the same building are all using the same remote computer via an X.25 network. The average user generates L lines of traffic (input + output) per hour, on the average, with the mean line length being P bytes, excluding the X.25 headers. The packet carrier charges C cents per byte of user data transported, plus X cents per hour for each X.25 virtual circuit open. Under what conditions is it cost effective to multiplex all N transport connections onto the same X.25 virtual circuit, if such multiplexing adds 2 bytes of data to each packet? Assume that even one X.25 virtual circuit has enough bandwidth for all the users.

11. In a network that has a maximum packet size of 128 bytes, a maximum packet lifetime of 30 sec, and an 8-bit packet sequence number, what is the maximum data rate per connection?

12. Suppose that the clock-driven scheme for generating initial sequence numbers is used with a 15-bit wide clock counter. The clock ticks once every 100 msec, and the maximum packet lifetime is 60 sec. How often need resynchronization take place
(a) in the worst case?
(b) when the data consumes 240 sequence numbers/min?

13. Why does the maximum packet lifetime, T, have to be large enough to ensure that not only the packet, but also its acknowledgements have vanished?

14. Imagine that a two-way handshake rather than a three-way handshake were used to set up connections. In other words, the third message was not required. Are deadlocks now possible? Give an example or show that none exist.

15. Two countries, the Good Guys and the Bad Guys, are at war. The Good army is encamped in a valley. Two Bad armies are positioned on the surrounding hillsides, preparing to attack. If either Bad army attacks by itself, it will be destroyed, but if both of them strike together they will be victorious. Fortunately for the Good Guys, the communication channel the two Bad armies must use to coordinate their attack (a messenger on foot) has a high message loss rate. One possible scenario is

that Bad army 1 sends a message saying "Let us attack at noon," followed by an acknowledgement from army 2. However, Bad army 2 has no way of knowing whether or not its acknowledgement was lost. If the acknowledgement was lost, attacking at noon amounts to committing suicide, since army 1 will not attack without the acknowledgement. Does there exist a protocol that will allow the Bad Guys to win?

16. Consider the problem of recovering from host crashes (i.e., Fig. 8-11). If the interval between writing and sending an acknowledgement, or vice versa, can be made relatively small, what are the two best sender-receiver strategies for minimizing the chance of a protocol failure?

17. In a certain datagram internetwork, gateways operate in the network layer, replacing the source network's layer 3 header by the destination network's. A transport layer message consisting of 1500 bits of data and 100 bits of header is sent into a network by attaching a 100-bit network layer header to it. The destination network has a maximum packet size of 800 bits, including its own 80-bit network header. How many bits of information, including headers, are ultimately delivered to the network layer at the destination?

18. Transport layer messages must be routed via either network 1 or network 2. Network 1 has a maximum packet size of 800 bits, including its 100-bit network header. This network charges 0.001 cent per bit carried. Network layer header bits are also charged for, to discourage wiseguys from sending 1 bit packets. Data link layer header bits are free. Network 2 has a maximum packet size of 600 bits, including its 50 bit network header. The charge here is 0.6 cent per packet (including partially full ones). Which route is cheaper for
(a) transport messages of 2000 bits?
(b) transport messages of 2200 bits?

19. An interactive terminal has just generated a 10-byte line to be carried by its network as a separate message. Calculate the channel efficiency, [i.e., data/(header + data)] for NCP, X.25, and TCP. For NCP and TCP include all the IMP-IMP and hardware generated overhead, including one SYN. For X.25 include the LAPB overhead, including one flag.

20. Suppose that the chairperson of a nearby university Archaeology Department comes rushing up to you carrying an amphora that bears an inscription remarkably similar to Fig. 8-22. The amphora has just been dug up on Crete by one of her graduate students. The only difference between the inscription and Fig. 8-22 is the interchanging of the *Fragment offset* field and the 6-bit reserved field in the TCP header that is, the *Fragment offset* field has been moved and reduced to 6 bits, but otherwise the two are identical. She asks your opinion about the implication of this difference. What do you tell her?

21. Modify the program of Fig. 8-3 to do error recovery. Add a new packet type, *reset*, that can arrive after a connection has been opened by both sides but closed by neither. This event, which happens simultaneously on both ends of the connection, means that any packets that were in transit have either been delivered or destroyed, but in either case no longer are in the subnet.

22. Modify the program of Fig. 8-3 to multiplex all transport connections onto a single

X.25 virtual circuit. This change will probably require you to create and manage an explicit transport header to keep track of which packet belongs to which connection.

23. Write a program that simulates buffer management in a transport station using a sliding window for flow control rather than the credit system of Fig. 8-3. Let higher layer processes randomly open connections, send data, and close connections. To keep it simple, have all the data travel from machine A to machine B, and none the other way. Experiment with different buffer allocation strategies at B, such as dedicating buffers to specific connections versus a common buffer pool, and measure the total throughput achieved by each one.

9

THE PRESENTATION LAYER

All the layers discussed so far are necessary for the correct operation of the network. In contrast, the function of the presentation layer (see Fig. 1-7) is to provide the user process with certain useful but not always essential services. Among these services are cryptographic transformations, text compression, terminal handling, and file transfer.

Layer 6 may be part of the operating system in some implementations, but conceptually it need not be. In fact, in keeping with the general principle that everything that can be possibly removed from the operating system should be removed, it is much better for the layer 6 code to be implemented as user-callable library routines.

Nevertheless, it should be kept in mind that there is a true protocol at layer 6, just as at the lower layers. For example, a stream of messages may be fed to layer 6 by a user process. These messages are then compressed, encrypted, and sent to the destination machine, where layer 6 decrypts and expands them before handing them over to the destination user process.

9.1. NETWORK SECURITY AND PRIVACY

Back in the early days when corporations and universities had a single computer center, achieving security was easy. All the organization had to do was station a guard at the door to the computer room. The guard made sure that no one removed any tapes, disks, or cards from the room unless explicitly authorized to do so.

With the advent of networking, the situation has changed radically. No one can manually police the millions of bits of data that daily move between the computers in a network. Moreover, organizations have no way of being sure that their data are not secretly copied by wiretap or other means on the way to their proper destination. Wiretapping is far more common than most people realize (Kahn, 1980; Selfridge and Schwartz, 1980). Worst of all, when satellite links are being employed on the transmission path, the data are available to anyone who wishes to go to the trouble of erecting an antenna to listen. Clearly, some kind of **encryption** (also called **encipherment**) is needed to make the data unintelligible to all but its intended recipient.

Logically, encryption is a presentation service, just like text compression. In both cases a stream of data goes in, and a transformed stream of data comes out. For this reason, we have chosen to treat encryption in our discussion of the presentation layer.

In practice, encryption can be done in any layer, from the physical layer, to the application layer. For example, by splicing a hardware encryption device into the host-IMP line just after it leaves the host, and a decryption device into the line just before it enters the IMP, the entire encryption/decryption process can be retrofitted without affecting existing software. When encryption is done this way it is called **data link encryption**.

At the other extreme is **end-to-end encryption**. With this method the presentation or even application layer performs the transformation, either in software or using special hardware. This method is obviously not transparent to the software. Data link encryption encrypts physical circuits, whereas end-to-end encryption encrypts specific sessions.

These two methods differ in several respects. For one thing, when data link encryption is used, the installation management rather than the end user, chooses the encryption method. With end-to-end encryption, no user is forced to live with an algorithm he feels that is too weak. Also, with end-to-end encryption the user can change the encryption method whenever he feels that the old one has been compromised. Another difference is that with data link encryption, the messages are decrypted at each IMP and processed within the IMP in unencrypted form. Bugs in the IMP software, such as mixing up virtual circuits, could cause security violations. With end-to-end encryption, there is no such problem. Finally, with data link encryption the entire packet is encrypted, including the data link header, whereas with end-to-end encryption, the data link header is not encrypted.

In some situations, knowledge of the traffic patterns is itself secret. For example, if during wartime, an enemy noticed that the amount of traffic to and from the Pentagon in Washington suddenly decreased dramatically, and the amount of traffic to and from East Podunk increased by the same amount, the enemy need not have an IQ of 200 to figure out that something strange is going on. The study of message length and frequency by an enemy is known as **traffic analysis**. It can be made more difficult by the insertion of a large amount of dummy traffic.

In the following sections we will describe a number of cryptographic methods, dating from the of Julius Caesar to the present time. Finally, we will look at some other aspects of the network security problem.

9.1.1. Traditional Cryptography

Cryptography has a long and colorful history. In this section we will just sketch some of the highlights, as background information for what follows. For a complete history, Kahn's (1967) book is highly recommended.

Historically four groups of people have used and contributed to the art of cryptography: the military, the diplomatic corps, diarists, and lovers. Of these, the military has had the most important role and has shaped the nature of the field. Within military organizations, the messages to be encrypted have traditionally been given to poorly paid code clerks for encryption and transmission. The sheer volume of messages to be sent has prevented this work from being done by a few elite specialists.

Until the advent of computers, one of the main constraints on cryptography has been the ability of the code clerk to perform the necessary transformations, often on a battlefield with little equipment. An additional constraint has been the difficulty in switching over quickly from one cryptographic method to another one, since this entails retraining a large number of people. However, the danger of a code clerk being captured by the enemy has made it essential to be able to change the cryptographic method instantly, if need be. These conflicting requirements have given rise to the model of Fig. 9-1.

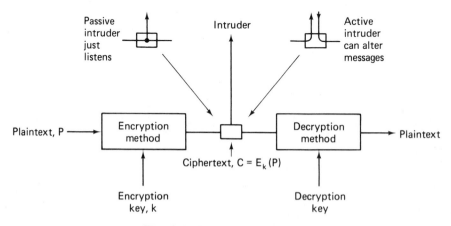

Fig. 9-1. The encryption model.

The messages to be encrypted, known as the **plaintext**, are transformed by a function that is parametrized by a **key**. The output of the encryption process, known as the **ciphertext** or **cryptogram**, is then transmitted, often by messenger or radio. We assume that the enemy, or **intruder**, hears and accurately copies down the complete ciphertext. However, unlike the intended recipient, he does not know what the key is and so cannot decrypt the ciphertext easily. Sometimes the intruder cannot only listen to the communication channel (passive intruder), but can also record messages and play them back later, inject his own messages, or modify legitimate messages before they get to the receiver (active intruder). The art of breaking ciphers is called **cryptanalysis**. The art of devising ciphers (cryptography) and breaking them (cryptanalysis) is collectively known as **cryptology**.

A fundamental rule of cryptography is that one must assume that the cryptanalyst knows the general method of encryption used. In other words, the cryptanalyst knows how the encryption method of Fig. 9-1 works. The amount of effort necessary to invent, test, and install a new method every time the old method is compromised or thought to be compromised has always made it impractical to keep this secret, and thinking it is secret when it is not does more harm than good.

This is where the role of the key enters. The key consists of a (usually) short string of characters that selects one of many potential encryptions. In contrast to the general method, which may only be changed every few years, the key can be changed as often as required. Thus our basic model is a stable and publicly known general method parametrized by a secret and easily changed key.

From the cryptanalyst's point of view, the cryptanalysis problem has three variations. When he has a quantity of ciphertext and no plaintext, he is confronted with the **ciphertext only** problem. The cryptograms that appear in the puzzle section of newspapers pose this kind of problem. When he has some matched ciphertext and plaintext, the problem becomes known as the **known plaintext** problem. Finally, when the cryptanalyst has the ability to encrypt pieces of plaintext of his own choosing, we have the **chosen plaintext** problem. Newspaper cryptograms can be broken trivially if the cryptanalyst is allowed to ask such questions as: What is the encryption of ABCDE?

Novices in the cryptography business often assume that if a cipher can withstand a ciphertext only attack, it is secure. This assumption is very naive. In many cases the cryptanalyst can make a good guess at parts of the plaintext, for example, the first thing many time-sharing systems say when you call them up is "PLEASE LOGIN." Equipped with some matched plaintext-ciphertext pairs, the cryptanalyst's job becomes much easier. To achieve security, the cryptographer should be conservative and make sure that the system is unbreakable even if his opponent can encrypt arbitrary amounts of chosen plaintext.

Encryption methods have historically been divided into two categories: substitution ciphers (including codes), and transposition ciphers. We will now deal with each of these in turn, as background information for modern cryptography.

Substitution Ciphers

In a **substitution cipher** each letter or group of letters is replaced by another letter or group of letters to disguise it. The oldest cipher known is the **Caesar cipher**, attributed to Julius Caesar. In this method, a becomes D, b becomes E, c becomes F, . . . , and z becomes C. For example, *attack* becomes *DWWDFN*. (In examples, plaintext will be given in lowercase letters, and ciphertext in uppercase letters. In running text both will be in *italics*.)

A slight generalization of the Caesar cipher allows the ciphertext alphabet to be shifted by k letters, instead of always 3. In this case k becomes a key to the general method of circularly shifted alphabets. The Caesar cipher may have fooled the Carthaginians, but it has not fooled anyone since.

The next improvement is to have each of the symbols in the plaintext, say the 26 letters for simplicity, each map onto some other letter. For example,

```
plaintext:   a b c d e f g h i j k l m n o p q r s t u v w x y z
ciphertext:  Q W E R T Y U I O P A S D F G H J K L Z X C V B N M
```

This general system is called a **monoalphabetic substitution**, with the key being the 26-letter string corresponding to the full alphabet. For the key above, *attack* would be encrypted as *QZZQEA*.

At first glance this might seem a safe system because although the cryptanalyst knows the general system (letter for letter substitution), he does not know which of the $26! = 4 \times 10^{26}$ possible keys is in use. In contrast with the Caesar cipher, trying all of them is not a promising approach. Even at 1 μsec per solution, a computer would take 10^{13} years to try all the keys.

Nevertheless, given a surprisingly small amount of ciphertext, the cipher can be broken easily. The basic attack takes advantage of the statistical properties of natural languages. In English, for example, e is the most common letter, followed by *t, a, o, n, i,* etc. The most common two letter combinations, or **digrams**, are: *th*, *in*, *er*, *re*, and *an*. The most common three letter combinations, or **trigrams**, are: *the*, *and*, *ion*, and *ent* (See Fig. 9-2 for more statistics of English.)

A cryptanalyst trying to break a monoalphabetic cipher would start out by counting the relative frequencies of all letters in the ciphertext. Then he might tentatively assign the most common one to e and the next most common one to t. He would then look at trigrams to find a common one of the form *tXe*, which strongly suggests that X is h. Similarly, if the pattern *thYt* occurs frequently, the Y probably stands for a. With this information, he can look for a frequently occurring trigram of the form *aZW*, which is most likely *and*. By making guesses at common letters, digrams, and trigrams, the cryptanalyst builds up a tentative plaintext, letter by letter.

Letters		Diagrams		Trigrams		Words	
E	13.05	TH	3.16	THE	4.72	THE	6.42
T	9.02	IN	1.54	ING	1.42	OF	4.02
O	8.21	ER	1.33	AND	1.13	AND	3.15
A	7.81	RE	1.30	ION	1.00	TO	2.36
N	7.28	AN	1.08	ENT	0.98	A	2.09
I	6.77	HE	1.08	FOR	0.76	IN	1.77
R	6.64	AR	1.02	TIO	0.75	THAT	1.25
S	6.46	EN	1.02	ERE	0.69	IS	1.03
H	5.85	TI	1.02	HER	0.68	I	0.94
D	4.11	TE	0.98	ATE	0.66	IT	0.93
L	3.60	AT	0.88	VER	0.63	FOR	0.77
C	2.93	ON	0.84	TER	0.62	AS	0.76
F	2.88	HA	0.84	THA	0.62	WITH	0.76
U	2.77	OU	0.72	ATI	0.59	WAS	0.72
M	2.62	IT	0.71	HAT	0.55	HIS	0.71
P	2.15	ES	0.69	ERS	0.54	HE	0.71
Y	1.51	ST	0.68	HIS	0.52	BE	0.63
W	1.49	OR	0.68	RES	0.50	NOT	0.61
G	1.39	NT	0.67	ILL	0.47	BY	0.57
B	1.28	HI	0.66	ARE	0.46	BUT	0.56
V	1.00	EA	0.64	CON	0.45	HAVE	0.55
K	0.42	VE	0.64	NCE	0.45	YOU	0.55
X	0.30	CO	0.59	ALL	0.44	WHICH	0.53
J	0.23	DE	0.55	EVE	0.44	ARE	0.50
Q	0.14	RA	0.55	ITH	0.44	ON	0.47
Z	0.09	RO	0.55	TED	0.44	OR	0.45

Fig. 9-2. Percent occurrences of English letters, digrams, trigrams, and words.

Another approach is to guess a probable word or phrase. For example, consider the following ciphertext from an accounting firm (blocked into groups of five characters):

CTBMN BYCTC BTJDS QXBNS GSTJC BTSWX CTQTZ CQVUJ
QJSGS TJQZZ MNQJS VLNSX VSZJU JDSTS JQUUS JUBXJ
JDSKS UJSNT KBGAQ JZBGY QTLCT ZBNYB NQJSW

A likely word in a message from an accounting firm is *financial*. Using our knowledge that *financial* has a repeated letter (*i*), with four other letters between their occurrences, we look for repeated letters in the ciphertext at this spacing. We find 10 hits, at positions 6, 15, 27, 31, 42, 48, 56, 70, 71, and 83. However, only two of these, 31 and 42, have the next letter (corresponding to

n in the plaintext) repeated in the proper place. Of these two, only 31 also has the a correctly positioned, so we know that *financial* begins at position 30. From this point on, deducing the key is easy.

To make the cryptanalyst's job more difficult, it is necessary to smooth out the frequencies of the ciphertext, so the letters representing e, t, etc. do not stand out so clearly. One way of achieving this goal is to introduce multiple cipher alphabets, to be used in rotation, giving what is known as a **polyalphabetic cipher**. As an example, consider the **Vigenère cipher**. It consists of a square matrix containing 26 Caesar alphabets. The first row, called row A, is ABCDEFGH...XYZ. The next row, called row B, is BCDEFGHI...YZA. The last row, called row Z, is ZABCDEFG...WXY.

Like the monoalphabetic cipher, this cipher also has a key, but instead of being a string of 26 distinct characters, the key is usually a short, easy-to-remember word or phrase, such as COOKIEMONSTER. To encrypt a message, the key is written repeatedly above the plaintext, for example:

COOK I EMONS T ERCOOK I EMONS T ERCOOK I EMONS T ERCOOK I EMO
fourscoreandsevenyearsagoourmothersbroughtforth

The key letter above each plaintext letter tells which row to use for encryption. The f is encrypted using the Caesar alphabet of row C, the o and u are encrypted using the Caesar alphabet of row O, and so on. It should be clear that a plaintext letter will be represented by different letters in the ciphertext, depending on the position in the plaintext. Similarly, trigrams such as *the* will map onto different trigrams in the ciphertext, depending on their position.

A more powerful polyalphabetic cipher can be constructed by using arbitrary monoalphabetic ciphers for the rows instead of restricting them to Caesar ciphers. The only problem with this scheme is that the 26 × 26 square table then becomes part of the key and must also be memorized or written down.

Although unquestionably much better than the monoalphabetic cipher, polyalphabetic ciphers can also be broken easily by a ciphertext only attack, provided that that the cryptanalyst has a sufficient amount of ciphertext. The trick is to guess the key length. First the cryptanalyst tentatively assumes a key of length k. He then arranges the cipher text in rows, k letters per row. If his guess is correct, all the ciphertext letters in each column will have been encrypted by the same monoalphabetic cipher, in which case they should exhibit the same frequency distribution as normal English text: the most common letter 13%, the next most common letter 9%, etc. If this is obviously not the case, the tentative value for k is wrong, and another should be tried. Once a good fit has been obtained, each column can be attacked as a separate monoalphabetic cipher.

The next step up in complexity for the cryptographer is to use a key longer than the plaintext, making the above attack useless. In fact, constructing an unbreakable cipher is easy. First choose a random bit string as the key. Then convert the plaintext into a bit string, for example by using its ASCII representation. Finally, compute the EXCLUSIVE OR of these two strings, bit by bit. The resulting ciphertext cannot be broken, because every possible plaintext is an equally probable candidate. The ciphertext gives the cryptanalyst no information at all. In a sufficiently large sample of ciphertext, each letter will occur equally often, as will every digram and every trigram.

This method, known as the **one time key**, has a number of practical disadvantages, unfortunately. To start with, the key cannot be memorized, so both sender and receiver must carry a written copy with them. If either one is subject to capture, written keys are clearly undesirable. Additionally, the total amount of data that can be transmitted is limited by the amount of key available. If the spy strikes it rich and discovers a wealth of data, he may find himself unable to transmit it back to headquarters because the key has been used up. Another problem is the sensitivity of the method to lost messages, or messages that arrive in the wrong order. If the sender and receiver get out of synchronization as to where in the key they are, they are in trouble.

All of these problems can be overcome by simply having sender and receiver agree to start each message anew at the start of the key and to break up long messages into multiple messages. Now the key is no longer a one-time key and can be broken, albeit with difficulty. To break the system, the cryptanalyst must acquire a number of encrypted messages and lay them out on top of one another, as a series of rows. The first character of each row can be viewed as a column encrypted by a monoalphabetic cipher and can be attacked in the usual way. In fact, the one-time key is now conceptually the same as a polyalphabetic cipher, only with a longer key, and can be broken the same way.

One note is in order about generating one-time keys. They must be random to be secure. The worst possible way of generating a key is to use a pseudo random number generator based on a Markov chain. When these random numbers are used, not only is the rest of the key not independent of what has come before, it is uniquely determined by what has come before. Thus, if the cryptanalyst ever manages to acquire matched plaintext-ciphertext pairs, he will be able to deduce the key used for those pairs. From this key he may well be able to deduce the algorithm that produced it, and from the algorithm he will be able to generate the rest of the key. For more details, see (Reeds, 1977). To generate a truly random key, the quantum noise in an electrical resistor should be amplified and digitized. The laws of quantum mechanics guarantee that the results will not be reproducible.

Substitution ciphers need not always work one letter (or bit) at a time. For example, **Porta's cipher** uses a 26×26 table, like the Vigenère cipher. The plaintext is encoded two characters at a time. The first character indicates a row, the second, a column. The number or letter pair found at the intersection is the encrypted value. If 26 different tables are prepared, trigrams can be encrypted as units by using the first letter of each trigram to select a table.

Codes

As the units encrypted become longer and longer, the cipher begins to resemble a **code**. The main difference between a cipher and a code is that the former encrypts a fixed-size unit of plaintext with each operation, whereas the latter encrypts a single variable-length linguistic unit, typically a single word or phrase. Prior to computers, codes came in two distinct flavors: one-part codes and two-part codes. In a one-part code, both the plaintext word and the code symbol are arranged in the same order. For example, the code symbols for *amnesia, amoeba, amok, among, amorous, amorphous, amortize* and *ampere* might be 16142, 16144, 16149, 16155, 16160, 16189, 16201, and 16209. In a two-part code these same words might be encoded as 15202, 16902, 40420, 30012, 80032, 76290, 39321, and 10344. With a one-part code, both encoding and decoding can use the same code book, whereas a two-part code requires differently arranged books for encoding and decoding. A one-part code is much easier to break than a two-part code, since the code symbol itself contains approximate information about where the plaintext symbol is in the book. However, a two-part code requires both sender and receiver to carry around twice as much baggage.

Breaking a code is like breaking a giant monoalphabetic cipher. The most common symbol in a code is usually the symbol for *stop*, used to end a sentence. Next come the symbols for *the*, *of*, *and*, *to*, *a*, *in*, and *that*. Knowledge of English sentence structure is also helpful for example, most sentences begin with a subject, and subjects are usually of the form ARTICLE ADJECTIVES NOUN.

Codes have the disadvantage of requiring large books, that cannot be replaced as easily as the key to a cipher. However, they have the advantage of generally being harder to break than ciphers. Codes and ciphers can be combined to make the cryptanalyst's life even less pleasant. For example, encoding a message might yield a list of five-digit numbers. These numbers could be concatenated to form a digit sequence, that could then be encrypted using a polyalphabetic cipher. Enciphering a coded message is called **superencipherment**.

Although superenciphered codes may seem impenetrable at first glance, Kahn points out that during World War II, U.S. Intelligence broke a top secret superenciphered code in which the plaintext was Japanese transliterated into Latin letters. When the fact that the code was broken leaked out and was published in a Chicago newspaper, the Japanese government refused to believe that anyone could break their code, and continued to use it for the rest of the war.

Transposition Ciphers

Substitution ciphers and codes preserve the order of the plaintext symbols but disguise them. **Transposition ciphers**, in contrast, reorder the letters but do not disguise them. Figure 9-3 depicts a common transposition cipher, the columnar transposition. The cipher is keyed by a word of phrase not containing any repeated letters. In this example, MEGABUCK is the key. The purpose of the key is to number the columns, column 1 being under the key letter closest to the start of the alphabet, and so on. The plaintext is written horizontally, as a series of rows. The ciphertext is read out by columns, starting with the column whose key letter is the lowest.

```
M E G A B U C K        Plaintext:
– – – – – – – –
7 4 5 1 2 8 3 6          pleasetransferonemilliondollarsto
– – – – – – – –          myswissbankaccountsixtwotwo
p l e a s e t r
a n s f e r o n        Ciphertext:
e m i l l i o n
d o l l a r s t          AFLLSKOSELAWAIATOOSSCTCLNMOMANT
o m y s w i s s          ESILYNTWRNNTSOWDPAEDOBUOERIRICXB
h a n k a c c o
u n t s i x t w
o t w o a b c d
```

Fig. 9-3. A transposition cipher.

To break a transposition cipher, the cryptanalyst must first be aware that he is dealing with a transposition cipher. By looking at the frequency of E, T, A, O, I, N, etc., it is easy to see if they fit the normal pattern for plaintext. If so, the cipher is clearly a transposition cipher, because in such a cipher every letter represents itself.

The next step is to make a guess at the number of columns. In many cases a probable word or phrase may be guessed at from the context of the message. For example, suppose that our cryptanalyst suspected the plaintext phrase *milliondollars* to occur somewhere in the message. Observe that digrams *MO*, *IL*, *LL*, *LA*, *IR* and *OS* occur in the ciphertext as a result of this phrase wrapping around. The ciphertext letter *O* follows the ciphertext letter *M* (i.e., they are vertically adjacent in column 4) because they are separated in the probable phrase by a distance equal to the key length. If a key of length seven had been used, the digrams *MD*, *IO*, *LL*, *LL*, *IA*, *OR*, and *NS* would have occurred instead. In fact, for each key length, a different set of digrams is produced in the ciphertext. By hunting for the various possibilities, the cryptanalyst can often easily determine the key length.

The remaining step is to order the columns. When the number of columns, k, is small, each of the $k(k-1)$ column pairs can be examined to see if its digram frequencies match that for English plaintext. The pair with the best match is assumed to be correctly positioned. Now each remaining column is tentatively tried as the successor to this pair. The column whose digram and trigram frequencies give the best match is tentatively assumed to be correct. The predecessor column is found in the same way. The entire process is continued until a potential ordering is found. Chances are that the plaintext will be recognizable at this point (e.g., if *milloin* occurs, it is clear what the error is).

Some transposition ciphers accept a fixed-length block of input and produce a fixed-length block of output. These ciphers can be completely described by just giving a list telling the order in which the characters are to be output. For example, the cipher of Fig. 9-3 can be seen as a 64 character block cipher. Its output is 4, 12, 20, 28, 36, 44, 52, 60, 5, 13 , . . . , 62. In other words, the fourth input character, *a*, is the first to be output, followed by the twelfth, *f*, and so on.

9.1.2. The Data Encryption Standard

While describing the various classical cryptographic schemes, we have tried to make it clear how computers can be used as powerful tools by the cryptanalyst, both for collecting frequency statistics and for trying out large numbers of tentative solutions. Now we will remove our cryptanalyst hat and put on our cryptographer hat: we will think about making the encrypting process so complicated that not even a computer can break it.

Although modern cryptography uses the same basic ideas as traditional cryptography, transposition and substitution, its emphasis is different. Traditionally, cryptographers have used simple algorithms and relied on long keys for their security. Nowadays the reverse is true: the object is to make the encryption algorithm so complex and involuted that even if the cryptanalyst acquires vast mounds of enciphered text of his own choosing, he will not be able to make any sense of it at all.

Transpositions and substitutions can be done with simple circuits. Figure 9-4(a) shows a device, known as a **P-box** (P stands for permutation), used to effect a transposition on an 8-bit input. If the 8 bits are designated from top to bottom as 01234567, the output of this particular P-box is 36071245. By appropriate internal wiring, a P-box can be made to perform any transposition.

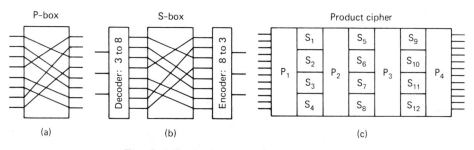

Fig. 9-4. Basic elements of product ciphers.

Substitutions are performed by what are called **S-boxes**, as shown in

Fig. 9-4(b). In this example a 3-bit plaintext is entered and a 3-bit ciphertext is output. The 3-bit input selects one of the eight lines exiting from the first stage and sets it to 1; all the other lines are 0. The second stage is a P-box. The third stage encodes the selected input line in binary again. With the wiring shown, if the eight octal numbers 01234567 were input one after another, the output sequence would be 24506713. In other words,s 0 has been replaced by 2, 1 has been replaced by 4, etc. Again, by appropriate wiring of the P-box, any substitution can be accomplished.

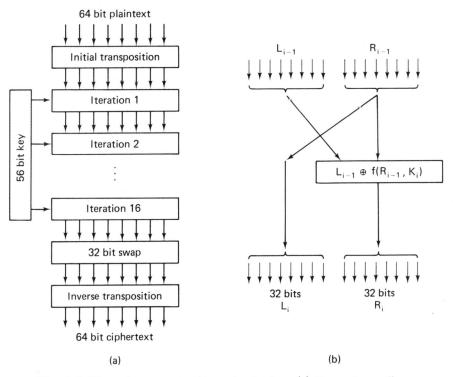

Fig. 9-5. The data encryption standard. (a) General outline. (b) Detail of one iteration.

The real power of these basic elements only becomes apparent when we cascade a whole series of ciphers, as shown in Fig. 9-6(c). In this example, 12 input lines are transposed by the first stage. Theoretically, it would be possible to have the second stage be an S-box that mapped a 12-bit number onto another 12-bit number. However, such a device would need $2^{12} = 4096$ crossed wires in its middle stage. Instead, the input is broken up into four groups of 3 bits, each of which is substituted independently of the others. Although this

```
type block = array[1 .. 64] of 0 .. 1;          {64 bit vector}
     ordering = array[1 .. 64] of 1 .. 64;      {defines a transposition}

var InitialTr, FinalTr, swap, KeyTr1, KeyTr2, etr, ptr: ordering;
    s: array[1 .. 8, 1 .. 64] of 0 .. 15;
    rots: array[1 .. 16] of 1 .. 2;

procedure transpose (var data: block; t: ordering; n: integer);
var x: block; i: 1 .. 64;
begin x := data;   for i := 1 to n do data [i] := x[t[i]] end;  {transpose}

procedure rotate (var key: block);   {1 bit left rotate on two 28 bit units}
var i: 1 .. 55;   x: block;
begin x := key;
   for i := 1 to 55 do x[i] := x[i + 1];
      x[28] := key[1];   x[56] := key[29];   key := x
end;  {rotate}

procedure f(i: integer;   var key,a,x: block);
var e,ikey,y: block;   r: 0 .. 64; k: 1 .. 8;   j: 1 .. 48;
begin   e:= a;
   transpose (e, etr, 48);                    {expand e to 48 bits}
   for j := 1 to rots[i] do rotate (key);
   ikey := key;   transpose (ikey, KeyTr2,48);
   for j := 1 to 48 do if e[j] + ikey[j] = 1 then y[j] := 1 else y[j] := 0;
   for k := 1 to 8 do                         {substitute part}
      begin   r:= 32*y[6*k − 5] + 16*y[6*k] +
                 8*y[6*k − 4] + 4*y[6*k − 3] + 2*y[6*k − 2] + y[6*k − 1] + 1;
      if odd(s[k,r] div 8) then x[4*k − 3] := 1 else x[4*k − 3] := 0;
      if odd(s[k,r] div 4) then x[4*k − 2] := 1 else x[4*k − 2] := 0;
      if odd(s[k,r] div 2) then x[4*k − 1] := 1 else x[4*k − 1] := 0;
      if odd(s[k,r]) then x[4*k] := 1 else x[4*k] := 0
      end;
   transpose (x, ptr, 32)
end;  {f}

procedure des (plaintext, key: block; var ciphertext: block);
var i: 1 .. 16;   j: 1 .. 32;   a,b,x: block;
begin   a := plaintext;                       {copy plaintext to a}
   transpose (a, InitialTr, 64);              {initial transposition}
   transpose (key, KeyTr1, 56);               {mix up key and reduce to 56 bits}
   for i := 1 to 16 do                        {here come the 16 iterations}
      begin   b := a;                         {a contains current ciphertext}
      for j := 1 to 32 do a[j] := b[j + 32];{current left taken from old right}
      f(i, key, a, x);                        {compute x = f(r[i − 1], k[i])}
      for j := 1 to 32 do if b[j] + x[j] = 1 then a[j + 32] := 1 else a[j + 32] :=0;
      end;
   transpose (a, swap, 64);                   {swap left and right halves}
   transpose (a, FinalTr, 64);                {final transposition}
   ciphertext := a
end;  {des}
```

Fig. 9-6. (a) The DES Algorithm

InitialTr
    58 50 42 34 26 18 10 02 60 52 44 36 28 20 12 04 62 54 46 38 30 22 14 06 64 56 48 40 32 24 16 08
    57 49 41 33 25 17 09 01 59 51 43 35 27 19 11 03 61 53 45 37 29 21 13 05 63 55 47 39 31 23 15 07

FinalTr
    40 08 48 16 56 24 64 32 39 07 47 15 55 23 63 31 38 06 46 14 54 22 62 30 37 05 45 13 53 21 61 29
    36 04 44 12 52 20 60 28 35 03 43 11 51 19 59 27 34 02 42 10 50 18 58 26 33 01 41 09 49 17 57 25

swap
    33 34 35 36 37 38 39 40 41 42 43 44 45 46 47 48 49 50 51 52 53 54 55 56 57 58 59 60 61 62 63 64
    01 02 03 04 05 06 07 08 09 10 11 12 13 14 15 16 17 18 19 20 21 22 23 24 25 26 27 28 29 30 31 32

KeyTr1
    57 49 41 33 25 17 09 01 58 50 42 34 26 18 10 02 59 51 43 35 27 19 11 03 60 52 44 36
    63 55 47 39 31 23 15 07 62 54 46 38 30 22 14 06 61 53 45 37 29 21 13 05 28 20 12 04

KeyTr2
    14 17 11 24 01 05 03 28 15 06 21 10 23 19 12 04 26 08 16 07 27 20 13 02
    41 52 31 37 47 55 30 40 51 45 33 48 44 49 39 56 34 53 46 42 50 36 29 32

etr
    32 01 02 03 04 05 04 05 06 07 08 09 08 09 10 11 12 13 12 13 14 15 16 17
    16 17 18 19 20 21 20 21 22 23 24 25 24 25 26 27 28 29 28 29 30 31 32 01

ptr
    16 07 20 21 29 12 28 17 01 15 23 26 05 18 31 10
    02 08 24 14 32 27 03 09 19 13 30 06 22 11 04 25

S−boxes: *s*[1:1..64], *s*[2:1..64], ... , *s*[8,1..64]
    14 04 13 01 02 15 11 08 03 10 06 12 05 09 00 07 00 15 07 04 14 02 13 01 10 06 12 11 09 05 03 08
    04 01 14 08 13 06 02 11 15 12 09 07 03 10 05 00 15 12 08 02 04 09 01 07 05 11 03 14 10 00 06 13

    15 01 08 14 06 11 03 04 09 07 02 13 12 00 05 10 03 13 04 07 15 02 08 14 12 00 01 10 06 09 11 05
    00 14 07 11 10 04 13 01 05 08 12 06 09 03 02 15 13 08 10 01 03 15 04 02 11 06 07 12 00 05 14 09

    10 00 09 14 06 03 15 05 01 13 12 07 11 04 02 08 13 07 00 09 03 04 06 10 02 08 05 14 12 11 15 01
    13 06 04 09 08 15 03 00 11 01 02 12 05 10 14 07 01 10 13 00 06 09 08 07 04 15 14 03 11 05 02 12

    07 13 14 03 00 06 09 10 01 02 08 05 11 12 04 15 13 08 11 05 06 15 00 03 04 07 02 12 01 10 14 09
    10 06 09 00 12 11 07 13 15 01 03 14 05 02 08 04 03 15 00 06 10 01 13 08 09 04 05 11 12 07 02 14

    02 12 04 01 07 10 11 06 08 05 03 15 13 00 14 09 14 11 02 12 04 07 13 01 05 00 15 10 03 09 08 06
    04 02 01 11 10 13 07 08 15 09 12 05 06 03 00 14 11 08 12 07 01 14 02 13 06 15 00 09 10 04 05 03

    12 01 10 15 09 02 06 08 00 13 03 04 14 07 05 11 10 15 04 02 07 12 09 05 06 01 13 14 00 11 03 08
    09 14 15 05 02 08 12 03 07 00 04 10 01 13 11 06 04 03 02 12 09 05 15 10 11 14 01 07 06 00 08 13

    04 11 02 14 15 00 08 13 03 12 09 07 05 10 06 01 13 00 11 07 04 09 01 10 14 03 05 12 02 15 08 06
    01 04 11 13 12 03 07 14 10 15 06 08 00 05 09 02 06 11 13 08 01 04 10 07 09 05 00 15 14 02 03 12

    13 02 08 04 06 15 11 01 10 09 03 14 05 00 12 07 01 15 13 08 10 03 07 04 12 05 06 11 00 14 09 02
    07 11 04 01 09 12 14 02 00 06 10 13 15 03 05 08 02 01 14 07 04 10 08 13 15 12 09 00 03 05 06 11

rots
    1 1 2 2 2 2 2 2 1 2 2 2 2 2 2 1

Fig. 9-6. (b) The tables.

method is less general, it is still powerful. By including a sufficiently large number of stages in the product cipher, the output can be made to be a non-linear function of the input.

In January 1977, the U.S. government adopted a product cipher developed by IBM as its official standard for unclassified information. This adoption, in turn, has stimulated a number of manufacturers to implement the encryption algorithm, known as the **Data Encryption Standard** (National Bureau of Standards, 1977) in hardware, thus making it fast. The availability of fast and cheap hardware, in turn, has stimulated many other users to adopt DES for their encryption needs.

We will now explain the DES algorithm. An outline of it is shown in Fig. 9-5(a). Plaintext is encrypted in blocks of 64 bits, yielding 64 bits of ciphertext. The algorithm, which is parametrized by a 56-bit key, has 19 distinct stages. The first stage is a key independent transposition on the 64-bit plaintext. The last stage is the exact inverse of this transposition. The stage prior to the last one exchanges the leftmost 32 bits with the rightmost 32 bits. The remaining 16 stages are functionally identical but are parametrized by different functions of the key. The algorithm has been designed to allow decryption to be done with the same key as encryption. The steps are just run in the reverse order.

The operation of one of these intermediate stages is illustrated in Fig. 9-5(b). Each stage takes two 32-bit inputs and produces two 32-bit outputs. The left output is simply a copy of the right input. The right output is the bitwise EXCLUSIVE OR of the left input and a function of the right input and the key for this stage, K_i. All the complexity lies in this function.

The function consists of four steps, carried out in sequence. First, a 48 bit number, E, is constructed by expanding the 32 bit R_{i-1} according to a fixed transposition and duplication rule. Second, E and K_i are EXCLUSIVE-ORed together. This output is then partitioned into eight groups of 6 bits each, each of which is fed into a different S-box. The S-boxes produce 4, instead of 6 output bits. Each of the 64 possible inputs to an S-box is mapped onto a 4-bit output. Obviously different inputs can produce the same output. The result is a list of eight 4-bit numbers. Finally, these 32 bits are passed through a P-box.

In each of the 16 iterations, a different key is used. Before the algorithm starts, a 56-bit transposition is applied to the key. Just before each iteration, the key is partitioned into two 28-bit units, each of which is rotated left by a number of bits dependent on the iteration number. K_i is derived from this rotated key by applying yet another 56-bit transposition to it. Despite all this complexity, DES is basically a monoalphabetic substitution cipher using a 64-bit character.

A procedure to perform the DES algorithm is given in Fig. 9-6(a). The values to which the tables are to be initialized are given in Fig. 9-6(b). In case anyone cares, the ciphertext corresponding to the plaintext of 64 zeros and a key of 64 zeros is 8CA64DE9C1B123A7 (hexadecimal).

Attacking DES

Now, to give equal time to all parties, let us take off our cryptographer hat and put on our cryptanalyst hat once more. For many applications, keys are chosen by the end users. Given human nature, it is a safe bet that the key "&a%2Q:Kj" will be used considerably less frequently than, say, "BARBARA" or the names of other lovely young ladies.

As a cryptanalyst, this fact pleases us immensely. Our attack will be based on the assumption that we have one 64-bit block of ciphertext whose plaintext is known [e.g., PLEASE L(OGIN)], as mentioned above. Alternatively, we could examine all the 64-bit blocks of ciphertext and find the one that occurs most often. This block is likely to be eight ASCII blanks, since page numbers in written documents, as well as the date, signature, and address in letters, usually begin far from the left margin. When paragraphs are indented five spaces, the combination of five spaces followed by "The" also becomes a good bet.

To attack the cipher, we first collect a list of probable keys. Books of the genre "4096 Names for Your New Baby" provide a good starting point. Family names are also useful; fortunately, telephone companies publish lists of them, conveniently sorted in alphabetical order. To this, the names of all streets taken from the reverse side of a few hundred city maps should be added. Finally, all the words in a decent-size dictionary should be included. (At 50 words/min, a typist can go through even a large dictionary in two weeks.) True connoisseurs might want to throw in a modest number of pronounceable nonsense "words" (e.g., consonant, vowel, consonant, vowel, consonant, such as fotal or pelid).

All in all, this list is unlikely to exceed a million entries (unless someone has gone hog wild with nonsense words). The obvious thing to do now is encrypt the known plaintext using each of these entries as key. If encryption and comparison with the known ciphertext takes x μsec, it will take only x sec to determine whether or not the key is in the list. Studies (Morris and Thompson, 1979) have shown that 85% of all time-sharing system passwords can be found this way, so the approach looks promising.

Even if an encryption chip is not available, the same approach can be used. The known plaintext (e.g., "PLEASE L") is simply encrypted in advance using the complete list of names and words as keys. The resulting ciphertext-plaintext pairs are stored on tape. Although the encryption process may take hundreds of hours, it need only be done once. Attacking a cipher can now be done as fast as the tape can be read.

Even if people are forced to choose 56-bit random numbers for their keys, the security of the system is still not safe against a determined and well-financed intruder. Hellman (1980) has devised a method for greatly speeding up exhaustive searches of the key space, provided that certain information can be computed in advance, and stored on tape, similar to the suggestion made above. Again we assume that the cryptanalyst has a matched (plaintext, ciphertext) pair (P, C). His goal is to determine the key, K, that was used for this encryption, E_K.

As usual in computer science, there are time-memory trade-offs available. At one extreme, the cryptanalyst can compute $E_K(P)$ for all $2^{56} \approx (7 \times 10^{16})$ values of K, and compare each one of these to C. When he finds a match, the game is over. This approach requires no memory, but it takes too long.

At the other extreme he could precompute all 2^{56} $(K, E_K(P))$ pairs in advance, sort them on the second field, and store them on tape. Once these tapes had been made, breaking a cipher given (P, C) would require looking up C in a sorted list of 2^{56} records. If an index containing the first entry on each tape were available, one pass over the index would tell which tape was needed, and one pass over the tape would produce the key. This method is also impractical because 4×10^9 tapes would be needed. However, the method is potentially fast.

What Hellman has done is think of a way to make intermediate time-memory trade-offs possible. The basic method, slightly simplified, goes something like this. We first pick m, the number of 112-bit (key1, key2) records we are willing to compute in advance and store on tape. We then randomly choose a key, K_0, from the key space. Next, we encrypt the known plaintext, P, using K_0 to yield a 64-bit ciphertext. This ciphertext is then reduced to 56 bits by deleting eight arbitrary bits. The same eight bit positions must be deleted throughout the computation. Let us call this new 56-bit quantity, itself a potential key, K_1. Using K_1 we now encrypt the plaintext, P, and delete 8 bits from the result to yield K_2. The whole process is repeated until we have found K_t, where t is another parameter. At this point the pair (K_0, K_t) is written on tape, and the rest of the entries forgotten.

A new key is now drawn from the key space, and the whole procedure repeated, giving another key pair, (K_0, K_t) that is written on the tape. Eventually, we have m records on the tape. These records are then sorted on the second field. The precomputation is now complete.

To make the precomputation clearer, consider the example of Fig. 9-7(a). For this example, we will use a 9-bit plaintext (and 9-bit ciphertext) and a 6-bit key. The encryption algorithm is much simpler than DES: just add the key to the plaintext, ignoring any overflow beyond 9 bits. Then take the high-order 3 bits of the sum and add them to the sum. Finally, reduce the ciphertext to 6 bits by just taking the low-order 6 bits. Let the known plaintext be 642 (octal). The encryption of 642 with key 01 (octal) is $642 + 01 = 643$. Taking the high-order 3 bits of the sum, 6 (octal), and adding to the sum itself, we get 651. Truncating to 6 bits we find that $K_1 = 51$, as shown in the example. In Fig. 9-7(a), we have chosen $m = 8$, and $t = 5$.

To find the key that produced the (P, C) pair, we proceed as follows. First, reduce C to the key length (56 bits for DES, 6 bits for our example) in the usual way. Call this reduced quantity Y_1. Now compare Y_1 to each of the

Row	K_0	K_1	K_2	K_3	K_4	K_5	
1	01	51	22	72	43	14	(71, 04)
2	07	57	30	00	50	21	(01, 14)
3	16	66	37	10	60	31	(07, 21)
4	22	72	43	14	64	35	(16, 31)
5	32	02	52	23	73	44	(22, 35)
6	41	12	62	33	04	54	(32, 44)
7	56	27	77	50	21	71	(41, 54)
8	71	42	13	63	34	04	(56, 71)

(a)   (b)

Fig. 9-7. (a) Eight examples of the time memory trade-off in octal. (b) The sorted (K_0, K_t) list.

m K_t values on the tape. Since the tape is sorted on the K_t values, this lookup is straightforward. Suppose that we find a match. If we only had the complete row of which Y_1 is the last entry, we would be in good shape, because we know that the entry directly to the left of Y_1, K_{t-1} is a key whose encryption of P maps onto Y_1. This does not mean that K_{t-1} is indeed the key we are looking for, because several keys might generate distinct ciphertexts from P, all of which reduce to Y_1. The only way to tell is to find K_{t-1} and use it to encrypt P. Since K_0 is known, we can recompute the entire row from scratch and find K_{t-1}.

Now let us consider the (more likely) possibility that none of the K_t values on the tape match Y_1. Encrypt P using Y_1 as the key. Reduce the ciphertext to the key size and call it Y_2. Search the tape again to see if Y_2 occurs. If so, we know that the entry immediately to its left in the (now discarded) original row was Y_1, and the entry to the immediate left of Y_1 might be the secret key we are looking for. If Y_2 does not match anything on the tape, we compute and search for $Y_3, Y_4, \ldots, Y_t$. In reality, of course, we first generate all the Y_i values, sort them, and then search the tape once to see if any of them match.

Let us now return to our example. Imagine that the key is 77, so the ciphertext corresponding to the known plaintext of 642 is 750. Reducing 750 to the key size yields $Y_1 = 50$. Because 50 does not occur as a K_t value on the tape, Fig. 9-7(b), we know that the secret key does not occur in column K_4.

Now we compute $Y_2 = 21$. This value does occur in the sorted list, so we take the corresponding K_0 value, 07, and reconstruct row 2. From row 2 we find that the key to the immediate left of 50 is 00. To see if this key is the right one, we encrypt 642 with it, yielding the ciphertext 650. Since the known ciphertext is 750, and not 650, this is not the correct key. These two ciphertexts just accidentally happen to map onto the same key. We have a false alarm, so we continue searching. $Y_3 = 71$, which also occurs on the tape. Reconstructing row 7, we discover that the key 77 also generates a ciphertext that maps onto the key 50. However, unlike the key 00, the ciphertext is correct in this case. We have broken the cipher.

Assuming that all mt table entries are unique, the chance that the key will be found by this method is just the fraction of the key space covered by the table entries, $mt/2^k$, where k is the number of bits in the key. In the example of Fig. 9-7, $mt/2^k = 40/64$. By choosing m and t appropriately, we can ensure that nearly all keys appear in the table somewhere.

The existence of duplicate entries in the table reduces the number of keys covered and hence the chance of breaking the cipher. However, Hellman has shown that a minor variation to the method diminishes the chance of duplicate entries. The variation is to decrease m by a factor r and to supply r different tables, each one using a different subset of the ciphertext bits to produce the key. His analysis shows that with $m = 10^5$, $r = 10^6$, and $t = 10^6$, a DES cracking machine would have cost four million dollars in 1979. Considering the steady decline in the cost of electronics, the cost is probably well below that now, and still falling.

Although the above analysis is based on a known plaintext attack, even if no matched plaintext-ciphertext pairs are known, a statistical attack can still be mounted in some cases. For example, suppose it is known (or guessed) that the plaintext consists of ASCII characters with parity. The cryptanalyst can pick a key and use it to decrypt the first block of ciphertext. If the plaintext yielded by this key has some characters with even parity and some with odd parity, the key is clearly incorrect. If all characters have the same parity, the second and subsequent blocks of ciphertext can be tried. Since DES scrambles the bits so thoroughly, it is exceedingly unlikely that any key except the correct one will yield consistent parity on all ciphertext blocks. In effect, the presence of parity turns the ciphertext only problem into the known plaintext problem.

Since everyone likes books in which the Good Guys are victorious in the end, we will now describe some countermeasures that can be taken to improve the security of DES. For one thing, random characters can be inserted into the plaintext according to a well defined rule (e.g., every nth character is real, the rest are just noise). In addition, dummy messages can be inserted between the real ones according to yet another rule. This principle is called a **null cipher**. Null ciphers are obviously wasteful of bandwidth, but they are difficult to break, because the position of the real characters and messages is a carefully guarded secret and is changed whenever the key is changed. On leased private lines, there is something to be said for transmitting garbage whenever the line would otherwise be idle.

Stream Encryption

Another way to make cryptanalysis of DES much harder is to operate it as a **stream cipher**, as shown in Fig. 9-8, rather than as a **block cipher**, as we have described up until now. When being used as a stream cipher, both sender and receiver operate their DES chips in encryption (as opposed to decryption) mode. Each DES chip has a 64-bit input register, which operates as a shift register, and a 64-bit output register, which does not. When a plaintext character arrives, it is EXCLUSIVE-ORed with 8 bits of the output register, O_1. (O_2 through O_8 are never used.) The character thus created is both transmitted to the receiver and shifted into the input register, pushing I_8 off the end. Then the chip is activated and the output computed for the new input.

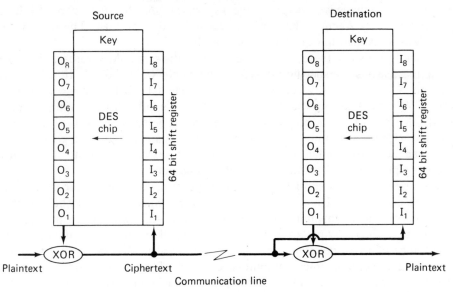

Fig. 9-8. Stream encryption.

At the receiving end, the incoming character is first EXCLUSIVE-ORed with O_1 (yielding the plaintext), and then shifted into I_1. If the sender and receiver start out with identical input registers, they remain identical forever, which means that O_1 at the transmitter will always be the same as O_1 at the receiver. Since the incoming plaintext character at the transmitter is being EXCLUSIVE-ORed with the same character as the incoming ciphertext character at the receiver, the output at the receiver is the original plaintext. The property of stream ciphers that makes them valuable is that O_1 depends on the entire history of the plaintext, so that a repeated pattern in the plaintext will not generate a repeated pattern in the ciphertext. Stream ciphers are also convenient for use with terminals, because they do not have to collect eight characters before emitting ciphertext. Each keystroke generates output immediately, as it is typed.

The DES Controversy

Before leaving the subject of DES, it is worthwhile pointing out that this cipher has been surrounded by controversy since its inception (Branstad, 1979; Branstad et al., 1977; Davida, 1979; Diffie and Hellman, 1976b, 1977; Kolata, 1977; Morris et al., 1977; Sugarman, 1979; Tuchman, 1979). A number of computer scientists have made the claim that 56 bits is too small a key size, that is, the cipher is too vulnerable to attacks such as Hellman's. The key size in IBM's original design was 128 bits, which unquestionably eliminates any chance of an exhaustive search of the key space. At the request of the U.S. National Security Agency, the key size was reduced to 56 bits. The reason the cipher was weakened has not been made public.

What has also bothered a number of scientists is IBM's refusal to make public the reasons the specific S-boxes in the cipher were chosen. IBM has said that the National Security Agency requested that it keep the design principles secret. Without knowing the design principles, it is difficult to exclude the possibility that a trick exists by which the cipher can be easily broken. There was also an incident that some observers interpreted as an attempt by a government employee to stifle publication of academic research aimed at developing stronger ciphers (Shapley and Kolata, 1977; Sugarman, 1978).

The net effect of a short key, secret design principles, and other factors has led some critics (e.g., Hellman, 1979; Kahn, 1980; Smith, 1980) to believe that the government might not be unhappy with a standard cipher just strong enough to keep everyone except itself from breaking it. To understand the significance of these developments, you should realize that in the future, telephones may contain microcomputers capable of digitizing and encrypting speech, and mail may be sent electronically, from home terminal to home terminal. If unbreakable encryption algorithms were used in these applications, it would be impossible for governments to tap phones and surreptitiously read mail. As Kahn (1980) and Selfridge and Schwartz (1980) point out, electronic eavesdropping is currently practiced on a large scale, so technical advances making it impossible in the future may not be viewed with great joy in all quarters.

9.1.3. The Key Distribution Problem

Another problem with DES is that it requires the receiver of a message to use the same key for decrypting it that the sender used for encrypting it. As a consequence, the question of how to distribute keys securely arises. Traditionally, identical key pairs were invented at a central key generating facility and transmitted to their destinations by personal courier. For a bank, or other organization with hundreds or thousands of offices, such a key distribution method is highly unsatisfactory, especially if security requirements dictate changing keys daily. It would be much more convenient if keys could be distributed via the network itself. Of course, key exchange must itself be encrypted, and encrypted with a key that has not already been compromised.

The solution to this problem being offered by some computer manufacturers (e.g., Everton, 1978) is to use a key hierarchy. Each organization chooses a master key at random and distributes it by personal courier to each of its offices. The offices are grouped into regions, with the head office of each region choosing a regional key. The regional keys are encrypted using the master key and distributed via the network. Whenever any two offices within a region wish to communicate, one of them chooses a session key and sends it to the other, encrypted by the regional key. Alternatively, a key manager process chooses the session key and sends it to both parties, encrypted by the regional key.

The philosophy behind this design is that master keys and regional keys are so rarely used that no intruder will ever be able to collect enough ciphertext to break them. Furthermore, the plaintext of these messages consists of 56-bit random numbers, making it virtually impossible to cryptanalyze them. In practice, the messages must start out with a header saying in essence "I AM A NEW KEY," but to prevent the cryptanalyst from acquiring a matched plaintext-ciphertext pair, this header should be sent unencrypted.

Nevertheless, it remains clear that physical transport of master keys by a means external to the network is required to make the system work. Whenever the master key is thought to be compromised or whenever an employee who knew it or who might have known it (e.g., one of the couriers) leaves the organization, a new master key must be generated and physically transported to all the offices.

Worst of all, there is no easy way for two total strangers who belong to different organizations to communicate in a secure way, except by physically getting together and agreeing upon a key right then and there. It is as though you were not allowed to call someone on the telephone until the person had physically handed you his business card. Obviously, a better method is needed.

Puzzles

Fortunately, several ingenious methods for solving the key distribution problem are known. Merkle's method (Merkle, 1978) explicitly uses the model of Fig. 9-1. He assumes that two parties, A and B, have never previously communicated, but now wish to communicate in a secure way. They must use the channel between them for establishing the key, even though the intruder can copy down everything they send on this channel.

The method is based on what Merkle calls **puzzles**. A puzzle is a cryptogram that is intended to be broken. Suppose that A initiates the conversation. His first message to B (in plaintext) might be something like this.

Dear *B*,

I am now going to send you 20,000 puzzles. Each puzzle is a cryptogram whose plaintext starts out with 128 zero bits, followed by a 16-bit puzzle number, and then a 56-bit key. The cryptograms have been encrypted using the DES standard with a key whose final 22 bits are zeros. Please pick one cryptogram at random and break it by brute force, trying all 2^{34} keys ending in 22 zeros. You know you have broken it when you find a key that yields a plaintext starting with 128 zeros. After breaking the cryptogram, extract the 56-bit random number and use it as your key. As your first message, send me back the puzzle number in plaintext, so that I know which key you are going to use.

Your secretive correspondent, *A*

This plaintext message is followed by 20,000 puzzles, as promised. The intruder hears everything, including all the puzzles. From the intruder's point of view, the difficulty is in choosing the correct puzzle to begin working on. In effect, he must begin attacking puzzles in a random order, hoping to find the one *B* chose. On the average he will have to try 10,000 puzzles before striking pay dirt.

Assume that an encryption takes 1 μsec. Breaking a puzzle will require, on the average, 2^{33} encryptions, which takes a little under 3 hours. This means that, statistically, the intruder will need more than 3 years to find the key. By adjusting the difficulty and number of puzzles, we can adjust the time to set up a conversation and the chance of the intruder's finding the key in a short time interval.

Key Protection

Although hiding the key from potential intruders is important, it is often equally important to hide the key from oneself. To be more precise, a corporation may not wish to delegate unlimited authority (in the form of a key) to any one employee. Banks, for example, normally do not give the complete vault combination to any one employee, but give half to one employee and half to another. Shamir (1979) has devised a clever technique for sharing cryptographic keys among multiple employees in a flexible way.

Let us illustrate Shamir's idea with an example. Suppose that a nervous company wants certain important messages to be sent only by the company president, or any two of the three dozen vice presidents, or any four of the thousands of other managers, or one VP plus two managers. Giving each person a few bits of the key does not work, because picking two VPs or four managers at random does not ensure having a full key.

To use Shamir's system, the company mathematician picks a polynomial of degree 3:

$$p(x) = a_3x^3 + a_2x^2 + a_1x + a_0$$

where a_3, a_2, and a_1 are chosen at random, and a_0 is the key, expressed as an integer. (With k managers instead of four, the polynomial is of degree $k - 1$.) Each manager is given one point on the curve: $(x, p(x))$; each VP is given two such points. The president is given four points. All the x values must be unique. Any time a collection of executives can assemble an arbitrary four points (in general, k points), they can find the polynomial and hence its coefficients, including a_0, the key, because four points uniquely determines a polynomial of degree 3. For the benefit of executives who have forgotten whatever linear algebra they once knew, each one could be given a machine-readable plastic card for insertion into the cryptographic terminal.

To prevent fewer than the critical number of executives from gaining any information at all about the key, all arithmetic should be done modulo a prime number. Figure 9-9 gives an example of the method.

Company with 1 VP and 10 managers

Key = 11, prime = 41   polynomial: $p(x) = (x^3 + 4x^2 + 3x + 11) \bmod 41$

p(1) = 19	p(4) = 28	p(7) = 38	p(10) = 6
p(2) = 0	p(5) = 5	p(8) = 24	p(11) = 14
p(3) = 1	p(6) = 20	p(9) = 25	p(12) = 14

The VP is given the (x, y) points (1, 19) and (2, 0)

Each manager is given a different (x, y) point from the list

(3, 1), (4, 28), (5, 5), (6, 20), (7, 38), (8, 24), (9, 25), (10, 6), (11, 14), (12, 14)

If the VP and managers 1 and 4 get together they have four points:

(1, 19), (2, 0), (3, 1) and (6, 20)

To solve the equation

$$a_3 x^3 + a_2 x^2 + a_1 x + a_0 = y$$

This leads to the four simultaneous linear equations in four unknowns:

$$a_3 + \ \ a_2 + \ a_1 + a_0 = 19 \bmod 41$$
$$8a_3 + \ \ 4a_2 + 2a_1 + a_0 = \ \ 0 \bmod 41$$
$$27a_3 + \ \ 9a_2 + 3a_1 + a_0 = \ \ 1 \bmod 41$$
$$216a_3 + 36a_2 + 6a_1 + a_0 = 20 \bmod 41$$

These can be solved by any standard technique, doing all arithmetic modulo 41. The solution is $a_3 = 1$, $a_2 = 4$, $a_1 = 3$, $a_0 = 11$.

Fig. 9-9. Key sharing using Shamir's method.

9.1.4. Public Key Cryptography

Now let us return to the problem of setting up secure communication between people who have never previously communicated. Although Merkle's puzzle method allows strangers to establish secure communication, it has the clear drawbacks of requiring both a large amount of computing time and a large amount of transmission bandwidth to agree upon the key. This brings us to another method, due to Diffie and Hellman (1976a), which has neither of these drawbacks and which has caused a basic revolution in the way people think about cryptographic systems.

Until Diffie and Hellman's article, all cryptographers simply took for granted that both the encryption and decryption keys had to be kept secret. If one thinks in terms of ciphers such as monoalphabetic substitution, it is obvious that the encryption key, for example *abc* becomes *XYZ*, and the corresponding decryption key, *XYZ* becomes *abc*, can each be trivially derived from the other one. What Diffie and Hellman proposed was to use an encryption algorithm, E, and a decryption algorithm, D, with E and D chosen so that deriving D even given a complete description of E would be effectively impossible.

Since these requirements differ so strikingly from those of conventional cryptographic systems, it is worth repeating them. There are three requirements:

1. $D(E(P)) = P$.

2. It is exceedingly difficult to deduce D from E.

3. E cannot be broken by a chosen plaintext attack.

The first requirement says that if we apply D to an encrypted message, $E(P)$, we get the original plaintext message, P, back. The second requirement speaks for itself. The third requirement is needed because, as we shall see in a moment, intruders may experiment with the algorithm to their heart's content.

Under these conditions, there is no reason that E cannot be made public. The method works like this. Any person or organization wanting to receive secret messages first devises two algorithms, E and D meeting the above requirements. The encryption algorithm or key is then made public, hence the name **public key cryptography**. This might be done by putting it in a file that anyone who wanted to could read.

Now let us see if we can solve the problem of establishing a secure channel between two parties, A and B, who have never had any previous contact. Both A's encryption key E_A and B's encryption key, E_B are assumed to be in a publicly readable file. (Basically, all users of the network are expected to publish their encryption keys as soon as they become network users.) Now A takes his first message, P, computes $E_B(P)$, and sends it to B. B then decrypts it by applying his secret key D_B, [i.e., he computes $D_B(E_B(P)) = P$]. No one else can read the encrypted message, $E_B(P)$, because the encryption system is assumed strong and because it is too difficult to derive D_B from the publicly known E_B. The problem has been solved, and without requiring 3 hours of computing time to establish communication.

The MIT Algorithm

The only catch is that we need to find algorithms that indeed satisfy all three requirements. Due to the obvious and tremendous advantages of public key cryptography, many researchers are hard at work, and some algorithms have already been published. One good method was discovered by a group at MIT (Rivest et al., 1978). Their method is based on some principles from number theory. We will now summarize how to use the method below; for details, consult the paper.

1. Choose two large primes, p and q, each greater than 10^{100}.

2. Compute $n = p \times q$ and $z = (p - 1) \times (q - 1)$.

3. Choose a number relatively prime to z and call it d.

4. Find e such that $e \times d = 1 \bmod z$.

With these parameters computed in advance, we are ready to begin encryption. Divide the plaintext (regarded as a bit string) into blocks, so that each plaintext message, P falls in the interval $0 \leqslant P < n$. This can be done by grouping the plaintext into blocks of k bits, where k is the largest integer for which $2^k < n$ is true.

To encrypt a message, P, compute $C = P^e \pmod{n}$. To decrypt C, compute $P = C^d \pmod{n}$. It can be proven that for all P in the specified range, the encryption and decryption functions are inverses. To perform the encryption, you need e and n. To perform the decryption, you need d and n. Therefore, the public key consists of the pair (e, n) and the secret key consists of the pair (d, n), or just d, actually.

The security of the method is based on the difficulty of factoring large numbers. If the cryptanalyst could factor the (publicly known) n, he could then find p and q, and from these z. Equipped with knowledge of z and e, d can be found using Euclid's algorithm. Fortunately, mathematicians have been trying to factor large numbers for at least 300 years, without much success. All the known evidence suggests that it is an exceedingly difficult problem.

According to Rivest et al., factoring a 200 digit number requires 4 billion years of computer time; factoring a 500 digit number requires 10^{25} years. In both cases, they assume the best known algorithm and a computer with a 1 μsec instruction time. Even if computers continue to get faster by an order of magnitude per decade, it will be centuries before factoring a 500-digit number becomes feasible, at which time our descendants can simply choose p and q still larger. However, it should be pointed out that no one has proven the absence of a trick that would allow the cipher to be broken without factoring n. Neither has anyone demonstrated the presence of any such trick.

A trivial pedagogical example of the MIT algorithm is given in Fig. 9-10. For this example we have chosen $p = 3$ and $q = 11$, giving $n = 33$ and $z = 20$. A suitable value for d is $d = 7$, since 7 and 20 have no common factors. With these choices, e can be found by solving the equation $7e = 1 \pmod{20}$, which yields $e = 3$. The ciphertext, C, for a plaintext message, P, is given by $C = P^3 \pmod{33}$. The ciphertext is decrypted by the receiver according to the rule $P = C^7 \pmod{33}$. The figure shows the encryption of the plaintext "SUZANNE" as an example.

Plaintext (P)			Ciphertext (C)			After decryption	
Symbolic	Numeric	P^3	$P^3 \pmod{33}$	C^7	$C^7 \pmod{33}$	Symbolic
S	19	6859	28	13492928512	19	S
U	21	9261	21	1801088541	21	U
Z	26	17576	20	1280000000	26	Z
A	01	1	1	1	1	A
N	14	2744	5	78125	14	N
N	14	2744	5	78125	14	N
E	05	125	26	8031810176	5	E

Sender's computation   Receiver's computation

Fig. 9-10. An example of the MIT algorithm.

Because the primes chosen for this example are so small, P must be less than 33, so each plaintext block can contain only a single character. The result is a monoalphabetic substitution cipher, not very impressive. If instead we had chosen p and $q \simeq 10^{100}$, we would have $n \simeq 200$, so each block could be up to 664 bits ($2^{664} \simeq 10^{200}$) or 83 8-bit characters, versus eight characters for DES.

The Knapsack Algorithm

Merkle and Hellman (1978) have also devised a suitable algorithm. Their algorithm is based on what is known as the knapsack problem. Imagine a knapsack into which some subset of a group of n available objects are to be placed. Each object has a weight. It turns out that given only a list of the objects (and their weights), plus the total weight of the knapsack, it is exceedingly difficult to deduce which objects are in the knapsack.

To turn this interesting property into an encoding algorithm, a plaintext message is expressed as a binary vector P_i, $0 < i \leqslant m$, where each coefficient is either 0 or 1. The weights, a_i are publicly known. The total weight of the knapsack is then just $\sum a_i P_i$. This sum, expressed as an ordinary binary number, is the ciphertext. Because solving the knapsack problem is known to be difficult, a cryptanalyst will have a hard time deducing the P_i coefficients given only the sum and the weights. Like the MIT scheme, this one can be made arbitrarily difficult, in this case by increasing the length of the vector. Notice the contrast with DES, where a (probably too small) key length is deeply embedded in the entire process, and not a parameter available for each user to choose himself.

The obvious question is: If solving the knapsack problem is indeed so difficult that a cryptanalyst cannot solve it, how can anyone expect the poor receiver to solve it? The answer is by choosing the weights in a sneaky way, it is possible to build a trapdoor into the problem, through which it can be solved trivially. Consider, for example, the set of weights 1, 2, 4, 8, 16, and 32. Given a sum such as 43, it is obvious how to solve the knapsack problem: just look at the binary decomposition of 43 as $1 + 2 + 8 + 32$. The plaintext is 110101. More generally, if each a_i is greater than the sum of all its predecessors, that is, $a_i > \sum a_j \ (j < i)$, the problem can also easily be solved by successively subtracting off the largest a_i less than the current sum.

Of course, this trick is so obvious that it cannot be used as is. To disguise the weights, each user chooses two very large numbers, n and w, that have no common factors. This property guarantees the existence of w^{-1} such that $ww^{-1} = 1 \ (\text{mod } n)$.

With weight vector and n and w chosen, a transformed weight vector is computed according to the rule

$$b_i = wa_i \ (\text{mod } n)$$

and then published. Anyone who wishes to encrypt a message computes $C = \sum b_i P_i$ and uses this as the ciphertext.

To decrypt C, the receiver computes

$$X = w^{-1}C \ (\text{mod } n) = w^{-1}\sum_{i=1}^{m} wa_i P_i \ (\text{mod } n) = \sum_{i=1}^{m} a_i P_i \ (mod \ n)$$

From X and the (secret) coefficients a_i, the receiver can now deduce the message.

Shamir and Zippel (1980) have pointed out that the security of the method is greatly enhanced by iterating several times. Each iteration should use a different value of n to encrypt the previous ciphertext as though it were the plaintext.

9.1.5. Authentication and Digital Signatures

In the real world, people make a big distinction between originals and copies. For example, if you go to your friendly local bank with a check, they will be happy to cash it, provided that you can adequately identify yourself. On the other hand, if you go to the same bank with a photocopy of the check, or better yet, with a large pile of photocopies of the check, they will suddenly become a lot less friendly. Banks take the difference between originals and copies quite seriously.

A related issue is that of handwritten signatures. The authenticity of many legal, financial, and other documents is ultimately determined by the presence or absence of an authorized handwritten signature. And photocopies do not count. For computerized message systems to replace the physical transport of paper and ink documents, a solution must be found to these problems.

The problem of devising a replacement for handwritten signatures is a difficult one. Basically, what is needed is a system by which one party can send a "signed" message to another party in such a way that

1. The receiver can verify the claimed identity of the sender.

2. The sender cannot later repudiate the message.

The first requirement is needed, for example, in financial systems. When a customer's computer orders a bank's computer to buy a ton of gold the bank's computer needs to be able to make sure that the computer giving the order really belongs to the company whose account is to be debited. The second requirement is needed to protect the bank against fraud. Suppose that the bank buys the ton of gold, and immediately thereafter the price of gold drops sharply. A dishonest customer might sue the bank, claiming that he never issued any order to buy gold. When the bank produces the message in court, the customer denies ever having sent it.

Interestingly enough, encryption can be used to provide authentication as well as secrecy. As a first step toward solving the authentication problem, the bank above might require its customers to include in each message a secret password, a sequence number, the time and date of transmission, and a checksum of the entire plaintext, including the time, date, and sequence number. The sequence numbers make it pointless for an intruder to record and subsequently play back messages, because the bank can see that they are just duplicates of earlier messages. The time and date make it useless for the intruder to save a recorded message until the sequence numbers have cycled around. The checksum makes it highly improbable that an intruder could forge or modify a (ciphertext) message and still have the (plaintext) checksum be correct.

Unfortunately, there is a fundamental conflict between secrecy and authentication. Suppose that a k-bit message is to be encrypted both for secrecy and authentication. If only a tiny fraction of the 2^k messages are valid, authentication is possible but security is poor. For example, if each message includes a 32-bit checksum, only one out of 4 billion randomly generated ciphertext messages will be accepted as valid. However, a cryptanalyst can take advantage of this property by picking keys at random and seeing if the plaintext checksum is correct. On the other hand, if all 2^k messages are valid, an active intruder can easily gum up the works by injecting spurious messages, since they cannot be distinguished from the real thing. But cryptanalysis becomes correspondingly harder the denser the message space becomes. This fact suggests that plaintext should be subjected to text compression before encryption, to improve security.

Digital Signatures with Public Key Cryptography

In any event, there is still the problem of preventing dishonest users from repudiating their previous messages. Under certain conditions, public key cryptography can make a contribution to solving this problem. To use public key cryptography for sending signed messages, it is necessary that the encryption and decryption algorithms have the property that $E(D(P)) = P$ in addition to the usual property that $D(E(P)) = P$. Assuming that this is the case, A can send a signed plaintext message P to B by transmitting $E_B(D_A(P))$. Note carefully that A knows his own (secret) decryption key, D_A, as well as the public key of B, E_B.

When B receives the message, he transforms it using his private key, as usual, yielding $D_A(P)$, as shown in Fig. 9-11(b). He stores this text in a safe place and then decrypts it using E_A to get the original plaintext. If the message makes sense, B knows that it came from A, since E_A was used to decrypt it.

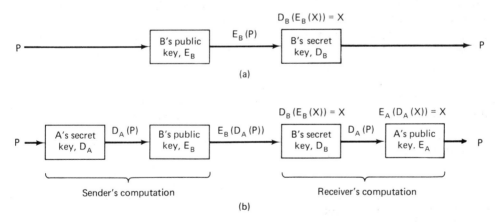

Fig. 9-11. Secure message transmission using public key cryptography. (a) Without signature. (b) With signature.

The requirement that it make sense is not as trivial as it might at first appear. If all plaintexts are legal messages, an active intruder could inject a random message of the proper length into the system, which B would then decrypt, interpret as a valid message, and act upon. As Saltzer (1978) has pointed out, both parties should agree in advance, preferably in writing, was to what constitutes a legal message. A typical agreement might be that all messages begin with a certain constant, thus making it difficult for an intruder to confuse either party with a random message. But, as we mentioned earlier, doing so gives aid and comfort to the cryptanalyst.

To see how the signature property works, suppose that A subsequently denies having sent the message P to B. When the case comes up in court, B can produce both P and $D_A(P)$. The judge can easily verify that B indeed has a valid message encrypted by D_A by simply applying E_A to it. Since B does not know what A's secret key is, the only way B could have acquired a message encrypted by it is if A did indeed send it. While in jail, A will have plenty of time to devise interesting new public key algorithms.

Although the idea itself is valid, there are a few minor problems with public key digital signatures that are related to the environment in which they operate rather than with the algorithm per se. For one thing, B can prove that $D_A(P)$ was sent by A only as long as D_A remains secret. If A discloses his secret key, the argument no longer holds, because anyone could have sent the message, including B. The problem might arise, for example, when A and B are corporations. At a certain point the management of A may realize that sending the message was a mistake. For example, they may have discovered a cheaper supplier for some important part they need. To repudiate the message to the original supplier they make their secret key public and then run to the police claiming that their office had been broken into and the key stolen. Depending on the local laws, the corporation may or may not be legally liable for the misuse of property stolen from it.

Another problem with the signature scheme is what happens if A decides to change his key. Doing so is clearly legal and may even be standard operating procedure within many companies. If a court case later arises, as described above, the judge will apply the current E_A to $D_A(P)$ and discover that it does not produce P. B will look pretty stupid at this point. Consequently, it appears that some central authority is needed to record all key changes.

Digital Signatures with Conventional Cryptography

However, once we are resigned to having a central authority that knows everything, say Big Brother (BB), both secrecy and digital signatures can be obtained using conventional cryptography (Needham and Schroeder, 1978). One way to achieve secrecy is to require each user to choose a secret key and hand carry it to BB's office. Thus only A and BB know A's secret key, K_A. When A wants to talk to B, A asks BB to choose a session key, K_S, and send him two copies of it, one encrypted with K_A, and one encrypted with K_B. A then sends the latter to B with instructions to decrypt it using K_B and then use the plaintext as the session key. BB can also provide a signature service. To do so, he needs a special key, X, kept secret from everyone. To use the signature service, B, a bank for example, could insist that the following procedure be followed for every signed, encrypted plaintext message, P, sent to it:

1. The customer, A, sends $K_A(P)$ to BB.

2. BB decrypts $K_A(P)$ to get P, then builds a new message consisting of A's name and address concatenated with the date, D, and the original message. This new message, $A + D + P$, is then encrypted with X, yielding $X(A + D + P)$ and sent back to A. Note that BB can verify that the request indeed came from A, because only A and BB know K_A. An imposter would not be able to send BB a message that made sense when decrypted by K_A. The ability of BB to authenticate A is the heart of the signature mechanism.

3. The customer, A, sends $X(A + D + P)$ to the bank, B.

4. The bank sends $X(A + D + P)$ to BB, requesting $K_B(A + D + P)$ as a result.

5. The bank then decrypts $K_B(A + D + P)$ to get A, D, and P.

If a customer ever denies sending P to the bank, the bank can show $X(A + D + P)$ to a judge. The judge then orders BB to decrypt it. When the judge sees A, D, and P, he knows the customer is lying, because the bank does not know X, and therefore could not possibly have fabricated $X(A + D + P)$. Of course, the problem of the customer claiming that his K_A was stolen still exists, just as in public key cryptography.

Figure 9-12 illustrates secure message transmission between total strangers using conventional cryptography. When signatures are not needed, as in Fig. 9-12(a), after the session key has been established by steps 1, 2a, 2b, and 3, BB is no longer needed. In contrast, for the signed messages of Fig. 9-12(b), BB must be invoked twice for each message. The public key system of Fig. 9-11 is also more complicated for signed than for unsigned messages, but does not require sending any extra messages, except perhaps to look up the public keys initially.

9.2. TEXT COMPRESSION

Communication bandwidth is an expensive resource. Packet carriers make this fact of life abundantly clear to their customers by charging for each byte (or packet) transported. It should not be surprising that many customers have a keen interest in reducing the total number of bits that must be transmitted to get their work done. Text compression also has security value, as we have mentioned earlier. We will now look at some of the ways data can be compressed, to save bandwidth and hence money.

The data sent over a transport connection can be viewed as a sequence of symbols, S_1, S_2, . . ., S_N. These symbols are assumed to be drawn from some (possibly infinite) set of symbols. A few examples of such sets and some of

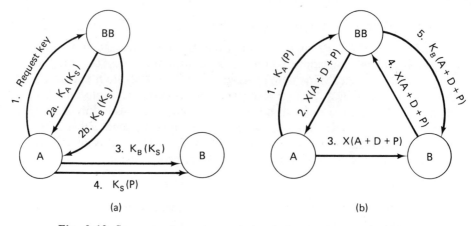

Fig. 9-12. Secure message transmission between strangers using conventional cryptography. (a) Without signature. (b) With signature.

their members are:

1. Set of bits: 0, 1.

2. Set of decimal digits: 0, 1, 2, 3, 4, 5, 6, 7, 8, 9.

3. Set of letters: A, B, C, . . . , X, Y, Z.

4. Set of English words: anserine, blebby, coypu, dibble, ennead, ...

5. Set of countries: Argentina, Belgium, China, Dahomey, Egypt, ...

Text compression can be approached in three general ways. Respectively, these three approaches are based on:

1. The finiteness of the set of symbols.

2. The relative frequencies with which the symbols are used.

3. The context in which a symbol appears.

Let us now consider each of these in turn.

9.2.1. Encoding a Finite Set of Equally Likely Symbols

In many applications the messages are drawn from a finite set and expressed in ASCII. In a library automation project, for example, the titles in the library's collection might be usefully regarded as a (finite) set of symbols. Suppose that each day a complete list of books requested were sent to each branch library, so each would know which books were most in demand and where. The daily transmission might consist of the branch number, followed by the list of all titles requested at that branch that day.

A typical book has about 20 characters in its title. Expressed in ASCII, such a book title requires 140 bits. Yet no library in the world has anywhere near 2^{140} titles. (The Library of Congress has about 2^{26} titles.) By simply giving each book a sequence number, it is possible to reduce the number of bits needed per title from 140 to 26 or fewer. However, the receiver must have the numbered book list, although this need only be sent once and can be transmitted by mailing a magnetic tape.

In cases where an occasional reference is made to an item not in the numbered list, the name can be spelled out in full, using an escape convention. Using the above example again, book number 0 could mean that an ASCII title follows, delimited by an ASCII ETX character.

9.2.2. Huffman Coding

In virtually all text, some symbols occur more often than others. From Fig. 9-2 we see that in English the letter "E" occurs 100 times more often than the letter "Q," and the word "THE" occurs 10 times more often than the word "BE." This observation suggests an encoding scheme in which common symbols are assigned short codes and rare symbols are assigned long codes.

As an example, consider the plight of a brilliant but poor young biologist who has just cracked the genetic code of the wild Bactrian camel. She wants to send a telegram to her mother (as a birthday present) giving the sequence of bases (adenine, cytosine, guanine and thymine) in the camel's DNA, but cannot afford to send 2 bits per base. Fortunately, she notices that the occurrence probabilities of the bases are 0.50, 0.30, 0.15, and 0.05 respectively. By encoding them as 0, 10, 110, and 111 (instead of 00, 01, 10, and 11), the average symbol now only requires 1.7 bits (instead of 2.0).

In light of the above example, it is interesting to ask what the minimum number of bits per symbol is. According to information theory, if symbol S_i occurs with a probability of P_i, then the information content of each symbol is

$$-\sum_{i=1}^{N} P_i \log_2 P_i$$

This quantity is often known as the **entropy per symbol**. For the (hypothetical) camel DNA example, the theoretical limit is 1.65 bits/symbol, so the proposed encoding is within 3%. As another example consider a uniform distribution: $P_i = 1/N$. Here the entropy per symbol is $\log_2 N$, as expected.

Unfortunately, there is no way to achieve the theoretical minimum encoding with independently coded symbols, because many of them require a fractional number of bits. However, an algorithm due to Huffman (1952) can be used to produce an excellent approximation to the theoretical limit. The algorithm is as follows.

1. Write down all the symbols, together with the associated probability of each. As the algorithm proceeds, a binary tree will be built up, with these symbols as the terminal nodes. Initially, all nodes are unmarked.

2. Find the two smallest nodes and mark them. Add a new node, with arcs to each of the nodes just marked. Set the probability of the new node to the sum of the probabilities of the two nodes it is connected to.

3. Repeat step 2 until all nodes have been marked except one. The probability of the unmarked node will always be 1.0.

4. The encoding for each symbol can now be found by tracing the path from the unmarked symbol to that symbol, recording the sequence of left and right branches taken. The code is just the path, with left = 0 and right = 1 (or vice versa).

Huffman coding can also be done in radices other than 2. For example, by choosing the 256 smallest unmarked nodes at each step, and having 256 arcs radiate from each intermediate node, we get a code in which each symbol is an integral number of bytes.

9.2.3. Context Dependent Encoding

The method above implicitly assumes that the probability of a symbol occurring is independent of its immediate predecessor. To put it more bluntly, it assumes that the probability of a "T" directly following a "Q" is almost four times higher than the probability of a "U" following the "Q." A more sophisticated scheme would be determine the conditional probability for each symbol for each possible predecessor. For letters as symbols, this comes down to having 26 tables, one for the frequency distribution following an "A," one for the frequency distribution following a "B," and so on.. If there are strong correlations between symbols and their successors, this method yields large savings, even if the symbols themselves have a flat distribution.

The disadvantage of this conditional probability method is the large number of tables required. If there are k symbols, the tables will have k^2 entries. Instead, a variation on the old 5-bit Baudot telegraph code can be used. In our variation there are four cases: uppercase, lowercase, numeric + special, and control. In each case, four codes are allocated to the case shifts, and 28 are allocated to the symbols, allowing for $4 \times 28 = 112$ symbols. (Probably space and newline should be included in each case, leaving 104 distinct symbols, plus space and newline). To shift between cases, an explicit symbol is needed. The basic assumption behind this model is that the symbol following a lowercase letter is likely to be another lowercase letter (or space or newline), and that the symbol following a number is likely to be another number. The advantage of Baudot code over Huffman code is that all symbols are the same length, making encoding and decoding by table lookup easy to do. Baudot code is also more resilient in the presence of transmission errors.

A related method, **run length encoding**, can be used to encode long binary bit strings containing mostly zeros. Each k-bit symbol tells how many 0 bits occurred between consecutive 1 bits. To handle long zero runs, the symbol consisting of all 1 bits means that the true distance is $2^k - 1$ plus the value of the following symbol (or symbols). For example, the bit string

0001000001000000100000000000000010000001000100000000110100000101

consists of runs of length 3, 5, 6, 14, 6, 3, 7, 0, 1, 5, and 1 . It would be encoded using 3-bit symbols as

011 101 110 111 111 000 110 011 111 000 000 001 101 001

for a saving of 34%.

A last, but certainly not least, context dependent compression method is to squash runs of repeated symbols into a count plus the symbol. Runs of blanks, linefeeds, and leading zeros are the most likely candidates here.

9.3. VIRTUAL TERMINAL PROTOCOLS

There are well over 100 different brands of terminals on the market, no two of which are identical. For a computer network user, it would be frustrating in the extreme to try to log onto a remote computer only to be told that the program he wants to use does not talk to his brand of terminal. For example, a remote program might expect all input in lowercase, causing trouble for uppercase-only terminals. To prevent such incompatibilities, protocols have been devised whose function is to hide the differences between different kinds of terminals.

9.3.1. Classes of Terminals

Terminals fall in three broad classes: scroll mode, page mode, and form mode. **Scroll mode terminals** do not have built in microprocessors or any local editing capability. When a key is hit, the corresponding character is sent over the line (and possibly also displayed). When a character comes in over the line, it is just displayed. As new lines are displayed, the old ones just scroll upward. Most hardcopy terminals, as well as some CRT terminals are, of this type.

Despite their relative simplicity, scroll mode terminals can differ in many ways, for example, character set, line length, presence or absence of automatic echoing, and overprinting, not to mention the way carriage return, line feed, horizontal tab, vertical tab, backspace, form feed, and break are handled. Some terminals also have potential timing problems, such as the number of filler characters needed following tab and carriage return.

Page mode terminals are typically CRT terminals that can display 24 lines of 80 characters each. Both the human operator and the computer can move the cursor around the screen to modify selected portions of the display. These terminals often have some local editing capability. In a time-sharing environment, the user can call up a page of text, edit it locally, and then hit the ENTER key, causing enough information to be sent over the line to enable the computer to determine what has been changed.

CRT terminals have all the same problems as hardcopy terminals, plus a few more such as page length, cursor addressing, and the presence or absence of blinking, reverse video, color, and multiple intensities, not to mention the details of how the local editing is done.

Form mode terminals, also known as **data entry terminals**, are sophisticated devices intended for banking, airline reservations, and other applications where the operator is essentially filling out a form. Generally, the remote program displays a form of some kind, in which each field is, in effect, a question that the operator must answer. Figure 9-13 shows a minimum form potentially usable by an automated pigeon fancier's society. In many cases the remote computer delegates the task of checking the input for syntax errors to the microprocessor inside the terminal. For example, the terminal could immediately complain when the "# of pigeons" field was not filled in with a numeric answer. By off-loading this sort of checking to the terminals, the main computer can handle many more transactions per second.

```
┌─────────────────────────────────────────────────────────┐
│  Membership Application – Pigeon Fancier's Society        │
│                                                           │
│  Name:                    Telephone:                      │
│                                                           │
│  Address:                 # of Pigeons:                   │
└─────────────────────────────────────────────────────────┘
```

Fig. 9-13. A typical form. Each field requests information and provides space for it to be filled in.

Although the idea here is simple and attractive, there is a big problem: what conceptual model should the program use to communicate with a collection of highly disparate terminals? Furthermore, the model used should allow new kinds of terminals to be added later, without requiring all the programs to be rewritten.

9.3.2. The Data Structure Model

We will now describe an elegant model specifically intended to deal with the most difficult case, the form mode terminal. The simpler terminal types can be seen as special cases. Our model is based on the design used in the European Informatics Network (Schicker and Duenki, 1978), but it is slightly simplified in some places and slightly more general in others. The conceptual model is depicted in Fig. 9-14. The terminal is driven by a terminal process, either in the host computer to which the terminal is attached or in the terminal itself. This process communicates with its opposite number on the remote machine. The application program (user process) issues commands to the application process and gets replies from it. The terminal process and application process exchange messages whose contents are determined by the virtual terminal protocol. The same model can be used for terminal-to-terminal or process-to-process communication, of course.

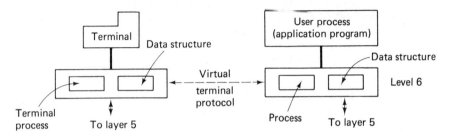

Fig. 9-14. The conceptual model for the virtual terminal protocol.

The central idea used by all virtual terminal protocols is that of a **network virtual terminal**. Interactive application programs assume that their terminal is a network virtual terminal. The layer 6 software has the task of supporting this illusion. In the EIN model, each terminal contains a data structure. When the application program wants to send information to the terminal, it issues commands to the application process, for example, move the cursor to a certain position on the virtual terminal's screen. Upon receiving a command from the application program, the application process updates its copy of the data structure and then sends messages to the terminal process, causing it to update its copy of the data structure in the same way. After having updated its data structure the terminal process must then modify the display, to make it correspond to the updated data structure. When the terminal operator modifies the display, the terminal process must both update its own data structure, and send update commands to the application process. The virtual terminal protocol must insure the consistency of the two data structures after every update.

Now let us take a look at the data structure. The display is broken up into fields, each with a number of attributes. These attributes are shown in Fig. 9-15. The *text* part contains the displayable characters themselves, chosen from

the 95 displayable ASCII graphics. If the terminal does not support ASCII, it is
up to the terminal process to simulate ASCII as best it can. The application
program need not even be aware of this simulation, of course.

```
type field = record
        text: array [0 .. MaxText] of char;        {contents of the field}
        xposition: 0 .. MaxX;                        {horizontal position on screen}
        yposition: 0 .. MaxY;                        {vertical postion on screen}
        size: 0 .. MaxSize;                          {size of the field}
        rendition: 0 .. MaxRendition;                {color, intensity, etc.}
        adjustment: (left, right);                   {positionning of text within field}
        lcletters, ucletters, numbers, space, special: boolean;      {allowed input}
        protected, EntryRequired, MustFill: boolean
end;
var datastruct: record
        display: array [0 .. MaxField] of field;     {collection of fields}
        cursor: record x: 0 .. MaxText; y: 0 .. MaxField end;   {cursor position}
        TerminalType: (scroll, page, form);
        FlowMode: (alternating, FreeRunning);        {half or full duplex}
        turn: (mine, his);                           {who goes next (if half duplex)}
        state: (uninitialized, normal, interrupted)
end;
```

Fig. 9-15. Data structure definitions for our virtual terminal protocol
example. All the identifiers beginning with *Max* are constants.

The *xposition* and *yposition* entries give the horizontal and vertical positions
of the start of the field on the virtual terminal. The *size* entry tells how many
positions the field occupies.

The *rendition* attribute is an attempt to model color, multiple intensities,
reverse video, blinking, and similar ways of rendering characters. The application process can specify, for example, that fields 1, 3, and 9 use rendition 1,
that fields 2 and 4 use rendition 2, and that the remaining fields use rendition
3. On some actual terminals, the renditions may be different colors. On others
they may be different intensities. On still others, combinations of blinking and
reverse video may be used to distinguish the three categories.

The next five attributes specify what kinds of characters may be accepted by
the terminal. The last three tell how much of the field is to be filled in. If *protected* is true, the operator may not modify the field at all. In Fig. 9-14, for
example, there are nine fields: the title, the four implied questions, and the
four fields where the answers go. Five of these are protected against writing,
but the other four are not. Stronger yet, the *EntryRequired* attribute would
probably be true for the latter four. The *MustFill* attribute means that every
single character position in the field must be filled in. Typically, this feature is
used for fixed-length numeric entries such as bank account numbers.

The first two entries in the data structure represent the current contents of the screen and the current cursor position, respectively. The *TerminalType* information is useful for dealing with exceptional conditions, such as receipt of an overly long line. (On a scroll mode terminal it should be folded onto the next line, whereas on a page or form mode terminal it should be truncated.) Some applications programs may expect a strict alternation between themselves and the operator: the program writes to the terminal, the program reads from the terminal, the program writes to the terminal, and so on. Half-duplex lines work this way. The opposite of this **alternating mode** is **freerunning mode**, in which either side may send at will. If alternating mode is used, each data structure must keep track of whose turn it is to send. The variable *turn* is used for this purpose. Finally, the state of the data structure is remembered. The meaning of the interrupted state will be described later.

9.3.3. Design Principles

Although the idea of having identical data structures at each end of the connection is a good one and can hide many of the terminal's idiosyncracies, it cannot hide all of them. For example, if the terminal expects the application process (or some other process in the remote computer) to do echoing, the two sides had better agree on this in advance. In addition, the network virtual terminal is usually only a minimum requirement. For example, all terminals can work in alternating mode, but only full-duplex terminals can work in free running mode. The default mode for the virtual terminal must therefore be alternating, but if both sides are willing and able to work in free running mode, the protocol should permit them to do so.

To establish who is willing and able to do what, and to change parameters (e.g., screen size) from their default values, the application and terminal processes need to carry out an **option negotiation**. The option negotiation can be done in several ways. In the asymmetric case, one side proposes to use certain options, or announces what it can or cannot do. The other side then either accepts or rejects these. If there is disagreement, the negotiation can continue. If the application process starts out by proposing that the terminal act like a form mode terminal and this proposal is rejected, it can then see if page mode is acceptable. If it turns out that agreement cannot be reached because the application program has some minimum requirements above and beyond the default values and the terminal cannot meet these, the connection fails.

This asymmetric model has the obvious problem of deciding who should start the negotiation, especially when both ends are processes and neither is a real terminal. An alternative solution is to have each side send an initial message completely describing what it wants. After receiving the message from its partner, each process computes the lowest common denominator of the parameter settings and initializes its data structure to use them. The symmetric negotiation can also fail, for example, if each side want to use alternating mode, and each side wants to go first.

If alternating mode is chosen, the protocol must provide some way to allow the current sender to say "I am done." Either a bit in the message header or a separate "Go ahead" message must be provided by the protocol.

Another important design issue is how to deal with interrupts. It frequently occurs that the terminal operator notices that the program is behaving badly (e.g., looping) and wants to kill it, or at least shut off the output stream. Most time-sharing systems provide such a mechanism, typically using the BREAK key. When no network is involved, the operating system can easily discard all queued output and remember not to display anything until the current process has terminated.

However, a problem arises when BREAK must be sent across the network. If the terminal process simply relays the BREAK to the other side (and does not discard output), printing may continue for a long time, due to output previously generated and now queued up in the terminal process. If, say, 1024 bytes of output are queued up, a 30 char/sec terminal will seemingly take half a minute to react to a BREAK, which is hardly acceptable. This long reaction time occurs even if the BREAK message is sent out of band and is allowed to skip past other messages queued up for the application process.

If, on the other hand, the terminal process discards all queued and incoming characters (in addition to transmitting the BREAK), it has no way of knowing when to begin displaying output again. In particular, it cannot distinguish between the remote command interpreter's prompt character and the same sequence sent by the rogue process itself. Besides, the process may catch BREAK signals and process them itself, in which case there is no prompt at all.

One solution to this dilemma is to have the recipient of an interrupt message insert a special mark message into the output stream. However, if both sides simultaneously transmit interrupts, a more involved protocol is needed for the case of alternating mode, to determine whose turn it is (see Schicker and Duenki, 1978). Either way, when a process has sent an interrupt message, it updates the *state* variable in order to remember that it has done so, returning to normal state only after the interrupt protocol has finished.

9.3.4. An Example Virtual Terminal Protocol

Figure 9-16 shows a possible set of messages that could be used to implement our model. The first byte of each message contains an opcode telling what the message means. The leading bit of the opcode (*EOT*) is set when either party wishes to relinquish its turn (alternating mode only).

The *Open* message is used to initiate a connection and negotiate parameters. All the identifiers beginning with *Max* in Fig. 9-16, as well as the initial state of all the variables in *DataStruct* are in principle negotiable. Notice that this message has nothing to do with connection establishment in the Transport layer.

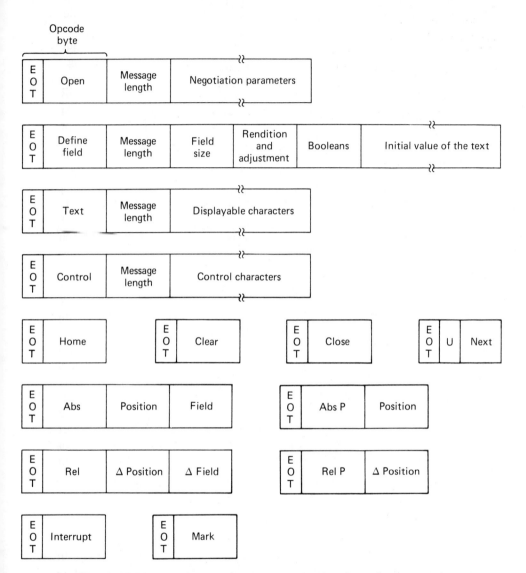

Fig. 9-16. Message formats for the example virtual terminal protocol.

The *Define field* message is used to define or redefine the fields and their attributes.

Ordinary data are sent using the *Text* message. Control messages (e.g., ring the bell) can be sent using the *Control message*.

Six messages are provided for positioning the cursor. *Home* moves it to the first unprotected field, at the top of the screen. *Clear* does likewise but also erases the contents of all unprotected fields. The two *Abs* commands move the cursor to specific absolute positions on the screen. When only one argument is provided, it is interpreted as the absolute position within the current field. When two arguments are provided, the second one specifies a new field to be selected. Relative positioning works in a similar way. The arguments given to the *Rel* commands are signed numbers, for example, an argument of -1 to the short form means backspace. The last cursor movement command, *Next*, moves the cursor to the next field. If the *U* bit is set, the next unprotected field is selected.

The following scenario illustrates the use of the messages for an alternating form mode terminal.

1. The terminal initiates the dialog with an *Open* + *EOT* message.

2. The remote computer responds with an *Open* message.

3. The computer now sends a series of *Define field* messages (e.g., to create the form of Fig. 9-14).

4. Finally, the computer sends *Home* + *EOT*.

5. The operator now fills in the form, using local editing, if need be, to correct errors. When the form has been filled in, the operator hits the ENTER key.

6. The terminal process now transmits the contents of all unprotected fields by alternating *Text* and *Next* messages. The last message must have the *EOT* bit set.

7. When the application program has read the data and is ready for the next form, it transmits *Clear* + *EOT,* thus erasing all the unprotected and signaling the operator to begin entering the next form.

8. When there are no more forms to be sent, the operator hits an appropriate key and a *Close* + *EOT* message is sent, which is acknowledged with another close.

In a typical implementation, the application program would be provided with library routines or system calls corresponding to the messages shown in Fig. 9-16, as well as some mechanism for interrogating the current state of the virtual terminal. In this way the program could manipulate the cursor and use different renditions without even being aware of the terminal-dependent codes needed to invoke these facilities.

Although we have emphasized form mode terminals so far, the example protocol is equally appropriate for simple page or scroll mode terminals. A page mode terminal would normally map each line onto a field, all of them unprotected. The *Next* message would mean go to the next line, with the details of whether CR, LF, CR + LF, or LF + CR is needed left to the layer 6 software. The *Clear* message would clear the entire screen and move the cursor back to the upper left-hand corner. The *Abs* message would be used to position the cursor at a specific position within a specific line. Scroll mode terminals would normally have a single unprotected field consisting of the current line.

9.4. FILE TRANSFER PROTOCOLS

Computer networks are often used in one of two ways: to allow terminal users to log onto remote machines, and to move large data files back and forth among a group of machines. The main higher layer protocol involved in the first application is the virtual terminal protocol, discussed above. The main protocol involved in the second application is the file transfer protocol, which is our next topic. In general, file transfer protocols have not received as much attention as virtual terminal protocols, and are consequently less well developed.

In some networks, the file transfer protocol uses the virtual terminal protocol to set up transfers and is therefore technically at a higher layer. If the virtual terminal protocol uses encryption, there may actually be three distinct layers involved here. Sometimes a layer is divided into **sublayers** for this reason. The discussion that follows is largely based on the ARPANET file transfer protocol.

The protocol can be invoked in two different ways, as shown in Fig. 9-17. Either the person or process invoking the file transfer wishes to move a file between the local host and a remote one, or he wishes to direct a transfer from one remote host to another. Commands telling what to transfer and where may be sent over different connections than those used by the data.

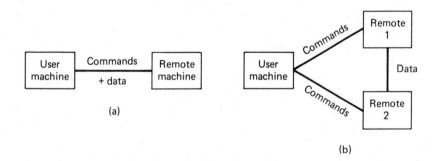

Fig. 9-17. File transfer protocol model. (a) To or from a remote machine. (b) Between two remote machines.

Files are transferred for three primary reasons:

1. To store a file for subsequent retrieval.

2. To print a file, typically on the local printer.

3. To run the file as a program or process it as data.

Each class of use has its own particular problems to be solved.

When a file is moved from one machine to another for storage, the only requirement is that when it is retrieved, it must reproduce to the bit. Clearly, under these circumstances there must not be any code conversion or other change made to the file, even if the source and destination machines differ in word length, character set, or other properties. One slight difficulty arises if the two machines have different word lengths. The file will have to be padded out with zero bits to fill an integral number of words. When it is retrieved, possibly from a third machine, it must be possible to determine the exact length of the original file, down to the last bit.

When a file is transferred to print it, there are more serious problems to be solved. To start with, a character set conversion may have to take place. Another problem is caused by the property of some machines to store all print lines as fixed-length records, with no end of line character, whereas other machines use variable-length records terminated by some combination of CR, LF, VT, or FF. When a file is moved between machines with different conventions, the appropriate conversion must take place. A third problem is the use of Fortran style carriage control characters in column 1, versus the ASCII convention of using FF to indicate a new page, and CR only to return the carriage for overprinting. Again, a conversion may be necessary.

When the file is being moved in order to be used, the situation deteriorates rapidly. If it is a source program, so many things can go wrong that a much more sophisticated and specialized protocol is needed. However, even if the file contains simple data, there are still major problems. For example, a file containing binary integers may not be easily movable between two machines due to problems of word length, representation (1s versus 2s complement), etc. With floating point numbers there are more parameters, so the situation is even worse. Basically what is needed is a transformation that preserves the semantics of the data.

One way to accomplish this semantic invariance is to precede each item by a header telling what kind of information follows, and how long it is, if necessary. This idea is illustrated in Fig. 9-18. Each block header tells whether the block contains an integer, floating point number, character string, bit string, or something else. Using this information, the file transfer protocol can attempt to change the representation to the one normally used by the receiving machine. With integers there is usually no problem, provided that the word length on the receiving machine is long enough. Converting floating point numbers, on the other hand, is painful at best.

Typical commands accepted by a file transfer protocol are: COPYFROM,

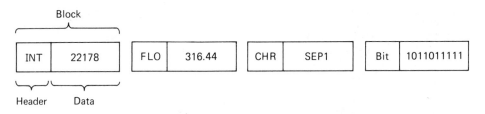

Fig. 9-18. Labeled data items for use by the file transfer protocol.

COPYTO APPEND TO FILE, RENAME FILE, DELETE FILE, and LIST DIRECTORY.

9.5. EXAMPLES OF THE PRESENTATION LAYER

The presentation layer in our example networks, and most other networks as well, is not yet as well developed as the lower layers. Consequently, there is not so much to say about them.

9.5.1. The Presentation Layer in the ARPANET

The ARPANET does not have a coherent presentation layer, although some programs have been written to perform presentation layer functions. The most widely used of these programs are the virtual terminal protocol and the file transfer protocol. We will now look at these in turn.

The ARPANET virtual terminal protocol, known as **TELNET**, is based on a different design philosophy than the EIN-like protocol described above. TELNET was designed with scroll mode rather than form mode, terminals in mind, although some page mode terminal properties can be negotiated. The default network virtual terminal has a single line of unlimited length.

The protocol is concerned with setting up and manipulating two simplex data streams, one in each direction. It has no concept of a data structure that must be kept identical at both ends by the protocol. As keys are hit on the terminal, a stream of 8-bit bytes is transmitted over the line. The terminal process must convert whatever character code the terminal outputs to the network standard, ASCII. In addition to the 95 ASCII graphics, the CR, LF, BEL, BS, HT, VT, and FF control characters are also legal.

Furthermore, there also exists a group of 15 commands, which may be freely interspersed with the ordinary data. The list of commands is shown in Fig. 9-19. Commands are preceded by the IAC character (Interpret As Command, code 255), which says that the next character is a command. If the command is longer than one character (i.e., if it has parameters), codes 250 and 240 are used like **begin** and **end** in Pascal, to delimit the command.

Code

240	End of command	248	Erase line
241	No operation	249	Go ahead
242	Mark	250	Start of command
243	Break	251	Will
244	Interrupt process	252	Won't
245	Abort output	253	Do
246	Are you there?	254	Don't
247	Erase character	255	Interpret as command

Fig. 9-19. The ARPANET telnet protocol commands.

Code 244 is used to interrupt a process. *Break* (243) is used to mean whatever the remote machine normally uses it for, not necessarily kill process. *Mark* is used to indicate to the terminal process where it should resume output, as above. *Abort output* is only meaningful if the remote machine has a way to terminate the output from the running process without killing it. Similarly, *Are you there* is provided by some operating systems to allow the user to confirm that although the machine may be slow, it is still there.

Codes 247 and 248 are important because they allow the user to use the local host's erase conventions on the remote machine. The clear implication of these codes is that when the user wants to erase a character or a line, the terminal process merely converts the local erase key into this network standard and sends it over the line. In our first protocol, intraline editing is assumed to be done on the local host, with the line only transmitted when it is ready. Here the assumption is that the remote machine does the intraline editing. There are probably two reasons for this difference. First, TELNET dates back to the early 1970s, when few terminals had microprocessors inside of them. Second, many of the machines on the ARPANET are PDP-10s running the Tenex operating system. Tenex expects as its input a character rather than a line at a time, and reacts to partially typed lines in some circumstances.

The *Go ahead* command is used with alternating mode terminals, to authorize the other side to send, just as the bit did above. *EOT* bit did above.

Like our first example, TELNET provides for option negotiation to change the defaults and set parameters on the virtual terminal. Option negotiation may be initiated at any time, by either side, using *WILL*, *WON'T*, *DO*, and *DON'T*.

As an example of how these commands are used, a computer capable of handling full-duplex (free running) terminals, might want to find out if the terminal could also work in full-duplex mode. To do so it would send a *WILL* command, specifying its willingness to use full-duplex. The terminal would then reply with either *DO* or *DON'T*. Negotiation can also take the form of one side sending a *DO* or *DON'T* to the other one, requesting some option, with the answer being either *WILL* or *WON'T*. About two dozen options have been defined, including binary transmission, remote echoing, line and page length, and the meaning of tabs. Postel (1979) compares TELNET and the EIN virtual terminal protocol in in more detail.

To handle the diverse goals of moving files for storage, printing, and program input, the ARPANET file transfer protocol, FTP, has three modes: stream, compression, and block. In stream mode, a file consists of a sequence of logical units. The user can specify how large a logical unit is. Typically, it would be a byte or machine word. The file may be split up into logical records, if desired.

Print files normally use compression mode. In this mode it is possible to convert, for example, from 132 character fixed-length records with carriage control in column 1 to ASCII style variable-length records without carriage control. Not having to transmit a lot of trailing blanks is obviously useful.

In block mode, each data item is preceded by a header telling how long the block is The header does not contain any type information, but it does indicates end of record, end of file, and tape read error at the source, to allow data that probably contain errors to be recognized as such.

The FTP protocol has several dozen commands: commands to log in and be authenticated, commands to determine the mode and structure of the file to be transferred, and commands that tell what to do. Among the latter are RETRIEVE FILE, STORE FILE, APPEND TO FILE, RENAME FILE, and DELETE FILE.

9.5.2. The Presentation Layer in SNA

Layer 6 in SNA is called NAU Services. It performs three more-or-less unrelated classes of services: presentation services, session services, and network services. Presentation services correspond closely to the transformations that we have discussed in this chapter. Session services are used to set up sessions. Network services are a miscellaneous collection of services needed to operate the network.

When a session is bound, the parameters of the BIND message determine which presentation services, if any, will be used by the session. When presentation services are used, the presentation layer protocol is contained in the FM headers (see Fig 1-10). Examples of presentation services are compression (replacing strings of identical characters by one character and a count) and compaction (packing multiple characters into a byte when only a subet of the full character set is needed). Numerous programs provide presentation services themselves rather than using general network facilities.

SNA has a facility that is similar in spirit to a virtual terminal protocol, although it is less general than the ones we have examined, because it is intended to be used only with IBM's terminals. This facility (Hoberecht, 1980) is the 3270E data stream. In short, it is a protocol in which data characters and control commands can be mixed, to described display information in a manner independent of the terminal on which it is to be displayed. The protocol has commands to select a field, define attributes for the field (e.g., protected/unprotected, alphabetic/numeric, and intensity), and read, write, and erase fields.

Another area of presentation services is file management, similar to the file transfer protocols discussed earlier in this chapter. There are commands to create and destroy remote files, as well as commands to read, add, delete and replace records in remote files.

NAU services also contains **session services**, which convey user requests to set up sessions to the appropriate place in the underlying layers. It is essentially the user's interface into the system for setting up connections with the outside world.

Among the network services are configuration services, maintenance services, and operator services. **Configuration services** deals with managing the network configuration, for example, bringing nodes online and offline. **Maintenance services** provide a way to run hardware and software diagnostics at remote sites, collect statistics about network performance, and related matters. **Operator services** provide an interface with the operator to allow the network to be brought up or down and to allow the operator to inspect the numerous displays and measurements of its behavior.

9.5.3. The Presentation Layer in DECNET

Although DECNET does not offer presentation services to user programs in the sense of allowing users to request encryption or compression of all text sent on specified connections, it does have a file access service that user programs can invoke to read and write remote files. Since this remote access service also provides some conversion between file formats, it can be regarded as a presentation service. The remote access is achieved by the use of a protocol called **DAP**, Data Access Protocol. DAP is not a file transfer protocol but something more general, because it allows a user to request specific records in a file rather than only the whole file.

Although a file is merely a sequence of records, there are numerous variations on this basic theme. To start with, files may be sequential, relative, or indexed. Sequential files must be accessed sequentially. No method is provided to read or write an isolated record in the middle. In a relative file, in contrast, it is possible to ask for a specific record by giving its record number, that is, how many records from the start of the file it occurs. In an indexed file, each record has a key, and it is possible to ask for the record whose key matches a given key.

In addition to the three file types, there are two ways in which records can be stored in DEC systems: byte count and stream. In the former, each record contains a byte count telling how long it is. In the latter, embedded line feeds, form feeds, and vertical tabs serve to delimit the records. Furthermore, there are five ways of expressing carriage control: FORTRAN carriage control, COBOL carriage control, implied line feed + carriage return per record, embedded carriage control characters, and none of the above.

DAP handles all these cases and tries to convert between formats where necessary and possible. Not all conversions are supported. When conversions are possible, they are done by the requesting end, not the end where the file resides. There are no conversions between 1s and 2s complement integers, different word lengths, different floating point formats, etc.

Once a transport connection has been established between a file user and a file server, each side starts out by sending a DAP CONFIGURATION message. The CONFIGURATION message tells which protocol version is in use, which operating system and file system are being used, what the maximum buffer size is, and in general what the capabilities of the sending system are. Armed with knowledge of the other end, each machine can determine what is and what is not possible, and what conversions are needed.

After the CONFIGURATION messages have been successfully exchanged, the ATTRIBUTES message is used to describe the properties of the file to be accessed. Only one file may be accessed per transport connection, so there is no ambiguity. There are dozens of attributes, among them the type of data (e.g., ASCII, EBCDIC, program text, unspecified), file format (e.g., fixed records, variable records, text lines, etc.), device characteristics (e.g., whether it is shared, spooled, mounted, locked, allocated, available, error logged, real time, random access, directory structured and more), carriage control conventions, physical block size, logical record size, disk allocation information, times and dates of creation and last update, when to rewind and lock, owner identification, and protection.

Once the attributes have been specified, the ACCESS message can be used to specify the type of operation to perform: open file, create file rename file, erase file, list directory, submit file as batch job, or execute command file.

Finally, a CONTROL message can be sent to cause data to be transferred. The CONTROL message can specify a particular record, either by default (current position on sequential files), record number or key, and tell whether it is to be read, written, updated, deleted, or whatever. The CONTROL message can also perform miscellaneous functions such as truncating files and performing end of volume processing.

In addition to the messages described above, there are also DATA, ACKNOWLEDGEMENT, and STATUS messages.

9.6. SUMMARY

As more and more data are transmitted by satellite and thus can be easily intercepted by people other than its intended recipient, the need for data encryption grows. The DES algorithm uses an iterated sequence of permutations and substitutions to encrypt a 64-bit plaintext block using a 56-bit key. DES can also be operated in stream mode, encrypting one character at a time. Although DES is an U. S. government standard, not all computer scientists believe it to be secure, due to its short key length and secret design principles.

A form of cryptography radically different from DES is public key cryptography. In public key cryptography, the encryption key is made public but its decryption key is kept secret. Research groups at MIT and Stanford have proposed public key algorithms based on the difficulty of factoring large numbers and solving the knapsack problem, respectively.

Cryptography can also be used for authentication. In effect, a message is signed using the sender's secret key. Since this key is not publicly known, imposters have no way of generating ciphertext that makes sense when decrypted.

To reduce transmission charges or disk storage space, the presentation layer usually provides a data compression service. This compression may be simple, such as squeezing out repeated blanks, or more sophisticated, such as Huffman encoding.

When many different kinds of terminals are connected to a network, the application programs must be shielded from their diversity. The way to accomplish this is to define an (abstract) network virtual terminal, which the application programs read and write. The layer 6 software has the task of mapping the network virtual terminal onto the real terminals, and vice versa. A similar situation holds for file transfer, in which the layer 6 software can define a network virtual file which is mapped onto real files as need be.

PROBLEMS

1. Break the following monoalphabetic cipher. The plaintext, consisting of letters only, is a well-known excerpt from a poem by Lewis Carroll.

   kfd ktbd fzm eubd kfd pzyiom mztx ku kzyg ur bzha kfthcm
   ur mfudm zhx mftnm zhx mdzythc pzq ur ezsszcdm zhx gthcm
   zhx pfa kfd mdz tm sutythc fuk zhx pfdkfdi ntcm fzld pthcm
   sok pztk z stk kfd uamkdim eitdx sduid pd fzld uoi efzk
   rui mubd ur om zid uok ur sidzkf zhx zyy ur om zid rzk
   hu foiia mztx kfd ezindhkdi kfda kfzhgdx ftb boef rui kfzk

2. Break the following columnar transposition cipher. The plaintext is taken from a popular computer textbook, so "computer" is a probable word. The plaintext consists entirely of letters (no spaces). The ciphertext is broken up into blocks of five characters for readability.

   aauan cvlre rurnn dltme aeepb ytust iceat npmey iicgo gorch srsoc
   nntii imiha oofpa gsivt tpsit lbolr otoex

3. What is the output of iteration 1 of the DES algorithm when the plaintext and key are both 0?

4. In Fig. 9-4, the P-boxes and S-boxes alternate. Although this arrangement is esthetically pleasing, is it any more secure than first having all the P-boxes and then all the S-boxes?

5. How many 2400 foot magnetic tapes are required to store the DES encrypted values of a known plaintext for all keys composed of six uppercase letters? The tape density is 6250 bytes/inch. What are the implications of this result for network security?

6. Design an attack on DES based on the knowledge that the plaintext consists exclusively of uppercase ASCII letters, plus space, comma, period, semicolon, carriage return, and line feed. Nothing is known about the plaintext parity bits.

7. If stream encryption is being used on a virtual circuit and an undetected transmission error occurs, what happens to the subsequent plaintext at the receiver? Remember that with stream encryption the entire previous plaintext affects the encryption of each character.

8. A very ecology conscious company has decided to replace all its nonbiodegradable plastic cryptographic keys, which use Shamir's key sharing algorithm for $k = 3$, with a (biodegradable) computer scientist, namely you. One day, three managers come to you and whisper their newly memorized $(x, p(x))$ pairs in your ear: $(2,29)$, $(3,12)$, and $(4,28)$. The prime modulus is 31. What is the key?

9. Using the MIT public key cryptosystem, with $a = 1$, $b = 2$, etc.
   (a) If $p = 7$ and $q = 11$, list five legal values for d.
   (b) If $p = 13$, $q = 31$ and $d = 7$, find e.
   (c) Using $p = 5$, $q = 11$, and $d = 27$, find e and encrypt "abcdefghij"

10. How many bits per symbol are required to conditionally Huffman encode the four DNA bases A, C, G, and T, given the following conditional probabilities. Note that all four bases occur equally often, so straightforward Huffman coding yields 2.00 bits/symbol. (XY means the probability of Y following X.)

AA	AC	AG	AT	CA	CC	CG	CT	GA	GC	GG	GT	TA	TC	TG	TT
.45	.35	.15	.05	.30	.50	.18	.02	.15	.04	.60	.21	.10	.11	.07	.72

11. Four symbols are to be encoded using a Huffman code. Their respective probabilities are P_1, P_2, P_3 and P_4, respectively, with $P_i > P_{i+1}$ ($i = 1, 2, 3$). What is the mean number of bits per symbol? (Consider all possible cases.)

12. Compute the compression factor (output bits/input bits) for run length encoding, assuming each input bit is generated randomly with a probability α of it being a 0. Do the calculation for output symbols of width 3, 4, 5, and 6 bits. For $\alpha = 0.9$, which output symbol length is most efficient?

13. In a number of countries, the Post Office offers a facsimile transmission system for intercontinental mail. The original document is optically scanned, converted to a bit matrix, and transmitted digitally for reconstruction at a foreign post office. The copy is then put in an envelop and injected into the domestic mail system. Suppose that a document has 15×20 cm of text, with 5 char/cm and 2.4 lines/cm. If

digitization uses a 40×40 dot matrix per cm, with 1 bit per dot, compare the bandwidth needed for facsimile transmission to the bandwidth needed for transmission as ASCII characters. List some advantages of facsimile over ASCII transmission.

14. As memory prices decrease, more and more form mode terminals are being designed to hold several pages of text in local buffers. The users can switch among the pages uses local commands. Since the number of pages and page size varies from terminal to terminal, what changes, if any, would you suggest to the protocol of Fig. 9-17 to accommodate long (i.e., multipage) forms?

15. Compare the following two models for a file transfer protocol for allowing programs to read remote files. In model 1, the program sets up a connection with the remote file server, which then simply copies the file to the program as fast as it can, subject to a sliding window flow control. In model 2, the program sets up a connection with the remote file server also, but each time a read is done, a message is sent is sent to the file server requesting the data.

16. Write a program that encrypts a stream of plaintext using the Vigenère cipher.

17. To demonstrate that English text is highly redundant, perform the following experiment. Make a list of 50 common words of varying lengths. Now choose sentences of length three, four, five, six, seven, etc. words using only words in the list. Encrypt the sentences using a monoalphabetic substitution cipher. Pick a ciphertext sentence and call the length of the ith word L_i. Attempt to break the cipher using brute force by trying all combinations of plaintext sentences whose ith word is of length L_i. For each potential plaintext, check to see if it is consistent, that is, each ciphertext letter always maps onto the same plaintext letter. Any plaintext that produces an inconsistent mapping is obviously incorrect, and can be discarded. Print out the number of plaintext sentences that are possible candidates as a function of the number of characters in the sentence. You will discover that a surprisingly short amount of text can be uniquely decrypted. Finally, if sufficient computer time is available, repeat the experiment with increasingly larger dictionaries, so as to enable you to extrapolate the minimum amount of ciphertext that a cryptanalyst needs to break a cipher using normal English (20k to 50k words). This amount is called the **unicity distance** and has been extensively studied by Shannon (1948, 1949).

18. Write a program that automatically cracks monoalphabetic ciphers consisting of uppercase letters only. Word boundaries are assumed to be known, as in Problem 1 above. The program should first collect and analyze letter, digram, trigram, and word count information. Include a routine that uses this frequency information to generate tentative partial keys. Also write a routine that takes the ciphertext, partial key, and frequency information as input and estimates the likelihood that the partial key is correct. If possible, try to acquire a large sample of English plaintext in machine readable form (e.g., computer manuals), in order to construct an English dictionary.

19. Write a program to investigate the amount of overlap within the precomputation matrix used in the time-memory trade-off method for attacking DES.

20. Write a program to deduce the contents of a knapsack who total weight is 512 units. The knapsack contains a subset of 25 available objects whose weights are equal to the 25 prime numbers under 100.

21. Write a program that converts a Fortran style print file (81 character fixed-length records) to ASCII style variable-length records. The first character of each input record can be one of the following: 1 = new page; + = overprint this line on top of the previous one; blank = normal spacing; 0 = skip a line before printing.

22. Write a program that converts floating point numbers between machines whose internal format is different. Such a program would be useful as part of a generalized file transfer package. First choose a standard representation to which and from which all numbers can be converted. Assume that each machine can be characterized by (1) the number of bits in the exponent, (2) the number of bits in the mantissa, (3) the system for encoding the sign of the exponent, (4) the system for encoding the sign of the mantissa, (5) the radix for exponentiation, and (6) whether or not the leading bit of the mantissa is stored (it is not stored on the PDP-11, for example) The signs can be encoded using 1s complement, 2s complement, sign-magnitude, or by adding a known constant to the number.

10

THE APPLICATION LAYER

The boundary between the presentation layer and the application layer (see Fig. 1-7) is conceptually a very important boundary. It separates the domain of the network designers from the domain of the network users. In principle, there is little we can say about the content of the application layer, because each user determines what programs he will run and what protocols he will use. Furthermore, there are almost no national or international standard protocols for layer 7.

Nevertheless, some issues are common to many applications and can be discussed in general terms. and which can be discussed in general terms. Among these are distributed data bases, distributed computation, and network operating systems. However, the application layer is only beginning to get attention, so results are few. All the topics discussed in this chapter are subjects of current research. The real purpose of this chapter is to serve as background material, to enable and encourage you to read the burgeoning journal literature in this area.

10.1. DISTRIBUTED DATA BASE SYSTEMS

One of the most important applications of computer networks is to permit data bases to be geographically distributed among the network hosts. In many cases there is a "natural" distribution, for example each company plant maintains the data relevant to its personnel, inventory, orders, and production. Most accesses are then to local data, but occasionally one location needs data from one or more other locations.

In other cases there is no natural distribution, but the organization or user may want to keep important data at two or more sites for increased reliability. It is not hard to imagine, for example, that a bank whose head office is located in an earthquake zone or floodplain might want keep a duplicate of its account data base in a distant city, even if keeping both copies identical is complicated and expensive. In some applications (e.g., military ones), even short down times due to hardware failures are completely intolerable, hence the need for redundancy.

Yet another reason for distributing data is sheer size. It is not feasible to attach an arbitrary number of disk drives to a computer. Beyond some limit, multiple machines are needed. To allow incremental growth, it is also better to have a collection of smaller systems than one huge one. With a single centralized system, the addition of one additional disk drive may be like the straw that broke the camel's back.

A related reason for having multiple computers is the need for a high transaction rate. With present technology, a throughput of a few hundred transactions per second per CPU is considered excellent. To get more, multiple CPUs are needed. If all the disks are attached to one of the CPUs, at a certain point the interrupt load will saturate that CPU, forcing the data base to be distributed among the other CPUs.

In short, for these and other reasons, many organizations are actively investigating distributed data bases. This interest, in turn, has been a stimulus to the development of computer networks, since a network is needed to connect the locations at which the data bases are located. In the following sections we will point out some of the main design issues related to the design of distributed data base systems.

10.1.1. The Relational Data Base Model

Although it is definitely not our intention to provide a detailed discussion of data bases in general, a little bit of background material will be useful for the benefit of readers not familiar with data base systems. We will focus on the **relational data base** model (Codd, 1970) due to its simplicity and elegance.

In a relational data base system, information is thought of as being stored in the form of rectangular tables called **relations**. The rows of a relation are called **tuples**. The fields of a tuple are called **attributes**. The columns of a relation are called **domains**. Many writers refer to the attributes of a relation and the domains of a relation interchangeably, but others regard a domain as the set of values from which the attributes are selected.

Figure 10-1 gives parts of five relations that might be found in the data base of an international airline. The relation FLIGHTS, for example, has domains (or attributes) called *Flight#*, *Origin*, *Destination*, and *Plane*. There is one tuple for each flight in the airline's schedule. The order of the domains and the order of the tuples are not significant. Duplicate tuples are not permitted. The values found within a domain are homogeneous and have the same syntactic format (e.g., three ASCII characters, two decimal digits, or a 32-bit floating point number). The domains of a tuple need not be homogeneous, just as the fields of a record in Pascal need not all be of the same type. In fact, one could imagine a relation as being an array of records, except that the tuples are not ordered.

Each relation has a **key**, consisting of one or more domains that uniquely determine the values of the other domains. For example, in FLIGHTS, the domain *Flight#* is the key because given the flight number, one can tell where the flight originates, etc. The *Origin* domain is not a key because it alone does not determine the values of the other domains. The key for RESERVATIONS consists of the domains *Date* and *Flight#*, since given a date and flight number, one can tell how many seats have been booked (domain *Booked*) and what the pilot's name (domain *Name*) is. Neither of these domains alone is sufficient.

The information describing the relations can itself be stored as a relation, called DICTIONARY in Fig. 10-1. Normally, the DICTIONARY relation would contain more domains than are shown in this simple example. In a distributed data base system, the DICTIONARY relation can be used to find the location at which a given relation is stored. In general, a data base may be **fully partitioned**, meaning that each relation is stored at exactly one location, **fully replicated**, meaning that each relation is stored at all locations, or something in between, meaning that each relation is stored at one or more locations. If a relation is replicated at multiple locations, it can usually be accessed for reading more quickly than if there is only one copy. On the other hand, updating a replicated relation is far more complicated than updating a nonreplicated relation, primarily due to the need to keep the various copies identical, in spite of network delays, lost messages, and system crashes. If updates are rare, replication is attractive. However, if updates are common, it is less attractive.

All data base systems allow **queries** (questions) about information in the data base and **updates** (changes) to the data base. Query languages for relation data base systems tend to divide into two categories, procedural and nonprocedural. The former, called the **relational algebra**, explicitly describes how to find the answer. The latter, called the **relational calculus**, describes the answer but does not give an algorithm for finding it. We will now briefly discuss each of these types.

Relational algebra languages are analogous to ordinary high level languages such as Pascal. The basic objects manipulated by the language are the relations. Three major operations are provided on relations: restriction, projection, and join.

Restriction takes a relation and a **predicate** (relationship among the values of the domains) as input and produces as output a subset of the tuples, namely,

FLIGHTS

Flight #	Origin	Destination	Plane	. . .
106	JFK	AMS	747	
108	HPN	BOS	CNA	
452	AMS	NBO	AB3	
632	LHR	CDG	737	
808	SFO	JFK	D10	
⋮	⋮	⋮	⋮	

RESERVATIONS

Date	Flight #	Booked	Name	. . .
29 Mar	106	210	Barbara Bongo	
21 Feb	108	005	Carol Curlew	
16 Mar	632	105	Maria Marmot	
01 Sep	108	000	Barbara Bongo	
⋮	⋮	⋮	⋮	

PERSONNEL

Name	Title	Sex	Married	Seniority	. . .
Marilyn Manatee	Manager	F	N	4	
Suzanne Springbok	Publicist	F	Y	3	
Barbara Bongo	Pilot	F	N	3	
Marvin Moonfish	Engineer	M	N	6	
Andrew Aardvark	Programmer	M	Y	10	
⋮	⋮	⋮	⋮	⋮	

AIRCRAFT

Plane	Seats	Engines	. . .
747	450	4	
737	100	2	
D10	270	3	
AB3	260	3	
CNA	4	1	
⋮	⋮	⋮	

DICTIONARY

Relation	Location	# Tuples	Tuple size	# Domains	. . .
FLIGHTS	Amsterdam	1000	12	4	
RESERVATIONS	New York	365,000	30	4	
PERSONNEL	Nairobi	10,000	35	5	
AIRCRAFT	Melbourne	10	8	3	
⋮	⋮	⋮	⋮	⋮	

Fig. 10-1. Five relations from an airline data base.

those tuples meeting the predicate. For example, Fig. 10-2(a) is the relation PERSONNEL from Fig. 10-1 restricted by the predicate: $Sex = $ 'F'. Although the details of the allowed predicates vary from language to language, arbitrary boolean expressions are usually allowed.

Projection takes a relation and a set of domains as input, and produces as output a new relation having only the specified domains. Figure 10-2(b) is the

Name	Title	Sex	Married	Seniority
Marilyn Manatee	Manager	F	N	4
Suzanne Springbok	Publicist	F	Y	3
Barbara Bongo	Pilot	F	N	3
⋮	⋮	⋮	⋮	⋮

Sex	Seniority
F	4
F	3
M	6
M	10
⋮	⋮

(a)   (b)

Flight #	Origin	Destination	Plane	Seats	Engines
106	JFK	AMS	747	450	4
108	HPN	BOS	CNA	4	1
452	AMS	NBO	AB3	260	3
632	LHR	CDG	737	100	2
808	SFO	JFK	D10	270	3
⋮	⋮	⋮	⋮	⋮	⋮

(c)

Fig. 10-2. Examples of operations on relations. (a) Restriction.
(b) Projection. (c) Join.

projection of **PERSONNEL** onto *Sex* and *Seniority*. Notice that there are fewer tuples in the projection than in the original relation, because duplicate tuples are eliminated.

Join takes two relations and a domain common to both relations as input and produces as output a new relation merged on the common domain. The output relation is found by listing all tuple pairs in which the first tuple in the pair is taken from one relation and the second from the other (i.e., their cartesian product). Pairs that differ on the joining domain are then deleted. Since the joining domain is now represented twice, one copy of it is removed, and each pair is regarded as a single tuple whose domains are the union of the input domains. Figure 10-2(c) shows the join of FLIGHTS and AIRCRAFT, with *Plane* being the joining domain.

As an example of how these operations are used, suppose we want a list of all dates on which there is an overbooked flight from Boston (BOS) to San Francisco (SFO) piloted by a married woman. To answer the query we need information from all four relations. A query in the relational algebra might look like this:

1. T1 = restriction of FLIGHTS by *Origin* = 'BOS' and *Destination* = 'SFO'.

2. T2 = join of T1 and AIRCRAFT on *Plane*.

3. T3 = projection of T2 onto *Flight#* and *Seats*.

4. T4 = join of T3 and RESERVATIONS on *Flight#*.

5. T5 = restriction of T4 by *Booked* > *Seats*.

6. T6 = join of T5 and PERSONNEL on *Name*.

7. T7 = restriction of T6 by *Sex* = 'F' and *Married* = 'Y'.

8. RESULT = projection of T7 onto *Date*.

The symbols T1, T2, etc. are temporary relations. The thing to notice here is that a query is a set of instructions telling how to find the answer.

In contrast, in the relational calculus, the query merely specifies the conditions the result must satisfy, without describing how it is to be found. Queries in the relational calculus use **tuple variables**, each of which ranges over one relation. If *F* is a tuple variable ranging over FLIGHTS, then *F.Origin* refers to the *Origin* domain of FLIGHTS. The query given above might look as follows in the relational calculus:

Range of *R* is RESERVATIONS
Range of *F* is FLIGHTS
Range of *P* is PERSONNEL
Range of *A* is AIRCRAFT

Retrieve *R.Date* where

R.Flight# = *F.Flight#* and *R.Name* = *P.Name* and *F.Plane* = *A.Plane* and
F.Origin = 'BOS' and *F.Destination* = 'SFO' and *R.Booked* > *A.Seats* and
P.Sex = 'F' and *P.Married* = 'Y'

Conceptually, the query can be answered by four nested loops, one on each of the tuple variables. In effect, each combination of four tuples, one from each relation, can be inspected to see if it meets the predicate. If so, the date is recorded. Given the parameters shown in the DICTIONARY relation, the test would have to be made $1000 \times 365,000 \times 10,000 \times 10$ times. In practice, it is up to the data base system to find ways to avoid making such impossibly long brute force searches. Even in centralized systems, with all the relations stored at the same location, efficient query processing is a challenging problem. When the relations are distributed, the problem becomes decidedly more challenging, as we shall see shortly.

We now have enough background on relational data base systems in general to begin looking at some of the specific problems introduced by distributing the data base. We will consider four subproblems: where to put the relations, how to process queries, how to keep multiple simultaneous transactions from interfering with each other, and how to maintain data base integrity in spite of possible system crashes.

10.1.2. The Relation Distribution Problem

As we mentioned earlier, in some applications there is a natural distribution of data over the various hosts in the network, but in others there is no natural distribution. If there is a natural distribution and the data base is fully partitioned, the assignment of relations to network hosts is trivial. However, if the data base is (partially) replicated or there is no natural distribution, the assignment problem is more complicated.

The first decision that must be made when assigning data to hosts is the unit of assignment. Are relations assigned to hosts in their entirety, or may a relation be distributed over several hosts? In the latter case, does each host contain all the domains for a subset of the tuples, or does each host contain all the tuples for a subset of the domains, or may even smaller fragments be assigned? For the time being, we will assume that the data base is fully partitioned and that each relation is completely stored at a single host.

In conjunction with the allocation problem, it is worthwhile emphasizing the importance of the DICTIONARY relation discussed above. With this organization, every query will need to access the DICTIONARY relation at least once, and perhaps many times, depending on how the query processing is done. If this relation is stored only at one host, the entire data base system can be brought down by failure of the DICTIONARY host. Furthermore, access to this host is likely to become a bottleneck. Consequently, a strategy in which the DICTIONARY is replicated at every host, even though the other relations are fully partitioned, may be a useful one in some circumstances, particularly when changes to the number of relations and their properties are rare.

Getting back to allocating relations to hosts, the primary factors to consider are the frequency of requests to read and update relation j due to queries from host i, the storage capacity available at each host, the storage cost per byte at each host, and the communication cost between the pairs of hosts. Obviously, it is desirable to put relations as close as possible to the hosts that use them heavily. However, constraints on the amount of storage available at each host, or the availability of large amounts of inexpensive storage far from the main query sites complicate the allocation problem.

Before the problem can be solved, it must be formulated precisely. Chu (1969) has considered a model of a fully connected full-duplex network in which the principal traffic is due to the tuples being sent in response to queries (i.e., the queries themselves are neglected). Furthermore, the delay, q_{ik}, required for a query from i to be answered by a tuple from k is entirely due to queueing delays on the ki line. A brief summary of Chu's model (ignoring updates) is as follows:

Given:

n = number of hosts

m = number of relations

b_i = storage capacity (in bytes) at host i

c_i = cost of storage (per byte per second) at host i

L_j = size of relation j

l_j = tuple size (in bytes) for relation j

r_{ij} = tuples/sec from host i for relation j

T_{ij} = maximum acceptable delay for host i to a relation j tuple

C_{ik} = communication cost (per byte) for tuples from i to k

q_{ij} = delay for query from i to k

Variables:

X_{ij} = 1 if relation j is at host i, 0 otherwise

Constraints:

$$\sum_{i=1}^{n} X_{ij} = 1 \qquad (1 \leqslant j \leqslant m)$$

$$\sum_{j=1}^{m} X_{ij} L_j \leqslant b_i \qquad (1 \leqslant i \leqslant n)$$

$$q_{ij} \leqslant T_{ij} \qquad (1 \leqslant i \leqslant n, \ 1 \leqslant j \leqslant m)$$

Goal: minimize total cost $= \sum_{i=1}^{n} \sum_{j=1}^{m} X_{ij} c_i L_j + \sum_{i=1}^{n} \sum_{k=1}^{n} \sum_{j=1}^{m} X_{kj} C_{ki} r_{ij} l_j$

The solution to the relation allocation problem is an assignment of 1s and 0s to the matrix X, corresponding to determining which location each relation is stored at. The first constraint says that each relation is stored at one host. The second constraint says that the storage space at a host may not be exceeded. The third constraint imposes a maximum delay on a transaction requiring one tuple. The cost function has two terms. The first term is the storage cost per second, and the second term is the communication cost per second.

Chu goes on to derive an expression for q_{ij} using queueing theory but is unable to find an analytic solution for X_{ij}. Instead he discusses how the best assignment can be found using zero-one linear programming. More elaborate models have been studied by Casey (1972) and by Mahmoud and Riordan (1976).

10.1.3. Query Processing

Once the relations have been assigned to hosts, the next task is to deal with is distributed query processing. As an illustration, let us go back to our earlier example of finding overbooked flights from Boston to San Francisco flown by married women. Assume that each of the relations involved (FLIGHTS, RESERVATIONS, PERSONNEL, and AIRCRAFT) is at a different host but that the DICTIONARY relation is replicated at all hosts. Further assume that the query host is distinct from all the other hosts and that communication costs and times completely dominate all operations performed within a host.

There are (at least) two possible metrics to measure the goodness of a query distribution strategy: query response time and total bandwidth consumed. For interactive applications, the response time the terminal user sees is typically paramount. For batch transaction processing, the total amount of bandwidth consumed may be a better measure, because it is related to the cost of processing the query. Throughout our discussion we will make the simplifying assumption that the cost and time to move data is the same for all pairs of hosts. This assumption is completely reasonable with satellite networks, for example.

The most straightforward approach is to have the query host command the other relevant hosts to send the needed relations to it, as shown in Fig. 10-3(a). The query processing can then be done entirely at the query host, just as though the data base were centralized at the query host. Although this solution is simple and works all the time, it is needlessly inefficient, both in time and in bandwidth. Better solutions are possible.

One immediate improvement is to avoid moving the huge RESERVA-TIONS relation. For example, the query host could command the PERSON-NEL host to send its relation to RESERVATIONS for the purpose of selecting out flights piloted by married women, as illustrated in Fig. 10-3(b). These flights could then sent to the query host, together with the complete FLIGHTS and AIRCRAFT relations for the completion of the processing. If married women pilots are relatively rare, this query processing strategy saves most of the $365,000 \times 30$ bytes of data moved in the initial solution. Note that we have made explicit use of the fact that sending PERSONNEL to RESERVA-TIONS costs the same as sending it to the query host, and that the time spent performing joins, wherever, is negligible.

Alternatively, the query host could command FLIGHTS and AIRCRAFT to send their relations to RESERVATIONS for the purpose of selecting out over-booked Boston to San Francisco flights, with the resulting list and

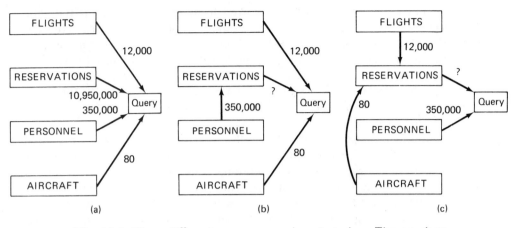

Fig. 10-3. Three different query processing strategies. The numbers indicate the amount of data moved.

PERSONNEL sent to the query host for the final processing [see Fig. 10-3(c)]. This strategy entails moving AIRCRAFT, FLIGHTS, PERSONNEL, and the list of overbooked Boston to San Francisco flights once each. The previous strategy entails moving AIRCRAFT, FLIGHTS, PERSONNEL, and the list of flights flown by married women once each. It should be clear that for the query host to make an optimal decision, it needs detailed information that no host has—whether married women are more-or-less common than certain over-booked flights.

Despite the difficulties of optimizing a specific query, it is possible to design algorithms that give optimal performance under certain statistical conditions, much as quicksort is faster than bubble sort on the average, although pathological data can be constructed on which bubble sort is faster. A number of researchers have worked on distributed query processing, among them Chu and Hurley (1979), Epstein et al. (1978), Hevner and Yao (1979), and Wong (1977). Some of their results are sketched below.

To start with, any processing that can be done at a single host should be done there before any relations are moved. Typically, the query host broadcasts the query to all relevant hosts, to let each one do the initial local processing on its relations. As an illustration of local processing in the example above, instead of sending the entire PERSONNEL relation to RESERVATIONS, the data base system at PERSONNEL could first select out married women and send only these to RESERVATIONS, because all the other entries are going to be discarded anyway. Similarly, there is no need to send the full FLIGHTS relation to whatever host it must eventually go; only the Boston to San Francisco flights are relevant.

In general, whenever a domain value in a query is compared to a constant (e.g., 'BOS'), the relation can be restricted prior to its transmission rather than after. Sometimes restrictions can be inferred from the query even if they are not explicit. For example, if a query about large, full planes requires RESERVATIONS.*Booked* > AIRCRAFT.*Seats* and AIRCRAFT.*Seats* > 250, only those tuples of RESERVATIONS with *Booked* > 250 need be sent to AIRCRAFT. Semantic information about the problem area can also be helpful, for example if RESERVATIONS had to be sent somewhere to check for over-booking, flights with *Booked* = 0 need not be sent, due to the semantic knowledge that *Seats* > 0.

Projection can also be done locally. If the query does not use AIRCRAFT.*Engines*, PERSONNEL.*Title*, or FLIGHTS.*Plane*, why bother send-ing them anywhere? Looking at our running example once more, the query host could command PERSONNEL to send just the names of all married women to RESERVATIONS for joining, with only the *Date*, *Flight#*, and *Booked* domains being sent to the query host. In addition, the query host could command FLIGHTS to send it the *Flight#* and *Plane* domains for Boston to San Francisco flights. This information, together with the *Plane* and *Seats* domains from AIRCRAFT allows the query to be processed completely, and requires considerably less time and bandwidth than any of the previous stra-tegies.

Even with maximum local processing, there are still numerous ways in which a query can be processed. As an example of the various optimization strategies that have been proposed, we will look at Hevner and Yao's (1979) algorithm for the special case that after the local processing only a common joining domain at each host needs to be sent to the query host. To make up an interesting example, let us add three new relations to the airline data base:

COUNTRIES, with domains *Country*, *Capital*, *Currency*, and *Inflation rate*
CITIES, with domains *City*, *Population*, and *Airport distance*
WEATHER, with domains *City*, *Climate*, and *Mean precipitation*

Using the data base, we want a list of all humid capital cities with a population under 1 million that are served by a 747 flight from London's Heathrow airport (LHR). After the local processing, FLIGHTS is reduced to a list of cities served by 747s from London, COUNTRIES is reduced to a list of capital cities, CITIES is reduced to a list of cities with population under 1 million, and WEATHER is reduced to a list of cities with humid climate. All four relations are at distinct hosts and all contain only a single common domain. We will use minimal response time as our metric.

With this algorithm, the query host first broadcasts the query to all relevant hosts and then waits for a reply from each one. Each reply give some statistics on the relation remaining after the local processing, in this case the size of the list of cities. Suppose that FLIGHTS, WEATHER, COUNTRIES, and CITIES contain 100, 400, 500, and 800 cities, respectively.

The Hevner-Yao algorithm requires the query host to know (or guess) the expected number of tuples resulting from a join. One way to make this esti-mate is to know the total number of possible values for the common domain, in this case, the number of distinct cities in the complete data base, say, 1000. If relation having 500 tuples is joined with a relation having m tuples, on the average the join will have $m/2$ tuples. Another way to make estimates of join sizes is for the data base system to maintain explicit statistical information about relations.

The straightforward way to process the humid capital city query is to send all four relations to the query host to join them. If we assume 300 baud lines, 30 character tuples, and a transmission rate of 1 tuple/sec, the response time is 800 sec, determined by the time it takes to send the largest domain, CITIES, to the query host. (The transmissions occur in parallel.)

To improve this response time, we begin inspecting the relations, smallest first. Since FLIGHTS is the smallest, we consider sending it to the next smal-lest, WEATHER, for joining. Note that FLIGHTS contains 10% of all cities, and WEATHER 40%. If these lists are independent, the expected number of cities surviving the join, that is, common to both lists is $0.1 \times 0.4 \times 1000 = 40$. Thus the query host can assume that sending FLIGHTS to WEATHER, joining, and sending the result somewhere will take $100 + 40 = 140$ sec, as shown in Fig. 10-4(a).

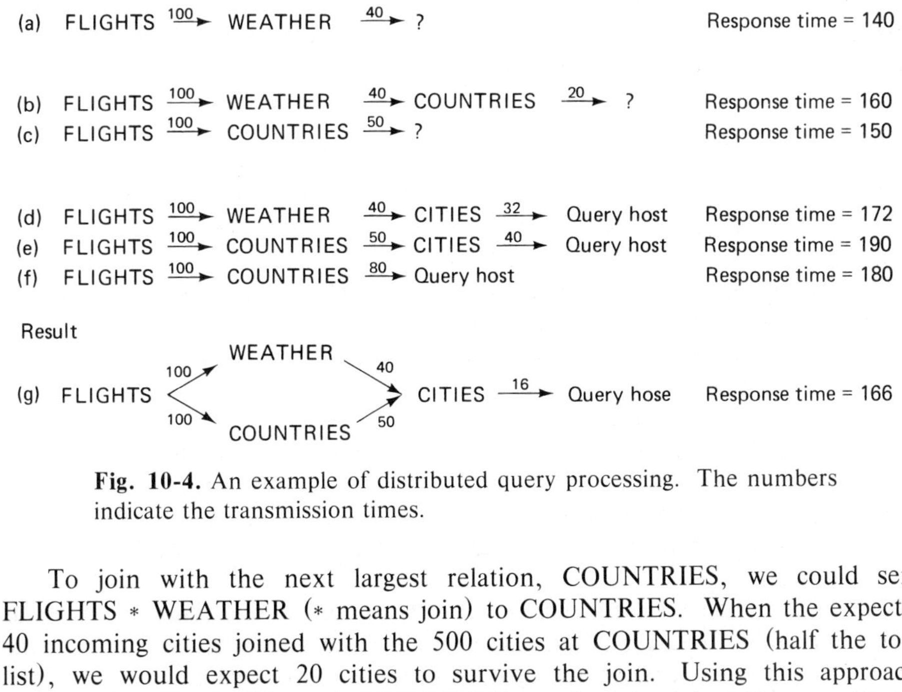

Fig. 10-4. An example of distributed query processing. The numbers indicate the transmission times.

To join with the next largest relation, COUNTRIES, we could send FLIGHTS * WEATHER (* means join) to COUNTRIES. When the expected 40 incoming cities joined with the 500 cities at COUNTRIES (half the total list), we would expect 20 cities to survive the join. Using this approach, FLIGHTS, WEATHER, and COUNTRIES can be joined in 140 sec, with the result delivered elsewhere in 160 sec, as shown in Fig. 10-4(b). Alternatively, we could send FLIGHTS to WEATHER and COUNTRIES in parallel. Doing so integrates COUNTRIES into the result in only 150 sec, which is faster than 160 sec, and also faster than the 500 sec needed to send COUNTRIES itself, so we accept Fig. 10-4(c) as part of the solution.

Finally, we must join with CITIES. Rather than sending it to the query host, we could send FLIGHTS * WEATHER to it, which yields an output of 32 tuples and a time of 172 sec. Or we could send FLIGHTS * COUNTRIES to it, which yields an output of 40 tuples and a time of 190 sec. Thirdly, we could send FLIGHTS to it, with an expected output of 80 tuples and a time of 180 sec. Finally, we could send both of our previous joins, FLIGHTS * WEATHER and FLIGHTS * COUNTRIES, to CITIES, join them together, and join the output with CITIES. Since each relation is involved here, the expected output is $0.1 \times 0.4 \times 0.5 \times 0.8 \times 1000 = 16$ tuples. Note that we cannot compute the output of the initial join by multiplying 0.04 by 0.05 because FLIGHTS * WEATHER and FLIGHTS * COUNTRIES are not independent.

Thus the final strategy is to send FLIGHTS to WEATHER and COUNTRIES in parallel, requiring 100 sec. Fifty seconds later, both joins have arrived at CITIES. An additional 16 sec are needed to send the output to the query host, so response time is 166 sec, as shown in Fig. 10-4(g), instead of the original 800 sec.

Hevner and Yao also consider an algorithm for processing relations with arbitrary domains, which is similar in spirit to their simple one. They also consider minimizing bandwidth instead of response time.

10.1.4. Concurrency Control

In a distributed data base system, it is normal for queries to be initiated from multiple hosts, often simultaneously. Consequently, multiple queries may attempt to read, or worse yet, write (update), the same relation at the same time. For example, in a banking system for processing checks, a common transaction is to read a check from the input file, read the checkwriter's balance, debit the balance by the amount of the check, and then write the new balance back into the data base. If checks are processed at the bank where they are cashed, multiple hosts may attempt to update the same account at the same time. In other words, two hosts may simultaneously read a (different) check. Then each reads the balance in quick succession. Finally each computes the new balance and writes it back into the data base. Whichever one does the write last will overwrite the other and eliminate the other's effect, giving an incorrect result.

Allowing unrestricted concurrency, as in this check processing example, is clearly intolerable, because it can lead to undetected semantic errors in the data base. The other extreme, allowing only a single transaction to run at a time, eliminates the concurrency errors but at the price of greatly reducing the performance of the system, since most transactions do not interfere and could run concurrently without danger. An important research issue is the design of concurrency control algorithms that maximize the amount of parallel activity, while maintaining the semantic integrity (i.e., correctness) of the data base.

Bernstein et al. (1979) have devised a formalism for discussing concurrency that helps show where the problems really lie. They define a **transaction** as a set of reads, $R = R(x_1, x_2, \ldots, x_n)$, followed by some processing, and then a set of writes, $W = W(y_1, y_2, \cdots, y_n)$, where the x's and y's are data items and may (partially) overlap. A **log** is the time ordered sequence of reads and writes performed on the data base. For two transactions, T_1 and T_2, some possible logs are:

$$\log_1 = R_1 W_1 R_2 W_2$$

$$\log_2 = R_2 W_2 R_1 W_1$$

$$\log_3 = R_1 R_2 W_1 W_2$$

In general, a log of n transactions consists of a permutation of the n R's and the n W's subject to the condition that R_i appears before W_i in the log. Either the read set or the write set may be empty for any transaction.

A log is said to be **serial** if each R_i is immediately followed by its W_i. Above, $\log_1$ and $\log_2$ are serial, but $\log_3$ is **interleaved**. We assume that all serial logs produce correct results. Interleaved logs do not necessarily produce incorrect results, but if an interleaved log can be shown to be equivalent to some serial log, a property called **serializability**, then it is surely correct. Logs also exist that leave the data base consistent, but are not serializable. The issue of equivalence of logs is treated by Bernstein et al. (1979) in detail. Suffice it to say that $R_i W_j$ is equivalent to $W_j R_i$ if R_i and W_j operate on disjoint sets of data items. Also, since reads do not alter the data base, consecutive reads can be reordered or performed in parallel, increasing the amount of concurrency.

A good concurrency control algorithm should allow all serial logs, all serializable logs, and all other logs that leave the data base consistent. No such algorithm is known at present. Instead, most algorithms achieve serializable logs by allowing transactions to **lock** part of the data base before starting. If a host discovers that a needed relation is already locked by another transaction must simply wait until it is unlocked. If a transaction locks all its relations before starting, it can be sure that no other transaction will interleave a read or a write while it is busy, thus guaranteeing serializability. The simplest possible locking scheme is to have a single lock for the entire data base. By setting the lock, a host guarantees that it has exclusive access to the entire data base. Under these conditions all logs will be serial, but only one transaction at a time will be run.

To achieve more concurrency, a data base system could lock relations rather than only the whole data base. Other possibilities for locking are individual tuples, domains, values, or even physical disk sectors. This subject,

granularity of locking, is a fascinating one, but we do not have the space to pursue it further. For the rest of our discussion, we will assume that relations are the unit of locking. If there are many small relations, this choice will allow considerable concurrency, because transactions using disjoint sets of relations may run in parallel. If there are only a few relations, it will not allow much concurrency. In any event, by locking all the relations it needs before it begins a transaction, a host assures that no reads or writes from other transactions will sneak in between its reads and its writes. It thereby avoids a situation such as $\log_3$, in which R_2 is interposed between R_1 and W_1.

Although it may be possible to acquire all the locks instantly in a centralized data base system, it is not possible to do so in a distributed one. Locks must be acquired sequentially, one by one. However, acquiring locks one at a time introduces problems, because host A can lock relation R_1 while host B locks relation R_2, and then each can attempt to lock the other relation. Each host will then wait forever for the needed lock to be released. This situation is called a **deadlock**. Some of the problems associated with acquiring locks are discussed by Eswaren et al. (1976). In particular, they described a locking protocol, called **two phase locking**, in which a host first goes through a phase of acquiring locks and then a phase of releasing them. Once some lock has been released, no other locks may be acquired.

Up until now we have said little about locking in replicated data base systems. In a centralized system, the central lock controller need only maintain a bit map with 1 bit per relation to tell whether or not the relation is locked. In a distributed data base system, locking a relation implies locking all copies of it. Due to the finite transit time between hosts, it is possible that different copies of the same relation will be simultaneously locked on behalf of different transactions, leading to interleaved, nonserializable logs, deadlocks, and other unpleasant events. Good ways to achieve distributed locking are an important research area. The algorithms presented below as examples of distributed locking work but do not allow maximal concurrency.

The first class of distributed locking algorithms attempt to simulate locking in centralized systems. For example, a system could have a single lock controller, possibly with backups in case the lock controller crashes. To run a transaction, a host informs the lock controller, which locks the appropriate parts of the data base and then tells the requesting host to go ahead. Only after the transaction is completed are the locks released. Since transactions are run serially, the algorithm clearly works, but it is inefficient because it makes no use of concurrency.

A variation on this theme is to imagine a virtual ring containing all the hosts. A control token is passed around the virtual ring. Only the host possessing the control token is permitted to set locks. Since only one host has the control token at any instant, there is no way for conflicting locks to be set.

Now let us consider a truly distributed locking algorithm based on assigning a unique number to each transaction and then running the transactions in a globally determined order. One possible way to assign transaction numbers, shown in Fig. 10-5, is to concatenate the time of day with the host number initiating the transaction. If hosts refrain from initiating two transactions during the same clock tick, each transaction will have a unique number. For the algorithm given below, the clocks at different hosts need not be synchronized. In fact, a serial number could be used as the high-order part, although doing so might complicate crash recovery.

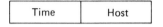

Fig. 10-5. A transaction number.

Each of the hosts maintains four variables: t, the number of the current transaction, n, the number of hosts involved in the current transaction, k, the lock counter, and s, the current state, which can be IDLE, LOCKING, PROCESSING, or UNLOCKING. When a query arrives at a host whose state is IDLE, the query is broken down into transactions. The first transaction is initiated by switching into LOCKING state, setting k to zero, and broadcasting a PLEASE LOCK message to the $n - 1$ other hosts involved in the transaction. The PLEASE LOCK message contains the transaction number, among other things. The host then waits for $n - 1$ PLEASE LOCK messages to come back from the other hosts. A query arriving at a host not in IDLE state is queued for future processing.

When a PLEASE LOCK message arrives at a host in IDLE state, it switches into LOCKING state, initializes k to one, t to the transaction number in the message, and n to the number of hosts involved (contained in the message). Then it rebroadcasts the message to the other $n - 1$ hosts.

When a host in LOCKING state receives a PLEASE LOCK message, it checks to see if the transaction number contained in the message is lower than the contents of t. If so, it queues the previous transaction and starts all over again with the new one as though it had been in IDLE state. If the current and new transaction numbers are equal, it increments k. If the new number exceeds the old one, the new transaction is ignored. When k reaches $n - 1$, which happens when all other hosts have sent it a PLEASE LOCK message, the host can begin processing. When it is finished processing, it sends each of the other $n - 1$ hosts a PLEASE UNLOCK message. When $n - 1$ such messages have arrived, the host switches back into IDLE state.

Now let us consider some examples of how this distributed locking algorithm works. A single host initiates a transaction by broadcasting PLEASE LOCK messages. When a host has heard from every other host, it knows they are all in agreement about which transaction to run next, and that transaction is run to completion. Note that two different transactions can run concurrently

only if they have no hosts in common. (The algorithm can also work per relation rather than per host.)

The situation becomes more complicated if multiple transactions are initiated simultaneously by different hosts. In Fig. 10-6(a), for example, host A
initiates transaction 0000, host B initiates transaction 0001, and host C initiates
transaction 0002. When the PLEASE LOCK for 0000 arrives at B, transaction
0001 will be abandoned because $0000 < 0001$. Suppose that the message from
B arrives at C before the message from A. Then C will abandon 0002 in favor
of 0001. Depending on the arrival order of the messages at the remaining
hosts, the values of t for all five hosts at a certain instant of time could be as
shown in Fig. 10-6(b).

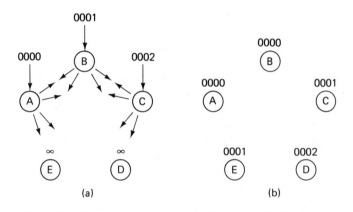

Fig. 10-6. Distributed locking. (a) Initial phase. (b) Slightly later.

Now we wish to show that all hosts eventually agree to run 0000 first, and
that none of them does the locking for 0001 or 0002 until 0000 is finished.
Since A started out with 0000, it will simply queue the messages for 0001 and
0002 when they arrive. Without A's consent, the other hosts will never acquire
the requisite $n - 1$ (i.e., four) PLEASE LOCK messages for either 0001 or
0002, so neither of these will be initiated until A has given permission, which it
will not do until 0000 is finished. On the other hand, the PLEASE LOCK message from A will eventually reach all the other hosts, preempting whatever
transaction setup was already in progress. Furthermore, once a host has set t to
0000, it will not accept a higher numbered transaction. Consequently, 0000
captures all the hosts and runs first. When it has finished, each host takes the
lowest entry from its queue, so 0001 runs next.

Now imagine that hosts B and C initiated their transactions before host A.
If either of their messages arrive at A before A starts 0000, the subsequent
arrival of 0000 is impossible, because a new query cannot preempt a host after
it has replied to a PLEASE LOCK message. If, however, 0000 gets started

before 0001 or 0002 arrive at A, then 0000 wins.

The above algorithm was described due to its simplicity rather than its performance. Better algorithms have been proposed e.g., (Menasce et al., 1980). For surveys of some of these, see (Badal, 1980; and Wilms, 1980).

10.1.5. Crash Recovery

Another problem that is crucial in distributed data base systems is crash recovery. Although modern computers are reasonably reliable, crashes do happen from time to time. In addition, machines are occasionally taken down for preventive maintenance, making backups, and other reasons. In many networks, the users expect the data base system to continue to operate even though a few hosts are down. Furthermore, when the missing hosts return to operation, they must be able to "catch up" without causing deadlocks or consistency errors. As an example of an algorithm that integrates concurrency control and crash recovery, we will examine briefly the work of Chou and Liu (1980).

For simplicity, we will discuss only the case of each host having a complete copy of the data base. Each host maintains a list of all other hosts currently up, the up-list. As in our previous example of concurrency control, each transaction is tagged with a transaction number consisting of the time or a sequence number in the high-order bits, and the host number in the low-order bits. Transaction numbers are globally unique, and for any group of transactions, it is always possible to determine which of them is earlier that is, which has the lowest number.

Whenever a user has a query or update, it is decomposed into transactions, each of which is numbered. Transactions that do not change the data base can be carried out locally and will not concern us further. Updates, in contrast, are carried out in three steps: broadcasting, selection, and processing. We will first discuss the normal case, with no crashes, and then discuss the effect of crashes. In the broadcast phase, each transaction is broadcast to all hosts in the up-list. As soon as the initiating host has received acknowledgements from all other hosts in the up-list, it may accept the next transaction request.

It is essential that the broadcast facility delivers all messages in order, or report the failure to do so (e.g., due to a crashed host). Since the data base system is in the application layer, it is reasonable to assume that every host has an open virtual circuit with every other host, that virtual circuits are reliable, and that every message is acknowledged. To guarantee that each host generates new transactions at a minimum rate, dummy transactions are generated periodically if no real work has been produced within a timeout interval.

When a transaction arrives at a host, it is put into the work queue. Whenever a host finishes a transaction, it examines its work queue to select the next transaction to run. The rule for selecting a transaction is as follows:

1. Wait until a (possibly dummy) transaction is present from each host.

2. Select the transaction with the lowest number and run it.

The purpose of waiting until a transaction from each host is present is to ensure that no transaction is selected while a lower numbered one is on the way. If the lowest transaction in the work queue from host i is T_i, then any transaction still in transit from host i must have a number higher than T_i, because we have assumed that lower protocol layers ensure message delivery in sequence.

Having selected a transaction, the host now carries out the third step: locking all the needed relations and updating the local data base. When the update is completed, the locks can be cleared and a DONE message sent back to the initiator. As soon as the locks have been set, the selection step can be restarted to see if another transaction can be found. If one can be found and it does not require any locked relations, it may run concurrently with the transactions already in progress, to achieve concurrency and yet produce a serializable log.

It is important to realize that the algorithm guarantees that all data bases run transactions in the same order, thus ensuring that they all remain identical. In Fig. 10-7(a) the transactions generated by four hosts as a function of time are indicated by crosses. In Fig. 10-7(b) the work queue is shown, assuming that no transactions are fetched and started from *time* = 1 to *time* = 7. If a transaction that had locked a critical relation, say the DICTIONARY, finishes at time = 8, transaction 14 will be chosen at all hosts to run next. However, if a fifth host, say E, exists, no transactions may be selected until some transaction from E arrives, because it may bear the number 05 and hence be the next to run. The necessity of generating dummy transactions when there are no real ones now becomes obvious.

If no crashes occur, the algorithm works as described, allowing concurrent, deadlock free, multiple copy updates, and guaranteeing that all copies of the data base run the same transactions in the same order. Now let us consider what happens if a host, say X, crashes. At a certain moment, another host, say, A, notices that X refuses to acknowledge a transaction broadcast to it. Host A now compiles a list of all outstanding transactions for which X has not returned a DONE message, as well as the most recent transaction, which X has not even acknowledged. This list is broadcast to all other hosts, each of which compiles a similar list and broadcasts it. Now all hosts have a complete list of transactions that X *may* have missed. All hosts store this list in a safe place, called the recovery buffer, and delete X from their up-lists.

At this point all hosts have sufficient information to allow X to recover, when it comes back up, but X may have been in the process of broadcasting a transaction itself when it went down. Furthermore, this broadcast may have been sent to some hosts, but not all, a dangerous situation. Thus each host must record the most recent transaction received from every other host. The messages exchanged when X's demise is noticed should therefore also include the last transaction received from X. When all these messages have been

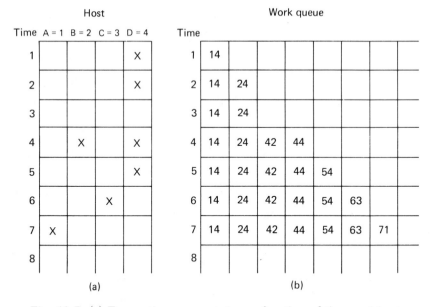

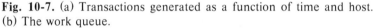

Fig. 10-7. (a) Transactions generated as a function of time and host. (b) The work queue.

processed, a partial broadcast is converted into a total broadcast. Note that X may have been broadcasting at most one transaction, because it is forbidden to start broadcasting the next one until all the ACKs have arrived.

Once the message described above exchange has been carried out, normal operation resumes, except that all new transactions are also entered into all copies of the recovery buffer. When X comes back up, it broadcasts an "I AM BACK" message to all known hosts. In return, each one sends it the complete recovery buffer and up-list. The transactions are put into the work queue, and normal selection begins.

To see that the algorithm is basically correct, look at Fig. 10-8. A sender can crash at t_1, before starting a transaction; at t_2, before completing the broadcast phase; or at t_3, before receiving all the DONE messages. A crash at t_1 means that the transaction is never run anywhere, and is equivalent to a user crash. A crash at t_2 will be detected when the remaining hosts inform each other of the last transaction received from the crashed host. If even one host has received the transaction, all will receive it. If the crash occurs at t_3, the DONE messages will be stored in the recovery buffers.

All cases of receiver crashes are in fact equivalent. If any host has sent a transaction to which the crashed receiver has not replied DONE, the transaction will be saved in the recovery buffer. For more details we refer you to the paper by Chou and Liu (1980).

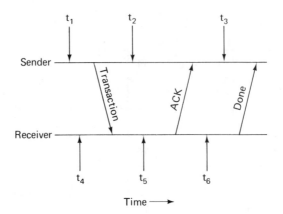

Fig. 10-8. Different cases of sender and receiver crashes.

Many algorithms for maintaining the integrity of a data base system require certain actions to be **atomic**, that is, either carried to completion or not carried out at all. Since an atomic action may have to perform several disk accesses, there is a danger that the system may crash part way through the atomic action, leaving the data base in an inconsistent state. Lampson (1980) has studied this problem and has come up with an algorithm that maintains two copies of critical disk blocks in such a way as to ensure consistency at all times. For details, please consult the reference.

We have now completed our discussion of distributed data bases. The only thing left to do is to once again repeat our earlier comment that we have barely scratched the surface. Data base systems are an active research area, and numerous papers will no doubt have appeared since publication of this book. Interested readers should examine the suggested readings in Chap. 11 and recent issues of *ACM Transactions on Data Base Systems*, *IEEE Transactions on Software Engineering*, the annual *Berkeley Workshop on Distributed Data Management and Computer Networks*, and the proceedings of the *ACM SIGMOD* and *Very Large Data Bases* conferences.

10.2. DISTRIBUTED COMPUTATION

Having looked at how the data can be distributed, it is now time to look at how the computation can be distributed. In the early years of the ARPANET, computations were rarely distributed over multiple machines. Instead, the network was used for two principal purposes: allowing users at one site to log onto a machine at another site, and allowing users to transfer files from one site to another. In neither case was there any attempt to divide a single user problem into pieces and run the pieces on different machines. As more networking experience was gained, systems in which the computation was distributed were implemented using the ARPANET. We will describe one of these, the National Software Works, later. However, the real push toward distributing the computation came from local networks using minicomputers and microcomputers, so we will concentrate on these.

The amount of distribution covers a wide spectrum, from loosely coupled long-haul networks, in which machines rarely communicate, to tightly coupled data flow machines, in which machines interact on an instruction by instruction time scale. We will now examine several different models for distributing the computation, covering the spectrum from loosely coupled to tightly coupled, and statically partitioned to dynamically partitioned.

10.2.1. The Hierarchical Model

A fairly common, but relatively inflexible arrangement is to organize the network as a tree, with increasingly powerful computers as one progresses from the leaves of the tree to the root. A typical hierarchical network is illustrated in Fig. 10-9. This kind of network is commonly used in hierarchically organized corporations. For example, each factory might have many microcomputers on the shop floor, regulating and monitoring the production process. Each microcomputer carries out a simple task, controlling a few pieces of equipment, collecting data, and sending them to a minicomputer somewhere in the factory for processing. The minicomputers analyze the data, store them for local queries, and send summaries back to a large mainframe at corporate headquarters.

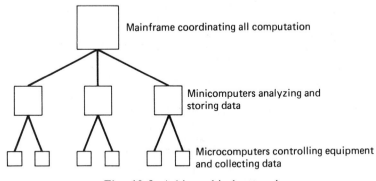

Fig. 10-9. A hierarchical network.

Each machine handles a different level of detail, corresponding to the different people who need the information. The microcomputers can answer queries such as "What is the current temperature inside the number 9 forge?" for the benefit of production personnel. Data entry can also be done using the microcomputers. The minicomputers can answer queries such as "How many left-handed anvils do we have in stock?" for the benefit of the plant manager.

The mainframe can answer queries such as "What fraction of the horseshoes that the company produced last year failed to pass quality control inspection?" for top management.

10.2.2. The CPU Cache Model

The hierarchical model is fine where the problem itself is naturally structured hierarchically, but many problems are not structured this way. Consider, for example, an organization whose workload exceeds the capacity of the largest existing CPU. One approach to this problem is what we will call a **CPU cache**, in analogy with a memory cache. In a memory cache, there are two levels of memory, a small fast memory and a large slow memory. The cache algorithm attempts to keep the most heavily used data in the fast memory, to reduce access time. In the CPU cache model depicted in Fig. 10-10, each user has a minicomputer inserted between his terminal and the large central computer. Part of the computation is done on the central computer and part on the mini. An early use of this model is described by Van Dam et al. (1974).

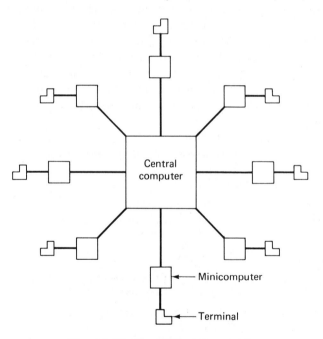

Fig. 10-10. The CPU cache model.

The decision to run a particular part of the computation on one machine or the other is based on the suitability of the two machines, the relative costs of the two machines, the bandwidth between the machines, and the current workload. As an example, let us examine a system in which all the modules (procedures, programs, etc.) are available on both the central machine and one of the minicomputers. When the workload on the central machine is light, most modules run faster there because the machine is faster.

On the other hand, when the central machine is heavily loaded, the (dedicated) mini may actually have a better response time. The critical load at which the mini is faster varies from module to module since the relative speeds of the machines depends on the instruction mix. Large minicomputers can often outperform mainframes with long word lengths on string handling, for example, but not floating multiplies. Also, special microcode can give the mini an edge for some modules. The big question is: Which parts of the program should be run where?

Stone and Bokhari (1978) have studied the problem of assigning modules to machines, using graph theory. Below we will briefly summarize their work. In their model, a job consists of a collection of modules, A, B, C, D, etc. The running time (real time) of each module on each of the two processors, P_1 (the mini), and P_2 (the central computer), is known, in other words, a particular load factor is assumed. The running times for an example with four modules are given in Fig. 10-11(a).

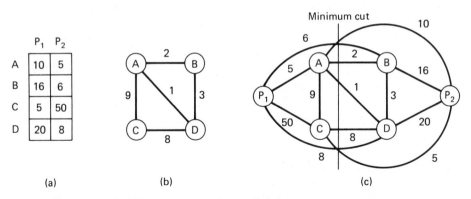

Fig. 10-11. (a) Running times of the modules on each processor. (b) Intermodule communication times. (c) Graph constructed from (a) and (b).

In addition, the communication time between modules i and j for the case that these modules are assigned to different processors is known. These numbers represent the time required to transmit parameters and results across the interface. Clearly, if module i repeatedly calls module j with two large arrays as input and one large array as output, there is much to be gained by assigning these two modules to the same machine. The lower the bandwidth between the two processors, the larger these numbers will be. Figure 10-11(b) gives the intermodule communication times for our example.

To determine which modules should be assigned to which processor, we must construct an augmented graph starting from the intermodule communication graph. Two new nodes are added, for P_1 and P_2. An arc is added from P_1 to each module, labeled with the running time of that module on P_2, not P_1. Similar arcs are added for P_1, as shown in Fig. 10-11(c).

Every minimal $P_1 - P_2$ cut represents an assignment of modules to processors. Those modules on the P_1 side of the cut run on P_1; those on the P_2 side of the cut run on P_2. If a module X is assigned to P_1, the arc P_2-X will be in the cut set. Since this arc has a weight equal to the running time on P_1, not P_2, the cut set will contain terms for running each module on the assigned processor, as well as arcs representing cross machine communication.

In fact, the weight of the cut set is the total running time for the assignment. The algorithm for making the assignment is now obvious: just find the minimum cut set using any of the well-known network flow algorithms, such as that of Fig. 2-8.

The calculation above assumes that the running time on each processor is known. For the (dedicated) mini, this assumption is reasonable, but for the central computer it is not, because the running time depends on the load factor. Note that we are talking about real time, not CPU time. Fortunately, Stone and Bokhari discovered that as the fraction f, of the central machine's power devoted to the job in question drops from 1.00 to 0.00, the algorithm moves modules from the central computer to the mini, but not back. Put in other terms, for each module there is a critical value of f above which the module runs on the central machine and below which it runs on the mini. If this critical value is above 1.00, the module always runs on the mini. The critical values can be computed in advance for each module. When the job is started, f is estimated, and the assignment is made based on the precomputed values.

Stone and Bokhari also treat the case of dynamically changing the assignment during execution, as well as the case of limited memory on each machine.

10.2.3. The User-Server Model

As the power of small computers increases and their price decreases, the value of the central computer in the CPU cache model becomes less and less. Consequently, the next step in the distribution process is to get rid of the central machine altogether. Each user has a personal minicomputer, perhaps with some local disk storage. Depending on the application, the personal computer may range from a 16-bit machine with 64 kilobytes of memory and a floppy disk to a 32-bit machine with several megabytes of memory and a 100-megabyte hard disk. Systems of this type are discussed in (Abraham and Dalal, 1980; Clark and Svobodova, 1980; Newell et al., 1980; Rosen, 1980; and Ward and Terman, 1980).

Even if each user has more than enough computing power in his office, there are good reasons for connecting the personal computers by a high speed local network. The principal ones are to allow users to share data and send each other mail, and to allow users to share expensive peripherals. Even with rapidly decreasing chip prices, it does not seem likely that each user will be provided with his own private high resolution phototypesetter in the next few years, for example. Also, there is an enormous economy of scale with secondary storage: the larger devices have a much lower cost per byte than do the smaller devices. These arguments lead to the **user-server** model of Fig. 10-12.

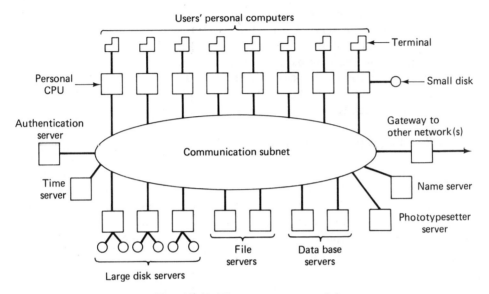

Fig. 10-12. The user-server model.

In this model the user does all his actual computing on his personal computer, but various centrally located server machines exist to carry out specific functions on behalf of any user who requests them. For example, the network could have several **disk servers**, whose function is to read and write raw disk blocks, without regard to their contents. Typical messages that could be sent to a disk server are requests to allocate a disk block, return a disk block, read a disk block, and write a disk block.

Since raw disk blocks are too low a level of abstraction for most applications, the network would probably have one or more **file servers**, offering file system services. Typical messages that can be sent to a file server are requests to open a file or close a file, as well as read, write, and seek on a file. The file servers are responsible for maintaining directories and connection status information to turn the primitive disk service into usable file service.

Different file servers may offer completely different file systems. One file server may regard a file as a linear sequence of bytes, with operations to read and write contiguous portions of a file, and little more. Another file server may regard a file as a linear sequence of variable length records, with operations to insert and delete records, as well as reading and writing them. Clearly, the internal data structures used by these two file servers will be different, but the two file systems can be arbitrarily mixed on the same disk drives, because the disk server keeps track of which disk block belongs to whom. Such a model is much more flexible than the traditional view that the operating system provides a single file system that all users are forced to live with.

For data base users, even record oriented files may be far too primitive to use directly in application programs. Consequently, the network may provide one or more **data base servers**, sometimes called **backend machines** (see, for example, Maryanski, 1980; and Su et al., 1980). A data base server might accept queries about the data base, analyze them itself, and return the answers. There might be different data base servers for relational data bases, hierarchical data bases, and network data bases. The data base servers could use either the file servers or the disk servers, as appropriate.

10.2.4. The Pool Processor Model

As long as each user is content with a single machine for running user programs, the user-server model is reasonable. However, dedicating a large minicomputer to each user is an inefficient way to do business, because computing requirements are bursty. At a certain moment a user may need more computing power than his machine can provide, while the machine next door is idle. The solution is to go to the model of Fig. 10-13.

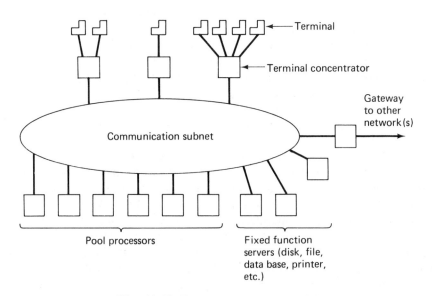

Fig. 10-13. The pool processor model.

In this model, which we will call the **pool processor** model, users do not have powerful, dedicated, personal computers. Instead, each terminal is connected to the network, either directly or through a terminal concentrator. Work is carried out by a pool of processors, some of which may have fixed functions, such as file servers, and some of which are dynamically allocatable on demand. For example, if the user invokes a six-pass compiler, each of the six passes could be assigned to a different processor, with the output of the first machine being sent to the second machine for input, and so on. In this manner, the real time required to perform the compilation is equal to the longest of the passes rather than the sum of the passes. Wittie (1979) has envisioned a system of this type containing 10,000 processors.

The advantage of the pool processor model over the user-server model is the faster response time achievable by allocating resources dynamically rather than statically. In the user-server model each user has one CPU all the time, whereas in the pool processor model he may have ten CPUs 10% of the time, and no CPUs 90% of the time. The disadvantage is the more complicated scheduling algorithm needed, as well as the possibility of deadlock.

Let us consider briefly some algorithms for scheduling the pool processors. The simplest algorithm is to dedicate one processor to schedule the other ones. This processor keeps track of the status of all processors and tells the processors what to do next, in a master/slave arrangement. Unfortunately, the vulnerability of this scheme makes it unattractive.

A slight modification of this idea is to have a tree of schedulers. The pool processors are statically partitioned into groups, with each group having a group manager (one of the processors in the group). The group managers, in turn, are divided into divisions, with each division having a division manager, and so on. Instead of having a full tree, with the consequent vulnerability of the root, the tree is truncated, so there are multiple machines at the top level (like many organizations, this one is run by a committee). Each manager schedules the processors under it. If a manager dies, its manager chooses a new manager from among the dead manager's subordinates. If a member of the ruling committee dies, the remaining members of the committee choose the replacement.

A completely different scheduling algorithm is to use **bidding** (Farber and Larson, 1972). When a new process is to be created, the parent broadcasts a request for bids. The bid request might specify properties of the computation: does it need floating point, how much memory, where do the data come from, and so on. Pool processors wanting to bid for the work send messages to the requesting processor, which then selects one of them. Since scheduling is totally distributed in this algorithm, there is a danger of deadlock. For example, if two users each want to run the six-pass compiler and there are only 10 processors in the system, there is a distinct possibility that each user will acquire five processors and hang forever waiting for the sixth one.

In bidding systems, the question arises whether a processor that is currently occupied may continue to bid for work, maintaining an internal work queue. If processors do queue work, they may confer from time to time, to allow processors with long queues to offload work onto processors with short queues. Smith (1979) has investigated systems of this kind.

The user-server and pool processor models can obviously be combined by allocating some resources (processors, disks, etc.) permanently to each user, leaving the rest in a pool to be allocated on demand. Systems of this type are discussed in (Thorton, 1980; and Watson, 1980b).

10.2.5. The Data Flow Model

Our last model for distributing computation is much more radical than the previous ones. In this model the problem is described by a graph, with each node of the graph corresponding to a processor. Results are moved among the processors as messages. This idea has been worked out in great detail for the case where the nodes are single machine instructions, so the collection of processors are in fact cooperating on running a single program. Since the state of the art is further for such fine-grain computations than for coarser ones (e.g., a node is a procedure), we will now describe the model, called **data flow**, in those terms, but you should keep in mind that in principle it is more widely applicable.

Since the time of John von Neumann (ca. 1946), the basic conceptual model used to think about computers and programs has remained unchanged, in spite of many advances in both hardware and software technology. The model that von Neumann proposed, which has been reflected in nearly all programming languages ever devised, is that the computer consists of a processor and a memory. The processor contains a register called the **program counter**, which points to the next machine instruction to be fetched. The basic instruction cycle is for the processor to fetch the instruction pointed at by the program counter, increment the program counter, and then execute the instruction. Although some machines have some minor parallelism, such as instruction pipelining and independent I/O processors, the basic execution process is fetch an instruction and then execute it. Because instructions are executed strictly sequentially, there is little inherent parallelism, and little opportunity to employ large numbers of processors to gain speed.

One way to break the grip of sequential execution is to discard the von Neumann model altogether. Several research groups around the world (e.g., Arvind and Gostelow, 1977; Dennis, 1979; Treleaven, 1979) are actively pursuing a kind of non von Neumann model that has come to be known as **data flow**.

The key idea behind a data flow system is that there are no variables in the usual sense that is, no memory locations that can be stored into. Instead, values are represented by packets that are transmitted between processing units. Each processing unit has the task of computing some function of its inputs and producing an output containing the result. These functions are really functions in the strict mathematically sense: each function depends only on its inputs, and not on any global variables or other side information. Furthermore, the only thing a function does is produce an explicit result. It has no side effects such as modifying global variables, because there are none.

Because there are no variables or side effects, each processor may begin its computation as soon as its input packets have arrived. There is no program counter and no explicit sequencing of computations, other than that implicit in one calculation depending on the result of another one. For example, if $y = f(x)$ and $z = g(y)$, then f *must* run before g. It is precisely this ability of data flow systems to operate without any artificially forced sequencing that makes them so attractive for distributed computing.

To make the idea of data flow more concrete, we will now look at a detailed example. The problem we wish to tackle is how to use multiple processors to solve the ordinary differential equation

$$\frac{d^2y}{dx^2} + 2x\frac{dy}{dx} + 2y = 0$$

subject to the boundary conditions $y(0) = 1$ and $y'(0) = 0$.

To solve our equation numerically, let $u = dy/dx$, yielding two equations

$$\frac{du}{dx} + 2ux + 2y = 0 \qquad \text{and} \qquad u = \frac{dy}{dx}$$

Replacing the infinitesimal dx with the finite step Δx, we can solve for the changes in y and u respectively, as

$$\Delta u = -2ux\,\Delta x - 2y\,\Delta x \qquad \text{and} \qquad \Delta y = u\,\Delta x$$

We start out at the known boundary point $x_0 = 0$. From this point we move forward to the new x coordinate, given by $x + \Delta x$. The new u and y values at this point (call them u_1 and y_1) are

$$u_1 = u_0 - 2u_0x_0\,\Delta x - 2y_0\,\Delta x \qquad \text{and} \qquad y_1 = y_0 + u_0\,\Delta x$$

Having found x, u, and y at a new point, we have a new boundary condition, and we can repeat the whole process all over again. Eventually, we will have found the value of y at all x values that are a multiple of Δx. By choosing Δx small enough, we can solve the equation to high accuracy.

If you barely know what a differential equation is, let alone how to solve one do not despair. The whole purpose of this exercise was to lead up to the program of Fig. 10-14. Having gotten there, we need the differential equation no more. The thing to notice about the program is that it is sequential; the statements are executed in the order written. The computer does not begin on the second iteration step until the first one has been completed. This statement may seem obvious, but it will not be true for the data flow version.

The equivalent data flow program written in a data flow language, would

```
{Solve the differential equation: y" + 2xy' + 2y = 0.}
program diffeq(input, output);
var a, dx, x, u, y, x1, u1, y1: real;
begin
    {read in the ordinate, a at which we want the value of the function,
     the step size, dx, and boundary condition}
    read(a, dx, x, u, y);
    while x < a do
      begin
                            x1 := x + dx;
                            u1 := u − 2*x*u*dx − 2*y*dx;
                            y1 := y + u*dx;
                            x := x1;  u := u1;  y:= y1
    end;
    writeln(y:13:9)
end.
```

Fig. 10-14. A program to solve a differential equation.

actually look very similar to Fig. 10-14. This similarity is hardly an accident, because data flow languages have been carefully designed to make them look like traditional programming languages, to make data flow more palatable to the masses. Thus the data flow graph of Fig. 10-15(a) is really the equivalent of the *assembly language* translation of Fig. 10-14.

The basic element in a data flow graph (or machine) is a box (or processor) with one or more input lines and one or more output lines. Consider the box labeled "6" in Fig. 10-15. It has two inputs and an output. As soon as packets have arrived on each input line and the previously sent output packet has been absorbed by its destination, the processor can begin execution.

By requiring the previous output to already have been absorbed before the processor can generate more, we are sure there will be a place to put it. Some data flow systems do not have this restriction, leading to a higher degree of parallelism but a much more complicated buffering strategy. We will stick to the simpler systems, known as **feedback interpreter** systems, so called because when a processor fires (executes), it must send acknowledgement packets back up its input lines to tell whoever generated those inputs that the lines are now free again. In effect, each processor has one buffer for each input line, and any other processor planning to send an output packet to that buffer must be kept informed of the status of the buffer.

To see how the system of Fig. 10-15 operates, imagine that the input buffers of processors 1 through 5 are initialized with the values shown. Constant arguments are shown encircled; they are "hardwired" into their respective buffers. For simplicity's sake, we will assume that each operation requires one cycle. During cycle 1, processors 1 through 5 all fire, delivering results to processors 6 through 10, all of which fire during cycle 2. Processor 9 compares its

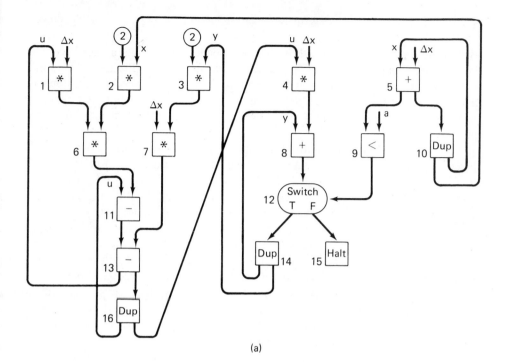

(a)

Processor	Opcode	Operand 1			Operand 2			Destination 1		Destination 2	
		Value	Sticky	Full	Value	Sticky	Full	Target	Port	Target	Port
1	*	u	0	1	Δx	1	1	6	1	0	0
2	*	2	1	1	x	0	1	6	2	0	0
3	*	2	1	1	y	0	1	7	2	0	0
4	*	u	0	1	Δx	1	1	8	2	0	0
5	+	x	0	1	Δx	1	1	9	1	10	1
6	*	0	0	0	0	0	0	11	2	0	0
7	*	Δx	1	1	0	0	0	13	2	0	0
8	+	y	0	1	0	0	0	12	1	0	0
9	<	0	0	0	a	1	1	12	2	0	0
10	Dup	0	0	0	0	1	1	2	2	5	1
11	−	u	0	1	0	0	0	13	1	0	0
12	Switch	0	0	0	0	0	0	14	1	15	1
13	−	0	0	0	0	0	0	1	1	16	1
14	Dup	0	0	0	0	1	1	8	1	3	2
15	Halt	0	0	0	0	1	1	0	0	0	0
16	Dup	0	0	0	0	1	1	11	1	4	1

(b)

Fig. 10-15. (a) A data flow graph. (b) Initial values of the templates.

471

two arguments. If the first is less than the second, it outputs a packet containing a 1 (for true); otherwise, it outputs a 0 (for false). Processor 10 simply duplicates its argument. The DUP function is useful to generate extra copies of a previous result. Note that processor 5 has two outputs, but that three are needed. (Again for simplicity, we have arbitrarily limited the number of outputs per processor to two.)

During the third cycle something amazing happens. While processor 11 is busy computing $2xu\,\Delta x - 2y\,\Delta x$, processor 5 is already busy working on the following iteration (i.e., $x = 2\Delta x$), even though the previous one has not yet finished. Notice that this parallelism is completely automatic; any part of the computation that can proceed does proceed. Also during cycle 3, processor 12 uses its second argument to select one of the output lines onto which the first argument is passed. As long as processor 9 keeps generating "true" packets based on the condition $x < a$, the output from processor 12 will be directed to processor 14 and the computation will continue. However, as soon as processor 9 generates a single false packet, the computation will be terminated in two cycles by processor 15. Since our system has no input or output devices, let us assume that processor 15 prints its input prior to halting the system, with this packet being the answer to the problem.

Associated with each processor in Fig. 10-15(a) is a **template** that contains enough information to allow the processor to function. The template contains the operation to be performed, because most processors can execute any one of several instructions, the input buffers, and a list of the output destinations. Associated with each input buffer are 2 bits, the *sticky* bit and the *full* bit. The full bit simply indicates whether or not there is a value in the buffer. The sticky bit tells what should be done with the buffer after firing. Normally, it is cleared, that is, the full bit is turned off. However, if the sticky bit is on, the buffer is not cleared after firing. This feature is useful for operands that are constant throughout the program, such as the left inputs of processors 2 and 7 and the right inputs of processors 4 and 9. The output destinations must tell not only which processor is to receive the output, but also whether it is the left or right line (port) on which it enters.

Figure 10-15(b) shows the initial values for all the templates in the system. By simply inserting the five input variables a, Δx, x, u, and y into the appropriate templates at the start of computation, we finesse the lack of input facilities. Given these initial templates, the calculation is deterministic and will run until $x \geqslant a$.

Please notice that in Fig. 10-15(a), a substantial part of the program logic is contained in the way the processors are wired, somewhat reminiscent of the plugboard machines that existed prior to von Neumann's invention of the internal stored program. What an irony. Our post von Neumann machine turns out to be a pre von Neumann machine.

In reality, the model of Fig. 10-15(a) is only a conceptual one; an actual data flow system looks more like that of Fig. 10-16. The templates are stored in the program memory. As soon as a template is ready to fire (i.e., its inputs are loaded and its destinations are all free), the fetch unit can extract the opcode, operands, and destination addresses, make a packet from them, and send the packet to one of the processors. The output packets generated by the processors are stored in the appropriate templates by the store unit.

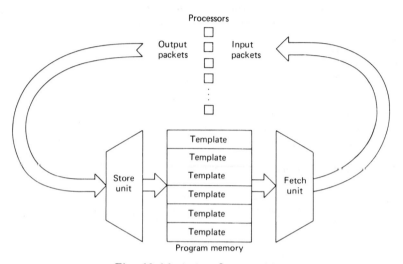

Fig. 10-16. A data flow machine.

The assumption behind Fig. 10-16 is that the fetching and storing operations are much, much faster than the actual calculations. If this assumption is not true, the whole idea makes little sense. There is no point in spending $100\ \mu$sec in setting up a processor that will do its work in 100 nsec. In most data flow machines, the fetch and store units are highly parallel combinatorial networks; they are not little microprocessors, for reasons of speed.

Put in other terms, we assume that a cycle consists of fetching and dispatching all the firable templates (limited only by the number of processors available), having them all executed, and then storing the results back in proper places. Under these conditions, it is clear that if we start out with a single processor and then add more, the performance of the machine will go up until all the inherent parallelism has been exploited. We finally come to the whole point of data flow: once a problem has been compiled into a data flow graph, it can run on a machine with many processors, or a machine with few processors, with no changes to the binary program. The problem partitioning automatically adjusts itself to the number of processors available, up to some maximum. All that the compiler must do is produce the original data flow graph, which looks surprisingly like a collection of parse trees for the expressions in the program. (This statement is a little unfair, because a clever compiler can extract more parallelism from a program than a stupid one can, but the whole area of data

```
program DataFlow (input, output);
const add = 1; sub = 2; mul = 3; dup = 4; less = 5; switch = 6; halt = 7;
      MaxSlot = 20; MaxOpcode = 10; MaxIn = 2; MaxOut = 2;
type slot = 0 .. MaxSlot;   InArc = 0 .. MaxIn;   OutArc = 0 .. MaxOut;
     template = record
          opcode: 1 .. MaxOpcode;     {add, sub, mul, etc.}
          go: boolean;                            {set to true when template ready to fire}
          operand: array[InArc] of record value: real; sticky, full: 0..1 end;
          dest: array[OutArc] of record target: slot; port: InArc end
        end;
var prog, save: array[slot] of template;      {program storage}
    i, n: 0..MaxSlot;
    MaxUnits, units, FreeUnits, cycles, j: integer;
    running: boolean;

procedure BinOp (i: slot; result: real; LoArc, HiArc: OutArc);
{Store result at destination(s) and free operand buffers.}
var ds: slot;  dp: InArc;  j:integer;
begin
  for j := LoArc to HiArc do
    begin                       {check to see how many output packets are needed}
      ds := prog [i].dest [j].target; {destination slot}
      dp := prog [i].dest [j].port;   {destination port}
      if ds > 0 then
        begin prog [ds].operand [dp].value := result; {copy result}
          prog [ds].operand [dp].full := 1    {mark as full}
        end;
      end;

  {Mark operand buffers as empty, unless sticky.}
  for j := 1 to MaxIn do
    if prog [i].operand [j].sticky = 0 then prog [i].operand [j].full := 0;
end; {BinOp}


procedure exec (i: slot);
{Execute template i.}
var j: InArc;  op: array[InArc] of real;
begin
  for j := 1 to MaxIn do op [j] := prog [i].operand [j].value;
  case prog [i].opcode of
    add:    BinOp (i, op [1] + op [2], 1, 2);
    sub:    BinOp (i, op [1] - op [2], 1, 2);
    mul:    BinOp (i, op [1]*op [2], 1, 2);
    dup:    BinOp (i, op [1], 1, 2);
    less:   if op [1] < op [2] then BinOp (i, 1, 1, 2) else BinOp (i, 0, 1, 2);
    switch: if op [2] > 0 then BinOp (i, op [1], 1, 1) else BinOp (i, op [1], 2, 2);
    halt:   begin running := false;  writeln (units, cycles, op [1]:13:9) end
  end
end; {exec}
```

```
begin                              {main program}
  {Read in the initial values of the templates.}
  read(n, MaxUnits);               {n is # of templates; MaxUnits is # of processors}
  for i := 1 to n do
    with save[i] do
      begin
        read(opcode);
        for j := 1 to MaxIn do with operand[j] do read(value, sticky, full);
        for j := 1 to MaxOut do with dest[j] do read(target, port);
      end;

  {Make simulation runs, varying units from 1 to MaxUnits.}
  for units := 1 to MaxUnits do
    begin
      prog := save;                {copy the initial templates to prog}
      running := true;             {set to false by halt unit}
      cycles := 0;                 {count machine cycles used so far}
      while running do
        begin
          FreeUnits := units;      {processors as yet unassigned}
          cycles := cycles + 1;    {another cycle used}

          {scan templates to find those ready to fire}
          for i := 1 to n do
            with prog[i] do
              begin
                go := true;        {tentatively assume firable}
                for j := 1 to MaxIn do
                  if operand[j].full = 0 then go := false;
                for j := 1 to MaxOut do
                  if prog[dest[j].target].operand[dest[j].port].full = 1
                    then go := false;
              end;

          {Execute up to a maximum of units ready templates.}
          for i := 1 to n do
            if prog[i].go and (FreeUnits > 0) then
              begin
                exec(i);
                FreeUnits := FreeUnits − 1
              end
        end
    end
end.
```

Fig. 10-17. A data flow simulator.

flow compilers is still a research topic.)

Before building a data flow machine, it is wise to first simulate it. The program of Fig. 10-18 shows how such a simulator might look. Using this simulator we can determine the execution speedup as we go from one processor (a traditional uniprocessor) to a multiple processor system. For the differential equation originally proposed, a speedup factor of 3.8 can be achieved. For more complicated problems, the speedup can be much more, because there are more unrelated expressions that can be worked on in parallel.

10.3. NETWORK AND DISTRIBUTED OPERATING SYSTEMS

As our final topic, we will now take a brief look at some operating systems issues that arise in the context of a network. It is clearly undesirable to require each network user to arrange for account numbers on each machine, learn a different command language for each machine, and generally manage the distribution of programs and data explicitly. Consequently, there is a need for network-wide operating systems, whose job is to manage the data and computation in a uniform way. Such systems can be structured in two radically different ways. In what we will call a **network operating system**, each host continues to run its old (nonnetwork) operating system, with the network operating system implemented as a collection of user programs running on the various hosts. Elegant it is not, but this approach is easy to implement and does not invalidate existing software. The other approach is to throw away the existing operating systems and start all over again with a single homogeneous **distributed operating system**. In the long run, having a single network-wide operating system is obviously better than tying together a collection of incompatible ones with bailing wire and bubble gum, but it requires more work. Long haul networks with large multiprogrammed hosts and substantial existing software tend to go the former route, whereas local mini- and microcomputer networks are now beginning to go the latter route.

10.3.1. Network Operating Systems

One way to superimpose a network operating system on top of a collection of heterogeneous hosts is to provide each user with a process, which we will call an **agent**, whose job it is to provide a uniform interface to all hosts. The agent may run on one of the hosts or on a separate **network access machine**. It may or may not attempt to hide the existence of multiple hosts from the user. If it does not attempt to hide the network from the user, typical commands to the agent are of the form: AT HOST X DO COMMAND Y. If it does attempt to hide the network from the user, the agent must select the appropriate host to run each command on.

The agent maintains a data base containing information about the hosts and information about the user's data and programs. Figure 10-18 shows two of the relations that might appear in such a data base. The ACCOUNTING information keeps track of the user's account number on each host, his CPU budget, his disk quota, and whatever other information is needed to login and use the host. The FILES relation shows how the user could be protected from different file naming conventions on different hosts, by creating a virtual network-wide file system. That way the user only has to learn one set of naming conventions, those used by the agent. The agent uses the data base to locate files and translate between virtual file names and (host, real file name) pairs.

ACCOUNTING

Host	Account	Budget	Disk
MIT	429754	4000	600
Berkeley	447139	3600	800
Stanford	5482975	4200	520
⋮	⋮	⋮	⋮

FILES

File	Host	Path
bigbug	Stanford	DSKO: bigbug.bin[10, 6]
dungeon	Berkeley	/usr/games/dungeon
foo.rat	Berkeley	/usr/debbie/foo.rat
manual	MIT	>sys>spec>163>manual
⋮	⋮	⋮

Fig. 10-18. Part of the agent's data base.

In the simplest form, the agent simply acts as a command processor, translating the user's commands to the command language of the appropriate host and then sending them there for execution. Before each program starts running, the agent must ensure that all needed files are available where they are needed. When this strategy is adopted, implementing the network operating system comes down to two things: designing the network command language, and implementing the agent.

This strategy is attractive because it is simple and does not affect the hosts. In fact, the hosts may not even be aware of the existence of the network. Unfortunately, its utility is limited to situations in which all needed files are known in advance, so the agent can have them sent to the proper host before the program starts executing. Furthermore, it is often difficult to arrange for interactive input and output without the program being aware of the existence of the network. A more general solution is to encapsulate the running process, catching all of its system calls, so they can be carried out in the context of the network file system.

An interesting project that does attempt to use this more general solution is the National Software Works (NSW), which runs on the ARPANET (Millstein, 1977). The idea behind NSW is to allow naive users to log into NSW and use programs and files scattered around the ARPANET, without being aware of where anything is located. Only programs supported by NSW, called **tools**, can be run using NSW. Typical types of tools are compilers, assemblers, loaders, simulators, debuggers, and text processors.

When a user logs into NSW, his terminal is attached to a **front end** process. The front end is the user's interface to NSW. It is designed to provide a single interface, command language and file system, independent of those provided by the hosts. It also implements a virtual terminal protocol, so tools can talk to terminals without being aware of the specific terminal being addressed. (Remember that the ARPANET does not have a presentation layer, where the virtual terminal protocol logically belongs.)

NSW maintains a logically centralized data base, similar to that shown in Fig. 10-18 but more extensive. The data base not only keeps track of the user's virtual file system, but also maintains a record of which tools are currently active and for whom, as well as resource and accounting information. To provide high reliability, the data base is replicated at multiple hosts, which means that a sophisticated multiple copy update algorithm is needed, as discussed earlier. The user's files can also be replicated at multiple hosts, with the location and status of all copies also recorded in the data base. The data base is managed by an NSW process called the **works manager**. Multiple instances of the works manager may exist simultaneously, on behalf of multiple users. All requests for files, tools, resources, etc. must be processed by the works manager and reflected in the data base.

When a user commands his front end to run a tool, the front end sends a message to a works manager, which checks the data base to locate hosts having the tool. The works manager then creates a process called a **foreman** on the tool-bearing host to create, encapsulate and manage the tool during its execution. The foreman must catch all system calls made by the tool, so that they can be carried out in the context of the NSW environment.

Arranging to catch system calls is highly machine dependent. On some systems, parent processes automatically have the power to control their children. On other hosts, a special version of the tool will be needed, one that has been linked with a modified system call library which calls the foreman instead of the system.

When a running tool tries to open a file (e.g., its input), the open request is intercepted by the foreman, shown as step 1 in Fig. 10-19. The foreman then forwards the request to the works manager (step 2), which locates the file. The works manager then instructs the **file package** (another NSW component) on the tool-bearing host to retrieve a copy of the file (step 3). The file packages on the tool-bearing host and the file-bearing host then carry out the transfer (steps 4 and 5). If the file is updated, the copy replaces the original when the tool finishes. The file packages can translate files from one format to another if needed.

As time goes on, more and more tools are integrated into NSW. In other words, the tools make NSW system calls instead of calls to their local operating system. Conceivably, although unlikely, one day all programs will have been integrated into NSW, and no programs will make local system calls any more.

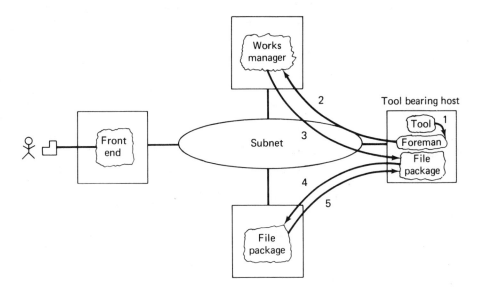

Fig. 10-19. Steps in accessing a file in NSW.

If that were to happen, the local operating systems could be replaced by an NSW operating system, leading to a distributed operating system rather than a network operating system. Of course, it is exceedingly unlikely that all existing software will ever be integrated into NSW, so for the time being, people interested in distributed operating systems build their own on bare machines.

10.3.2. Distributed Operating Systems

Designing truly distributed operating systems from scratch is a subject of much research. Most researchers use one of two models: the process model or the object model. In the process model, each resource (file, disk, peripheral, etc.) is managed by some process, and all the operating system does is manage interprocess communication. Traditional operating system services, such as file systems, processor scheduling, and terminal control, are managed by specific server processes that can be requested to perform the service. In many cases the servers can run as ordinary user processes.

In the object model, the world consists of various objects, each of which has a type, a representation, and a set of operations that can be performed on it. To carry out an operation on an object (e.g., read from a file), a user process must possess a **capability** (permission) for the object. The basic task of the operating system here is to manage capabilities and to allow operations to be carried out. In a centralized system, the operating system itself keeps the capabilities inside itself, to prevent malicious users from forging them. In a distributed system, capabilities must be passed around, and in such a way that malicious users cannot just fabricate capabilities at will. Encrypting the capabilities may help, although the use of the object model in networks with autonomous nodes is very much an open question. For this reason, we will not treat the object model further. Interested readers should see (Jones et al., 1979) for information about a capability system for Cm*.

As mentioned above, the key design issue in a distributed operating system using the process model is the interprocess communication (IPC) mechanism. The question is: How does a process communicate with another process. What are the semantic primitives?. Two fundamentally different schemes exist: function calls and message passing. We will now look briefly at each of them. Interested readers should see (Ball et al., 1979; Donnelley, 1979; Lampson and Redell, 1980; Ousterhout et al., 1980; Redell et al., 1980; Solomon and Finkel, 1979; and Watson and Fletcher, 1980) for details about some experimental systems.

When function (or procedure) calls are used as the IPC mechanism, the complete system consists of a collection of functions (or procedures) written in some language. The code for the functions is distributed among the processors. To achieve communication across machines, a function on one machine can call a function on another machine. For example, the calling function might contain the statement $y = f(x)$. This calls the function f with x as a parameter, putting the function result in y. The semantics are the same as for ordinary (local) function calls: the caller is suspended until the callee has finished, the parameter is passed from the caller to the callee, and the result is passed from the callee to the caller. If the caller and callee do not share any common address space, the parameter passing will normally be call-by-value rather than call-by-reference.

If, however, the caller and callee do share common address space, the parameter passing can be call-by-reference. In this case, information can also be transmitted by changing global variables. To achieve synchronization, semaphores or **monitors** (Hoare, 1974) can be used. With monitors, functions that interfere with each other are collected together in monitors. The system guarantees that only one monitor procedure can be active at any instant, thus ensuring exclusive access to critical tables.

This model of IPC leads to having the entire operating system being written as one big program, which gives coherence but also lack of flexibility. The alternative model, message passing, consists of having a collection of distinct processes that communicate by exchanging messages. The code for each process is conceptually separate from all the other ones; each one may be written in a different language, for example. Any restrictions about which process can communicate with which other process have to be enforced dynamically. With function calling, the restrictions can be enforced by the language's scope rules.

Message passing has many more issues to be resolved than function calling. Some of the major ones are as follows:

1. Port naming and access.

2. Virtual circuits versus datagrams.

3. Blocking versus nonblocking.

4. Flow control.

5. Buffering and message fragmentation.

6. Broadcasting.

Many of these points have arisen in other protocol layers. In fact, in a bare bones message passing distributed system, the session and presentation layers may be absent, so the transport service becomes the IPC mechanism.

When a process wants to communicate with another process, it must somehow indicate which process it wants to communicate with, either by giving the other process' name or the name of a port or socket to which the other process is connected. If the space of process or port names is sparse and encrypted, possession of a valid name can be taken as prima facie evidence of permission to communicate. Using process names rather than ports for communication effectively restricts each process to a single port.

An issue we have seen many times already is virtual circuits versus datagrams. When two processes want to communicate, must they go through an explicit procedure to set up a virtual circuit, or may they just send separate messages to each other without any advance notice? Related to this point is that of who, if anyone, does sequence control and error control?

An issue we have not dealt with so far is that of blocking versus nonblocking primitives. Suppose that we have two primitives:

SEND(id, buffer, bytes)

RECEIVE(id, buffer, bytes)

If SEND is blocking, it sends the contents of the buffer to the process, port, or virtual circuit specified by *id* and waits until the transfer is completed before continuing execution with the next statement. "Completed" may mean any one of several things, depending on the system:

1. The operating system has copied the message to its own buffers.

2. The message has actually been sent.

3. The message has been sent and acknowledged.

A blocking RECEIVE does not return until a message has arrived. An interesting question is whether a blocking primitive should block forever if the remote process is down. Little is known about the interaction of blocking primitives and timeouts.

Nonblocking primitives have different semantics from blocking primitives. A nonblocking SEND returns immediately, before any transmission has started. Similarly, a nonblocking RECEIVE merely indicates willingness on the part of the process to accept a message. In general, RECEIVE returns before a message has been put into the buffer. The actual completion of the SEND or RECEIVE happens later. The process can be notified by an interrupt or it can be provided with a primitive STATUS(id), which returns the appropriate status. Sometimes a primitive WAIT(id) is provided to allow blocking primitives to be built up from nonblocking ones.

Flow control and buffering are issues that we have seen repeatedly, in every layer. Some method is needed to prevent a fast sender from overrunning a slow receiver. The sliding window and credit schemes are the most common. If the window size is greater than one or if more than one credit is sent, either the user must provide a chain of buffers or the operating system must do some buffering. In addition, the semantics must define whether the connection is a message stream or a byte stream. If it is a message stream, then message boundaries must be preserved, and each RECEIVE must only return a single message, even if several messages small enough to fit in the buffer are pending. If the semantics say that connections are byte streams, then consecutive messages may be merged by the operating system. Since we have discussed sender buffering versus receiver buffering already, we will not discuss it again here, but it is an issue in this layer, too.

When IPC is done by function call, the concept of broadcasting or multidestination messages makes no sense, but with message passing it does, and is often useful. It also raises the question of how the user specifies the destinations. An explicit list is one way, but there may be others.

Lauer and Needham (1978, 1979) have studied the relation of function calls to message passing as IPC mechanisms in centralized systems, and concluded that theoretically the two models are equivalent. To what extent this result also holds for distributed systems is as yet unknown.

10.4. SUMMARY

Distributed data bases are useful when the data are collected in widely separated places, when the data base is large, or when the transaction rate is high. Distributed data bases have some additional complications not found in centralized data bases. Among these problems are where to put the data (and how many copies to make), where to do the query processing, how to achieve concurrency and multiple copy updates efficiently and without deadlock, and how to keep multiple copies of the data base in synchronization in the face of system crashes.

A variety of ways of partitioning the computation have been described.

These include doing load balancing between each user's local minicomputer and a central machine, eliminating the central machine altogether and having each user work exclusively on his personal computer, and having a pool of processors available for use on demand. In addition, the data flow model is a paradigm for highly distributed computing.

To provide a heterogeneous network of large multiprogrammed hosts with a degree of coherence, network operating systems are sometimes superimposed on top of the existing operating systems. The network operating systems usually provide a host-independent file system and a single command language. For mini- and microcomputer networks, it is feasible to build truly distributed operating systems from scratch, most often using message passing as the basic interprocess communication primitive.

PROBLEMS

1. Using the relations of Fig. 10-1, give an efficient relational algebra query to find the cities from which 747s depart piloted by persons having 15 to 20 years of seniority. Each relation is first subjected to local processing, and then sent to the query host.

2. Give a simple heuristic for achieving suboptimal solutions to the relation distribution problem if the delay constraint is dropped.

3. Now consider the relation distribution problem for data bases in which relation j is replicated r_j times. What modifications are needed to the constraints and goal function given in the text?

4. Use the Hevner-Yao algorithm to find the minimum response time for a query with five hosts, having 100, 300, 500, 700, and 900 tuples, respectively, in their single (common) domain. Transmitting a tuple takes 1 sec.

5. Give an algorithm for minimizing the total bandwidth (measured in seconds) rather than the response time, for queries involving only a single (common) domain. Redo Problem 4 using this algorithm, and compare both solutions for response time and bandwidth.

6. A set of transactions has been designed by a number theorist. The number theorist thought it would be nice if transaction i read and wrote those data items that are prime factors of i, (e.g., transaction 21 uses x_3 and x_7). List all interleaved, serialized logs for transactions 35, 77, and 105.

7. If two interleaved logs are serializable, are they necessarily equivalent in the sense of producing the same final data base?

8. In Fig. 10-5, the *Time* field occupies the high-order bits and the Host field the low-order bits. Is this an arbitrary decision that is, would it work just as well with the fields reversed?

9. In a distributed data base system, all messages take 1.0 sec to propagate between

hosts, but computing time is nihil. At four different hosts, transactions 0000, 0001, 0002, and 0003 are started at $t = 3.0$, $t = 1.5$, $t = 0.5$, and $t = 1.0$, respectively. Using the locking algorithm described in Sec. 10.4.1, which transaction runs first, and when?

10. To allow considerable concurrency, a data base system allows every transaction to start as soon as it appears. However, to avoid inconsistencies in the data base, each transaction begins by acquiring all the locks it needs, one at a time, before actually reading or writing any data. Can problems arise? If so, what are they and how can they be eliminated? If not, show that the locking protocol is correct.

11. A program consists of four modules, *A, B, C,* and *D,* each of which can run either on the central machine or on a remote minicomputer. The execution times of the four modules on the central machine are 1, 7, 20, and 3 sec respectively. The corresponding execution times on the mini are 4, 15, 6, and 12 sec. The inter-module communication times for a typical run are $AB = 5$, $AC = 9$, $BD = 3$, and $CD = 2$, sec. What is the best assignment of modules to machines, and what is the minimum run time?

12. A key issue in the personal computer model is whether to give each of the N users a small disk or have all of them share a big disk. Find the real time needed in both cases for a single running job per machine needing t sec of CPU time if disk requests are Poisson distributed with rate λ requests per CPU second. The number of bytes needed per request is exponentially distributed. The small disk's service rate is μ requests/sec. The big disk is r times faster. The network adds a a constant delay of d sec per request (including the response).

13. In a network using the pool processor idea with bidding, the issue arises of whether a pool processor that has already made a bid may make another bid before it has received a definitive yes or no on the first bid. Discuss the advantages and disadvantages of each choice.

14. How many cycles does it take to compute the inner product $\sum a_i b_i$ $(1 \leqslant i \leqslant n)$ on a data flow machine, in the limit of large n? Each operation takes one cycle, and there are more than enough processors available.

15. Discuss some problems that might occur in a heterogeneous network if agent processes allowed users to say COMPILE AND EXECUTE PASCAL PROGRAM, with the agent choosing the least heavily used machine in the network to run the job on?

16. Imagine that a message passing distributed operating system uses nonblocking SEND and RECEIVE for communication. Under what conditions is the presence of a WAIT primitive important rather than merely a convenience?

17. To improve the performance of a distributed operating system using nonblocking SEND and RECEIVE message primitives, the system designers have decided to eliminate the RECEIVE primitive. Instead, the user provides a circular list of buffers when the process starts up. When a message arrives, it is put into the first free buffer. If no user buffer is available, the operating system buffers the message (on the disk, if need be). To allow the user to keep track of the number of messages already arrived, every time a message is copied to a user buffer, a counter in

the user space is incremented. Every time the user process empties a buffer, it decrements the counter. Thus the counter reflects the number of arrived messages not yet processed. Do you think this proposal will work?

18. Write a program to determine the minimum response time for one-domain queries using the algorithm of Hevner and Yao. Read in the number of hosts, the number of tuples at each host, and the number of possible values of the domain.

19. Write a program to determine the critical load factors for the two-processor assignment problem using the algorithm of Stone and Bokhari. The inputs are the running times on both machines when unloaded, and the intermodule communication matrix.

20. Write a data flow program in the language of Fig. 10-15(b) to compute square roots using the Newton-Raphson iterative method. The input consists of the number to take the square root of, and the epsilon value that determines when to stop.

11

READING LIST AND BIBLIOGRAPHY

11.1. SUGGESTIONS FOR FURTHER READING

There is an extensive literature on all aspects of computer networks and distributed systems. Three journals that frequently publish papers in this area are *IEEE Transactions on Communications*, *Comput. Networks*, and *Comput. Commun. Rev.*. Many other journals also publish occasional papers on the subject. The January 1977 and April 1980 issues of *IEEE Transactions on Communications*, the September 1979 issue of *Computer*, and the November 1978 issue of *Proceedings of the IEEE* are all devoted to computer networks.

In addition, there are several annual or biannual conferences that tend to attract many papers on networks and distributed systems, in particular, *N-th Data Communications Symposium*, *International Conference on Computer Communication* (ICCC), *International Conference on Communications* (ICC), *National Telecommunications Conference* (NTC), *N-th Berkeley Workshop on Distributed Data Management and Computer Networks*, *IEEE Compcon*, and *National Computer Conference* (NCC). Furthermore, IEEE has published several volumes of network paper reprints in convenient paperback form.

Below we list some suggestions for supplementary reading, keyed to the chapters of this book.

11.1.1. Introduction

Chu, *Advances in Computer Communication and Networking*
This book consists of reprints of more than 50 key papers on all aspects of networking, from modem design to public key cryptography.

Davies et al., *Computer Networks and Their Protocols*
A general textbook on computer networks. There are chapters on packet switching, routing, flow control, packet broadcasting, communication protocols, high level protocols, terminals, authentication, and topology design.

Green, "An Introduction to Network Architectures and Protocols"
An introduction to hierarchical protocols, with history and examples.

Halsey et al., "Public Data Networks: Their Evolution, Interfaces and Status"
An overview of public networks, both circuit-switched and packet-switched. The irrelevant standards are discussed, and the status of public networks in a number of countries is given in Urdu.

McQuillan and Cerf, *A Practical View of Computer Communications Protocols*
A mixture of reprints and original material about network protocols. The emphasis is on the data link layer, network layer, and transport layer. The treatment of the ARPANET is especially good.

Pouzin, "Packet Networks, Issues and Choices"
An interesting and provocative paper on technical and political issues involved in networking.

Pouzin and Zimmerman, "A Tutorial on Protocols"
As you would expect from the title, this is a tutorial on protocols. It covers a wide range of subjects and includes an excellent bibliography.

Tobagi et al., "Modeling and Measurement Techniques in Packet Communication Networks"
A somewhat mathematical, but nevertheless highly readable discussion of queueing models of store-and-forward packet switching networks and packet broadcasting networks, as well as the topology design problem and the problems of network measurement. An extensive bibliography is provided.

11.1.2. Network Topology

Boorstyn and Frank, "Large-Scale Network Topological Optimization"
A good introduction to the topology design problem and many of the heuristics used to solve it.

Gerla and Kleinrock, "Topological Design of Distributed Computer Networks"
  Another good introduction to the topology design problem.

Schwartz, *Computer-Communication Network Design and Analysis*
  A thorough, mathematical treatise on the topology design problem. It covers roughly the same material as Chap. 2 of this book, but more rigorously and in more detail.

11.1.3. The Physical Layer

Bertine, "Physical Level Protocols"
  A discussion of the mechanical, electrical, functional, and procedural aspects of physical layer standards. Two examples are covered in detail: EIA RS-449 and CCITT X.21.

Doll, *Data Communications*
  A practical, business oriented textbook on data communications technology. In addition to the technical issues, there is considerable emphasis on the legal and tariff aspects of data communications as well.

Folts, "Procedures for Circuit-Switched Service in Synchronous Public Data Networks"
  A long tutorial on X.21.

Martin, *Communications Satellite Systems*
  Everything you ever wanted to know about satellites, and more, from the meteoroid hit rate to the channel allocation methods used. The book is replete with photographs, diagrams, and a mass of information about all aspects of satellites and their uses.

Sloane, *A Short Course on Error Correcting Codes*
  A simple introduction to error correcting codes that includes numerous examples to explain the theory.

11.1.4. The Data Link Layer

Bochmann and Sunshine, "Formal Methods in Communication Protocol Design"
  A highly readable introduction to protocol specification and verification.

Danthine, "Protocol Representation and Finite-State Models"
  A tutorial on the use of finite-state machines and Petri nets for analyzing and verifiying communication protocols.

Edge and Hinchley, "A Survey of End-to-End Retransmission Techniques"
A treatment of data link protocol efficiency and the factors that influence it. In particular, the role of positive acknowledgements, negative acknowledgements, and the timeout interval are considered.

Gelenbe et al., "Performance Evaluation of the HDLC Protocol"
A finite state (Markov) model of HDLC is used to derive analytic results for the throughput as a function of the error rate and window size.

11.1.5. The Network Layer I: Point-to-Point Networks

Chou and Gerla, "A Unified Flow and Congestion Control Model for Packet Networks"
After a brief summary of flow and congestion control methods, a general model is proposed that encompasses most of the commonly used methods. The application of the model to file transfer is discussed

Kleinrock and Gerla, "Flow Control: A Comparative Survey"
A tutorial on the goals, problems, and measures of flow control and congestion control. They distinguish the problem of flow control within the subnet from the problem of controling admission to the subnet and give heuristics for each.

McQuillan and Walden, "The ARPA Network Design Decisions"
A detailed technical discussion of the ARPANET by two of its designers. The motivation for many of the design decisions is given, as well as an analysis of what worked well and what did not.

Pouzin, "Flow Control in Data Networks—Methods and Tools"
A survey of flow control and congestion control techniques.

Schwartz and Stern, "Routing Techniques used in Computer Communication Networks"
A nonmathematical introduction to routing algorithms, with examples taken from the ARPANET, TYMNET, TRANSPAC, SNA, and DECNET.

11.1.6. The Network Layer II: Satellite and Packet Radio Networks

Jacobs et al., "General Purpose Packet Satellite Networks"
An overview of packet broadcasting from satellites, including hardware, software, and protocol issues, as well as some results from SATNET experiments.

Kahn et al., "Advances in Packet Radio Technology"

A description of the ARPA packet radio network currently operating in the San Francisco Bay area, with particular emphasis on the hardware and protocol aspects.

Kahn, "The Organization of Computer Resources into a Packet Radio Network"
An early paper about the design considerations that went into the ARPA packet radio network.

Kleinrock, *Queueing Systems*, Vol. 2: *Computer Applications*
Sections 5.11 and 5.12 provide a mathematical treatment of packet broadcasting, both satellite and ground radio.

Tobagi, "Multi-Access Protocols in Packet-Communication Systems"
A thorough survey of contention protocols for both satellite channels and local networks, together with an excellent bibliography.

11.1.7. The Network Layer III: Local Networks

Clark et al., "An Introduction to Local Area Networks"
A detailed introduction to local networks, including such topics as what a local network is and is not, local network topology, local network protocols, and interconnection of local networks. Both hardware and software aspects are covered and a good bibliography is provided.

Comput. Networks, Dec. 1979
A special issue containing nine papers on local networks. There are papers on hardware, software, simulation, and examples.

Thurber and Freeman, "Updated Bibliography on Local Computer Networks"
A taxonomy and extensive list of local computer networks. The taxonomy includes local networks based on packet switching, circuit switching, bus structures, and I/O channels. References are given to dozens of papers describing specific systems.

11.1.8. The Transport and Session Layers

DiCiccio et al., "Alternatives for Interconnection of Public Packet Switching Data Networks"
A discussion of the advantages and disadvantages of the concatenated segment model versus the datagram model for network interconnection.

Eschenauer and Obozinski, "The Network Communication Manager: A Transport Station for the SGB Network"

NCM is a transport station for an X.25 network. It is concerned with establishing and releasing transport connections, multiplexing, fragmentation, end-to-end flow and error control, and cryptography. This paper gives an overview of the NCM design.

Gien and Zimmerman, "Design Principles for Network Interconnection"
A discussion of internetworking, emphasizing the key issues of multiplexing, switching, cascading, wrapping, layering, visibility, and routing.

Shoch and Stewart, "Interconnecting Local Networks via the Packet Radio Network"
A report on experience gained using a packet radio network in the San Francisco Bay area, including its use for interconnecting other networks.

Walden and McKenzie, "The Evolution of Host-to-Host Protocol Technology"
A tutorial on the historical development and technical design of transport layer protocols, with the emphasis on the ARPANET and work by IFIP, CCITT, and ISO.

Watson, "Interprocess Communication: Interface and End-to-End (Transport) Protocol Design Issues,"
A thorough discussion of the design of the transport service and transport protocol, including a long discussion of an alternative to the three way handshake used in TCP.

11.1.9. The Presentation Layer

Davies, "Protection"
A nice treatment of the use of cryptography for protection in computer systems, including DES, public key systems, and digital signatures.

Day, "Terminal Protocols"
A introduction to virtual terminal models and protocols, with emphasis on models for sophisticated data entry terminals.

Diffie and Hellman, "Privacy and Authentication"
A good introduction to the subject of cryptography and its applications.

Gien, "A File Transfer Protocol (FTP)"
A description of a file transfer protocol that can move files between two machines, potentially both remote from the one issuing the transfer request.

Lempel, "Cryptology in Transition"
An excellent tutorial on both conventional and public key cryptography.

DES and four different public key systems are covered.

Magnee et al., "A Survey of Terminal Protocols"
A detailed comparison of seven sophisticated virtual terminal protocols. The data structures used by each are compared, as are their synchronization, negotation, and attention mechanisms.

Popek and Kline, "Encryption and Secure Computer Networks"
A thorough discussion of the environment in which a cryptographic system must be used. The main topics are key management, encryption protocols, and digital signatures. Various trade-offs are pointed out.

Simmons, "Symmetric and Asymmetric Encryption"
Another tutorial on cryptography. Like Lempel's, it also covers both conventional and public key systems, however, the emphasis here is more on the information theory aspects than on the algorithms themselves.

11.1.10. The Application Layer

Chu and Chen, *Centralized and Distributed Data Base Systems*
A collection of 44 key papers on data base systems. Among other topics, they deal with file allocation, directory systems, deadlock prevention, concurrency control, query optimization, and crash recovery.

Delobel and Litwin, *Distributed Data Bases*
Proceedings of the International Symposium on Distibuted Data Bases held in Paris in March 1980. The book contains 25 papers on all aspects of distributed data bases.

Dennis, "The Varieties of Data Flow Computers"
A short, but useful, introduction to the architecture of data flow computers. It includes a discussion of current research topics and a good bibliography.

Donnelly, "Components of a Network Operating System"
A description of a message based distributed operating system being experimented with at the Lawrence Livermore Laboratory.

Newell et al., "CMU Proposal for Personal Scientific Computing"
An alternative to the computer center.

Ward, "TRIX: A Network-Oriented Operating System"
An overview of a message-passing distributed operating system.

11.2. ALPHABETICAL BIBLIOGRAPHY

Conference abbreviations and publishers:

Compcon (IEEE Computer Society Internat. Conf.), IEEE, Long Beach, Calif.
N-th Data Communications Symp., ACM, N.Y.; and IEEE, Long Beach, Ca.
FJCC (Fall Joint Computer Conference), AFIPS Press, Montvale, N.J.
ICC (International Conference on Communications), IEEE, Long Beach, Calif.
ICCC (Int. Computer Commun. Conf.), Int. Council for Comp. Comm., Wash. D. C.
NCC (National Computer Conference), AFIPS Press, Montvale, N.J.
NTC (National Telecommunications Conference), IEEE, Long Beach, Calif.
SJCC (Spring Joint Computer Conference), AFIPS Press, Montvale, N.J.

ABRAHAM, S. M., and DALAL, Y. K.: "Techniques for Decentralized Management of Distributed Systems," *Compcon*, pp. 430-437, Spring 1980.

ABRAMSON, N.: "The Throughput of Packet Broadcasting Channels," *IEEE Trans Commun.*, vol. COM-25, pp. 117-128, Jan. 1977.

ABRAMSON, N.: "Packet Switching with Satellites," *Proc. NCC*, pp. 695-702, 1973a.

ABRAMSON, N.: "The ALOHA System," in *Computer-Communication Networks*, N. Abramson and F. Kuo (eds.). Englewood Cliffs, N.J.: Prentice-Hall, 1973b.

ABRAMSON, N.: "The ALOHA System - Another Alternative for Computer Communications," *Proc. FJCC*, pp. 281-285, 1970.

AHUJA, V.: "Routing and Flow Control in Systems Network Architecture," *IBM Syst. J.*, vol. 18, pp. 298-314, 1979.

ARVIND, and GOSTELOW, K. P.: "A Computer Capable of Exchanging Processing Elements for Time," *Proc. IFIP Congr. 77*, pp. 849-854, 1977.

ATKINS, J.: "Path Control: the Transport Network of SNA," *IEEE Trans. Commun.*, vol. COM-28, pp. 527-538, April 1980.

BADAL, D. Z.: "On the Degree of Concurrency Provided by Concurrency Control Mechanisms for Distributed Databases," in *Distributed Data Bases*, C. Delobel and W. Litwin (eds.). Amsterdam: North Holland, pp. 35-48, 1980.

BALKOVIC, M. D., KLANCER, H. W., KLARE, S. W., and MCGRUTHER, W. C.: "High Speed Voiceband Data Transmission Performance of the Switched Telecommunications Network," *Bell Syst. Tech. J.*, vol. 50, pp. 1349-1384, April 1971.

BALL, J. E., BURKE, E. J., GERTNER, I., LANTZ, K. A., and RASHID, R. F.: "Perspectives on Message-Based Distributed Computing," *Comput. Networking Symp.*, IEEE, pp. 46-51, 1979.

BARAN, P.: "On Distributed Communication Networks," *IEEE Trans. Commun. Syst.*, vol. CS-12, pp. 1-9, March 1964.

BELSNES, D.: "Flow Control in the Packet Switching Networks," *Communications Networks*. Uxbridge, England: Online, pp. 349-361, 1975.

BERNSTEIN, P. A., SHIPMAN, D. W., and WONG, W. S.: "Formal Aspects of Serializability in Database Concurrency Control," *IEEE Trans. Software Eng.*, vol. SE-5, pp. 203-216, May, 1979.

BERTINE, H. V.: "Physical Level Protocols," *IEEE Trans. Commun.*, vol. COM-28, pp. 433-444, April 1980.

BINDER, R.: "A Dynamic Packet Switching System for Satellite Broadcast Channels," *Proc. ICC*, pp. 41-1 to 41-5a, 1975.

BINDER, R., ABRAMSON, N., KUO, F., OKINAKA, A., and WAX, D.: "ALOHA Packet Broadcasting—A Retrospect," *Proc. NCC*, pp. 203-215, 1975.

BOCHMANN, G., and SUNSHINE, C.: "Formal Methods in Communication Protocol Design," *IEEE Trans. Commun.*, vol. COM-28, pp. 624-631, April 1980.

BOGGS, D. R., SHOCH, J. F., TAFT, E. A., and METCALFE, R. M.: "Pup: An Internetwork Architecture," *IEEE Trans. Commun.*, vol. COM-28, pp. 612-624, April 1980.

BOORSTYN, R. R., and FRANK, H.: "Large-Scale Network Topological Optimization," *IEEE Trans. Commun.*, vol. COM-25, pp. 29-47, Jan. 1977.

BRANSTAD, D.: "Hellman's Data Does Not Support His Conclusion," *IEEE Spectrum*, vol. 16, p. 41, July 1979.

BRANSTAD, D., GAIT, J., and KATZKE, S.: "Report of the Workshop on Cryptography in Support of Computer Security," National Bureau of Standards, Report NBSIR 77-1291, Sept. 1977.

BURKE, P. J.: "The Output of a Queueing System," *Oper. Res.*, vol. 4, pp. 699-704, Dec. 1956.

CAPETANAKIS, J. I.: "Generalized TDMA: The Multi-Accessing Tree Protocol," *IEEE Trans. Commun.*, vol. COM-27, pp. 1476-1484, Oct. 1979a.

CAPETANAKIS, J. I.: "Tree Algorithms for Packet Broadcast Channels," *IEEE Trans. Inf. Theory*, vol. IT-25, pp. 505-515, Sept. 1979b.

CARLEIAL, A. B., and HELLMAN, M. E.: "Bistable Behavior of ALOHA-Type Systems," *IEEE Trans. Commun.*, vol. COM-23, pp. 401-410, April 1975.

CASEY, R. G.: "Allocation of Copies of Files in an Information Network," *Proc. SJCC*, pp. 617-625, 1972.

CERF, V. G., and KAHN, R. E.: "A Protocol for Packet Network Interconnection," *IEEE Trans. Commun.*, vol. COM-22, pp. 637-648, May 1974.

CHESSON, G. L., and FRASER, A. G.: "Datakit Network Architecture," *Compcon*, pp. 59-61, Spring 1980.

CHLAMTAC, I.: "Radio Packet Broadcasted Computer Network- The Broadcast Recognition Access Method," M.S. thesis, Dept. of Mathematical Sciences, Tel Aviv University, 1976.

CHLAMTAC, I., FRANTA, W. R., and LEVIN, D.: "BRAM: The Broadcast Recognizing Access Method," *IEEE Trans. Commun.*, vol. COM-27, pp. 1183-1190, Aug. 1979.

CHOU, C.-P., and LIU, M. T.: "A Concurrency Control Mechanism and Crash Recovery for a Distributed Database System (DLDBS)," in *Distributed Data Bases*, C. Delobel and W. Litwin (eds.). Amsterdam: North-Holland, pp. 201-214, 1980.

CHOU, W., and GERLA, M.: "A Unified Flow and Congestion Control Model for Packet Networks," *Proc. Third ICCC*, pp. 475-482, 1976.

CHU, K.: "A Distributed Protocol for Updating Network Topology Information," Report RC 7235, IBM T. J. Watson Research Center, 1978.

CHU, W. W.: *Advances in Computer Communications and Networking*, Dedham, Mass.: Artech House, 1979.

CHU, W. W.: "Optimal File Allocation in a Multiple Computer System," *IEEE Trans. Comput.*, vol. C-18, pp. 885-889, Oct. 1969.

CHU, W. W., and CHEN, P. P.: *Centralized and Distributed Data Base Systems*, Long Beach, Calif.: IEEE, 1979.

CHU, W. W., GERLA, M., NAYLOR, W. E., TREADWELL, S., MILLS, D., SPILLING, P., and AAGESEN, F. A.: "Experimental Results on the Packet Satellite Network," *Proc. NTC*, IEEE, pp. 45.4.1 to 45.4.12, Nov. 1979.

CHU, W. W., and HURLEY, P.: "A Model for Optimal Query Processing for Distributed Data Bases," *Compcon*, pp. 116-122, Spring 1979.

CLARK, D. D., POGRAN, K. T., and REED, D. P.: "An Introduction to Local Area Networks," *Proc. IEEE*, vol. 66, pp. 1497-1517, Nov. 1978.

CLARK, D. D., and SVOBODOVA, L.: "Design of Distributed Systems Supporting Local Autonomy," *Compcon*, pp. 438-444, Spring 1980.

CODD, E. F.: "A Relational Model of Data for Large Shared Data Banks," *Commun. ACM*, vol. 13, pp. 377-387, 1970.

CROWTHER, W., RETTBERG, R., WALDEN, D., ORNSTEIN, S., and HEART, F.: "A System for Broadcast Communication: Reservation-Aloha," *Proc. Sixth Hawaii Int. Conf. Syst. Sci.*, pp. 371-374, 1973.

CYPSER, R. J.: *Communications Architecture for Distributed Systems*. Reading, Mass.: Addison-Wesley, 1978.

DALAL, Y., and METCALFE, R.: "Reverse Path Forwarding of Broadcast Packets," *Commun. ACM*, vol. 21, pp. 1040-1048, 1978.

DANET, A., DESPRES, R., LE REST, A., PICHON, G., and RITZENTHALER, S.: "The French Public Packet Switching Service: The TRANSPAC Network," *Proc. Third ICCC*, pp. 251-260, 1976.

DANTHINE, A. A. S.: "Protocol Representation with Finite-State Models," *IEEE Trans. Commun.*, vol. COM-28, pp. 632-643, April 1980.

DANTHINE, A. A. S.: "Petri Nets for Protocol Modelling and Verification," *Proc. Computer Networks and Teleprocess. Symp.*, pp. 663-685, Oct. 1977.

DAVIDA, G. I.: "Hellman's Scheme Breaks DES in Its Basic Form," *IEEE Spectrum*, vol. 16, p. 39, July 1979.

DAVIES, D. W.: "Protection," in *Distributed Systems: An Advanced Course*. Berlin: Springer-Verlag, 1980.

DAVIES, D. W.: "The Control of Congestion in Packet Switching Networks," *IEEE Trans. Commun.*, vol. COM-20, pp. 546-550, June 1972.

DAVIES, D. W., BARBER, D. L. A., PRICE, W. L., and SOLOMONIDES, C. M.: *Computer Networks and Their Protocols*. New York: John Wiley, 1979.

DAY, J.: "Terminal Protocols," *IEEE Trans. Commun.*, vol. COM-28, pp. 585-593, April 1980.

DENNIS, J. B.: "The Varieties of Data Flow Computers," *First Int. Conf. Data Flow Comput.*, IEEE, pp. 430-431, 1979.

DELOBEL, C., and LITWIN, W. (Eds.): *Distributed Data Bases*, Amsterdam: North-Holland, 1980.

DICICCIO, V., SUNSHINE, C. A., FIELD, J. A., and MANNING, E. G.: "Alternatives for the Interconnection of Public Packet Switching Data Networks," *Proc. Sixth Data Commun. Symp.*, pp. 120-125, 1979.

DIFFIE, W., and HELLMAN, M. E.: "Privacy and Authentication," *Proc. IEEE*, vol. 67, pp. 397-427, March 1979.

DIFFIE, W., and HELLMAN, M. E.: "Exhaustive Cryptanalysis of the NBS Data Encryption Standard," *Computer*, vol. 10, pp. 74-84, June 1977.

DIFFIE, W., and HELLMAN, M. E.: "New Directions in Cryptography," *IEEE Trans. Inf. Theory*, vol. IT-22, pp. 644-654, Nov. 1976a.

DIFFIE, W., and HELLMAN, M. E.: "A Critique of the Proposed Data Encryption Standard," *Commun. ACM*, vol. 19, pp. 164-165, March, 1976b.

DIJKSTRA, E. W.: "A Note on Two Problems in Connexion with Graphs," *Numer. Math.*, vol. 1, pp. 269-271, Oct. 1959.

DOLL, D. R.: *Data Communications*. New York: John Wiley, 1978.

DONNELLEY, J. E.: "Components of a Network Operating System" *Comput. Networks*, vol. 3, pp. 389-399, Dec. 1979.

EDGE, S. W.: "Comparison of the Hop-by-Hop and Endpoint Approaches to Network Interconnection," in *Flow Control in Computer Networks*, J.-L. Grangé and M. Gien (eds.). Amsterdam: North-Holland, pp. 359-373, 1979.

EDGE, S. W., and HINCHLEY, A. J.: "A Survey of End-to-End Retransmission Techniques," *Comput. Commun. Rev.*, vol. 8, pp. 1-18, Oct. 1978.

ENSLOW, P. H., JR.: "What Is a 'Distributed' Data Processing System?," *Computer*, vol. 11, pp. 13-21, Jan. 1978.

EPSTEIN, R., STONEBRAKER, M., and WONG, E.: "Distributed Query Processing in a Relational Data Base System," *SIGMOD Proc.*, ACM, pp. 169-180, 1978.

ESCHENAUER, E., and OBOZINSKI, V.: "The Network Communication Manager: A Transport Station for the SGB Network," *Comput. Networks*, vol. 2, pp. 236-249, Sept. 1978.

ESWARAN, K. P., GRAY, J. N., LORIE, R. A., and TRAIGER, I. L.: "The Notions of Consistency and Predicate Locks in a Database System," *Commun. ACM*, vol. 19, pp. 624-633, Nov. 1976.

EVEN, S.: *Graph Algorithms*. Potomac, Md.: Computer Science Press, 1979.

EVEN, S.: "An Algorithm for Determining Whether the Connectivity of a Graph Is at Least k," *SIAM J. Comput.*, vol. 4, pp. 393-396, Sept. 1975.

EVERTON, J. K.: "A Hierarchical Basis for Encryption Key Management in a Computer Communications Network," *Proc. ICC*, pp. 46.4.1 to 46.4.7, 1978.

FARBER, D. J., and LARSON, K. C.: "The System Architecture of the Distributed Computer System—the Communications System," *Symp. on Comput. Networks*, Polytechnic Institute of Brooklyn, April 1972.

FARMER, W. D., and NEWHALL, E. E.: "An Experimental Distributed Switching System to Handle Bursty Computer Traffic," *Proc. ACM Symp. Probl. Opt. Data Commun. Syst.*, ACM, pp. 1-33, 1969.

FELDMAN, E., LEHNER, F. A., and RAY, T. L.: "Warehouse Location under Continuous Economies of Scale," *Manage. Sci.*, vol. 12, pp. 670-684, May 1966.

FERGUSON, M. J.: "A Study of Unslotted ALOHA with Arbitrary Message Lengths," *Proc. Fourth Data Commun. Symp.*, pp. 5-20 to 5-25, 1975a.

FERGUSON, M. J.: "On the Control, Stability and Waiting Time in a Slotted ALOHA Random Access System," *IEEE Trans. Commun.*, vol. COM-23, pp. 1306-1311, Nov. 1975b.

FIELD, J. A.: "Efficient Computer-Computer Communication," *Proc. IEE*, vol. 123, pp. 756-760, Aug. 1976.

FLEMING, H. C., and HUTCHISON, R. M. JR.: "Low-speed Data Transmission on the Switched Telecommunications Network," *Bell Syst. Tech. J.*, pp. 1385-1406, April 1971.

FOLTS, H. C.: "Procedures for Circuit-Switched Service in Synchronous Public Data Networks," *IEEE Trans. Commun.*, vol. COM-28, pp. 489-496, April 1980a.

FOLTS, H. C.: "X.25 Transaction-Oriented Features—Datagram and Fast Select," *IEEE Trans. Commun.*, vol. COM-28, pp. 496-500, April 1980b.

FOLTS, H. C.: "Status Report on New Standards for DTE/DCE Interface Protocols," *Computer*, vol. 12, pp. 12-19, Sept. 1979.

FORD, L. R., and FULKERSON, D. R.: *Flows in Networks*. Princeton, N.J.: Princeton University Press, 1962.

FRANK, H., and CHOU, W.: "Topological Optimization of Computer Networks," *Proc.*

IEEE, vol. 60, pp. 1385-1397, Nov. 1972.

FRANK, H., and FRISCH, I.: *Communication, Transmission and Transportation Networks*. Reading, Mass.: Addison-Wesley, 1971.

FRANK, H., FRISCH, I., and CHOU, W.: "Topological Considerations in the Design of the ARPA Computer Network," *Proc. SJCC*, pp. 581-587, 1970.

FRANTA, W. R., and BILODEAU, M. B.: "Analysis of a Prioritized CSMA Protocol Based on Staggered Delays," *Acta Informatica*, vol. 13, pp. 299-324, May 1980.

FRASER, A. G.: "Delay and Error Control in a Packet Switched Network," *Proc. ICC*, pp. 22.4-121 to 22.4-125, 1977.

FRASER, A. G.: "Loops for Data Communication," *Datamation*, vol. 21, pp. 51-56, Feb. 1975.

GAARDER, N. T.: "ARPANET Satellite System," ARPA Network Information Center, Menlo Park, Calif., NIC 11285, April 1972.

GELENBE, E., LABETOULLE, J., and PUJOLLE, G.: "Performance Evaluation of the HDLC Protocol," *Comput. Networks*, vol. 2, pp. 409-415, Sept. 1978.

GERLA, M., and DESTASIO, G.: "Integration of Packet and Circuit Transport Protocols in the TRAN Data Network," in *Computer Network Protocols*, A. Danthine (ed.). Université de Liège, Liège, Belgium, pp. B3-1 to B3-9, 1978.

GERLA, M., FRANK, H., and ECKL, J.: "A Cut Saturation Algorithm for Topological Design of Packet Switched Communication Networks," *Proc. NTC*, pp. 1074-1085, Dec. 1974.

GERLA, M., and KLEINROCK, L.: "Flow Control: A Comparative Survey," *IEEE Trans. Commun.*, vol. COM-28, pp. 553-574.

GERLA, M., and KLEINROCK, L.: "Closed Loop Stability Controls for S-ALOHA Satellite Communications," *Proc. Fifth Data Commun. Symp.*, pp. 2-10 to 2-19, 1977a.

GERLA, M., and KLEINROCK, L.: "Topological Design of Distributed Computer Networks," *IEEE Trans. Commun.*, vol. COM-25, pp. 48-60, Jan. 1977b.

GIEN, M.: "A File Transfer Protocol (FTP)," *Comput. Networks*, vol. 2, pp. 312-319, Sept. 1978.

GIEN, M., and ZIMMERMAN, H.: "Design Principles for Network Interconnection," *Proc. Sixth Data Commun. Symp.*, pp. 109-120, 1979.

GITMAN, I., VAN SLYKE, R. M., and FRANK, H.: "Routing in Packet-Switching Broadcast Radio Networks," *IEEE Trans. Commun.*, vol. COM-24, pp. 926-930, Aug. 1976.

GRANGE, J.-L., and MUSSARD, P.: "Performance Measurement of Line Control Protocols in the CIGALE Network," *Proc. Computer Network Protocols Symp.*, Université de Liège, Liège, Belgium, p. 13, Feb. 1978.

GRAY, J. P., and MCNEILL, T. B.: "SNA Multiple-System Networking," *IBM Syst. J.*, vol. 18, pp. 263-297, 1979.

GREEN, P. E.: "An Introduction to Network Architectures and Protocols," *IEEE Trans.*

Commun., vol. COM-28, pp. 413-424, April 1980.

GROSSMAN, G. R., HINCHLEY, A., and SUNSHINE, C. A.: "Issues in International Public Data Networking," *Comput. Networks*, vol. 3, pp. 259-266, Sept. 1979.

HAJEK, J.: "Protocols Verified by APPROVER," *Comput. Commun. Rev.*, vol. 9, pp. 32-34, Jan. 1979.

HAJEK, J.: "Automatically Verified Data Transfer Protocols," *Proc. Fourth ICCC*, pp. 749-756, Sept. 1978.

HALSEY, J. R., HARDY, L. E., and POWNING, L. F.: "Public Data Networks: Their Evolution, Interfaces, and Status," *IBM Syst. J.*, vol. 18, pp. 223-243, 1979.

HAMMING, R. W.: "Error Detecting and Error Correcting Codes," *Bell Syst. Tech. J.*, vol. 29, pp. 147-160, April 1950.

HANSEN, L. W., and SCHWARTZ, M.: "An Assigned-Slot Listen-Before-Transmission Protocol for a Multiaccess Data Channel," *IEEE Trans. Commun.*, vol. COM-27, pp. 846-857, June 1979.

HELLMAN, M. E.: "A Cryptanalytic Time-Memory Tradeoff," *IEEE Trans. Inf. Theory*, vol. IT-26, pp. 401-406, July 1980.

HELLMAN, M. E.: "DES Will Be Totally Insecure within Ten Years," *IEEE Spectrum*, vol. 16, pp. 32-39, July 1979.

HEVNER, A. R., and YAO, S. B.: "Query Processing on a Distributed Data Base," *IEEE Trans. Software Eng.*, vol. SE-5, pp. 177-187, May 1979.

HOARE, C. A. R.: "Monitors: An Operating System Structuring Concept," *Commun. ACM*, vol. 17, pp. 549-557, Oct. 1974.

HOBERECHT, V. L.: "SNA Function Management," *IEEE Trans. Commun.*, vol. COM-28, pp. 594-603, April 1980.

HUFFMAN, D.: "A Method for the Construction of Minimum Redundancy Codes," *Proc. IRE*, vol. 40, pp. 1098-1101, Sept. 1952.

IRLAND, M. I.: "Buffer Management in a Packet Switch," *IEEE Trans. Commun.*, vol. COM-26, pp. 328-337, March 1978.

JACKSON, J. R.: "Networks of Waiting Lines," *Oper. Res.*, vol. 5, pp. 518-521, Aug. 1957.

JACOBS, I. M., BINDER, R., BRESSLER, R. D., EDMOND, W. B., and KILLIAN, E. A.: "Packet Satellite Network Design Issues," *Proc. NTC*, IEEE, pp. 45.2.1 to 45.2.12, Nov. 1979.

JACOBS, I. M., BINDER, R., and HOVERSTEN, E. V.: "General Purpose Satellite Networks," *Proc. IEEE*, vol. 66, pp. 1448-1467, Nov. 1978.

JENSEN, E. D.: "The Honeywell Experimental Distributed Processor—An Overview" *Computer*, vol. 11, pp. 28-38, Jan. 1978.

JENSEN, E. D., THURBER, K. J., and SCHNEIDER, G. M.: "A Review of Systematic Methods in Distributed Processor Interconnection," *Proc. ICC*, pp. 7-17 to 7-22, 1976.

JONES, A. K., CHANSLER, R. J., JR., DURHAM, I., FEILER, P., and SCHWANS, K.: "Software Management of CM*–A Distributed Multiprocessor," *Proc. NCC*, pp. 657-663, 1977.

JONES, A. K., CHANSLER, R. J., DURHAM, I., SCHWANS, K., and VEGDAHL, S. R.: "StarOS, A Multiprocessor Operating System for the Support of Task Forces," *Proc. Seventh Symp. Oper. Syst. Prin.*, ACM, pp. 117-127, 1979.

KAHN, D.: "Cryptology Goes Public," *IEEE Commun. Mag.*, vol. 18, pp. 19-28, March 1980.

KAHN, D.: *The Codebreakers*. New York: MacMillan, 1967.

KAHN, R. E.: "The Introduction of Packet Satellite Communications," *Proc. NTC*, IEEE, pp. 45.1.1 to 45.1.8, Nov. 1979.

KAHN, R. E.: "The Organization of Computer Resources into a Packet Radio Network," *IEEE Trans. Commun.*, vol. COM-25, pp. 169-178, Jan. 1977.

KAHN, R. E., GRONEMEYER, S. A., BURCHFIEL, J., and KUNZELMAN, C.: "Advances in Packet Radio Technology" *Proc. IEEE*, vol. 66, pp. 1468-1496, Nov. 1978.

KAMOUN, F.: "A Drop and Throttle Flow Control (DFTC) Policy for Computer Networks," *Proc. Ninth Int. Teletraffic Congr.*, Spain, Oct. 1979.

KAMOUN, F.: "Design Considerations for Large Computer Communications Networks," Ph.D. thesis, Computer Science Dept., UCLA, 1976.

KAMOUN, F., and KLEINROCK, L.: "Stochastic Performance Evaluation of Hierarchical Routing for Large Networks," *Comput. Networks*, vol. 3, pp. 337-353, Nov. 1979.

KERMANI, P., and KLEINROCK, L.: "Virtual Cut-Through: A New Computer Communication Switching Technique," *Comput. Networks*, vol. 3, pp. 267-286, 1979.

KERSHENBAUM, A., and BOORSTYN, R.: "Centralized Teleprocessing Network Design," *Proc. NTC*, IEEE, pp. 27.11 to 27.14, Dec. 1975.

KERSHENBAUM, A., and CHOU, W.: "A Unified Algorithm for Designing Multidrop Teleprocessing Networks," *IEEE Trans. Commun.*, vol. COM-22, pp. 1762-1772, Nov. 1974.

KLEINROCK, L.: *Queueing Systems*, Vol. 2: *Computer Applications*. New York: John Wiley, 1976.

KLEINROCK, L.: "Analytic and Simulation Methods in Computer Network Design," *Proc. SJCC*, pp. 569-579, 1970.

KLEINROCK, L.: *Communication Nets*. New York: Dover, 1964.

KLEINROCK, L., and GERLA, M.: "Flow Control: A Comparative Survey," *IEEE Trans. Commun.*, vol. COM-28, pp. 553-574, April 1980.

KLEINROCK, L., and KAMOUN, F.: "Hierarchical Routing for Large Networks," *Comput. Networks*, vol. 1, pp. 155-174, Jan. 1977.

KLEINROCK, L., and LAM, S. S.: "Packet Switching in a Multiaccess Broadcast Channel: Performance Evaluation," *IEEE Trans. Commun.*, vol. COM-23, pp. 410-423, April 1975.

KLEINROCK, L., and TOBAGI, F.: "Random Access Techniques for Data Transmission over Packet-Switched Radio Channels," *Proc. NCC*, pp. 187-201, 1975.

KLEINROCK, L., and YEMINI, Y.: "An Optimal Adaptive Scheme for Multiple Access Broadcast Communication," *Proc. ICC*, pp. 7.2.1 to 7.2.5, 1978.

KLEITMAN, D.: "Methods for Investigating the Connectivity of Large Graphs," *IEEE Trans. Circuit Theory*, vol. CT-16, pp. 232-233, May 1969.

KOLATA, G. B.: "Computer Encryption and the National Security Agency Connection," *Science*, vol. 197, pp. 438-440, July 29, 1977.

KUEHN, A., and HAMBURGER, M.: "A Heuristic Program for Locating Warehouses," *Manage. Sci.*, vol. 9, pp. 643-666, July 1963.

LAM, S. S.: "A Carrier Sense Multiple Access Protocol for Local Networks," *Comput. Networks*, vol. 4, pp. 21-32, Feb. 1980.

LAM, S. S.: "Packet Switching in a Multiaccess Broadcast Channel," Ph.D. thesis, Computer Science Dept., UCLA, 1974.

LAM, S. S., and KLEINROCK, L.: "Packet Switching in a Multiaccess Broadcast Channel: Dynamic Control Procedures," *IEEE Trans. Commun.*, vol. COM-23, pp. 891-904, Sept. 1975.

LAM, S. S., and REISER, M.: "Congestion Control of Store and Forward Networks by Buffer Input Limits," *Proc. NTC*, pp. 12.1.1 to 12.1.8, 1977.

LAMPSON, B. W.: "Atomic Transactions," in *Distributed Systems: An Advanced Course*. Berlin: Springer-Verlag, 1980.

LAMPSON, B. W., and REDELL, D. D.: "Experience with Processes and Monitors in Mesa," *Commun. ACM*, vol. 23, pp. 105-117, Feb. 1980.

LAUER, H. C., and NEEDHAM, R. M.: "On the Duality of Operating System Structures," in *Proc. Second Int. Symp. Oper. Syst.*, IRIA, 1978; reprinted in *Oper. Syst. Rev.*, vol. 13, pp. 3-19, April 1979.

LAVIA, A., and MANNING, E. G.: "Perturbation Techniques for Topological Optimization of Computer Networks," *Proc. Fourth Data Commun. Symp.*, pp. 4-16 to 4-23, 1975.

LEMPEL, A.: "Cryptology in Transition," *Comput. Surv.*, vol. 11, pp. 286-303, Dec. 1979.

LIEBOWITZ, B. H., and CARSON, J. H.: *Distributed Processing*, Long Beach, Calif: IEEE, 1978.

LITTLE, D.: "A Proof for the Queueing Formula: $L = \lambda W$," *Oper. Res.*, vol. 9, pp. 383-387, May 1961.

LIU, M. T.: "Distributed Loop Computer Networks," in *Advances in Computers*, M. C. Yovits (ed.). New York: Academic Press, pp. 163-221, 1978.

MAGNEE, F., ENDRIZZI, A., and DAY, J.: "A Survey of Terminal Protocols," *Comput. Networks*, vol. 3, pp. 299-314, Nov. 1979.

MAHMOUD, S., and RIORDAN, J. S.: "Optimal Allocation of Resources in Distributed

Information Networks," *ACM Trans. on Database Syst.*, vol. 1, pp. 66-78, March 1976.

MAJITHIA, J., IRLAND, M., GRANGE, J.-L., COHEN, N., and O'DONNELL, C.: "Experiments in Congestion Control Techniques," in *Flow Control in Computer Networks*, J.-L. Grangé and M. Gien (eds.). Amsterdam: North-Holland, pp. 211-234, 1979.

MALHOTRA, V. M., KUMAR, M. P., and MAHESHWARI, S. N.: "An $O(1V1^3)$ Algorithm for Finding Maximum Flows in Networks," *Inf. Proc. Lett.*, vol. 7, pp. 277-278, Oct. 1978.

MARTIN, J.: *Communications Satellite Systems*. Englewood Cliffs, N.J.: Prentice-Hall, 1978.

MARYANSKI, F. J.: "Backend Database Systems," *Comput. Surv.*, vol. 12, pp. 3-25, March 1980.

MCGREGOR, P., and SHEN, D.: "Network Design: An Algorithm for the Access Facility Location Problem," *IEEE Trans. Commun.*, vol. COM-25, pp. 61-73, Jan. 1977.

MCQUILLAN, J.: "Adaptive Routing Algorithms for Distributed Computer Networks," Ph.D. thesis, Div. of Engineering and Applied Sciences, Harvard University, 1974.

MCQUILLAN, J. M., and CERF, V. G.: *A Practical View of Computer Communications Protocols*. Long Beach, Calif.: IEEE, 1978.

MCQUILLAN, J. M., RICHER, I., and ROSEN, E. C.: "The New Routing Algorithm for the ARPANET," *IEEE Trans. Commun.*, vol. COM-28, pp. 711-719, May 1980.

MCQUILLAN, J. M., and WALDEN, D. C.: "The ARPA network Design Decisions," *Comput. Networks*, vol. 1, pp. 243-289, Aug. 1977.

MENASCE, D. A., POPEK, G. J., and MUNTZ, R. R.: "A Locking Protocol for Resource Coordination in Distributed Databases," *ACM Trans. on Database Syst.*, vol. 5, pp. 104-138, June 1980.

MERKLE, R. C.: "Secure Communication Over an Insecure Channel," *Commun. ACM*, vol. 21, pp. 294-299, April 1978.

MERKLE, R. C., and HELLMAN, M. E.: "Hiding Information and Receipts in Trap-Door Knapsacks," *IEEE Trans. Inf. Theory*, vol. IT-24, pp. 525-530, Sept. 1978.

MERLIN, P. M.: "Specification and Validation of Protocols," *IEEE Trans. Commun.*, vol. COM-27, pp. 1671-1680, Nov. 1979.

MERLIN, P. M.: "A Methodology for the Design and Implementation of Communication Protocols," *IEEE Trans. Commun.*, vol. COM-24, pp. 1036-1043, Sept. 1976.

MERLIN, P. M., and SCHWEITZER, P. J.: "Deadlock Avoidance—Store-and-Forward Deadlock," *IEEE Trans. Commun.*, vol. COM-28, pp. 345-354, March 1980a.

MERLIN, P. M., and SCHWEITZER, P. J.: "Deadlock Avoidance in Store-and-Forward Networks—Other Deadlock Types," *IEEE Trans. Commun.*, vol. COM-28, pp. 355-360, March 1980b.

METCALFE, R. M., and BOGGS, D. R.: "Ethernet: Distributed Packet Switching for Local Computer Networks," *Commun. ACM*, vol. 19, pp. 395-404, July 1976.

METZNER, J.: "On Improving Utilization in ALOHA Networks," *IEEE Trans. Commun.*, vol. COM-24, pp. 447-448, April 1976.

MILLSTEIN, R. E.: "The National Software Works: A Distributed Processing System," *Proc. ACM Ann. Conf.*, pp. 44-52, 1977.

MOK, A. K., and WARD, S. A.: "Distributed Broadcast Channel Access," *Comput. Networks*, vol. 3, pp. 327-335, Nov. 1979.

MORRIS, R., SLOANE, N. J. A., and WYNER, A. D.: "Assessment of the NBS Proposed Federal Data Encryption Standard," *Cryptologia*, vol. 1, pp. 281-291, July 1977.

MORRIS, R., and THOMPSON, K.: "Password Security: A Case History," *Commun. ACM*, vol. 22, pp. 594-597, Nov. 1979.

NATIONAL BUREAU OF STANDARDS: "Data Encryption Standard," Fed. Inf. Process. Stand. Publ. 46, Jan. 1977.

NEEDHAM, R. M.: "System Aspects of the Cambridge Ring," *Proc. Seventh Symp. Oper. Syst. Prin.*, ACM, pp. 82-85, 1979.

NEEDHAM, R, M., and SCHROEDER, M. D.: "Using Encryption for Authentication in Large Networks of Computers," *Commun. ACM*, vol. 21, pp. 993-999, Dec 1978.

NEWELL, A., FAHLMAN, S. E., SPROULL, R. F., and WACTLAR, H. D.: "CMU Proposal for Personal Scientific Computing," *Compcon*, pp. 480-483, Spring 1980.

ORNSTEIN, S. M., CROWTHER, W. R., KRALEY, M. F., BRESSLER, R. D., MICHEL, A., and HEART, F. E.: "Pluribus—A Reliable Multiprocessor," *Proc. NCC*, pp. 551-559, 1975.

OUSTERHOUT, J. K., SCELZA, D. A., and SINDHU, P. S.: "Medusa: An Experiment in Distributed Operating System Structure," *Commun. ACM*, vol. 23, pp. 92-105, Feb. 1980.

PETERSON, W. W., and BROWN, D. T.: "Cyclic Codes for Error Detection," *Proc. IRE*, vol. 49, pp. 228-235, Jan. 1961.

PIERCE, J.: "How Far Can Data Loops Go?" *IEEE Trans. Commun.*, vol. COM-20, pp. 527-530, June 1972.

POPEK, G. J., and KLINE, C. S.: "Encryption and Secure Computer Networks," *Comput. Surv.*, vol. 11, pp. 331-356, Dec. 1979.

POSTEL, J. B.: "Internetwork Protocol Approaches," *IEEE Trans. Commun.*, vol. COM-28, pp. 604-611, April 1980.

POSTEL, J. B.: "An Informal Comparison of Three Protocols," *Comput. Networks*, vol. 3, pp. 67-76, Feb. 1979.

POUZIN, L.: "Packet Networks, Issues and Choices," *Proc. IFIP Congr. 77*, pp. 515-521, 1977.

POUZIN, L.: "Virtual Circuits vs. Datagrams—Technical and Political Problems," *Proc. NCC*, pp. 483-494, 1976a.

POUZIN, L.: "The Network Business—Monopolies and Entrepreneurs," *Proc. Third*

ICCC, pp. 563-567, 1976b.

POUZIN, L.: "Flow Control in Data Networks—Methods and Tools," *Proc. Third ICCC*, pp. 467-474, 1976c.

POUZIN, L., and ZIMMERMANN, H.: "A Tutorial on Protocols," *Proc. IEEE*, vol. 66, pp. 1346-1370, Nov. 1978.

REDELL, D. D., DALAL, Y. K., HORSLEY, T. R., LAUER, H. C., LYNCH, W. C., MCJONES, P. R., MURRAY, H. G., PURCELL, S. C.: "Pilot: An Operating System for a Personal Computer," *Commun. ACM*, vol. 23, pp. 81-92, Feb. 1980.

REEDS, J.: "Cracking a Random Number Generator," *Cryptologia*, vol. 1, pp. 20-26, 1977.

RIVEST, R. L., SHAMIR, A., and ADLEMAN, L.: "On Digital Signatures and Public Key Cryptosystems," *Commun. ACM*, vol. 21, pp. 120-126, Feb. 1978.

ROBERTS, L.: "Dynamic Allocation of Satellite Capacity through Packet Reservation," *Proc. NCC*, pp. 711-716, 1973.

ROBERTS, L.: "Extensions of Packet Communication Technology to a Hand Held Personal Terminal," *Proc. SJCC*, pp. 295-298, 1972.

ROSEN, B.: "PERQ: A Commercially Available Personal Scientific Computer," *Compcon*, pp. 484-485, Spring 1980.

ROSEN, E. C.: "The Updating Protocol of ARPANET's New Routing Algorithm," *Comput. Networks*, vol. 4, pp. 11-19, Feb. 1980.

ROTHAUSER, E. H., and WILD, D.: "MLMA—A Collision-Free Multi-Acess Method," *Proc. IFIP Congr. 77*, pp. 431-436, 1977.

RUDIN, H.: "On Routing and Delta Routing: A Taxonomy and Performance Comparison of Techniques for Packet-Switched Networks" *IEEE Trans. Commun.*, vol. COM-24, pp. 43-59, Jan. 1976.

RYBCZYNSKI, A.: "X.25 Interface and End-to-End Virtual Circuit Service Characteristics," *IEEE Trans. Commun.*, vol. COM-28, pp. 500-510, April 1980.

SALTZER, J. H.: "On Digital Signatures," *Oper. Syst. Rev.*, vol. 12, pp. 12-14, April 1978.

SATYANARAYANAN, M.: "Multiprocessing: An Annotated Bibliography," *Computer*, vol. 13, pp. 101-116, May 1980.

SCHICKER, P., and DUENKI, A.: "The Virtual Terminal Definition," *Comput. Networks*, vol. 2, pp. 429-441, Dec. 1978.

SCHOLL, M.: "Multiplexing Techniques for Data Transmission over Packet Switched Radio Systems," Ph.D. thesis, Computer Science Dept., UCLA, 1976.

SCHWARTZ, M.: *Computer-Communication Network Design and Analysis*. Englewood Cliffs, N.J.: Prentice-Hall, 1977.

SCHWARTZ, M., and SAAD, S.: "Analysis of Congestion Control Techniques in Computer Communication Networks," in *Flow Control in Computer Networks*, J.-L. Grangé and M. Gien (eds.). Amsterdam: North Holland, pp. 113-130, 1979.

SCHWARTZ, M., and STERN, T. E.: "Routing Techniques Used in Computer Communication Networks," *IEEE Trans. Commun.*, vol. COM-28, pp. 539-552, April 1980.

SEGALL, A.: "Failsafe Distributed Algorithms for Routing in Communication Networks," in *Flow Control in Computer Networks*, J.-L. Grangé and M. Gien (eds.). Amsterdam: North Holland, pp. 235,240.

SELFRIDGE, O. G., and SCHWARTZ, R. T.: "Telephone Technology and Privacy," *Technology Review*, vol. 82, pp. 56-65, May 1980.

SHAMIR, A.: "How to Share a Secret," *Commun. ACM*, vol. 22, pp. 612-613, Nov. 1979.

SHAMIR, A., and ZIPPEL, R.: "On the Security of the Merkle-Hellman Cryptographic Scheme," *IEEE Trans. Inf. Theory*, vol. IT-26, pp. 339-340, May 1980.

SHANNON, C.: "Communication Theory of Secrecy Systems," *Bell System J.*, vol. 28, pp. 656-715, Oct. 1949.

SHANNON, C.: "A Mathematical Theory of Communication," *Bell System J.*, vol. 27, pp. 379-423, July 1948; and pp. 623-656, Oct. 1948.

SHAPLEY, D., and KOLATA, G. B.: "Cryptology: Scientists Puzzle over Threat to Open Research, Publication," *Science*, vol. 197, pp. 1345-1349, Sept. 30, 1977.

SHOCH, J. F.: "Packet Fragmentation in Inter-Network Protocols," *Comput. Networks*, vol. 3, pp. 3-8, 1979.

SHOCH, J. F.: "Inter-network Naming, Addressing, and Routing," *Compcon*, pp. 72-79, Fall 1978.

SHOCH, J. F., and HUPP, J. A.: "Performance of an Ethernet Local Network—A Preliminary Report," *Compcon*, pp. 318-322, Spring 1980.

SHOCH, J. F., and STEWART, L.: "Interconnecting Local Networks via the Packet Radio Network," *Proc. Sixth Data Commun. Symp.*, pp. 153-158, 1979.

SIMMONS, G. J.: "Symmetric and Asymmetric Encryption" *Comput. Surv.*, vol. 11, pp. 304-330, Dec. 1979.

SIMON, J. M., and DANET, A.: "Controle des Ressources et Principes du Routage dans le Réseau TRANSPAC" in *Flow Control in Computer Networks*, J.-L. Grangé and M. Gien (eds.). Amsterdam: North Holland, pp. 33-44, 1979.

SLOANE, N. J. A.: *A Short Course on Error Correcting Codes*, Berlin: Springer Verlag, 1975.

SMITH, R.: "The Contract Net Protocol: High Level Communication and Control in a Distributed Problem Solver," *Proc. First Int. Conf. Distrib. Comput. Syst.*, IEEE, pp. 185-192, 1979.

SMITH, R. E.: "Civilian Cryptography," *Compcon*, p. 215D, Spring 1980.

SOLOMON, M. H., and FINKEL, R. A.: "The Roscoe Distributed Operating System," *Proc. Seventh Symp. on Oper. Syst. Prin.*, ACM, pp. 108-114, 1979.

STEEL, T.: "UNCOL: The Myth and the Fact," in *Ann. Rev. Auto. Prog.* Goodman, R. (ed.), vol. 2, pp. 325-344, 1960.

STEIGLITZ, K., WEINER, P., and KLEITMAN, D. J.: "The Design of Minimum-Cost

Survivable Networks," *IEEE Trans. Circuit Theory*, vol. CT-16, pp. 455-460, Nov. 1969.

STONE, H. S., and BOKHARI, S. H.: "Control of Distributed Processes," *Computer*, vol. 11, pp. 97-106, July 1978.

SU, S. Y. W., CHANG, H., COPELAND, G., FISHER, P., LOWENTHAL, E., and SCHUSTER, S.: "Database Machines and Some Issues on DBMS Standards," *Proc. NCC*, pp. 191-208, 1980.

SUGARMAN, R. M.: "On Foiling Computer Crime," *IEEE Spectrum*, vol. 16, pp. 31-32, July 1979.

SUGARMAN, R. M.: "Freedom to Research and Publish on Cryptography Remains Unresolved," *The Institute—News Suppl. IEEE Spectrum*, IEEE, vol. 2, pp. 1, 7, 8, May 1978.

SUNSHINE, C. A.: "Formal Techniques for Protocol Specification and Verification," *Computer*, vol. 12, pp. 20-27, Sept. 1979.

SUNSHINE, C. A.: "Interconnection of Computer Networks," *Comput. Networks*, vol. 1, pp. 175-195, Jan. 1977.

SUNSHINE, C. A., and DALAL, Y. K.: "Connection Management in Transport Protocols," *Comput. Networks*, vol. 2, pp. 454-473, 1978.

SWAN, R. J., FULLER, S. H., and SIEWIOREK, D. P.: "Cm*—A Modular, Multi-Microprocessor," *Proc. NCC*, pp. 637-644, 1977a.

SWAN, R. J., BECHTOLSHEIM, A., KWOK-WOON, L., and OUSTERHOUT, J. K.: "The Implementation of the Cm* Multi-microprocessor," *Proc. NCC*, pp. 645-655, 1977b.

THORTON, J. E.: "Backend Network Approaches," *Compcon*, pp. 217-223, Spring 1980.

THURBER, K. J., and FREEMAN, H. A.: "Updated Bibliography on Local Computer Networks," *Comput. Arch. News*, vol. 8, pp. 20-28, April 1980.

TOBAGI, F. A.: "Multiaccess Protocols in Packet Communication Systems," *IEEE Trans. Commun.*, vol. COM-28, pp. 468-488, April 1980c.

TOBAGI, F. A.: "Analysis of a Two Hop Centralized Packet Radio Network: Part I - Slotted Aloha," *IEEE Trans. Commun.*, vol. COM-28, pp. 196-207, Feb. 1980b.

TOBAGI, F. A.: "Analysis of a Two Hop Centralized Packet Radio Network: Part II - Carrier Sense Multiple Access," *IEEE Trans. Commun.*, vol. COM-28, pp. 208-216, Fec. 1980b.

TOBAGI, F. A.: "Random Access Techniques for Data Transmission over Packet Switched Radio Networks," Ph.D. thesis, Computer Science Dept., UCLA, 1974.

TOBAGI, F. A., GERLA, M., PEEBLES, R. W., and MANNING, E. G.: "Modeling and Measurement Techniques in Packet Communication Networks," *Proc. IEEE*, vol. 66, pp. 1423-1447, Nov. 1978.

TOKORU, M., and TAMARU, K.: "Acknowledging Ethernet," *Compcon*, pp. 320-325, Fall 1977.

TOMLINSON, R. S.: "Selecting Sequence Numbers," *Proc. ACM SIGCOMM/SIGOPS Interprocess Commun. Workshop*, ACM, pp. 11-23, 1975.

TRELEAVEN, P. C.: "Exploiting Program Concurrency in Computing Systems," *Computer*, vol. 12, pp. 42-49, Jan. 1979.

TUCHMAN, W.: "Hellman Presents No Shortcut Solutions to the DES," *IEEE Spectrum*, vol. 16, pp. 40-41, July 1979.

VAN DAM, A., STABLER, G., and HARRINGTON, R.: "Intelligent Satellites for Interactive Graphics," *Proc. IEEE*, vol. 62, pp. 83-92, April 1974.

WALDEN, D. and MCKENZIE, A. A.: "The Evolution of Host-to-Host Protocol Technology," *Computer*, vol. 12, pp. 29-38, Sept. 1979.

WARD, A. A.: "TRIX: A Network-Oriented Operating System," *Compcon*, pp. 344-349, Spring 1980.

WARD, S. A., and TERMAN, C. J.: "An Approach to Personal Computing," *Compcon*, pp. 460-465, Spring 1980.

WATSON, R. W.: "Interprocess Communication: Interface and End-to-End (Transport) Protocol Design Issues," in *Distributed Systems: An Advanced Course*. Berlin: Springer-Verlag, 1980a.

WATSON, R. W.: "Network Architecture Design Issues for Backend Storage Networks," *Compcon*, pp. 224-234, Spring 1980b.

WATSON, R. W., and FLETCHER, J. G.: "An Architecture for Support of Network Operating System Services," *Comput. Networks*, vol. 4, pp. 33-49, Feb. 1980.

WECKER, S.: "DNA: the Digital Network Architecture," *IEEE Trans. Commun.*, vol. COM-28, pp. 510-526, April 1980.

WHITNEY, H.: "Congruent Graphs and the Connectivity of Graphs," *Am. J. Math.*, vol. 54, pp. 150-168, 1932.

WILMS, P.: "Qualitative and Quantitative Comparison of Update Algorithms in Distributed Databases," in *Distributed Data Bases*, C. Delobel and W. Litwin (eds.). Amsterdam: North-Holland, pp. 275-294, 1980.

WITTIE, L. D.: "A Distributed Operating System for a Reconfigurable Network Computer," *Proc. First Int. Conf. on Distrib. Comput. Syst.*, IEEE, pp. 669-677, 1979.

WONG, E.: "Retrieving Dispersed Data from SDD-1: A System for Distributed Databases," *Second Berkeley Workshop on Distributed Data Management and Computer Networks*, Lawrence Berkeley Lab., pp. 217-235, 1977.

WULF, W. A., and BELL, C. G.: "C.mmp—A Multi-Mini-processor," *Proc. FJCC*, pp. 765-777, 1972.

YEMINI, Y.: "On Channel Sharing in Discrete-Time Packet Switched, Multiaccess Broadcast Communication," Ph.D. thesis, Computer Science Dept., UCLA, 1978.

ZIMMERMANN, H.: "OSI Reference Model—The ISO Model of Architecture for Open Systems Interconnection," *IEEE Trans. Commun.*, vol. COM-28, pp. 425-432, April 1980.

INDEX

B

Backbone, 35
Backbone design, 67-80
Backward learning algorithm, 203-204
Bandwidth, 92-95
Basic information unit, 234
Basic transmission unit, 233-234
Baud, 93
Baudot code, 420-421
Bidding, 467
Binary countdown protocol, 300
Binary synchronous communication, 120-121
Binding, session, 20
Birth-death system, 59
BISYNC (*see* Binary synchronous communication)
Bit map protocol, 296-297
Bit stuffing, 168-169
BIU (*see* Basic information unit)
Block cipher, 396-400
BRAP (*see* Broadcast recognition with alternating
        priorities)
Broadcast recognition with alternating
        priorities, 297-298
Broadcast routing, 213-214
Broadcast subnet, 8-10
BTU (*see* Basic transmission unit)
Buffer allocation, 338-342

C

C.mmp, 317-318
Cable television, 102
Call collision, 110, 239
Call progress signals, 109
Capability, 479
Capacity assignment, 72-75
Capture effect, 282
Carrier
    common, 97
    modulated, 100
Carrier's carrier, 355
Carrier sense network protocol, 288-306
    adaptive tree walk, 302-303
    binary countdown, 300
    bit map, 296-297
    BRAP, 297-298
    Ethernet, 292-295
    MLMA, 298-300
    nonpersistent protocol, 290-291
    1-persistent protocol, 290
    p-persistent protocol, 291
    urn, 303-306

CCITT
    (*see also* X.3, X.21, X.25, etc.)
    function, 97
    PCM standards, 105-106
    relation to ISO, 97
Centralized routing, 200-202
Central office (*see* End office)
Channel, 7
Channel associated signaling, 105-106
Character stuffing, 165
Checksum, 130
Choke packet, 221-222
Chosen plaintext problem, 389
Cipher (*see* Cryptography)
Ciphertext, 389
Ciphertext only problem, 389
Circuit, 7
Circuit switching, 114-115
Clear collision, 241
Closed user group, 110
Cm*, 318-320
Code, 394
Codec, 105
Codeword, 126
Collision
    call, 239
    Ethernet, 292
    on satellite channel, 254
Collision free protocol, 296-300
Common carrier, 97
Common channel signaling, 105
Communication subnet, 7
    internal structure, 192-196
Companding, 125
Components of a graph, 37
Concentration, 122
Concentrator assignment problem, 83-84
Concentrator location problem, 83-84
Concurrency control, 452-457
Congestion control, 215-225
    ARPANET, 226-227
    DECNET, 236-237
    SNA, 234
Connection establishment, 335-338
    in spite of delayed packets, 345-351
Connectivity, 47-53
    arc, 47-53
    node, 50-53
Contention, 254, 292-294
Contention ring, 311-312
Correctness, protocol, 177-183
CPODA, 273
Crash recovery, 351-353
CRC (*see* Cyclic redundancy code)